D0164037

Sybase Performance Tuning

Shaibal Roy
Marc Sugiyama

For book and bookstore information

http://www.prenhall.com

Prentice Hall PTR
Upper Saddle River, NJ 07458

Editorial/production supervision: bookworks/Karen Fortgang
Cover design director: Jerry Votta
Manufacturing manager: Alexis R. Heydt
Acquisitions editor: Mark L. Taub

© 1996 by Prentice Hall P T R
Prentice-Hall, Inc.
A Simon & Schuster Company
Upper Saddle River, NJ 07458

The publisher offers discounts on this book when ordered in bulk quantities. For more information, contact: Corporate Sales Department, Prentice Hall P T R, One Lake Street, Upper Saddle River, New Jersey 07458, Phone: 800-382-3419, FAX: 201-236-7141, e-mail: corpsales@prenhall.com

SYBASE, the Sybase logo, Data Workbench, and VQL are registered trademarks of Sybase, Inc. SYBASE SQL Server, SYBASE SQL Toolset, Transact-SQL, DB-Library, Net-Library, APT Workbench, APT Library, APT-SQL, APT-Build, APT-Execute, APT-Edit, Report Workbench, Report-Execute, SYBASE Embedded SQL, Hyper DB-Library, PC-APT Execute, PC DB-Library, PC Net-Library, Open Client, SYBASE Developer's Workbench, SYBASE User Workbench, Replication Server, Open Server, Client/Server Interfaces, SYBASE Server-Library, SYBASE Open Gateway, Tabular Data Stream, SQL Server/DBM, SQL Server/CFT, SYBASE Secure SQL Server, Sybase Synergy Program, Adaptable Windowing Environment, and SYBASE Virtual Server Architecture are trademarks of Sybase, Inc.

Any other company and product names used herein may be the trademarks or registered trademarks of their respective companies.

All rights reserved. No part of this book may be reproduced, in any form or by any means, without permission in writing from the publisher.

Printed in the United States of America

10 9 8 7 6 5 4 3 2 1

ISBN 0-13-442997-4

Prentice-Hall International (UK) Limited, *London*
Prentice-Hall of Australia Pty. Limited, *Sydney*
Prentice-Hall Canada Inc., *Toronto*
Prentice-Hall Hispanoamericana, S.A., *Mexico*
Prentice-Hall of India Private Limited, *New Delhi*
Prentice-Hall of Japan, Inc., *Tokyo*
Simon & Schuster Asia Pte. Ltd., *Singapore*
Editora Prentice-Hall do Brasil, Ltda., *Rio de Janeiro*

Table of Contents

List of Figures

List of Tables

Foreword

Many people are attracted to Sybase SQL Server for its ability to get the maximum performance out of any computer regardless of size. With the invention of System 11, both total performance and the developer's ability to influence that performance have increased. This book, *Sybase Performance Tuning*, contains state-of-the-art information and insight into nearly every factor that determines performance. It is written in a "just the facts" manner by two very gifted engineers who are part of the SQL Server development team.

This book gives the new developer an overview of what affects performance and how the underlying concepts of data management work. It also gives the experienced database designer the underlying details of how SQL Server is implemented, what every "knob" does, and where every byte of data resides.

While three generations of Sybase technology are covered (versions 4.9, 10, and 11), the reader will be particularly interested in understanding and exploiting the new concepts and capabilities of SQL Server 11. At this time, no other book provides the reader with the depth of knowledge for getting the maximum value out of version 11. Version 11 has established new definitions of performance excellence and it has accomplished this with new concepts such as named caches, table partitions, and so on. The reader learns first hand how these capabilities work and how to use them for maximum advantage.

So don't just read the foreword, dig in! Your own customers will appreciate the speed of your database and your finance department will love the fact that all you did was buy a new book instead of a new computer!

Bob Epstein
Executive Vice President
Sybase, Inc.

Preface

As the architect or developer of a high-performance database application, you must weigh the desire for performance against the cost of achieving that performance. Given the constraints imposed by business requirements, the problem of tuning performance is best described as a multivariate optimization problem involving several constraints.

Cost of Hardware

Throwing more hardware at the problem is a proven technique to improving performance. Often, it is also the most appropriate, given all other constraints. However, a clever, elegant solution that uses hardware intelligently is always more attractive than a solution that relies on brute force. This is exactly what this book is all about. However, the performance of hardware components does impose an upper bound on the performance of your application. You need to recognize the point of diminishing returns in your efforts to maximize the utilization of hardware resources.

Cost of Development and Maintenance

If you splurge on hardware, you may be able to get by with a simple design involving few special optimizations. With limited hardware, you may need to spend more time using every trick in the book to get the most out of the limited hardware. However, the few dollars saved on the cost of CPUs, memory, or disks may end up costing a lot more in the development and maintenance of the application. The optimal point in this trade-off lies somewhere between the two extremes and depends on the nature of your business. If you are developing for the mass market, splurging on hardware may not be an option — you may need to tune for the hardware configuration that comprises the least common denominator of a large installed base. If you are implementing a special-purpose application for a limited number of installations, you may want to trade cost of development for additional hardware. If the performance requirements of your special-purpose application are so demanding as to have reached the limit of hardware capabilities, your only option may be to put additional effort into tuning.

Need for Generality

The performance of a custom-built system can exceed that of a general-purpose system customized or programmed to perform the same tasks. However, the cost of a custom-built system can be very high and may be difficult to justify unless the performance requirements of your application far exceed the performance available from commercially available systems. There are database systems in operation today whose performance is beyond the reach of any commercially available database system. However, advances in the performance of hardware and relational database software have caught up with the performance requirements for the vast majority of database systems that still employ custom-built proprietary software.

Importance of Deadlines

A design that meets all the performance requirements but fails to meet the deadlines imposed by the business requirements is not the right design. Like many aspects of the design of a complex system, performance tuning is an iterative process. Instead of trying to achieve the maximum possible performance out of the gate, you may want to break up the performance features of your application into multiple phases.

SQL Server Performance Tuning

Much of what you need to build a high performance Sybase SQL Server database system is good intuition and some common sense. In this book we emphasize design and implementation of the application over the acquisition of additional hardware. We do so by focusing on the distribution of the workload among the components of the system and on eliminating points of contention. Much of what is needed to accomplish these two tasks follows from a very basic understanding of the architecture of Sybase SQL Server and some of its performance features. To that end, we start with a description of the architecture of Sybase SQL Server and the features that are the most influential in its performance.

Perhaps the most important step in performance tuning is the identification of the performance bottlenecks. These are components whose performance is a limiting factor in the performance of the overall system. The discussion on monitoring the performance of Sybase SQL Server may assist you in identifying bottlenecks. Another important step in designing a well-balanced system is assessing the performance requirements of individual components. For example, you may need to measure the network throughput or the utilization of a particular disk or CPU to be able to estimate the performance of your application under varying workload conditions. The monitoring tools can help you assess the demands placed by your application on individual components of the system.

Audience

The audience for this book includes:

- **Project Managers** who need to understand resource and capacity planning for their SQL Server system. We define performance requirements and metrics. We provide information to help project managers decide how many disk drives, how much memory, and how much CPU power are needed to achieve the performance goals of the application.

- **Database Architects** who lay out the logical and physical database designs. We provide tips on table and index definitions and physical layout.

- **Application Developers** who need to understand SQL Server query processing. We help application developers decide on the best way to implement the queries needed by the application. We explain how query optimization is performed in Sybase SQL Server and how developers can code queries to get the best performance from the query optimizer.

- **Database Administrators** who monitor application performance and field complaints about performance from their customers. We explain how to monitor the performance of applications and provide methods to improve the performance of existing applications.

- **System Administrators** who monitor system-wide performance metrics. We describe operating system and Sybase monitoring tools that can help pinpoint performance bottlenecks in the system.

The prerequisites for reading this book are a working knowledge of Sybase Transact-SQL (T-SQL) and an understanding of the basic operation of Sybase SQL Server as described in the Sybase User Documentation.

Developers new to Sybase will find our discussion of Sybase architecture and basic performance tips interesting. This book includes a glossary of common performance tools and techniques and example code segments, all designed to accelerate the learning process.

Experienced application programmers and database developers who address performance issues early in the design cycle will find this book a useful resource. We include sections describing how to take advantage of unique (and in some cases not so unique) Sybase features. We discuss the trade-offs between complementary features and show how to tailor the choice and usage of performance features to the application requirements.

On the other hand, developers often have to work with applications where performance problems are addressed later in the design cycle. While we strongly discourage developers from treating performance as an afterthought, we recognize that unforeseen changes in business requirements and the application environment can, and often do, affect performance. This book presents techniques for diagnosing performance problems in existing applications, and tools for improving performance within the confined specifications of a mature design.

SQL Server Versions

In this book we refer to three versions of SQL Server: **4.9**, **System 10**, and **System 11**. 4.9 SQL Server refers to 4.9.x versions of SQL Server. Many of the performance characteristics of 4.9 apply to 4.8 as well. System 10 SQL Server refers to all 10.0.x versions of SQL Server, and System 11 to the 11.0.0 version of SQL Server.

System 10 SQL Server enhanced the functionality of SQL Server with several features, including ANSI SQL compatibility and the availability of a family of related products such as Replication and Backup Servers. System 11 SQL Server improves the performance and scalability of SQL Server and adds new functionality, including configuration management tools, isolation level 0, and capability to handle very large databases.

Our discussion of System 11 SQL Server examples, commands, and procedures where they differ from System 10, are based on the Beta and pre-Beta versions of System 11 SQL Server. While we do not expect many significant changes between

Beta and general availability of System 11 SQL Server, some changes are inevitable. In all cases, refer to the documentation that came with your version of SQL Server.

The primary focus of this book is System 10 and System 11 SQL Server. Application developers migrating from 4.9 or System 10 SQL Server to System 11 SQL Server will find our discussion of System 11 SQL Server performance enhancements of special interest. By appropriately configuring System 11 SQL Server features, such as named data caches and buffer pools, it is possible to see significant performance gains without changing any application code.

We have emphasized performance aspects in our discussion of Sybase SQL Server commands and options. Our explanations of commands may slight or not even mention other aspects of the commands. Your Sybase documentation is your complete reference to SQL Server commands and should be considered the final reference when information in the documentation conflicts with the contents of this book.

While the common architectural heritage shared by Sybase SQL Server and Microsoft SQL Server often encourages developers to assume commonality of features and functionalities between the two products, we must discourage the readers from assuming that the material in this book applies to Microsoft SQL Server.

As much as possible, we have tried to remain platform neutral and rely on platform information only when a discussion of operating system behavior or tools is required. In such cases, we tend to favor the Unix operating system, as this is the operating environment most familiar and available to us. The performance techniques we discuss, for the most part, make no assumptions about the homogeneity of your computing environment. We try to avoid network protocol and hardware architectural issues.

Organization

This book is divided into thirteen chapters. The first three chapters provide an overview of performance issues, hardware and software systems, and the Sybase product set. These chapters establish some basic ground rules and set the stage for a discussion of SQL Server performance issues.

The next two chapters discuss the architecture of SQL Server. In these two chapters we discuss how SQL Server is put together and how it works inside. Here, we try to avoid too many performance issues, relying instead on later chapters to discuss these issues.

With the background material behind us, the remaining chapters discuss various aspects of the design and development of a high performance Sybase SQL Server client/server application. Each chapter focuses on a particular aspect of the application — client/server organization, on-line transaction processing, complex query processing, batch processing, etc.

Tuning for Performance — Defines performance and provides general tips for performance tuning.

Hardware and System Software — Describes the hardware and software components that make up a client/server system.

Sybase Product and Feature Overview — Runs through the Sybase product set as it relates to SQL Server performance.

SQL Server — Form and Structure — Provides an architectural overview of SQL Server, focusing on the organization of information inside SQL Server and the way SQL Server organizes and represents databases.

SQL Server — Methods and Features — Completes the architecture overview of SQL Server, focusing on the features of SQL Server and how SQL Server processes queries.

Physical Database Design — Discusses the optimal organization of tables, choice of indexes, and methods for maintaining data integrity.

Application Development — Describes the organization of work between client and server, how to send queries to SQL Server, how to form queries, and other T-SQL programming techniques.

Monitoring SQL Server — Discusses various tools for monitoring the performance of SQL Server. Topics include system stored procedures, operating system tools, and SQL Monitor.

Instrumenting SQL Code — Describes various mechanism to instrument T-SQL code to gather more information about the performance of your application. Particular attention is given to showplan output.

Transaction Processing Performance — Discusses various aspects of transaction processing performance for SQL Server.

Query Processing Performance — Describes various aspects of query processing performance for SQL Server.

Batch Processing Performance — Discusses a variety of batch operations that are commonly performed with SQL Server, including backup and load, create index, and BCP loads.

Advanced Topics — Covers many of the features new to System 11 SQL Server.

The following appendices consolidate some information found in the main body of the book, give extra details about configuration of SQL Server, and describe some useful commands.

General Configuration Practices — Provides general performance tips for SQL Server.

SQL Server Configuration — Describes the configuration parameters for SQL Server and their performance implications.

Network Configuration — Discusses the Sybase interfaces file and the performance implications of the interfaces file.

DBCC Commands — Details the DBCC commands and discusses their performance implications.

Troubleshooting — Provides some general tips for identifying the source of a SQL Server performance problem. Several common situations are covered.

Industry Standard Benchmarks — Gives a description of the industry standard database benchmarks defined by the Transaction Processing Council.

Reference and Scripts — Lists SQL data types, useful functions, and provides some useful stored procedures.

Glossary — Defines various terms used throughout the book and in the relational database industry.

Notational Conventions

`Text in this font` is used to indicate SQL Server keywords, commands, and output. Words in **bold** introduce special terms. Emphasis is given by using *italics*. Footnotes are used throughout the book to provide incidental or anecdotal information that would otherwise interrupt the flow of the text.

Acknowledgments

Creating a book requires the time and effort of many people. The authors would like to thank everyone who helped in small and in large part with the completion of this work. As with any project, there are always some individuals or organizations who stand out. In particular, the authors would like to thank the following people and organizations: Sybase, Inc. for giving us permission to use their equipment to create the examples, run tests, etc.; Byron Servies for his excellent, thoughtful, and copious comments on the early drafts of this book; Sandy Emerson and Garudapura Madhusudan for taking the time to review the material; Jerry Brenner, Ignacio Huerta, Jeff Lichtman, Peter Thawley, Matthias Bergeroff, and Charles Levine for their contributions to this book; Brijesh Agarwal, Jerry Brenner, Robert Mihalyi, Mohan Shankaran, Eric McCormick, and Allyn Randall for reviewing chapters from this book; Brijesh Agarwal, Sunil Agarwal, Max Berenson, Jerry Brenner, Yongmin Chen, Dwayne Chung, Dan Debrunner, Sangeeta Doraiswamy, Clark French, Ron Hu, Ganesan Gopal, Aditya Gurajada, Hanuma Kodavalla, Vaikom Krishnan, Jeff Lichtman, Scott McCargar, Sethu Meenakshisundara, Francois Orisini, Sapan Panigrahi, Madhavan Rangarao, T. K. Rengarajan, Dave Rubin, Peter Schneider, Edwin Seputis, and Srinivasan Suresh for educating us about the features and characteristics of the System 11 family of products; and finally, Mark Taub, our editor, for his never ending patience as we missed deadline after deadline.

Shaibal Roy would like to thank his wife, Yin Ling Leung, and his parents, Prativa and Narendra Nath Roy, for their patience and encouragement.

Marc Sugiyama would like to thank Orson Scott Card for his early encouragement.

Chapter 1

Tuning for Performance

An application tuned for performance is a competitive edge. The less time your sales staff spends waiting for your order-entry system to respond, the more time they can spend selling your product. The more efficient your application, the less hardware you need. The money you save can be used to improve your product. On the other hand, performance tuning can easily become a never-ending process. It is almost always true that there is no optimal configuration for a database system. No matter how well you tune your database and your application there is always something in it that can be improved further.

Objective goals are a must for performance tuning. You stop tweaking the performance of the system when either the goals are met or the project deadline expires. Our objective is to provide you with tools and techniques that enable you to make the former precede the latter. This chapter addresses some of the issues faced in the early stages of a project, including assessment of performance requirements, and some of the choices you may face in order to succeed with them. Largely, these issues are not exclusive to SQL Server.

Changes in design that improve performance in one area influence other aspects of the system. For example, changing the order of rows in a table may change the order of rows in the result of a query or replacing a fat unique index by a trim non-unique index may eliminate a useful integrity constraint. Such changes may not be acceptable to the functional requirements of the system being tuned; performance tuning should never compromise any essential aspect of the system. Among aspects of the system that should not be compromised by performance tuning are availability, durability, ease of use, functionality, interoperability, maintainability, portability, reliability, and scalability. This chapter includes a discussion on the compromises a designer is often tempted to make while tuning performance, and how some of them can be avoided.

1.1 WHAT IS PERFORMANCE?

Metrics for performance surround us in our personal and professional lives. Pick up any car magazine and you see performance figures for new cars: 0-60 mph time ratings, average mpg, horsepower, torque, engine size. Computer manufacturers announce MIPS, SPEC, scalability, and backplane bandwidth figures. Database vendors promulgate TPC benchmark throughput, cost per transaction rate, etc. Everyone has an intuitive notion of performance, but in different contexts performance can mean different things to different people.

1.1.1 Basic Performance Metrics

For database applications, there are three important performance metrics: **response**, **throughput**, and **cost**.

- **Response** measures the time taken by the system to execute commands. Response measures performance from the point of view of individual users of the system.[1]

- **Throughput** measures the number of jobs executed by the system per unit of time. Throughput measures performance from the point of view of the system.

- **Cost** measures the incremental financial and/or human resource cost of improving the performance of the system. Cost is measured from the point of view of the organization using the system.

Throughput is an excellent measure of the capacity of a database system and is easy to relate to business requirements such as number of orders processed per day or per hour. Throughput is often very closely related to the raw power of the computer system, especially in multi-user environments. Consequently, it is the metric chosen by most hardware vendors for showcasing their best and newest products.

Cost is often combined with throughput and expressed as a ratio of throughput to cost. Although throughput almost never scales linearly with cost, the throughput to cost ratio is useful in comparing systems of disparate capacities. The throughput to cost ratio is often used to rationalize the decision to partition an application.

---

[1] In some situations the term **elapsed time** denotes what we mean by **response,** and the term **response** denotes the time taken by the system to return the first byte of the result. The latter is not a well-defined concept. For example, do the column headers qualify as the first bytes of the result? We use response to mean the time taken by the system to complete the execution of a command.

Often, you can split a large application into smaller applications by replacing a large, centralized system based on propriety hardware with multiple smaller, commodity products based on industry standard components. The cost-justification to do so is best indicated by a comparison of the throughput to cost ratio between large, centralized systems and smaller, commodity products. Typically, this ratio tends to favor small, commodity products.

Response is often the metric of greatest interest to end-users. An order-entry system that processes thousands of transactions per second but takes five minutes to respond to commands will be considered a poor performer by most. However, once response is fast enough to satisfy most users, there is no strong motivation to reduce it further. As a result, response is often not emphasized in reports of industry-standard benchmarks.

If your performance objectives include multi-user transaction processing or batch processing, then overall throughput is of interest to you. Throughput of components such as networks and disk subsystems is crucial to the overall performance of the system. If your only concern is response to complex queries from a single user, overall throughput of the database system is of little interest.

Most standard benchmarks and some real applications aim to maximize throughput or minimize cost without violating preset limits on response. However, achieving an acceptable response is often more difficult in real applications than the lackadaisical attitude toward response would imply. Standard benchmarks always show reasonable response time because they are based on unrealistically short transactions and run on hardware overconfigured to emphasize performance. Depending on the characteristics of your application, you may find your goals on response very demanding rather than just a formality.

1.1.2 Performance Metrics

A coherent set of metrics and requirements is essential in assessing performance and in selecting products and components. The choice of the metrics themselves (e.g., response, throughput, cost) is the easy part. The hard part is avoiding the pitfalls in combining different metrics into a coherent set. Here are some of the common mistakes.

- **Lack of relevance** — The number of transactions per second is at best a poor indicator of performance on complex queries. The amount of cache on a disk controller is not very relevant to the performance of writes to the disk that cannot be cached. Your choice of metrics should be based on your performance requirements and on how you intend to use the product. If this happens to differ from the performance data that is readily available from the vendor, the time and effort necessary to obtain the right information may be well justified.

- **Lack of objectivity** — Subjective metrics such as ease of use and programmer productivity are open to interpretation. The values of your metrics should not depend on who is performing the measurements.

- **Lack of generality** — The primary criteria for selecting a RISC processor should not be its performance in emulating the x86 instruction set. It is unfair to measure the performance of one product in emulating the functionality of another.

- **Lack of reproducibility** — The time to insert a row into a table may depend on the number of rows already present in the table and the activity that precedes the insert. The performance of an update transaction may be artificially high during the warm-up period (e.g., soon after a checkpoint). Often, the performance of a system varies over time.

- **Interpolation** — While there is no guarantee that the throughput of a 75 MHz processor is the average of that of the 50 and 100 MHz processors, you do have the comfort of knowing that the claimed throughput is no larger than a demonstrated throughput (for whatever that is worth). The hazard here is in assuming performance of the system scales linearly with the value you are interpolating.

- **Extrapolation** — In some cases extrapolation is clear, the claim that a four processor system is twice as fast as a two processor system. In other cases extrapolation may be more subtle. For example, you may see claims about the transaction processing power of a system listed next to claims about its prowess in processing read-only queries. It would be wrong to deduce the performance of the system in a mixed workload environment from the two claims.

- **Cost of measurement** — How long does it take to delete one billion rows? The cost and time to construct the table to conduct this test is prohibitive. A metric should not be prohibitively expensive to measure and the effects of taking the measurement on other aspects of the system should be minimal. Instrumenting a program with a software profiler provides excellent information about the time spent in every line of code but the performance of the program is seriously impacted, making the profiling results of questionable value.

- **Mixing incomparable metrics** — Some obvious tricks in mixing metrics include listing the price of an entry-level system along with the performance of a fully configured system.

- **Combining multiple metrics** — It is difficult, but tempting, to distill all the performance aspects of a complex system into one or two numbers. Some benchmarks that measure the performance of database systems on multiple queries use the average of the response of individual queries and transactions as the overall performance metric. Other benchmarks combine results from single and multi-user tests, and some others combine query, transaction, and batch processing. In such cases, combining the results by arithmetic mean tends to overemphasize the slowest parts of the tests, whereas combining the results by geometric mean tends to underemphasize the slow parts. It is better to acknowledge the multi-dimensional nature of performance than to risk oversimplification in mapping a multi-dimensional quantity into a single dimension.

1.1.3   Relevance of Benchmarks

You want the most efficient database system for your application to make the most of your hardware budget. Industry standard benchmarks like TPC-C measure the performance of a specific application, making it possible to compare competing database and hardware systems against one another. The fact that the benchmark is standard means that the workload run against each system is identical, so the application itself is not a variable in the comparison. Appendix F, *Industry Standard Benchmarks*, describes a number of industry standard benchmarks. There are several factors that determine the relevance of benchmarks to your application.

Type of Workload

The workload used in the benchmark should bear some similarity to the expected workload in your system. Of course, an on-line transaction processing (OLTP) benchmark result is relevant only for an OLTP system, and not for a decision-support system. However, sometimes you need to look beyond the broad classifications to determine relevance. A benchmark result stating that Whizbang Server 5000 can do 100 transactions per second on a standard benchmark means just that, and not that it will do 100 transactions per second in your environment.

Comparative Evaluation

When using benchmark results to compare two products, you should attempt to make the two tests as similar as possible. Ideally, the only difference between the two benchmarks should be the products being tested. For example, if you are comparing two hardware systems, you should compare the results from the same benchmark, with the same number of users, and using the same database software. When comparing database software, the results should be obtained using the same hardware system.

System Utilization

You should avoid extrapolating standard benchmark results to size your database system. Most standard benchmark results are obtained with near 100% utilization of most system resources. Such benchmarks excel as stress-tests, but are poor indicators for performance on real-world applications, where most system resources are less than fully utilized. Good designs underutilize system resources on purpose. If your disks are 100% utilized on an average day, you are likely to have a lot of frustrated customers during peak seasons.

In general, it is worth keeping in mind that vendors are allowed to publish the best recorded numbers. The best results for SQL Server might come when twenty users are on the system, but a competing vendor might have peak performance with only 10 users. This can make direct comparisons difficult because vendors seldom publish data on exactly the same systems and configurations. Cynics might say that this is done on purpose to complicate direct comparisons.

1.2 WHAT IS PERFORMANCE TUNING?

Performance tuning is the process of configuring your database system to meet performance objectives. Defining your performance objectives, in measurable quantities, makes it easy to assess your success or failure. If your goals are poorly defined, or defined in quantities that are impossible to measure, it is hard to say if you have succeeded in delivering a well performing system or even that the system is ready for delivery.

1.2.1 Project Development

The task of tuning takes various shapes and forms during different phases of a project. It is important to start thinking about performance as early and as often as possible. It is also important to define your performance goals in quantities that can be measured objectively and reliably.

Specification Phase

During the specification phase, you need to assess the performance requirements of your system. You may find that the performance requirements given to you are incomplete. Now is the time to document all of the important performance measures of the system.

An essential, but often overlooked part of requirements is the need for growth and scalability. Requirements change over time and you need to plan for projected changes in the usage of the database system. If your requirements have very specific performance metrics, you should consider specifying the appropriate system monitors at this time.

This is a good time to set appropriate performance expectations.

Planning Phase

During the planning phase, you need decompose the overall performance requirements of the system into its components in order to identify components critical to performance. In most applications, you will find that certain components limit the overall performance of the system. Improving these **critical path** components improves the system as a whole. Clearly, you need to focus your energy on critical path components. Improving a component that is not on the critical path might be fun and interesting, but it does not improve the overall performance of the application. Different features of your application may have different critical paths. Within SQL Server the components in the critical path for dump and load differ from the components in the critical path for updating a row in a table.

Product Selection

During the product selection phase, you need to identify products that can deliver the required performance. Knowledge of the requirements beforehand eliminates guesswork and enables you to order the right size and options for each component. Through an understanding of your own performance requirements, you can correctly interpret the performance information given to you about products you are considering. For some products, the information you need about their performance is readily available. For example, the size and throughput of disk drives are usually well documented. For some other components, you need to make estimates based on industry standard benchmarks. For others, you may need to run your own tests to determine whether they can meet the performance requirements.

Design Phase

During the design phase, you need to ensure that each component meets its performance requirements. Often, you will find it useful to instrument critical components. For example, if you expect that the performance of writes to the log disk is critical to the application's performance, you may want to include instrumentation that monitors throughput of writes to the log disk. Being able to observe the behavior of individual components enables you to identify bottlenecks quickly.

During design it is important to document all design assumptions. For example, if you assumed that the log will be located on an exclusive drive, it is better to document this assumption than to risk having it violated by subsequent changes.

Analysis Phase

During the analysis phase, you need to test components, as well as the overall system, to ensure that the performance requirements are met. Unit tests can be used to exercise individual components and features in isolation to measure the limits of their performance. However, a greater challenge is to find a realistic workload before the system is put into production. A simulated workload is helpful, but may be a poor substitute for real usage if your application has a complex usage pattern. In some cases, you may have the option of deploying the system in multiple phases. If the design is properly instrumented, you can collect a wealth of information on the performance of components and the overall system during earlier phases of deployment.

Documentation Phase

During the documentation phase, you should document information regarding performance of components, including performance observed during unit tests. Compare the expected performance with the observed performance. Document any anomalies. Include assumptions, if any, that were made about the usage and performance of the component.

Maintenance

Once a project goes into a maintenance phase, many performance tuning choices are no longer available to you. You need to tune the performance of the system without adversely affecting the functional behavior of the system. In many cases, a system in maintenance cannot tolerate extended down time, to implement a new physical database design for example. On the positive side, with a complete design you have a limited number of unknowns. A limited number of choices makes it easier to make a decision and act.

1.2.2   Server and Hardware Configuration

Within the bounds of physics, almost any performance problem can be solved with an unlimited budget. Most applications are constrained by cost. The result is a compromise. Once the application is fast enough, the extra cost of making it faster is difficult to justify. Buying undersized hardware frustrates your ability to achieve your performance objectives. Savings in hardware are eroded over time by excessive user wait time and the programming effort to get every last ounce of performance from the system. Oversized hardware imposes extra costs on your organization reducing your competitiveness.

Deciding on the right amount of hardware for your application is more art than science. There are several moving targets in this equation, including the hardware, the system software, your application, and system usage. Improvements in hardware performance and capacity have been rather dramatic in recent years. Processors double in performance every 18 months or so. Disk and memory sizes are not lagging far behind. Notwithstanding a slow start, network and system bus bandwidths are picking up. System software, on the other hand, seems to have addressed functionality and scalability more than raw performance. Sybase provides new releases of SQL Server at regular intervals, some with significantly different performance characteristics. Most applications also undergo significant changes during their lifetime. Last, but not the least, for most database systems, usage is unpredictable.

What criteria should you use to select a system? Listed below are some of the basic parameters that are generally important when defining database applications.

- **Disk** — Disk drives hold the data for your application. What are the disk input/output requirements for your application? How much data is stored? How much data needs to move between the disk drives and SQL Server? Obviously, the more data you have, the more disks you need. With disk drive capacity surpassing 8 Gigabytes, it might be difficult imagining the need for a large number of drives. However, more important than capacity is throughput. A disk drive can find and transfer information only so quickly. Your application might benefit from a large number of smaller drives.

- **Network** — How much data must move between the clients and SQL Server? The choice of network protocol is largely irrelevant to performance. In general, there are other considerations that weigh more heavily. What is the capacity of your network? Can you transfer the information quickly enough to your clients? It might be necessary to put more than one network adapter in the server.

- **CPU Capacity** — How much computation does SQL Server perform in your application? Computation for a database is more than figuring numbers. The CPU is heavily involved in string manipulations, pattern searches, query optimization, buffer scans, and resource management. Hardware and software vendors talk about scalability. This is a measure of how much extra *oomph* you get out of the server by adding another CPU. In a perfect world, adding a second CPU to a system would double the capacity of the system. Statements by hardware and software vendors notwithstanding, scaling by CPU is not assured and it is dangerous to extrapolate on the basis of CPU count. Just because one CPU can handle 100 transactions per second, adding a second CPU to the machine does not give you 200 transactions per second. Very few applications achieve 100% scaling. The physical and algorithmic limitations in the hardware, the operating system, the database system, and your application all conspire to reduce the scalability.

- **Log Throughput/Transactions per Second** — How quickly is data updated, inserted, or deleted from tables? What is the volume of data involved? All versions of SQL Server log changes to data in the database's transaction log and use a single database device for the transaction log.[2] You should make sure that your application does not overwhelm the transaction log device.

- **Large Table Scans, Index Scans** — Does SQL Server need to scan large tables? Can index scans be used in place of table scans? You need to construct the database to minimize SQL Server's use of the disk drives. Reading the disk

---

[2.] While you can create a database that uses more than one log device, at any given time SQL Server is writing log records to only one of those devices.

for data is expensive. Reading all of a large table to find one row of data is prohibitive resulting in a severe bottleneck on this operation. Hence, you should place appropriate indexes on your tables and write your queries to take advantage of the table and index schema.

- **Batch Operations** — How do you plan to backup your database? How often do you dump the transaction log? When do you run the database consistency checks? There is more to running your application than just fielding queries. You should make sure the data is available and recoverable. Dump operations are important and can negatively impact performance if not planned well. System 10 SQL Server uses an Open Server application called Backup Server to perform database dumps. Performance of System 10 SQL Server dumps far exceeds that of previous versions of SQL Server. Backup Server can simultaneously dump your database or transaction log to more than one tape drive using a device striping strategy.

Unfortunately, there are no good rules of thumb for figuring these parameters for the general case. You need to think about these issues as you plan your application.

1.2.3 Maximizing Hardware Utilization

SQL Server and the hardware to run it are probably the most expensive and critical components of your Sybase database application. Unfortunately, SQL Server or the underlying operating system and hardware often throttle the maximum performance of your application. Collecting the pieces, and getting them to work together effectively is part of the challenge. There are a number of tasks that can help make SQL Server maximize the hardware you make available:

- **Load Balancing Disk Utilization** — You want to take advantage of all of the disk drives on your system. If you put all of the frequently used tables and indexes on one disk drive, that one disk drive is a bottleneck. Spreading the work over several disk drives can improve the performance of your application.

- **Load Balancing Disk Controllers** — Spreading the data over many disk drives often is not enough for high throughput applications. Often you need to spread the load over multiple disk controllers as well.

- **Load Balancing Network** — As with disk drives, you want to load balance between network adapters. A single network card can be a bottleneck if you have a lot of data that flows between the clients and SQL Server.

- **Using Multiple Processors** — SQL Server's *Virtual Server Architecture* allows SQL Server to take advantage of multiprocessor computer systems. For multi-user applications, adding more processors can significantly improve the performance.

- **Maximizing Memory** — Reading data out of RAM is much faster than reading data from a disk drive. Adding more memory to your system often means that more data can temporarily reside in RAM, and SQL Server has to read data from disk drives less frequently.

1.2.4 Application Development

SQL Server employs a client/server architecture. This means the client programs that provide the look and feel of the application are separate from SQL Server, which stores the data and enforces data integrity and consistency rules. This inherent modularity allows you to tune SQL Server separately from the client front ends. Examples of tasks involved in tuning applications are:

- **Understanding how SQL Server stores and retrieves data** — The algorithms SQL Server uses to lock, record, and read data have many performance implications. Understanding these implications allows you to plan your application so that it works with SQL Server rather than at cross purposes.

- **Working with SQL Server's query optimizer** — The SQL Server query optimizer tries to find the fastest route to your data. Understanding how the optimizer interprets the query makes it possible for you to coerce the optimizer into giving you the best query plan or at worst avoid mediocre plans.

- **Taking advantage of performance optimizations in SQL Server** — Many operations in SQL Server have optimized special cases. Sometimes, these are optimizations that proved useful in improving the performance of SQL Server in certain customer applications or industry standard benchmarks. Your application should take advantage of these optimizations whenever possible.

While we focus on tuning the SQL Server part of your application, it is possible that the client is a bottleneck in your application. If your clients are running at 100%, but SQL Server is not fully utilized, you need to look at your clients as a possible bottleneck. In Chapter 8, *Monitoring SQL Server*, we discuss ways of monitoring SQL Server.

1.2.5 Troubleshooting

Even the perfect plan and execution may require some firefighting. That is, you may often find yourself fixing problems that you wish somebody had seen coming. There are several reasons why firefighting is almost inevitable, some justifiable and some not. The most common reason is oversight. In a complex system, it is easy to make an error in estimating the performance required of some component and have this component show up as an unexpected bottleneck at a very late stage. Another reason is incomplete specification of requirements. Yet another is a change in the way the database system is used.

Working with a mature design can be both challenging and rewarding. Typical challenges include incomplete specifications, poor documentation, unreasonable expectations, limits on permissible changes, and a demanding schedule. Suppose the application is already in production and its performance is deemed unacceptable. Your challenge is to work within the confines of the current specifications and produce dramatic improvements in performance. The reward is in doing just that. Sometimes, you may find and fix the one bottleneck in the system that is solely responsible for the performance problems. Sometimes, you may be able to redesign parts of the system without breaking anything else, and still meet the performance requirements. And then there are times when the only viable solution is a major redesign of the entire system.

Finding the Problem

The first half of the problem is identifying the components critical to performance. Does each component of the system meet the performance requirements outlined in the functional specifications? If not, is the component on the critical path? The techniques discussed in Chapter 8, *Monitoring SQL Server*, and Chapter 9, *Instrumenting SQL Code*, will assist you in answering these questions.

Often, the source of the problem is an assumption about the application, SQL Server, or the client that is no longer valid. It helps to start by checking whether the features and components of the system agree with the assumptions made about them. Some of this information can be obtained by monitoring SQL Server. For other information, you need to instrument the application and gather statistics on its usage.

Another common source of problems is a change in the use of the system. You need to check whether the current workload matches the workload used to justify design decisions. Has the volume of data and the number of users changed? How about the distribution or arrival rate of jobs?

Yet another common source of problems is a failure that activates a failover mechanism. Most database systems have a large number of failover mechanisms built-in to protect against possible component failures. Typically, a single failure causes the system to keep functioning properly, albeit at a reduced performance.

Solving the Problem

You may be faced with just a few or a plethora of options once you have identified the problem. Examples of options that may be available to you are: rewriting queries, creating new tables, triggers, stored procedures and indexes, relocating data on disks, changing the configuration of SQL Server, redesigning the client applications, and upgrading hardware. Your challenge is to find the option that compromises neither the functionality of the system nor the performance of unrelated features or components, and still has the required improvement in performance.

The path to the correct solution may involve several failed attempts. Two simple precautions can make the process easier: **instrumentation** and **change control**. Instrumenting the application enables you to observe the behavior of the components affected by the change and verify that effect of the change is as intended. If that is not the case, or if some other untoward effect of the change surfaces at some later stage, a change control mechanism enables you to undo the change with minimal effort. Document the reason, assumptions, justifications, and observed effect of each change, including the changes you undo. Having such documentation makes the system easier to maintain. In addition, proper documentation may prevent the effects of your change from being nullified unintentionally by a change in some other part of the system.

1.3   STRATEGIES FOR SUCCESS

The best time to start tuning a database application for performance is before it is implemented. A dollar or minute spent in addressing performance in the early stages of design and development can save many in later stages. We cannot overemphasize the importance of addressing performance in all phases of a project, including specification of requirements, design, development, testing, and maintenance.

1.3.1   How to Do It Right

There is no easy, surefire process for performance tuning. However, here are some hints that may make your task a little easier.

Set Goals and Expectations

Listen to end-users. Understand what your users expect and formulate performance goals and requirements that meet those expectations. If you are planning for a new application, you should understand what your users expect out of the application. If you are troubleshooting, this information may be readily available in relation to the current performance (e.g., "We need to process queries twice as fast."). In either case, users undoubtedly tell you that they expect applications to respond "faster." Unfortunately, terms like "faster" are difficult to measure. You need to turn these expectations into quantified requirements that relate to the metrics in your system.

- How long are users willing to wait for a response from the system?
- How many transactions are going to be processed per minute?
- What is the expected workload on the system? Frequency of transactions? Batch operations?
- Which of these factors is the most important?

It pays to be conservative in your estimates and design for probable under estimates.

Address Performance Early in the Design Cycle

Plan with performance in mind. Turn the performance goals and requirements into metrics and apply the metrics to your application. Verify that meeting the metrics allows you to meet the system's performance goals. It is too late to think about performance after the application is deployed. Post-production tuning gives you some gains, but extensive tuning is more akin to reverse-engineering, re-implementing, and firefighting. Once an application is in the field, it is difficult to make extensive changes.

Source Code Control System

Firefighting can lead to more firefighting. It is often the case that enhancing the performance of one component or feature degrades that of another, or, even worse, breaks some essential functionality. Users complain, management points fingers, and no one is happy. It helps to use a change control system that enables you to rollback code changes individually. When a change does not have desired effect you can quickly back out the change.

Plan for Growth

Your application may need to grow with the demands of the business. Consider the sources of growth. Is the company growing? Is the scope of the application expanding? Is the application a historical database? How much data is added each day? each month? each year? Is your customer base growing?

As you plan your application, you need to consider how you will grow your application to meet demand. Does the design of your application scale with expected growth in its scope or usage? Will you need to buy a bigger server, more network capacity, more client machines? Can you partition the application so that some of the clients talk to one server and other clients talk to a different server?

Verify and Document Performance

As components are implemented and tested, verify that each component meets its target metric. Include performance metrics as part of your quality process. An application that is too slow can be just as damaging to your organization as an application that gives you the wrong answers.

Recognize Trade-offs

Performance metrics often have complementary requirements. The trade-off between cost and throughput and between cost and response are obvious. Less obvious is the trade-off between throughput and response. For example, consider multiple concurrent transactions, where each transaction accesses a few pages from a disk in random order. One way to improve throughput is to have SQL Server group multiple transactions into a single large transaction, thus enabling optimizations such as escalation of page locks to table locks and reordering page accesses to replace random I/O by sequential I/O. However, this also degrades response, since the earlier transactions are put on hold until a large enough group of transactions has arrived at SQL Server.

Given the complementary requirements of response, throughput, and other metrics, you are often faced with a multivariate optimization. For example, one application may require you to maximize throughput without violating constraints on response and total cost, another may require you to minimize response with constraints on cost and throughput, and yet another may require you to minimize cost with constraints on response, but without any concern for throughput. The important thing is to know what the constraints are and which metric is being optimized.

1.3.2   How to Do It Wrong

Learning from your mistakes is a valuable skill. Learning from others' mistakes is even better. Here are some lessons we learned the hard way.

Tune Everything in Sight

Often, only a few components are critical to the performance of a large, complex system. Trying to get the most performance out of a component that is not critical to overall performance is, of course, fruitless. Also, you need to recognize the point of diminishing returns. Suppose you identify a component as being critical to performance and start improving its performance. Soon, it is no longer critical to performance. Now, it is in your interest to reorder your priorities and move onto the next task, no matter how tempting it is to keep improving this component now that you know how to do it better.

Overlook Fundamental Limitations

At some point, a major redesign is the only way to meet the performance objectives. Avoid the temptation to keep making small, incremental improvements in performance, while ignoring the fundamental limitations of the current design or approach. For example, if your throughput requirements far exceed the limits of a centralized server, your best option may be to redesign the application so that the workload is partitioned across multiple servers. The hard part is to recognize when the requirements exceed the fundamental limitations of the current design.

Beyond design limitations are the physical limitations of the real world. The laws of physics put an absolute limit on the performance of computer hardware. Light travels about one foot in a nanosecond and it is impossible to make a single component smaller than an atom. While most commercial systems are far from reaching these limitations, the existing hardware and software database technology effectively limits the size and performance of your application. An ambitious application should be firmly rooted in the realities of current technology.

Tuning before Stability

While performance issues should be addressed at all stages of a project, it is nearly impossible to add performance tweaks to an application unless the functionality of the application is stable. Is the response time poor because the access to a table is not performing as expected or because the query is joining the wrong tables together? A complete test suite for the application simplifies the job of the performance engineer. After tweaking the application, you can see if the application still operates according to the required functionality.

Rely on Prototypes

Prototypes can help you verify your performance assumptions, but do not be tempted to skip the performance design stage because you have a working prototype. How do you know that the prototype's performance scales to the full system? Are you using the same hardware? What are the limitations of the design? Are the bottlenecks in the prototype the same as the bottlenecks in the completed system?

Work with Incompatible Components

Fast components do not necessarily add up to a fast system. They need to work with each other. How often have you been told that a vendor has the solutions to all of your requirements, but in separate and incompatible products? Or that the solution is available in the new release of the product, which happens to be incompatible with other products already in your design?

There is no silver bullet for the problem of incompatibility. But there are measures you can take to protect yourself. You can always insist on the highest level of compatibility by requiring that each component and feature abide by the most conservative industry standard. But that may lead you to a least common denominator solution, which works with the largest variety of products, but not well with any one product. On the other hand, you could bet your business on the products from a single vendor, or those based on a marginal standard. But that could lead you to a dead-end in terms of the longevity of your design. Your best bet is to start with a layered, modular design that allows the interaction between components to be changed without a major redesign. For example, you can use vendor-specific, non-standard features in components critical to performance in a manner that allows their replacement by industry standard features at a later time.

1.4   MORE PRECIOUS THAN PERFORMANCE

While achieving your performance goals is important, there are some aspects of SQL Server systems that are even more important. You should never trade getting the right answer for getting the wrong answer quickly.

1.4.1   Assuring Availability

A high-performance system should also be highly available. A system that is frequently down does not render answers at all quickly. On the other hand, building a 100% uptime system is very difficult and extremely expensive. There are about 9,000 hours in a year. A 99% reliable system is allowed 90 hours of downtime per year. That is more than three and a half days. 99.9% gives you nine hours of downtime per year, or an entire business day. You should consider the trade-offs. Adding reliability adds cost. Can you afford a complete copy of your hardware installation for backup? Can you afford not to?

The key to reliability is recoverability. You should devise a plan to make recovery quick and painless. It is possible to improve the reliability of a SQL Server application by anticipating possible failures.

Hardware Failure

Computer systems have lots of parts. We have personally experienced a variety of failures:

- Utility line power
- Power supply unit
- Disk drive/Disk controller

- CPU unit/Floating point unit[3]
- Memory card
- Network adapter

Some systems have built in redundancy. The cabinet might include two power supplies. If one fails, the other takes over and the computer continues to run. Such systems are expensive, so most systems rely on non-redundant hardware. A compromise might be to have spare parts on hand in case of failure. If a component like the power supply fails, you have a backup unit available to swap in.

For most applications, the data is the most valuable component of the application. As a result, many systems allow you to "mirror" disk data. This means the same information is stored on more than one physical disk. If one disk fails, the data can be recovered from the other.

Operating System Failure

On Unix they are called "system panics," on Microsoft Windows a "general protection violation," but the real meaning is that something is wrong and the operating system has no way of correcting the problem. These happen more frequently when the system is pushed to its limit, or some highly unusual sequence of events occurs. We rarely see operating system failures on our benchmarking systems. You can protect yourself by running stable, tested versions of the operating system. Upgrade the operating system on your development or quality assurance systems before you upgrade your production system. Verify that your application performs as expected on the new operating system before you deploy it on your production system.

SQL Server Failure

All programmable applications are difficult to test, more so are database systems. It is impossible to test comprehensively every combination of datatype, access method, and transaction. Hence, SQL Server is not perfect and it occasionally makes a mistake. In general, the mistakes do not corrupt your data, though on occasion you must resort to backup tapes to recover a database. Errors in the database are generally detected well after the error actually occurred. The database

---

[3.] This led to a curious problem on a four processor system. Roughly every fourth floating operation had the wrong result. A program in a tight loop calculating 2.0*2.0 gave 4.0 3/4 of the time and 0.0 1/4 of the time.

consistency check (DBCC) commands are the tools you use to verify the state of your database. By running these commands periodically, you are assured that your database is in a consistent state.

Sybase certifies each version of SQL Server against a particular operating system version. Sometimes the operating system includes patches from the vendor to provide important last minute fixes to problems. Make sure you are running the certified version of the operating system with the correct patches. Sybase and the hardware vendor can help you determine if you are running a certified combination. While its generally possible to run SQL Server on a "compatible" but not certified operating system version, we strongly advise against the practice except for experimental or developmental systems.

1.4.2   Recovery Time

For mission-critical applications, availability is just as important as throughput and response time. In the event of a system failure, you want to minimize the amount of time it takes to restart your application. SQL Server allows you to control how long it takes to recover from a system failure.

Recovery is the process of reading the log and verifying that the changes recorded in the log are stored in the database. Complete transactions are recorded in the database (i.e., rolled forward) and transactions that are not completely represented in the log are removed from the database (i.e., rolled back). The amount of time it takes to run recovery depends on how much change history is stored in the log since the last checkpoint. The more change history, the longer it takes to run recovery. Some applications have very strict availability requirements, that is, the application must be available every minute of every day. When SQL Server is running recovery on a database, applications cannot use the database, so the application is unavailable.

SQL Server periodically checkpoints the database to limit the time it takes to run recovery. The `recovery interval in minutes` configuration value sets the maximum amount of time you are willing to wait for recovery of the database to complete. Unfortunately, checkpoints are not free. During a checkpoint, SQL

Server briefly suspends activity in the database and applications that need to update the database are suspended until the checkpoint is complete.[4] This means the application's throughput declines while SQL Server checkpoints the database.

You can avoid frequent automatic checkpoints by setting a large `recovery interval in minutes`. This means you may have to wait a long time for recovery to complete if SQL Server shuts down unexpectedly. If your application cannot tolerate extended downtime, consider writing a separate program that logs into SQL Server at regular intervals and manually checkpoints the database with the `checkpoint` command. This strategy is particularly useful if your application has bursts of activity at predictable intervals. This is not as useful for applications with a steady stream of database activity. For applications with a steady flow of changes it is best to let SQL Server automatically checkpoint the database and suffer the periodic drops in application performance.

1.4.3 Hot Standby

Reliability is an important performance metric. A system that is down has zero throughput and infinite response time. A hot standby is a system that is "waiting in the wings" to stand in for the primary system. Depending on your application, it might be a complete duplicate of the primary system or you might get by with your development system. If you are worried about natural disasters (e.g., earthquakes, floods) or office emergencies (e.g., fires, bomb threats, terrorists, government coups) your hot standby might be in a different building, a different city, or perhaps even a different country. Building a reliable system requires careful planning. Sybase provides a number of features that make it easier.

Companion Server

Applications running on VMS and OpenVMS can use Companion Server. With Companion Server, the primary SQL Server runs your application, while Companion Server stands by waiting to run recovery on the databases. If the primary SQL Server goes down, the Companion Server runs recovery on the databases and is up and running very quickly. There are no adverse performance implications to using Companion Server with your VMS or OpenVMS SQL Server. Future versions of SQL Server extend this capability to more operating systems and reduce the time it takes to complete the fail-over from the primary to the backup system.

---

4. This is a simplification. For more details, see Chapter 5, *SQL Server — Methods and Features*.

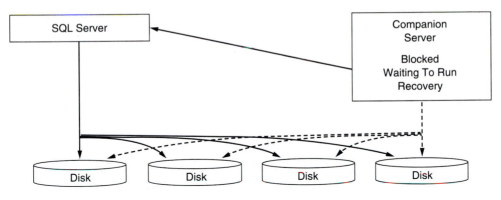

Figure 1.1   Companion Server -

Replication Server

4.9.2, System 10, and later versions of SQL Server applications can use Replication Server to replicate transactions made in one SQL Server into another SQL Server. Replication Server reads the transaction log of the primary SQL Server and mimics the changes in the subscriber SQL Servers. Transactional integrity is maintained, so partial transactions are not replicated. Replication Server is useful if you need to keep many copies of a database synchronized with one another. Because Replication Server uses the transaction log of SQL Server, using Replication Server has some subtle performance implications (see Chapter 6, *Physical Database Design*).

It is possible to build your own Replication Server-like software. You can use dump and load to dump databases and transaction logs periodically and load them into your hot standby. System 10 SQL Server dump and load performance is significantly better than in previous versions of SQL Server. You can also use bcp to dump and load particular tables. These approaches are not without their drawbacks. Dump database takes a heavy toll on disk activity. Dump tran affects database logging operations. The bcp operation acquires read locks on the source table. Chapter 12, *Batch Processing Performance*, discusses these issues.

With careful and clever planning you can build a reliable system that also meets your performance requirements. Depending on your application, you may find that a home-grown solution is a better fit to your performance and reliability needs than commercial packages. But whatever path you take, in a mission-critical application reliability concerns must outweigh performance considerations.

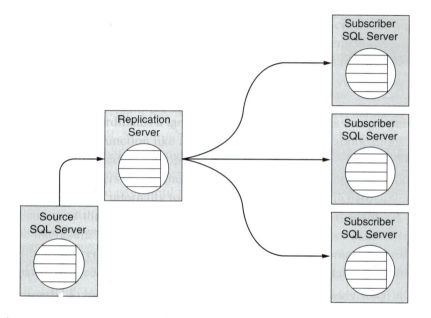

Figure 1.2   Replication Server- -

1.4.4   Modularity

A well designed, modular application is a pleasure to maintain and enhance. A poorly designed monolithic application is everyone's worst nightmare. Unfortunately, good modularity often gets in the way of maximum performance.

Modular code generally employs abstraction layers to isolate one part of the application from the operational details of another. The abstraction layers act like translators. They translate requests made through a "generic" interface into operations that are specific to the module being called. The translations and the function calls themselves impose an operational overhead on the application. Graphical applications are a good example. The interface to the screen generally has some abstraction layer so that the same application will work on a variety of displays. As long as the application uses only the "generic" interface and does not try to use a feature specific to only one kind of video hardware, the application works on any video system.

There are many significant benefits to modular development. Application construction can go more quickly since you have pre-built modules at your disposal. Good modular programs are easy to maintain because of the isolation between the modules. Changes to one module do not affect the behavior of another, a useful characteristic if your application needs to evolve quickly. You can plan the modules to help isolate your application from the hardware, operating system, and commercial software that your application relies on.

If the application is deployed at more than one site you may want to plan your modules to isolate the application from installation-specific information. For example, you might create a module that communicates with SQL Server. Only that module knows the name of SQL Server, the login name, and password. This is the only part of the application that needs to change if this information varies from installation to installation. This kind of isolation makes it easy to bring new sites on-line quickly and is useful for disaster recovery.

The purpose of modular design is to isolate one component of the system from the operational details of the other components. As a result, one component cannot optimize for the other by putting requests in the proper order or the like. An individual component can optimize requests that it receives, but it must anticipate the requests in advance. This is not necessarily optimal and can involve a lot of extra logic to work well. All of this extra processing is more overhead that slows down the application.

Considering the benefits of modularity: ease of maintenance, portability, simplicity of design, and rapid development, the advantages of modularity generally outweigh the performance drawbacks.

1.4.5 Transactional Semantics

Loosening the isolation between transactions can improve the throughput of your application, but changing the isolation level without careful analysis of your application invites disaster. ANSI SQL defines the following four levels of isolation between concurrent transactions. These are listed in Table 1.1.

Table 1.1   ANSI Isolation levels

Isolation Level	Description
0	Prevent dirty writes. No isolation. All is fair. Transactions can read uncommitted data.
1	Prevent dirty reads. Transactions cannot read uncommitted data.
2	Serializable repeatable reads. Reads are repeatable and transactions serializable.
3	Eliminate phantoms.

The higher isolation levels include the isolation characteristics of the lower levels. Isolation between transactions is enforced by acquiring and holding locks on the tables or rows of tables that participate in the transactions. Isolation level influences performance primarily by dictating how long locks are held. While it is important to study the relation between isolation levels and performance, we do not believe that isolation level is a commodity to be traded for performance.

1.4.6 Recommendations

As the application planner, you have to make decisions about performance trade-offs. Perhaps your application can accept a long recovery time, or the lack of a hot standby, or a monolithic program, or transactional errors while reading a table. Then again, perhaps not.

Chapter 2

Hardware and System Software

The challenge of building a client/server application is understanding the interaction of all the pieces:

- The front end, or client, application that communicates with users

- The computers to run the front end applications

- The SQL Server and other back end, server programs

- The hardware to run the back end processing

- The network to glue all the pieces together

- Getting all the operating systems to communicate with one another

For clients, you can develop your own using Sybase's Open Client or Embedded SQL products, develop in a programming language like Visual Basic, or use an application builder like PowerBuilder from PowerSoft. Alternatively you can purchase complete application suites from companies like Peoplesoft, etc.

This chapter describes some of the choices you have to make for hardware, operating system, and software given an emphasis on your application's performance.

2.1 SERVER SYSTEM

Building a fast database application requires a good design, fast computer hardware, an efficient operating system, and performance database software. Several components of the server system conspire to limit SQL Server's performance. These are:

- **Disk drives and controllers** — Limit how quickly SQL Server (or any database product) can access and update information.

- **Memory** — Limits how much information SQL Server can store in its cache in order to avoid reading the disks.

- **Central processing units** — Limit how quickly information is found and processed.

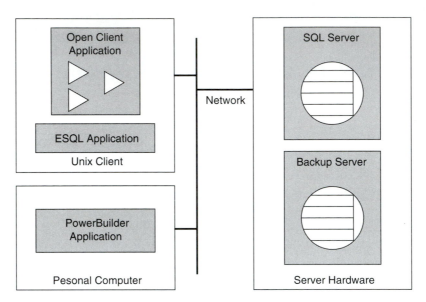

Figure 2.1   Client-Server application -

- **Network** — Limits the rate at which data is exchanged between the client and server.
- **Operating system** — Limits how efficiently programs like SQL Server use the hardware.
- **The efficiency of SQL Server itself** — The algorithms and implementation of SQL Server imposes limits on how efficiently it locates, updates, and processes information.

Everyone would like to buy the fastest, biggest, most powerful computer system for their application. However, in the real world, money spent on hardware and software reduces money spent on other areas such as research, development, manufacturing, and sales. You should size your hardware to your application and budget. Ideally, you should purchase only as much system as you need to run your application.

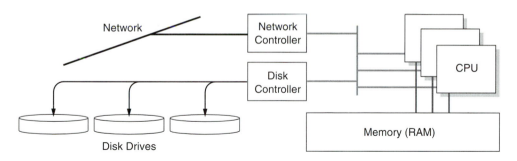

Figure 2.2   Block diagram of a computer system -

2.1.1   Disk Drives

Disk drives use rotating platters coated with magnetic media to store information. A single disk drive may have several platters on a common spindle. An armature moves the disk drive's read/write heads across the platters to playback and record data stored in the magnetic media. The operating system uses disks to store data files, executable images, libraries, and the like. SQL Server uses disks to store tables, indexes, stored procedures, configuration information, etc.

There are two primary roles for disks in a database system. First, they provide a persistence store for data. In case of a power failure or a system reset, the contents of main memory are lost, but the contents of the disk drive survives most failures. Database systems rely on the persistence of writes to disks to ensure the integrity of the databases. Second, they provide a low-cost alternative to main memory. A megabyte of main memory costs orders of magnitude more than a megabyte of disk drive. This encourages us to put multiple gigabytes of data on disks and access it with only a few megabytes of main memory, caching only the most frequently accessed portions of the data.

The performance of disks is often a determining factor in the overall performance of a database system. Let us discuss some of the factors that limit the performance of disks. There is a limit to how quickly a disk drive locates and transfers data. Disk drives have limited capacity for fielding requests to read and write data. You can work around these limitations by spreading the work over many disk drives. Thus, for performance work, it is often more important to have a lot of disk drives than to maximize the space utilization on each drive.

Performance Characteristics

The performance of disk drives may be characterized by several measures. The following sections describe the more important performance characteristics of disk drives for SQL Server.

RPM

Revolutions Per Minute; this is how quickly the disks are spinning. Typical speeds are 3600 and 7200 RPM. The disk's RPM rate affects how quickly data becomes available and how quickly data is transferred to and from the disk. The faster the disk is spinning, the less you have to wait for information to show up under the read/write head and the more information moves under the head in a given amount of time.

Seek Time

The average amount of time it takes the disk's read/write head to move from one part of the disk to another. Most large disk drives have average seek times around 10ms. The faster the head moves from one part of the disk to another, the less time you have to wait for the drive to find the information you need.

Transfer Speed

The rate at which the drive can transfer information to the disk controller. Transfer speeds generally depend on the disk drive's communications interface. The SCSI-2 disk interface has a transfer rate of about 10 Megabytes per second.

Cache Size

Disk drives and disk controllers often have their own cache memory, and use the memory for read-ahead buffering. When the drive is asked for data from a particular part of the disk, it reads that data plus information that is a little ahead of it on the disk. This costs little as the disk drive's read/write head is already positioned to read that information. Read-ahead is done under the assumption that the next request is for information physically located just after the last request. When this happens, the drive sends the information from its cache memory rather than waiting for the information to appear under the read/write head. This saves time if the information you need has just passed the head and you would otherwise have to wait for a complete rotation. Read-ahead buffering helps the performance of sequential scans, but not that of random accesses.

The disk and controller caches can also be used for write-caching. However, write-caching has implications on the ability of the database to recover from failures and should not be enabled indiscriminately. SQL Server assumes that data written to disk is stored on the disk. For this reason, write-caching should be used with caution. Databases can be corrupted if the cache does not have a mechanism to ensure that all writes always make it to persistence media, even in case of a power failure or other disaster.

Transaction Rate

A disk transaction is a read or write of a chunk of data at a particular location on the disk. Disk drives can only field a certain number of transactions per second. A conventional drive can field 50 transactions per second and a good performance drive might handle 100. For example, if each transaction in a database requires one disk operation, a database created on a single high-performance drive can do no more than 100 transactions per second. If each transaction requires two disk operations, you can only get 50 transactions per second. If your application has more ambitious performance goals or more complicated transactions, you must create the database over more than one disk drive and spread your data cleverly over all of the disk drives in the database.

System 10 and previous versions of SQL Server read and write data to disk drives in 2 Kb chunks.[1] Each read or write of a 2 Kb chunk is a disk transaction. So, with conventional disk drives, this limits you to 100 Kb transfer per second, no where near the theoretical transfer rate limit of a SCSI-2 disk drive. System 11 SQL Server reads and writes data in larger chunks. This makes better use of the disk drives as more data is read or updated per disk transaction. For example, with reads and writes of 16 Kb chunks a conventional disk drive can transfer 800 Kb per second. With even larger chunks it is possible to approach the theoretical limit of the disk drive's transfer rate.

[1.] Some platforms, notably Stratus, read and write data in 4 Kb chunks.

Sequential versus Random Access

Disks are generally organized into tracks and sectors. A track is a ring around the disk and each track is divided into a number of sectors. Most Unix systems expect 512 byte sectors.[2] In a disk drive with multiple platters, the same track on each platter is called a cylinder.

The way an application uses a disk drive is characterized by the organization of the data. Sequential access means the data is organized linearly on the drive. The start of one transfer is near the end of the previous transfer. Random access means the data is scattered throughout the drive. Reading or writing data requires we make several requests; the drive asking for data in various places.

Sequential access is much more efficient than random access:

- **Less head movement** — Because sequential data is either in the same cylinder or adjacent cylinders, there is very little motion of the read/write head.

- **No latency** — With sequential data, the read/write head is active continuously and there is no need to wait for information to come around and appear under the read/write head.

- **Better cache utilization** — Disk drives and controllers with cache memory optimize for sequential disk reads.

2.1.2   Disk Controllers

Disk drives require special "glue" to attach them to a computer system. This "glue" is called a disk controller. On one side, the controller communicates with the CPU and main memory and on the other side with the disk drives. The controller receives requests from the CPU to read or write information on one of the disk drives. The controller, in turn, sends the request to the disk drive.

Disk controllers generally include cache memory to hold recently used data. As with a caching disk drive, a caching disk controller can significantly improve performance for reading data from the disks. Some caching controllers also cache writes of data. The controller gets data from the computer's memory and stores it

---

[2]   At this point, we are walking around on terminological quicksand. Disk drive sectors may not correspond with operating system file system blocks (called sectors by some operating systems). The disk drive sectors identify storage for the communication between the disk drive and the operating system. The operating system may, or may not, choose to expose the raw sector information to user applications. Changing the sector size typically requires that the user perform a physical format on the disk drive. This differs from a logical format whereby the operating system places control information (e.g., partitions and file systems) on the disk drive.

in the write cache instead of sending it directly on to the disk drive. After the controller has a copy of the data, it tells the CPU that the data is written. The program that wrote data thinks that the data is written to disk, when in fact, the data is still stored in the memory of the controller. When convenient, the controller schedules the write of the data from its cache to the disk drive. The controller can consolidate read/write requests to minimize the number of disk transactions and to optimize the read/write head movement for optimum performance of the disk drives. The use of write-caching by disk controllers has the same implications on the recoverability as the use of write-caching by disks. However, some controllers employ uninterruptible power supplies to ensure persistence of writes. If the power fails, a battery on the controller maintains power to the controller's cache until the main power is restored.

2.1.3 Disk I/O

SQL Server spends most of its time writing to and reading from disk drives. As a result, optimization of disk I/O is crucial to the performance of SQL Server.

Raw Partitions, File Systems, and Logical Volumes

Typically, the operating system divides disks into disk partitions.[3] Depending on the operating system, partitions may be distinct or overlap. File systems are built in raw partitions and are responsible for managing the files and directories. For most Unix-variants, Sybase recommends using unbuffered raw partitions for database devices rather than buffered files like file system files.[4] If the operating system buffers writes to a Sybase database device file, SQL Server is not assured that data written to disks is actually stored on the disks when the write system call returns. This can make database recovery impossible in the event of a power failure or operating system crash.[5]

On non-Unix operating systems (e.g., OpenVMS, Windows/NT) SQL Server normally uses file system files. In this case, SQL Server asks the operating system not to buffer data transfers between SQL Server and the disks.

---

[3] On Unix, raw partitions are accessed through the character special device files.

[4] The notable exception is Hewlett-Packard HP-UX, where the asynchronous I/O driver requires the block (i.e., buffered) device files. Nevertheless, the asynchronous I/O driver performs all I/O without buffering.

[5] A common misconception is that killing SQL Server may cause corruption of data. This is not generally true. Any data buffered by the operating system is written out when SQL Server is killed. The only way data may be lost is during a system crash, when the operating system does not have an opportunity to write out all of the buffered data.

Several operating system vendors provide logical volumes. A logical volume is a collection of disks that the operating system treats as a single disk device. These collections are called logical volumes to avoid terminological confusion. Logical volumes simplify system administration by allowing you to add and remove disk drives from the logical volumes, to reconfigure the size and quantity of logical volumes without completely re-partitioning the disks. In general, SQL Server performance is not severely affected by using logical volumes. If the system administration ease of logical volumes appeals to you, there is no reason not to use them with SQL Server.[6]

Many customers discover that SQL Server runs faster when database devices are stored on buffered files such as file system files. Response time is improved because the operating system buffers data. When SQL Server requests information, the operating system may find it in one of the buffers and the disk is not accessed. However, for applications with large databases, the performance advantage of file systems is limited. Throughput is limited by the speed of the disk drives and I/O channel. In this case, operating buffering actually impedes performance because the operating system must scan its buffers before accessing the disks.

SQL Server buffering algorithms are improved between System 10 and System 11 SQL Server. We believe that the careful use of the buffer manager in System 11 SQL Server can help reduce the perceived performance gains of using file system files for database devices. We do not recommend using file system files for database devices for any production database system (although there are some exceptions, see Chapter 13, *Advanced Topics*).

Asynchronous Disk I/O

When an operating system process makes a call to an operating system utility function (e.g., read block of data from disk), the process waits for the operating system to complete the request. When the operating system function returns, the process can continue to execute. In programmer terminology, the process **blocks** on the operating system call. These are **synchronous** calls because the process is synchronized with the operating system routines.

[6.] Ensure that SQL Server is certified with logical volumes on your platform.

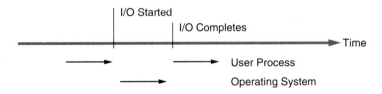

Figure 2.3   Timeline for synchronous I/O -

Asynchronous routines allow the process to continue executing while the operating system function completes the request. For asynchronous disk I/O, the process can ask for a block of data and continues processing while the operating system reads the block of data into memory. When the request is complete, the operating system notifies the process of the completion. The method of notification varies by operating system. Processes running on Unix either receive a signal from the operating system on I/O completion or the process must explicitly poll for completion. VMS and Windows/NT use a call back mechanism. When the I/O request is complete, the operating system calls a routine in your program passing the routine enough information that it can tell which I/O completed.

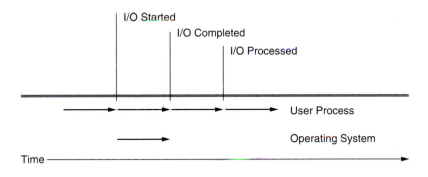

Figure 2.4   Timeline for asynchronous I/O -

Because SQL Server is a single operating system process, asynchronous I/O is very important to good performance. If SQL Server blocks on disk I/O operations, no other useful work can go on until the I/O completes. Threads in SQL Server doing work that does not involve disk I/O must wait for the one thread that needs data read or written from disk. For this reason, SQL Server runs faster when asynchronous I/O is used. All versions of SQL Server support asynchronous I/O, although the support might be limited to certain kinds of files by the operating system or SQL Server. Most Unix operating systems require you to use character special device files to use asynchronous I/O but there are exceptions. This is normally documented in the SQL Server installation guide. By default, Windows/NT and VMS always use asynchronous disk I/O.

SQL Server `errorlog` indicates whether or not asynchronous I/O is used on each database device. Figure 2.5 is a part of an `errorlog` file from a SunOS 4 System 10 SQL Server that contains the asynchronous I/O start-up message.

```
00:95/02/27 13:38:32.41 server  Activating disk 'mpd_log'.
00:95/02/27 13:38:32.41 kernel  Initializing virtual device 1, '/dev/rid012d'
00:95/02/27 13:38:32.41 kernel  Virtual device 1 started using asynchronous i/o.
```

Figure 2.5   Asynchronous I/O messages -

Asynchronous disk I/O is not standardized across Unix operating systems. It is also not a frequently used feature. Many data corruption errors experienced by SQL Server customers are actually errors in the operating system's asynchronous I/O routines. Possible errors include:

- reading the wrong block of data into memory
- writing the wrong block of memory to disk
- indicating that I/O is complete, when in fact it is not
- reading in all zeros rather than the expected data
- failing to report a disk drive error (e.g., bad sector)

SQL Server typically responds with a 605 error (e.g., the object on the database page is not the object that SQL Server expected on the page). If 605 errors are frequent, consider running with asynchronous I/O disabled to see if the problems go away. The 1603 trace flag disables asynchronous I/O. Make sure you report any problems to Sybase technical support so they can be corrected.

2.1.4   Disk Mirroring

Disk drives are mechanical devices and as such are prone to mechanical failure. Information stored on the drive becomes unavailable when it no longer functions properly. As a result it is useful to have copies of your data on more than one drive in the event of a drive failure. Disk mirroring is an automatic way of making an extra copy of the data. When a disk is mirrored all of the information from one drive is copied as it changes onto another drive. This significantly improves reliability. The chances of both drives failing at the same time is far more remote than the chance of only one drive failing. Since your data is on both drives, your application can continue to run even when one of the drive fails.

Disk mirroring is supported at a number of levels within a server system. Some hardware vendors provide controller mirroring. The disk controller is responsible for mirroring the data between drives. You must generally mirror an entire drive. Failover is normally transparent to applications. Mirroring controllers are becoming more common as applications start using many disk drives. Some systems allow you to remove and install mirrored disks without turning off the computer.

Many operating systems now provide for mirroring. At this level, the operating system knows to duplicate a write to a drive to the drive's mirror. You must generally mirror an entire disk drive, although some operating systems allow you to mirror a disk partition. Operating system mirroring imposes more overhead than controller mirroring. Failover is normally transparent to applications.

Controller and operating system mirroring generally allow you to mirror more than two devices together. For extremely critical data, you might want to mirror three devices together. Data is written to all three devices simultaneously and the information on each drive is identical to the others.

SQL Server also supports mirroring. At this level SQL Server duplicates writes to one database device to the device's mirror. You can only have one mirror per device. SQL Server sometimes has trouble detecting disk errors if the operating system shields SQL Server from minor disk errors.

Mirroring all of your data can be expensive for a large application. You need to weigh the trade-offs between the cost of the additional hardware and the expense of system down time.

2.1.5   Disk Striping

Given the performance limitations of a single disk drive to field I/O requests and transfer data, many computer systems allow you to combine several disk drives into a single **logical** drive. This technique is called **disk striping**. The disks that are participating in the logical drive are generally called a **stripe set**.

When the stripe set is created, you can often choose a striping size. This is the amount of sequential data that is stored on each disk in the stripe set. For example, if the striping size is 16K, the first 16K of the stripe set is stored on the first disk, the next 16K on the second, and so forth. When a program needs to write 32K to the stripe set, the first 16K goes to one disk, the second 16K to another.[7]

Because of this organization, stripe sets can help with both random and sequential I/O. For random I/O, any one of the disks in the stripe set may be asked to perform I/O. Thus, the load of processing the random I/O is spread evenly over all of the disks in the stripe set. While individually a disk may be able to field 100 operations per second. A stripe set with four disks can field 400 operations per second, assuming the I/O pattern is truly random.

The benefits to sequential I/O are seen only if the amount of I/O exceeds the striping size. For example, if a program reads 512K from a single disk, the amount of time it takes to retrieve the 512K is limited by the speed of the single disk. If, instead, the read is performed against a stripe set with four disks, and a 16K striping size, then the I/O is spread across all four disks, each disk returning only 128K. The total time taken is the time needed to read 128K from a single disk, rather than 512K.

From the point of view of SQL Server, disk striping is implemented in one of three ways:

1. **Hardware** — Many disk controllers support disk striping.

2. **Operating System** — Several operating systems support disk striping, either directly as part of the disk partitioning system or through logical volume managers.

3. **Physical Database Design** — SQL Server allows you to create tables and indexes on segments. To stripe the table or index over several devices, you can place appropriately sized database devices into the segments (see Chapter 4, *SQL Server — Form and Structure*). Alternatively, you can use the `vstart`

[7.]   This assumes that the I/O operation started on a 16K boundary.

option on the `disk init` command to place several database device files on the same disk drive. Either way, it is possible to spread the I/O for a single table or index across several disks.

2.1.6   Memory

The computer's memory, also called Random Access Memory (RAM), is used to hold transient information. When the computer is turned off, all information stored in RAM is lost. In general, operating systems use RAM to hold data that needs to be accessed quickly: the executing programs, their data, the operating system (which is really just a large program), and any data relevant to the operation of the computer (e.g., process information, data buffers, etc.).

Performance Characteristics

The performance of RAM is generally measured in terms of response time. This is the amount of time it takes the RAM chips to return information after the CPU asks for data. Response times are typically measured in tens of nanoseconds. A modern Pentium-based PC requires RAM with 70ns response time. In general, you do not have much of a choice when selecting RAM for your computer. The manufacturer decides what the best RAM is for your machine. Putting in RAM that is faster than recommended does not necessarily make the computer run any faster and might cause the computer to behave unpredictably.

Most 32 bit computers (e.g., SPARC, PowerPC) can accommodate up to 2Gb RAM. 64 bit computers (e.g., Digital AXP OSF/1) can accommodate more.

Virtual Memory

Given the expense of RAM over disk drives, operating systems provide a mechanism, called **virtual memory**, to substitute disk space for RAM space.[8] There are two basic algorithms generally used by operating systems to implement virtual memory (paging and swapping), but the overall effect in both cases is to take unused information in RAM and store it on disk so the RAM can be used for something else. In this way, a computer with a limited amount of RAM can appear to applications to have much more memory. There is, of course, a significant performance penalty for this charade. Disk drives are much slower than RAM and

---

[8.]   A few operating systems do not provide for virtual memory support, the notable example being Novell Netware.

there is the overhead of planning and executing the substitution. Although not technically accurate in the strictest sense, we will refer to this substitution as **paging** and a block of RAM that is on disk as **paged**.

In a paging environment, the RAM is called **physical memory** and the total memory available to the system because of the disk storage is called **virtual memory**. Computer jargon, having evolved differently at the various companies that founded computing, has other terms for a computer's memory: **main memory**, **core**, **RAM**, etc.

SQL Server's Use of Memory

SQL Server uses memory to hold state information about the users logged into SQL Server and to buffer information read from databases. When a user queries a database, SQL Server reads the information that is needed from disks into its buffers. If other users ask for the same information, SQL Server returns the information in the buffers rather than reading the information again from the disk drives. Since reading RAM is faster than accessing a disk drive, the information comes back much more quickly. The cost of reading the disk drives is born only by the first user to access the data.

For fastest access you should strive to keep all of the active portion of the database buffered in RAM. This is probably reasonable for an application with a small amount of data, but in most cases, it is not possible to have enough RAM to buffer all of the data for your application. Thus, old information in the buffers must "make way" for new information requested by users. SQL Server cannot predict when the information will be needed again, so it uses a fairly simple aging algorithm. The information that is purged first is the information that was least recently used. When information is loaded from disk it is the most recently used information. Any time this same information is used again it is once again made the most recently used information. If the information is not used for a while, it eventually becomes the least recently used information. The more memory you have allocated to buffers, the longer it takes information to migrate from most recently used to least recently used. Thus, information can stay in RAM for more time and there is a greater chance that someone else will use the information before it gets purged.

The benefits of SQL Server buffering data from databases is lost if SQL Server is paged out of RAM by the operating system. SQL Server expects information in buffers to be available very quickly. If the buffers are paged by the operating system onto disks, SQL Server must wait for the buffers to be paged back into RAM before it can use them. Because SQL Server can use asynchronous disk I/O to load data from disk, SQL Server is better off purging a buffer and loading the information from the database on its own. In general, you want to avoid operating system paging when SQL Server is running. You can check for paging using operating system utilities (see Chapter 8, *Monitoring SQL Server*). You can also adjust how much memory SQL Server consumes by changing the `total memory` configuration value. Make sure you adjust this parameter so SQL Server uses almost, but not quite all, of the physical memory available on the system (assuming SQL Server is the only application running on this machine).

Some operating systems allow you to lock a process into RAM. This is usually called **locking physical memory**. SQL Server benefits from being locked into RAM in an environment when other processes on the system might cause the operating system to page SQL Server. This ensures that all of SQL Server's buffers are always in RAM and readily available.

2.1.7 Central Processing Unit

The Central Processing Unit (CPU) of the computer is responsible for coordinating the activity inside the computer. It handles all of the data processing, calculating, and manipulation. For a database application, CPU performance is not as important as disk and network performance. The purpose of a database is to store information and make it available to applications. As a result, databases do not generally do much processing or manipulation of data. That is the responsibility of the client programs.

Cache Memory

Modern CPUs often have instruction and data cache associated with them. This is special memory that is tied closely to the CPU. Accessing information in the cache is much faster than accessing information in the computer's main memory. The instruction cache stores recently used memory pages that include CPU instructions (e.g., the executing program). Data cache stores recently used memory pages that contain data (e.g., something other than the program's instructions).

The larger the cache, the more likely needed program instructions or data can be found in the cache. In computer terms, finding information in cache is called a **cache hit**. If the information that is needed it not in the cache, the CPU must wait for main memory to make the information available. This is called a **cache miss**. The information we need was not found in the cache.

CPUs sometimes have many **levels** of cache. These are referred to as L1, L2, etc., cache. L1 cache is normally built into the CPU's chip and is very fast. L2 cache is normally "further away," located in a separate chip. L2 cache is still faster than main memory, but is slower than L1 cache.

RISC versus CISC

Computer vendors divide the world of CPUs into two broad categories, Reduced Instruction Set Computers (RISC) and Complex Instruction Set Computers (CISC). RISC chips use a relatively small set of simple instructions that are designed to be easy to implement by chip designers but a little harder to program by compiler writers. CISC chips have larger more complex instruction sets that are easier to program but are more difficult to implement in silicon.

RISC chips include Silicon Graphic's MIPS, Sun's SPARC, Digital's AXP, HP's PARISC, and IBM's RS/6000 and PowerPC. CISC chips include Digital's VAX, Motorola's 68000 series, and Intel's 386, 486, and Pentium processors. The newest CISC chips are incorporating various components of RISC technology in a bid to improve performance.

Hardware vendors may not agree with this statement, but the choice of CPU is largely irrelevant to achieving strong database performance. What is more important is disk and network performance.

2.1.8   Network

In a client/server application, the network is the webbing that holds all the pieces together. The capacity of the network eventually limits the rate of data transfer between clients and servers. In general, the greater the distances between sites and the higher the capacity of the network, the higher the cost to maintain the connection.

Your choice of network protocol and hardware, more likely than not, is dictated by factors other than performance. For example, the computers running your application may need to co-exist with computers already at your facility.

For the purposes of understanding network protocols in relation to SQL Server, we can divide the description of a network in the following layers:[9]

- **Tabular Data Stream (TDS)** — Specification for the dialog used to transfer data between Sybase clients and servers.

- **Application Programming Interface (API)** — Operating system provided functions a program (e.g., SQL Server) uses to communicate with other programs through the network. In the Unix environment, the two primary programming models are Berkeley sockets and the Transport Layer Interface (TLI).

- **Network Protocol** — Description of how the information is communicated through the network. Examples are TCP/IP, DECnet, and SPX/IPX (Novell Netware).

- **Physical Network** — What information looks like in the network (e.g., signalling patterns, voltage levels, etc.) and how the parts of the network are physically plugged into one another. Examples are ethernet and token ring.

The networking layers are largely independent of one another. Sybase TDS works equally well with the socket API or the TLI API. Either interface is used to communicate with a variety of network protocols. A network protocol like TCP/IP works equally well through a coaxial cable as it does over serial lines using Serial Line IP (SLIP) or Point to Point Protocol (PPP).

All versions of SQL Server support TCP/IP. Some SQL Server implementations also support SPX/IPX, DECnet, and Named Pipe. Check with your Sybase sales representative if you have special networking requirements.

The quality of the network implementation varies from vendor to vendor. You may find that one vendor's TCP/IP is robust and performs well, while another seems to mysteriously crash the computer. Sybase has found performance differences of up to 20% when comparing the performance of network protocols on otherwise identical systems. If your application involves transferring large amounts of data between the clients and SQL Server, make sure you run your own tests or get results from the vendors that are easily comparable. Remember to

---

[9.] The International Standards Organization (ISO) defines the Open Systems Interconnection (OSI) model for networking, which is useful for defining networking standards. This model incorporates more detail than is described here.

check on the network protocol used for any benchmarks you are using for comparisons. Make sure the benchmarks use the network protocol you are planning to use or at least that all of the benchmarks use the same network protocol.

When planning a high performance application it is important to consider the throughput and response time of the network. Consider the amount of data flowing through each segment of the network. If you concentrate all of your network traffic onto one piece of wire, make sure that wire has enough capacity to handle all of the traffic. Balancing the load between various parts of the network can help improve performance. In some cases, the performance of a computer can be adversely affected by an extremely busy network. For this reason, for example, Sybase uses an isolated network for performance testing of SQL Server. We find that the benchmark results are much more consistent when the benchmark machine is on the isolated network.

A number of companies provide products and services to help you find bottlenecks in your network. Your network hardware provider can probably get you in touch with these companies.

As with disk drives, the computer needs a network adapter to communicate with the network. Larger computer systems can accommodate more than one network adapter allowing the system to talk to more than one network at a time. Adding more network adapters to a computer significantly increases the network bandwidth of the machine. By judiciously placing clients on different networks, you can balance the load across the network so that no one network is overloaded.

2.2 SYSTEM SOFTWARE

The operating system is the interface between the hardware and applications. By providing an operating system, application programs are largely isolated from a detailed understanding of the physical resources that are running the program. Application programs, for example, do not care if your computer is using SCSI disk drives or IDE disk drives.

Sybase runs on a variety of operating systems including several Unix-variants (SunOS 4, SunOS 5, AIX, HP-UX, Digital Unix, SCO Unix, UnixWare, Irix, etc.), Windows/NT, Novell Netware, OS/2, and OpenVMS. Check with your Sybase sales representative for SQL Server availability on the systems you are considering.

For small and intermediate systems, the choice of operating system should be based on factors other than performance. For example, administration, application availability, and system reliability might be justifiably more important than performance at your site. At the high end, operating system choice is important. Hardware/Operating system vendors have taken different approaches to solving the problem of high-end scalability. Here it is wise to shop carefully. In this section we discuss issues related to operating systems that may help you choose the right operating system for your application.

2.2.1 Operating System Symmetry

An efficient multiprocessor system implements symmetric multiprocessing. All processes can execute on any of the CPUs and no CPU is dedicated to a particular operation of the computer. In an asymmetric arrangement, one CPU is dedicated to some operation, disk I/O for example. Whenever a process needs to execute a disk I/O, the process must run on the CPU dedicated to disk I/O. This slows down the program because the program must change processors whenever it needs to run on one of the dedicated processors. In a disk intensive application, the processor dedicated to disk I/O becomes a bottleneck. Only one process can do I/O at a time. You do not want the dedicated processor to always run your program because that would starve other processes that need to use the resources devoted to that one processor.

2.2.2 Operating System Efficiency

The application's view of the computer system is through the operating system. If the operating system is slow, so is your application. System efficiency relates to:

- **How efficiently it fields requests from application programs** — Application programs communicate with the hardware through the operating system. If SQL Server wants to write data to a disk drive, it sends a request through the operating system. How quickly the operating system can respond to and complete the request dictates the maximum performance of SQL Server.

- **How quickly it responds to requests from the hardware** — The disk drives and network controllers may require the attention of the operating system as I/O requests complete or data arrives from a client. If the operating system can only field a limited number of requests at a time, SQL Server is starved for data and the operating system is a bottleneck.

- **Number of CPU instructions required to perform basic operations** — Time spent by the operating system to field requests is processor time stolen from SQL Server. The fewer instructions the operating system needs for itself is less overhead for the system and better performance for SQL Server.

- **Amount of memory required** — Physical memory used by the operating system is memory that is not available to run application programs. The more memory you give SQL Server, the more data it can buffer from database devices. The less memory taken by the operating system, the more memory is available to SQL Server.

2.3   MULTIPROCESSORS AND BEYOND

A single processor has a limited capacity to process data. If you need to process more data, you can buy another processor. The problem then, is moving the data around in an efficient manner.

2.3.1   Shared Memory Systems

Most multiprocessor systems use a shared-architecture. This means several CPUs share the other resources of the computer: disk drives, memory, network adapters, etc. SQL Server takes advantage of this kind of multiprocessor platform. Sybase calls this the **Virtual Server Architecture** (VSA). SQL Server version 4.8 was the first SQL Server to implement VSA. System 10 supports VSA on a variety of platforms including: SunOS 4, SunOS 5, HP-UX, AIX, Digital Unix, OpenVMS, and Windows/NT.

SQL Server implements multiprocessor support by running multiple copies of SQL Server on the same machine. The SQL Server processes, called **engines** in Sybase jargon, cooperate with one another and appear to applications as a single SQL Server. The engines communicate with one another through shared memory segments. Shared memory is memory that is simultaneously accessed by more than one process at a time.

On Unix variants and VMS, SQL Server uses operating system processes for engines. On Windows/NT, SQL Server uses operating system threads.

The main differentiators in shared memory systems are:

- **Scalability of the operating system** — As CPUs are added to the system, how much more processing power does each CPU add to the complete system? Ideally, one achieves 100% scalability. In the real world, synchronization issues get in the way of perfect scaling. The scalability of the operating system measures how well the operating system copes with added processors. The better the scalability of the hardware and operating system, the better scalability you can achieve with SQL Server as you add engines.

- **Cache management** — Each CPU has its own cache memory, but if memory is shared between processes, some mechanism must make sure that a CPU's cached copy of the information stays synchronized with main memory when another CPU changes the data. Hardware vendors have taken different approaches to solving this problem, with various degrees of success. A good CPU cache management approach benefits shared memory application programs like SQL Server by minimizing the cost of synchronizing activity among SQL Server's engines. A poor CPU cache management strategy limits the overall scalability and performance of SQL Server.

- **CPU memory bus utilization** — In a system with many CPUs, the communication channel between the main memory and the CPUs can become a bottleneck. This measure describes how quickly data can be transferred between the CPUs and memory, usually in terms of megabytes per second. The bigger the number the better.

SQL Server does not yet support parallel query processing. A single query is processed by a single CPU even on an MP system.

2.3.2 Clusters

Clusters are a group of machines typically connected with a high speed network. Clusters share disks, but do not share memory or network adapters. Implementations of clusters differ from vendor to vendor. In some implementations, disks are associated with one computer, but the other machines in the cluster are allowed to access the disks. In other implementations, the disks are connected to a special cluster controller. There are advantages to both approaches. In the first, access to the disks local to the machine is no slower in the cluster than in a stand-alone system. Accessing a non-local disk is slower. If a machine goes down, the disks on that machine are not accessible from any of the other machines. In the second implementation, all machines must route disk I/O through the cluster controller, but the disks are available as long as the cluster controller is running. If one machine goes down, the others can still access the disks on the cluster controller. SQL Server does not support clusters directly.

2.3.3   Massively Parallel Processing

Massively Parallel Processing (MPP) systems generally implement a shared-nothing architecture. Each processor in the system has its own memory, disk, and network channel. SQL Server does not take advantage of MPP systems directly. Sybase MPP uses multiple SQL Servers running on individual processors. Data is partitioned among the SQL Servers. For example, a telephone directory might be partitioned by surname. A-G on the first SQL Server, H-P on the second, Q-Z on the third. When an application asks for Michael Practical's phone number, Sybase MPP knows to route the query to the second SQL Server (the SQL Server handling H-P). The optimal partitioning scheme depends on the data and the applications. It is possible that a query accesses all of the SQL Servers simultaneously. For example, when an application asks for all the surnames of the people with the phone number prefix 345, Sybase MPP routes the request to all three SQL Servers. Each SQL Server selects the appropriate names, and Sybase MPP merges and returns the results to the application. Such a query runs faster on Sybase MPP than a conventional SQL Server because there are three SQL Servers running the query simultaneously.

Chapter 3

Sybase Product and Feature Overview

Performance requires that you use the right tool for the job. If the hardware and software components of your system are not right for the purpose they serve, or if their ability to interact and coexist with each other is fundamentally limited, then the job of performance tuning can easily turn into a frustrating and futile endeavor. This chapter familiarizes you with the performance-related aspects of some products from Sybase and their interaction with SQL Server. Our intent is to provide you with criteria for the selection of the right set of components for your performance requirements.

A key issue in the interaction between components of any system is how well they share resources. This issue is especially important when it comes to having another application share hardware with SQL Server. The way SQL Server shares CPUs, memory, and disks with other concurrent applications is critical to its performance. There are products and classes of applications that are designed to share hardware with SQL Server, and there are applications and products that should never share a CPU or memory with SQL Server. A proper understanding of the issues and opportunities underlying these properties will ensure that the components that are critical to the performance of your system work well together.

One of the strengths of the products from Sybase is their ability to work with products from other database vendors as well as they work with each other. You may find yourself combining products from many vendors with products from Sybase. Our discussion in this chapter is limited to a few products from Sybase, simply because of the sheer number of products and vendors that work with the open architecture of Sybase. It is not our intent to imply that these are the only or necessarily the best choices for performance. You should always select the components that best meet the performance needs of your application.

System 11 is a collection of Sybase products that work together to complement and enhance each others functionality. The System 11 family includes: client libraries, server libraries, SQL Server, Replication Server, gateway systems, and other connectivity tools. To take best advantage of this product set, you must use the products as they were intended. If the products are used inappropriately, they can adversely affect each others performance.

3.1   RDBMS ENGINES

Sybase provides a variety of database engines targeted at different audiences. SQL Server for on-line transaction processing and complex query support. Sybase MPP for extremely large applications, and SQL Anywhere for smaller applications.

Figure 3.1 contains an oversimplified view of the options available to you in selecting an RDBMS engine.

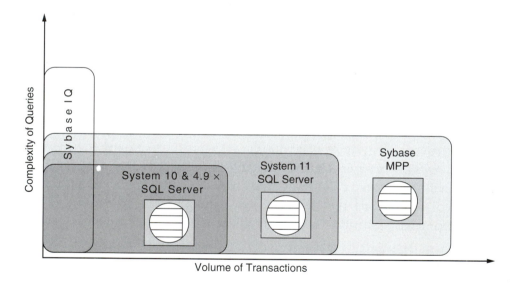

Figure 3.1   Sybase RDBMS capabilities- -

The System 11 SQL Server enhances the capability of the 4.9 and System 10 SQL Servers in both the throughput of transaction processing and the processing of complex queries in very large databases while maintaining complete functional compatibility. Sybase MPP retains most of the functionality of SQL Server, while extending performance in terms of volume of data, transaction throughput, and the complexity of queries. Sybase IQ provides support for high volume, read-only decision support queries.

3.1.1   Sybase SQL Server

SQL Server was originally designed for high throughput, high availability, on-line transaction processing. These applications are characterized by frequent, small, short duration transactions. Recent versions of SQL Server have added features that improve the performance of complex, decision support style queries. This trend is likely to continue in future versions. The architecture of SQL Server is flexible enough to continue to provide high throughput for on-line transaction processing, while accommodating decision support applications.

Clearly, SQL Server is an evolving product. The material in this book covers three major versions of SQL Server: 4.9.x, System 10, and System 11. Each of these has added substantial improvements in performance, functionality, or both, to the previous major versions. Your choice among major versions of SQL Server influences the functionality, performance, and maintainability of your application.

Another choice you face is deciding whether or when to upgrade to the next major version. Generally speaking, the later versions subsume the functionality and performance features of the former versions. However, an upgrade to a major version of a complex software product always deserves a careful analysis of all the options and trade-offs. This section familiarizes you with most of the major differences in performance and some of the differences in functionality among the major versions of SQL Server.

SQL Server 4.9

SQL Server versions 4.8, 4.9, and 4.9.1 added a number of performance related features to SQL Server versions 4.0 and 4.2:

- `create database ... for load` — Create database zeros all of the pages in the created database to ensure recoverability of the database. Most of the time spent in create database is in zeroing the pages. If the database is created as a pre-cursor to a load, there is no reason to zero the pages. Load writes over the pages as it loads data. The `for load` option on `create database` tells SQL Server to by-pass the page zeroing and only blank out the pages that control page allocation. As there is only one control page for every 256 database pages, `create database for load` is roughly 256 times faster than a regular `create database`.

- `smallmoney`, `smalldatetime`, **and** `real` **datatypes** — These datatypes are smaller versions of `money`, `datetime`, and `float`. With these smaller datatypes, you can put more rows of data on a single page, reducing the number of pages read in order to locate information. This improves throughput.

- **Support for Symmetric Multiprocessor Computers** — Starting with version 4.8, SQL Server takes advantage of multiprocessor computer systems. Using multiple CPUs can improve the throughput and response time of a multi-user application.

- `dbcc tablealloc`, `dbcc indexalloc` — These dbcc commands are similar to `checkalloc`, only they check individual tables and indexes rather than the entire database. This makes it possible to check a database selectively, saving time over a complete `checkalloc`.

- **Stack Size Configuration** — Certain queries require a lot of stack space. The stack space configuration lets you adjust the amount of stack space allocated to each thread in SQL Server. Memory used for thread stack space is memory that cannot be used for other purposes. By making the stack size as small as possible for your application, you save memory for buffering data inside SQL Server.

System 10 SQL Server

System 10 SQL Server provides a number of enhancements over previous versions of SQL Server. These are covered in detail in the Sybase manual *What's New in SYBASE SQL Server Release 10.0*. Here we highlight some of the more interesting changes:

- **Server-side Cursors** — Application programmers can now use cursors defined inside SQL Server. This can significantly simplify writing stored procedures and SQL scripts that must process data in a non-relational way. For example, with cursors it is very easy to loop over each row of a result set and do processing on each row. Before System 10 SQL Server, the only way to do this was with temporary tables and aggregate calculations.

- **Auditing** — The auditing capabilities built into SQL Server can help you monitor the use of your application. It might be possible for you to correlate information from the audit with other system statistics to help identify performance bottlenecks. The audit record may also help you tune your system to match the expected loads.

- **Declarative Constraints and Referential Integrity** — System 10 SQL Server supports declarative and referential integrity constraints. The implications of the use of these features on performance are discussed in Chapter 6, *Physical Database Design*.

- **Backup Server** — System 10 SQL Server uses Backup Server to perform database dumps and loads. In the past, SQL Server managed the dumps on its own. Because dump and load are I/O intensive, decoupling Backup Server from SQL Server has significantly improved the performance of dumps and loads by eliminating the need for SQL Server to manage dump devices.

- **Identity** — System 10 SQL Server includes an identity mechanism that automatically assigns a unique value to each row inserted into a table. This eliminates a difficult implementation problem for Sybase application developers. In the past, developers had to come up with their own schemes to produce unique values. In general, simple schemes limited the concurrency of the application and complex schemes were difficult to implement and manage effectively.

- **Limits on Size of Stored Procedures** — The limits on the sizes of stored procedures is effectively eliminated in System 10 SQL Server.[1]

- **Subquery Processing Changes** — System 10 SQL Server includes a variety of changes to subquery processing, mostly to eliminate a number of nagging problems with subquery processing in previous versions. For example, previous versions of SQL Server do not return the correct results for certain queries that contain quantified and correlated subqueries involving NULL values in the correlation column. System 10 SQL Server corrects this error in functionality, but not without changes in the performance of such queries.

- **Chained Transactions and Isolation Level** — Chained transactions and isolation levels are required for ANSI SQL compliance and backward compatibility for existing Sybase applications. Changing modes can have a significant impact, both positive and negative, on the performance of your application. But to change modes safely, you must understand the trade-offs between maintaining proper transactional semantics and higher performance.

[1.] To be technically accurate, there remains a limit to the size of a stored procedure, but the limit is high enough that it is unlikely any application developer would create stored procedures of that size.

- **Create Index Enhancements** — Creating an index is disk I/O intensive. SQL Server must read and write data pages, intermediate sorting results, and the index pages. Previous versions of SQL Server did these reads and writes one page at a time. Configuring extra `extent i/o buffers` allows System 10 SQL Server to read and write information an extent at a time.[2] This can significantly improve the performance of `create index`.

- **Index Statistics Improvements** — Previous versions of SQL Server recorded statistics only on the set of all the columns in an index. System 10 SQL Server records statistics on each non-empty prefix of the index. For example, suppose the index key has four columns, A, B, C and D. Previous versions of SQL Server recorded statistics on the composite key: A-B-C-D. System 10 SQL Server stores statistics on A, A-B, A-B-C, and A-B-C-D. This means the optimizer can make a better prediction about selectivity when only the first part of the index key is used.

System 11 SQL Server

System 11 SQL Server includes a variety of performance related changes, but very little new user-level functionality. This makes it somewhat different than System 10 SQL Server that included a significant amount of new feature-functionality. The major subsystems in SQL Server were reviewed and roadblocks to improved multiprocessing scalability were identified. Much of the significant engineering work in System 11 is directed at eliminating these roadblocks:

- **Large Memory** — System 11 SQL Server supports more than 2 Gb of memory on platforms with 64 bit addressing (e.g., Digital Unix). This means SQL Server can cache more than 2 Gb of data.

- **Optimizer, Locking, and Buffer Replacement Hints** — The SQL language parser of System 11 SQL Server supports an improved mechanism for providing hints to the query optimizer. See Chapter 11, *Query Processing Performance* for more details.

- **Large Database Device Files** — On platforms that support asynchronous I/O on large device files, System 11 SQL Server allows you to create and use database device files larger than 2 Gb. This increases the theoretical maximum size of a database.

---

[2] There are eight pages in an extent.

- **Cache Manager** — The new cache manager requires less synchronization in a multiprocessor environment, improving its scalability. In addition, system administrators can configure the cache manager to read and write data in power of two multiples of the page size. For example, 2k, 4k, 8k, and 16k reads and writes are possible. SQL Server's cache space is organized into named caches and particular tables, indexes, or databases may be bound to a named cache. With this capability, you can force SQL Server to keep a table entirely in memory. SQL Server never needs to access a disk to read values from the table. This improves performance for uniprocessor and multiprocessor systems.

- **Lock Manager** — Like the cache manager, the lock manager is modified to eliminate a number of synchronization points in a multiprocessor environment. This significantly improves performance in multiprocessor systems and does not affect single-processor performance. SQL Server's deadlock detection strategy also changes significantly.

- **Data Partitioning** — Appending data to the end of a table makes the last page of the table a point of contention. Transactions must synchronize with one another on the page. Data partitioning eliminates this point of contention by creating many "ends" to append to. Each "end" is a partition. This improves performance in multiprocessor and single-processor systems by eliminating the synchronization between transactions.

- **Subquery Changes** — System 11 SQL Server introduces a method for processing queries involving subqueries that is radically different from all those used in the previous versions of SQL Server. In a nutshell, System 11 SQL Server processes subqueries **outside-in**; that is, it evaluates the values for the correlation columns, if any, by processing the outer block of the query before evaluating the inner block (i.e., the subquery). If your application involves subqueries that are critical to performance, System 11 may provide you with significantly better performance. We discuss these changes in greater detail in Chapter 11, *Query Processing Performance*.

- **Dirty Reads** — When you read data in System 10 SQL Server, you are assured that the data is transactionally consistent (ANSI isolation level 1). System 11 SQL Server adds dirty reads. This means, applications are permitted to read data that may not be transactionally consistent. This is useful in some decision support queries, where the occasional transactional error may not be all that important. If you are calculating the average of a column over a large number of rows, one or two mistakes may not be significant. Dirty reads improves performance by eliminating the synchronization between transactions reading data and transactions modifying data. Not only is the synchronization eliminated, the overhead needed to maintain the synchronization structures is also eliminated.

3.1.2   Sybase MPP

Sybase MPP extends most of the functionality of SQL Server to a highly scalable, **shared-nothing** environment. If the disk or CPU requirements of your application are truly huge, or if your application requires scalability beyond the reach of shared-memory multiprocessors, Sybase MPP provides you with an option to scale to massively parallel processors.

Sybase MPP coordinates a large number of SQL Servers using Control Servers that make them function like a single SQL Server to all applications. Data is partitioned or replicated as appropriate among the SQL Servers. On receiving a query, the Control Servers determine which SQL Servers need to participate in the query, rewrite the query internally to divide workload among the participants, coordinate execution of the query fragments among the SQL Servers involved, and consolidate the results. The SQL Servers do not share memory or disks (hence the attribute **shared-nothing**). By sharing nothing, synchronization problems are greatly reduced, resulting in almost linear scaling for a large class of queries.

Currently, Sybase MPP provides functionality comparable to SQL Server 4.9.x, with some enhancements and a few restrictions. Sybase MPP's inability to support triggers limits its applicability to applications that make extensive use of triggers. The query optimizer used by Sybase MPP is, naturally, significantly different to that of SQL Server. Therefore, the discussion on query optimization techniques in this book is not necessarily applicable to Sybase MPP. Further, the enhancements to query optimization made in System 11, including the new subquery processing techniques, are not yet available in Sybase MPP.

3.1.3   Sybase IQ

The Sybase IQ provides very high performance query processing to decision-support type applications that do not need to query data that is updated concurrently. Sybase IQ uses some very innovative indexing techniques, some very efficient techniques for storing tabular data, and data compression to greatly reduce the workload of query processing.

The model of updates in Sybase IQ is significantly different from that of SQL Server. Each database in Sybase IQ must always be in one of two states, one allows multiple users to query the database, and the other allows a single user to update the database. A database can only be updated in an exclusive mode.

The Sybase IQ can also operate in a **pass-through** mode as a front for SQL Server. In this mode, Sybase IQ stores a read-only copy of a the database in SQL Server. The clients communicate with the Sybase IQ instead of communicating directly with SQL Server. Sybase IQ culls the commands from the clients to decide which queries it can handle itself and executes them. The rest of the commands are passed through to SQL Server. This mode of operation improves the functional compatibility between SQL Server and Sybase IQ. However, you are still responsible for the transactional integrity between the two databases.

Besides the lack of concurrent updates, there are other significant differences in functionality between SQL Server and Sybase IQ. Subsequent versions of Sybase IQ are likely to improve the level of compatibility between the two products.

3.2 CLIENT AND SERVER LIBRARIES

You have several choices of client libraries and/or languages each of which provide different capabilities. In part the decisions you make here may have little to do with performance. You may find ESQL a convenient Sybase interface if your environment includes other relational database systems that require an embedded SQL interface. DB-Library and Client-Library, while they have similar capabilities, present substantially different faces to application programmers. The functional differences, for example in cursors, asynchronous programming, or the presence of two phase commit, may be enough to sway the balance in favor of one library over the other.

Sybase Open Client libraries allow you to write client programs that communicate with Sybase SQL Server and other server products. With Sybase Open Server library you can develop your own specialized servers. These clients and servers communicate through a Sybase defined protocol that allows you to mix and match different products, or different versions of the same product from Sybase. Even more importantly, the open availability of these libraries has encouraged many other vendors to use these libraries in their products. Thus, use of these interfaces enables you to access not only a wide range of products from Sybase, but also products from a large number of other vendors. We should note that these are certainly not the only standards followed by Sybase products; most Sybase products follow the major industry-standard interfaces that exist in their domain of applicability.

3.2.1   Client Libraries and Language Preprocessors

Sybase supports several client libraries and language preprocessors for application programmers:

- Open Client DB-Library
- Open Client Client-Library[3]
- Open DataBase Connectivity (ODBC) Library
- Embedded SQL (ESQL)

All the Sybase client interfaces share a common set of basic functionality:

1. **Manage Connections to the Server** — Log on and off the Sybase server.
2. **Process Errors** — Handle errors returned by the Sybase server or generated within the client library itself.
3. **Submit Queries** — Send T-SQL or other commands to the Sybase server.
4. **Remote Procedure Calls** — Make a remote procedure call to a server.
5. **Read Results** — Read data rows, columns, and format information from the Sybase server.
6. **Datatype Conversion** — Convert server datatypes to client datatypes and vice-versa.
7. **Client-side Cursors** — Implementation of cursors built into the client library.
8. **Browse Mode** — Predecessor to cursors. Largely superseded by server-side cursors.
9. **Asynchronous Programming** — Allows the client program to continue processing while SQL Server executes the query.

A more detailed discussion of cursors and asynchronous program follows this section.

Client-Library includes some capabilities not found in DB-Library:

- **Dynamic SQL** — Used primarily to support embedded SQL pre-compilers.

[3.] At one time called CT-Library.

- **Array Binding** — Ability to read more than one row of results at a time.
- **Asynchronous Callback Functions** — The application programmer may register functions for Client-Library to call when certain events occur.

Client-Library does not include support for two phase commit. If your application requires two phase commit, you must use DB-Library.

ODBC

ODBC is typically used with PC applications that must communicate with many different database servers. ODBC presents a standard interface to all brands of database servers. Most ODBC drivers translate between the ODBC standard interface and the interface particular to the database system being accessed. This enables programmers to write database applications or shrink wrap software without concerning themselves with the individual characteristics of each database system. There are several ODBC drivers for Sybase. They translate ODBC calls into Client-Library calls. The translation imposes a certain amount of overhead and is, in general, a little slower than using a client library directly.

ESQL

Sybase ESQL allows you to embed or mix together SQL with another programming language such as C, Cobol, or Ada. ESQL uses a pre-compiler to translate the SQL statements into the appropriate Client-Library calls to interact with the database server. Results from the SQL can be stored in variables that are accessible in the other programming language. Sybase ESQL is ANSI-89 compliant and might be a good choice where multi-vendor database compatibility is required in the client programs.

For example:

```
exec sql begin declare section
CS_INT columna;
CS_INT columnb;
exec sql end declare section;

exec sql select a into :columna where b = :columnb
printf("a has the value %d for b = %b\n", columna, columnb);
```

The Sybase ESQL pre-compiler must take a conservative approach to using Client-Library. The pre-compilers cannot make any assumptions about the form of your data. By writing with DB-Library or Client-Library directly, you have complete control over the flow of execution within the client program. This gives you more flexibility in how to handle returns and allows you to optimize your client program to the commands you expect to send to SQL Server and the data you expect to read back. For example, if none of the client program's queries involve `compute` clauses, there is no reason to check for compute rows in the returned data. ESQL cannot know the result of your queries at compile time and must assume that every query includes the most complicated result set possible.

Using Cursors

Cursors allow programmers to process results from a query in small batches rather than all at once. With cursors you can read a single row of the result set at a time and do processing on the row before moving onto the next row. This kind of processing violates the relational data model, but is provided in most relational database systems because many "real world" applications are not entirely relational. Among the client libraries and SQL Server, Sybase provides four different implementations of cursor functionality:

- Browse mode
- Native (language) cursors built into SQL Server
- Client-Library cursors
- DB-Library cursors

The functionality provided by browse mode is superceded by native cursors and the use of browse mode is now discouraged by Sybase. Native cursors were introduced in System 10 SQL Server. You declare and use native cursors with T-SQL commands. DB-Library cursors are implemented in the library and do not rely on the T-SQL implementation of cursors. Client-Library cursors take advantage of T-SQL cursors, but use an interface not available to T-SQL programmers.

3.2.2   Open Server

Sybase Open Server library enables developers to write servers. With Open Server, an application can masquerade as a SQL Server, accepting and processing commands from Open Client applications. Client applications send commands to Open Server applications just as they send SQL to SQL Server. In addition, client applications and SQL Server can use remote procedures calls (RPCs) to send instructions to Open Server applications.

Several vendors use Open Server to develop products that work along side SQL Server, appearing like SQL Servers to clients. Several System 10 products, including Backup Server, Monitor Server, and Replication Server are built using Open Server Library.

Open Server is SQL Server's gateway to C functions and shell scripts. As SQL Server cannot execute a developer's C function or shell script directly, SQL Server must rely on an Open Server **agent** to do the work and then report the results. Most Open Server applications serve functions that are significantly different from that of SQL Server.

Some Open Server developers have chosen to implement functionality that are radically different from the common notion of database applications. Typical end-user applications include specialized data replication systems, electronic mail delivery systems, and alert systems. If your application can benefit from having a server that provides some **non-database** functionality, and you would like to make that functionality available through a widely-used, standard interface, you should consider Open Client/Open Server libraries.

3.3 AUXILIARY SERVERS

Not all applications can share CPU or memory with SQL Server without hurting its performance. (Yes, this includes SQL Server itself.) The primary reason for this is that SQL Server acts as its own operating system in scheduling CPU cycles and memory among the tasks that are running concurrently. This may conflict with the real operating systems scheduling policies, should there be a process that shares CPU and memory with the SQL Server process. Therefore, you need to be very careful about having SQL Server share a CPU or memory with other applications.

A major exception to the above rule of thumb is the class of **auxiliary servers**. These are Open Server applications that are designed to share hardware with SQL Server and other auxiliary servers. The auxiliary servers augment the functionality of SQL Server without actually being part of the SQL Server executable. Examples of auxiliary servers include Backup Server and Monitor Server. Figure 3.2 depicts a typical configuration for some auxiliary servers.

Some auxiliary servers are not directly accessible to the clients and can only be accessed through SQL Server. In the figure, auxiliary servers #1 and #2 are not directly accessible to clients. This section outlines three auxiliary servers that are frequently used in conjunction with SQL Server.

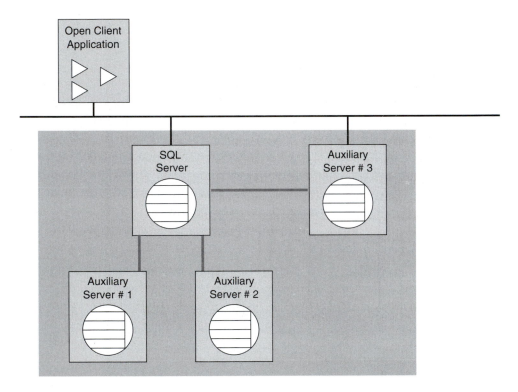

Figure 3.2   Auxiliary Servers -

3.3.1   Backup Server

Starting with System 10, SQL Server no longer manages database dumps and loads on its own. Instead, it relies on a Backup Server. Figure 3.3 depicts the architecture of Backup Server.

Backup Server is not directly accessible from the clients. Instead, users initiate a backup or restore operation with a `dump` or `load` command on SQL Server. SQL Server then communicates with Backup Server via the RPC interface.

Backup Server can directly access the database devices. The flux of data to and from the backup devices is unencumbered by costly protocol stacks. Further, Backup Server reads and writes data in larger units than the SQL Server page size. Consequently, Backup Server is able to perform dumps on-line with minimal impact on SQL Server performance.

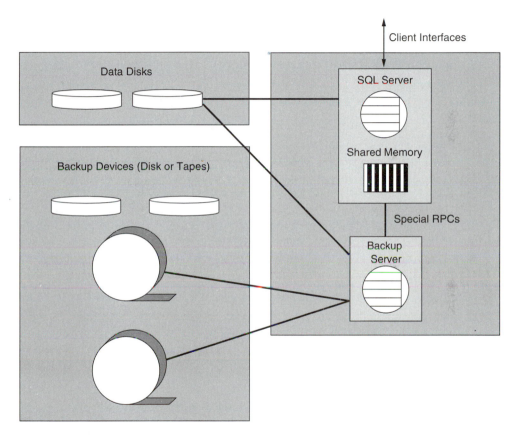

Figure 3.3   Backup Server architecture -

Backup Server can write database dumps to raw partitions, operating system files, or tape drives. In general, Backup Server reads and writes data to tape drives as quickly as the drives can handle data. Thus, the more tape drives you dump to or load from simultaneously, the faster the dump or load can happen. In Sybase terminology, Backup Server allows you to **stripe** the dump of a database across many devices. Loads can also be **striped** and there is no requirement that you use the same number of devices to read the dumps as to write them.

3.3.2   Monitor Server

SQL Server maintains a number of monitor counters and an event log in its shared memory. These counters and events track the state of affairs inside the running SQL Server. Monitor Server is an auxiliary server built using Open Server that connects to SQL Server's shared memory to access the monitor counters.

SQL Monitor is an Open Client application that allows you to monitor some of SQL Server internal counters. SQL Monitor reads the counters from Monitor Server at regular intervals and lets you plot the values as they change over time. Changing which values you monitor does not affect the performance of SQL Server. Monitor Server is only one of several ways to read the monitor counters and events. However, as of writing this book, it is the only way supported by Sybase.

Sybase chooses to keep some counters and the event system proprietary. Hence, only some of the monitor counters and none of the monitor events can be accessed through SQL Monitor. Nevertheless, Monitor Server is a great asset in performance tuning. Among its biggest strengths is its ability to observe the state of SQL Server without significantly changing it in the process. This differentiates it from less subtle means of instrumenting software, such as compilation with special profiling options (an option not available to endusers).

3.3.3   Replication Server

Sybase Replication Server is another Sybase application based on Open Server. Replication Server copies transactions from one SQL Server to another. When a transaction updates data in the source SQL Server, Replication Server reconstructs the transaction from the log records and replicates the transaction to SQL Servers subscribing to the changes.

Replication Server uses a store and forward approach. If the link to one of the subscriber servers is down, replication server stores the replicated transactions until the link is restored. Then all of the missed transactions are sent to the server receiving replicated data.

The Sybase Replication Server technology differs somewhat from other methods typically used to synchronize disparate data storage systems: two phase commit and snap shot replication.

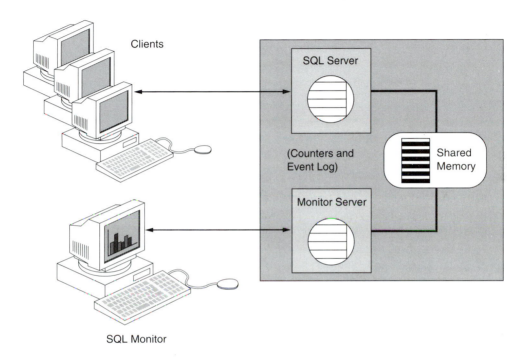

Figure 3.4   Monitor Server architecture -

Two phase commit involves synchronizing the commit of the transaction in two servers. The transaction is not allowed to commit in one server until it is assured that the transaction can commit in both. This synchronization can be a big performance problem. The transaction commits at the rate of the slowest system. If either system is down, neither can commit any transactions. If the link between the systems is down, then no transactions can commit. Replication Server avoids these problems by allowing the transaction to commit in one server before it commits in another. The performance and failure problems are eliminated by the store and forward approach.

Snap shot replication involves taking a "picture" of the database at some instant in time and replicating that snap shot to all of the other data servers. This system avoids the two phase commit bottleneck by ignoring the transactional semantics of the source database. The problem, then, is that the snap shot may not include complete transactions. This means the copy of the database may not be a transactionally consistent picture of the original database. Replication server maintains the transactional integrity of the changes made to the source database. Because the changes are applied to the copies of the database just as they were applied to the original, any triggers or other semantic checks can take place on the copies as well as the original.

3.4   PUTTING IT ALL TOGETHER

If you are using System 11 SQL Server, you are probably using one or more of the other members of the System 11 family. Let us refresh our acquaintance with some select members of the family. Figure 3.5 depicts a typical use of some of the System 11 family of products.

In Figure 3.5, the clients are communicating with two SQL Servers, a Monitor Server, an OmniSQL Gateway, which allows Sybase client applications to communicate with other database systems, and an Open Server application. Monitor Server is communicating with SQL Server #1 and reporting the SQL Server's activity to a client. OmniSQL gateway allows Sybase clients to communicate with database servers from other vendors. Open Server allows Sybase clients to access C functions implemented by customers.

3.5   USING OTHER PEOPLE'S SOFTWARE

For optimal performance, it is important that any Value Added Retailer (VAR) or Computer Aided Software Engineering (CASE) tools you use are optimized for the version of SQL Server you are using. Many applications are written first for other data vendors and ported to SQL Server. SQL Server has different strengths than the other vendors and many applications may not work properly until they are tuned and optimized to SQL Server.

When you are using software development tools, you must be aware of how the tool is using your database. If possible, inspect the SQL generated by the tool. Is the tool generating good, high performance, SQL? Keep your eyes open. Many tools generate code for a variety of database systems. Make sure your tool is generating code that is good for Sybase. Good Sybase SQL is not necessarily the same as good Informix SQL and good Oracle SQL.

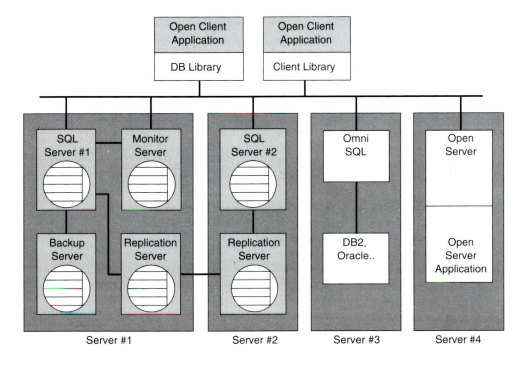

Figure 3.5   Typical organization of Sybase products - - - - - - - - - - - - - - - - - - -

Graphical User Interfaces (GUIs) are slick and often easier to use than textual, command based data entry systems. Their drawback is the high amount of processing power generally required to keep a GUI looking snappy. GUI interfaces can become a bottleneck in database applications in which case the computers running the clients are at 100%, but SQL Server still has reserves. In this situation, making SQL Server faster does not help your overall system. Monitoring tools described in Chapter 8, *Monitoring SQL Server*, can help you determine if SQL Server is the bottleneck in your application.

Chapter 4

SQL Server — Form and Structure

SQL Server's architecture differs somewhat from the other RDBMS products. If you are already familiar with the architecture of another RDBMS product, you need to understand the differences in the architectures to take best advantage of SQL Server. This first chapter about SQL Server's architecture describes how SQL Server uses the computer's physical resources: CPUs, memory, and disk drives. Understanding how SQL Server uses the computer's physical resources makes it easier to master the query optimizations described in later chapters because you have an understanding of the logic behind them. For example:

- How SQL Server divides the computer's CPU time over the user connections impacts the concurrency of transactions.
- How memory is used may affect disk I/O rates.
- Organization of tables and indexes into databases and database devices directly affects disk utilization and application throughput.
- Table and Index allocation methods affect locality of access and has implications for very large databases.

The following chapter on SQL Server's architecture describes how the physical resources are managed.

4.1 TASK SCHEDULING

A single instance of SQL Server may be a single operating system process or, in a multiprocessor environment, a set of tightly coupled cooperating processes.[1] Each process represents a thread of execution to the operating system. Sybase calls these **engines** to avoid confusion with **processes** and **threads**. Engines are num-

---

[1.] On Windows/NT, a set of threads within a single process are used rather than a set of tightly coupled processes.

bered starting from zero in the order in which they start. Engine 0 is responsible for bootstrapping SQL Server and recovering the databases. After database recovery, engine 0 starts the other engines.

As shown in Figure 4.1, all engines attach to a common shared memory segment, which contains information about the state of SQL Server. The engines synchronize their activity using spinlocks and locking mechanisms built on top of spinlocks.

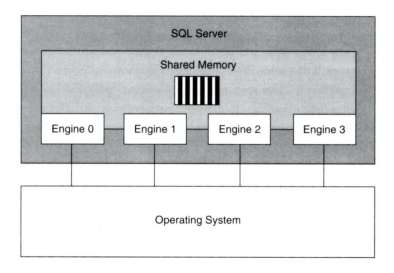

Figure 4.1   SQL Server engines -

Each connection to SQL Server is assigned a **task** by SQL Server.[2] A **task** represents a thread of execution to SQL Server. Sybase calls these threads **tasks**, to distinguish them from light-weight operating system threads. SQL Server performs its own task scheduling by assigning runnable tasks to the engines. The operating system is responsible for managing the execution of the engines. Execution of the task is non-preemptive. This means the task must explicitly yield control of the engine to another task.

A task can be in any one of several states:

[2.]   This is an oversimplification. The work for any one user connection may be shared among more than one task. However, this simplification aides the ensuing discussion.

- **Running** — Task is currently executing and doing something useful.
- **Runnable** — Task is not running but is not waiting to synchronize with other activity. The task can do useful work if it is scheduled onto an engine.
- **Sleeping** — Task has yielded control of the engine to other tasks and is waiting to synchronize with other activity in SQL Server. The task cannot be scheduled onto an engine until the activity blocking the thread informs the task that it is free to execute.

A task goes to sleep when it must synchronize with another task in SQL Server. For example, a task that is waiting for a command from the client cannot do useful work until a command arrives. Hence, the task is "put to sleep" or "blocked" until a command arrives. When the scheduler notices that commands have arrived for the task, the scheduler makes the task "runnable." When an engine is available to run the task, the scheduler assigns the task to the engine and the task is now "running."

Normally, any task can be scheduled on any engine.[3] Periodically it is important for a task to run on a particular engine. Tasks can dynamically develop affinity to specific engines, in which case they are scheduled only on the specified engine. There are two reasons for affinity:

1. Certain activities can be performed only on certain engines. For example, in UNIX, a disk I/O started by an engine must be completed by the same engine.
2. For best performance, a task that sleeps only briefly should be scheduled to run on the engine it was most recently using. For most platforms, this improves the hardware cache hit ratio and the performance of the system.

Figure 4.2 outlines the task management in SQL Server. A task can be sleeping on any one of several events: completion of an I/O request, arrival or acknowledgment of a network packet, or availability of a lock. When the specified event happens, the scheduler wakes up the task and the task is added to either the global queue of runnables, or to the queue of the engine to which it has an affinity. The engines, in turn, look for runnable tasks first in their own run queue, and then in the global run queue, both in descending order of task priority.

---

[3] This is known as **Symmetric Multiprocessing**.

The context switching among tasks is non-preemptive. In most multiprocessing operating systems[4] the operating system scheduler measures out processor time to each process, giving the process only a certain amount of processor time. When the time is up, the scheduler interrupts, or **preempts**, the process and gives the processor to another process. SQL Server's non-preemptive scheduler requires that the tasks **yield** the engine so that other tasks can run on the engine. For most database operations, yields happen naturally when the task must wait for network or disk I/O or for a lock. Long running operations need explicit yields.

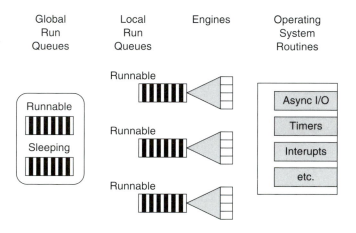

Figure 4.2   Global and local run queues- -

A **clocktick** is a unit of time measured in milliseconds. The `cclockrate` configuration parameter controls the length of a clocktick. The length of the clocktick controls how frequently a long running task considers explicitly yielding to other tasks.

A time slicing mechanism acts as a watchdog to verify that a thread yields periodically. If a thread uses more than its fair share of the engine's time, SQL Server assumes that something has gone wrong, kills the thread, and reports a timeslice error in the errorlog. You can adjust the "fair share" by changing the **time slice** configuration value. The time slice mechanism is an important safety system.

[4.]   The primary exception is Netware.

Because an engine runs only one task at a time, if a task goes into an infinite loop, the engine cannot run any other tasks and SQL Server appears to hang. The time slice mechanism kills the "jammed" task and frees the engine to run other tasks in its queue.

Traditionally it has been the prerogative of the operating system to dominate the hardware, not application programs. Nevertheless, SQL Server's scheduler works best when the engine has complete control over the CPU. Consequently, a SQL Server engine is not very graceful about sharing the CPU with most other applications. You can configure the number of engines to limit the number of CPUs dedicated to SQL Server on your server hardware. SQL Server does not use more CPUs than configured engines. For example, on an 8 CPU server, you can run a SQL Server with 6 engines, keeping 2 CPUs free for other applications.

We strongly recommend against running any applications on a single CPU server while SQL Server is running or on a multi-CPU server when the number of engines is equal to the number of CPUs, with the exception of programs that must share server hardware with SQL Server to be useful. For example:

- Auxiliary Servers like Backup Server and Monitor Server
- Lightweight monitoring tools such as the Unix utilities `sar`, `vmstat` and `iostat`

You should not rely on operating system monitors to measure the availability of free cycles in SQL Server. Engines often resort to **busy waiting** to improve system response time. An engine in busy wait loops through a routine looking for work to do. While the engine is doing this, it is consuming CPU time, but it is not doing any useful work.

The alternative is to put the engine to sleep and allow other operating system processes to execute. When there is work to do, say an I/O finishes, the operating system wakes up the engine, the engine figures out what happened, and the scheduler identifies the appropriate task to field the activity. The time it takes the operating system to wake up the engine and the engine to figure out what to do adds to the response time. If the engine is already running, there is no time delay and the response time is shorter. Because of the busy waits, SQL Server can appear almost 100% busy to the operating system, even when it is doing useful work less than half the time.

4.2   MEMORY ALLOCATION

Along with task management, SQL Server does its own memory management. All of the memory required by SQL Server is allocated up front when SQL Server boots. Tasks can allocate memory for their purposes from a memory manager built into SQL Server.

Most of the memory allocated by SQL Server is shared memory. This means more than one operating system process can view and change the memory at the same time.[5] Normally, the operating system prevents one process from viewing or changing memory allocated to another process. The process's memory is said to be protected.

SQL Server's memory management strategy assumes it never allocates more memory than the physical memory available on the server. Therefore, its reaction to page faults is less than graceful. We strongly recommend eliminating all paging activity from SQL Server engines. On some operating systems, SQL Server locks its address space into physical memory at boot time. On some others, SQL Server provides an option to do so. On the rest, you should configure SQL Server with less memory than available on the server, leaving enough physical memory for the operating system, auxiliary servers, and occasional DBA activities.

As Figure 4.3 suggests, SQL Server uses memory for a number of different purposes. There are two primary uses for memory: state information for tasks and buffer space. The state information for tasks includes the task's stack, the locks held by the task, tables the task is currently reading or updating, etc. This information is overhead. Allocating more memory to store state information does not make SQL Server run any faster. You should configure SQL Server with enough connections to accommodate the number of simultaneous users you expect, and no more. The fewer configured connections, the fewer tasks are allocated, and the less memory is consumed to store task state information.

Buffer space is divided into two sections: data cache and procedure cache. Data cache holds transient copies of data pages and index pages. Procedure cache holds transient copies of optimized stored procedure plans. In addition, various utilities built into SQL Server may "steal" memory from procedure cache to hold state

---

[5.]   This is not strictly required on Windows/NT as each engine is an operating system thread in the SQL Server process. Nevertheless, SQL Server on Windows/NT allocates shared memory. Only version 4 of Netware supports protected memory. Previous versions allow all Netware processes to modify the memory of the other processes running on the system.

information. Adding memory to buffer space makes SQL Server run faster. When SQL Server looks for a particular page of a table, access is much faster if it finds the page in buffer space (i.e., in memory) rather than on disk. Reading the disk is orders of magnitude slower than reading memory. The more memory available to buffer space, the more likely SQL Server will find the data or index pages it needs in memory, thus avoiding a trip to the disk drive.

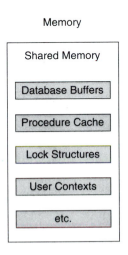

Figure 4.3   Memory allocation in SQL Server -

System 11 SQL Server further divides data cache into user-defined named caches. The SQL Server administrator may divide the data cache into regions. Each region is configured to consume a certain amount of memory. Particular databases or objects within a database may be assigned to a named cache. If table `titles` is assigned to a named cache, then pages of `titles` cached in SQL Server are only in the named cache. This is useful when you want to encourage particular tables or indexes to stay in memory, or restrict the amount of memory that can be consumed by certain tables or indexes.

4.3　MULTIPROCESSOR ISSUES

SQL Server can exploit multiple processors even when configured with only one engine. However, such parallelism is limited to concurrent I/O and network activities. The best way to exploit shared-memory parallelism with SQL Server is to configure SQL Server with more than one engine. The optimal number of engines depends on the operating system as well as the workload. The number of engines should never exceed the number of processors on the system. For certain operating systems, it pays to leave one or two processors free to field I/O requests by the operating system kernel.

A single query is processed by one task only. As a result, multiple engines help performance only if there are multiple runnable tasks and only multi-user applications stand to gain from use of multiple processors.

Certain operating systems allow you to bind processes to processors. Doing so may aid performance by improving the processor's data and instruction cache hit ratios. The degree of benefit depends on the workload and the operating system.

4.4　NETWORK I/O

All client programs communicate with SQL Server through the network. Clients initiate communication with SQL Server by connecting to a SQL Server listener port. The interfaces file gives the address of the listener port. After SQL Server acknowledges the connection, the communication is automatically transferred to another port. This transfer it transparent to the client. This makes the listener port available to accept another connection.

On System 10 and earlier versions of SQL Server, engine 0 is responsible for all network I/O. Engine 0 accepts the connections and any task that needs to read or write to the network must run on engine 0 for the duration of the network read or write. At other times, any other engine may run the task. This makes SQL Server processing in System 10 and earlier versions of SQL Server somewhat asymmetric in that one engine is responsible for work that other engines cannot perform.

System 11 SQL Server improves on the symmetry of processing and throughput by allowing any engine to perform network I/O. Engine 0 is still responsible for accepting connections. Once a connection is established, the connection is transferred to the engine that has the fewest open connections. Note that this may be the engine that originally accepted the connection. The engine the becomes responsible for the connection remains responsible for the connection for the duration of the session. When a task needs to perform network I/O, it must run on the engine that is responsible for its connection. At other times, for example, while the task is processing a join, the task may run on any engine.

The more symmetric System 11 SQL Server network I/O subsystem has a number of advantages over System 10 SQL Server subsystem:

- Improved network throughput because the burden of performing network I/O is spread over more processes.

- Increased number of simultaneous network connections. With System 10 and earlier versions of SQL Server the maximum number of simultaneous network connections is limited by the maximum number of file descriptors available per process. As each engine may now manage network connections, the maximum number of network connections per SQL Server is now the product of the maximum number of file descriptors permitted per process and the number of engines.

- Reduced number of context switches. A SQL Server task does not have to switch to engine 0 to perform network I/O. If the task is running on the engine responsible for its network connection, the task does not need a context switch. Worst case, the task must still context switch to the engine handling its network connection and performance is no worse than before.

4.5 DEVICES, SEGMENTS, AND PAGES

The basic unit of storage used by SQL Server is a 2 Kbyte page.[6] A database is a collection of pages that are allocated from database devices. **Segments** define groups of pages coming from sets of database devices. Segments are one of the basic tools in performance tuning SQL Server. They allow you to place a set of tables and indexes on specific disks. You can use this mechanism, for example, to spread a frequently accessed table across several disks while confining several infrequently accessed tables to one large disk. In order to do this effectively, you need to understand how SQL Server maps rows into pages, pages into segments, segments into database devices, and how tables and indexes share segments.

[6.] Some platforms use 4K pages. The Sybase page size has nothing to do with the platform's operating system or hardware page size. For convenience, the Sybase database page size is used for sizing database devices and SQL Server memory allocation.

4.5.1   Mapping Segments and Databases to Disks

Databases are created using pages from database devices. Each database device can be a part of many databases and many devices can participate in a single database. This many-to-many mapping is done via two intermediate units: **disk fragments** and **segments**. Figure 4.4 illustrates the relationship between devices, disk fragments, segments, and database.

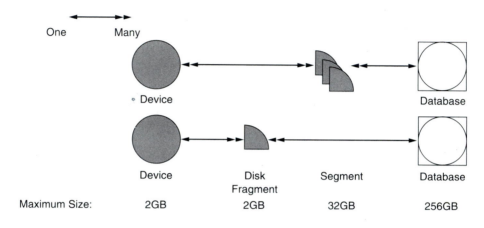

Figure 4.4   Devices, disk fragments, segments, and databases[7] - - - - - - - - - -

The `disk init` command creates database devices. SQL Server can use raw partitions, logical volumes, or operating system files as database devices.[8] In general:

- **Only one database device on each physical disk** — SQL Server assumes that disk activity to one database device does not impact disk activity to other database devices. If two database devices occupy the same physical disk, this assumption is invalid.

- **Devices that permit asynchronous I/O are preferred over devices that only allow synchronous I/O** — Asynchronous I/O improves the throughput of SQL Server by allowing engines to perform other work while the operating system performs the I/O operation. If only synchronous I/O is available, engines must

---

7.   The maximum device size is limited to 2Gb in System 10 SQL Server. System 11 SQL Server allows larger device files if such files are permitted by the operating system and support asynchronous I/O.

8.   The possible choices and the best choice depend on the operating system and your application.

wait while the operating system completes the I/O operation, preventing the engine from performing useful SQL Server work while the I/O is in progress.

- **Non-buffered devices (e.g., raw partitions via the character device special file) are preferred over buffered files (e.g., Unix file system files)** — SQL Server assumes that writes to a disk are persistent. Buffered files break this assumption by caching writes to the disk in operating system buffers. If the power fails before the operating system writes its buffers to disk, the information in the buffer is lost.

Your Sybase manuals describe the appropriate device files for SQL Server on your platform.

Database Device Fragments

In Figure 4.5 we create three database devices, each 100Mb in size using three raw partitions: `/dev/rdsk/0s0`, `/dev/rdsk/0s1`, `/dev/rdsk/0s2`.

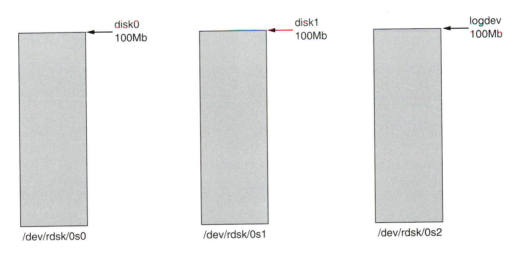

```
disk init name = "disk0", physname = "/dev/rdsk/0s0", vdevno = 4, size = 102400
disk init name = "disk1", physname = "/dev/rdsk/0s1", vdevno = 5, size = 102400
disk init name = "logdev", physname = "/dev/rdsk/0s2", vdevno = 3, size = 102400
```

Figure 4.5   Initialize database devices -

After you have all of the database devices you need, you use `create database` to create the database on the devices. The `on` keyword for `create database` tells SQL Server how much space to take from each device when creating the database. A database may contain as many as 128 devices, limiting the size of a database to 256Gb.[9] In Figure 4.6 we create a database called `public` using space from the database devices `disk0` and `disk1` for data, and `logdev` for the log.

create database public on disk0 = 25, disk1 = 50 log on logdev = 50

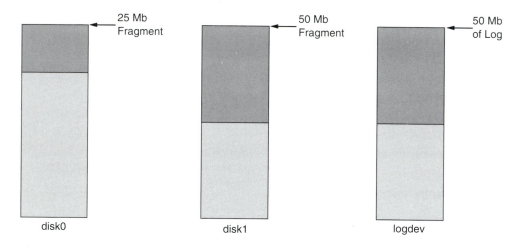

Figure 4.6   Creating the database -

Figure 4.7 shows that we can create more databases using the same database device files. The database `private` uses space on database device `disk0`. The database `sheltered` uses space on database device `disk1`. The part of the database device that is used by a database is called a **device fragment**, as it is only part of the complete database device. A database can consume all of a database device, in which case the device fragment is the same size as the database device.

---

9.   For systems with a maximum database device size of 2Gb.

Database Segments

You can organize a subset of the database devices participating in a database into a **segment**. This is an unfortunate name for this feature of SQL Server, as SQL Server segments are not really segments in the way we normally think about them. We find it easier to think of segments as a way of tagging database devices with a name. Within a database, a database device can be associated with more than one segment name and the same segment can be applied to more than one database device.

```
create database private on disk0 = 50
create database sheltered on disk1 = 25
```

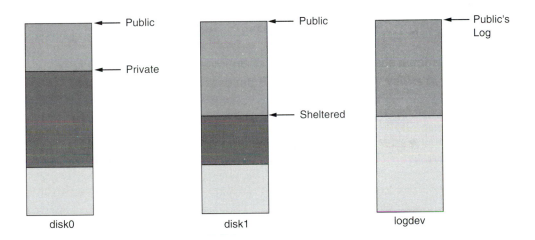

Figure 4.7   Creating more than one database on a database device- - - - - - - -

You create new segments in a database with the sp_addsegment stored procedure. As Figure 4.8 shows, SQL Server creates three segments when a database is created:

- **default** — Segment used when objects are created and no specific segment is given for placing the object.
- **system** — Segment used for system tables.
- **logsegment** — Segment used for transaction log.

For the database `public`, `logsegment` contains only the `logdev` database device. The `system` and `default` segments include both the `disk0` and `disk1` database devices.

At some point we may want to segregate our use of database device `disk0`, so we decide to create a segment called `d0segment` that includes only database device `disk0`. The `sp_addsegment` command lets you create new segments and add database devices to segments. As a result of the `sp_addsegment` command in Figure 4.9, the device fragment from `disk0` that is part of database `public` is now associated with three segments: `default` segment, `system` segment, and the segment we created called `d0segment`.

create database public on disk0 = 25, disk1 = 50 log logdev = 50

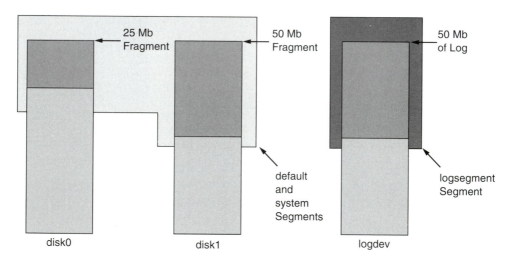

Figure 4.8   Pre-assigned segment arrangement -

We can use the `sp_dropsegment` stored procedure to remove a disk fragment from a segment. For example, in Figure 4.10 we drop `disk0` from the `default` segment for the database `public`.

The optimal number and sizes of segments is determined by your database schema. We could, size permitting, put all the database devices into the `default` segment, place all tables and indexes on the `default` segment, and never create another segment. But we would not be able to control the placement of tables and indexes on disks. In the next section, we will see how tables and indexes are mapped to segments. We should spread each segment across as many disks as necessitated either by the size of the objects placed in the segment or by the I/O requirements of the tables and indexes on the segment. This is discussed in more detail in Chapter 6, *Physical Database Design*.

sp_addsegment d0segment, public, disk0

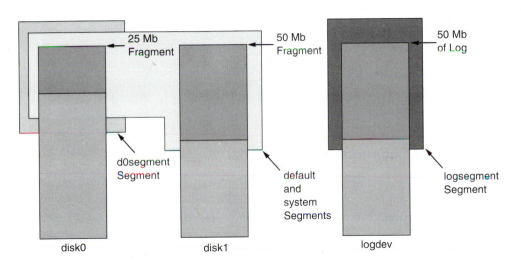

Figure 4.9   Defining a segment -

sp_dropsegment default, public, disk0
sp_dropsegment system, public, disk0

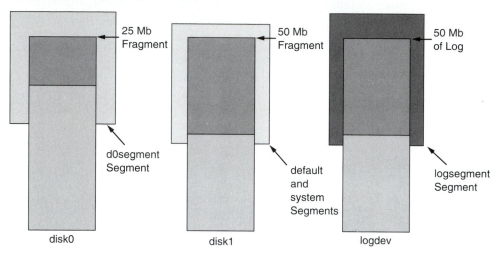

| 25 Mb Fragment | 50 Mb Fragment | 50 Mb of Log |

d0segment Segment

default and system Segments

logsegment Segment

disk0   disk1   logdev

Figure 4.10   Drop disk0 from the default segment- -

Placing Objects in Segments

You tell SQL Server to place tables and indexes on particular segments in the database when you create the table or index. The create table and create index commands have an on *segment* clause that identifies the segment. SQL Server allocates space for the object only from the database devices assigned to the named segment. If you do not use an on segment clause, SQL Server uses space from the segment default.

You can re-assign an existing table or index to a new segment with the sp_placeobject stored procedure. As the table or index grows, space comes from the new segment. sp_placeobject does not move the table or index from one segment to another. To do this, you must drop and recreate the table or index. When you recreate the table or index you can give the new segment name in the on segment clause.

4.5.2   Mapping Database Pages to Device Pages

The pages in a database are assigned sequential identification numbers starting at zero and ending with the last page of the database. These identification numbers are called the **logical page numbers**. SQL Server must translate the logical page number in a database into an offset on the appropriate database device. To assist in this translation, SQL Server organizes all of the database devices into a large *virtual* address space and assigns each page of every database device a **virtual page number**. As Figure 4.11 shows, the most significant byte of the virtual page number identifies the database device. The rest of the virtual page number gives the offset into the device in page sized units.

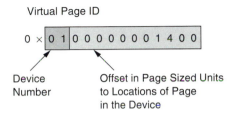

Figure 4.11   Decoding the virtual page ID -

As Figure 4.12 suggests, SQL Server consolidates the device fragments that make up a database into a continuous logical page space. The map between the virtual page space and the logical page space is described by the `master..sysusages` table.

As database users, you deal mostly with logical pages rather than virtual pages. In general, when we talk about a page ID, we mean a logical page ID.

4.5.3   Logical Page Organization

SQL Server organizes the pages in a database into **extents**. Each extent holds eight contiguous pages. All of the pages in an extent must belong to the same table or index. When any page from an extent is allocated to a table or index, the rest of the extent is reserved for that object. These are called **reserved pages**.

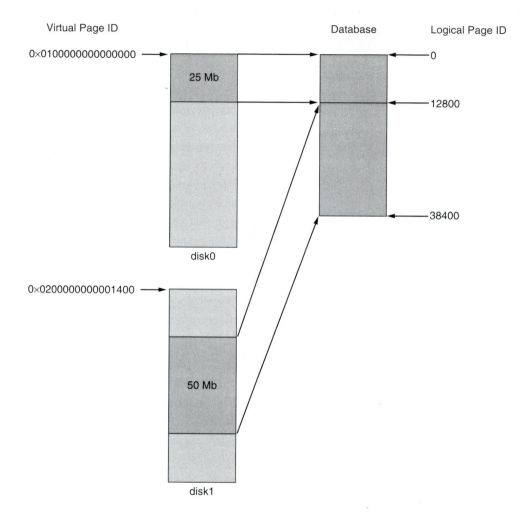

Figure 4.12   Mapping the virtual page ID to the database's logical page ID - - - -

Extents are organized into **allocation units**. There are 32 extents in each allocation unit. Hence, an allocation unit has 256 pages, or 512K of storage. A 100Mb database has 51,200 pages, organized into 6,400 extents, which in turn are managed as 200 allocation units.[10] The first page of an allocation unit is the **allocation**

[10.]   For these calculations assume that each database page is 2K.

page. The allocation page manages the pages in the allocation unit. SQL Server can figure out how much free space is available in each extent of the allocation unit by reading only the allocation page. As the first page of the allocation unit is also the first page of the first extent in the allocation unit, the first extent in an allocation unit has seven pages available for tables and indexes rather than eight. Figure 4.13 shows the relationship between pages, extents, and allocation units.

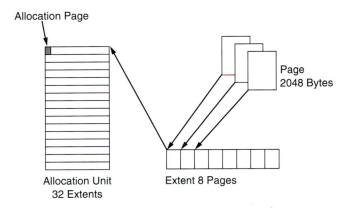

Figure 4.13   Pages, extents, and allocation units -

A database is made up of a collection of allocation units. Each allocation unit resides on a disk fragment and may participate in one or more segments. Figure 4.14 depicts the relationship between allocation units, segments, database devices, and databases.

Allocation units are managed by a Global Allocation Map (GAM). The GAM is a chain of pages. Each allocation unit is associated with a single bit on a GAM page. The bit indicates if there is any free space in the allocation unit. Figure 4.15 shows the relationship between the GAM and allocation units.

For each table and index, SQL Server maintains a list of allocation units that contains extents for that object. This is called the Object Allocation Map (OAM). The OAM differs from the GAM in that the GAM makes it easier to locate extents that are not assigned to any table or index and the OAM makes it easier to find the allocation units that contain a particular table or index. Figure 4.16 shows the relationship between the OAM and the allocation pages.

Database Accounts

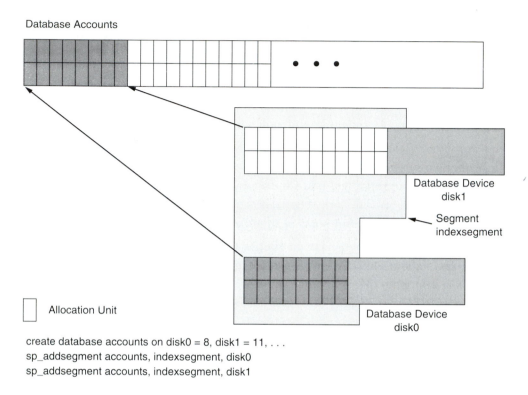

```
create database accounts on disk0 = 8, disk1 = 11, . . .
sp_addsegment accounts, indexsegment, disk0
sp_addsegment accounts, indexsegment, disk1
```

Figure 4.14   Allocation units, segments, database devices, and databases- - - -

Tables are chains of pages. The page chain is orthogonal to the allocation mechanism. That two pages for an object are allocated in adjacent database pages does not imply that the pages follow one another in the table. This fragmentation can cause performance problems and limit the effectiveness of large I/O operations in System 11 SQL Server. Chapter 12, *Batch Processing Performance*, and discusses ways to prevent fragmentation of a table.

The pages are linked together with next and previous page pointers in a doubly linked fashion. Figure 4.17 shows how pages are linked together.

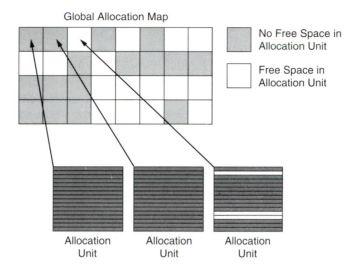

Figure 4.15   Relationship between GAM and allocation unit - - - - - - - - - - - - - -

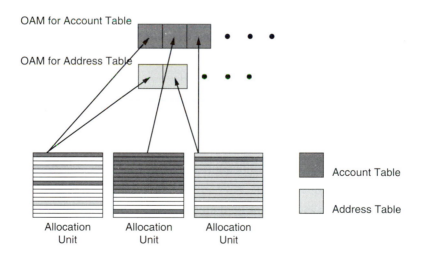

Figure 4.16   Object Allocation Map -

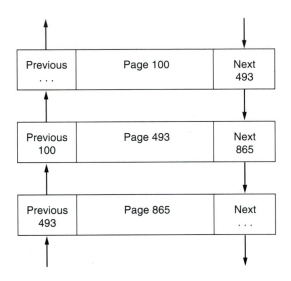

Figure 4.17   Doubly linked list of pages -

4.5.4   **How SQL Server Allocates Pages**

When the first row of data is inserted into a table, SQL Server allocates an extent to the table and puts the row onto a page in the extent. The table now has one allocated page and seven reserved pages. As more rows are added to the table, SQL Server first uses the reserved pages. When the reserved pages on the first extent are exhausted, SQL Server allocates a new extent for the table, and the process repeats as before. In allocating a new extent, SQL Server attempts to maintain object homogeneity in allocation units. That is, SQL Server prefers to allocate extents for a table from an allocation unit that already contains extents for the table that is growing. This is done in an attempt to keep the pages of a table close together. Allocation of pages for indexes works similarly.

When you delete rows from the table, pages are deallocated from the tables and indexes when there are no longer any rows left on the page. When all of the pages in an extent are deallocated, the extent is freed and is no longer assigned to the table or index.

When you assign tables and indexes to segments, you might put more than one table or index on a particular segment. If the tables and indexes grow concurrently, they share allocation units within the segment. For example, if you put a table and its three indexes on the same segment, some allocation units in the segment may contain a medley of extents belonging to the table and its three indexes. On the other hand, if we put the table in a segment by itself, all the extents in each allocation unit contain only the table and not the indexes.

If the database becomes fragmented because there are many small inserts and deletes to tables, SQL Server's heuristic for allocating database pages may not provide good homogeneity. Furthermore, homogeneity may not imply locality of reference for sufficiently large tables and indexes. Figure 4.18 demonstrates a table with good locality of reference and a straight page chain. Figure 4.19 illustrates that the order of the pages in the table may not correspond well to the placement of the pages in the database. The only way to de-fragment the table is to drop and recreate the table.

Because SQL Server does not free an extent until the last page on the extent is deallocated, you might be left with one page in each extent holding data and seven reserved pages. Such a table is using eight times more space than it really needs. The only way to recover the space is to insert more rows into the table or drop and recreate the table.

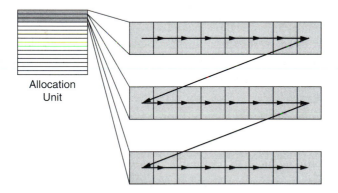

Allocation
Unit

Figure 4.18   Good locality of reference -

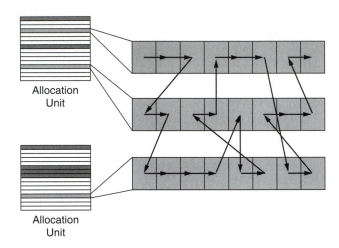

Figure 4.19   Table page chain in a heavily fragmented database - - - - - - - - - - -

Fragmentation can have a serious impact in System 11 SQL Server when large I/O is used. Large I/O reads adjacent pages into memory simultaneously. To get maximum advantage out of large I/O, logically adjacent pages in a table should also be physically adjacent. Then, with a single I/O operation, a larger, useful part of the table is read all at once. If the table is highly fragmented, then a single large I/O operation may bring in only one useful page. The rest of the I/O is wasted. We discuss large I/O in Chapter 13, *Advanced Topics* and table fragmentation in Chapter 12, *Batch Processing Performance*.

4.6   INDEXES

Proper indexing of data can significantly reduce the amount of time it takes to retrieve particular rows from a table. Locating a particular row of data with an index is a lot faster than reading the entire table looking for the row. However, the index consumes space in the database and must be maintained during updates, inserts, and deletes. SQL Server supports two kinds of indexes: clustered indexes and nonclustered indexes.[11]

[11.] Both clustered and nonclustered indexes are based on B-tree indexes. SQL Server does not currently support hash indexes or bitmap indexes.

4.6.1 Clustered Index

Figure 4.20 illustrates the structure of a clustered index. A clustered index physically orders the rows in a table by the order of the index. The leaf pages of the index are the table's data pages. The indexed columns from the first row of data of each leaf page are copied onto the first layer of non-leaf pages. The first row of each first layer non-leaf page is copied into the second layer non-leaf page, and so on. Each row of data in the non-leaf index pages has a pointer to the page that contains the row. The number of index rows in each index page depends on the size and number of columns participating in the index. As there can only be one physical ordering of the data, you can only have one clustered index per table.

In the example clustered index in Figure 4.20, the root index page contains the rows `abby` and `kimberly`. These are the first index rows for the index pages in the next layer of the index. For example, `abby` points to the index page containing `abby`, `bob`, and `george`, while `kimberly` points to the index page containing `kimberly`, `paul`, and `victor`. The second layer of the index points to the data pages. For example, the index row for `bob` points to the data page that begins with the row containing the name `bob`. The other rows on the page are ordered by the index.

Suppose SQL Server needs to find the row containing the name `eric` using this clustered index. Starting with the root index page, SQL Server finds that `eric` falls after `abby` but before `kimberly`, so it follows the link from `abby` to the next layer of the index. On this index page, SQL Server finds that `eric` falls between `bob` and `george`, so it follows the link from `bob` to the data page. It then searches the data page that starts with `bob` to find the row for `eric`.

4.6.2 Clustered Index and Duplicate Keys

Duplicate indexed columns somewhat complicate the structure of a clustered index. If there are many duplicates of the indexed columns, SQL Server creates an **overflow page** to contain the rows with the duplicate indexed columns. Only rows with the same indexed columns are stored in the overflow page. The overflow page is linked into the table's page chain, but is not linked into the non-leaf index pages. New rows are appended to the end of the overflow page. If the overflow page is full, a new page is linked into the table after the overflow page and the row added to the new page. Looking for a row with duplicate indexed columns requires SQL Server to scan the overflow pages. Figure 4.21 shows a clustered index with an overflow page.

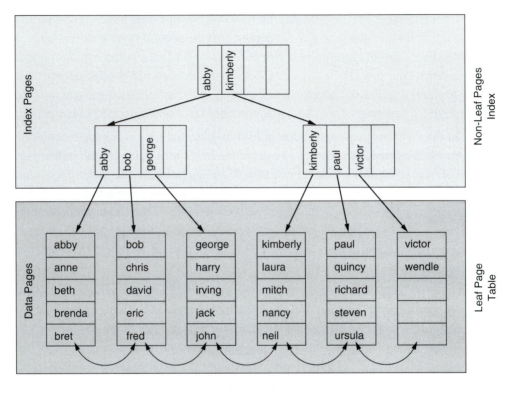

Figure 4.20   Clustered index on names: data pages ordered by index order - - -

In the example in Figure 4.21, the rows for irving are duplicated and stored in the overflow page. If the first irving row, the row that is not on the overflow page, is deleted, the overflow page is said to be **disconnected**. The values on the overflow page are no longer represented on a data page pointed to by a non-leaf page in the clustered index. Disconnected overflow pages may slow some queries because SQL Server must read the disconnected overflow page to find out what value is stored on it. Suppose irving is not disconnected and we query SQL Server looking for kelly. SQL Server knows that kelly is between george and kimberly so it reads the page headed by george and discovers there is no `kelly`. No rows qualify. Suppose `irving` is disconnected. When we perform the same query, SQL Server reads the page headed by `george` and then must read the disconnected overflow page to see if it contains `kelly`. Two page reads are needed rather than one.

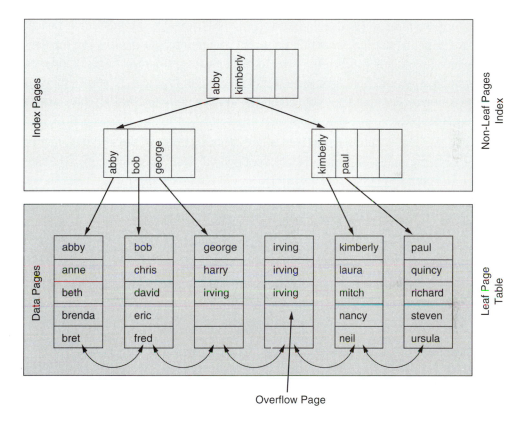

Overflow Page

Figure 4.21   Overflow page -

You can avoid duplicate keys altogether by manipulating the schema to allow for a unique index on the table. You can create a unique index or an index that ignores duplicate keys. Of course, this changes the semantics of the table schema as it can no longer hold duplicate keys. If this is not acceptable to your application, consider adding a column to the index so that the keys become unique. For example, if the table includes an unique column, you can include this column as the last key in the index to make the index keys unique. The trade-off is that adding a column to the index makes the index wider, reducing the number of index rows on each page, and increasing the I/O needed to scan the index.

4.6.3 Nonclustered Index

A nonclustered index does not physically order the data by the index. Instead, the leaf pages of the index contain page and row pointers to the rows in the data pages. In other respects nonclustered indexes are similar to clustered indexes. You can have several nonclustered indexes on a table. Figure 4.22 shows the structure of a nonclustered index. Not shown are the page pointers linking the data pages together.

The leaf pages of a nonclustered index contain copies of the columns that participate in the index. SQL Server does not need to read the data pages from the table if no columns outside those participating in the index are selected and the index is used to facilitate the query. This saves following the page and row pointers in the index leaf page to the data page and reading the data page.

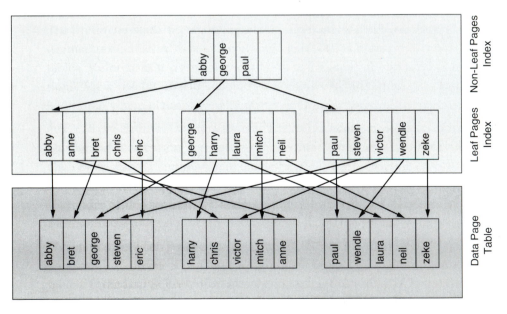

Figure 4.22   Nonclustered index on names: data pages are not ordered- - - - - -

4.6.4 Fill Factor

The index fill factor determines how full we make each index page when the index is created. For example, a fill factor of 50% means SQL Server only uses half the space in each index page before moving on to the next page. This means the index is twice as big as necessary but much more data can be added to the table before we must link new pages into the index (see Figure 4.23). For a clustered index, the fill factor also changes the amount of space left open in the data pages with the exception of overflow pages. Overflow pages are always 100% full.

SQL Server uses the fill factor only when the index is created. It does not maintain the specified fill factor over the life of the index. When SQL Server inserts a new page, it generally splits the rows 50:50 between the full page and the new page.[12] As a result, all of the pages in the table are somewhere between 50% full and 100% full, with the pages 75% full on average. This means indexes converge on a 75% fill factor.

100% Fill Factor		70% Fill Factor		50% Fill Factor	
abby		abby	bob	abby	bob
anne		anne	chris	anne	chris
beth		beth	david	beth	david
brenda		brenda	eric	brenda	eric
bret		bret	fred	bret	fred
bob		bob			
chris		chris			
david					
eric					
fred					

Figure 4.23   Fill factor -

[12.] There are two exceptions here: (1) on a clustered index where the last page of the table is split because we append a row to the end of the table SQL Server leaves the last page completely full and moves onto the next page; (2) overflow pages are left 100% full.

4.6.5   Maximum Rows per Page

System 11 SQL Server has a maximum rows feature that limits the number of rows per data page. Unlike fill factor, the maximum rows per page feature permanently limits the number of rows on each page. This can be a useful feature for applications ported to SQL Server that require locking with finer granularity than page locks.

The trade-off is that for small rows and small maximum row counts much of the space on the page is wasted. I/O time is also wasted because more pages must be read from disk to read the same amount of useful data. On the other hand, concurrency is improved if the ported application demands row level locking.

The `create table` command accepts the option:

```
with max_rows_per_page = <number>
```

that sets or changes the maximum number of rows per page. This attribute of the table can be changed at any time by using the command:

```
sp_chgattribute "<table>","max_rows_per_page",<number>
```

which does not change the number of rows on the pages already in the table, but sets the number of rows per page for all future inserts to the table.

4.6.6   Update Statistics

Using an index to find a particular row of data is a lot faster than reading the entire table and scanning for the row. On the other hand, if we are looking for a large set of rows, using the index might be more costly. To make intelligent decisions about the fastest way to access data, SQL Server keeps statistical information about the index. The idea is to characterize how evenly spread the values are in the index. Are the data clumped around certain values or are the data evenly spread over a wide range? This characterization is called the **distribution** of the index.

The values of the indexed columns are sampled at even intervals through the index. The number of intervals is inversely proportional to the size of the indexed columns, since the statistics for an index are stored in a single database page. The smaller the indexed column, the more detailed the statistics. In the example shown in Figure 4.24 there are 20 rows in the table and room for five values on the statistics page. We are indexing on an integer column.[13] We sample the table on every fifth row, also remembering the first row so we know the smallest value in the table. Each sampled row is called a **step**.

As we know there are five rows for each step of the distribution, from only the distribution we know there are ten rows in the table less than 176. We also know there are five rows between 539 and 2034. Besides the distribution, SQL Server stores additional information on the distribution of values within each interval through the use of the **density** function. The density function describes the number of duplicate values in the indexed column. A density of 100% means every row of the indexed column has the same value. In a 100 row table, a density of 1% means that each row has a different value. The table in Figure 4.23 has 20 rows with no repeated values, so the density is 5%. SQL Server has no mechanism to estimate statistics quickly and it does not incrementally adjust statistics as the contents of the index are changed.

SQL Server's method of recording statistics about indexes has advantages over a top ten or histogram approach. In a top ten approach, the statistics identify the ten most frequent values of the indexed column. For example, a travel agent's database may identify Honolulu, Orlando, and San Francisco as the most popular vacation destinations. However, such statistics fail to indicate the distribution of values in range queries. For example, it may be true for the same travel agent that the number of vacations starting between June 1 and June 7 far exceeds the number of vacations that start between September 10 and September 17. But this fact is not captured by the top ten method unless the individual days between June 1 and June 7 are enormously popular.

In a histogram approach, the range of data is divided into even intervals and we count how many rows fit into each range. This approach tends to clump several extremely frequent values with some not so frequent values in the same range, rendering them indistinguishable from one another. The SQL Server distribution statistics provide more information about data that is not evenly distributed. For example, if many rows are clustered around a single value, SQL Server can distinguish between very similar numbers. The details are lost in the histogram.

[13.] OK, so the example is not using a 2 Kbyte page. It is only an example after all.

SQL Server records statistics about a table when an index is created. Of course, the statistics are based on the data in the table when the index is created. If the table is empty, the statistics are not very interesting. The `update statistics` command makes SQL Server update the statistics for all indexes. You should do this after the data in indexed tables has changed significantly.

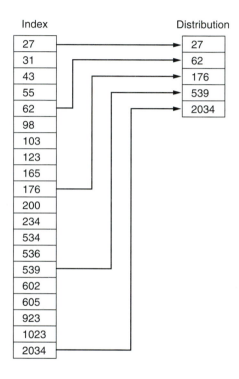

Figure 4.24   Distribution of values in indexes -

4.7   TEXT AND IMAGE DATA

SQL Server supports the text and image datatypes as a way of storing more than 255 bytes in a column. Text and image data are stored as a page chain separate from tables and indexes. There is one page chain for each table that has a text or image column. A 16 byte text page pointer is stored in the row that points to the text pages representing the value stored in the column for that row. Within a table, each row must have a unique text page pointer, hence duplicate rows are not allowed on the text or image columns.[14] Figure 4.25 shows a small table with an image column. The text page pointers in the image column point into the text page chain. Not shown are the previous page pointers that link the text pages in the reverse order.

Each text or image value is stored on its own page. If the value is too large to fit on a single page, more pages are added to the page chain after the first page of the value. This means the minimum amount of storage consumed by a text or image column is a single page. As the value grows, it is assigned additional space a page at a time. Text and image values do not share pages, so a value that is one byte too big for one page uses two pages. Each page holds 1800 bytes of text or image data.

As each text or image value uses at least one page of space, you can save a considerable amount of space by allowing NULLs on the text or image column. There is some additional programming complexity in allocating space for the value afterwards, but it may be to your advantage if space is a problem.

When you insert a row with a text or image value, SQL Server allocates space for the new text or image value at the end of the page chain and stores the page pointer in the table. If the value is too long to fit on one page, SQL Server allocates and links in additional pages. If you update the value, SQL Server deallocates all but the first page of the page chain, writes the new value over the first page, and allocates any new pages that are needed, linking them into the page chain as appropriate. When the row is deleted, SQL Server deallocates all of the pages associated with the value.

Because text and image data is not stored in the table, there are restrictions on how you can use text and image data in queries:

- Text or image data cannot be used as arguments to stored procedures.
- You cannot declare local variables of type text or image.
- Text or image columns can only be used with the `like` operator in a `where` clause. They cannot be used for joins or in `order by`, `compute`, or `group by` clauses.
- You cannot build an index on a text or image column.

[14.] If the text or image column allows NULLs then a NULL text or image column may be duplicated.

SQL Server does not use any data compression on `text` and `image` datatypes and it does not exploit the indirection it uses in storage of `text` and `image` to replace multiple occurrences of a duplicated value by pointers to the first occurrence. If your application can benefit from either of these two optimizations, you need to implement them in your application code.

The Transact-SQL commands `readtext` and `writetext` are useful when dealing with large text or image values. `writetext` can insert text or image values into the table without logging the change. This saves time and reduces the space requirements of the log if the values are large. You compromise recoverability, however.

The most efficient interface is through the client libraries. They interact directly with SQL Server at a level not available to Transact-SQL programmers, that bypasses some of the command interpretation and formatting routines in SQL Server. In DB-Library these are `dbwritetext` and `dbreadtext`, and for Client-Library these are `ct_send_data` and `ct_get_data`.

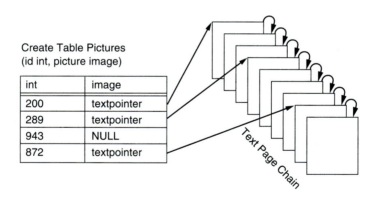

Create Table Pictures
(id int, picture image)

int	image
200	textpointer
289	textpointer
943	NULL
872	textpointer

Text Page Chain

Figure 4.25   Text and image data -

Chapter 5

SQL Server — Methods and Features

This second chapter on SQL Server's architecture discusses some of the important features and methods used to manage the physical resources controlled by SQL Server. Understanding how SQL Server manages physical resources is an important part of understanding how to tune your application to SQL Server and how SQL Server configuration changes the way it behaves toward your application. For example:

- How SQL Server optimizes access to data affects how you should organize your data into tables and your selection of indexes.

- SQL Server enforces concurrency controls with a locking mechanism. If not used properly, excessive locking can impact the throughput of your application, while insufficient locking can upset the transactional integrity of your application.

- How SQL Server implements important data integrity features affects your choice of triggers over declarative integrity constraints.

5.1   CACHE MANAGEMENT

SQL Server uses a portion of the shared memory segment to cache pages from the database devices. The cache is divided into buffers, each of which holds one page of the database. The primary purpose of the buffer cache is to reduce the number of I/O operations to the database devices. Some of the buffers are reserved for internal bookkeeping operations; others cache stored procedures. The rest (typically the lion's share) cache data, index, and log pages in memory. Let us discuss some essentials of the buffer replacement strategies used by SQL Server and how they influence performance.

5.1.1   Dirty Buffers

A buffer contains the image of a page in the database. An internal hash table locates the buffer holding the current image of the database page, if any. Two different buffers cannot contain images of the same page. A buffer can be in any one of several states, including **clean** and **dirty**. A buffer is clean if its contents agree with the contents of the corresponding page in the database device. An update, insert, or delete operation renders a buffer dirty. That is, the contents of the buffer differ from the contents of the page in the database device. A dirty buffer can be cleaned by writing its contents to the database device. However, doing so indiscriminately may violate the integrity of data. The buffer manager follows a variation of the traditional write-ahead log (WAL) policy[1] to ensure data integrity. In a nutshell, WAL policy requires that all log pages pertaining to a buffer are written to the disk before the buffer.

Clean buffers can be reused at virtually no cost. We can read in a different page into the same buffer without losing any information. This happens frequently in the course of SQL Server's normal operation as pages are either read off database devices or created as a result of inserts and updates. However, a dirty page must be cleaned before it can be reused. The reason for this is simple: A dirty page is the only image of the current contents of the page. Unless we write its contents to the database device, the contents of the page are lost.[2]

A supply of clean buffers is essential for database performance. Cleaning a dirty buffer is time consuming. Not only must you write out the contents of the dirty buffer, but you must ensure that all of the log records associated with the buffer are written. SQL Server maintains a supply of clean buffers through a mechanism called **buffer wash**. Buffer wash specifies a minimum number of buffers that must either be clean or in the process of becoming clean. When the supply of clean buffers dwindles below the threshold set by the buffer wash, the cache manager requires that every task requesting a new buffer wash the two least recently used buffers.

As inserts, updates, and deletes continue, the collection of dirty buffers left behind after committed transactions grows. Should SQL Server fail at this instant, these dirty buffers represent work that must be done during recovery. The change to the

---

[1]   For a detailed description of the Write-Ahead Log policy, see Section 10.3.7.6 in "Transaction Processing: Concepts and Techniques" by Jim Gray and Andreas Reuter, Morgan Kaufman 1993.

[2]   This is a simplification. There may already be a record of the changes made to the page in the transaction log.

page has not yet been written to the database device, so recovery must reconstruct the change from the transaction log. SQL Server may checkpoint the database to minimize the amount of work that needs to be done during recovery. In the context of the buffer manager, this means we need to clean all of the dirty buffers for the database. Should SQL Server fail when there are no dirty buffers, recovery should have very little work to do. Checkpoint forces all of the buffers dirtied before the checkpoint to be written to the database devices. This means looking at the transactions recorded in log since the last checkpoint (or boot, or `dump transaction`) and writing out the dirty buffers associated with those transactions.

Here are some of the impacts of the above strategies on performance:

1. Updates, deletes, and inserts need *not* be written to disk immediately, even after a commit operation. All we need to do is to enter all changes in the transaction log and require that all relevant log entries are written to database devices before the commit is complete. Actually writing the buffers to the database devices is done later as a result of one of several events including the reuse of the buffer, checkpoint, and shutdown.

2. Buffer wash is performed by all tasks, not just the tasks that dirty buffers. Thus, read-only operations can, and often do, require writing to the disk. On a side note, a lot of queries that appear to be read-only are not. For example, complex queries may involve creation of work tables (see Chapter 11, *Query Processing Performance*).

3. Running out of clean buffers will bring SQL Server down on its knees. We discuss diagnosis and remedy of this rare disease in Chapter 10, *Transaction Processing Performance*.

5.1.2 Named Caches and Buffer Pools

The cache manager in System 11 SQL Server has several new features that can significantly improve the performance of your applications. In System 10 SQL Server, all memory dedicated to data cache was monolithic. All tables and indexes accessed by users shared the single cache. A query that scans a large table can displace all other data in cache, disrupting the data caching for other users.

System 11 SQL Server allows you to divide the data cache into **named caches**. Tables and/or indexes are bound to the named caches. By binding a particular table or index to a named cache, you are assured that only that table or index is using the memory dedicated to the named cache and that no memory outside the named cache is used to cache the table or index.

With the named cache feature, you can cache an entire table or index in memory and only incur the cost of reading the disks once, to warm the cache. Once the data is in cache, it cannot be displaced by another table or index because the named cache is dedicated to caching only the table or index bound to the cache.

In addition to named caches, System 11 SQL Server allows you to divide the named cache into **buffer pools**. Each buffer pool has an I/O size associated with it. System 10 SQL Server performs all I/O in 2K chunks. System 11 SQL Server may perform I/O in 2K, 4K, 8K, and 16K chunks. This improves the performance of table scans and heap inserts as it allows more data to be transferred in a single I/O operation. Chapter 13, *Advanced Topics*, for more information about named caches and buffer pools.

5.1.3   Buffer Replacement Strategy

System 10 and earlier SQL Servers use a variant of the **Least Recently Used** (LRU) buffer replacement strategy to choose a buffer to reuse. LRU dictates that we reuse buffers that have not been used for the longest interval. This makes it very likely that the pages most frequently used by our application stay in memory.

Along with the LRU buffer replacement strategy, System 11 SQL Server may also choose to use the **Fetch-and-Discard** buffer replacement strategy. The fetch and discard strategy is helpful in situations where LRU works against you.

How use and discard is useful is not immediately intuitive. Consider a query that involves several tables, some of which need to be read many times in order to complete the query. The LRU buffer replacement strategy works against us if one or more of those tables is larger than the total amount of memory devoted to data cache. In reading one of the large tables, the database pages for the large tables displace buffered pages for the other tables participating in the query. Pages from the displaced tables must be read from disk the next time they are needed. If the use and discard strategy is used for the larger tables, the same buffers are used over and over again as the larger tables are read so the smaller tables stay in memory. Pages from the large tables must be read into memory each time they are needed. But, as these large tables are larger than the total amount of buffer space, even the LRU buffer replacement strategy requires that the pages are read each time they are needed. Fetch and discard saves reads overall by keeping the smaller tables cached.

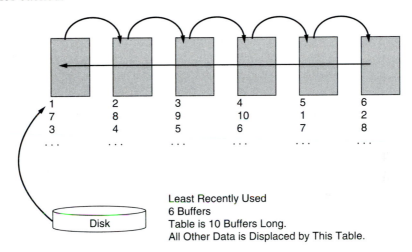

Least Recently Used
6 Buffers
Table is 10 Buffers Long.
All Other Data is Displaced by This Table.

Figure 5.1   LRU buffer replacement strategy -

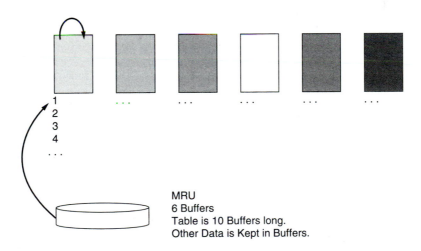

MRU
6 Buffers
Table is 10 Buffers long.
Other Data is Kept in Buffers.

Figure 5.2   Fetch and discard buffer replacement strategy- - - - - - - - - - - - - - -

5.2 LOCK MANAGEMENT

Locks are used to synchronize activity inside SQL Server. SQL Server uses locks on pages, tables, and page addresses to ensure transactional consistency. Lock contention can be a major stumbling block for performance. Very often, applications developed on another RDBMS using row-level locks exhibits severe lock contention when ported to SQL Server. Currently, SQL Server does not support row-level locks. Let us pay special attention to the granularity of locks as we explore the implications of lock management on performance.

Before we jump in, a short note on terminology is in order. The general computing community talks of **locks** and **latches**. In the traditional Sybase terminology, latches come in two flavors: **spinlocks** and **semaphore locks**. Latches are used to synchronize activities between the engines in a multi-engine SQL Server and between the threads in all SQL Servers. While latches are by no means irrelevant to lock management, they are better addressed elsewhere. Here we limit our discussion to transactional locks.

SQL Server uses page and table locks to synchronize transactions for the application. Only user tables are locked. No locks are needed to synchronize access to work tables and temporary tables because only one task can access these tables at a time.

5.2.1 Page-Level Locks

There are two types of page locks:

- **Address locks** — Used on non-leaf index pages.
- **Logical locks** — Used on leaf nonclustered index pages and data pages.

Address locks are always exclusive with System 10 and previous versions of SQL Server, even when a task only wants to read (and not update) a page protected by an address lock. If a task is holding an address lock on a page, no other task can access that page. System 11 SQL Server adds shared address locks to improve concurrency. If a task is only reading a page protected by an address lock, other tasks may also read the page.

Address locks are held while a task moves from one node of an index tree structure to another. This process, often called **crabbing** in database jargon, is highly optimized and the locks are not held for very long. Address locks can be a source of contention, but rarely affect performance quite as severely as a contention for logical locks.

Logical locks come in three types:

- **Shared** — The transaction reads the page and does not want the rows to change. The transaction holding the lock has no intention of modifying the page. No transaction may modify the page.

- **Update** — The transaction has read the page and may modify the page later. Update locks are promoted to exclusive locks when the transaction actually modifies the page. No other transaction may modify the page.

- **Exclusive** — Transaction wants to modify the page. No other transaction may read or modify the page.[3]

Suppose a transaction wants to read (but not modify) a page in the database. It acquires a shared lock on the page. A second transaction wants to read (but not modify) the same page. There is no reason to prevent the second transaction from also acquiring a shared lock on the page as neither transaction wants to modify the page. The purpose of shared locks is to prevent another transaction from modifying the page. Extrapolating, we can define lock compatibility rules that describe which locks can be acquired when other locks are already granted on the page. Table 5.1 shows the compatibility among different types of page locks.

Table 5.1   Compatibility between page-level locks

	Shared	**Update**	**Exclusive**
Shared	OK	OK	Conflict
Update	OK	Conflict	Conflict
Exclusive	Conflict	Conflict	Conflict

Let us examine how the lock compatibility synchronizes access to database pages:

[3.] System 11 SQL Server adds dirty reads, which allows tasks to read data on pages protected with an exclusive lock.

- **Many readers** — Each reader must acquire a shared lock on the page. A shared lock is compatible with another shared lock, so many transactions can read the page at the same time.

- **Many readers and a modifier** — The readers acquire shared locks on the page, but the modifier must acquire an exclusive lock. Shared locks and exclusive locks conflict, so the modifier waits until all of the shared locks are released from the page before proceeding.

- **Many modifiers** — Each modifier must acquire an exclusive lock on the page before modifying the page. Exclusive locks conflict with other exclusive locks, so the modifiers must queue up and must change the contents of the page one at a time.

Update locks are similar to shared locks, hence they are compatible. If the transaction holding an update lock decides to modify the page, it must first promote the update lock to an exclusive lock. If other transactions have shared or update locks on the same page, the transaction that wants to modify the page must wait for the other shared and update locks to be released before proceeding.

5.2.2 Table-Level Locks

Table-level locks control access to an entire table, including all indexes on the table. There are four kinds of table locks:

- **Shared intent** — Indicates that the transaction holds a shared page lock on a page in the table.

- **Exclusive intent** — Indicates that the transaction holds an exclusive page lock on a page in the table.

- **Shared** — Transaction does not want any row in the table to change. This is similar to a shared page lock except that it applies to the entire table.

- **Exclusive** — Transaction is modifying much or all of the table. This is similar to an exclusive page lock except that it applies to the entire table.

Intent locks simply reflect the status of page locks on a table. For example, if a transaction holds a shared lock on some page of a table, it also holds a shared intent lock on the entire table.

As with page locks, it is possible to describe the compatibility of table locks. Table 5.2 shows the compatibility between different types of table locks.

Table 5.2   Compatibility between table-level locks

	Shared Intent	Shared	Exclusive Intent	Exclusive
Shared Intent	OK	OK	OK	Conflict
Shared	OK	OK	Conflict	Conflict
Exclusive Intent	OK	Conflict	OK	Conflict
Exclusive	Conflict	Conflict	Conflict	Conflict

5.2.3   Lock Upgrades and Demand Locks

A transaction can promote its shared (or update) lock on a page or table to an exclusive lock, subject to the lock compatibility rules described in Table 5.1 and Table 5.2. There is, of course, no demotion of locks.

A task waiting for an exclusive lock on a page or table can be starved out by other tasks who take turns acquiring and releasing shared locks. For example, transaction A acquires a shared page lock. Transaction B wants to modify the page, so it tries to acquire an exclusive lock. As transaction A already holds a shared lock on the page, transaction B must wait until the shared lock is released. Transaction C comes along and also acquires a shared lock on the page. Transaction A completes and releases its lock, but transaction B still cannot continue because transaction C now holds a shared lock on the page. You can imagine this relay race running indefinitely with the shared lock passed like a baton from one transaction to the next.

To prevent this from happening, SQL Server limits the number of times a shared lock can be granted while a conflicting exclusive lock is waiting. Once this threshold is reached, the blocked transaction is said to hold a **demand lock** on the object. Requests for shared locks queue up behind the exclusive lock to be granted as soon as the exclusive lock is released. This prevents any further conflicting shared locks from being granted.

5.2.4   Lock Escalation

If a single SQL statement acquires many page locks on any table, SQL Server attempts to escalate the page locks to a table-level lock at every subsequent acquisition of a page lock on the same table by the query. The threshold is 200 page locks for System 10 SQL Server and can be configured for System 11 SQL Server. For System 10 SQL Server, for example, if a query scans 1000 pages of a table, SQL Server will try to acquire a table lock instead of another page lock once it reaches the 201st page.[4] If the lock escalation succeeds, no further locks are acquired for the remainder of the table scan. If there is a conflicting lock that prevents the query from acquiring a table lock, SQL Server grants the needed page lock and tries again the next time a page lock is requested. This might continue for the remaining 800 pages.

System 11 SQL Server has configuration parameters for a low water threshold mark, a high water threshold mark, and a lock percentage. If the product of the percentage and the number of pages in the table is less than the low water threshold mark, then the low water threshold mark is used as the lock escalation threshold. If the product of the percentage and the number of pages in the table is greater than the high water threshold mark, then the high water threshold mark is used as the lock escalation threshold. If the product of the percentage and the number of pages in the table falls between the two threshold marks, then that threshold is used as the lock escalation threshold.

It is during lock escalation that the intent table locks come in handy. If a transaction needs a shared table lock, the lock can be granted if other transactions hold only shared-intent table locks on the table. If a transaction holds an exclusive page lock on a page in the table, it also holds an exclusive-intent table lock, and a shared table lock cannot be granted.

5.2.5   Isolation Levels and Locks

When several changes to a database must be made as an indivisible set, the changes are bundled into a transaction. A transaction may want to believe that it is the only activity in the database. This means that any information read by the

---

4. This is a little misleading. In general, SQL Server holds a shared lock on a page only long enough to read the contents of the page. Once the scan has moved off the page, the lock is released. For this example, assume that SQL Server is holding the locks as it scans the table as is the case when `holdlock` is used or the scan is performed at isolation level 3.

transaction cannot change until the transaction is complete. Consider a banking scenario. A customer transfers $200 from a savings account to a checking account. The transaction is: verify that the customer has at least $200 in the savings account; if so, reduce the balance of the savings account by $200 and increase the balance of the checking account by $200. All three operations must exist in a single transaction.

If we allow the balance of the savings account to change during the transfer we could lose the $200 between the savings account update and the checking account update, or (worse for the bank) the customer's partner could withdraw all of the money from the savings account between the time the application checks the balance of the savings account and transfers the money (Figure 5.4).

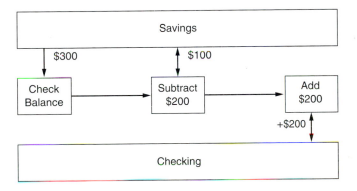

Figure 5.3   Simple two part transaction -

SQL Server uses read locks to protect data a transaction has read from changing while the transaction is in progress. One transaction is isolated from another. When the customer starts the transfer, the savings account balance is locked against changes until the transfer is complete. If the customer's partner tries to withdraw money from the savings account at the same time, the partner's transaction waits (or *blocks*) until the customer's transfer is complete. Then, the lock on the savings account balance is released and the partner's withdrawal can continue. Performance can suffer if many transactions need to access and change the same information at the same time.

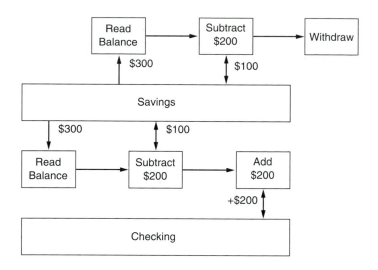

Figure 5.4   Concurrent transactions- -

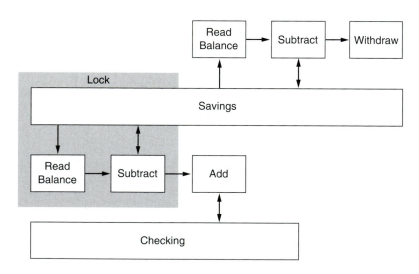

Figure 5.5   Concurrent transaction with appropriate locking- - - - - - - - - - - - - -

The term **isolation level** applies to how strongly isolated transactions are from one another. ANSI defines four levels of isolation. The higher the isolation level, the more isolated transactions are from one another. The higher isolation levels include the isolation characteristics of the lower levels.

- **Level 0: no isolation** — Allows dirty reads. When a transaction modifies data, other transactions can see the modified data even before the transaction modifying data commits the change. Transactions may get an inconsistent picture of the data. System 10 SQL Server version 10.0.3 and System 11 SQL Server implement dirty reads.

- **Level 1: does not allow dirty reads** — When a transaction modifies data in a table, other transactions are not allowed to see the change until the transaction modifying the data commits the change. SQL Server implements level 1 isolation by allowing only one transaction at a time to modify a particular row of data.[5] If a transaction is modifying data, no other transaction can access the data until the transaction commits.

- **Level 2: assures repeatable serializable reads** — When a transaction reads a row of data, it should see the same values in that row of data every time it reads the data. If non-repeatable reads are allowed, then the following is permitted: transaction A reads a row of data. Transaction B modifies that row and commits. Transaction A reads the same row of data and discovers that the values in the row have changed. SQL Server does not implement level 2 isolation.

- **Level 3: does not allow phantoms** — When a transaction reads a set of data from a table using a search criteria, it should see the same set of data every time it searches the table with the same search criteria. If phantoms are allowed, transaction A may read a set of data using a search criteria, another transaction may commit changes to rows such that a different set of rows now qualify for the search, and on reading the table with the same search criteria, transaction A gets a different set of rows. SQL Server implements level 3 isolation by allowing only one transaction to modify rows in a table at one time. If a transaction is modifying rows of data in a table, then no other transaction can access the table until the modification commits.

[5.] Note that SQL Server does not lock individual rows of data. It locks database pages. There might be more than one row of data on a page.

In its default mode of operation, called **cursor stability**, SQL Server supports all of the characteristics of level 1 isolation. In cursor stability mode, exclusive page locks are held until commit time, but shared locks are released as soon as SQL Server moves on to the next statement or page. This prevents reading of uncommitted data, but falls short of a guarantee for repeatability of reads or the serializability of transactions. The HOLDLOCK keyword on select statements causes SQL Server to hold onto all locks until commit. Compared against cursor stability mode with HOLDLOCK, shared locks are held much longer. This delay in releasing the locks may cause more lock contention with HOLDLOCK than without. HOLD-LOCK adds the repeatable read characteristic of isolation level 2 to cursor stability mode, but does not assure serializability of transactions.

You enable level 3 isolation with the T-SQL statement:

```
set isolation level 3
```

At this level of isolation, transactions acquire table locks and hold them until commit. This allows many transactions to read the tables concurrently, but only one transaction may modify data at a time, and no transaction is allowed to read data while a transaction is modifying data. This eliminates the possibility of non-repeatable reads, non-serialized transactions, and phantoms.

5.2.6 Deadlock

A deadlock, often more colorfully called a deadly embrace, describes a particular kind of lock contention situation. Deadlocks occur when two or more tasks try to acquire locks on the same set of locks, but each has acquired some of the locks that the other needs. All tasks are waiting for the others to release locks so they can continue. Figure 5.6 shows a deadlock between two tasks. **A** has a lock on resource **1** and is waiting for resource **2**. **B** has a lock on resource **2** and is waiting for resource **1**. **A** cannot proceed until **B** releases its lock on resource **2**, and similarly **B** cannot proceed until **A** releases its lock on resource **1**. No progress is possible until either **A** or **B** gives up and releases its lock.

In SQL Server, deadlocks can occur on both page and table locks. Referring to Figure 5.6, **A** and **B** are transactions and **1** and **2** are pages of a table. System 10 SQL Server checks for deadlocks whenever a task cannot acquire a lock because another task already has a lock on the resource. **A** checks for a deadlock situation when it tries to acquire a lock on **2** and discovers that **B** already has a lock on **2**. System 11 SQL Server uses a different strategy for detecting deadlocks. It checks for deadlocks on a periodic basis rather than every time a lock acquisition has to wait. This improves performance for transactions that do not deadlock, but it may take longer to detect that a deadlock has occurred. You should attempt to avoid deadlocks as much as possible. Chapter 10, *Transaction Processing Performance*, discusses deadlock avoidance in more detail.

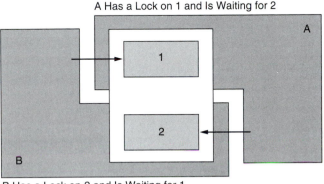

A Has a Lock on 1 and Is Waiting for 2

B Has a Lock on 2 and Is Waiting for 1

Figure 5.6   Deadlock -

5.3   TRANSACTION LOG

Each database has a transaction log. In general, any action that changes the data stored in the database is recorded in the transaction log.[6] The log is the most precious part of the database because from the transaction log and a recent database dump you can reconstruct your database right up to the point of system failure. Changes to the database are appended to the end of the log. SQL Server presents the transaction log as the `syslogs` table. It is a special table, optimized for append operations.

In a production database, the log is normally placed on a device separate from the data. The `logsegment` in the database defines the devices that participate in the transaction log. You can specify the location of the log when the database is cre-

---

[6]   Notable exceptions are text and image inserts and updates, `select into`, and bcp operations.

ated or altered with the `log on` clause. Keeping the log and data on separate devices makes it possible to dump the transaction log separately from the database.

During a boot after a system crash, SQL Server recovers the database by reading the transaction log and applying the changes recorded in the log to the database. At the completion of a transaction, the buffer manager may not have written out all of the dirty pages to the database. The transaction log records the changes so SQL Server can reconstruct the contents of the dirty pages and apply them to the database. **Timestamps** in the log records and on the database pages indicates whether or not the page needs to be modified. If the log record is younger than the database page, SQL Server knows to apply the changes recorded in the transaction log. If the timestamps are the same, or the timestamp of the database page is younger, then the change has already been applied.

On checkpoint, SQL Server writes out all of the dirty pages and places a marker in the transaction log. When SQL Server runs recovery, it knows that it is not necessary to update pages changed before the checkpoint record because all of those changes were written to the database during checkpoint.

On `dump database` or `dump transaction`, SQL Server truncates the transaction log so that the instance of the database in the dump reflects the state of the transaction log for the database. The instance of the database in the dump, plus any changes recorded in the transaction log after the truncation, are sufficient to reconstruct the database any time after the dump completes.

Replication Server reads the transaction log to reconstruct the transactions to apply to subscriber SQL Servers. If replication server is not well synchronized with database or transaction log dumps, it may not be ready for the dump to truncate the transaction log. To avoid this problem, Replication Server may place markers in the transaction log indicating how much of the log may be truncated. The part of the transaction log that Replication Server has not yet processed, must stay in the database until it is replicated.

5.4   DEFERRED VERSUS IN-PLACE UPDATES

An update involves modifying rows of data in a table. Update does not add or remove rows from the table. There are two ways we might consider updating a row in a table:

- **Update in-place** — Update data in the row in-place, that is, without moving it to another page.[7]
- **Deferred update** — Use the existing delete and insert mechanisms to delete the old row and insert the modified row.[8]

The first method is faster, as it involves locking and changing only the page that contains the row we want to update. The latter method involves locking and changing the page that currently contains the row to delete the row, then locking and changing the page that accepts the modified row. There are a number of limitations on in-place updates:

- The new row must fit on the same page as the old row. If the new row is too long, it may not fit on the page, causing the other rows to shift onto adjacent pages, defeating the purpose of an in-place update.
- None of the changed columns must participate in the clustered index. If any column participating in the clustered index changes, the row must move to keep the rows physically ordered by the clustered index.

SQL Server uses both methods to update rows, but places further restrictions on in-place updates. These are described in Chapter 10, *Transaction Processing Performance*.

5.5   EXAMPLE QUERIES

Let us go through some examples that may help solidify our understanding of SQL Server architecture. Here we describe what happens when we insert, delete, update, and select rows in a table.

5.5.1   Insert

Inserting a row into a table means adding a row to a page allocated to the table and fixing any index entries that might be affected by the insert. Suppose we have hired a new employee and need to add him to our employees table:

```
insert employees (fname, lname, empeeid) values ("Zack", "Key", 5532222)
```

---

[7]   An in-place update is also called a direct update.

[8]   Deferred updates also refer to an update that is written to the log before being applied to database pages. Such updates are used when the number of pages to change is larger than the amount of memory and when updating key columns.

If there is no index on employees, SQL Server appends the new row to the last page of the table. If the last page is full, SQL Server allocates a new page, and puts this row on the new page. If a new page is allocated to the table, SQL Server must update the allocation page, and associated GAM and OAM pages.

If there is a nonclustered index on `employees(empeeid)`, SQL Server still appends the new row to the end of the table, but it must also insert the index key on the appropriate leaf page of the nonclustered index.

If there is a clustered index on `employees(empeeid)`, SQL Server must insert the row on the appropriate page of the table so that the rows remain physically ordered by `empeeid`. SQL Server uses the non-leaf index pages to find the correct leaf page to insert the row. Then it inserts the row onto the page, allocating and linking in a new page if the existing page is too full to accommodate the new row.

In every case, SQL Server must acquire an exclusive lock on the page that it is going to modify before changing the page. This prevents another task from changing or reading rows from the page at the same time. No other task is allowed to read or update the page until the our transaction commits and we release our lock.

If there is no clustered index on the table, all inserts are made at the end of the table and the exclusive lock allows only one task to append to the table at a time. This can be a bottleneck if there are many concurrent tasks trying to insert rows into the table. You can alleviate this bottleneck by adding a clustered index on the table. Chapter 10, *Transaction Processing Performance*, discusses this issue in more detail.

Because inserts modify data pages, the insert must log the changes it is making to the affected database's transaction log. The insert transaction commits when all of the log pages are written to the database device. At this point, the page changed by insert may not yet be written to the database device. This is acceptable as the change is logged and committed in the transaction log. At some point, a checkpoint or the buffer wash mechanism may write this dirty buffer out to the database device.

5.5.2   Delete

Delete means removing rows from a table. Depending on the `where` clause on the delete, one or many rows may be deleted from the table. In the insert example we added Zack to our `employees` table. Unfortunately for poor Zack, things did not work out and he is being let go. Now we need to delete Zack from the `employees` table:

```
delete employees where empeeid = 5532222
```

Once we have identified the affected rows, we need to remove them from the table. If there is a clustered index on the table, the index pages may need to be updated to reflect the deleted rows. For a nonclustered index, the leaf pages need to be updated along with the data pages, and the non-leaf pages may need to be updated depending on the rows which are deleted.

Delete acquires exclusive locks on all of the affected pages and does not release the locks until the transaction commits. This prevents other tasks from reading or modifying the pages at the same time. As with insert, the deletes are logged in the affected database's transaction log. The transaction is considered committed when all of the log records pertaining to the delete are written to the log device.

When the last row on a page is deleted, the page is deallocated from the table. When that page is also the last page in an extent that is assigned to the table, the extent is also freed. When a page is deallocated, SQL Server must update the adjacent pages to fix the previous and next page pointers. When an extent is deallocated, SQL Server must update the allocation page. If the deallocated extent was the last extent assigned to the table in the allocation unit, SQL Server must update the GAM and the OAM pages.

5.5.3   Update

Sales were good this year, so everyone at the company gets a 5% raise:

```
update payschedule set salary = salary * 1.05
```

The salary column does not participate in any indexes and the width of the column does not change. As a result, in-place updates are possible. SQL Server updates the table one page at a time. It acquires an exclusive lock on the page and modifies the contents. If along the way we acquire more than 200 page locks, the lock manager will try to acquire a table lock instead.[9] The transaction commits and all locks are released when every page of the table is modified and the log records are written out successfully.

5.5.4 Select

Selecting rows from a table means reading pages from the database. Reading pages from database devices takes a long time, so ideally we read as few pages as possible to get the desired result set. If another query is accessing the same tables, some or all of the pages from the table may already be in memory. We cannot be assured of this, however, so we must make the pessimistic assumption that none of the pages we need are in memory. As our objective is to minimize reads from the database devices (called a **physical read**), finding that a page is already in memory (called a **logical read**) is "icing on the cake" and does not detract from our objective.

In each of the following examples, SQL Server acquires shared locks on the pages read from the table.[10] If the isolation level is 1, SQL Server acquires a shared lock on each page as it is read and holds the lock only long enough to extract the data from the page. This is to prevent another task from changing the contents of the page while we are reading it. If the isolation level is 3, SQL Server acquires a shared lock on each page as it is read and holds the lock until all of the pages are read and the transaction is complete. This means our transaction can read the pages again and be assured that the values on the pages have not changed.

No Where Clause

```
select * from employees
```

There is no `where` clause on the `select`, so the result set is all the rows in the `employees` table. Clearly, SQL Server must read every page of the table to return the desired results.

No Useful Index

```
select * from employees where empeeid = 5321145
```

---

9. Assume the lock escalation threshold is set at 200.

10. With isolation level 0 (i.e., dirty reads), SQL Server does not use locks to lock data and may read uncommitted data.

If there is no index on `employees`, we must still read the entire table looking for the rows that match the search criteria. Suppose `empeeid` is a unique key for the `employees` table and we have a unique index on `employees(empeeid)`. Following entries in the index pages, we can find the page containing the desired row without scanning the entire table. For a large table, using an index to find the desired row is much faster than scanning the entire table.

Where Clause Includes Between

```
select * from employees where empeeid between 400000 and 600000
```

This is more difficult. If the index on `employees(empeeid)` is a clustered index, the rows of the table are physically ordered by `empeeid`. We find the page containing the first row larger than 400000 and read the table until we get to `empeeid` 600000.

If the index is nonclustered we have to decide if its more efficient to use the index or scan the table directly. Suppose nearly all of the `empeeids` are between 400000 and 600000. In this case we are better off reading the table directly and discarding the few rows that do not qualify. In this way, we avoid the overhead of reading the index pages. On the other hand, if very few `empeeids` fall between 400000 and 600000, the index makes it easier for us to find those rows. We need to know something about the data in order to pick the optimal plan. The difference between guessing wrong and guessing right is execution time. It is the responsibility of SQL Server's optimizer to use index statistics and pick the optimal plan.

Index Covering

```
select fname, lname from employees where empeeid = 123456
```

Suppose there is a nonclustered index on `employees(empeeid, lname, fname)`. In this query, we do not need to read the data pages of the table, saving us a few reads from the database device. The leaf pages of the nonclustered index contain all of the information we need to satisfy the query. This optimization is called **index covering**.

Select Join

Joins are an important part of any relational database.

```
select e.fname, e.lname, p.salary
from employees e, payschedule p
where e.empeeid = p.empeeid
```

This query returns one row for each `empeeid` that is common to both the `employees` and `payschedule` tables, with `fname` and `lname` columns from `employees` and `salary` from `payschedule`.

A simple (and time consuming) approach to building the result set is to enumerate every combination of the rows in `employees` and `payschedule`, called the **cartesian product**, and then cull the result for the rows where employee's `empeeid` column matches payschedule's `empeeid` column. A more optimal approach is to iterate: read a row from `employees` and search `payschedule` for the row with the same `empeeid`.

In database jargon we say that the `employees` table is the **outer table** and `payschedule` is the **inner table**. Clearly we are searching the inner table many more times than the outer table. The choice of outer and inner tables can significantly affect performance. Queries can run very slowly if the inner table is difficult to search (say there is no index on the table). It is the job of the query optimizer to choose the optimal join order.

5.6 COMMAND INTERPRETATION

In most computer languages, programmers must describe, step by step, how to accomplish the desired operation. The SQL language differs in that SQL programmers describe only what they want done, not how to do it. It is up to the database engine to decide the optimal may to achieve the desired results. Sybase calls this process of changing a SQL statement into executable instructions **query compilation**.

Clients send the text of a query in Transact-SQL to SQL Server in batches. A SQL batch is delimited by the separator `go` in `isql` and by calls to `dbsqlexec()`, `dbrpcsend()` or `ctsend()` in the case of Open Client DB-Library and Client-Library programs.

Among the most frequent sources for performance problems on SQL Server are misconceptions regarding when and how a command is compiled and optimized (see Chapter 11, *Query Processing Performance*, "MYTH VERSUS REALITY" on page 368). There are four stages to SQL Server command interpretation:

- **Parse** — Converts the Transact-SQL statements into an internal format that is easier to manipulate than the text form of the statements. Sybase calls this internal data structure a **parse tree**. Syntax checks on the query are performed at this stage to verify that the statements conform to the rules of the Transact-

SQL language. Syntax errors are mistakes in the structure or organization of the command. For example, typical syntax errors are leaving the `from` clause out of a `select` statement or putting the `order by` clause before the `where` clause.

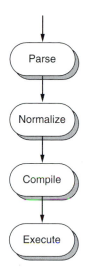

Figure 5.7   Executing a batch -

- **Normalize** — Organizes the parse tree into a more regular structure. This helps simplify the steps that follow by eliminating duplicated logic. For example, in expressions, it is not necessary to implement a `not` operator as the `not` operator can be removed by rewriting the expression using deMorgan's theorem. This eliminates the need to implement `not` processing in the steps that follow. During normalization, SQL Server checks that the objects referenced by the query exist and constructs the protection checks needed to verify permissions. The result of normalization is a **normalized parse tree**.[11]
- **Compile** — Reads the normalized parse tree, resolves views, flattens subqueries into joins (if possible), adds processing for defaults, rules, check constraints, and referential integrity, and generates a **query plan**. The query plan describes the steps SQL Server must follow to execute the Transact-SQL state-

---

[11] Note that this does not have anything to do with normalizing a database schema.

ments in the original query. Query optimization is performed as part of this phase (see "OPTIMIZER BASICS" on page 127).

- **Execute** — Runs the query plan and reports the results to the client.

Most data manipulation queries flow through this entire process. Data definition language and administration commands generally bypass compilation, jumping directly from normalization to execution.

5.7 STORED PROCEDURES

Stored procedures, triggers, rules, and defaults make it possible to encapsulate business rules in SQL and store the SQL statements in SQL Server rather than in client programs. A single stored procedure can represent many lines of SQL code. SQL Server preprocesses stored procedures, bypassing some of the overhead associated with ad hoc queries. Using stored procedures also cuts down on network traffic because fewer SQL statements must be conveyed from the client to SQL Server.

When procedural database objects such as stored procedures, triggers, and views, are created, the body of the procedural object is parsed, normalized, and stored in `sysprocedures`. When a stored procedure is executed, SQL Server reads the normalized parse tree from `sysprocedures`, completes the compilation (remember, compilation includes optimization), and executes the resulting query plan. The query plan is stored in the procedure cache and reused whenever the same stored procedure is executed. The optimizer uses the arguments passed into the stored procedure to select the optimal query plan.

Procedural objects are automatically renormalized if a referenced table, index, or stored procedure is altered, dropped, or recreated.

Procedural objects are automatically recompiled if:

- A rule, constraint, or default is added to a table referenced by the stored procedure, trigger, or view.
- The database containing the stored procedure, trigger, or view is loaded from a dump.
- The database containing the stored procedure, trigger, or view was just created.
- The character set changed since the last time the stored procedure or trigger was run.

The user is not notified when a procedural object is renormalized or recompiled.

5.8   OPTIMIZER BASICS

One of the most fundamental premises of the relational database systems is the separation of the semantics of the query from the access methods used to execute the query. The intent is to isolate the application developer from details of physical database design, thereby enabling designs that access data through semantics rather than though hardcoded access methods. The execution of a query often requires the formulation of a complex web of access methods, whose structure depends on the semantics of the query as well as on the physical design of the database. The result should be optimized to minimize the cost of executing the query.

The access methods used by SQL Server include table scan, scan through clustered and nonclustered indexes, scan through a list of row addresses, nested loop joins, creation of indexes and lists of row addresses on-the-fly, and several variations of table and index scans. Currently, SQL Server does not consider sort-merge joins or hash-joins, and considers only left-deep join orders (with few notable exceptions). We discuss these access methods in greater detail in Chapter 11, *Query Processing Performance.*

Most relational database systems employ an optimizer to translate the semantics of the query to this web of access methods. SQL Server uses a cost-based optimizer. Alternative approaches are to choose the optimal plan based on query syntax or heuristics. A cost-based optimizer enumerates a large number of execution plans, comparing alternative execution plans using estimated cost of execution. The optimal plan is selected and used to execute the query.

There are limits to the effectiveness of any query optimizer. A cost-based optimizer is limited by:

- **The availability of useful statistics** — The availability, accuracy, usability, and sheer complexity of statistics limit the accuracy of the estimates for execution costs.

- **The time needed to compute cost estimates for every possible query plan** — The number of alternative plans grows exponentially with several measures of the complexity of queries, including the number of tables. This forces the optimizer to forgo a vast majority of plans for complex queries. Optimizing the query is overhead. The time SQL Server spends optimizing the query is time it is not spending running the query. If the best plan takes 10 minutes to find and

5 minutes to run, but a mediocre plan takes 2 minutes to find and 10 minutes to run, the mediocre plan is better than the fastest plan.

- **Semantics of SQL** — The semantics of industry-standard SQL sometimes force the optimizer to generate plans for the worst-case scenario with respect to the domain of attributes (e.g., uniqueness constraints and presence of NULL values).

The application developer is often forced to assist the optimizer by providing more than just the semantics of the query. Let us discuss the basic principles of the optimizer and understand its limitations.

The following discussion assumes that we have communicated to the optimizer the semantics of the query completely and accurately. The optimizer makes extensive use of the semantics of the domains of attributes. A more precise definition of the domain of an attribute can often result in a more efficient plan. If a column is unique, we should declare it as such. We should not declare a column as allowing NULL values unless necessary. If multiple columns and local variables share a common domain, we should ensure that their definitions match on all counts, including whether or not they allow NULL values, length and type of character strings, and precision of numeric types.

The optimizer starts by resolving views and flattening subqueries into joins if deemed profitable. All views involving aggregates are materialized into work-tables. References to views not involving aggregates are replaced by their definitions. View resolution and subquery flattening can, and often do, contribute additional where clauses. Finally, the optimizer performs the two most crucial steps: index selection and join order selection.

During index selection, the optimizer classifies the where clauses as either join clauses or search clauses. A join clause is one that implies equality between columns from two different tables. All other where clauses are search clauses. For each table and for each relevant search or join clause, the optimizer consults the available statistics on indexes to choose an index for the table and the clause.

During join order selection, the optimizer enumerates a large number of join orders. If the number of tables is five or less, it considers all permutations of tables. If the number of tables exceeds five, it considers only a subset of all possible permutations.

The steps involving subquery processing, index selection and join order selection are of great significance to performance and are addressed in more detail in Chapter 11, *Query Processing Performance*.

5.9   CURSORS

Server-side cursors were introduced with the System 10 SQL Server. Cursors allow you to process data one row at a time. For example, you might want to call a stored procedure or make a remote procedure call on each row in a table. These are non-relational operations which cannot be done easily on a set of data.

To use a cursor you:

- `declare` **the cursor** — The declaration of the cursor includes a `select` statement. You also indicate if you plan to update any values in the table using the cursor.

- `open` **the cursor** — Tells SQL Server you are ready to use the cursor and sets the cursor to the beginning of the table.

- `fetch` **rows from the table** — Reads a row of data from the table and returns the results as `select` would (for processing by a client program) or into Transact-SQL variables (for processing in SQL).

- `close` **the cursor** — tells SQL Server you are finished using the cursor. The opposite of open.

- `deallocate` **cursor** — Frees resources associated with the cursor. The opposite of declare.

Typically, one loops on the cursor fetch command until all of the rows are read from the cursor. The global variable `@@sqlstatus` tells you when all of the results are read or an error occurs (see Table 5.3). The loop can be written in SQL using the `while` command, or in the client program using some appropriate programming idiom.

Table 5.3   @ @sqlstatus

@@sqlstatus value	Description
0	No error, more can be read from the cursor
1	Error occurred
2	No more results can be read from the cursor

The following example might be a fragment from a larger stored procedure.
utils.dbo.sendemail is a stored procedure that sends email to the person
named by the arguments:

```
declare @fname varchar(80)
declare @lname varchar(80)
declare @email varchar(80)
declare c_employee cursor for select fname, lname, email from employ-
ees, email where employees.empeeid = email.empeeid for read only
open c_employee
fetch c_employee into @fname, @lname, @email
if (@@sqlstatus = 2)
begin
        print "There are no employees"
        close c_employee
        return
end
while (@@sqlstatus = 0)
begin
        utils.dbo.sendemail @email, @fname, @lname
        fetch c_employee into @fname, @lname, @email
        if (@@sqlstatus = 1)
                begin
                print "Error"
                close c_employee
                return
        end
end
close c_employee
```

```
deallocate cursor c_employee
```

For read-only cursors, SQL Server locks the data read by the cursor with shared locks. For cursors that are used for update, SQL Server locks data read by the cursor with update locks. Exclusive locks are acquired for any pages that are actually changed. SQL Server assumes that a cursor is declared for update, unless it is told otherwise. If you do not plan to update through the cursor, you should declare the cursor for read only to improve concurrency in the affected tables. For cursors declared for update, you can add the `shared` keyword to the `from` clause before tables that are not updated through the cursor. This tells SQL Server that it can use shared locks rather than update locks when locking information read from these tables.

As with a conventional `select` statement, with isolation level 1, SQL Server only holds shared locks on pages while data is read from the page. Once all of the rows are read from a page, the shared lock is released and other transactions are free to modify the page. Exclusive locks (held on pages that were modified through the cursor) are released when the transaction commits. With isolation level 3, SQL Server holds onto shared (or update) locks for the pages read by the cursor until the transaction commits. Exclusive locks are handled with isolation level 3 similarly to isolation level 1.

Cursors can significantly simplify many programming problems in SQL Server, though you must use them carefully where performance is important. Chapter 10, *Transaction Processing Performance*, discusses the performance implications of using cursors in more detail.

5.10   CONSTRAINTS

System 10 SQL Server provides two mechanisms to enforce constraints and referential integrity:

- Rules, defaults, and triggers defined and bound to columns and tables.

- Check constraints and referential integrity checks declared when a table or schema is created.

Both mechanisms help maintain consistency in the database. Information in the wrong format is avoided and invalid foreign key references are not permitted.

5.10.1 Rules, Defaults, and Triggers

Before System 10 SQL Server, application programmers relied on rules, defaults, and triggers to manage constraints and referential integrity. Rules, created with the `create rule` statement, are bound to columns with the `sp_bindrule` stored procedure and define an acceptable format for the value of a column. Defaults, created with the `create default` statement, are bound to columns with the `sp_bindefault` stored procedure and define a value for the column during an insert if no value is provided. Triggers, created with `create trigger`, are bound to tables and fire on insert to, update on, or delete from the table. The trigger is told the action that has occurred (i.e., insert, update, or delete) and the rows and columns affected through the `inserted` and `deleted` tables and the `if update` construct. The trigger can then perform checks or even manipulate values in other tables. For example, a delete trigger on the `employees` table might delete all rows pertaining to the employee when the employee's record is removed from the `employees` table. This is called a **cascade delete**.

Information about rules, defaults, and triggers are stored in the `sysprocedures` table when they are created. When a query updates or inserts a table with a rule or default bound to it, the query's parse tree is augmented to include the commands needed to enact the default or rule. The augmented parse tree is compiled and executed. There is no reason to enforce defaults and rules on select and delete.

Triggers are fired during query execution. After a query's execution completes, but before changes are committed, SQL Server checks for triggers bound to the affected table. If any appropriate triggers are found, SQL Server executes the trigger much like it executes a stored procedure.

5.10.2 User-Defined Datatypes

You can create user-defined datatypes with the `sp_addtype` stored procedure. Rules and defaults can be bound to the user-defined datatype. When a table is created using the user-defined type the column inherits the rule and default bound to the user-defined type. For example:

```
sp_addtype ssntype, char(11),"not null"
create default ssndefault as "999-99-9999"
sp_bindefault ssndefault, ssntype
create rule ssnrule as @ssn like
        "[0-9][0-9][0-9]-[0-9][0-9]-[0-9][0-9][0-9][0-9]"
sp_bindrule ssnrule, ssntype
```

```
create table citizens
(fname char(20) not null,
lname char(20) not null,
ssn ssntype primary key)
```

creates a user-defined datatype called `ssntype` that only accepts valid Social Security Identification numbers and uses it in a table. The base (e.g., physical) datatype is `char(11)`. The base datatype defines how SQL Server actually stores the user-defined datatype in the database.

User-defined datatypes do not affect SQL Server query optimization. The query optimizer treats the user-defined type as identical to the base type. Explicit datatype conversions from a user-defined type to the base type are not required to help the optimizer. The citizen table in the above example is functionally identical to:

```
create table citizens
(fname char(20) not null,
lname char(20) not null,
ssn char(11) primary key)
sp_bindefault ssndefault, citizens.ssn
sp_bindrule ssnrule, citizens.ssn
```

As a result, how SQL Server treats rules and defaults bound to tables applies equally well to tables using user-defined datatypes.

5.10.3 Declarative Constraints and Referential Integrity

System 10 SQL Server allows you to declare constraints and define referential relationships between tables when tables are created or altered. On `create` or `alter table`, you can declare:

- **Declarative default** — Define a default value for the columns using the `default` keyword.

- **Check constraint** — Constrain the values in the column by a user-defined `constraint` with the constraint keyword or verify that the inserted value passes some search-like criteria with the `check` keyword.

- **Referential integrity constraint** — Ensure that the value already exists in another table through the `references` and `foreign key` keywords.

- **Uniqueness constraint** — Force a key to have only unique values with the `unique` and `primary key` keywords.

Declarative constraints are easier to understand than triggers, rules, and defaults because there are fewer database objects to manage. However, declarative constraints are not as versatile as triggers, they cannot do cascade deletes for example.

SQL Server handles declarative constraints similarly to rules and defaults. For declarative defaults and check constraints, information about the default or check constraint is stored in `sysprocedures`. When an update or insert affects a table with a declarative default or check constraint, SQL Server augments the parse tree with the appropriate commands to enforce the default or check constraint. The resulting parse tree is compiled and executed.

Information about referential integrity constraints is stored in `sysreferences`. SQL Server adds referential integrity checks to the parse trees for inserts and updates on tables with referential integrity constraints, and on deletes for tables referred to in referential integrity constraints. The resulting tree is compiled and executed. Note that referential integrity checks implicitly add accesses to more tables in order to verify the references.

SQL Server implements uniqueness by creating an index on the appropriate columns of the table. Everything we have said about indexes applies to uniqueness constraints.

5.11 REMOTE PROCEDURE CALLS

SQL Servers can communicate with one another through the Sybase remote procedure call interface. This mechanism is available to Open Server applications and is the only way that a SQL Server can send commands to an Open Server application. SQL Server uses remote procedure calls to communicate with Backup Server, for example.

When one SQL Server calls another for the first time, the two SQL Servers establish **site handlers** to manage the communication between the two servers. The site handlers continue to run until one of the Sybase servers is shutdown. Setting the `sp_serveroption` "timeouts" option to true makes the site handler stop running after a period of inactivity. This frees the resources associated with the site handler at the cost of re-establishing the connection between the two SQL Servers the next time a remote procedure call is made to SQL Server.

5.12   TWO PHASE COMMIT

Synchronizing transactions between two SQL Servers is possible through a two phase commit mechanism. Using two phase commit requires writing a DB-Library program. It cannot be done directly in Transact-SQL. The purpose of two phase commit is to ensure that transactions on two SQL Servers commit or rollback together. Either the transactions commit on both SQL Servers, or the transactions commit on neither.

The two phase commit algorithm is:

1. Start transactions on two SQL Servers.

2. Put transactions on both servers in a state where the transactions can either commit or rollback.

3. Verify that both transactions can commit.

4. If both transactions can commit, commit both transactions.

5. If one or both transactions cannot commit, rollback both transactions.

Sybase's two phase commit uses three SQL Servers. Two SQL Servers carry on the transactions and the third acts as a commit service. The commit service mediates between the SQL Servers performing the transactions and records whether or not the transactions committed. The record of committed transactions is important for recovery. When the SQL Servers run recovery, they communicate with the commit service with the `probe` utility to check whether or not the two phase commit transaction committed.

Chapter 6

Physical Database Design

The path from a logical database design to a physical design is fraught with trials and tribulations. As you start mapping logical entities such as tables and business rules into physical entities such as disks, indexes, constraints, and procedures, you are faced with a myriad of choices. Which columns belong in which tables? Is the `text` datatype as efficient as `varchar`? How many indexes is too many? How large should you make `tempdb`? Will integrity constraints hurt performance? Where should I put the log?

Most of these choices have implications for performance. Unfortunately, their implications are not limited to performance. Certain columns may have been assigned to particular tables to enforce access control. The purpose of an index may be to enforce an essential integrity constraint. This chapter will address only the performance-related aspects of the process of physical database design. We assume familiarity with the basics of database design and limit our discussion to the performance aspects only.

There is one aspect of the process of physical database design that deserves special recognition: the high cost of experimentation. Experiments in physical database design typically take hours, if not days. For example, an experiment in the vertical partitioning of a table may require you to load data, create indexes, and update statistics. An experiment in mapping of tables and indexes to disks may require you to rebuild large portions of the database. In contrast, other phases of performance tuning often measure cost of experimentation in seconds and minutes. For example, the process of tuning complex queries may allow you to try several alternative phrasings of a complex query in a few minutes. An experiment in lock escalation may involve little more than recompiling a stored procedure.

The excessive cost of experimentation in physical database design is a strong incentive to replace guesswork with careful analysis. It is essential that we start with a good understanding of the performance goals and requirements and detailed knowledge of the application, including the frequency and characteristics of transactions and queries and the volume and distribution of data. Certain design decisions trade performance on one query for that on another. Some decisions trade throughput for response time or vice versa. Such decisions can be justified only in the context of quantified performance objectives.

The decisions involved in physical database design are often at the very core of the database system and have far-reaching implications on almost all aspects of the system. Often, choices that are best for performance are not acceptable to the design. You may find yourself working with a mature design and against a hard deadline. Or you may be troubleshooting, with stringent limits on the portion of the application you may change. Sometimes choices are forced by business and compatibility requirements. The key is to recognize that such restrictions exist for a reason and see them as a technical challenge rather than as a hinderance.

Some techniques for physical database design that enhance performance may compromise other desirable properties of the design including integrity, maintainability, portability, and scalability. Such techniques should be used only when absolutely necessitated by performance requirements and only with proper caution and documentation. Few applications are truly static. Solving a performance problem today is good, but solving a performance problem and leaving the door open for enhancement tomorrow is better.

The design of the database schema and physical layout is often one of the most significant factors in the performance of SQL Server. A design optimized for performance can greatly reduce the processing workload on SQL Server, often improving throughput, response, and cost simultaneously. It can eliminate performance bottlenecks and improve resource utilization by balancing workload more evenly among available resources.

6.1   DESIGN OF TABLES

The logical design of the database entails the mapping of domains and entities in the application to tables and views in the database. Notwithstanding the significant number of hints, guidelines, and rules of thumb circulated on this topic, the process remains an art rather than a science. Although the primary focus of this chapter is physical rather than logical database design, let us revisit some of the choices available in the later stages of logical database design and their implications on performance.

6.1.1   To Normalize or Not?

Normalization eliminates redundancy from the logical model of the database by requiring that all functional dependencies be of the form $X \Rightarrow A$, where X is a set of columns that comprise a key of the table and A is a non-key column. The example in Figure 6.1, based on a minimal health-care database, illustrates some of the effects of normalization.

Not normalized

```
insured(insuredSSN, insuredAddress)
provider(providerSSN, providerAddress)
visit(insuredSSN, providerSSN, insuredName, providerName, amount)
```

Normalized

```
insured(insuredSSN, insuredName, insuredAddress)
provider(providerSSN, providerName, providerAddress)
visit(insuredSSN, providerSSN, amount)
```

Bold columns are the keys in the table

Figure 6.1   Example schemes: not normalized and normalized - - - - - - - - - - -

The first schema is not normalized because of the dependencies within the table `visit` that determine names from social security numbers. The key is a composite of `insuredSSN` and `providerSSN`. The key does not uniquely identify either the `insuredName` or the `providerName`. It does, however, uniquely identify the amount charged for the visit. We can normalize the schema by moving `insured-Name` to `insured` and `providerName` to `provider`. The second schema is normalized. Now, `insuredSSN` in `insured` uniquely identifies the name of the insured. Similarly the `providerSSN` in `provider` uniquely identifies the name of the provider. Let us study some of the implications of normalization.

- Normalization can reduce the volume of data and save space. The names of the insured and the provider are stored only once and not duplicated for every visit.

- Normalization can reduce the overhead of maintaining data integrity. The first schema requires an update trigger or check constraint on `visit(insured-Name)` and `visit(providerName)` to ensure that each SSN corresponds to the correct name. The normalized schema does not require a trigger to maintain data integrity.

- Normalization may increase the number of tables in joins.

As an example of the effect of normalization in the complexity of queries, consider listing the names of all the patients of a provider using the unnormalized `visit` table:

```
select distinct insuredName
from visit where providerName = "Welby"
```

With the second, normalized, schema we must join the `visit` table with the `insured` and `provider` tables to get the same result:

```
select distinct insuredName
from    visit v, insured i, provider p
where   v.insuredSSN = i.insuredSSN
and     v.providerSSN = p.providerSSN
and     p.providerName = "Welby"
```

The equi-joins `visit.insuredSSN = insured.insuredSSN` and `visit.providerSSN = provider.providerSSN` match up the rows we need from `visit`, `insured`, and `provider`.

A normalized schema has no duplicated information, so data integrity and consistency issues are easy to handle in your application. The cost of normalization is a large number of tables that must be joined together to get useful information out of the database. Joins can be difficult for users to formulate on the fly and time consuming to compute for the database engine.

A denormalized schema has redundant information you must keep synchronized and consistent. The benefit of some denormalization is avoiding joins in time critical queries. As you plan the physical design of your database schema, you should consider the cost of maintaining redundant data during inserts and updates against the cost of calculating joins when the database is queried.

You should start with a fully normalized schema and the list of time critical queries. Examine the queries and look for situations that might benefit from denormalization. Are there joins that are used frequently? Are the tables involved in the joins reasonably static, minimizing the cost of maintaining the duplicated information?

6.1.2 Datatypes and Permissibility of NULL Values

The choice of datatypes can have a significant impact on the performance. If two columns share a domain, or if the domain of one contains that of the other, you should make every effort to use the same datatype for both. The primary motivation is the efficiency of equi-joins involving those columns. The cost of data conversion is one reason to avoid data type mismatches. A more compelling reason is that data type mismatches often prevent the query optimizer from recognizing the clause as a join. As a result, the query optimizer may not select the optimal plan for the query.

For example, consider this query:

```
select *
from     T1, T2
where    T1.x = T2.y
```

If the datatypes of `T1.x` and `T2.y` differ, then the above query is effectively translated into

```
select *
from     T1, T2
where    T1.x = f(T2.y)
```

where `f(.)` is the datatype conversion function. In this case, the optimizer fails to recognize the fact that the query can be processed as an equi-join and may lead to an inefficient plan. More specifically, the optimizer does not consider use of an index on `T2(y)` and takes a very pessimistic view of the join order that uses `T1` as the outer table and `T2` as the inner table.[1]

Two datatypes that are otherwise identical but differ in the permissibility of NULL values are considered different datatypes. Therefore, you need to ensure that the datatypes of frequently joined columns match not only in the range of values, but also in the permissibility of NULL values. Further, the datatype `CHAR()` is internally translated to `VARCHAR()` whenever NULL values are permissible. The best way to verify that the datatypes of two columns match exactly is by comparing the corresponding rows in the output from `sp_help`.

---

[1] Of course, this property of the optimizer can potentially be used to force a join order. However, we strongly advise against such practices because they are very likely to backfire.

6.1.3   Impact of Variable Length Columns

Use of variable length columns can save space. A `varchar(n)` takes anywhere from one to *n* bytes of storage in the row. A `char(n)` always takes *n* bytes of storage. If your application contains a column whose size varies from one row to another, a variable length datatype may be your best option for performance. However, the use of variable length columns can have three adverse effects on performance.

1. Use of variable length datatypes may cause updates to be deferred rather than in place. Please see the section on access methods in Chapter 5, *SQL Server — Methods and Features*, for a discussion on deferred updates.

2. The presence of variable length columns in a row adds two bytes to the size of the row. This overhead is incurred only for the first variable length column in a table and not once every variable length column. The next section, "Reducing Unused Space in Pages", discusses how to compute the size of rows.

3. Variable length columns are not as processor efficient as fixed length columns. SQL Server works harder to read a row with variable length columns than a row containing only fixed length columns. As a result, accessing tables with variable length columns is more processor intensive.

Of the above three, deferred updates is potentially the most severe. The space-saving due to use of variable-length columns can rarely offset the adverse effect of deferred updates on performance. In all likelihood, your first priority is to avoid deferred updates and use variable-length columns to save space only if they do not necessitate deferred updates.

6.1.4   Reducing Unused Space in Pages

The number of bytes in a row can be computed as $x + \sum b_i$, where x, the overhead per row, is 4 if the row does not contain any variable length columns and 6 otherwise, and b_i is the number of bytes in the i-th column. An alternative method is to create the table, insert rows, and divide the number of rows by half the number of kilobytes used by data pages as reported by `sp_spaceused`.

SQL Server uses a page size of 2048 bytes. Rows do not span pages and hence most pages contain at least some unused space. This can, and often does, have adverse implications on the storage and I/O requirements, as well as on performance. SQL Server reads and writes data in pages. Therefore, the unused space on each page wastes not only disk space and bandwidth, but also main memory.

The amount of unused space on a page depends on several aspects of the database system, including sizes of the rows, presence of a clustered index, and the order of insertions, deletions, and deferred updates. Let us discuss the effect of row size on the amount of wasted space in pages. In some sense, the effect of row size is a lower bound on the amount of wasted space. We address space wasted due to clustered indexes, insertions, deletions, and deferred updates later in this chapter.

The number of rows in a data page is $max(\frac{2016}{n}, 256)$ where n is the average number of bytes in a row located in the page. Suppose a large table in our database has fixed-length rows of size 1009 bytes. Then we could fit only one row on each page, and use up almost twice as much storage and I/O as really necessary. We can improve performance either by trimming a few bytes off each row or by dividing the columns of the table into two tables, a technique called **vertical partitioning**. The example in Figure 6.2 illustrates the savings that can be realized by trimming and vertical partitioning. Trimming bytes off columns is an option available only to a lucky few. Often, vertical partitioning of tables is the only option for reducing unused space.

6.1.5   Vertical Partitioning of Tables

Vertical partitioning of tables can improve performance. By separating infrequently used columns from more frequently used columns, the number of I/O operations needed to access or scan the table is often reduced. Columns that are mostly read rather than updated can be separated from frequently updated columns to improve concurrency.

Infrequently Accessed Columns

Often, logical database design places columns of widely different access frequency into the same table. For example, suppose you have an application that accesses the street addresses of customers much less frequently than their phone numbers. You can improve performance by vertically partitioning the customer table into two tables, one of which contains the frequently accessed data such as the phone numbers, and the other which contains the less frequently accessed data, such as the street addresses. The benefit of vertical partitioning is positively correlated to the proportion of data that is accessed infrequently, as well as to the degree of imbalance in the frequency of access.

```
create table wide (
        x            int unique clustered,
        y1           char (250),
        y2           char (250),
        y3           char (250),
        y4           char (228))
```

Original Table Definition
100 Rows = 100 Pages

```
create table wide (
        x            int unique clustered,
        y1           char (250),
        y2           char (250),
        y3           char (250),
        y4           char (227))
```

Table after Trimming
100 Rows = 50 Pages

```
create table wide1 (
        x            int unique clustered,
        y1           char (250),
        y2           char (250)),

create table wide1 (
        x            int unique clustered,
        y3           char (250),
        y4           char (228))

create view wide as
        select wide1.x, y1, y2, y3, y4
                from    wide1, wide2
                where   wide1.x=wide2.x
```

Tables after Vertical Partioning
100 Rows = 68 Pages

Figure 6.2   Vertical partitioning -

Performance of Table Scans

The performance and resource consumption of table scans is directly related to the volume of data scanned. Therefore, the performance of table scans can be improved in the manner discussed in "Reducing Unused Space in Pages" on page 142 by effectively excluding the bulky columns that are not required by the query invoking the table scan. However, this optimization assumes that only a few small columns are accessed very frequently, which may not always be the case. Fortunately, your application can benefit from vertical partitioning even if all columns are accessed frequently, as long as not all are accessed by the same query. Suppose your table contains two disjoint groups of columns that are rarely accessed by the same query. You can improve performance by vertically partitioning the table into two smaller tables and have queries scan only one of the two. For example, it may be the case that no single frequently run query accesses both the phone number and the current balance of customers.

Reduce Contention and Deadlock

Often, a table may contain some columns that are never updated and others that are frequently updated. In such cases, you may be able to improve concurrency by vertically partitioning the read-only columns into a separate table. This enables transactions that access only the read-only columns in the table to avoid lock contention with those that update the table. For example, you may have the case that the phone number of a customer is rarely updated, whereas the customer's account balance undergoes frequent updates.

If your application permits, you may also benefit from using vertical partitioning to separate two columns that are generally updated by different transactions. In either case, verify that vertical partitioning preserves the transactional semantics of the application. You may need to add triggers or referential integrity to maintain consistency between the vertical slices of the table.

There are several ways to vertically partition a table into two or more tables. The obvious way is to distribute non-key columns among the new tables and then add the key columns to each new table. Less obvious ways reduce duplication by using other means to ensure that the original table can be reconstructed by a **loss-less** join of the vertical partitions.[2]

[2.] For more information on the semantics of vertical partitioning and lossless joins, see Section 7.4 in *Principles of Database and Knowledge-Base Systems*, Volume I by Jeffrey D. Ullman, Computer Science Press, 1988.

An indirect and yet safe method for vertical partitioning is through the creation of covering indexes. We discuss this option in more detail under "Index Covering" on page 154.

6.1.6 Impact of Text and Image Data

The text and image datatypes are used to store large strings and binary objects up to 2 gigabytes in size. Access to `text` and `image` datatypes is less efficient than access to other datatypes. There are several reasons for this.

1. The data for the `text` and `image` columns is stored in a separate page chain. This adds one level of indirection for each row for access to each such column. Specifically, each such column adds a 16 byte pointer to each row for each such column and potentially one more random access to the disk.

2. The smallest unit of allocation for a `text` or `image` is a page, which can hold up to 1800 bytes of data. If the size of your data is always smaller, the use of these datatypes wastes storage, I/O, and memory.

3. The separate page chain introduced by `text` and `image` datatypes is a potential source of lock contention.

4. The presence of `text` and `image` datatypes can turn the sequential scan of a table scan into random accesses that are far more demanding on the I/O subsystem.

There are cases when the `text` and `image` datatypes can be used to enhance performance. One example is to use these datatypes to effectively vertically partition a table to put large columns that are not accessed very frequently into a separate page chain. However, such cases are rare. More often than not, your reason for use of these datatypes is functionality rather than performance. The datatypes `char` and `varchar` can store strings of length up to 255. If your application permits, consider replacing your `text` column by an appropriate number of `char` or `varchar` columns.

6.2 CHOOSING YOUR INDEXES

Having a useful index is somewhat like knowing the spelling of the word you are looking for in a dictionary — it can make an enormous difference in performance of SQL Server by limiting the volume of data that it needs to sift through to satisfy the query. Unfortunately, the presence of an index does not always guarantee improved performance. In order to make a difference in performance, the index must satisfy several criteria:

1. The index must be beneficial to the query. That is, its use should improve the performance of the query, not degrade it.

2. The index must be usable by the query. Queries involving cursors and updates may not be able to use certain indexes because of the semantics of the query.

3. The optimizer must be able to deduce the above two facts at the time of query compilation. Often, the optimizer does not have access to some crucial information at the time of compilation, such as values of search arguments (i.e., because they are in variables), statistics on base tables and/or intermediate results, and whether your use of updates and cursors abides by certain constraints.

In this section, we focus on the first of the above three criteria, and save the other two for Chapter 11, *Query Processing Performance*. We also outline some of the adverse effects that indexes may have on performance of updates, deletes, and inserts.

The choice of indexes influences functionality as well as performance. The effects of indexes on functionality include enforcement of uniqueness constraints and implicit ordering of rows in results. You need to be aware of the effects of the choice of indexes on the functionality of your application.

6.2.1 Why Use Indexes?

The primary use of indexes is in limiting the scope of the search for rows in tables and thereby minimizing disk access. On a select with a clustered index, the last layer of the non-leaf index pages points to the page containing the interesting row. On a select with a nonclustered index, the last layer of the non-leaf index pages contains the indexed columns and a pointer to the row itself, which is located on a data page.

When Indexes Help Performance

Indexes are used in almost all stages of query and transaction processing. A `select`, `update`, `insert`, or `delete` operation on a single table can use an index to locate the data page or pages where the operation is to be performed. If the search clause specifies a unique row, the index points SQL Server at this row.

If the search clause specifies a set of rows, then the index points SQL Server to the point in the page chain which marks the beginning of the occurrences of such rows. The search clause need not specify the pages exactly for an index to be useful. For example, if the search clauses `name like "Jeff%"` and `age < 40` are used in conjunction to identify a set of rows, SQL Server has the option of using either an index on `name` with the first clause or an index on `age` with the second to identify a subset of rows in the table. It then uses the other clause to weed out the rows that do not qualify.

Of course, the use of indexes is not limited to single-table queries. Indexes can improve the performance of joins and subqueries by providing SQL Server with an efficient way to lookup all rows from the inner table that match the current row in outer table. This is used extensively in join computation by SQL Server. In fact, the availability and use of indexes is of such importance to performance of joins and subqueries that SQL Server considers creating a temporary index on tables that do not have usable indexes. Creation of temporary indexes is called **reformatting** in most Sybase documentation and is usually done in conjunction with another optimization involving the projection of only the interesting rows and columns of a table into the temporary table. When SQL Server uses reformatting, it typically indicates the absence of an index that is of substantial benefit to the performance of the query. The reformatted table is not visible to other queries or even to a separate instance of the same query. Thus, the same reformat operation may be repeated unnecessarily. Should this happen frequently, you should consider creating an index that obviates reformatting. Chapter 11, *Query Processing Performance*, contains details on how to detect and correct this situation.

We discuss two or more ways an index can improve performance in "Special Use of Indexes" on page 154.

When Indexes Regress Performance

Nothing comes for free and that holds true for the performance benefits of indexes as well. While improving the performance of select operations, an index may degrade that of `insert`, `delete`, and `update` that modify indexed columns. For nonclustered indexes, the leaf pages of the index contains copies of the indexed columns from the table. Any change to an indexed column results in updates to the leaf pages of the index. For clustered indexes, SQL Server keeps the table physically ordered by the indexed columns. Every time the indexed columns are modified, SQL Server shuffles rows and pages to maintain this order. Worse yet, if this table has a nonclustered index as well, SQL Server now needs to locate and update the appropriate leaf pages to reflect the shuffling of rows and pages.

It pays to drop indexes that are of questionable benefit to your application, especially those indexes that are updated frequently. The techniques in Chapter 9, *Instrumenting SQL Code*, can help you identify indexes that are not used by your queries. In general, you will find techniques such as denormalization of tables and indexing of greatest benefit in applications that are not update-intensive. For applications that do involve frequent updates and yet stand to benefit from indexes, you should be very wary of indexing any column that is updated frequently, especially when it comes to a clustered index on a table that also has multiple nonclustered indexes.

6.2.2   Which Columns Should be Indexed?

SQL Server's optimizer decides to use an index in a query if it believes using the index reduces the cost of executing the query. If you provide the query optimizer with a selection of useful indexes, it can pick the index that benefits the execution of the query the most. The trade-off is the cost of maintaining the indexes as the data is changed. In this section we introduce the query optimizer's decision making process. This is covered in more detail in Chapter 11, *Query Processing Performance*.

Know Your Queries

Because indexes hinder `insert`, `update`, and `delete` operations and use up space, you should strive to have the fewest number of indexes possible that allow you to meet our performance objectives. Doing this requires knowing and understanding the queries you are trying to optimize and the performance requirements for the queries. Understanding how SQL Server interprets your query is important to knowing what information and hints SQL Server needs to pick the optimal query plan.

After query normalization, the query optimizer analyzes the query and enumerates various plans that could be used to execute the query, estimates the cost of executing each query, and picks the query with the lowest cost. In enumerating plans, the optimizer examines the `where` and `having` clauses, looking at the search criteria and joins to help it decide which indexes might be useful.

As part of the query analysis, the optimizer assigns a selectivity to each search clause. For example:

```
select * from employees where empeeid between 400000 and 500000
```

If there is an index on `employees(empeeid)`, the optimizer consults the statistics page for the index to determine the selectivity of the expression `empeeid between 400000 and 500000`. If the expression is highly selective (e.g., only a small proportion of `empeeids` fall between 400000 and 500000), the optimizer chooses to use the index to access the table. If the expression is not selective (e.g., most of the `empeeids` fall between 400000 and 500000) the optimizer chooses not to use the index and instead scans the table directly.

Selectivity of Indexes

In the case of nonclustered indexes, the values or ranges specified in queries should be selective, in the sense that they should identify a small subset of rows in the table. The optimizer favors a nonclustered index if the selectivity on the column is high. It favors a full table scan over an index if it believes the selectivity is low. The selectivity of the tables depends on the data and your application. For example:

- In the United States, Social Security Numbers are highly selective. Everyone has a unique number. Many applications that deal with people use the Social Security Number as a primary key. An index on such a column is probably very useful.

- Gender is not selective. There are only two genders (for mammals anyway) and most population samples are evenly divided between them. An index on gender is not very useful and SQL Server's optimizer probably would never choose to use it.

- Postal Code[3] might be selective, depending on the scope of your application. For a nation-wide application, postal code probably is selective, assuming your database includes addresses scattered evenly across the country. Within a small city, postal code probably is not selective and would make a poor choice for an indexed column.

[3.] In the United States, the Zone Improvement Plan (ZIP) code.

For SQL Server to pick the optimal query plan, among other things, it must pick the most efficient indexes to use for the query. To do this, it needs to know the selectivity of each index with regards to the search criteria before it has actually performed the query. Indexes that SQL Server thinks are highly selective are chosen over table scans or indexes which are not selective. SQL Server relies on index statistics to estimate the selectivity of an index given the search criteria. For this reason, it is important to have up to date index statistics on all of your tables. If the statistics are out of date, SQL Server may choose to use an index when it is inappropriate to do so, or worse, choose a full table scan when using an index is beneficial.

A Case Study in Index Selection

The use of indexes by SQL Server is best illustrated by example. We use the set of tables, indexes, and queries in Figure 6.3 to illustrate the use of indexes in SQL Server.

```
create table department (
        deptno    int        unique clustered,
        name      char(32),
        address   char(32),
        manager   int        /* references employee(ssn) */)
create nonclustered index dept_name on department(deptname)


create table employee (
        ssn       int        unique,
        lastname  char(32),
        firstname char(32),
        gender    char(1),
        deptno    int        references department(deptno))
create clustered index emp_name on employee(lastname, firstname)
create nonclustered index emp_gender on employee(gender)
create nonclustered index emp_deptno on employee(deptno)
```

Figure 6.3   Example tables -

The keyword `unique` creates an index as well as a constraint. Thus, the example in Figure 6.3 has unique indexes on `employee(ssn)` and `department(deptno)`. In the ensuing discussion, we assume that the two tables contain 100 and 10,000 rows, respectively.

1. ```
   select lastname, firstname
     from employee
    where ssn = 9999999999
   ```

   Given there are more than a few pages of data in the `employee` table, this query benefits from the use of the nonclustered index on `employee(ssn)`. The optimizer uses the uniqueness condition to infer that at most one row can match this search. Notice that statistics are not necessary for this case.

2. ```
   select ssn
     from employee
    where lastname = "Roy"
   ```

   This query may benefit from the use of the index on `employee(lastname, firstname)`, assuming that the last name `Roy` does not occur very frequently. Notice that the use of the index does not require knowledge of the values for all the columns in the index; it suffices to know the values of a non-empty prefix. In this case, the optimizer needs to have the statistics for this index to decide whether or not to use the index. If up to date statistics are not available, the optimizer may err by not using this index.

3. ```
   select ssn
     from employee
    where firstname = "Shaibal"
   ```

   This query cannot benefit from the use of any of the indexes present. The index on `employee(lastname, firstname)` does not help because `firstname` is not a prefix of this index.

4. ```
   select ssn
     from employee
    where lastname like "Roy%"
   ```

   This query may benefit from the use of the index on `employee(lastname, firstname)`. A `like` clause involving a pattern that does not begin with the wildcard character `%` implies a `between` clause on the same variable. In this example, `lastname like "Roy%"` is the same as saying `lastname >="Roy" and lastname < "Roz"`. The optimizer uses this information, in conjunction with statistics, to evaluate use of the index.

5. ```
select ssn
from employee
where lastname like "%Roy%"
```

This query cannot use the index on `employee(lastname, firstname)` because the pattern in the `like` clause begins with the wildcard character, and hence cannot be reformulated by the optimizer to limit the scope of search. In this case, SQL Server scans the entire table searching for rows that match.

6. ```
select ssn
from employee
where lastname = "Roy" and gender = "M"
```

This query presents the optimizer with a choice of two indexes: `employee(lastname, firstname)` and `employee(gender)`. The optimizer may choose one of the two indexes, or none. It uses the former if the index on gender is not very selective (i.e., contains a large number of duplicates). In general, columns that contain many duplicates are not good candidates for indexes. There are, however, exceptions. Suppose such a column also contains some values that are highly selective. For example, suppose our example database has only 10 out of the 10,000 rows in `employee have gender = "M"`. Then, assuming statistics are up to date, SQL Server uses this information in evaluating the use of the index.

7. ```
select firstname
from employee
where lastname = "Roy"
```

This query is a slight variation on query 2 (above), which we use to illustrate the concept of **covering indexes**. In this case, the nonclustered index `employee(lastname, firstname)` contains not only pointers to the row, but also all the columns that are required in the query. In such cases, the index is said to cover the query and provides the optimizer with the option of not accessing the data pages at all. If the optimizer decides to use the index `employee(lastname, firstname)`, then SQL Server scans only the leaf level of the index and not the data pages themselves.
```

```
8. select dept.deptno, employee.lastname
   from dept, employees
   where dept.manager = employee.ssn
```

This query illustrates a simple case of the use of indexes in joins. Assume that the optimizer has chosen department as the outer table and employee as the inner table.[4] Then, for each row in department, SQL Server needs to look up all rows in employee that have matching values of ssn. It uses the unique index on employee(ssn) for this.

6.2.3 Special Use of Indexes

SQL Server can use indexes to reduce the volume of data scanned even when the search clause is not very selective. You can also use indexes to reduce lock contention or to fine-tune the allocation of pages in your database.

Index Covering

With a nonclustered index, the leaf index pages contain copies of index columns for every row of the table. If a query uses a nonclustered index and does not access any columns from the table other than the columns participating in the nonclustered index, SQL Server does not need to read the associated data pages. This can save a disk I/O if many rows are accessed through the index. We saw an example of index covering in query 7 in "A Case Study in Index Selection". Another very common usage of index covering is in select count(*) queries.

You may have the option of adding an extra column or two to an existing index to enable an index to cover a query whose performance is critical to your application. The query optimizer considers index covering when it evaluates the cost of the possible query plans. Therefore, you should not need to give any special directives to SQL Server to convince it to use it as a covering index. Of course, adding columns to an index for the sake of covering queries should always be weighed against the overhead of having more columns in indexes and especially its implications on the cost of updates.

---

4. How the optimizer chooses join order is discussed in Chapter 11, *Query Processing Performance*.

Heap Inserts and Clustered Indexes

If there is no clustered index on a table, SQL Server inserts new rows to the end of the table. In a high throughput, multi-user environment, the exclusive page lock on the last page of the table can become a performance bottleneck. This situation is often described as a **heap insert**, since tables that do not have any clustered indexes are called heaps. For example, consider an application where a thousand salespersons are entering orders into a single table. In the absence of a clustered index, each insert must commit before another can start. Thus, all the processing is serialized by the single point of insertion into the table.

A clustered index on the table can be used to reduce lock contention. Since a clustered index keeps the table physically ordered by the index, data is inserted in the appropriate place in the table and there is less contention for the pages that need to be modified. The inserts are not competing for the lock on the page at the end of the table. Instead, they lock pages somewhere in the middle of the table based on the data in the indexed columns.

For a clustered index to be effective, concurrent inserts must differ in values for the indexed columns. For example, we may be able to eliminate the bottleneck in the above example by creating a clustered index on the ID of the salesperson. This effectively provides each salesperson with their own point of insertion into the table. On the other hand, a clustered index on, say, the time of the day may not be as effective, since all the insertions at any given point in time go to the same page.

System 11 SQL Server offers an alternative approach. You can partition the table. See Chapter 13, *Advanced Topics*, for more information.

Granularity of Locks and Fill Factor

SQL Server uses page-level locks to lock rows. Sometimes, this causes artificial lock contention. For example, consider a manufacturing database which needs to maintain inventory at a thousand points in an assembly line. Suppose each such point is represented by a row that is a hundred bytes in length. SQL Server puts 19 such rows into each page. This may cause an artificial contention between concurrent updates to two points that just happened to be on the same page.

In such cases, you have the option of using a clustered index with the use of the fill factor feature to eliminate artificial contention. Fill factor specifies how full to make index pages, including data pages in a clustered index, when the index is created. A low fill factor puts fewer entries on each page, allowing your indexes space to grow. You can use this feature to put fewer of the highly contended rows on each page. You can even force each row to be put on a page by itself, thus eliminating artificial contention entirely.

You need to be aware that the fill factor option is effective only during the creation of an index and not during subsequent inserts, deletes, and updates. That is, the control you have over allocation of rows to pages during index creation may erode over time as either rows are inserted and deleted, or as indexed columns are updated.

If you are using System 11 SQL Server, you can take advantage of the `max_rows_per_page` feature. This is discussed further in Chapter 13, *Advanced Topics*.

Page Splits and Tuning Page Allocation

One of the issues in using clustered indexes on a table subject to frequent inserts is the unused space in pages created as a result of page splits. In the presence of a clustered index, when we insert a row into a page that does not have enough empty space, SQL Server splits the page into two pages. Unless the row being inserted belongs at the very end of the page, the page is split into two equal halves, each half empty.[5] This is frequently the case when you use a clustered index to provide multiple points of insertion into a table as described in "Heap Inserts and Clustered Indexes". However, it may also happen naturally whenever there is no correlation between the values of the indexed columns in successive inserts to a table having a clustered index — random inserts, for example. In such cases, the empty pages created as a result of the page split tend to remain unused.

You may be able to tune the clustered index to the order of insertions to reduce or even eliminate the space wasted by page splits. The key is to ensure that most page splits happen as the result of row inserts at the very end of a page, even if the page is not the last page of the table. We discuss this technique in greater detail in Chapter 10, *Transaction Processing Performance*.

[5.] Or half full, depending on your outlook.

6.2.4   Using Indexes

There are several aspects of the use of indexes that are not immediately obvious even to experienced developers. An oversight in the choice of indexes can sometimes have some rather unexpected effects on the performance of your application in a seemingly unrelated area. In this section, we discuss a few of the implications of some choices available to you in selecting your indexes.

Impact of Composite Indexes

A composite index, that is, an index made up of more than one column from a table, can be useful to the query optimizer. If we are looking for particular values in an indexed column, the optimizer can use the composite index if that column is the first column in a composite index. The index is even more useful if you are also searching for a particular value for the next column of the composite index.

- An index is useful to a query only if the values of a sufficiently long prefix of the index are known. For example, an index on (A,B,C) can be used to reduce the number of rows that need to be examined only if SQL Server knows the values for at least one of the three subsets (A,B,C), (A,B), or (A). On the other hand, knowledge of the values for the sets (B,C), (B), and (C) does not help.

- A range query may benefit from the use of a composite index; but all columns following the column on which a range is used are considered unknown. For example, an index on (A,B,C) can be used by the clauses A between 10 and 20 and B=5, but the index does not help with the clause B=5.

- Statistics on composite indexes are tricky. You may see some unexpected results when the first column contains a large number of duplicates. We discuss this issue in greater detail in Chapter 11, *Query Processing Performance*.

Size of Indexes

While you may be tempted to use indexes on a large number of columns, some of which may be very wide, you need to be aware of certain untoward effects of large indexes.

- **Caching of index pages** — The number of index pages can be an issue if you have lots of indexes, or if you index large columns. Formulas for the calculation of the number of index pages can be found in *Physical Database Design for SYBASE SQL Server* (Rob Gillette, Dean Muench, and Jean Tabaka). If the size of an index prevents leaf pages of an index from staying in cache, performance may degrade for both transaction processing and query processing.

- **A wide index means more index pages** — Index pages contain copies of the indexed columns. If a composite index contains many columns, fewer rows can fit on an index page, and more pages are needed to construct the index. SQL Server must read more pages to read the same number of rows. This increases the disk I/O requirements of your application.

- **A wide index results in a deeper index** — Fewer rows per index page also means a deeper index. A deep index has many non-leaf layers. The deeper an index the more pages SQL Server must read to traverse the index to the leaf page. This increases the disk I/O requirements of your application and slows retrieval of data.

- **Narrow index improves statistics** — Only one page is used to store index statistics. The wider the index, the fewer rows can be stored on the statistics page, the less detailed the statistics, and the less precise the query cost estimates calculated by the query optimizer. A narrow index provides more detailed statistics and improves the precision of the query optimizer's cost estimates. This improves the likelihood that the optimizer will choose a good plan over a mediocre plan.

Wide composite indexes should be avoided. Strive to keep indexes as narrow as possible. Of course, we cannot trim bytes off an index and we cannot vertically partition an index. But we can either trim bytes off the indexed columns in the indexed table or drop large columns from the index. The latter, of course, may have other unintended implications on performance. Rather than index several wide columns, consider creating a surrogate key and using the surrogate key rather than the columns for joins.

6.3   MAPPING TO DEVICES

Database devices form the foundation of the database system. These devices store and make available the data in the database. How you create and organize the database devices impacts the performance of the database system.

6.3.1   Basics of Using Devices

Here are some ground rules for creating database devices and databases:

- System 10 SQL Server limits the size of a database device to 2 Gb, even on systems that allow larger files. System 11 SQL Server supports larger database devices on those platforms that support large files. Check the documentation that comes with the version of SQL Server you are using.

- Do not use a buffered file like a Unix file system file as a database device. In particular, do not use a buffered file as a log device. Using buffered files as files as database devices may compromise the recoverability of your database. In addition, SQL Server generally does not use asynchronous I/O on operating system files, hence using buffered files may also affect performance. There are special situations where a buffered device can help performance without compromising recoverability (see Chapter 13, *Advanced Topics*).[6]

- Never put two database devices on the same physical disk. If a physical disk must be shared between two databases, create a single database device and share the database device among the databases. Several operations in SQL Server, for example `create database`, assume that each database device is on a separate physical disk. Having two or more devices on the same physical disk can lead to an I/O bottleneck if the two devices are used concurrently.

- Always put the transaction log on a database device separate from the data. This ensures high throughput for the largely sequential I/O to the log. If your application does a lot of updates, inserts, or deletes, you should pick the fastest disks for the log device.

- Consider protecting the contents of the log disk through mirroring.

6.3.2 How Many Devices?

One of the crucial steps in database design and performance tuning is choosing the right number of physical disks and assigning database devices to segments in a way that optimizes the SQL Server's use of the available hardware. Unfortunately, there are no formulas for the right number of disks or segment mapping and guessing wrong can be painful. The penalty for choosing poorly on a large database is a long rebuilding of the database. Nevertheless, the following guidelines may help you avoid some costly mistakes.

[6.] Some operating systems do not provide access to raw partitions as does Unix, in particular Windows/NT and VMS. On these operating systems it is safe to use an operating system file as the database device. Sybase documentation describes what kinds of files you can and should not use for your platform.

- A typical on-line transaction processing application performs a lot of random accesses to disks. Random accesses require more physical disks than may be dictated by the size of the database alone. We could put a 2GB table on a single disk, but that would be unfortunate if we needed to do more random accesses per second to this table than the disk drive can accommodate. You should consider configuring substantially more disks than the minimum dictated by the size of the database for on-line transaction processing applications. We discuss database segmenting in Chapter 4, *SQL Server — Form and Structure*.

- Complex queries often require large sequential reads. Most disks perform better on sequential access than on random access. If your application contains a lot of complex queries, design your schema to promote locality of reference and, therefore, sequential access. Plan a clustered index on the table that keeps rows likely to be accessed during the same query near one another in the table. Try to avoid fragmenting the table with many small inserts, updates, and deletes. Another option, if supported by your disk vendor, is hardware disk striping. See "Improve Locality of Access" on page 161 and "Disk Striping" on page 161.

- When spreading I/O load across multiple disk drives, also consider the load on the disk controllers. For example, while it is possible to chain several SCSI disk drives off a single SCSI controller, doing so may shift the bottleneck from the disk drives to the SCSI controller. Some controllers are better than others. Check with your hardware vendor for the optimal disk drive to SCSI controller ratio.

- The amount of data cache allocated by SQL Server is inversely related to the load on physical disks. The more data cache, the less often SQL Server needs to access the database devices to find data. If you suspect SQL Server's performance is limited by the performance of the physical disks, you should first verify that you are using the largest possible data cache.

- Often, reducing the number of database device accesses with a minor change in the database schema or in the phrasing of a query can be more effective than a ten-fold increase in the number of physical disks. Before you explore the limits of SCSI cables and disk controllers, you should investigate the possibility of reducing the number of random accesses to database devices by modifying the schema or queries. Such changes may be less painful than rebuilding a large database.

6.3.3   Disk Striping

Improperly distributing large, active tables across disk drives is one of the surest ways of jeopardizing the performance of your application. SQL Server allows you to map tables and indexes to segments within a database. A segment is a collection of database devices that are participating in the database. By cleverly assigning database devices to segments, you can segregate the disk activity for accessing one table from disk activity for accessing another. Indexes and tables can also be placed on different database devices to the advantage of performance.

By using multiple disk fragments in creating a database, you can stripe a database across multiple database devices. For example:

```
create database orders
on data1=2, data2=2, data1=2, data2=2, data1=2, data2=2
log on log1 = 4
```

creates a 16 Mb database with 6 Mb on database device `data1`, 6 Mb on database device `data2`, and 4 Mb on the log device `log1`. The database devices `data1` and `data2` are striped in 2 Mb chunks. If the database holds a single table, the first 2 Mb of the table comes from `data1`, the next 2 Mb from `data2`, the third 2 Mb from `data1`, etc. If access to the table is random, the disk activity is evenly spread between `data1` and `data2` and some performance gain is seen. Even if access to the table is sequential, concurrency can improve if many sequential scans must execute at the same time.

Some operating systems and hardware include a disk striping mechanism. In general, the large granularity of operating system or hardware disk striping does not benefit performance of SQL Server to any great extent over careful use of segments and disk fragments. There is no guarantee that the allocation structures of SQL Server will align themselves properly with the boundaries of the striping.

6.3.4   Improve Locality of Access

Segregating tables and indexes into different database devices with segments may help the performance of table and index scans. The issue again is sequential I/O. If a table and its indexes share a segment, the extents allocated to tables and indexes are mixed together. Scanning the table means skipping over the extents allocated to the index. Placing the table on its own segment helps ensure that scanning the table is sequential access, rather than random access. For example, a large table of customer data with the customer's name and account balance is on one database device. The index on the customer's name is on another database device. Disk activity for reading index pages does not interfere with disk I/O for the table. Locality of access is improved because the pages of the table are clustered together and the pages of the index are clustered together.

More to the point, do not put two frequently accessed objects on the same database device. This includes the table and its indexes, two tables that are accessed frequently, and indexes from different tables that are accessed frequently. This can be accomplished with separate segments, each with a disjoint set of database devices, for each frequently used table and index.

Make an effort to put a table or index that is frequently involved in large scans on a separate database device. This helps improve sequential I/O.

6.4 DATA INTEGRITY

SQL Server provides two classes of mechanisms for maintaining data integrity:

- **Triggers**, **rules**, **indexes**, **user-defined datatypes**, and **defaults** — Available in all versions of SQL Server.

- **Referential integrity constraints**, **check constraints**, **uniqueness constraints**, and **declarative defaults** — Available in System 10 SQL Server and later versions.

While the capabilities of the mechanisms are similar, implementation differences inside SQL Server make some more efficient than others depending on your needs. Understanding what happens when you add a referential integrity check to a table column, for example, is important to understanding these trade-offs.

6.4.1 Uniqueness Constraints

`create table` and `alter table` let you add a uniqueness constraint to a column or group of columns through the `unique` and `primary key` keywords. Doing so creates an index on the columns that does not allow duplicates. If not told otherwise, SQL Server creates a nonclustered index. As a uniqueness constraint is simply an index, all of the discussion about indexes applies here as well. Selecting columns for indexing involves different criteria, however, as here you are indexing to enforce uniqueness rather than improve query performance.

When selecting and using an index, SQL Server's query optimizer distinguishes unique and non-unique indexes. While the optimizer can provide certain optimizations if index statistics indicate the indexed columns are unique, declaring an index as unique provides opportunities for optimization beyond what can be derived from the use of statistics alone.

Do not add an index to enforce uniqueness if you already have an index on the same columns. See if it is possible to use the same index for both uniqueness and query optimization. Consider trade-offs that might be beneficial to both requirements if this is not immediately possible.

6.4.2 Referential Constraints

Referential integrity constraints are added to a table with the `references` and `foreign key` keywords. Tables mentioned in the `references` and `foreign key` clauses are the **referenced** tables. The table that refers to the referenced table is the **referencing** table.

`Select` is unaffected by a referential integrity constraint as it is not necessary to enforce referential integrity checks during a select. The optimizer does not use the presence or absence of referential integrity constraints in selecting a query plan. SQL Server automatically modifies `insert`, `update`, and `delete` statements to include commands that verify the statement does not violate the referential integrity constraints. `Insert` and `update` statements on the referencing table are augmented to verify that the key columns of the new row are already in the referenced table. `Delete` statements against the referenced table are augmented to verify that the key columns of the deleted rows are not used in any of the referencing tables.

Verifying the referential integrity constraint involves accessing the referenced or referencing table in addition to the insert, update, or delete already in the query. This adds overhead to every insert and update to a referencing table, and every delete from a referenced table. Performing the referential integrity check on every insert, update, and delete is to your advantage if the referenced and/or referencing table is changing frequently. If the referenced table is not changing, performing the referential integrity check on every insert and update to a referencing table may not be necessary. For example, if your application has already selected the key value from the referenced table, it is not necessary to perform a referential integrity check when the referencing table is updated as long as you know that the referenced table is not changing.

With 4.9 and previous versions of SQL Server, referential integrity checks are coded in triggers. You create two triggers:

- trigger for insert and update on a referencing table that accepts the change if the values for the key columns are present in the referenced table, and rolls back the change if the values are not present.

- trigger for delete on the referenced table that accepts the delete if the values for the key columns are not present in any referencing table, and rolls back the change if the values are present.

Triggers are more versatile than referential integrity constraints because they can be programmed in SQL. For example, a delete trigger can perform a cascade delete that removes all references to the rows deleted from a referenced table in all of the referencing tables. You cannot do this with referential integrity constraints. This versatility comes at a cost. Firing a trigger is similar to running a stored procedure and involves more overhead than executing a referential integrity constraint check.

We recommend using referential integrity constraints in situations where it is reasonable to do so. Use triggers if referential integrity constraints do not give you the flexibility you need to encapsulate your business processes.

6.4.3   Check Constraints and Declarative Defaults

You can add check constraints to a table with the `check` keyword on `create table` and `alter table` commands. Declarative defaults are added to a table with the `default` keyword. `Select` and `delete` statements are not affected by check constraints or declarative defaults, as it is not necessary to enforce check constraints or defaults when selecting and deleting data. SQL Server automatically adds code to perform check constraints or use the declared default value on the appropriate columns when inserting or updating the table.

Declarative defaults are similar to defaults created with the `create default` statement. Check constraints are similar to rules created with the `create rule` statement, although check constraints can be applied to more than one column of the table. Without using a check constraint, you need to use an update and insert trigger to enforce a multi-column rule. As with referential integrity, check constraints have less overhead than triggers. If you need to enforce a multi-column rule, we recommend using a table-level check constraint over a trigger.

With the exception of multi-column rules, we see no performance advantage to using declarative defaults over defaults and check constraints over rules. The primary issue here is schema maintenance. Declarative defaults and check constraints can be easier to maintain as all of the information is included in the create table command. On the other hand, rules and defaults are created separately and bound to columns and the same rule or default can be bound to many different columns and tables. Declarative defaults and check constraints must be repeated for each column and the relationship between the columns is not as obvious.

6.5   ORDER OF INSERTS

For a single table, query processing performance can benefit from improving the **locality of access**. That is, rows that are accessed at the same time should be located on the same or adjacent data pages. This can reduce the number of pages read from database devices and decreases lock contention. Whether or not this ends up being useful to you depends on your application. For example, an order entry system that generates hourly reports of activity may benefit from ordering the activities chronologically.

6.5.1   Inserts Without a Clustered Index

If there is no clustered index on the table, SQL Server always appends new rows to the end of the table. You can use this to your advantage by loading data so that locality of access is improved for your queries. For example, in the same order entry system, suppose you need to access all of the rows for a particular customer ID. Locality of access is improved by loading the table in the order of customer ID. All of the rows pertaining to a particular customer are near one another in the table. Remember, however, that they may not be near one another physically on the disk. The allocation of database device space depends on the insert, update, and delete pattern in the database. A large delete leaves holes that are filled in by later allocations. SQL Server makes some effort to reuse pages so that pages of a table remain contiguous.

Given SQL Server's page allocation scheme, the density of the data and delete performance improves if the order of deletes matches the order of inserts. For example, suppose the order entry application keeps a table of recent orders and delete orders that are older than 30 days. In this case, it is better if we insert the rows in chronological order. On delete, the pages containing the rows older than

30 days are removed from the table. The rest of the table is not affected. As a counter example, suppose we insert based on customer ID but delete on date. Potentially every page of the table may need to be updated, slowing the delete process and impacting concurrency. Many partially empty pages are left in the table after the delete. SQL Server does not consolidate pages as rows are deleted. When rows are deleted the page is simply left with empty space. This is particularly a problem for tables without a clustered index because fresh inserts are always appended to the end of the table. Pages may end up with only a single row, wasting space. Query processing is slowed because more pages must be read from the database devices to scan the table.

6.5.2   Inserts With a Clustered Index

When there is a unique clustered index on the table, the clustered index determines the locality of access, not the order of inserts. The density of the data does depend, however, on the order of insert. When compared to the index, if the order of inserts is random the density of the data remains relatively low. Pages are full if the insert is in the same order as the index. When you append to the end of a table with a clustered index SQL Server does not split the last page, but simply appends a new page to the table when the last page is full.

Deleting from a table with a clustered index is most efficient if the deletes are also clustered by the clustered index. For example, deleting all orders within a certain range in time is efficient if the table is clustered by time. The same reasons apply here as in the case without a clustered index.

If the clustered index allows duplicate keys and you are inserting duplicate key rows, the duplicates end up on overflow pages that are linked in a chain between leaf pages of the clustered index (the table's non-overflow data pages). New duplicate rows are added to the end of the chain of overflow pages. As the chain grows, inserts of the duplicate key slow because SQL Server must follow the overflow page chain to append the new row. Insert and delete order within the duplicate key helps manage the physical ordering of the rows within the duplicate. For example, an orders table with a clustered index on customer ID and purchase order number might allow duplicates to accommodate more than one item per purchase order. The pattern of inserts within each duplicate key should correspond to the pattern of deletes or updates. In addition, the rows inserted first are found more quickly than rows inserted later. Within each duplicate key, rows that are used more frequently should be inserted first. Of course, a useful nonclustered index could be employed in lieu of scanning the overflow pages.

6.6   DISK MIRRORING

Mirroring disk drives helps alleviate the danger of a disk drive failure from crippling your application. Operating system and hardware mirroring are usually faster and more efficient than SQL Server mirroring. Contrary to intuition, operating system mirroring sometimes performs better than hardware mirroring. This depends on the hardware, operating system, and usage characteristics. You should run your own tests if this is a concern.

SQL Server mirroring is started with the `disk mirror` command. With the command you can call for `serial` or `noserial` writes. When `serial` writes are specified, SQL Server waits for writes to the primary device to complete before initiating the write to the mirror device. The `noserial` option allows SQL Server to write data to both database devices simultaneously. Clearly, `serial` writes take about twice as long to complete as `noserial` writes, a significant performance disadvantage. Assuming your system can accommodate the disk I/O load, we see no reason to specify `serial` over `noserial` writes in disk mirroring. SQL Server does not optimize reads from mirrored devices. Under normal operation SQL Server always reads from the primary device.

A common misconception with SQL Server database device mirroring is that SQL Server somehow ensures that the two copies of the database device always remain identical. This is not the case. If you shutdown SQL Server, write random data over one of the mirrored database devices, and reboot, SQL Server does not notice there is a problem until you try to read data that is corrupted. Even then, SQL Server has no way of knowing which copy of the data is actually correct. SQL Server mirroring protects you from disk drive failures. Should one of the database device files become inaccessible, you have a usable copy in the mirror.

While mirroring outside SQL Server has its performance advantages, you are generally required to mirror complete disk drives rather than individual partitions or files. SQL Server lets you mirror individual database devices, but cannot ensure that you have placed the mirrored database devices on physically separate disk drives. Placing both halves of a mirror on the same physical disk drive defeats the purpose of mirroring and can significantly slow the disk drive's performance.

SQL Server mirror failover is sometimes complicated by operating systems that do not report hardware errors in a timely manner, panic when a hardware error occurs, or go catatonic when a disk drive fails to respond.

6.7   REPLICATION

Application developers that employ Sybase Replication Server should be aware of the performance implications to SQL Server:

- When data replication is enabled, updates on the replicated table are always deferred updates. In place updates are not allowed. If you are using data replication you cannot rely on the in-place update optimization. This either means, if you require data replication you are free to construct your database without regard to in-place update optimizations, or if in-place updates are essential to the performance of your application you must find a different way to replicate data.

- Replication of stored procedure execution causes SQL Server to wrap stored procedure executions in internal transactions. The execution of the stored procedure is logged. If your application uses many stored procedures and data replication, you may need to adjust upward your estimates of transaction log utilization.

- Replication Server reads the transaction log of SQL Server to reconstruct the transactions made against the primary database. It may place a marker in the transaction log that prevents the entire log from being truncated on `dump tran` or `dump database` to ensure that none of the log disappears before Replication Server has had a chance to get a copy of the transactions. This can be a problem if data replication is started and then stopped for some reason without telling SQL Server that replication is no longer required. The transaction log fills and there is no way to truncate the log without first telling SQL Server that replication of the transactions is no longer needed.

Chapter 7

Application Development

Client programs must not themselves become a performance bottleneck. They should display information quickly and process requests from users efficiently. The interface between the client and server should impose little overhead, using as little code as possible to send commands to SQL Server and read results from SQL Server. Ideally, the client and server are well matched in performance, with SQL Server giving data to the client at the moment the client needs it and the client sending data to SQL Server no faster than SQL Server can accept it. Unfortunately, hitting the bull's-eye is nearly impossible.

You can balance the load between the client and server by carefully considering the division of labor between the client applications and SQL Server. You may find ways to improve the performance of your application by moving computation or complex numerical analysis from SQL Server to the client programs.

Having decided on general themes for the division of work between your clients and servers, you need to find an efficient method for linking the client part of your application to the server part of your application. Large command batches reduce the number of exchanges between the clients and SQL Server, but may complicate your application programs. Smaller command batches result in more exchanges between the clients and SQL Server, but may improve concurrency. Stored procedures reduce network traffic by storing frequently used Transact-SQL (T-SQL) code on SQL Server, but only certain parts of T-SQL commands may accept parameters substitution. The Remote Procedure Call (RPC) mechanism saves the translation of parameters from text to native format. Embedded SQL (ESQL) and dynamic SQL are useful in environments where ANSI-compatible ESQL statements are needed.

Another challenge is writing optimal T-SQL commands. You should select only the columns you need, take advantage of expression short cuts, use joins instead of subqueries (where the semantics of your schema permit), avoid unnecessary expressions in search and join clauses, and write out join clauses completely (where appropriate).

Finally, you should understand that there is some overhead in forming a connection to SQL Server and in configuring SQL Server to accept a large number of simultaneous connections. Some tricks, such as replacing the name of the host running SQL Server with the host's network address, may improve performance in large networks.

In this chapter we discuss various topics related to writing client applications: how to divide workload between clients and SQL Server, techniques for writing T-SQL code, and issues concerning the communication between clients and SQL Server.

7.1   DIVISION OF WORKLOAD

The prospect of moving workload from the centralized servers to a multitude of client workstations is among the most commonly used justifications for client/server architectures. Intuitively, it makes sense to take advantage of all the computing power available to you whether the CPUs are in large server machines in the back office or in the clients on people's desktops. Unfortunately, dividing a big job into dozens or hundreds of smaller distributed jobs is not always the best solution. Let us investigate how distributing a job may translate into tangible benefits for your application.

7.1.1   Delegation of Work

SQL Server provides several options to divide workload among multiple clients and servers. Work can be divided functionally, dividing the applications tasks between the clients and SQL Servers. Stored procedures, for example, are a convenient way to define units of work on SQL Server. Similarly, functions, if the language you are using on the client provides them, define units of work on the clients. Alternatively, the division of labor can be data driven. Data for particular parts of the application or for different purposes is divided up among a collection of SQL Servers. Application programming interfaces and remote procedure calls enable clients and SQL Servers to communicate with each other.

When assigning workload to clients and SQL servers it is important to keep recoverability in mind. Processing data on a client's local disks does not guarantee data recovery in the event of systems failure. SQL Server is not managing the data once it is in the client. Transactional semantics are also important. Unless you lock data using SQL Server, other clients may change the data while the client is processing. Is this acceptable to your application?

SQL Server excels at managing data. Leaving SQL Server to process integrity and referential rules for your data is a valuable client/server division. Coding business rules into SQL Server is also rewarding. In this way, rules are placed on the data, where the data is stored, rather than where the data is processed. The various client programs that process data are ignorant of the constraints placed on the data by your organization's business rules. You can update the rules without managing the simultaneous upgrade of every application.

Move Work to Clients

Described here are some of the competing motivations for moving work from SQL Server to client.

Reduce Computation at SQL Servers

Unlike a language like C that is compiled into instructions the computer can execute directly, T-SQL is compiled into steps the computer must still interpret. As a result, T-SQL is not appropriate for long, complex computations. Generally, such computation performs significantly better when compiled into native computer instructions. As a result, certain types of computations are better done with clients than within SQL Server. Examples include most functions performed by statistical packages (in particular, non-relational operations such as time-series data reduction calculations), pattern matching, image processing, and certain specialized sort routines. You should consider off-loading computation to client workstations if your application requires SQL Server to perform significant computation that can be performed more easily by your client workstations. As an example, suppose you want to calculate the linear correlation between two sets of data. The linear correlation coefficient is given by the expression:

$$r = \frac{\left(\sum_i (x_i - \bar{x})(y_i - \bar{y}) \right)}{\left(\sqrt{\sum_i (x_i - \bar{x})^2} \sqrt{\sum_i (y_i - \bar{y})^2} \right)}$$

171

where $\bar{x}$ is the mean of the x_i values, and $\bar{y}$ is the mean of the y_i values. This expression can be implemented in T-SQL with the following statements:

```
declare @avgx double precision
declare @avgy double precision
select @avgx = avg(data) from table_x
select @avgy = avg(data) from table_y
select r = sum((table_x.data - @avgx)*(table_y.data - @avgy)) /
(sqrt(sum((table_x.data - @avgx)*(table_x.data - @avgx)) *
sqrt(sum((table_y.data - @avgy)*(table_y.data - @avgy)) from table_x,
table_y where table_x.pkey = table_y.pkey
```

This implementation involves the rather messy step to calculate r. Some parts of the expression are repeated (e.g., `table_x.data - @avgx`) and must be evaluated more than once for each row of data in the data sets we are comparing.[1]

Alternatively, the data in `table_x` and `table_y` can be read into the client, and the processing performed using a standard math library or through your own implementation. The query:

```
select table_x.data, table_y.data from table_x, table_y where
table_x.pkey = table_y.pkey
```

gets a copy of the data into the client. The client stores the data in two arrays, calculates the means and then the correlation coefficient.

```
double table_x[MAXLEN];
double table_y[MAXLEN];
int arraylen;
double avgx = 0.0, avgy = 0.0;
double sxx = 0.0, sxy = 0.0, syy = 0.0;
double xt, yt;

for (i = 0; i < arraylen; i++) {
        avgx += table_x[i];
        avgy += table_y[i];
}
avgx /= arraylen;
avgy /= arraylen;

for (i = 0; i < arraylen; i++) {
        xt = table_x[i] - avgx;
        yt = table_y[i] - avgy;
        sxx += xt*xt;
```

---

[1]. Temporary tables and variables could be used to reduce the amount of computation.

```
        syy += yt*yt;
        sxy += xt*yt;
}
r = sxy/sqrt(sxx*syy);
```

Because we control the computation inside the loop directly, we can simplify the steps and eliminate some of the redundant computation in the T-SQL implementation. The calculation of a linear correlation coefficient is straightforward enough, but other statistics computations, matrix manipulations, and linear programming are more difficult. There are many highly optimized and well tested statistical library functions available to C programmers. There is no reason for you to re-invent the wheel in T-SQL when a perfectly suitable routine already exists for the client.

Eliminate Communication between Clients and SQL Server

The fastest way to read results from SQL Server is to avoid doing so in the first place. If your application permits, make the clients keep local copies of information and go to SQL Server as infrequently as possible. This lightens load on SQL Server as it avoids the communication overhead associated with querying SQL Server. It also eliminates unnecessary operations against SQL Server. Of course, this strategy may not be appropriate in every situation. SQL Server provides data locking, recovery, and transactional integrity capabilities that may be important to your application and that you should avoid trying to implement in your client programs.

In the second example above, the client retrieves all of the data before calculating the linear correlation coefficient for the two data sets. Because the calculation is performed inside the client, the data may change while the client is crunching out the answer. This may not be appropriate for your application. On the other hand, if it is acceptable, perhaps other computations can piggy-back onto the same set of data. If many computations need to be performed on the same set of data, there is no reason to load a fresh copy of the data from SQL Server for each calculation.

Reduce Communication between Clients and SQL Server

Most applications involve some form of simple data reduction. Among the more obvious examples of data reduction are computation of averages, maximums and minimums, distinct values, detection of patterns, and summary generation. When generating reports, summary calculations are generally obvious and straightforward. However, data reduction may be hidden deep in the application logic. In either case, you may be able to reduce communication between client and SQL Server by performing the data reduction before rather than after communication.

For example, if your application accumulates incoming data in a temporary table in SQL Server over multiple procedures calls and then consolidates the data into a much smaller volume before permanently entering it into the database, you may be able to save communication by performing the consolidation of data at the clients that generate the data. Conversely, if your client workstation consolidates thousands of rows received from SQL Server into a few lines of summary data for display, you should consider computing the summary with SQL Server itself.

Client Can be Optimized

If you are rolling your own client programs using DB-Library or Client-Library, you have the source code to your client programs. You can instrument, profile, and improve the performance of the clients using well documented performance coding and troubleshooting techniques. You can choose efficient client libraries and communication protocols.

Exploit Cheaper Hardware on the Clients

Often client workstations offer more performance per dollar than larger server systems, where a premium is placed on reliability, durability, and I/O bandwidth. In this case, you may be able to improve the cost to performance ratio of your application by off-loading computation to the clients.

Partition Database Across Multiple SQL Servers

If your application logic allows you to partition data among multiple servers, you may be able to improve performance by replacing a large centralized server with a small number of decentralized servers. Your options include:

Partition by Databases or Tables

Putting two databases on two different servers is among the most accessible methods of decentralizing your application. However, SQL Server does not automatically support multi-server transactions. For this strategy to work successfully, you need to be keenly aware of the limitations in the transactional semantics of server-to-server remote procedure calls on SQL Server. Partitioning a database among multiple servers by dividing tables among SQL Servers is a more challenging task. If you choose this strategy, it is best to migrate in two steps: first partition the tables among two databases on the same server and then move databases to different servers.

Vertical Partitioning of Tables

Vertical partitioning of tables involves dividing the columns among multiple (not necessarily disjoint) subsets, each of which then comprises a separate table. A commonly practiced technique to prevent loss of information in vertical partitioning is to include the primary key in every subset. See Chapter 6, *Physical Database Design*, for more information.

Horizontal Partitioning of Tables

Horizontal partitioning of tables involves dividing the rows among multiple disjoint subsets. Each subset is stored in its own table. Such partitioning of data may follow naturally from application logic such as business units or geographic regions, or may involve artificial artifacts such as random, hash, or range partitioning.

Partition by the Purpose of the Data

Divide the data by how your application program uses it. For example, the same data might be used for an on-line transaction inventory control system and sales report generation. Rather than attempting to support both transaction processing and decision support on the same SQL Server, replicate the data from the on-line transaction system to the decision support system (in real time or periodically). Run inventory control against one of the SQL Servers and the sales reports against the other.

Whenever applicable, horizontal partitioning provides the most scalable performance of the above three methods of partitioning. Any or all of the above techniques may be useful in partitioning the workload of your application among multiple servers. If you see obvious strategies or advantages to partitioning your application, but are discouraged by the complexity of partitioning, you should consider Sybase MPP.

Common Pitfalls

While no more challenging than several other aspects of the design of any complex system, the division of workload among clients and SQL Server has its own set of common pitfalls.

Portability

One advantage of using stored procedures, triggers, and constraints to code application logic on SQL Server is the portability of SQL Server over a multitude of operating systems and hardware vendors. Shifting some of that logic into your clients may compromise portability. For example, if your client workstations use a medley of operating systems, the portion of your application logic you shifted from SQL Server now must be ported to and maintained on each of those operating systems.

Reliability and Availability

We often take for granted SQL Server's ability to provide a reliable, available, recoverable, transactionally consistent environment for storing and manipulating data. Shifting functionality from SQL Server to clients may require you to code some of these features into the client. These features are far from trivial to implement and coding your own implementation defeats the purpose of using a commercial database product.

Trading Computation for Communication

To perform computation on data, the computer needs both the data to work on and the instructions on how to manipulate the data. Moving data and/or computation from SQL Server to clients so that the data stays with the programs that know how to manipulate it has the potential for increasing communication. It does not pay to transfer a large volume of data from the client or SQL Server to the other if the cost of communication exceeds the savings in computation. Therefore, you should consider moving functionality across the client/server boundary only if the savings in computation are significant.

7.1.2   Granularity of Client-Server Interaction

One of the choices often overlooked by application developers is the granularity of interaction between the clients and SQL Servers. At one extreme, we can bundle multiple complex tasks into a single procedure call. At the other, we can employ hundreds or even thousands of exchanges between a client and SQL Server in performing a single task.

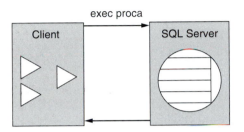
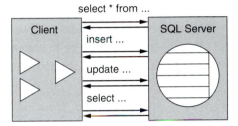

Figure 7.1   Client/Server interaction -

The choice of the appropriate level of granularity involves several trade-offs. There are four measures of granularity: the length of a session, the length of a transaction, the length of a stored procedure, and the length of a command batch (see Figure 7.2).

There are two important properties of SQL Server that constrain your choices in selecting the granularity of the client/server interaction:

1. A session cannot begin a transaction without terminating it. That is, the nesting level of transactions must be maintained by each session.[2]

2. A call to a stored procedure and the execution of a command batch are indivisible units of work. That is, the clients cannot use a stored procedure or a command batch as a co-routine and exchange data interactively with it. Once you exec a stored procedure, the stored procedure cannot ask you for any more information.

[2.] Stored procedures are allowed to start transactions without terminating them. You receive message 266 indicating that the number of begin trans does not match the number of commit trans. This is a warning and does not result in a rollback of the transaction that is open.

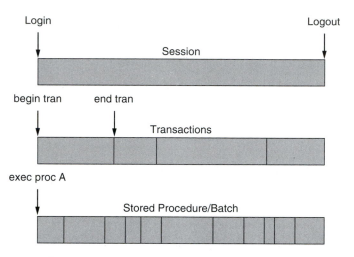

Figure 7.2   Client/Server interaction granularity -

How Long Should Clients Stay Logged into SQL Server?

It takes a certain amount of time to log into SQL Server. The overhead is high enough that it is impractical to log in and out for each query against the database. Given the overhead, you may be tempted to keep each client logged in as long as SQL Server stays up. Besides a host of security and administrative related reasons, there are two performance-related reasons to limit the duration of each session:

- **Memory** — Each configured user connection uses up some memory and other shared resources in SQL Server.

- **Heartbeat** — The server and an inactive client exchange messages to ensure that the other is alive.

SQL Server can handle a large number of connections. The maximum number of connections is set through the `number of user connections` configuration value. Ultimately, the maximum number of connections is generally limited by the amount of memory available on the system and the maximum number of file descriptors allowed per process by host operating system. The operating system uses a file descriptor for each open file whether the file represents a network connection or a database device. Many operating systems place an upper limit of a few thousand file descriptors per process. If you need to reconfigure the host operating system to allow more file descriptors, do not go overboard and configure the maximum number of file descriptors (per process or for the system as a whole) much larger than you need. Some operating systems require a small amount of memory for each potential file descriptor. Memory consumed by the operating system to store state information about the file descriptor is not available to user programs, like SQL Server.

Each potential connection to SQL Server needs a Sybase task. Whether or not the task is running, the task consumes memory for stack space and state information. This means less memory is available for buffering data and stored procedure plans.

Managing the maximum number of configured connections to SQL Server is important, particularly if your system is constrained by available memory. Configuring too many connections wastes memory. Configuring too few prevents users from logging into the system. While the users already on board experience better performance, users who cannot get on have infinite response time.

As a general rule, only the active clients should stay logged into SQL Server. You should have the client relinquish the connection when you do not expect the client to require any services from SQL Server for more than a few minutes. We discuss techniques to reduce the overhead of logging in and out of SQL Server later in this section.

Length of Transactions

An excessively long transaction hurts performance in several ways. First, it may reduce concurrency by adding to the lock contention with other transactions. Second, a long-running transaction makes it impossible to truncate the log. A **log full** condition brings SQL Server to a grinding halt. Third, if the duration of the transaction causes SQL Server to write uncommitted dirty pages to disk, the cost of rollbacks can be excessive.

Of course, it does not pay to make transactions excessively short either, since there is a fixed overhead for every transaction, even the short ones. There are two important factors to consider in striking the right balance:

Escalation of Page Locks to Table Locks

As discussed in Chapter 5, *SQL Server — Methods and Features*, SQL Server attempts to escalate page locks to table locks when the number of page locks held by a single statement on a table or index exceeds a threshold. In the absence of lock contention, this behavior works in favor of long transactions because there is a relatively fixed cost in acquiring a lock whether on a page or table.

To see this, consider dividing a transaction that scans 1000 pages of a table into five transactions, each of which scans 200 pages. Assuming SQL Server escalates page locks to a table lock after the first 200 pages, the long 1000 page transaction acquires 200 page locks, then receives a table level lock. No more page locks are needed. The five shorter 200 page transactions each acquire 200 page locks, never passing the threshold to acquire a table level lock. Whereas the 1000 page transaction needed 200 page locks, the five 200 page transactions need 1000 page locks in all, a five-fold increase.

On the one hand, if contention on this table is a problem in your application, you should keep transactions smaller to avoid escalating from page locks to table locks. On the other hand, if the overhead of acquiring locks is limiting the performance of your application, you should make transactions larger to encourage escalation from page locks to table locks.

Transaction Isolation Level

During select, SQL Server normally holds read locks on pages only long enough to read rows from the page. Using isolation level 3 or the HOLDLOCK keyword causes SQL Server to hold locks for the duration of the entire transaction. If the duration of locks is a performance bottleneck, you have two options to improving performance: lower the isolation level or divide the transaction into shorter transactions.

There are two cases of special interest when it comes to determining the length of transactions:

- **The batch size in bulk copying of data** — Each batch is treated as a separate transaction. Thus, the length of transactions in bulk copy is tuned easily by adjusting the batch size.

- **Conversational transactions** — Transactions that involve interaction with end-users may be excessively long. Such transactions may limit concurrency and transform an innocuous coffee break into a log-full condition.[3] Concurrency may be limited because SQL Server locks pages rather than rows. If several rows of data may occupy one page, when one row of the data is locked, all other rows of data on the same page are similarly locked. For example, If Joe acquires an exclusive lock on a page because he is updating a row on that page, no other users can select or update that page until Joe finishes the update. If Joe goes on a coffee break while he is holding the lock, everyone else who is trying to modify data on the same page might as well go with him.

Length of Stored Procedures and Command Batches

A single stored procedure call or command batch that performs several large tasks has obvious advantages in terms of minimizing communication overhead. Given the overhead in communication between the client and SQL Server, we should maximize the amount of work performed per exchange. Of course, there are practical limits to the size of a stored procedure or a command batch. A single, do everything stored procedure might need dozens of parameters or have a complicated flow of execution. Hence, there are certain advantages to having more frequent interactions between the client and SQL Server.

Optional Parameters

Often, your stored procedure may not need every parameter every time it is executed. For example, consider a stored procedure that computes eligibility of a loan applicant given the applicant's profile. If the profile includes either a triple-A rating or the history of bankruptcy (and hopefully not both), then the stored procedure does not need the rest of the profile to come up with an answer. In such cases, you may find it to your advantage to divide the stored procedure into two or more phases, especially if it saves your client the work of computing the values of parameters that are not used by the stored procedure in all cases.

Optional Functionality

The output of a stored procedure might depend on the parameters it is given. Many of the system stored procedures are good examples. `sp_help` with no arguments lists all of the objects in the database. When `sp_help` is given the name of an object, the information it gives you about the object depends on what kind of

---

3. Remember, SQL Server does not truncate the log beyond the first open transaction in the database.

object you have named. This requires a substantial amount of logic inside the stored procedure that must be executed every time an object name is given. If the programmer using the stored procedure already knows the object's type, there is no reason to have the stored procedure figure it out again. For performance, it is better to have separate procedures for each object type, eliminating the need for the stored procedure to rediscover the object's type. This may be inappropriate from a usability standpoint if the user is unlikely to know the object's type ahead of time.

Transactional Semantics

If a single logical unit of work against SQL Server involves more than one transaction, you may want to perform each transaction in a separate batch rather than executing them in a single batch. If the Nth transaction fails, you would like to restart from the Nth transaction and complete all of the transactions without redoing the first through N-1th transaction in the batch. Doing so in a single batch adds to the complexity of the application code.

7.2 QUERYING SQL SERVER

Once you have decided on your queries, you need to get the query to SQL Server and collect the results back to the client. There are several ways to deliver commands to SQL Server from clients:

- Send raw `select`, `insert`, `update`, `delete` statements to SQL Server as ad hoc queries using a login session.

- Encapsulate your selects, inserts, updates, and deletes into stored procedures and execute the stored procedures by name from a login session.

- Create stored procedures for your queries and execute the procedures through the remote procedure call (RPC) interface.

- Mix SQL code with another computer language using an Embedded SQL pre-compiler.

- Use the dynamic SQL feature of the Embedded SQL pre-compilers.

After SQL Server executes your commands, it needs to get the results back to the client. Your client application has several ways it can read results:

- **Use an `isql` session and process `isql`'s output with various text processing utilities (e.g., `sed`, `awk`, `perl`)** — This method is quick to implement in

simple cases, but can be difficult to modify and extend. It is also not very efficient as data must always be converted to text. If your client program needs to
manipulate the data as numbers, the value must be converted back into the
machine representation that is suitable for data manipulation.[4]

- **Compile the text of queries into your application code using an ESQL pre-compiler** — The pre-compiler converts embedded SQL into Client-Library
  calls. While more efficient than using a completely generic client program like
  `isql`, the pre-compiler cannot know exactly what data is expected. As a result,
  it must provide result processing code that is very general, and not optimal for
  the particular queries.

- **Code to Client-Library or DB-Library directly** — This is the most difficult,
  but likely to give the best performing program. You can code directly to your
  queries. If your query results in only one column of data of a known type, you
  can code with that in mind. You do not have code generally and discover the
  datatypes along the way.

In this section, we discuss the various ways queries can be delivered to SQL
Server, comparing the more common and efficient, and also some strategies for
reading results from SQL Server.

7.2.1   Stored Procedures versus Ad Hoc Queries

When delivering queries to SQL Server, you can either send all of the SQL statements you want to execute directly, or encapsulate the statements into stored procedures.

Advantages to Stored Procedures

Besides the application design strengths of using stored procedures (i.e., encapsu-
lating business rules in SQL Server rather than the clients) there are a host of performance reasons for choosing stored procedures over ad hoc T-SQL statements.

[4.] Slightly more flexible are extensions to popular public domain scripting languages such as sybperl for Perl and
sybtcl for TCL.

Stored Procedures Re-Use the Optimized Query Plan

When you first execute a stored procedure, SQL Server reads a partially compiled plan from `sysprocedures`, completes the compilation, optimizes, and then executes the query. The optimized query plan is cached. The next time you run the same stored procedure, SQL Server finds the query plan cached in memory. SQL Server re-uses the plan, eliminating the need to parse, compile, and optimize the query each time the query is executed.

Reduced Network Traffic

Using stored procedures reduces network traffic by eliminating the need to pass significant amounts of SQL code from the client to SQL Server. The client simply passes the name of the stored procedure and parameters rather than the code represented by the body of the stored procedure. Almost any ad hoc query is longer than the name of a stored procedure.

Disadvantages to Using Stored Procedures

There are also some disadvantages to stored procedures you should consider when designing your application:

Stored Procedures Use the Optimized Query Plan

SQL Server generates the query plan for a stored procedure based on the parameters passed into the stored procedure every time it is recompiled. A stored procedure is recompiled when it is invoked for the first time after a schema revision or it is executed with the recompile option. All subsequent users of the stored procedure get this copy of the optimized query plan.[5] This can cause performance problems if the invocation of the stored procedure that is optimized and cached creates an optimized query plan that is not optimal for all users of the stored procedure. For example, suppose one of the stored procedure parameters defines the search criteria for a query:

```
select fname, lname from addresses where zip = @zip
```

[5.] A single copy of an optimized query plan cannot be shared by many tasks running simultaneously. Each task has its own copy of the optimized query plan for the stored procedure, and each plan may be optimized differently based on the parameters passed into the various invocations of the stored procedure.

where the `select` appears in a stored procedure and `@zip` is one of the parameters to the stored procedure. Suppose further that there is an index on zip. There are very few customers in the 94804 zip code, but there are many customers in the 94618 zip code. With a highly selective search clause like `@zip = 94804`, SQL Server may choose to use the index to find the few rows with this zip code. With the relatively low selectivity of the index with `@zip = 94618`, SQL Server may choose to use a table scan. Suppose the first time the stored procedure is run, `@zip = 94618`. The plan that says "use a table scan to find the matching rows in addresses" is stored in the procedure cache. The next time the stored procedure is executed, SQL Server uses the cached plan, even if `@zip` is now 94804. In fact, from now on, every time the stored procedure is executed (until the plan is pushed out of the procedure cache), SQL Server uses a table scan to read addresses. This is undesirable, particularly if the `@zip` we choose does not appear in the table.

This problem is solved in one of three ways:

- **Create the stored procedure with the recompile option** — This causes SQL Server to compile and optimize the query each time before it is executed.

- **Execute the stored procedure with the recompile option** — SQL Server compiles and executes the stored procedure before it is executed this one time. The new optimized query plan is stored in the procedure cache.

- **Do not use a stored procedure** — Use an ad hoc query instead, giving SQL Server all of the SQL code rather than storing the code in a stored procedure. SQL Server now compiles and optimizes the query each time, without regard to its past experience with the query.

This issue is covered in more detail in Chapter 11, *Query Processing Performance*.

Table and Column Names Cannot Be Used As Parameters

You cannot make the name of a table or column a parameter to a stored procedure. For example:

```
create procedure p_select @tabname varchar(30)
as
select * from @tabname
```

is not a valid stored procedure. If you need to parameterize the table or column name in a stored procedure and there are a small number of possibilities, you might consider creating a stored procedure for each possibility. Alternatively, you can put if ... then .. else logic in your stored procedure for each case:

```
if @tabname = "table1" then
        select * from table1
else if @tabname = "table2" then
        select * from table2
else if @tabname = "table3" then
        select * from table3
else begin
        print "unknown table %1!",@tabname
        return 1
end
```

Neither solution is practical if the number of tables is large or unknown. In this case, you can create an ad hoc query in a C string and substitute in the name of the table:

```
char p_select[] = "select * from %s";
```

Then use the dbfcmd() function in DB-Library to submit the query:

```
dbfcmd(...,p_select,"mytable");
```

The same thing can be accomplished in Client-Library through sprintf() and ct_command():

```
char cbuf[BUFSIZ];
CS_COMMAND *command;
[...]
sprintf(cbuf,p_select,"mytable");
ct_command(command, CS_LANG_CMD, cbuf, CS_NULLTERM, CS_UNUSED);
```

7.2.2 Dynamic SQL

Dynamic SQL is used in compiled applications that cannot process ad hoc queries but still need to allow users to provide parameters, queries, etc. It is a feature of Client-Library and the ESQL pre-compilers. Dynamic SQL is useful primarily for applications migrating from or co-existing with database environments where there is a distinction between static, compiled SQL statements and dynamic SQL statements that cannot be known entirely when the application is compiled. SQL

Server does not make this distinction but other database environments may. Hence, with Sybase, you can implement dynamic SQL with simple string manipulation of T-SQL before sending the SQL statements to SQL Server.

Using the dynamic SQL feature of Client-Library or the ESQL pre-compilers involves two steps. In the first step, the **prepare** step, you provide a SQL statement with place holders for the dynamic information. For example:

```
select fname, lname from employees where empid = ?
```

The ? is a place holder for the empid in the query. Client-Library creates a temporary stored procedure with parameters in place of the place holders.

The second step, **execute**, executes the temporary stored procedure with the given parameters. As a result of this implementation, any query optimization issues discussed with stored procedures apply equally well to dynamic SQL. When the application is finished using the dynamic SQL statement, it deallocates the dynamic SQL descriptor. The deallocation drops the temporary stored procedure.

Dynamic SQL has some performance advantages over ad hoc queries if you are executing the same query over and over again with similar parameters. Because dynamic SQL stores the bulk of the statement in a stored procedure, the amount of data transmitted from the client to SQL Server is reduced and parse, compile, and optimization time is eliminated.

Dynamic SQL is not without its drawbacks. Contention on the system tables in tempdb can become a problem if many applications must prepare dynamic SQL statements concurrently. In addition, each dynamic SQL prepare generates log records in tempdb to record the create procedure command. These consequences are the result of the implementation of dynamic SQL using stored procedures in tempdb. You may want to avoid a lot of dynamic SQL prepare statements, particularly when maximum concurrency is desired. If dynamic SQL is a critical part of your application, consider putting tempdb on a fast disk to mitigate problems with the transaction log for tempdb.

7.2.3 Executing Stored Procedures

Stored procedures are generally written to take in and return one or more parameters. In this section we discuss issues regarding the performance of invoking stored procedures. There are three issues:

- Passing parameters to stored procedures

- Parameter datatype conversion
- Output parameters

Stored Procedure Parameters

Stored procedure parameters must be parsed by SQL Server, so there is a small amount of overhead associated with each parameter. As a result, a stored procedure with many parameters takes longer to execute than the same stored procedure with only a few parameters. As we discussed in "Length of Stored Procedures and Command Batches" on page 181, you should try to eliminate unnecessary parameters to your stored procedures by moving optional functionality into separate stored procedures. Rather than create one giant stored procedure taking all possible parameters, only some of which are needed at any one time, create several smaller stored procedures where every parameter is used all of the time.

SQL Server lets you pass stored procedure parameters either by position or by name. Suppose we have a stored procedure that takes three parameters, `@first`, `@second`, and `@third`:

```
create procedure example
        (@first int, @second char(10), @third datetime) as ...
```

When we invoke example, we can pass the parameters by position:

```
example 10,"string","jan 1, 1994"
```

or by name:

```
example @third = "jan 1 1994",
        @first = 10, @second = "string"
```

Passing parameters by position is more efficient than passing parameters by name. Passing parameters by position eliminates the need for SQL Server to match up the named parameters with the names of the variables in the stored procedure. The savings can be significant if the transaction is relatively short and there are many parameters.

Parameter Datatype Conversion

When you execute a stored procedure with the `execute` command, you pass the parameters to the stored procedure in text form. That is, the string that SQL Server processes includes the text of the parameters. Before SQL Server can execute the query, it must convert the text of the parameters into an internal representation that is easier and faster to manipulate. For example, the parameter @first in the previous example is an int. Before SQL Server executes example, it must translate the string "10" into the integer 10.

If there are a large number of parameters that need such conversion, or if you are trying to execute the stored procedure with minimal overhead, you would like to eliminate this conversion. This can be accomplished by executing the stored procedure via the Remote Procedure Call (RPC) mechanism. Client-Library provides the ct_command() type CS_RPC_CMD. DB-Library uses the dbrpcinit() routine. Executed this way, the stored procedure parameters are sent to SQL Server in native format and no conversion from text is needed. If the client and server have differing internal formats for the values, a data conversion is performed to accommodate the differences. In general, the primary differences between platforms is byte order and floating point representation (see "Cost of Communication" on page 208).

Because the RPC mechanism has the least amount of overhead for executing stored procedures, the fastest way to execute a stored procedure is as an RPC from the client. Other than a little extra coding on the client side, you do not lose any capabilities as compared to executing the stored procedure with the execute command.

Stored Procedure Output Parameters

Stored procedures can return data to clients in one of several ways:

- Row results from a select
- Print output
- Return status
- Output parameters

Row results appear as regular row results and can be retrieved in the same way that you read values from a select statement. Output from the print command is returned to the client as server messages with the error number set to 0. The return status is read in Client-Library as a CS_STATUS_RESULT result_type from ct_results() or in DB-Library with the dbretstatus() routine.

Output parameters are parameters that the stored procedure may return a value in. The parameter must be declared as an output parameter when the stored procedure is created and when the stored procedure is executed. For example:

```
create procedure outputexample
```

```
                    (@inparam int, @outparam char(10) output) as
                    select @outparam = convert(char(10),@inparam)
```

For `outputexample` to affect a change to `outparam`, it must be executed as:

```
declare @string char(10)
execute outputexample 10,@string output
```

`outputexample` then modifies `@string`. The client can read the new value of `@string` in one of two ways.

- **Explicitly select @string** — The client then reads the value by processing the row result from the select command.

- **Reading the changed parameter** — The client receives a message stating that the parameter has changed value. In Client-Library this appears as a `CS_PARAM_RESULT result_type` from `ct_results()` and in DB-Library you can use the `dbretdata()`.

The latter method is preferred as it eliminates extra SQL code that must be processed by SQL Server. SQL Server sends information about the changed parameter whether or not the client decides to do anything with the information.

If you execute the stored procedure with output parameters with the `execute` command, you must first declare a SQL variable to hold the returned parameter value. This is not necessary if you execute the stored procedure via the RPC mechanism. With the RPC mechanism you simply execute the stored procedure and the change parameter values are made available to you with the `CS_PARAM_RESULT result_type` in Client-Library or `dbretdata()` in DB-Library. You do not need to declare SQL variables ahead of time to hold the new return value.

7.2.4   Retrieving Results

Reading results from SQL Server is one of the biggest parts of a database application. Doing so efficiently is the responsibility of the client programmer. When your program processes results, it typically follows this pattern:

```
execute select statement
read results to get to the row data
bind columns
while (more results) {
        fetch row
        process row
}
```

You must bind variables in your client program to read results from SQL Server. When you do this, the client library copies of the appropriate values from the results read from SQL Server into the bound variables. Binding is a utility function and all overhead. It does nothing toward the processing of your data that the client must perform. As a consequence, you should bind variables only as absolutely necessary.

Binding Strings

Special consideration should be given to binding long char columns to char arrays in your program when you want to save copies of the strings. In many cases, it may be more efficient to bind a new string variable to the char column each time you fetch a row of results than to copy the string from the bound variable to the storage array in your program. For example:

```
bind string to char column
while (more results) {
        fetch row
        strcpy(storage[i],string)
}
```

may not be as efficient as:

```
while (more results) {
        bind storage[i] to char column
        fetch row
}
```

Of course, this is only an issue of the client program saves copies of the rows rather than processing the rows one by one as it reads them from SQL Server.

Array Bindings

Array binding allows programmers to grab more than one row of results at a time when fetching results from a query. This is a feature of Client-Library and is not available to DB-Library programmers. Array binding is useful when you need to process rows in small batches. It reduces program overhead because fewer library calls are needed to fetch results and the program spends less time traversing the Client-Library call stack. Network traffic is not affected as the same results are sent whether you read the results one row at a time or many rows at a time.

7.2.5 Added Parallelism: Asynchronous Programming

Asynchronous programming allows a client program to send a request to SQL Server and do other work while SQL Server processes the last command. If the client works synchronously with SQL Server, the client must wait for SQL Server to complete the command before doing any other processing. The client and server work in lock step. The client waits while SQL Server completes the query.

An asynchronous arrangement improves the overall performance of the application by allowing the client and SQL Server to process information in parallel. If your client does not support pre-emptive multitasking, you need to write your own scheduler, one that lets your client proceed with other tasks while it is waiting for SQL Server to complete a command. When SQL Server completes, the scheduler in the client knows to pick up the results of the command. Callback functions from Client-Library facilitate this style of application development. If your client supports pre-emptive multitasking, you have the option of multi-threading your client application so that while some threads are blocked on SQL Server, other threads can do some processing. The client's operating system takes care of the scheduling, thus relieving you of the task of asynchronous programming. However, you may still find it advantageous to write your own scheduler using the callback functions for these reasons:

- Some versions of Client-Library and DB-Library are not thread safe. You can get around this problem by using a separate operating system process for each thread. The complication then comes in getting the threads to communicate with one another.

- The pre-emptive multitasking on your client operating system may not be optimal for your application.

- You may need to write your application for multiple client operating systems, some of which do not support multi-tasking or multi-threaded applications.

Asynchronous Programming with Client-Library

Under Client-Library, programmers change a Client-Library property to enable asynchronous network I/O. Client-Library allows you to register functions that are called by Client-Library when certain events occur. These callbacks make it possible to use a truly asynchronous style of programming.

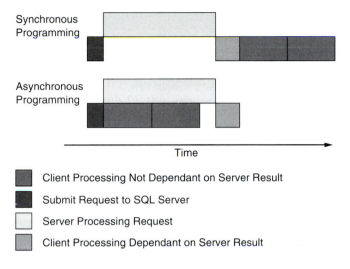

Synchronous
Programming

Asynchronous
Programming

Time

Client Processing Not Dependant on Server Result

Submit Request to SQL Server

Server Processing Request

Client Processing Dependant on Server Result

Figure 7.3   Asynchronous vs. synchronous programming - - - - - - - - - - - - - -

After calling:

```
ct_callback(NULL,
        connection,
        CS_SET,
        CS_COMPLETION_CB,
        &callbackfunction);
```

Client-Library calls `callbackfunction` whenever an asynchronous Client-Library function completes. `callbackfunction` must take the following arguments:

```
callbackfunction(CS_CONNECTION *connection,
        CS_COMMAND *command,
        CS_INT function,
        CS_RETCODE returncode)
```

where `connection` and `command` provide some context for the connection and command that completed, `function` indicates the Client-Library function that completed, and `returncode` is the return status from the function that completed. For example, if `ct_send` is used asynchronously and succeeds successfully, `function` is `CT_SEND` and returncode is `CS_SUCCEED`.

Asynchronous Programming with DB-Library

Under DB-Library, special routines are used to send commands to SQL Server and poll for completion. `dbsqlsend()` sends commands to SQL Server without waiting for any response from SQL Server. Next, you must call a routine to check if results are available. `dbpoll()` checks for results from any connection. `DBRBUF` can be used if you have many connections open and need to check for results on a particular connection. The program can perform other tasks while results are not available. You must remember to call `dbpoll` or `DBRBUF` periodically to look for results.

7.3 TRANSACT-SQL CODING TIPS

SQL is a high level language that is designed intentionally to isolate the SQL coder from the details of database access methods. You do not need to tell SQL Server which indexes to use and the appropriate join order. The query compiler and optimizer figure these things out for you. To produce an efficient query plan, the query optimizer relies on the information you have provided in the query and information it can glean about your data from index statistics and the schema.

Given the amount of optimization that is possible with certain simplifying assumptions, even minute changes to the query may alter the query optimizations considered by SQL Server. Changing the columns you are selecting may force SQL Server to read the data pages from the table when index covering was adequate before. Changing how you join tables together may alter the join orders SQL Server considers during join order optimization. SQL Server performs some optimization on expressions included in Transact-SQL commands. When you write expressions with complex mathematical or boolean operations, you should consider these optimizations in order to speed processing.

7.3.1 The Select List

When you express your queries, you should include only the columns you really need in the select list. There are two reasons for this. First, limiting the number of columns to only the columns you are interested in reduces the amount of data that must be sent from SQL Server to the client. This is particularly true if you expect a large number of columns and some of the columns you do not need are wide. Second, if the tables you are using include nonclustered indexes, the indexes may cover the query. Index covering improves performance because SQL Server does not need to read the data pages of the table. This saves disk I/O and buffer space. If you include columns you do not need, SQL Server may be forced to read the data pages of the table simply to provide the data in the columns.

For example, suppose we have the table and index:

```
create table testtable
          (a int, b char(10), c char(255), d float)
create nonclustered index i_testtable_ab on testtable(a,b)
```

Assuming SQL Server chooses to use the index i_testtable_ab on the query below, it is not necessary for SQL Server to read the data pages of testtable. The index i_testtable_ab contains all of the information needed to satisfy the query:

```
select b
from testtable
where a = 27
```

On the other hand, if the query is:

```
select *
from testtable
where a = 27
```

SQL Server must read the data pages from testtable in order to get the values for columns c and d. If the client using this query is only interested in column b, SQL Server has had to access database pages unnecessarily. This wastes buffer space and disk I/O time.

The SQL Server monitoring techniques in Chapter 9, *Instrumenting SQL Code*, can help you determine if the a nonclustered index is covering the query.

7.3.2 Joins

When you join on the same column between three or more tables, you should include all possible table joins, not just a unique set. For example, suppose you are joining tables ta, tb, and tc on the column empid as:

```
select *
from ta,tb,tc
where ta.empid = tb.empid and tb.empid = tc.empid
```

While this forms a complete join between the three tables, SQL Server does not recognize that ta.empid = tc.empid. As a result, it does not consider this a possible join strategy and may miss an opportunity to optimize the join order for this query. To be complete, you should state:

```
select *
from ta,tb,tc
where ta.empid = tb.empid and
        tb.empid = tc.empid and
        ta.empid = tc.empid
```

SQL Server does not care what order the joins appear in or which side of the equals sign the various tables appear on.

You can use this behavior to your advantage if you want to force SQL Server to consider only certain join strategies. For example, if you leave out `ta.empid = tc.empid` from the `where` clause, SQL Server does not consider joining `ta` to `tc`.

7.3.3   Where Clause

When you specify a join or search criteria in a `where` clause, you should avoid unnecessary expressions. For example:

```
select *
from ta,tb
where ta.value = tb.value+0
```

is functionally identical to:

```
select *
from ta,tb
where ta.value = tb.value
```

but the two queries are not optimized in the same way. SQL Server's query optimizer cannot use `ta.value = tb.value+0` as a join clause on `tb` because there is an expression involved in the equality. SQL Server assumes that it cannot determine the selectivity of the equality at compile time. This means SQL Server uses heuristics for selecting the best join order rather than taking advantage of any index statistics that might be available.

7.3.4   Join versus Subquery

Consider the following queries:

```
select intcolumn
from tinteger
where pkey in (select a from table1)
```

and:

```
select intcolumn
```

```
from tinteger, table1
where tinteger.pkey = table1.a
```

These two queries are functionally equivalent if `table1.a` is unique. Given their equivalence, it is better to express the query as a join than a subquery.

You can tell SQL Server that `table1.a` is unique by creating a unique index on `table1(a)`:

```
create index u_table1a on table1(a)
```

With this hint, System 11 SQL Server recognizes that the subquery is identical the join and optimizes the join order accordingly. System 10 and previous versions of SQL Server do not recognize the equivalence and miss an opportunity to optimize the join order.

7.3.5   AND and OR Processing

SQL Server takes advantage of `AND` and `OR` short cuts when expressions appear in `if` and `while` statements of T-SQL. For example, the expression:

```
X and Y and Z
```

where `X`, `Y`, and `Z` are boolean expressions (e.g., `@variable > 10`) is only true if `X`, `Y`, and `Z` are all true. If any of them is false, the expression as a whole is also false. This means if `X` is found to be false, there is no reason to evaluate `Y` and `Z` because we already know that the expression as a whole is false. You can take advantage of this by making `X` the expression that is most likely to be false. This minimizes the number of times `Y` and `Z` need to be processed. Alternatively, if `X`, `Y`, and `Z` are equally likely, you can order them by difficulty of evaluation. The easy to evaluate expressions come first, the more difficult later. This way, the likelihood of evaluating the most complex, and presumably time consuming expression is minimized.

Processing `OR` operators is similarly optimized. The expression:

```
A or B or C
```

where `A`, `B`, and `C` are boolean expressions is only true if one or more of `A`, `B`, or `C` is true. If `A` is true there is no need to evaluate `B` and `C` because we already know that the expression as a whole is true. As with `AND`, you can take advantage of this in `OR` by making `A` the expression that is most likely to be true. This minimizes the number of times `B` and `C` need to be evaluated. Again, like `AND`, if the expressions are equally likely to be true, you should order the expressions from least to most difficult to evaluate. This minimizes processing by increasing the chances that B and C are not evaluated.

7.3.6   Loop Invariants

SQL Server does not eliminate loop invariants. For example, in a while loop, SQL Server executes all of the commands in the loop, even if the results are not going to change:

```
declare @i int
declare @b float
select @i = 1000
while (@i > 0)
begin
        select @i = @i - 1
        select @b = 10.0 * pi() * log(23)
        select @b * colb from T where coli = @i
end
```

The while loop evaluates the value of @b for each iteration of the loop. This is a contrived example, and it is clear that moving the calculation of @b outside the loop reduces the amount of processing required of SQL Server. More subtle are statements such as:

```
select columnA, columnB * 2 * pi()/sqrt(10) from tableT
```

Here, the expression:

```
2 * pi()/sqrt(10)
```

is evaluated for every row of the table. Declaring a variable and calculating the constant part of the expression ahead of time is preferable:

```
declare @c float
select @c = 2 * pi()/sqrt(10)
select columnA, columnB * @c from tableT
```

Be wary of introducing variables in inappropriate places. For example:

```
declare @c float
select @c = 87 * sin(pi()/2.0 * 45)
select @d = 87 * sin(pi()/2.0 * 44)
select colA from T where colR between @c and @d
```

may not be an appropriate use of variable substitution. The query optimizer cannot use @c and @d to assess the selectivity of the where clause and may not choose the correct query plan. In this situation, it might be preferable to calculate @c and @d in the client or in a separate batch and read the values into the client, and use the values as constants in the query against T.

7.4 PROGRAMMING TECHNIQUES

T-SQL has certain limitations. For example, T-SQL lacks the case expression and arrays. Described here are some ways to work around these problems while also maintaining good performance.

7.4.1 Case Expression

The case expression in ANSI SQL-2 is a useful feature that can save coding effort as well as improve performance. You need to rephrase your queries if your application uses or requires the case expression.

Let us use the following query to outline alternative methods for rephrasing the case expression for T-SQL.

```
select w, (case    when B1(x) then x1
                   when B2(x) then x2
                   ..
                   when Bk(x) then xk
                   else x0
         end)
         from T
```

In the above, $Bi(x)$ (where i is 1 to k) are boolean predicates, x is a column of the table, and xi are other columns or expressions. There are several different ways you can express this query in T-SQL.

Rephrasing Case Expressions Using Union All

```
select w, x1 from T where B1(x)
union all
select w, x2 from T where B2(x)
union all
...
union all
select w, xk from T where Bk(x)
union all
```

```
select w, x0 from T where x not in (B1(x) .. Bk(x))
```

There are several disadvantages in this rephrasing. If the clauses `Bi(x)` do not include a useful search argument, we end up scanning the table multiple times, once for each `select`. The `union all` operation has limited applicability. For example, you cannot define a view on this rephrasing. Processing of `not in` for the default case requires a table scan. Processing of `union all` requires a work-table to accumulate results. Further, this technique may run into trouble because of the 16 table per statement limit of System 10 and earlier versions of SQL Server.

Rephrasing Case Expressions Using a Temporary Table

```
select w, x, x1 into #S from T where B1(x)
insert into #S select w, x, x2 from T where B2(x)
insert into #S select w, x, x3 from T where B3(x)
...
insert into #S select w, x, xk from T where Bk(x)
insert into #S select w, x, x0 from T where T.x not in (select x from
#S)
select w, x1 from #S
```

Here we have traded `union all` for a temp table, thus eliminating the fourth disadvantage in the above rephrasing. Processing of the default case is simplified somewhat by keeping track of the values of x that were already processed. However, this rephrasing maintains all the other disadvantages of the former rephrasing, and adds two new ones. We now have multiple statements instead of a single statement, which may change the behavior of the application because the transactional semantics differ. Second, unlike entries into a worktable, the `insert into` operations log the inserts into the temp table.

Rephrasing Case Expressions Using Arithmetic

In the special case that the boolean expressions $Ci(x)$ and xi can be evaluated as numeric values, you may be able to use rephrase the query as:

```
select w,
        C1(x) * x1
        + C2(x) * x2
        ...
        + Ck(x) * xk
        from T
```

where $Ci(x)$ is the numeric representation of $Bi(x)$. For example, the predicate:

```
x like "prefix%"
```

has a numerical equivalent in the T-SQL expression:

```
patindex(x,"prefix%")
```

This is a reasonably flexible approach that supports most comparison and boolean operations. Table 7.1 lists the equivalent numeric expressions for comparison operations between numeric values.

Table 7.1   Expressions for comparing numeric values

Comparison	Expression
A = B	1 - abs(sign(A - B))
A <> B	abs(sign(A-B))
A > B	1 - sign(1 - sign(A - B))
A < B	1 - sign(1 + sign(A - B))
A >= B	sign(1 + sign(A - B))
A <= B	sign(1 - sign(A - B))

Table 7.2 lists the equivalent numeric expressions for various comparison operations between datetime values.

Table 7.2   Expressions for comparing datetime values

Comparison	Expression
A = B	1 - abs(sign(datediff(dd, B, A)))
A <> B	abs(sign(datediff(dd, B, A)))
A > B	1 - sign(1 - sign(datediff(dd, B, A)))

Table 7.2   Expressions for comparing datetime values

Comparison	Expression
A < B	1 - sign(1 + sign(datediff(dd, B, A)))
A >= B	sign(1 + sign(datediff(dd, B, A)))
A <= B	sign(1 - sign(datediff(dd, B, A)))

Table 7.3 shows the equivalent numeric expressions for comparing two strings.

Table 7.3   Expressions for comparing character values

Comparison	Expression
A = B	charindex(A,B)*charindex(B,A)
A <> B	1 - charindex(A,B)*charindex(B,A)

Finally, Table 7.4 shows how you can combine the equivalent numeric expressions using arithmetic to simulate the boolean operations.

Table 7.4   Expressions for logical operators

Comparison	Expression
C1 AND C2	C1 * C2
C1 OR C2	sign(C1 + C2)[a]
NOT C1	1 - C1

a.   If C1 and C2 cannot be true at the same time, then
       C1 + C2 can be used instead.

While using the equivalent numeric expressions is straightforward for selecting numeric values, it is less clear how the equivalent numeric expressions might be useful for generating strings. You can use the `substring()` function to construct a string based on a value. For example, suppose you want to generate the strings "poor", "acceptable", and "excellent" based on the value of the column `sales`: "poor" for `sales` less than or equal to 10, "acceptable" for `sales` between 10 and 15, and "excellent" for `sales` greater than or equal to 15. You can do so with the following expression:

```
substring("poor",1,255*sign(1-sign(sales-10)))+
substring("acceptable",1,255*
         sign(1+sign(sales-10)*sign(1-sign(sales+15)))+
substring("excellent",1,255*sign(1+sign(sales-15)))
```

Using the equivalent numeric expressions can be computationally expensive and confusing. However, even with these limitations, this solution is the clear winner if you can use it. It processes the entire query as a single statement and does not, in itself, mandate a worktable.

7.4.2 Arrays as Parameters to Stored Procedures

Often you need to pass a variable length array as a parameter to a stored procedure. Unfortunately, T-SQL does not support array variables, only scalar values. One option is to pass the elements of the array as individual parameters to the stored procedure; but this approach has the disadvantage that the length of array is limited by the maximum number of parameters to a stored procedure. Here is an alternative for passing variable length arrays as parameters that relies on a table to hold the array of arguments across multiple procedure calls.

```
proc opt_proc
        int @v1 = <null value>,
        int @v2 = <null value>,
        int @v3 = <null value>,
        int @v4 = <null value>,
        int @v5 = <null value>,
        boolean @first_batch,   /* true if this is the first batch */
        boolean @last_batch     /* true if this is the last batch */
as ...
if (@first_batch and @last_batch) begin
        execute proc
end
else if (@first_batch and not @last_batch) begin
```

```
                begin transaction
                create table to hold array elements
                append values to table
        end
        else if (not @first_batch and not @last_batch) begin
                append values to table
        end
        else if (not @first_batch and @last_batch) begin
                append values to table
                execute proc using values from table
                commit transaction
        end
```

When the array has more than five elements, SQL Server reports error 266 because the procedure has an unbalanced number of begin transaction and commit transaction commands. This is a warning message and can be ignored in your client program. If there are fewer than five elements in the array the client sends only one command to SQL Server, passing all the elements of the array in one go. Of course, you can pass up to 255 elements in each batch, in which case a single command suffices for even larger arrays. There is, of course, no limit on the overall length of the array to be passed.

7.5   THE COMMUNICATION SUBSYSTEM

In a large, complex computer network, a vast conglomeration of computers, network adapters, routers, gateways, and wires connect your clients and your servers. Networks are generally described through various layers of abstraction to make them easier to understand. Figure 7.4 takes a simple view and shows a general structure.

Client programs communicate with servers through the DB-Library or Client-Library Application Programmer Interface (API). DB-Library and Client-Library translate the calls to the API into data that can be sent over the network to servers. Sybase servers and clients communicate using the Tabular Data Stream (TDS) protocol. This Sybase-defined protocol describes how information is organized and interpreted on both the server and client sides of the network connection between a Sybase client and Sybase server. TDS runs on top of several network protocols, including TCP/IP, SPX/IPX, and DECnet. The network protocols communicate through other lower level protocols that define how information, in general, is carried through the network. Finally, at the lowest level is the network hardware, the network adapters, wires, routers, gateways, phone lines, and microwave antennae that physically represent the network.

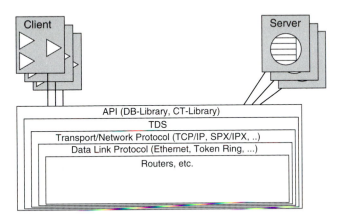

| Client | | Server |

| API (DB-Library, CT-Library) |
| TDS |
| Transport/Network Protocol (TCP/IP, SPX/IPX, ..) |
| Data Link Protocol (Ethernet, Token Ring, ...) |
| Routers, etc. |

Figure 7.4   Network protocol stack -

It takes time to make a connection between the client and SQL Server. Like any other kind of network (i.e., water pipes, highways), computer networks are bandwidth limited. Taken together, this means you as the application designer must consider trade-offs between connecting frequently or infrequently, between moving data to processors, or the processing to the data.

A client/server system generally consists of a small number of large server machines and an army of smaller client workstations.

Given the complexity of even a moderately sized computer network, it is impossible to include specific recommendations for improving the general flow of information through your network. To paraphrase: your throughput may vary depending on how you choose to configure each layer of your network. Optimizing the flow of information through your network can only help your client/server application.

Here we discuss the time it takes to log into SQL Server, special considerations for PC-based clients, and some testing ideas that can help you assess the performance of your communication subsystem.

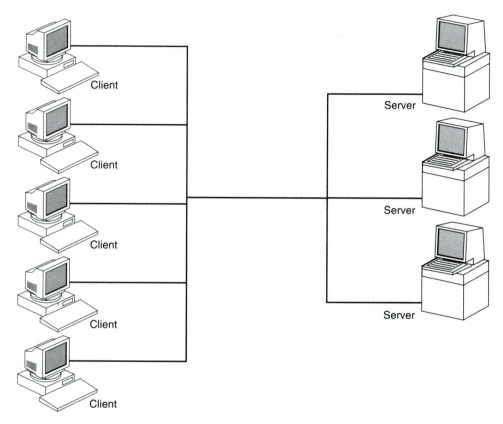

Figure 7.5   Servers and clients -

7.5.1   Cost of Connection

When the client needs to form a connection with SQL Server, the client looks up the interfaces file entry (or equivalent depending on the host operating system) for SQL Server and connects to the network address and port SQL Server is listening on (i.e., the hailing frequency). Once SQL Server acknowledges the connection, the client and SQL Server negotiate a switch to another network port, freeing the listening port for more connection attempts. Generally, the interfaces file stores the server machine's symbolic name rather than its actual network address number. In some large environments, translating the host name to a network address takes a long time.

If you suspect you are having this problem, check the performance of your network name server. If you are using yp-style services (e.g., Network Information Services), you can use the `ypmatch` command to see how long it takes to translate an address (e.g., `ypmatch <hostname> hosts`).

You can save the translation time by putting the network address into the interfaces file rather than the host name. For Unix systems with the socket-style interfaces file, you can use the dot notation for the host name (e.g., 192.214.1.34). There are some risks. If the network address of the host changes (e.g., it is moved to a different sub-network), you must update the interfaces file to reflect the new address. This problem is avoided if you use the symbolic name of the host instead.

Long delays in network name translation are a particular problem for SQL Server's forming connections to other SQL Servers to perform a server-to-server RPC. Because network name translation is a synchronous operation, we have seen cases where SQL Server timeslices because network name translation takes too long. The engine doing a name translation stops and any tasks running on that engine also stop running until the translation is complete. This is performance death on a single CPU SQL Server, as the whole SQL Server stops running while the networking software translates the name into a network address.

Sybase clients and servers read the interfaces file from top to bottom. You can save a little time by placing the frequently used entries at the top of the file. If you have an extremely large interfaces file, you might consider partitioning it and coding clients to look at only the interfaces file that holds the Sybase servers they will need. These optimizations are especially important if the client frequently logs into SQL Servers, or logs in many times to complete an operation.

Earlier versions of SQL Server can have trouble picking up many connections simultaneously. For example, everyone comes to work at 8 a.m. and tries to log into SQL Server at the same time. Clients see the connection failure as a time-out during connections. The time-out generally means SQL Server is too busy to acknowledge the connection in a reasonable amount of time. There is nothing you can configure in SQL Server to make it pick up connections faster. You can reduce the likelihood of time-outs by increasing the connection time-out parameter included in the interfaces file entry. Alternatively, you can somehow arrange to stagger client logins into SQL Server or code applications to retry connections that time out. More recent versions of SQL Server have better behavior in this regard.

Once connected, an idle connection to SQL Server imposes no load on SQL Server. If one user is running a query, the performance of SQL Server is no different if that is the only user logged in or if there are another hundred users logged in doing nothing. As a result of this characteristic, it is often better to have applications log in once and keep an open connection to SQL Server, rather than log in and out for each transaction. You must balance this with the memory consumed by each configured connection and whether memory might be better spent on buffer space.

7.5.2 Cost of Communication

In a homogeneous client/server environment, where client and server machines have the same basic architecture, both client and server encode information the same way. When a heterogeneous environment is deployed, for example Hewlett-Packard HP-UX servers and PCs running Microsoft Windows, some translation of information is needed between the client and server because the two platforms use different data encoding techniques. The characteristics of the machine that are relevant to Sybase client/server communication are the following:

- Byte order
- Floating point format
- Character set

Table 7.5 lists the byte order, floating point format, and default character set for a variety of platforms supported by Sybase SQL Server and Sybase clients.

Sybase clients and SQL Server communicate in the native format of the client. The burden of translating the format of the information is given to SQL Server. For example, if SQL Server is running on HP-UX and the clients are on PCs running Microsoft Windows, SQL Server must translate characters from Roman-8 to ISO-1 and reverse the byte order of all integer and floating point values.

These translations are relatively light weight and are simply the cost of accommodating a mix of client and server platforms. However, it is important to consider that such translations are also required when large volumes of information must be transmitted between heterogeneous clients and servers. If you are loading millions of rows of data, it is worth considering the cost of translating the data as it moves between client and server.

Table 7.5   Platform byte order, floating point format, and character set

Platform	Byte Order	Floating Point Format	Default Character Set
Digital Unix	little endian	IEEE	ISO-1
Hewlett-Packard HP-UX	big endian	IEEE	Roman 8
IBM AIX	big endian	IEEE	ISO-1 or Code Page 850
Sun Solaris 1.x and Solaris 2.x	big endian	IEEE	ISO-1
Digital VAX/VMS	little endian	VAX float	ISO-1
Digital Alpha VMS	little endian	IEEE	ISO-1
Windows/NT on Intel	little endian	reverse order IEEE	ISO-1
Microsoft Windows clients	little endian	reverse order IEEE	ISO-1

7.5.3   Special Considerations for PC Clients

PC clients running on DOS or Microsoft Windows can present some special challenges when connecting to a non-PC operating system server. Frequently there are problems with connections that do not disappear when the client machine crashes or is turned off. This may cause SQL Server unexpectedly to run out of connections or concurrency problems when a connection is stranded holding locks on tables.

Understanding the problem is part of the solution. Consider two machines, A and B, communicating with one another through a network. A is waiting for B to send data. How long should A wait? Is B dead? Is B just very slow in responding? Is the network so congested that B cannot get its messages onto the wire? Under TCP/IP, machines wait a certain amount of time before they decide the other machine is never going to respond. Once that decision is made, the connection is terminated and resources associated with the connection are freed. Suppose, in this example A is the machine running SQL Server and B is the client machine. SQL Server is waiting for the client to send data. How long does it wait? Is the client simply idle or has the client computer been turned off?

To solve this problem, TCP/IP periodically sends a message to the client. If the client machine responds in a timely manner, TCP/IP assumes the client is still alive and the connection is kept open. The application is not aware that this is happening. If the client does not respond, the connection is dropped. How long TCP/IP waits for a response is configurable. Most Unix systems use a fairly large value for this time-out (on the order of hours) so connections can hang around for a long time, even after the client machine is turned off. Shortening this time-out speeds the release of the connection but if the time-out value is too low, the server may drop connections to clients that are just taking a long time to respond. Long time-out values are historical. Networking has been a part of Unix for many years. Early wide-area networks were quite slow and long time-outs were essential to the smooth operation of the network.

This network time-out problem is compounded on PCs by Microsoft Windows hosted applications. The networking software is part of DOS, not Microsoft Windows. If the Microsoft Windows hosted application crashes and is restarted without closing the network connections, the machines on the other side of the connections have no way of knowing that the connections are now effectively dead. Suppose you are using a Microsoft Windows hosted application that opens connections to SQL Server. The application crashes and Microsoft Windows shuts down, leaving you at the DOS prompt. The application was never given an opportunity to close the connections. DOS is not aware that the connections are now useless and keeps them open. The SQL Server sees valid, but idle connections. You restart your Microsoft Windows hosted application without rebooting your system. The application makes fresh connections to SQL Server, not knowing that connections already exist (even it if knew the connections existed, there is no way for it to recycle the connections). Now you are using twice as many connections as before. SQL Server has no way to know that the new connections supercede the old connections. The only way to clean this up is to reboot the client or reboot SQL Server.

7.5.4 Performance of the Communication Subsystem

This section includes some simple tests that you can perform on your client/server system to measure the performance of your communication subsystem. The results of performance tests like these are more consistent if they are run on a quiet network with devoted client and server machines. Of course, you can also use tests like these to assess the impact of adding new applications to an existing network. Do not run the client and SQL Server on the same machine, as this generally bypasses some of the operating system networking software overhead.

The sample programs presented here are written using Open Client Client-Library and were tested against System 11 SQL Servers running on a variety of hardware. For the sake of clarity, very little error handling is included in the programs. Production quality programs should be more pedantic about checking the return codes from Client-Library calls.

Login Rate

You can test how quickly your client can log into your servers with a simple client program that logs into and out of a SQL Server without performing any queries. This measures how long it takes the client to read the interfaces file, open a connection to the appropriate network address, and negotiate the login with SQL Server. An extremely busy SQL Server might take its time acknowledging the login from the client. If forming many connections simultaneously is important, you can start many copies of this program running at the same time.

```
/*
** Example program for login rate test
*/
#include <stdio.h>
#include <ctpublic.h>

/* COUNT - number of times to login in
** USERNAME - username to use for logins
** PASSWORD - USERNAME's password
** DSQUERY - SQL Server to log into
*/
#define COUNT 100
#define USERNAME "sa"
#define PASSWORD ""
#define DSQUERY "SYBASE"
```

```
main()
{
        CS_CONNECTION *connection;
        CS_CONTEXT *context;
        CS_INT len;
        CS_RETCODE retcode;
        int i;

        printf("connecting %d times\n",COUNT);

        cs_ctx_alloc(CS_VERSION_100, &context);
        ct_init(context,CS_VERSION_100);
        ct_con_alloc(context,&connection);
        ct_con_props(connection, CS_SET, CS_USERNAME,
                USERNAME, CS_NULLTERM, NULL);
        ct_con_props(connection, CS_SET, CS_PASSWORD,
                PASSWORD, CS_NULLTERM, NULL);

        for (i = 0; i < COUNT; i++) {
                retcode = ct_connect(connection, DSQUERY,
                        CS_NULLTERM);
                if (retcode != CS_SUCCEED) {
                        perror("ct_connect failed");
                        exit(1);
                }

                ct_close(connection,CS_UNUSED);
        }

        ct_con_drop(connection);
        ct_exit(context, CS_UNUSED);
        cs_ctx_drop(context);

        exit(0);
}
```

Select 1

The select 1 benchmark tests command turnaround time in the client and SQL Server. select 1 is the simplest query you can execute against any SQL database engine. The result returned is one row with a single number. As no tables are accessed, there is no disk activity associated with the query. This test measures how long it takes the client to send a command to SQL Server, for SQL Server to turnaround the request, and the client to read the result. The `select 1` test is very network intensive because there is no disk I/O and very little processing involved. Because this is the simplest query you can perform against SQL Server, most of the time spent in this query is in communications overhead:

```c
/*
** Example program for select 1 test
*/
#include <stdio.h>
#include <ctpublic.h>

/* COUNT - number of times to do COMMAND
** USERNAME - username to user for logins
** PASSWORD - USERNAME's password
** DSQUERY - SQL Server to log into
** COMMAND - command to execute
*/
#define COUNT 1000
#define USERNAME "sa"
#define PASSWORD ""
#define DSQUERY "SYBASE"
#define COMMAND "select 1"

main ()
{
        CS_CONTEXT *context;
        CS_CONNECTION *connection;
        CS_COMMAND *command;
        CS_RETCODE retcode;
        CS_RETCODE fetchretcode;
        CS_INT result;
        int i;

        printf("\"%s\" %d times\n",COMMAND,COUNT);
        cs_ctx_alloc(CS_VERSION_100, &context);
        ct_init(context,CS_VERSION_100);
        ct_con_alloc(context,&connection);
        ct_con_props(connection, CS_SET, CS_USERNAME,
                USERNAME, CS_NULLTERM, NULL);
        ct_con_props(connection, CS_SET, CS_PASSWORD,
                PASSWORD, CS_NULLTERM, NULL);
        if (ct_connect(connection, DSQUERY, CS_NULLTERM) !=
```

```
            CS_SUCCEED) {
            perror("ct_connect failed");
            exit(1);
}
ct_cmd_alloc(connection, &command);

for (i = 0; i < COUNT; i++) {
        if (ct_command(command, CS_LANG_CMD, COMMAND,
                CS_NULLTERM, CS_UNUSED) !=
                CS_SUCCEED) {
                perror("ct_command failed");
                exit(1);
        }
        ct_send(command);
        while ((retcode =
                ct_results(command, &result)) ==
                CS_SUCCEED) {
                switch (result) {
                case CS_CMD_SUCCEED:
                case CS_CMD_FAIL:
                case CS_CMD_DONE:
                        break;

                case CS_ROW_RESULT:
                        while ((fetchretcode =
                                ct_fetch(command,
                                CS_UNUSED,CS_UNUSED,
                                CS_UNUSED, NULL)) ==
                                CS_SUCCEED ||
                                (fetchretcode ==
                                CS_ROW_FAIL))
                                ;
                        break;
                default:
                        perror("ct_results wrong");
                        exit(1);
                        break;
                }
        }
        if (retcode != CS_END_RESULTS) {
                perror("ct_results failed\n");
                exit(1);
        }
```

```
            }

            ct_cmd_drop(command);
            ct_close(connection,CS_UNUSED);
            ct_con_drop(connection);
            ct_exit(context, CS_UNUSED);
            cs_ctx_drop(context);

            exit(0);
    }
```

Select Large Amount of Data

Selecting from large tables tests the network's capacity to transmit data and the client's ability to accept and format the data. For this test to successfully measure the performance of the communications subsystem, other factors such as disk I/O limits in SQL Server must be eliminated. The easiest way to generate a lot of data quickly is to generate the cartesian product of two or more moderately sized tables. For example:

```
select * from tableA, tableB
```

where `tableA` and `tableB` each contain 1000 rows. The result of this query is the cartesian product of the two tables, that is, every row of `tableA` combined with every row of `tableB`. This is a result set with one million rows. SQL Server can easily cache all of `tableA` and `tableB` in memory, eliminating the need for disk I/O.

This test measures how long it takes to read lots of data from SQL Server. Whereas the `select 1` test measures turnaround time, the select large amount of data test measures the throughput of the client/server connection.

There are two programs here. The first creates and loads two tables with data. The second program selects the cartesian product of the two tables and counts the number of rows in the result.

```
/*
** Example program to load data for large select test
*/
#include <stdio.h>
#include <ctpublic.h>

/* COUNT - number of rows for each table
** USERNAME - username to user for logins
```

```
** PASSWORD - USERNAME's password
** DSQUERY - SQL Server to log into
** TABLEA - name of the first table
** TABLEB - name of the second table
*/
#define COUNT 100
#define USERNAME "sa"
#define PASSWORD ""
#define DSQUERY "SYBASE"
#define TABLEA "a"
#define TABLEB "b"

void sql_exec(CS_COMMAND *command, char *query)
{
        CS_RETCODE retcode;
        CS_RETCODE fetchretcode;
        CS_INT result;

        if (ct_command(command, CS_LANG_CMD, query,
                CS_NULLTERM, CS_UNUSED) != CS_SUCCEED) {
                perror("ct_command failed");
                exit(1);
        }
        ct_send(command);
        while ((retcode = ct_results(command, &result)) ==
                CS_SUCCEED) {
                switch (result) {
                case CS_CMD_SUCCEED:
                case CS_CMD_FAIL:
                case CS_CMD_DONE:
                        break;

                case CS_ROW_RESULT:
                        while ((fetchretcode =
                                ct_fetch(command, CS_UNUSED,
                                        CS_UNUSED, CS_UNUSED,
                                        NULL)) ==
                                CS_SUCCEED ||
                            (fetchretcode == CS_ROW_FAIL))
                                ;
                        break;
                default:
                        perror("ct_results:resultunexpected");
```

```
                        exit(1);
                        break;
                }
        }
        if (retcode != CS_END_RESULTS) {
                perror("ct_results failed\n");
                exit(1);
        }
}

main ()
{
        CS_CONTEXT *context;
        CS_CONNECTION *connection;
        CS_COMMAND *command;
        char cbuf[255];
        int i;

        printf("populating tables \"%s\" and \"%s\" with %d rows\n",
                TABLEA, TABLEB, COUNT);

        cs_ctx_alloc(CS_VERSION_100, &context);
        ct_init(context,CS_VERSION_100);
        ct_con_alloc(context,&connection);
        ct_con_props(connection, CS_SET, CS_USERNAME,
                USERNAME, CS_NULLTERM, NULL);
        ct_con_props(connection, CS_SET, CS_PASSWORD,
                PASSWORD, CS_NULLTERM, NULL);
        if (ct_connect(connection, DSQUERY, CS_NULLTERM) !=
                CS_SUCCEED) {
                perror("ct_connect failed");
        }
        ct_cmd_alloc(connection, &command);

        /* create tables */
        sprintf(cbuf, "create table %s (a int, ac char(128))",
                TABLEA);
        sql_exec(command, cbuf);
        sprintf(cbuf, "create table %s (b int, bc char(128))",
                TABLEB);
        sql_exec(command, cbuf);

        /* populate tables */
```

```
            for (i = 0; i < COUNT; i++) {
                    sprintf(cbuf, "insert %s values(%d,'x')",
                            TABLEA, i);
                    sql_exec(command, cbuf);
            }
            sprintf(cbuf, "insert %s (b, bc) select a, ac from %s",
                    TABLEB, TABLEA);
            sql_exec(command, cbuf);

            ct_cmd_drop(command);
            ct_close(connection,CS_UNUSED);
            ct_con_drop(connection);
            ct_exit(context, CS_UNUSED);
            cs_ctx_drop(context);

            exit(0);
}


/*
** Example program to perform large select test
*/
#include <stdio.h>
#include <ctpublic.h>

/* COUNT - number of rows for each table
** USERNAME - username to user for logins
** PASSWORD - USERNAME's password
** DSQUERY - SQL Server to log into
** TABLEA - name of the first table
** TABLEB - name of the second table
*/
#define USERNAME "sa"
#define PASSWORD ""
#define DSQUERY "SYBASE"
#define TABLEA "a"
#define TABLEB "b"

main ()
{
            CS_CONTEXT *context;
            CS_CONNECTION *connection;
            CS_COMMAND *command;
            CS_RETCODE retcode;
```

```
CS_RETCODE fetchretcode;
CS_INT result;
char cbuf[255];
int rowcount = 0;

cs_ctx_alloc(CS_VERSION_100, &context);
ct_init(context,CS_VERSION_100);
ct_con_alloc(context,&connection);
ct_con_props(connection, CS_SET, CS_USERNAME,
        USERNAME, CS_NULLTERM, NULL);
ct_con_props(connection, CS_SET, CS_PASSWORD,
        PASSWORD, CS_NULLTERM, NULL);
if (ct_connect(connection, DSQUERY, CS_NULLTERM) !=
        CS_SUCCEED) {
        perror("ct_connect failed");
        exit(1);
}
ct_cmd_alloc(connection, &command);

sprintf(cbuf,"select a.ac, b.bc from %s a, %s b",
        TABLEA, TABLEB);
if (ct_command(command, CS_LANG_CMD, cbuf,
        CS_NULLTERM, CS_UNUSED) !=
        CS_SUCCEED) {
        perror("ct_command failed");
        exit(1);
}
ct_send(command);
while ((retcode = ct_results(command, &result)) ==
        CS_SUCCEED) {
        switch (result) {
        case CS_CMD_SUCCEED:
        case CS_CMD_FAIL:
        case CS_CMD_DONE:
                break;

        case CS_ROW_RESULT:
                while ((fetchretcode =
                        ct_fetch(command, CS_UNUSED,
                                CS_UNUSED,CS_UNUSED,
                                NULL)) ==
                                CS_SUCCEED ||
                        (fetchretcode == CS_ROW_FAIL))
```

```
                                rowcount++;
                        break;
                default:
                        perror("ct_results:resultunexpected");
                        exit(1);
                        break;
                }
        }
        if (retcode != CS_END_RESULTS) {
                perror("ct_results failed\n");
                exit(1);
        }
        printf("read %d rows\n",rowcount);

        ct_cmd_drop(command);
        ct_close(connection,CS_UNUSED);
        ct_con_drop(connection);
        ct_exit(context, CS_UNUSED);
        cs_ctx_drop(context);
        exit(0);
}
```

Chapter 8

Monitoring SQL Server

It is difficult to predict accurately the performance characteristics of a system as complex as SQL Server. Adding to this the complexity of your own application and computing environment, predicting the performance becomes nearly impossible. When you approach a complex performance problem, various tools and techniques can help you work through the difficulties: modelling, analysis, simulation, and monitoring. These are all useful when it comes to understanding how a complex system works. These tools and techniques complement each other. In this chapter we focus only on monitoring.

Analytic prediction of SQL Server applications is problematic. We need tools to monitor the performance of SQL Server to determine the performance characteristics empirically. Monitoring tools help to identify bottlenecks when performance becomes a problem. During the design of the application, monitoring an experimental system helps in measuring and estimating the impact of changes in workload, hardware, and software configurations.

SQL Server and operating system monitoring tools let you peer inside SQL Server and see how much time is consumed by various components of the system. We have divided monitoring tools into three categories:

- Information you can gather by interactively querying SQL Server with `isql` or some other client program
- Operating system tools
- Monitor Server and SQL Monitor

8.1 ANALYSIS AND MONITORING

SQL Server monitoring tools help you understand how the system behaves under various conditions. With enough experience you can predict how SQL Server is going to behave when the workload changes. With enough data from the monitors, you can build a model describing how SQL Server operates. When the performance of the system is unexpectedly poor, you can measure SQL Server against your expectations to find out why SQL Server is not performing as you anticipated.

The performance of SQL Server depends on a multiple of variables including:

- Performance of disk drives
- Number of disk drives devoted to database devices
- Amount of memory configured for SQL Server
- Presence and usefulness of your indexes
- Complexity and phrasing of your queries
- Volume and distribution of your data
- Number of CPUs
- Performance of the network
- Number of users
- Performance of the part of your application that does not reside on SQL Server (i.e., client programs, gateways)

Often, one of these factors has a disproportionately significant influence on the performance of your application. For example, the performance of your application may be limited by the throughput of a single disk or the lack of an index. We refer to such factors as performance bottlenecks. Monitoring SQL Server simplifies the task of discovering and eliminating bottlenecks. Doing so requires analysis of the monitoring data you have collected and perhaps some experimentation.

Eliminating bottlenecks allows your application to run faster. In general, eliminating one bottleneck simply reveals another. The new bottleneck may be easy to eliminate, or it may be extremely difficult. The cost of eradicating the bottleneck must be weighed against the cost of accommodating the performance limitations of your application.

8.1.1   Analysis

In some situations the bottleneck is easy to identify. Client bottlenecks are often a problem in benchmark situations. For example, you might have one or two workstations acting as clients for a large server machine. Performance of SQL Server is not as high as expected. The situation is made clear by monitoring the CPU utilization of the clients and SQL Server. If the clients are running at 100% and SQL

Server is running at less than 100%, the performance of the system is limited by the clients. The benchmark is measuring the performance of the clients rather than SQL Server.[1]

More complex problems require more difficult analysis and experimentation. Suppose you have a system where there are three types of actions processed by three different components of the system. Action A uses component d1, action B uses component d2, and action C uses component d3. d1 needs 10 ms to complete a action, d2 needs 15 ms, and d3 needs 40 ms. The mix of actions is fixed: 50% are action A, 40% B, and 10% C. Which action is the bottleneck in the system? Is it action A, because actions of type A out number both B and C? Is it C because it is using the slowest disk? Is it B because its performance is between A and C?

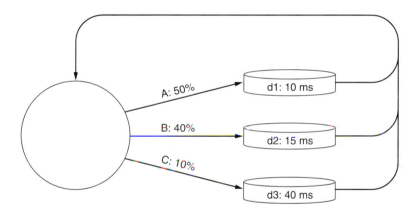

Figure 8.1   Analysis example -

Here is an intuitive, albeit somewhat less than accurate analysis of the given scenario that will help us identify the bottleneck. Consider the expected time to process 100 actions. From the given mix of actions, we expect the number of A actions is 50, hence the expected time to process the action at d1 is 500 ms. Similarly, we decide that the expected times at d2 and d3 for B and C actions is 600 ms

---

[1]   In this situation you can get by without actually measuring CPU utilization of SQL Server and the clients. Here you can use indirect evidence. You can add more client machines to see if the performance of SQL Server improves. If you measure an improvement, this suggests that the client machines are the bottleneck in the benchmark.

and 400 ms respectively. As B actions take the longest to process, the overall performance is determined by the time to process B actions at d2. The performance of d2 is the current bottleneck.

The example shows that the result is not always obvious. Improving the performance of d3 does nothing to improve the overall performance of the system even though d3 is the slowest component. Improving the performance of d1 does not improve the overall performance of the system even though most of the actions use d1. Reducing d2's time from 15 ms improves the performance of the system to a point. When d2's performance reaches 12.5 ms the overall performance improvements stop. The system is then limited by the performance of d1. If d1 is reduced to 8 ms and d2 to 10 ms, the limiting factor becomes d3.

None of these conclusions were obvious from the description of the problem. Spending the time to analyze the problem before or at design time may save a lot of work. We now know that the system's performance is limited by d2. Our optimization efforts can focus on reducing the time it takes d2 to process transaction B.[2] Furthermore, we know that there is an upper limit to our optimization work. Reducing d2's processing time below 12.5 ms is pointless, unless we can afford to improve the performance of d1 as well.

This example benefits from oversimplification. In the real world, there is rarely a one-to-one relationship between the workload and the system components. In the example, the processing times and workload mix are constant. The real world has far more variability. Analysis at the component level is rarely possible. However, it is often valuable to analyze a simplified model of the system that captures only a few essential aspects of the system.

8.1.2   Solving a Performance Problem

Described below are the basic steps to solving a performance problem:

- **Define the problem** — Get a comprehensive list of all of the symptoms, but be prepared for red herrings. The symptoms tell you what is wrong, but not why it is wrong. If you have a performance specification, verify that the system still operates within the bounds of the performance specification. If so, there is not a problem, at least as defined by the specification. Perhaps the requirements have changed and the specification needs to be updated to reflect a more aggressive

---

[2.]   An alternative approach is to reduce the proportion of transaction B in the transaction mix.

performance criteria. Is this a new problem? Is it possible the problem has existed since the system was installed but was only just now discovered? If the problem is new, what has changed in the system since the problem appeared? New uses of the system? New users? Changes to the schema? More data? Software or hardware upgrades? Can the symptom be mapped clearly into queries against the database? It is possible that some modification to the system has changed the critical path for this operation?

- **Formulate a hypothesis about the cause of the problem** — Try to figure out why the system is not working as expected. At this stage it is important to avoid analysis paralysis. If you need more information, devise an experiment to get the information you need.

- **Experiment to determine the root cause** — From the symptoms alone, you might not know enough about the problem to state definitively the source of the problem. Conduct experiments that confirm or contradict the hypothesis.

- **Confirm the hypothesis** — Once you have a working hypothesis of the problem, test it against the symptoms. Are all of the symptoms explained by the proposed cause of the problem? Keep in mind there might be more than one problem. Some unseen problems might hide behind symptoms you have observed.

- **Determine a solution to the problem** — Now that you understand the cause of the problem, you can work toward a solution. What are the constraints on the solution? Can you afford to completely rebuild your database, buy more memory, restrict the number of users, restrict the times certain queries are run? As you look for a solution, keep in mind that sometimes the phrase *hit it with a bigger hammer* describes the best or only solution.

- **Implement the solution and verify** — Implement your solution and loop back to the beginning to close the loop. Was your solution effective? Did it resolve the original problem? Are there new problems to be solved?

Diagnosing a performance problem sometimes requires some experimentation. Experimenting on a production system is dangerous as it can impact the performance of other applications or in extreme cases bring down the system. Spending the time to recreate the problem in a non-production system is often rewarding. We have seen situations where hours are spent trying to understand the behavior of the problem on the production system, generally without success. Within minutes of recreating the problem on a system that permitted experimentation, the exact nature of the problem became obvious and we moved from identifying the problem to working on the solution. Reproducing the problem in a simpler, easy to understand environment is helpful.

It is tempting to investigate performance only when performance is not as good as expected. It can also be valuable to investigate situations where performance is much better than expected. Perhaps there is some aspect of SQL Server's performance characteristics you have misunderstood. See what you can learn and apply to other parts of the application.

8.2 QUERYING ABOUT PERFORMANCE

Sybase includes a variety of system stored procedures you can use to monitor the performance of SQL Server. You can run these stored procedures anytime you are logged into SQL Server.

The system stored procedure `sp_monitor` and `sp_sysmon` give you a quick snap shot about the operation of SQL Server. `sp_monitor` reports how busy the CPU is, the total amount of network and disk activity, and the number of connections that have been made. `sp_sysmon` monitors activity on SQL Server for a period of time and generates a comprehensive report. `sp_who` reports who is logged into SQL Server. There is one row for every currently open connection. The `sp_who` report also includes some information about the command the connection is running and whether the connection is blocked by a lock held by another connection. `sp_lock` lists the locks given to connections. `sp_lock` combined with `sp_who` are useful tools for identifying connections, and hence users and applications, that may be blocking other users or applications.

8.2.1 Using sp_monitor

The `sp_monitor` system stored procedure reports a variety of information about the operation of SQL Server. Table 8.1 lists the values given in the report.

The `sp_monitor` system stored procedure relies on a variety of global variables and the `master..spt_monitor` table to generate the report. Each time `sp_monitor` is run, it records the current values of these variables in the `master..spt_monitor` table. When `sp_monitor` is run again, it uses the values stored in the table to calculate the changes in the values since the last time the report was run. Then it stores the new values in the table.

The report in the example output was run on May 16, 1995 at 10:38pm. Before that, the last time `sp_monitor` was run was 3:39pm. 25,153 seconds elapsed between the two runs. During that time, the SQL Server was not very busy. Many of the values appear as $N(M)$. In this display, N is the value of the measure since SQL Server was last started. M is the value of the measure since the last time `sp_monitor` was run, in this case, since 3:39pm. For example, there were 143 connections made to SQL Server since SQL Server was started, and 140 connections since 3:39pm.

Table 8.1   Values reported by the sp_monitor system stored procedure

Value	Equivalent Global Variable	Description
cpu_busy	@@cpu_busy	Amount of time CPU reported as busy averaged over all engines.
io_busy	@@io_busy	Amount of time CPU reported as doing I/O averaged over all engines.
idle	@@idle	Amount of time CPU reported as idled averaged over all engines.
packets_received	@@pack_received	Number of network packets read by SQL Server.
packets_sent	@@pack_sent	Number of network packets sent by SQL Server.
packet_errors	@@pack_errors	Number of network errors encountered by SQL Server.
total_read	@@total_read	Number of disk reads made by SQL Server.
total_write	@@total_write	Number of disk writes made by SQL Server.
total_errors	@@total_errors	Number of disk errors encountered by SQL Server.
connections	@@connections	Number of connection attempts made to SQL Server.

```
1> sp_monitor
2> go
 last_run                       current_run                 seconds
 ------------------------       ------------------------    -----------
         May 16 1995  3:39PM           May 16 1995 10:38PM        25153

 cpu_busy                       io_busy                     idle
 ------------------------       ------------------------    ------------------------
 250(240)-0%                    0(0)-0%                      24862(24857)-98%

 packets_received               packets_sent                packet_errors
 ------------------------       ------------------------    ------------------------
 7347(7077)                     5162(4933)                  9(9)

 total_read         total_write         total_errors        connections
 ------------------ ------------------  ------------------  ------------------
 2702(2490)         48625(47867)        0(0)                143(140)

(return status = 0)
1>
```

Figure 8.2   sp_monitor output -

If you intend to rely on this report, you should consider running it periodically. If the counts get too large, you may encounter arithmetic overflow while some of the values are calculated.

This report gives you a quick look at how hard your SQL Server is working. More useful than the totals since SQL Server was started are the measures since the last time the report was run. If you run the report on a regular basis, you can create a chart showing how busy your SQL Server is at various times of day. It might also be useful to run this report when SQL Server appears to be very slow to see if there is significant network or disk activity.

8.2.2   sp_sysmon

System 11 SQL Server adds a system stored procedure sp_sysmon to monitor system activity. Details of this stored procedure were not available at the writing of this book. We expect this stored procedure to be extremely valuable in monitoring the performance of SQL Server.

8.2.3   Using sp_who

The sp_who system stored procedure lists all of the connections open against SQL Server. The report includes the following columns:

- **spid** — Server process identification number. This is the number used to identify the task inside SQL Server that represents the connection to SQL Server. Process in this context means task.

- **status** — State of the task.

- **loginname** — Name of the login associated with the task.

- **hostname** — Name of the host running the client application as reported by the client. Some client applications may not set the hostname properly or at all.

- **blk** — Task that is blocking this task. In general the value here is 0. If the status is `lock sleep`, this column tells you the `spid` of the task blocking this task. `sp_lock` lists all of the locks that have been acquired. If the status is `lock sleep` and `blk` is 0, the task is sleeping on a semaphore. Semaphores are used to control access to the transaction log and index pages.

- **dbname** — Name of the database the task is currently using.

- **cmd** — Command the task is currently running.

The task status is one of:

- **recv sleep** — Waiting to read data from the network.

- **send sleep** — Waiting to write data to the network.

- **alarm sleep** — Waiting for an alarm (e.g., the waitfor command).

- **lock sleep** — Waiting to acquire a lock.

- **sleeping** — Waiting for input from the client or for disk activity.

- **running** — Running a command. There is only one running task for each engine in SQL Server.

Figure 8.3 shows the output for `sp_who`.

`sp_who` lists all of the tasks running on SQL Server. Most tasks are associated with connections from client programs. For example, there are 12 regular users logged into this SQL Server and 2 users logged in as sa. Some tasks in SQL Server are not associated with a network connection. These tasks perform utility functions within SQL Server, much like operating system daemons like `inetd` in Unix perform utility operating system functions. The NETWORK HANDLER is the network listener. There is one NETWORK HANDLER for each `master` line in the interfaces file entry for SQL Server. The MIRROR HANDLER takes care of disk mirroring. This task appears whether or not you are have mirrored any disks. The

CHECKPOINT SLEEP task is the task that takes care of checkpointing your data-bases. Not shown here is a SITE HANDLER that appears when SQL Server is con-nected to another server to perform a server to server RPC.

```
1> sp_who
2> go
spid   status        loginame     hostname    blk   dbname      cmd
------ ------------- ------------ ----------- ----- ----------  ----------------
     1 recv sleep    sa           srvr1        0    example     AWAITING COMMAND
     2 sleeping      NULL                       0    master      NETWORK HANDLER
     3 sleeping      NULL                       0    master      MIRROR HANDLER
     4 sleeping      NULL                       0    master      CHECKPOINT SLEEP
     5 recv sleep    rob          srvr1        0    example     AWAITING COMMAND
     8 recv sleep    lisa         srvr1        0    example     AWAITING COMMAND
     9 recv sleep    toni         srvr1        0    example     AWAITING COMMAND
    10 lock sleep    katrina      srvr1        5    example     UPDATE
    11 recv sleep    rick         srvr1        0    example     AWAITING COMMAND
    12 lock sleep    maria        srvr1       11    example     UPDATE
    13 recv sleep    mark         srvr1        0    example     AWAITING COMMAND
    14 lock sleep    paul         srvr1       13    example     SELECT
    15 recv sleep    ben          srvr1        0    example     AWAITING COMMAND
    16 recv sleep    judy         srvr1        0    example     AWAITING COMMAND
    17 running       sa           srvr1        0    master      SELECT
    18 recv sleep    david        srvr1        0    example     AWAITING COMMAND
    19 recv sleep    steve        srvr1        0    example     AWAITING COMMAND

(17 rows affected, return status = 0)
1>
```

Figure 8.3   sp_who example output- -

In the sp_who output shown in Figure 8.3, the tasks with the cmd NETWORK HAN-DLER, MIRROR HANDLER, and CHECKPOINT SLEEP are all sleeping. They are not using CPU time and are waiting until they can be useful. The sa user on spid 17 is running. This was the user who ran the sp_who command. Most of the other tasks have the status recv sleep. They are waiting for input from the client. The tasks with the spids 10, 12, and 14 have the status lock sleep. These tasks are trying to acquire locks, but are blocked by other tasks. 10 (katrina) is blocked by 5 (rob), 12 (maria) is blocked by 11 (rick), and 14 (paul) is blocked by 13 (mark). Notice that the users katrina and maria are trying to UPDATE a table. rob is blocking katrina, but is AWAITING COMMAND. This suggests that rob has a transaction open that is modifying or holding a shared lock on the same page of the table that katrina wants to modify. We can say the same for maria and rick. paul is trying to SELECT from a table. paul's blocker is mark, who is AWAITING COMMAND. paul is probably trying to read a page that mark is modifying inside a transaction.

New to System 11 SQL Server are a variety of utility tasks. DEADLOCK TUNE assists user tasks in detecting deadlocks. HOUSEKEEPER writes out dirty buffers to help minimize checkpoint time. Other utility tasks may be added in future versions of SQL Server.

8.2.4 Using sp_lock

The sp_lock system stored procedure generates a report listing all of the locks currently granted and pending inside SQL Server. The report includes:

spid — SQL Server process identification number. This number matches the spid reported in sp_who and indicates the owner of the lock.

locktype — The kind of lock that is owned by the task.

table_id — Object identification number of the table containing the page that is locked, for page locks, or the table that is locked.

page — The number identifying the page that is locked.

dbname — The name of the database containing the page or table that is locked.

class — Indicates if the lock is for a cursor. If the lock is for a cursor, class indicates the name of the cursor for locks owned by the spid running sp_lock, and an identification number for locks owned by a different spid.

Here are possible values for locktype (see Chapter 5, *SQL Server — Methods and Features*, for a complete description of SQL Server locking):

- **Ex_intent** — Exclusive intent lock; the task holds an exclusive intent lock on a table if it also holds an exclusive lock on a page in the table.

- **Ex_page** — Exclusive page lock; the task is changing a page in the table.

- **Ex_table** — Exclusive table lock; the task is changing a large number of pages in the table, so it has acquired a table lock rather than locks on each page.

- **Update_page** — Update lock; the task is upgrading a shared lock to an exclusive lock. Acquiring an update_page lock is the first step in upgrading a shared lock to an exclusive lock.

- **Sh_intent** — Shared intent lock; the task holds a shared lock on a table if it also holds a shared lock on a page in the table.

- **Sh_page** — Shared page lock; the task is reading data from a page and does not want the contents of the page to change.

- **Sh_table** — Shared table lock; the task does not want any page in the table to change. This probably means the task is selecting from the table with holdlock or isolation level 3 is being used.

Figure 8.4 shows the `sp_lock` output taken at the same time as the example `sp_who` output in Figure 8.3. The `sp_who` output indicates that spids 5, 11, and 13 are blocking 10, 12, and 14 respectively. Let us examine the `sp_lock` output for these spids carefully. To keep the example reasonably uncomplicated, all of the locks for these tasks are against the same table with the object ID number (e.g., table_id) 16003088.

The task with spid 5 holds a shared intent lock, a shared page lock on 722 and a shared page lock on 384 that is blocking another lock. Spid 10 is blocked by 5. It is trying to acquire update_page locks on pages 722 and 384. From the `sp_who` output, we know that spid 10 is trying to perform an update, but it is not clear what spid 5 is doing. From the `sp_lock` output, we can see spid 5 is reading the pages of the table and holding onto the shared locks on those pages. A similar situation exists between spids 11 and 12.

Spid 13 holds a variety of exclusive page locks. It is modifying the table. Spid 14 wants to read some part of the table, but it cannot acquire shared locks on the pages until 13 releases its exclusive locks. As a result, spid 14 is blocked.

Not shown in the example is a lock with the demand attribute, generally called a **demand lock**. Demand locks are indicated when the lock type includes the suffix -demand. A demand lock means that other tasks cannot acquire locks ahead of this task. This generally happens when a task wants to acquire an exclusive lock and other tasks already have shared locks on the page or table. See Chapter 5, *SQL Server — Methods and Features* for more information about how SQL Server manages locking. The following example is a fragment of output from `sp_lock` that shows an exclusive table demand lock that has not yet been granted. Note that this lock is itself preventing other locks from being acquired.

Locks blocked behind a demand lock are sometimes shown as being blocked by the lock blocking the demand lock. This is potentially confusing because it appears as though a shared lock is blocking other shared locks.

```
1> sp_lock
2> go
The class column will display the cursor name for locks associated with a cursor
for the current user and the cursor id for other users.
 spid    locktype              table_id     page         dbname
         class
------  ---------------------  -----------  -----------  ---------------  ----------------
     5  Sh_intent              16003088               0 example          Non Cursor Lock
     5  Sh_page                16003088             722 example          Non Cursor Lock
     5  Sh_page-blk            16003088             384 example          Non Cursor Lock
     6  Sh_intent              16003088               0 example          Non Cursor Lock
     7  Sh_intent              16003088               0 example          Non Cursor Lock
     8  Sh_intent              16003088               0 example          Non Cursor Lock
     8  Sh_page                16003088             722 example          Non Cursor Lock
     8  Sh_page-blk            16003088             384 example          Non Cursor Lock
     9  Sh_intent              16003088               0 example          Non Cursor Lock
     9  Sh_page                16003088             722 example          Non Cursor Lock
     9  Sh_page-blk            16003088             384 example          Non Cursor Lock
    10  Ex_intent              16003088               0 example          Non Cursor Lock
    10  Update_page            16003088             384 example          Non Cursor Lock
    10  Update_page            16003088             722 example          Non Cursor Lock
    11  Sh_intent              16003088               0 example          Non Cursor Lock
    11  Sh_page                16003088             720 example          Non Cursor Lock
    11  Sh_page-blk            16003088             145 example          Non Cursor Lock
    12  Ex_intent              16003088               0 example          Non Cursor Lock
    12  Sh_intent              16003088               0 example          Non Cursor Lock
    12  Sh_page                16003088             145 example          Non Cursor Lock
    12  Sh_page                16003088             720 example          Non Cursor Lock
    12  Update_page            16003088             145 example          Non Cursor Lock
    12  Update_page            16003088             720 example          Non Cursor Lock
    13  Ex_intent              16003088               0 example          Non Cursor Lock
    13  Ex_page                16003088             429 example          Non Cursor Lock
    13  Ex_page                16003088             682 example          Non Cursor Lock
    13  Ex_page                16003088             688 example          Non Cursor Lock
    13  Ex_page                16003088             723 example          Non Cursor Lock
    13  Ex_page                16003088             725 example          Non Cursor Lock
    13  Ex_page                16003088             726 example          Non Cursor Lock
    13  Ex_page-blk            16003088             689 example          Non Cursor Lock
    14  Sh_intent              16003088               0 example          Non Cursor Lock
    17  Sh_intent             384004399               0 master           Non Cursor Lock

(33 rows affected, return status = 0)
1>
```

Figure 8.4   sp_lock output -

```
 spid    locktype              table_id     page         dbname           class
------  ---------------------  -----------  -----------  ---------------  ----------------
     8  Ex_table-demand-blk    16003088               0 example          Non Cursor Lock
```

Figure 8.5   sp_lock demand lock example -

8.2.5   Useful Global Variables

SQL Server has a number of global variables that contain useful performance information. Some are used and stored by `sp_monitor`. The command `sp_helptext sp_monitor` shows you how they are used in that stored procedure. You can build your own stored procedures or scripts to read and store these values. For example, you can write a simple cron job that logs into SQL Server periodically and retrieves these values. Over time, you can create a strip graph to see how these values change. This is useful for figuring out usage patterns.

The values in many of the global variables are stored in clockticks. You can convert clockticks into wall time using:

```
select @engcount = count(*) from master..sysengines
select @@cpu_busy * @@timeticks / 1000000 / @engcount
```

The results is the amount of CPU busy time in seconds. You may need to experiment with the order of the calculation to avoid arithmetic overflow errors or excessive round off. If you are using System 10 or later, you can convert the values to the numeric datatype.

- **@@cpu_busy** — Number of time ticks engine was busy since start-up. An engine is considered busy if it is working on a user task. If it is not working on a user task, the engine is considered idle. This value is incremented by every engine. You must divide this value by the number of engines (`select count(*) from sysengines`) in order to normalize it to the average CPU busy time per engine.

- **@@idle** — Number of time ticks engine was idle since start-up. An engine is idle if there is no runnable user task. Some I/O processing is counted as idle time. An engine that is idle from the point of view of SQL Server is still consuming CPU time and will appear to be busy on operating system statistics. Engines that are idle for a long time eventually sleep, becoming idle from the operating system's point of view. You must divide this value by the number of engines to normalize to the average CPU idle time per engine.

- **@@connections** — Total number of login attempts, successful and failed, since start-up.

- **@@io_busy** — Number of time ticks engines spent doing I/O since start-up. This value is incremented by every engine. You must divide this value by the number of engines to normalize to the average CPU time spent doing I/O per engine.

- **@@max_connections** — Maximum number of simultaneous connections permitted into SQL Server. This is essentially the same as the `user connections` configuration value.

- **@@pack_received** — Number of network packets read by SQL Server since start-up.

- **@@pack_sent** — Number of network packets written by SQL Server since start-up.

- **@@pack_errors** — Number of network errors encountered by SQL Server since start-up.

- **@@timeticks** — Number of microseconds per time tick. Use this value to normalize **@@cpu_busy**, **@@idle**, and **@@io_busy** into seconds.

- **@@total_errors** —Number of database device errors encountered by SQL Server since start-up.

- **@@total_read** — Number of database device reads since start-up.

- **@@total_write** — Number of database device writes since start-up.

8.3 OPERATING SYSTEM TOOLS

Operating systems generally provide some tools to monitor the performance of the system as a whole. These give you a way to monitor performance from the system's point of view rather than SQL Server's. For example, this might be valuable if you are using operating system disk striping or mirroring. SQL Server is unaware that the operating system is manipulating the way it interacts with disk drives, so it cannot provide you with the same level of monitoring information as the operating system.

On Unix, various programs such as `ps`, `sar`, `vmstat`, `iostat`, and `netstat` are used to monitor system activity. The availability and exact format, options, and capabilities of these programs depends on the variety of Unix running on your system. Windows/NT includes a performance monitor tool that displays colorful bar graphs and strip charts. NetWare includes a variety of performance monitoring screens you can access to check up on your system.

The optimization of computer systems as a whole is a broad topic. Included here is some basic information about the tools available on Unix, with a particular attention on how the tools tell you information about SQL Server.

8.3.1   CPU Utilization

In general, the operating system performance monitoring tools report reliable statistics about SQL Server with the exception of CPU utilization. SQL Server consumes CPU even while it is idle (see Chapter 4, *SQL Server — Form and Structure*). In other words, even though SQL Server has no work to do, it still consumes CPU time from the point of view of the operating system. SQL Server polls for new activity while it is idle to shorten the response time to new queries and logins. This is often referred to as **spinning**. If SQL Server is spinning it takes much less time to respond to new activity than if it is sleeping.

Most operating systems can report the amount of system time, user time, and idle time of the CPU.

System time is time the CPU spends running code inside the operating system kernel. This means reading and writing to devices such as the network and disk drives, managing the processes on the system, and attending to a variety of other housekeeping needs of the computer. Many of these tasks are done by the request of user programs.

User time is the time the CPU spends running programs for users. SQL Server, Backup Server, and client programs fall into this category. User programs spend time by performing calculations or searching through memory for data. When a user program asks for data from a disk drive, the CPU time it takes to read and write the file is system time.

Idle time is time the CPU spends doing nothing. A busy system has 0% idle time. A system that is very busy with disk activity might have 70% system time and 30% user time.

The CPU can process information much more quickly than disk drives and networks can make it available. As a result, the CPU must often wait for information to become available from these devices. Time the CPU spends waiting for data is considered idle time. If a computer system is constrained by disk and network speed, the CPU may report a certain amount of idle time, even while the system appears to be very busy. This is an indication that you should spread the disk activity (typically) or network activity (less common) across more devices. During I/O intensive benchmarks on a computer with a very fast CPU, it is difficult to achieve 100% CPU utilization. Generally such applications are bound by the speed of the disk drives.

For Unix, the useful commands are ps, uptime, and certain fields from vmstat and iostat. The ps command lists all of the processes running on your system. SQL Server has one process for each engine. If you configure your SQL Server with three engines, there are three SQL Server processes running on your system. Backup Server requires several processes, the backup server program itself and one helper process for each local device you are dumping to. Monitor server is a single process.

The ps command takes a number of command line flags to change the information it displays about the processes. The available flags and their semantics vary depending on which version of Unix you are using. For example, ps from a Berkeley-derived version of Unix takes the flags aux. When ps aux is used, the output is organized by CPU utilization. Processes consuming the most CPU time are listed first. %CPU is the amount of percentage of the CPU's time this process is currently consuming. %MEM is the percentage of physical memory the process is currently consuming. SZ is the number of pages of non-shared virtual memory consumed by the process. This is the total amount of non-shared memory the process has ever addressed. Non-shared memory is memory given to the process's data and stack. The text (i.e., executable binary portion) is shared. SQL Server uses shared memory for most of its data and this also does not appear in SZ. RSS is the resident set size, or the number of physical memory pages allocated to the process. The Unix kernel decides on the RSS for the process. In general, it tries to set the RSS large enough to avoid paging and swapping for the process. STAT is the process's status. In general, SQL Server appears as R (runnable), P (waiting for a page-in), D (waiting for disk I/O), or I (process is idle). A second letter, W, means the process is swapped out. It is normal to see many idle processes swapped out. This is the Unix kernel's way of re-organizing and managing physical memory. START is the time the process was started. TIME is the amount of CPU time already consumed by the process. Finally, COMMAND is the argument list passed into main().[3]

A busy SQL Server is a heavy consumer of CPU time. Once SQL Server is up and running, SZ does not change appreciably as SQL Server allocates all of the memory it needs up front. RSS changes as SQL Server "settles in" to running your

---

[3.] In some versions of Unix, it is possible to change the argument list passed into main() and have the modified argument list appear as COMMAND. Some versions of isql uses this trick to hide the password. Some Unix games use this trick to make themselves look like useful programs so managers think their individual contributors are actually contributing something.

operation. Unix generally uses a "lazy read" strategy for loading programs. Only the bit of the program that is needed immediately is loaded into memory. If you only exercise certain parts of the program, only those parts are consuming physical memory. When a new bit of program is needed, the Unix kernel reads the appropriate pages from the executable file into memory. In addition, as you touch more and more buffer space, Unix grows the RSS to accommodate the memory needs of SQL Server.[4] For this reason, its a good idea to let the system "warm up" for a while before running benchmarks. The Unix kernel needs a little time to understand the characteristics of the SQL Server process and adapt itself accordingly.

The uptime command reports the load average of the system. This is a vaguely useful number that relates to how busy the system is, averaged over a short amount of time. uptime measures how busy a machine is by counting the number of processes which are runnable, but not currently running. These are processes that are ready to continue executing, but must wait for the CPU to service them.

For client programs, the Unix time command reports how much CPU and real time was consumed by the program during its run. This is not particularly useful for servers, but is an easy way to measure the efficiency of short lived client programs.

CPU time consumed by the system, user processes, and idle time are reported by vmstat and iostat. iostat includes the columns: us (user time), ni (nice time), sy (system time), and id (idle time).

- **user time** — percentage of time CPU spent running user programs
- **nice time** — percentage of time CPU spent running niced (i.e., lower priority) user programs
- **system time** — percentage of time CPU spent running in the operating system kernel (generally handling I/O and other system calls)
- **idle time** — percentage of time the CPU spent doing nothing

The vmstat command provides a similar set of output, but does not distinguish between user time and nice time. Both are included in the column headed us.

The fact that these programs report these statistics is useful although almost incidental. Below, we talk about the other useful information these programs provide.

---

[4] Other operating systems use similar strategies. Windows/NT, for example, has its equivalent of RSS.

```
% ps aux
USER        PID %CPU %MEM    SZ  RSS TT STAT START   TIME COMMAND
sugiyama   9479 60.6 37.4 78810172 p6 R    21:25   1:52 /usr/u/sybase/dataserver
sugiyama   9513  3.9  1.9  264  520 pc R    21:28   0:00 ps aux
sugiyama   6685  0.0  0.0  216    0 p3 IW   09:35   0:02 /bin/csh
root          2  0.0  0.0    0    0 ?  D    May  5  0:09 pagedaemon
...
```

Figure 8.6   Example output from the ps aux command - - - - - - - - - - - - - - - - -

```
% uptime
  9:31pm  up 17 days,   7:40,   13 users,   load average: 2.77, 1.85, 1.22
```

Figure 8.7   Example output from the uptime command - - - - - - - - - - - - - - - - -

```
% time isql -Usa -P -is10 -oout -e
       2.4 real        0.1 user        0.1 sys
```

Figure 8.8   Example output from the time command - - - - - - - - - - - - - - - - - -

```
% iostat 5 5
           tty            dk0            cpu
  tin tout bps tps msps   us ni sy id
    0   22   7   1  0.0     2  0  1 97
    0    7   6   1  0.0    70  0 30  0
    0    7   2   0  0.0    67  0 33  0
    0    7  87  12  0.0    64  0 33  3
    0    7  31   2  0.0    66  0 33  1
```

Figure 8.9   Example output from the iostat command - - - - - - - - - - - - - - - - - -

```
% vmstat 5 5
 procs      memory              page                disk         faults       cpu
 r b w   avm   fre  re at  pi  po  fr  de  sr d0 d1 d2 d3   in   sy  cs us sy id
 3 0 0     0  2060   0  8   2   2   1   0   1  1  0  0  0   18  267 109  2  1 97
 0 0 0     0  2044   0  3  20   0  28   0   8  1  0  0  0  453903 103 84 13  3
 2 0 0     0  2044   0  0   0   0   4   0   1  0  0  0  0  214787  97 85 15  0
 2 0 0     0  2072   0  0  16   0  24   0   6  2  0  0  0  152041 109 94  3  3
 2 1 0     0  1924   0 84  12   8 236   0  56  9  0  0  0  593359 110 77 22  1
```

Figure 8.10   Example output from the vmstat command - - - - - - - - - - - - - - - -

8.3.2   Disk Activity

There should be good correspondence between the operating system tools and SQL Server monitoring for disk I/O measures. In the simple case that a single database device uses a single physical disk drive and no other program uses the disk drive, correlating the operating system and SQL Server measures is simple. The I/O measures reported by the operating system tools for the disk drive should match exactly with the I/O measures reported by SQL Server. Correlating database device I/O to physical disk I/O can be more complicated if you are using logical volumes to split a SQL Server database device across more than one physical disk drive. In this case, a two step mapping is useful. First correlate the I/O measures between the database device file and the logical volume, then correlate the I/O measures between the logical volume and the physical disk drives used by the volume.

If you have more than one database device on the same disk (not a good idea, but it can happen), make sure you sum the activity across all of the database devices on the same disk. Using the operating system's measure of disk activity is more accurate than SQL Server's if the disks are used for more than database devices. For example, if you share a disk between a raw partition devoted to Sybase and a file system containing some programs, the operating system measure of activity on the disk includes both SQL Server's and the file system's use of the disk. SQL Server is not aware of the file system and only reports it's own activity.[5]

On Unix, the `iostat` command shows the I/O count and average transfer rate by disk. The example output in Figure 8.11 shows a machine with only one disk drive, `dk0`.

```
% iostat 5 5
          tty              dk0            cpu
tin tout bps tps msps  us ni sy id
  0   22   7   1  0.0    2  0  1 97
  0    7   6   1  0.0   70  0 30  0
  0    7   2   0  0.0   67  0 33  0
  0    7  87  12  0.0   64  0 33  3
  0    7  31   2  0.0   66  0 33  1
```

Figure 8.11   Example output from the iostat command - - - - - - - - - - - - - - - - - -

---

[5]   SQL Server is also not aware of Backup Server disk activity.

8.3.3 Memory Use

The amount of memory consumed by SQL Server generally does not change once SQL Server is up and running. SQL Server allocates all of the memory it needs up front as part of the start-up sequence. The most important factor about memory is that SQL Server performs very poorly if the system is paging (or worse swapping). Excessive paging or swapping of runnable processes on Unix is an indication of a memory shortage. If this happens, you should kill any unnecessary programs running on the SQL Server machine. If the machine continues to page or swap, you should configure SQL Server to use less memory.

The `vmstat` command shows number of pages paged in, paged out, disk operations per second by disk, percent CPU time spent in system calls, user processes, and idle.

```
% vmstat 5 5
 procs     memory            page            disk          faults      cpu
 r b w   avm   fre  re at pi  po  fr  de  sr d0 d1 d2 d3   in  sy  cs us sy id
 3 0 0     0  2060   0  8  2   2   1   0   1  1  0  0  0   18 267 109  2  1 97
 0 0 0     0  2044   0  3 20   0  28   0   8  1  0  0  0 453903 103 84 13  3
 2 0 0     0  2044   0  0  0   0   4   0   1  0  0  0  0 214787  97 85 15  0
 2 0 0     0  2072   0  0 16   0  24   0   6  2  0  0  0 152041 109 94  3  3
 2 1 0     0  1924   0 84 12   8 236   0  56  9  0  0  0 593359 110 77 22  1
```

Figure 8.12   Example output from the vmstat command - - - - - - - - - - - - - - - -

Most versions of SQL Server running on a variant of Unix use shared memory segments to hold state information about SQL Server. This allows the multiple engines in an SMP SQL Server to communicate with one another as well as Monitor Server to gather statistics about SQL Server. Some versions of Unix let you find out about the shared memory segments with the `ipcs` command.[6]

```
% ipcs -mob
IPC status from srvr1 as of Fri May 26 18:05:06 1995
T     ID    KEY         MODE       OWNER     GROUP NATTCH  SEGSZ
Shared Memory:
m  27648 0x2d055ad5 --rw------- sugiyama   sybase       11527808
m  27649 0x2d055b2f --rw------- sugiyama   sybase       16107136
```

Figure 8.13   Example output from the ipcs -mob command

---

6. IPC stands for Inter-Process Communication.

In the output from `ipcs`, `ID` is the process ID that created the shared memory segment. `KEY` identifies the shared memory segment. `MODE` indicates access permissions for user, group, and other. `OWNER` and `GROUP` are the user and the user's group that own the segment. `NATTACH` is the number of times processes have attached to the shared memory segment. In general, this is the number of engines running in your SQL Server. `SEGSZ` is the size of the segment. In the example output, `SEGSZ` has run into the `NATTCH` column, so they appear as a single number. In fact, the two segments have the sizes 1527808 and 6107136.[7] Each is being accessed by a single process.

SQL Server creates at least two shared memory segments when the system boots. Under certain circumstances, SQL Server does not clean up its shared memory segments.[8] Shared memory segments with no programs attached report an `NATTACH` of 0. There are no processes connected to the shared memory segments. These shared memory segments consume resources on your machine and should be removed. When you boot SQL Server again, it is unaware that shared memory segments already exist and goes about creating new segments, consuming even more resources. You can use the `ipcrm` command to remove unwanted shared memory segments. You must be the owner of the segment or root to remove it.[9]

8.3.4   Network Statistics

Operating system network statistics are useful for identifying bottlenecks and high error rates. The occasional error is expected on an even moderately busy network. Extremely busy networks may experience regular errors. A high error rate impedes performance by slowing the machine's access to the network. If SQL Server is periodically blocked from reading or writing to the network because of errors, your client applications will see slower performance.

For Unix, `netstat` shows all network connections and summary reports of network activity. For monitoring SQL Server, the important networking information is listed under the heading `Active Internet connections`. There is one row

---

[7.] The actual number of shared memory segments used by SQL Server varies by platform and SQL Server version.

[8.] This may happen if SQL Server shuts down in a highly unexpected way or is killed with `kill -9`.

[9.] Shared memory segments may live longer than the programs that create them. This characteristic is used in certain applications. Applications that consist of a sequence of programs processing a large amount of data can create a shared memory segment for the data, load the data with the first program, and tell subsequent programs the key to the shared memory segment. The subsequent programs process the data and the final program writes the data into a file. This saves reading and writing the data to disk for each program.

for each active network port on the machine. `Proto` is the protocol being used for the connection. `tcp` means TCP/IP. `Recv-Q` and `Send-Q` is how much data is queued up waiting to be written to the network or read by application programs. `Local Address` and `Foreign Address` are the addresses of the two ends of the network connection. `Local Address` is always on the host that ran the `netstat` command. `Foreign Address` may be the same machine or another host. For each, the format of the address is `hostname.portnumber`. For example, `srvr1.4455` means the host `srvr1` has a connection open on port `4455`, `srvr1.telnet` means the host `srvr1` has a connection open on the `telnet` port. Port numbers may be named in the `/etc/services` file. `(state)` describes what state the network connection is in. There are a variety of network states that you might see in `netstat`'s output. The most common are:

- **LISTEN** — The host is listening for connections on this port. This corresponds to the master line in an interfaces file entry for SQL Server. The `Foreign Address` is shown as `*.*` because no connection really exists.

- **ESTABLISHED** — There is a connection established between the `Local Address` and `Foreign Address`. A variety of network connections may exist on your system. For example, `rlogin`, `telnet`, and `sendmail` all use network connections to transfer information from one machine to another. Of course, all active Sybase connections are listed here as well.

- **CLOSE_WAIT, FIN_WAIT_2** — The two sides of the connection are negotiating a shutdown of the connection.

```
% netstat
Active Internet connections
Proto Recv-Q Send-Q  Local Address          Foreign Address         (state)
tcp        0      0  srvr1.1557             *.*                     LISTEN
tcp        0      0  srvr1.5570             srvr1.4455              CLOSE_WAIT
tcp        0      0  srvr1.4455             srvr1.5570              FIN_WAIT_2
tcp        0      0  srvr1.5570             srvr1.4454              CLOSE_WAIT
tcp        0      0  srvr1.4454             srvr1.5570              FIN_WAIT_2
tcp        0      0  srvr1.4201             srvr1.1557              CLOSE_WAIT
tcp        0      0  srvr1.5570             *.*                     LISTEN
tcp        0      0  localhost.1127         localhost.1129          ESTABLISHED
tcp        0      0  localhost.1129         localhost.1127          ESTABLISHED
Active UNIX domain sockets
Address    Type    Recv-Q Send-Q  Vnode      Conn     Refs  Nextref Addr
ff66020c   stream       0      0         0 ff66d48c       0        0
ff671b8c   stream       0      0         0 ff65250c       0        0
ff656e8c   stream     800      0         0 ff649f8c       0        0
ff64fe0c   stream       0      0         0 ff65af0c       0        0
ff64b00c   stream       0      0         0 ff66368c       0        0
```

Figure 8.14   Example output from the netstat command - - - - - - - - - - - - - - - - - -

The `netstat -i` command lists errors and collisions. A chronically high collision rate suggests that the network is over utilized. The `netstat -i` output lists:

- **Name** — The name of the network interface. Ethernet adapters usually appear as `leN`, where `N` is the adapter's number. `lo0` is the loopback interface and can be used when connections are made locally (the client and server processes are running on the same machine).

- **Mtu** — Maximum transfer unit. This is the largest amount of information that can be transferred at one time with this network interface.

- **Net/Dest** — The name of the network this network interface is attached to. The machine running `netstat -i` is attached to the network named `net1`.

- **Address** — The name of the host on that network interface. This machine is called `srvr1`. Hostnames are generally recorded in the `/etc/hosts` file.

- **Ipckts** — Input Packets. The number of network packets received by the host through this interface since the system was started.

- **Ierrs** — Number of errors received while reading packets from the network.

- **Opkts** — Output Packets. The number of network packets written by the host through this interface since the system was started.

- **Oerrs** — Number of errors received while writing packets to the network.

- **Collis** — Number of network collisions encountered since the system was started.

- **Queue** — Amount of information pending in the network interface.

```
% netstat -i
Name  Mtu   Net/Dest      Address       Ipkts     Ierrs Opkts    Oerrs Collis Queue
le0   1500  net1          srvr1         10191344  518   1521710  90    314336 0
lo0   1536  loopback      localhost     1514075   0     1514075  0     0      0
```

Figure 8.15   Example output from the netstat -i command - - - - - - - - - - - - - - - -

8.4   SQL MONITOR

SQL Monitor provides a powerful and convenient porthole into the operation of SQL Server. You can use SQL Monitor to find out disk and network I/O rates, the transaction rate, process details, and how quickly data is being inserted, updated, and deleted from tables. SQL Monitor is a client application that communicates with Monitor Server. Monitor Server is an auxiliary server (see Chapter 3, *Sybase Product and Feature Overview*) that reads the internal data structures of SQL Server's shared memory at regular intervals.

The process of instrumenting the internals of a complex software system often run into a variant of the Hiesenberg Uncertainty Principal: It is impossible to observe the state of the system without perturbing it. Monitor Server's architecture minimizes the impact of the monitoring tools on the performance of SQL Server. Monitor Server minimizes the impact on SQL Server by having a separate process do the work. SQL Server does not process any additional interrupts or handle any more synchronization operations as a result of monitoring. The only impact of Monitor Server on SQL Server is that Monitor Server and SQL Server must share the computer. On a single CPU system the CPU must split its time between SQL Server and Monitor Server. Monitor Server is very lightweight, so even here the performance impact is small.

System 10 SQL Server does not execute any additional code when using Monitor Server to read SQL Server's monitor counters. System 11 SQL Server only updates its monitor counters when they are being used. As a result, performance of System 11 SQL Server drops slightly when Monitor Server is used to read the monitor counters.[10]

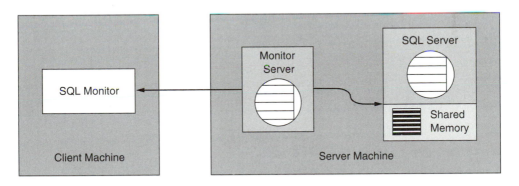

Figure 8.16 SQL Monitor, Monitor Server, SQL Server relationship - - - - - - - - -

---

[10.] The actual amount of the drop depends on the platform. Most systems experience a 1% to 5% performance drop during periods of high throughput or low idle time.

This section is based on SQL Monitor Release 10.0. SQL Monitor documentation refers to SQL Server tasks as processes inside SQL Server.

8.4.1   Main Window

The Main Window gives you access to the other windows and shows the proportion of memory given to different purposes by SQL Server.

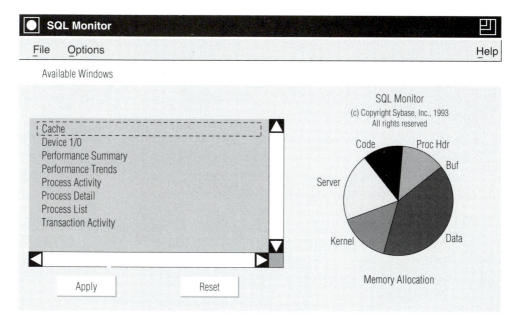

Figure 8.17   SQL Monitor Main Window -

The memory is divided into the following parts:

- **Kernel** — Memory assigned to SQL Server's kernel. The SQL Server kernel is the interface between the part of SQL Server that is the database and the operating system. The kernel is also responsible for task management, the scheduling of runnable tasks to engines, queuing of tasks for networking and disk I/O, etc. The memory given to the kernel includes stack space for each task and other state information. Increasing the maximum number of user connections or the stack size for each thread increases the amount of memory needed by the kernel.

- **Server** — Memory assigned to the part of SQL Server that constitutes the database engine. This part of SQL Server manages buffers, locking, tables, indexes, etc. and knows how to execute T-SQL commands. It includes the query parser, compiler, and optimizer. The memory given to SQL Server is used to store state information about the various components of SQL Server. For example, logical locks are represented in memory as data structures. Increasing the maximum number of locks increases the amount of memory needed by SQL Server.

- **Code** — Memory consumed by the executable code of the SQL Server binary is assigned to code. There is nothing you can do to change this value. Each version of SQL Server consumes a slightly different amount of memory in code.

- **Procedure buffer** — Memory assigned to procedure buffers is used to cached compiled and optimized stored procedure plans. You can adjust how much memory is devoted to procedure buffers with the procedure cache configuration variable. The more memory devoted to procedure buffers, the less likely SQL Server needs to read the sysprocedures table to load stored procedures. Some utilities, such as sort for `order by` and `create index` also use procedure buffer memory.

- **Data** — Memory assigned to data is used to buffer data and index pages from database devices. The more memory devoted to data cache, the more likely it is that SQL Server can find the data it needs in memory and avoid reading data from the database devices.

You adjust the total amount of memory devoted to SQL Server with the `total memory` configuration value. Note that the meaning of this value differs from platform to platform and version to version of SQL Server. In general, for System 10 SQL Server and earlier versions, the memory configuration value is the total amount of memory devoted to SQL Server, including all of the parts described above. In System 11 SQL Server and later, the `memory` configuration value excludes the code part.

Picking the best way to partition memory is one of the ways you can tune the performance of SQL Server. From the pie chart, it is clear that any memory used for increasing the stack size of tasks is memory taken away from something else, probably procedure cache and data cache. Some parts that consume memory cannot be configured. You cannot change the amount of memory devoted to code, for example. But you can configure for fewer users, locks, or maximum number of open objects. This leaves you more memory for procedure and data cache. You can adjust the ratio of memory devoted to procedure cache and data cache.

SQL Monitor provides the data you need to make informed and intelligent decisions about configuring memory. The cache window shows how often SQL Server is reading data from database devices, rather than finding the memory in cache. The device I/O window provides more detail, showing database device I/O rate on a device basis.

8.4.2   Cache Window

The Cache Window shows the number of logical reads from memory, physical reads from database devices, writes to database device files, procedure reads from `sysprocedures`, procedure executions, the data cache hit rate, and the procedure cache hit rate.

When SQL Server needs to access a data page and finds the page in cache, this is counted as a logical read. When SQL Server must read the data from the database device (i.e., the data page was not in cache), this is counted as a physical read. When SQL Server writes a data page to a database device, this is counted as a write. There is no notion of a logical write. SQL Server always writes out changed database pages eventually. A logical write implies a physical write. A data page can be read into cache and used many times. A logical read does not imply a physical read.

Note that the read and write count given here assumes that SQL Server's memory is not being paged or swapped by the operating system. SQL Server does not know when its memory is being paged out to make room for another process. If the operating system must page in SQL Server's data cache memory, it defeats the purpose of having a large data cache. The cost of a logical read and physical read from SQL Server's perspective become identical (i.e., the page is either read in from the database device or the operating system's paging space).

The ratio of logical reads to the total number of reads is the cache hit rate. If SQL Server always finds data in cache, then the cache hit rate is 100%. This is a reasonable expectation for applications with only a small amount of data running on SQL Servers configured with a lot of memory. To avoid constraining your application by disk I/O, you need to assure that the disk I/O to any one device does not exceed the capacity of that device. The Device I/O window details how much I/O goes to each database device.

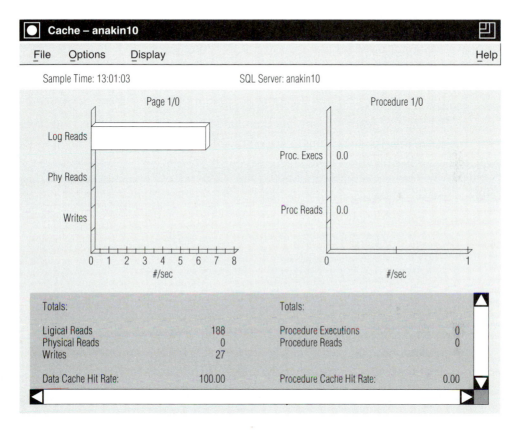

Figure 8.18   SQL Monitor Cache Window -

When SQL Server reads a stored procedure plan from `sysprocedures`, this is counted as a **procedure read**. **Procedure execute** is a count of the number of times stored procedures are executed. If the stored procedure plan is found in cache, SQL Server does not need to read the plan from `sysprocedures`. This is called a **cache hit**. If the cache hit rate is low, you should consider increasing the amount of memory devoted to procedure cache. Ideally, the procedure cache hit rate should be near 100%. If the hit rate is 100% and the data cache hit rate could stand improvement, you can consider reducing the amount of memory devoted to procedure cache. This leaves you more data for data cache.

8.4.3   Device I/O

SQL Monitor provides two views of SQL Server device I/O. The summary view indicates the total amount of I/O, whether read or write, on each database device as well as the device I/O hit rate. The device I/O hit rate the percentage of I/O requests that did not have to wait. If the I/O hit rate is not 100%, SQL Server has an I/O that it is ready to start, but that the device is not yet willing to accept. This indicates that you are trying to do too much I/O to this device.

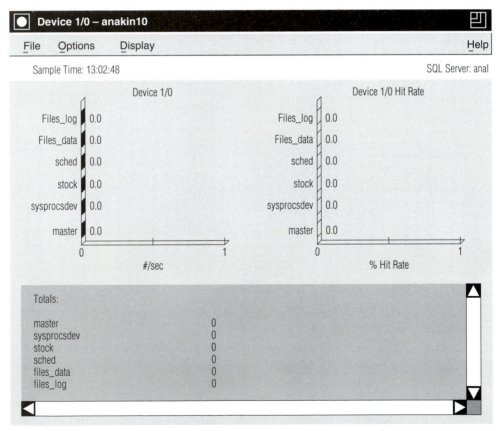

Figure 8.19   SQL Monitor Device I/O Summary Window - - - - - - - - - - - - - -

The detail view breaks the I/O requests down by reads and writes as well as giving more detail about the device I/O hit rate. Rather than presenting the percentage hit rate, the detail view shows the actual number of I/O requests that were made to the device and the number that were refused.

SQL Monitor reports on the I/O performed only by SQL Server. It does not include Backup Server. Backup Server performs its own I/O to database devices and tape drives. You must use the operating system's performance monitoring tools to see the impact of backup server on device I/O. Replication Server I/O is included in the SQL Monitor I/O statistics. SQL Server reads the transaction log on behalf of Replication Server. Replication Server does not read or write database devices directly.

The summary view lets you quickly identify the database devices that are heavily utilized by your application. Looking at the detail view can give you some idea about what is happening on that database device.

8.4.4 Performance Summary

The Performance Summary window shows a variety of summary information: transaction rate, SQL Server CPU utilization, data cache hit rate (percentage), procedure cache hit rate (percentage), I/O start success rate (percentage), successful lock rate (percentage), network read rate, network write rate, device I/O rate averaged over all database devices, I/O rate of the most active database device, and the requested and granted locks by type.

Much of the information here is also displayed in other windows, so here we focus on the information that is unique to this window.

The network read and write rate tell you how much data is being transferred through the network.

The Performance Summary window also shows a bar graph of the number of locks requested and granted, separated by type. The lock types are:

- **Ex_Page** — Exclusive lock on a page. A task is changing a page.

- **Ex_Int** — Exclusive intent lock. A task has an exclusive lock on a page in the table.

- **Ex_Tab** — Exclusive lock on a table. A task is changing a large number of pages in the table.

- **Up_Page** — Update lock on a page. A task is upgrading a shared lock to an exclusive lock.

- **Sh_Page** — Shared lock on a page. A task is reading a page and does not want the data on the page to change.

- **Sh_Int** — Shared intent lock. A task has a shared lock on a page in the table.

- **Sh_Tab** — Shared lock on a table. A task does not want any page in the table to change.

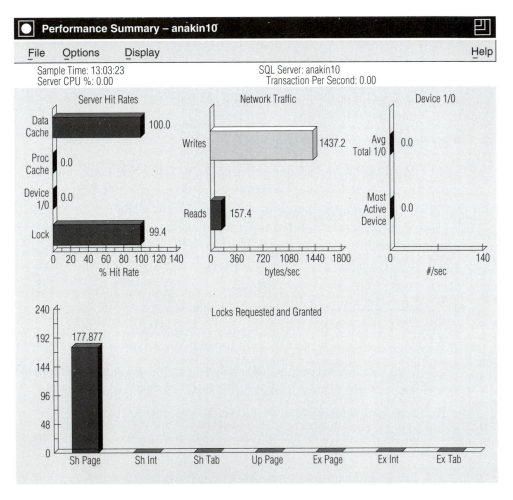

Figure 8.20   SQL Monitor Performance Summary Window - - - - - - - - - - - -

This window does not display other important information about locking performance:

- The length of time a task had to wait for a lock.
- The pages, tables, or tasks that account for most of the lock contention.

For this information, you need to rely on the `sp_lock` and `sp_who` system stored procedures. The `sp_lock` stored procedure lists all of the locks currently requested and granted in SQL Server. The `sp_who` stored procedure lists all of the tasks running on SQL Server, and which task, if any, they are waiting on before proceeding. See the discussion of `sp_lock` and `sp_who` in "QUERYING ABOUT PERFORMANCE" on page 226.

8.4.5 Performance Trends

In the Performance Trends window you can set up strip chart-style graphs of: CPU utilization

- Data cache hit rate
- Device I/O
- Ratio of successfully started device I/O to all I/O requests
- Ratio of granted locks to all lock requests
- Lock request rate
- Network I/O
- Procedure cache hit rate.

Strip charts are useful in several of ways, including:

- Seeing trends over time.
- Identifying busy and idle times for your application.
- Assessing the impact of running a new query or adding another application to your SQL Server.

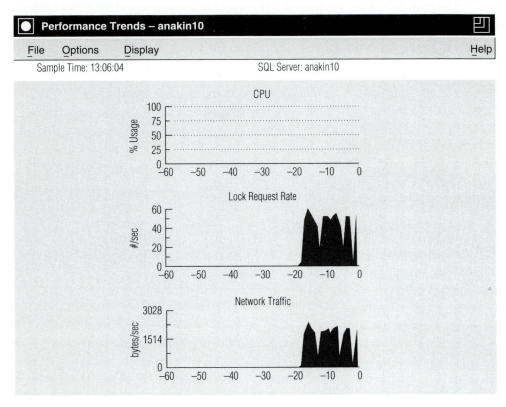

Figure 8.21   SQL Monitor Performance Trends Window- - - - - - - - - - - - - - -

8.4.6   Process Windows

The Process Activity window, Process Detail window, and Process List window allow you to examine individual tasks inside SQL Server. Whereas the performance summary window displays information for SQL Server as a whole and the device windows give information organized by database device, the process windows organize information by task.

The process activity window gives you significant control over which tasks are displayed. It presents information about the amount of CPU utilized by the task and the number of logical reads, physical reads, and writes by task. Operationally, this is useful if your system suddenly slows down and you need to identify the user who is running a big query.

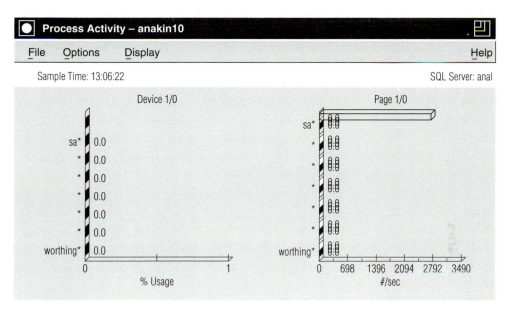

Figure 8.22   SQL Monitor Process Activity Window - - - - - - - - - - - - - - - -

The process detail window shows

- The name of task (generally the login name)
- spid (SQL Server Process Identifier)
- Connect time
- Task State
- Current engine
- CPU time
- Logical reads
- Physical reads
- Writes

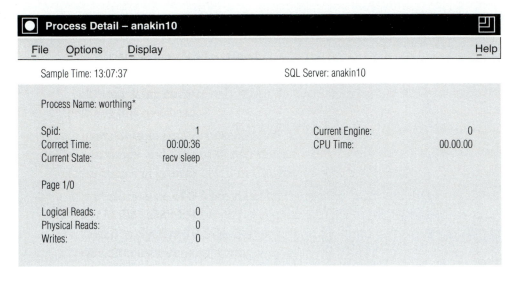

Figure 8.23   SQL Monitor Process Detail Window   -

The state can be:

- **infected** — The task has detected an internal error in SQL Server. SQL Server is no longer running this task. Infected tasks generally result in a stack trace in SQL Server's errorlog.

- **runnable** — There is nothing blocking the task from running, however, it is not currently scheduled to run on an engine. When an engine becomes available, this task can be run.

- **running** — The task is currently executing on an engine. It continues to execute until it is blocked by network or disk I/O, must wait for a lock, or yields the engine to another task.

- **sleeping** — The task is waiting for network or disk I/O or is waiting to acquire a lock.

- **terminating** — The task is in the process of exiting. The user is either disconnecting from SQL Server or the task is being killed.

- **yielding** — The task has used up its slice of time on the engine and is yielding the engine to another runnable task.

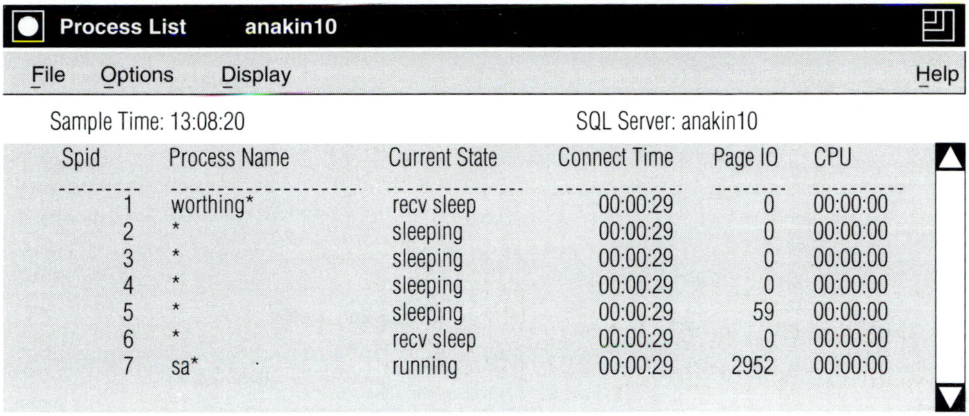

```
┌──────────────────────────────────────────────────────────────────────┐
│ ●  Process List        anakin10                                   ⊐    │
├──────────────────────────────────────────────────────────────────────┤
│  File    Options    Display                                    Help    │
├──────────────────────────────────────────────────────────────────────┤
│   Sample Time: 13:08:20                    SQL Server: anakin10         │
│   Spid     Process Name        Current State    Connect Time  Page IO  CPU    ▲
│  -------   ---------------     --------------   ------------  -------  --------
│        1   worthing*           recv sleep          00:00:29        0   00:00:00
│        2   *                   sleeping            00:00:29        0   00:00:00
│        3   *                   sleeping            00:00:29        0   00:00:00
│        4   *                   sleeping            00:00:29        0   00:00:00
│        5   *                   sleeping            00:00:29       59   00:00:00
│        6   *                   recv sleep          00:00:29        0   00:00:00
│        7   sa*      ·          running             00:00:29     2952   00:00:00
│                                                                              ▼
└──────────────────────────────────────────────────────────────────────┘
```

Figure 8.24   SQL Monitor Process List Window -

For design and experimentation, the process detail window is useful because you can isolate statistics about a particular application or query from the rest of the system. The Process List window displays the spid, task name, current state, connect time, database device I/O, and CPU time consumed.

The Process List Window displays all of the logins on SQL Server, their current state, and a few other useful bits of information.

8.4.7   Transaction Activity

The Transaction Activity window displays the rate of transactions, updates, direct updates (i.e., updates in place), deletes, and inserts to tables.

A transaction is identified by a matching part of `begin transaction` and `commit transaction` commands. Transactions that are rolled back are not counted. This window gives you an idea of the rate at which work is accomplished in SQL Server.

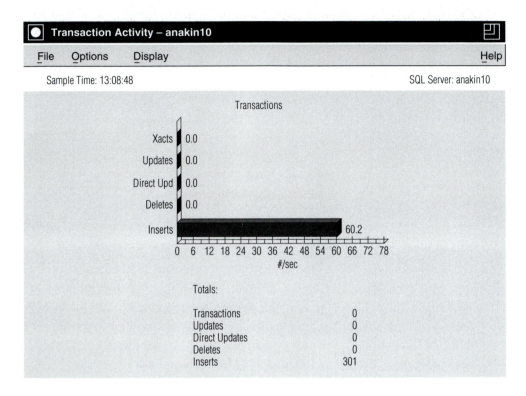

Figure 8.25   SQL Monitor Transaction Activity Window - - - - - - - - - - - - - -

Chapter 9

Instrumenting SQL Code

Monitoring SQL Server provides excellent information about the state of SQL Server and how it is processing your queries. You can learn quite a bit about how your application behaves from monitoring, but much of the evidence is indirect. You can deduce that you are taking advantage of an index because the I/O rate on the database device containing the index is relatively high. When you need more direct information about how SQL Server is processing your queries, you need to instrument your SQL code.

This chapter discusses various ways in which you can instrument your SQL code to get more information about how SQL Server is executing your queries. The output generated by the `set showplan on` command is the most powerful tool here, giving you insight into how SQL Server actually goes about processing your query. I/O and timing information is reported with `set statistics io on` and `set statistics time on`. Finally, there are ways in which you can instrument your stored procedures to give you better information about how often the procedures are run and how long they take to execute.

9.1   SHOWPLAN

You have probably spent some time crafting the physical design of your database. Carefully chosen indexes should optimize your queries. In running the queries, you may find that there is more disk I/O than you expect. Perhaps the query takes far longer to execute than anticipated. Turning on showplan output with the `set showplan on` command makes SQL Server tell you the query plan chosen by the query optimizer. Using this output, you can compare the plan chosen by the optimizer with the plan you were expecting. Showplan is a powerful and useful analysis tool when queries do not behave the way you think they should.

You activate showplan output with the command:

```
set showplan on
```

From then on, SQL Server produces showplan output for every command executed in the session. You can turn showplan output off with the command:

```
set showplan off
```

SQL Server sends the showplan output to the client as messages. These messages are handled like errors, only the severity of the message is set to indicate they are informational messages. Other informational messages are sent at other times. For example, when you change the current database with the `use` command, SQL Server sends message number `5701, Changed database context to 'database'`. This message is routinely filtered out. For example, `isql` does not report this message.

This section describes the messages you might see in showplan output and then goes through several examples.

9.1.1   4.9 and System 10 SQL Server

SQL Server 4.9 and System 10 have a similar format for showplan output. The messages come in a stream with very little formatting and you must read them carefully. Listed below are the messages that can be produced in showplan output, and a brief statement of the message's meaning:

- **STEP** *n* — Ordinal count of steps. The steps are performed in ascending order.

- **The type of query is** *X* — *X* is a SQL command such as `SELECT` or `INSERT`.

- **The update mode is direct|deferred** — Says which update mode SQL Server is using. Direct update mode for `insert` and `delete` means the database pages are changed directly, without first logging the entire operation. For `update`, the row is changed in place. Deferred update mode for `insert` and `delete` means the database pages are changed only after the entire operation is written to the database transaction log. For `update`, the row is changed by deleting the old row and inserting the new row.

- **GROUP BY** — A `group by` is being performed.

- **Vector Aggregate** — Calculate an aggregate function (e.g., `avg`) where the result is a more than one value. A vector aggregate is the result of an aggregate function used with `group by`.

- **Scalar Aggregate** — Calculate an aggregate function where the result is a single value. For example, `count(*)`, `sum(x)`, and `min(y)` are examples of scalar aggregates when they are used with a `group by` clause. A `group by` clause and subquery flattening convert scalar aggregates into vector aggregates.

- **This step involves sorting** — The data is sorted during this step.

- **Worktable created** *X* — Create a worktable to assist in the processing of the query. A worktable is something like a temporary table that SQL Server uses to hold intermediate results from the query. *X* indicates the reason for the worktable. Possible values for *X* are: **by ORDER BY**, **for DISTINCT**, **for REFORMATTING**, and **for SELECT_INTO**. **By ORDER BY** means the worktable temporarily holds results so they can be properly sorted before sending them to the client. **For DISTINCT** means the worktable was created to perform `select distinct` processing. The unique rows are stored temporarily in the worktable. **For REFORMATTING** means results are stored in the worktable so SQL Server can create an index on the results. This generally indicates that an extremely useful index is missing from your schema. **For SELECT_INTO** means the worktable was created in order to select results into the worktable.

- **TO TABLE** — Send the results of this step to this table.

- **FROM TABLE** — Read rows from the indicated table.

- **Worktable** — If Worktable appears instead of a table name, SQL Server is reading or writing a worktable rather than a named table. A worktable is a temporary table created by SQL Server in the process of executing the query. Worktables are created in the temporary database and generally hold intermediate results. We discuss work tables in more detail in Chapter 11, *Query Processing Performance*.

- **DISJOINT TABLE : nested iteration** — The query requires the creation of a cartesian product. Every row of one table is joined with every row of another table.

- **Nested Iteration** — Rows are read from a table, or tables are joined together. This indicates that SQL Server is using a loop to read rows from the table. This is the only access method SQL Server has for computing joins.

- **EXISTS TABLE : nested iteration** — Scan the table, but only so far as to discover that a particular row exists. It is not necessary to find all such rows.

- **Table Scan** — SQL Server is scanning the entire table rather than using an index.

- **Using GETSORTED** — Get the data from the table and rely on the fact that the data is already sorted.

- **Using Dynamic Index** — Indicates that an index on row identifiers is used to construct the list of rows to be retrieved from a table. The index may be scanned more than once. Dynamic indexes are used internally to process certain kinds of queries. For example, a `select` statement with a search clause containing `or` may use a dynamic index to generate the union of the results from both sides of the `or` operator.

- **Using Clustered Index** — The clustered index is being used to find rows in the table. SQL Server does not give the name of the clustered index because there can only be one clustered index on a table.

- **Index : *X*** — Index *X* is used to find rows in the table. This only appears when a nonclustered index is used.

9.1.2   System 11 SQL Server

For System 11 SQL Server, Sybase has enhanced the showplan output to make it easier to read and more useful:

- The output is indented to show the nesting of the information. This makes it easier to read the messages.

- The I/O size is indicated. In 4.9.1 and System 10 SQL Servers there is only one possible I/O size, so this information was unnecessary.[1] System 11 allows for different I/O sizes and it may be useful to know what size is being used for the query.

- The buffer replacement strategy is indicated. System 11 SQL Server can use either the Least Recently Used (LRU) or Fetch-and-Discard (indicated as MRU) buffer replacement strategy. System 10 and 4.9.1 SQL Servers can only use the LRU buffer replacement strategy, so there is no need to indicate which strategy was chosen.

- Worktables are identified by number, rather than just indicating a worktable is used. In place of `Worktable` in the showplan output is `WorktableN`, where *N* is a number that identifies the particular worktable throughout the showplan output.

---

[1]   Some utilities like `create database`, `create index`, and BCP use 16K I/O under certain circumstances.

- Covering indexes are identified.

In addition to 4.9.1 and System 10 SQL Server showplan messages, System 11 SQL Server includes the following messages:

- **Using I/O Size N Kbytes** — I/O size of N Kbytes is being used. If you have not configured caches with larger I/O sizes, this is probably 2K.

- **With MRU|LRU Buffer Replacement Strategy** — Indicates which buffer replacement strategy is being used by the query: Fetch and discard (identified by MRU) or Least Recently Used (LRU).

- **Evaluate Grouped X** — Calculate the vector quantity indicated by X.

- **Evaluate Ungrouped X** — Calculate the scalar quantity indicated by X.

- **Ascending scan** — Read rows in ascending order. This is the default behavior of SQL Server.

- **Descending scan** — Read rows in descending order.

- **Positioning at start of table** — Move to the beginning of the table.

- **Positioning at end of table** — Move to the end of the table.

- **Positioning by Row IDentifier (RID)** — Find a row of the table using the Row Identifier.

- **Positioning by key** — Use the values of an indexed column to limit the scope of an index scan.

- **Positioning at index start** — Move to the beginning of the index.

- **Positioning at index end** — Move to the end of the index.

- **Scanning only the last page of the table** — Check only the last page of the table.

- **Scanning only up to the first qualifying row** — Scan the table up to the first qualifying row. This is used for exists processing.

- **Index contains all needed columns. Base table will not be read** — The non-clustered index has all of the columns needed to acquire the results. It is not necessary to read the data pages. This is called index covering.

- **Keys are:** — Which indexed columns are being used in this query.

- **QUERY PLAN FOR STATEMENT N (at line M)** — Identify the query (N) and line number (M) that this showplan output corresponds to. This is useful when many queries are submitted in the same batch.

- **Update mode is** X — System 10 and earlier versions of SQL Server had only two modes for performing updates — direct and deferred. System 11 SQL Server has 4 modes for performing updates. They are, in increasing cost:

1. **direct** — Update is performed in-place. A nonclustered index is modified only if a column in the index is modified.

2. **deferred_varcol** — A variable-length column is modified. Update is done in-place whenever the new row still fits in page and in deferred mode otherwise. In the former case, only the affected nonclustered indexes are modified. In the latter case, all indexes are modified.

3. **deferred_index** — Update modifies the data page in-place, but affected indexes are modified in deferred mode.

4. **deferred** — Update is performed as a delete followed by an insert. All indexes are modified.

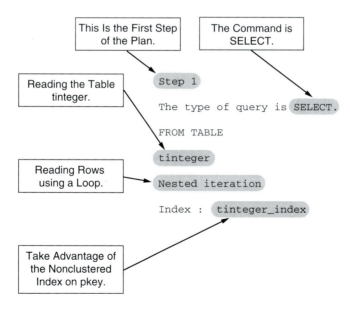

Figure 9.1   System 10 SQL Server showplan: the simple query - - - - - - - - - - -

The following sections describe a variety of showplan output examples from System 10 and System 11 SQL Servers. The examples are provided to help you understand showplan output and should not be used to predict the best plan generated by SQL Server's query optimizer. The exact plan that is generated by the query optimizer may differ in your situation depending on the exact schema (e.g., fixed length columns, variable length columns, uniqueness constraints), statistics (e.g., distribution of data and number of rows), and exact version of SQL Server.

9.1.3 Select Query

For this example, we query a single table `tinteger`. The table `tinteger` has two columns, a unique key `pkey` and the integer column `int`. There is a unique nonclustered index on `pkey`, `tinteger_index`.

```
create table tinteger (pkey numeric, int int)
create unique nonclustered index tinteger_index on tinteger(pkey)
```

Suppose we want to find the row with `pkey` equal to 45:

```
select pkey,int from tinteger where pkey=45
```

Because values for `pkey` are unique, we expect only one row from the table to qualify for the result. We expect this query to take advantage of the index `tinteger_index` because the search clause is highly selective on `pkey`. As the showplan output from System 10 SQL Server in Figure 9.1 shows, SQL Server properly chooses to use the index `tinteger_index`.

System 11 SQL Server generates the same query plan, but provides showplan output in a more readable form. Figure 9.2 shows the System 11 SQL Server showplan output. In addition to the information provided by the System 10 SQL server showplan output, System 11 SQL Server tells us that it is using `pkey` as the key for searching `tinteger`, that it is using 2K I/O and the Least Recently Used (LRU) buffer replacement strategy.

Suppose we use the same table, but instead of selecting on `pkey` we select on `int`. There is no index on `int`, so we expect SQL Server to read the entire table (e.g., perform a table scan) to find all rows in tinteger that match the search criteria.

```
select pkey, int from tinteger where int = -10633
```

Figure 9.3 lists the System 11 SQL Server showplan output for this query. Notice that we perform a table scan on the table, in ascending order, starting from the beginning of the table. The index on `pkey` is not useful in this query, so it is not used.

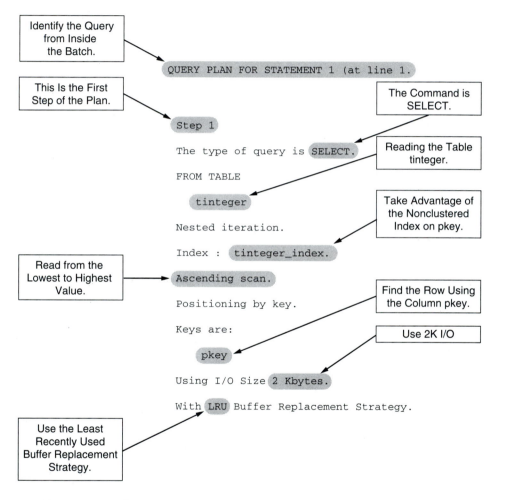

Figure 9.2   System 11 SQL Server showplan: the simple query - - - - - - - - - - -

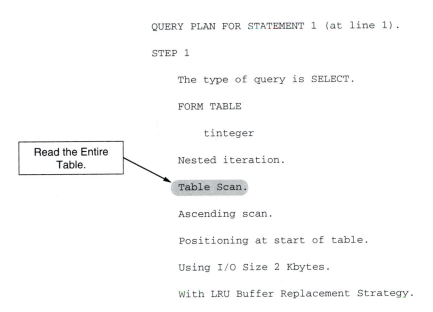

```
QUERY PLAN FOR STATEMENT 1 (at line 1).

STEP 1

    The type of query is SELECT.

    FORM TABLE

        tinteger

    Nested iteration.

    Table Scan.

    Ascending scan.

    Positioning at start of table.

    Using I/O Size 2 Kbytes.

    With LRU Buffer Replacement Strategy.
```

Read the Entire Table.

Figure 9.3   System 11 SQL Server showplan: another simple example- - - - - -

9.1.4   Join Query

Building on the previous example, now we join two tables together. The first table is `tinteger` from the previous example. The second table is `tmoney`, containing two columns: a `pkey` that joins with the `pkey` in `tinteger`, and `money`, a column of type `money`. `tmoney` has a unique nonclustered index on `pkey` named `tmoney_integer`:

```
create table tmoney (pkey numeric, money money)
create unique nonclustered index tmoney_integer on tmoney(pkey)
```

The following query joins `tinteger` and `tmoney` on `pkey`.

```
select money, int from tmoney, tinteger
        where tmoney.pkey = tinteger.pkey
```

We expect SQL Server to process this query by reading every row of one of the tables and finding the matching row in the other table. The showplan output given in Figure 9.4 shows that SQL Server reads every row of `tinteger` and then scans `tmoney` for the needed row. The scan of `tmoney` takes advantage of the `tmoney_index` index on `tmoney(pkey)`. The order of FROM TABLE lines in the showplan output indicates the join order. The first FROM TABLE mentioned is the outer most table of the join. The last FROM TABLE mentioned is the inner most table of the join.

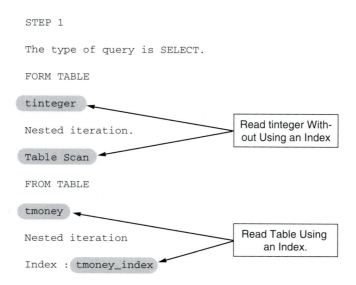

```
STEP 1

The type of query is SELECT.

FORM TABLE

   tinteger

   Nested iteration.

   Table Scan

   FROM TABLE

   tmoney

   Nested iteration

   Index : tmoney_index
```

Read tinteger Without Using an Index

Read Table Using an Index.

Figure 9.4   System 10 SQL Server showplan: a simple join - - - - - - - - - - - - - -

As before, the System 11 SQL Server showplan output provides more details. The System 11 showplan output explicitly states which key columns from the index tmoney_index are used to find rows in the tmoney. In addition, the output states that tinteger scan starts from the beginning of the table and that the scan of tmoney depends is based on the value of the key.

Adding an order by clause to the query causes SQL Server to sort the result. Suppose we want to order by the money column:

```
select money, int from tmoney, tinteger
        where tmoney.pkey = tinteger.pkey
        order by money
```

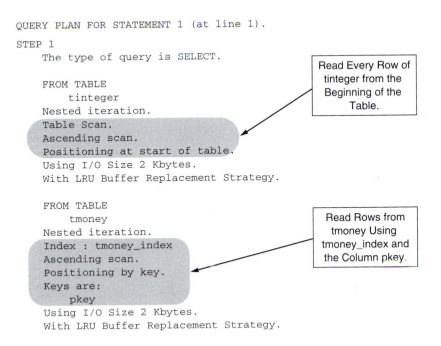

```
QUERY PLAN FOR STATEMENT 1 (at line 1).

STEP 1
    The type of query is SELECT.

    FROM TABLE
        tinteger
    Nested iteration.
    Table Scan.
    Ascending scan.
    Positioning at start of table.
    Using I/O Size 2 Kbytes.
    With LRU Buffer Replacement Strategy.

    FROM TABLE
        tmoney
    Nested iteration.
    Index : tmoney_index
    Ascending scan.
    Positioning by key.
    Keys are:
        pkey
    Using I/O Size 2 Kbytes.
    With LRU Buffer Replacement Strategy.
```

Read Every Row of tinteger from the Beginning of the Table.

Read Rows from tmoney Using tmoney_index and the Column pkey.

Figure 9.5   System 11 SQL Server showplan: simple join - - - - - - - - - - - - - - -

We expect SQL Server to choose the same query plan to find the rows we want, then sort the results so they appear in the correct order in the output. The sort operation requires a worktable. Hence, we expect SQL Server to find the rows we want using the same plan as before, insert the results into a worktable, then sort the worktable and return the results to the client.

System 10 SQL Server showplan output for this query shows the insert into a worktable in the first step. The second step of the plan has SQL Server sorting the worktable and returning the results to the client. Notice that although the type of query that was submitted by the client is SELECT, the type of query reported in the showplan output is INSERT. If you have a stream of showplan output, it might not be obvious which plan relates to which query.

The final step of the showplan example in Figure 9.6 represents the step sending data to the client. The absence of a TO TABLE line means that the results are being returned either to the client or to T-SQL variables.

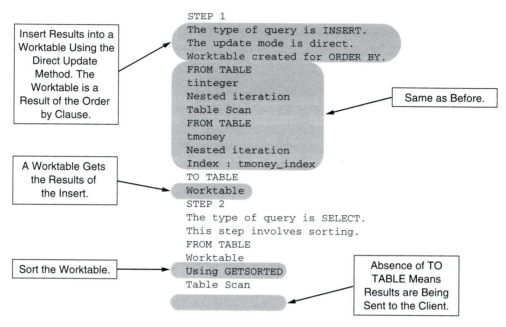

Figure 9.6 System 10 SQL Server showplan: join with order by- - - - - - - - - -

System 11 SQL Server produces a similar plan, although the showplan output has a different appearance. In the example output in Figure 9.7 notice that the worktable is identified as Worktable1. This makes interpreting showplan output much easier when there is more than one worktable involved in the query. In addition, because System 11 SQL Server indicates which query and the line number of the query in the batch, it is much easier to match up the query plan output with the queries in a large batch.

Notice that System 11 SQL Server chooses to use the Fetch and discard (MRU) buffer replacement strategy when it reads Worktable1. Because Worktable1 is dropped right after the query completes, there is no reason to cache the pages of this table with the LRU strategy. This means reading Worktable1 does not displace data from other tables from the data cache.

QUERY PLAN FOR STATEMENT 1 (at line 1).

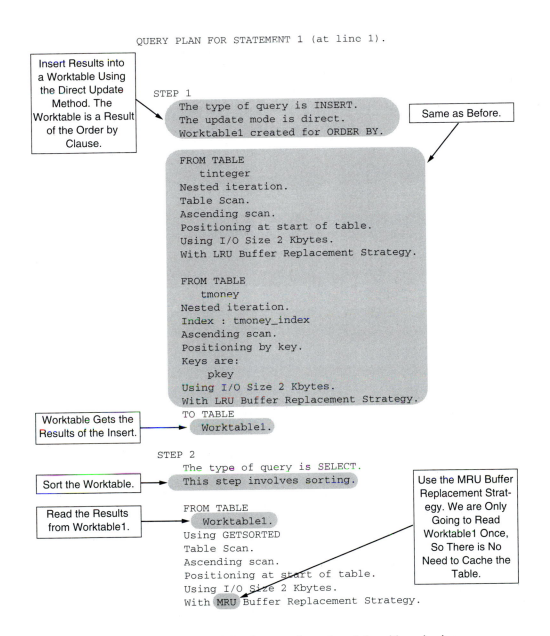

Insert Results into a Worktable Using the Direct Update Method. The Worktable is a Result of the Order by Clause.

STEP 1

    The type of query is INSERT.
    The update mode is direct.
    Worktable1 created for ORDER BY.

Same as Before.

    FROM TABLE
        tinteger
    Nested iteration.
    Table Scan.
    Ascending scan.
    Positioning at start of table.
    Using I/O Size 2 Kbytes.
    With LRU Buffer Replacement Strategy.

    FROM TABLE
        tmoney
    Nested iteration.
    Index : tmoney_index
    Ascending scan.
    Positioning by key.
    Keys are:
        pkey
    Using I/O Size 2 Kbytes.
    With LRU Buffer Replacement Strategy.

Worktable Gets the Results of the Insert.

    TO TABLE
        Worktable1.

STEP 2

    The type of query is SELECT.
    This step involves sorting.

Sort the Worktable.

Read the Results from Worktable1.

    FROM TABLE
        Worktable1.
    Using GETSORTED
    Table Scan.
    Ascending scan.
    Positioning at start of table.
    Using I/O Size 2 Kbytes.
    With MRU Buffer Replacement Strategy.

Use the MRU Buffer Replacement Strategy. We are Only Going to Read Worktable1 Once, So There is No Need to Cache the Table.

Figure 9.7   System 11 SQL Server showplan: join with order by- - - - - - - - - - -

271

9.1.5 Subquery

Consider the following select statement that includes a subquery:

```
select int from tinteger
        where pkey in (select a from t)
```

The table `tinteger` is the same as in the previous examples. The table `t` has a single integer column, `a`:

```
create table t (a int)
```

There are no indexes on `t`.

The obvious way to process this query is to read every row from `tinteger` and check for the existence of the `pkey` value in table `t`. Figure 9.8 and Figure 9.9 show showplan output for System 10 and System 11 SQL Servers processing the query in this way.

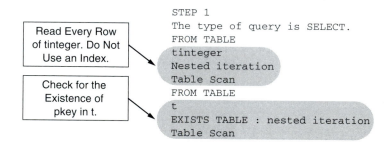

Figure 9.8   System 10 SQL Server showplan: simple subquery - - - - - - - - - - -

9.1.6 Correlated Subquery

A correlated subquery is a subquery that refers to tables from the outer query. For example:

```
select count(*)
        from tinteger ti1, tinteger ti2
        where ti1.int != ti2.int and
                not exists
                        (select 1 from t where t.a = ti1.int)
```

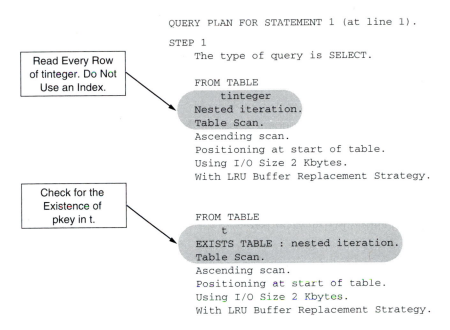

```
                    QUERY PLAN FOR STATEMENT 1 (at line 1).

                    STEP 1
                        The type of query is SELECT.

                    FROM TABLE
                            tinteger
                    Nested iteration.
                    Table Scan.
                    Ascending scan.
                    Positioning at start of table.
                    Using I/O Size 2 Kbytes.
                    With LRU Buffer Replacement Strategy.


                    FROM TABLE
                            t
                    EXISTS TABLE : nested iteration.
                    Table Scan.
                    Ascending scan.
                    Positioning at start of table.
                    Using I/O Size 2 Kbytes.
                    With LRU Buffer Replacement Strategy.
```

Read Every Row of tinteger. Do Not Use an Index.

Check for the Existence of pkey in t.

Figure 9.9   System 11 SQL Server showplan: simple subquery - - - - - - - - - - -

We use tables `tinteger` and `t` from the previous examples. This query counts the number of `int` pairs formed from `tinteger.int` where the first member of the pair is not in `t`.[2] A brief read through the query makes this clearer. We join `tinteger` with itself and exclude the pair of a value with itself (`ti1.int !=` `ti2.int`). Next, we use the subquery to exclude rows where the first `int` is in `t`.

As you can see from the showplan output for System 10 and System 11 SQL Servers, the two versions of SQL Server take very different approaches to processing this query. System 10 SQL Server takes the following approach:

1. Find all of the distinct `tinteger.int` values and put them in a worktable.

2. Join `tinteger` with `t` to identify which values of `tinteger.int` are disqualified by the `not exists` clause. Mark those values of `tinteger.int` as disqualified in the worktable. Now we have a list of the `tinteger.int` values we need to exclude from the `tinteger, tinteger` self join.

[2.] To make this a bit more concrete: Count all of the employees who do not share offices (office number is tinteger.int) where the first employee of the pair is not in a particular building (t.a are offices in a particular building).

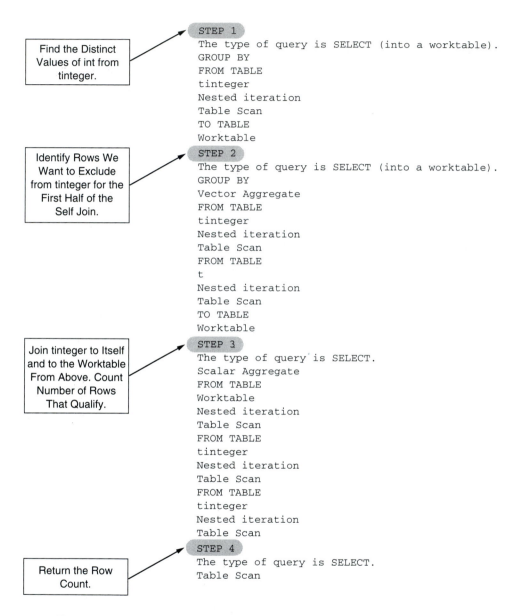

Find the Distinct Values of int from tinteger.

```
STEP 1
The type of query is SELECT (into a worktable).
GROUP BY
FROM TABLE
tinteger
Nested iteration
Table Scan
TO TABLE
Worktable
```

Identify Rows We Want to Exclude from tinteger for the First Half of the Self Join.

```
STEP 2
The type of query is SELECT (into a worktable).
GROUP BY
Vector Aggregate
FROM TABLE
tinteger
Nested iteration
Table Scan
FROM TABLE
t
Nested iteration
Table Scan
TO TABLE
Worktable
```

Join tinteger to Itself and to the Worktable From Above. Count Number of Rows That Qualify.

```
STEP 3
The type of query is SELECT.
Scalar Aggregate
FROM TABLE
Worktable
Nested iteration
Table Scan
FROM TABLE
tinteger
Nested iteration
Table Scan
FROM TABLE
tinteger
Nested iteration
Table Scan
```

Return the Row Count.

```
STEP 4
The type of query is SELECT.
Table Scan
```

Figure 9.10   System 10 SQL Server showplan: correlated subquery - - - - - - - -

3. Join all but the disqualified rows of the worktable with `ti1` and `ti2` (i.e., the self join) to compute the final row count.

4. Return the number of rows.

Subquery optimizer changes made to System 11 SQL Server improve the performance of this query (see Chapter 11, *Query Processing Performance* for a more complete explanation of the differences between System 11 SQL Server and previous versions of SQL Server in the handling of subqueries). To do so, System 11 SQL Server uses a more direct method to perform the correlated subquery. The general organization of the plan is much more like a regular join and does not involve a worktable. System 11 SQL Server scans the `tinteger` table, along the way executing the subquery for each row. If the subquery indicates that the row still qualifies for the query, the row is joined with every other row from `tinteger` (the self join). Along the way, we count up the number of rows that qualify.

The System 11 SQL Server showplan output is divided into two parts. The first part, in Figure 9.11, shows the query plan for the outer part of the query. The second part in Figure 9.12 shows the query plan for the subquery. The first part indicates when the second part is executed.

9.1.7 Update Statement

Up to now, all of the showplan examples have used the `select` command. This last set of examples focuses on the `update` command. As discussed in Chapter 5, *SQL Server — Methods and Features*, SQL Server has two different modes for updating data: direct mode and deferred mode. The showplan output indicates which mode is being used.

In the following examples, the table `tf` is created as:

```
create table tf (pkey numeric, float float, nfloat float null)
```
There is a unique nonclustered index on pkey.

```
create unique nonclustered index unci_tf on tf(pkey)
```

update tf set pkey = pkey + 1

This `update` statement is changing the key column. SQL Server must use a deferred update in order to avoid violating the uniqueness constraint on the `pkey` column imposed by the index. If the update mode were direct, the uniqueness constraint might prevent the update from succeeding. For example, suppose there are three rows in tf, with pkeys 1,2,3. If the update mode is direct, when the first pkey = 1 is updated to pkey+1 = 2, the new pkey = 2 cannot be inserted into the table because there is already a row with pkey = 2. With a deferred update, the entire update is written to the transaction log before any of the database pages are changed. This means the uniqueness can be checked after all of the changes are made, rather than while the change is underway.

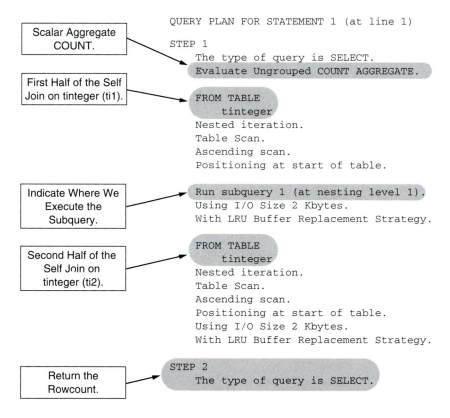

Figure 9.11   System 11 SQL Server showplan: correlated subquery (part 1)- - -

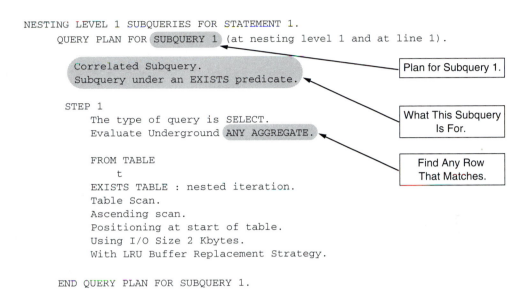

```
NESTING LEVEL 1 SUBQUERIES FOR STATEMENT 1.
      QUERY PLAN FOR SUBQUERY 1 (at nesting level 1 and at line 1).
```

Plan for Subquery 1.

```
      Correlated Subquery.
      Subquery under an EXISTS predicate.
```

What This Subquery Is For.

```
      STEP 1
            The type of query is SELECT.
            Evaluate Underground ANY AGGREGATE.
```

Find Any Row That Matches.

```
            FROM TABLE
                t
            EXISTS TABLE : nested iteration.
            Table Scan.
            Ascending scan.
            Positioning at start of table.
            Using I/O Size 2 Kbytes.
            With LRU Buffer Replacement Strategy.


      END QUERY PLAN FOR SUBQUERY 1.
```

Figure 9.12   System 11 SQL Server showplan: correlated subquery (part 2) - - -

System 10 SQL Server: 3955 Logical Reads

```
Table: tinteger  scan count 162,  logical reads 1134,  physical reads: 0
Table: tinteger  scan count 160,  logical reads 1120,  physical reads: 0
Table: t  scan count 400,  logical reads 400,  physical reads: 0
Table: Worktable  scan count 1,  logical reads 1301,  physical reads: 0
Table: writes for this command: 0
```

System 11 SQL Server: 1527 Logical Reads

```
Table: tinteger  scan count 1,  logical reads 7,  physical reads: 0
Table: tinteger  scan count 160,  logical reads 1120,  physical reads: 0
Table: t  scan count 400,  logical reads 400,  physical reads: 0
Table: writes for this command: 0
```

Figure 9.13   Comparison of statistics io output for correlated subquery - - - - - - -

277

```
STEP 1
The type of query is UPDATE.
The update mode is deferred.
FROM TABLE
tf
Nested iteration
Table Scan
TO TABLE
tf
```

Using the Deferred
Update Mode.

Figure 9.14   System 10 SQL Server showplan: unique key update- - - - - - - - - -

```
QUERY PLAN FOR STATEMENT 1 (at line 1).

    STEP 1
        The type of query is UPDATE.
        The update mode is deferred.

        FROM TABLE
            tf
        Nested iteration.
        Table Scan.
        Ascending scan.
        Positioning at start of table.
        Using I/O Size 2 Kbytes.
        With LRU Buffer Replacement Strategy.
        TO TABLE
            tf
```

Using the Deferred
Update Mode.

Figure 9.15   System 11 SQL Server showplan: unique key update- - - - - - - - - -

update tf set float = float * pkey

The second update is modifying the column `float`. The column `float` is a fixed length column, so SQL Server may use the direct update mode and update the row in place.

```
STEP 1
The type of query is UPDATE.
The update mode is direct.
FROM TABLE
tf
Nested iteration
Table Scan
TO TABLE
tf
```

Using the Direct
Update Mode.

Figure 9.16   System 10 SQL Server showplan: direct update - - - - - - - - - - - - -

```
QUERY PLAN FOR STATEMENT 1 (at line 1).

    STEP 1
        The type of query is UPDATE.
        The update mode is direct

        FROM TABLE
            tf
        Nested iteration.
        Table Scan.
        Ascending scan.
        Positioning at start of table.
        Using I/O Size 2 Kbytes.
        With LRU Buffer Replacement Strategy.
        TO TABLE
            tf
```

Using the Direct
Update Mode.

Figure 9.17   System 11 SQL Server showplan: direct update - - - - - - - - - - - - -

update tf set nfloat = nfloat / pkey

The third update is similar to the second, but the column `nfloat` allows nulls. A column that allows nulls is a variable length column and cannot be updated in place. As a result, SQL Server uses the deferred update mode and deletes the old row and inserts new rows.

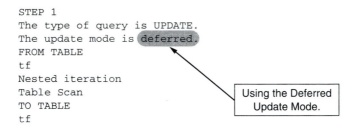

```
STEP 1
The type of query is UPDATE.
The update mode is  deferred.
FROM TABLE
tf
Nested iteration
Table Scan
TO TABLE
tf
```

Using the Deferred
Update Mode.

Figure 9.18   System 10 SQL Server showplan: variable length column update -

```
QUERY PLAN FOR STATEMENT 1 (at line 1).

    STEP 1
        The type of query is UPDATE.
        The update mode is  deferred_varcol.

        FROM TABLE
            tf
        Nested iteration.
        Table Scan.
        Ascending scan.
        Positioning at start of table.
        Using I/O Size 2 Kbytes.
        With LRU Buffer Replacement Strategy.
        TO TABLE
            tf
```

Using the Deferred
Update Mode.

Figure 9.19   System 11 SQL Server showplan: variable length column update -

9.1.8 Stored Procedure

Showplan displays the query plan for statements inside a stored procedure when the stored procedure is executed. This can be a problem sometimes if you have turned on showplan and then execute a long system stored procedure, `sp_help` for example. Most of the time, however, this is exactly the behavior that you want. Consider the following simple stored procedure:

```
create proc exproc (@a int) as begin
        print "input value: %1!",@a
        select * from tinteger where pkey = @a
end
```

The steps of the plan are in the same order as the statements in the stored procedure. Figure 9.20 shows the showplan output for executing this stored procedure on System 10 SQL Server. Figure 9.21 shows the similar output from System 11 SQL Server.

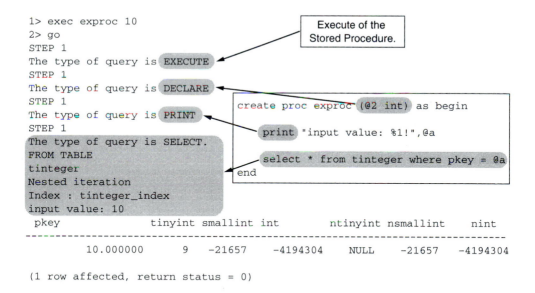

```
1> exec exproc 10
2> go
STEP 1
The type of query is EXECUTE         ┌─────────────────────┐
STEP 1                               │ Execute of the      │
The type of query is DECLARE         │ Stored Procedure.   │
STEP 1                               └─────────────────────┘
The type of query is PRINT          create proc exproc (@2 int) as begin
STEP 1
The type of query is SELECT.           print "input value: %1!",@a
FROM TABLE
tinteger                               select * from tinteger where pkey = @a
Nested iteration
Index : tinteger_index          end
input value: 10
  pkey            tinyint smallint int        ntinyint nsmallint    nint
------------------------------------------------------------------------
        10.000000       9   -21657   -4194304   NULL    -21657   -4194304

(1 row affected, return status = 0)
```

Figure 9.20   System 10 showplan execute stored procedure example - - - - - - -

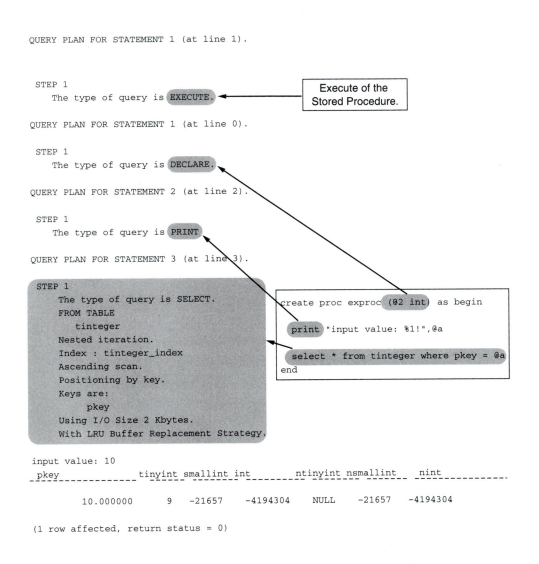

```
QUERY PLAN FOR STATEMENT 1 (at line 1).


    STEP 1
        The type of query is EXECUTE.              Execute of the
                                                   Stored Procedure.

QUERY PLAN FOR STATEMENT 1 (at line 0).

    STEP 1
        The type of query is DECLARE.

QUERY PLAN FOR STATEMENT 2 (at line 2).

    STEP 1
        The type of query is PRINT

QUERY PLAN FOR STATEMENT 3 (at line 3).

    STEP 1
        The type of query is SELECT.         create proc exproc (@2 int) as begin
        FROM TABLE
            tinteger                          print "input value: %1!",@a
        Nested iteration.
        Index : tinteger_index                select * from tinteger where pkey = @a
        Ascending scan.                      end
        Positioning by key.
        Keys are:
            pkey
        Using I/O Size 2 Kbytes.
        With LRU Buffer Replacement Strategy.

input value: 10
 pkey               tinyint smallint int        ntinyint nsmallint   nint
 ------------------ ------- -------- ---------- -------- --------- ----------------

         10.000000      9   -21657   -4194304    NULL    -21657    -4194304

(1 row affected, return status = 0)
```

Figure 9.21   System 11 SQL Server showplan: executing a stored procedure - -

9.1.9   Update with Trigger

When there is a trigger on a table, the plan for the trigger is included in the show-plan output for queries that manipulate data in the table. For example, suppose we create the following trigger on the table `tinteger`:

```
create trigger ut_tinteger on tinteger for update as
begin
        if update(int)
        begin
                print "inserted:"
                select * from inserted
                print "deleted:"
                select * from deleted
        end
end
```

Updating the table `tinteger` causes the trigger `ut_tinteger` to execute. The trigger's query plan is attached to the showplan output for any updates against `tinteger`. For example, the following query changes one row of `tinteger`:

```
update tinteger set int=50 where pkey = 1
```

It results in the output in Figure 9.22.

```
inserted:
 pkey                 tinyint smallint int          ntinyint nsmallint      nint
 -------------------- ------- -------- ----------- -------- --------- -----------
            1.000000       0   -31656          50     NULL    -31656 -2147483647
deleted:

(1 row affected)
 pkey                 tinyint smallint int          ntinyint nsmallint      nint
 -------------------- ------- -------- ----------- -------- --------- -----------
            1.000000       0   -31656 -2147483647     NULL    -31656 -2147483647

(1 row affected)
```

Figure 9.22   Output from update on a table with an update trigger - - - - - - - - - -

As with stored procedures, the steps of plan representing the trigger are ordered as are the statements in the trigger. Figure 9.23 shows showplan output for this update. Notice that the selects of inserted and deleted in the trigger involve scanning the log, not the table. The before and after images of the rows are stored in the transaction log.

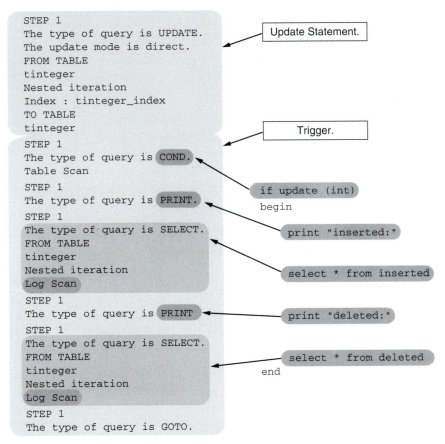

```
STEP 1
The type of query is UPDATE.            Update Statement.
The update mode is direct.
FROM TABLE
tinteger
Nested iteration
Index : tinteger_index
TO TABLE
tinteger
                                        Trigger.
STEP 1
The type of query is COND.
Table Scan
STEP 1                                  if update (int)
The type of query is PRINT.            begin
STEP 1
The type of quary is SELECT.
FROM TABLE                              print "inserted:"
tinteger
Nested iteration
Log Scan                                select * from inserted

STEP 1
The type of query is PRINT              print "deleted:"
STEP 1
The type of quary is SELECT.
FROM TABLE                              select * from deleted
tinteger
Nested iteration                        end
Log Scan
STEP 1
The type of query is GOTO.
```

Figure 9.23   System 10 showplan trigger example -

Figure 9.24 shows the first part of the showplan output for the same query and trigger in System 11. This part of the output represents the update statement. Figure 9.25 and Figure 9.26 show the rest of the showplan output. These two figures represent the trigger.

```
QUERY PLAN FOR SUBQUERY 1 (at line 1).

        STEP 1
            The type of query is UPDATE.
            The update mode is direct.

            FROM TABLE
                tinteger
            Nested iteration.
            Index : tinteger_index
            Ascending scan.
            Positioning by key.
            Keys are:
                pkey
            Using I/O Size 2 Kbytes.
            With LRU Buffer Replacement Strategy.
            TO TABLE
                tinteger
```

> Update Statement.

Figure 9.24   System 11 showplan trigger example (part 1) - - - - - - - - - - - - - - -

```
QUERY PLAN FOR STATEMENT 1 (at line 3).

    STEP 1
        The type of query is COND.
QUERY PLAN FOR STATEMENT 2 (at line 5).

    STEP 1
        The type of query is PRINT.

QUERY PLAN FOR STATEMENT 3 (at line 6)

    STEP 1
        The type of query is SELECT.

    FROM TABLE
        tinteger
    Nested iteration.
    Log Scan.
    Ascending scan.
    Positioning at start of table.
    Using I/O Size 2 Kbytes.
    With MRU Buffer Replacement Strategy.
```

```
if update (int)
  begin

    print "inserted:"

    select * from inserted
    print "deleted:"
    select * from deleted

  end
```

Figure 9.25   System 11 showplan trigger example (part 2) - - - - - - - - - - - - - - -

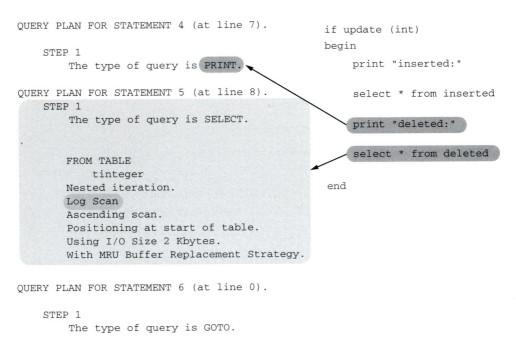

```
QUERY PLAN FOR STATEMENT 4 (at line 7).          if update (int)
                                                 begin
    STEP 1
        The type of query is PRINT.                  print "inserted:"

QUERY PLAN FOR STATEMENT 5 (at line 8).              select * from inserted
    STEP 1
        The type of query is SELECT.                 print "deleted:"


                                                     select * from deleted
    FROM TABLE
        tinteger
    Nested iteration.                            end
    Log Scan
    Ascending scan.
    Positioning at start of table.
    Using I/O Size 2 Kbytes.
    With MRU Buffer Replacement Strategy.


QUERY PLAN FOR STATEMENT 6 (at line 0).

    STEP 1
        The type of query is GOTO.
```

Figure 9.26 System 11 showplan trigger example (part 3) - - - - - - - - - - - - - - -

9.1.10 Constraints

Referential integrity constraints make SQL Server check that new data inserted into a table has the appropriate matching data in other tables.[3] For example:

```
create table tex
          (pkey numeric references tinteger(pkey), b int, c int)
```

---

3. This feature is available in System 10 and later versions of SQL Server.

When data is inserted into the table `tex`, SQL Server checks that the value for the column `pkey` is in `tinteger.pkey`. If the value is in `tinteger.pkey` the insert is allowed to go through. Otherwise the insert is rejected. Figure 9.27 lists the System 10 SQL Server showplan output for inserting a row into `tex`. Figure 9.28 is the similar showplan output from System 11 SQL Server.

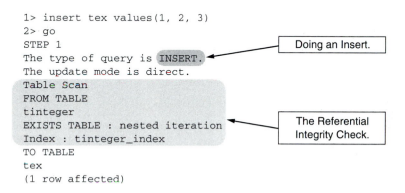

```
1> insert tex values(1, 2, 3)
2> go
STEP 1
The type of query is  INSERT.         ◄──── Doing an Insert.
The update mode is direct.
Table Scan
FROM TABLE
tinteger
EXISTS TABLE : nested iteration       ◄──── The Referential
Index : tinteger_index                        Integrity Check.
TO TABLE
tex
(1 row affected)
```

Figure 9.27   System 10 SQL Server showplan: referential integrity constraints -

9.1.11 Cursor

When cursors are used, SQL Server reports the query plan for the cursor when the cursor is declared. The cursor `open`, `fetch`, `close`, and `deallocation` are reported simply as those statements. Figure 9.29 shows the System 10 SQL Server showplan output for a cursor.

```
1> insert tex values(1, 2, 3)
2> go

QUERY PLAN FOR STATEMENT 1 (at line 1).

    STEP 1
        The type of query is INSERT.
        The update mode is direct.
```

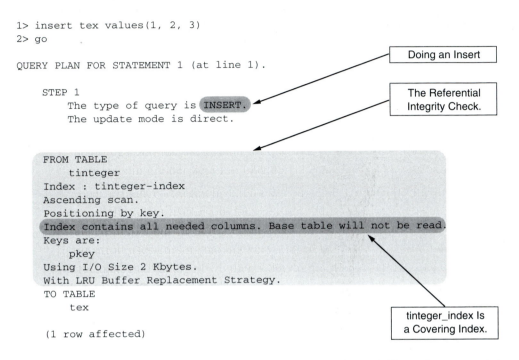

Doing an Insert

The Referential Integrity Check.

```
FROM TABLE
    tinteger
Index : tinteger-index
Ascending scan.
Positioning by key.
Index contains all needed columns. Base table will not be read.
Keys are:
    pkey
Using I/O Size 2 Kbytes.
With LRU Buffer Replacement Strategy.
TO TABLE
    tex

(1 row affected)
```

tinteger_index Is a Covering Index.

Figure 9.28   System 11 SQL Server showplan: referential integrity constraints -

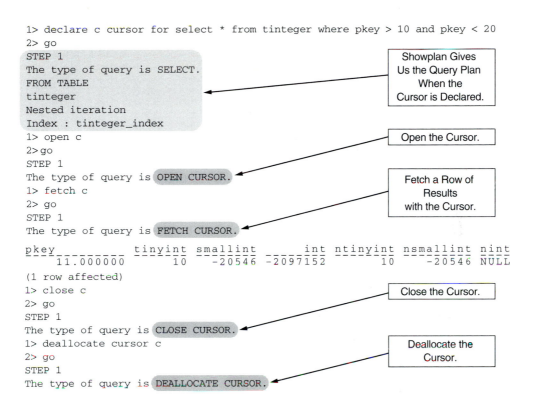

```
1> declare c cursor for select * from tinteger where pkey > 10 and pkey < 20
2> go
STEP 1
The type of query is SELECT.
FROM TABLE
tinteger
Nested iteration
Index : tinteger_index
1> open c
2> go
STEP 1
The type of query is OPEN CURSOR.
1> fetch c
2> go
STEP 1
The type of query is FETCH CURSOR.
pkey           tinyint  smallint       int  ntinyint  nsmallint  nint
  11.000000         10    -20546  -2097152        10     -20546  NULL
(1 row affected)
1> close c
2> go
STEP 1
The type of query is CLOSE CURSOR.
1> deallocate cursor c
2> go
STEP 1
The type of query is DEALLOCATE CURSOR.
```

Showplan Gives Us the Query Plan When the Cursor is Declared.

Open the Cursor.

Fetch a Row of Results with the Cursor.

Close the Cursor.

Deallocate the Cursor.

Figure 9.29   System 10 showplan cursor -

```
1> declare c cursor for select * from tinteger where pkey > 10 and pkey < 20
2> go

QUERY PLAN FOR STATEMENT 1 (at line 1)

STEP 1
    The type of query is SELECT.

    FROM TABLE
        tinteger
    Nested iteration.
    Index : tinteger_index
    Ascending scan.
    Positioning by key.
    Keys are:
        pkey
    Using I/O Size 2 Kbytes.
    With LRU Buffer Replacement Strategy.
```

Declaring the Cursor Produces the Showplan Output.

Figure 9.30   System 11 showplan cursor declaration - - - - - - - - - - - - - - - - - - -

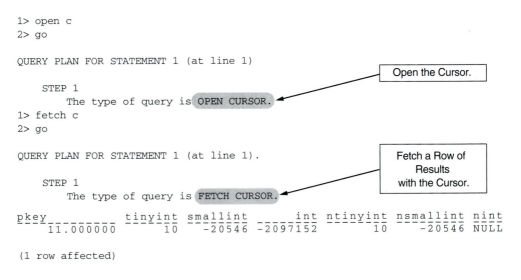

```
1> open c
2> go

QUERY PLAN FOR STATEMENT 1 (at line 1)

    STEP 1
        The type of query is OPEN CURSOR.
1> fetch c
2> go

QUERY PLAN FOR STATEMENT 1 (at line 1).

    STEP 1
        The type of query is FETCH CURSOR.
```

Open the Cursor.

Fetch a Row of Results with the Cursor.

```
pkey            tinyint smallint      int ntinyint nsmallint nint
     11.000000      10   -20546 -2097152      10    -20546 NULL

(1 row affected)
```

Figure 9.31   System 11 SQL Server showplan: cursor open and fetch - - - - - - -

```
1> close c
2> go

QUERY PLAN FOR STATEMENT 1 (at line 1)

    STEP 1
        The type of query is CLOSE CURSOR.
```

Close the Cursor.

```
1> deallocate cursor c
2> go

QUERY PLAN FOR STATEMENT 1 (at line 1).

    STEP 1
        The type of query is DEALLOCATE CURSOR
```

Deallocate the Cursor.

Figure 9.32   System 11 SQL Server showplan: cursor close and deallocate - - -

9.2   SET STATISTICS COMMANDS

9.2.1   Time Statistics

The set statistics time on command tells SQL Server to display the number of CPU ticks and milliseconds needed to parse and compile the query, and ticks and milliseconds needed to execute each step of the command. The execution time includes the amount of CPU time needed as well as the amount of real time needed to execute the command. When you set statistics time on, the first set of time statistics that SQL Server gives you, the statistics for the set statistics time on command itself, are sometimes wrong.

The example statistics time output in Figure 9.33 shows a query that required virtually no time to parse and compile, a total of 2 CPU time ticks (200 milliseconds on this machine) to execute the command. From the client's point of view (e.g., real time), the query needed 1033 milliseconds to execute. Notice that this query returned 2877 rows of results. Most of the real time was probably spent in transmitting the results from SQL Server to the client.

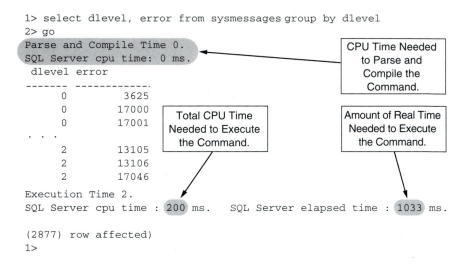

```
1> select dlevel, error from sysmessages group by dlevel
2> go
Parse and Compile Time 0.
SQL Server cpu time: 0 ms.
 dlevel error
------- ------------
      0         3625
      0        17000
      0        17001
 . . .
      2        13105
      2        13106
      2        17046
Execution Time 2.
SQL Server cpu time :  200  ms.   SQL Server elapsed time :  1033  ms.

(2877) row affected)
1>
```

CPU Time Needed
to Parse and
Compile the
Command.

Total CPU Time
Needed to Execute
the Command.

Amount of Real Time
Needed to Execute
the Command.

Figure 9.33 `set statistics time` **example output**- - - - - - - - - - - - - - - - -

When cursors are used, SQL Server returns the time statistics for each fetch individually.

```
1> declare c cursor for select * from tinteger where pkey > 10 and pkey < 20
2> go
Parse and Compile Time 1.
SQL Server cpu time: 100 ms.

Execution Time 0.
SQL Server cpu time: 0 ms.  SQL Server elapsed time: 0 ms.
1> open c
2> go
Parse and Compile Time 0.
SQL Server cpu time: 0 ms.

Execution Time 0.
SQL Server cpu time: 0 ms.  SQL Server elapsed time: 0 ms.
1> fetch c
2> go
Parse and Compile Time 0.
SQL Server cpu time: 0 ms.
 pkey                  tinyint smallint int          ntinyint nsmallint       nint
 -------------------- ------- -------- ----------- -------- --------- -----------
            11.000000      10   -20546    -2097152       10    -20546        NULL

Execution Time 1.
SQL Server cpu time: 100 ms.  SQL Server elapsed time: 0 ms.

(1 row affected)
1> fetch c
2> go
Parse and Compile Time 0.
SQL Server cpu time: 0 ms.
 pkey                  tinyint smallint int          ntinyint nsmallint       nint
 -------------------- ------- -------- ----------- -------- --------- -----------
            12.000000      11   -19435    -1048576       11      NULL    -1048576

Execution Time 0.
SQL Server cpu time: 0 ms.  SQL Server elapsed time: 0 ms.

(1 row affected)
1> close c
2> go
Parse and Compile Time 0.
SQL Server cpu time: 0 ms.

Execution Time 0.
SQL Server cpu time: 0 ms.  SQL Server elapsed time: 3 ms.
1> deallocate cursor c
2> go
Parse and Compile Time 1.
SQL Server cpu time: 100 ms.

Execution Time 0.
SQL Server cpu time: 0 ms.  SQL Server elapsed time: 3 ms.
```

Figure 9.34 `set statistics time` **example output for cursors** - - - - - - - - -

9.2.2   IO Statistics

The `set statistics io on` command tells SQL Server to report the number of table scans, logical reads, physical reads, and writes for each table used in the query. The write count includes the number of log pages written.

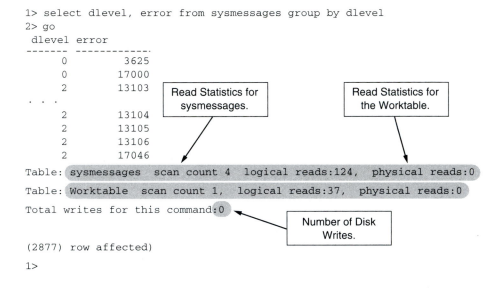

```
1> select dlevel, error from sysmessages group by dlevel
2> go
 dlevel error
 ------- -------------
      0          3625
      0         17000
      2         13103
  . . .
      2         13104
      2         13105
      2         13106
      2         17046
Table: sysmessages   scan count 4   logical reads:124,   physical reads:0
Table: Worktable   scan count 1,   logical reads:37,   physical reads:0
Total writes for this command:0

(2877) row affected)

1>
```

Read Statistics for sysmessages.

Read Statistics for the Worktable.

Number of Disk Writes.

Figure 9.35 `set statistics io` output -

When cursors are used, the I/O statistics are cumulative for the duration of the cursor. The statistics reset when you close and open the cursor again. Each time you fetch with the cursor, the I/O statistics are updated and displayed. This differs from the time statistics which give you information about each fetch individually.

System 11 `statistics io` output identifies worktables similarly to the way worktables are identified in System 11 showplan output.

Some select statements include writes. In many cases the writes are for worktables. If you find worktables in the showplan output, chances are the writes are for the worktable. In some cases a worktable is not involved. These writes result from:

- Dirty pages from the pervious command being written because select needs clean buffers.

- Begin tran and commit tran log records.

- Some internal processing of the pages.

```
1> declare c cursor for select * from tinteger where pkey > 10 and pkey < 20
2> go
Total writes for this command: 0
1> open c                                        ┌─────────────────────┐
2> go                                            │ No pages Read Yet.   │
Table: tinteger scan count 0, logical reads  0,  physical reads: 0
Total writes for this command: 0
1> fetch c
2> go
pkey           tinyint smallint      int ntinyint nsmallint nint
   11.000000        10  -20546 -2097152       10    -20546 NULL
Table: tinteger scan count 1, logical reads:  3,  physical reads: 0
Total writes for this command: 0                 ┌─────────────────────┐
                                                 │ Read Three Pages    │
(1 row affected)                                 │ to Fetch First Result.│
1> fetch c
2> go
pkey           tinyint smallint      int ntinyint nsmallint      nint
   12.000000        11  -19435 -1048576       11      NULL -1048576
Table: tinteger scan count 1, logical reads:  4,  physical reads: 0
Total writes for this command: 0
                                                 ┌─────────────────────┐
(1 row affected)                                 │ Read One Pages      │
1> fetch c                                       │ to Fetch Next Result.│
2> go
pkey           tinyint smallint      int ntinyint nsmallint    nint
   13.000000        12  -18324 -524288     NULL    -18324 -524288
Table: tinteger scan count 1, logical reads:  5,  physical reads: 0
Total writes for this command: 0
                                                 ┌─────────────────────┐
(1 row affected)                                 │ Read Another Page   │
1> close c                                       │ to Fetch Next Result.│
2> go
Total writes for this command: 0
1> deallocate cursor c
2> go
Total writes for this command: 0
1>
```

Figure 9.36 set statistics io output for cursor - - - - - - - - - - - - - - - - - - -

9.2.3 Subquery Cache Statistics

System 11 SQL Server introduces the command:

```
set statistics subquerycache on
```

to monitor the usage of the subquery cache. The subquery cache plays an important role in the outside-in subquery processing strategy used by System 11 SQL Server. This is discussed in more detail in Chapter 11, *Query Processing Performance*, "Subquery Processing: System 11 SQL Server" on page 422. Figure 9.37 shows a sample session using the set statistics subquerycache on command and Figure 9.38 shows the statistics output.

```
set statistics subquerycache on
go
select c_d_id, avg(c_balance)
        from customer c
        where     c_w_id = 10
        and       c_d_id not in
                  (select d_id from district
                                where     d_w_id = c.c_w_id
                                and       d_id   = c.c_d_id
                                and       d_ytd  >= 1000000.00)
        group by c_d_id
   go
```

Figure 9.37   Set subquerycache query -

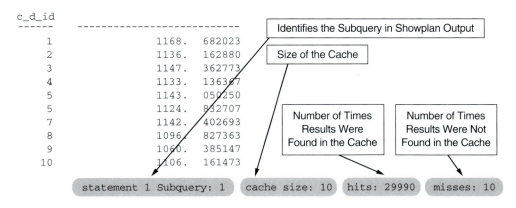

Figure 9.38   Set subquerycache output -

9.3   STORED PROCEDURES

Instrumenting stored procedures can tell you how often the procedures are being used and how long they take to execute. As with most instrumentation techniques, it is difficult to get accurate measurements without perturbing the thing you are trying to measure. You should use these techniques carefully and consider the ramifications of the instrumentation on your queries.

The instrumentation is implemented by creating two tables. One holds the start time of the stored procedure and the other the end time. An identity column on the start table allows us to match up the start and end times in the two tables. SQL Server automatically provides us with a number that uniquely identifies the particular execution of the stored procedure. We use this as the key value in the finish table.

```
create table
        start_history (id numeric identity, date datetime)
create table
        finish_history(id numeric, date datetime)
```

Add the following lines to the beginning of each stored procedure you want to measure:

```
declare @id numeric
insert start_history(date) values(getdate())
select @id = @@identity
```

on finish:

```
insert finish_history(id,date) values(@id,getdate())
```

Figure 9.39 shows how to include these statements in a stored procedure.

```
create procedure exproc (...) as
begin
        declare @id numeric
        insert start_history(date) values(getdate())
        select @id = @@identity

        -- body of stored procedure exproc

        insertfinish_history(id,date)values(@id,getdate())
end
```

Figure 9.39   Instrumenting stored procedures -

There is some performance penalty associated with this instrumentation. Stored procedures become single threaded on the insert to `start_history` and `finish_history`. You can reduce contention by using different history tables for each stored procedure. If you have one stored procedure that is used very frequently, you can consider partitioning the history tables by creating extra copies of the stored procedure, each of which uses a different history table. The performance penalty is not severe if the stored procedure is already single threaded at some other point in the processing. Changes to the two history tables are logged, so there is some increase on the amount of data logged during the execution of the stored procedure.

A relatively simple query matches the start and finish times and creates a histogram of the time taken to execute the procedure.

```
select
        duration = datediff(second,f.date,s.date),
        times = count(*)
from
        start_history s, finish_history f
where
        s.id = f.id
group by 1
order by 1
```

Each row of the result has the amount of time it took to execute the stored procedure and the number of times the stored procedure took that long to execute. You can change the granularity of the histogram by adjusting the units in the `datediff`. If your stored procedures run very quickly, you can use millisecond; if they take longer, perhaps minute (or per hour) is the more appropriate time unit.

You can make the analysis more sophisticated by creating histograms for various times of the day by adding a time restriction to the where clause:

```
... and datepart(hour,s.date) between 8 and 9
```

To get a more visual display, you can use the string function `replicate()` to produce a character bar chart:

```
select
        duration = replicate("X",
                datediff(second,f.date,s.date))
from
        start_history s, finish_history f
where
        s.id = f.id
```

```
group by 1
order by 1
```

The history tables grow whenever the instrumented stored procedure is executed. You need to truncate the history tables now and then. A good time might be just after summary data is collected.

Chapter 10

Transaction Processing Performance

Transaction processing applications are often the backbone of business computing environments. High performance, reliability, and availability are not just desirable in such applications — they are essential to the very survival of the business. One cannot overemphasize the importance of performance, reliability, and availability in operations as indispensable as banking, customer service, inventory control, order-entry, reservation systems, trading, and the like.

The level of reliability and availability required varies over a wide range. For example, an hour of scheduled maintenance may be acceptable for a World Wide Web server or an electronic BBS, but absolutely unacceptable for an on-line trading system or an ambulance service. Similarly, the range of performance required of the transaction processing application varies over a wide range. Systems for large applications, such as those typically found in telephone companies, credit card agencies, overnight shipping services, and pay-per-view cable television services, may need to handle thousands of customer interactions simultaneously. On the other hand, small transaction processing applications such as a bookstore or a chain of restaurants may never see more than ten concurrent users. The challenge in tuning the performance of a transaction processing application lies in providing the required performance *without* compromising the requirements on reliability and availability.

Typical transaction processing applications are characterized by:

1. Large number of users
2. Large number of short to medium-length transactions
3. Large number of update, insert, and delete operations
4. Emphasis on reliability, availability, and performance of recovery
5. High degree of contention for resources
6. Emphasis on data and transactional integrity
7. Canned procedures, not ad hoc queries

Transaction processing systems can be **on-line** or **batch-processing**. An on-line transaction processing (OLTP) system services multiple concurrent users, often interactively. Hence, response time is an extremely important aspect of the performance of OLTP systems. Probably the best-known examples of OLTP systems are the airline reservation systems.

Batch-processing systems process transactions in large batches, instead of catering to users interactively. Examples of batch-processing systems include the credit card operations of some gas companies. Instead of verifying the balance of a customer interactively, they collect all transactions that have taken place at a single gas station or for a small region over a period of time and then transmit the transactions to a central location to be processed as a batch.

Batch processing systems can provide higher throughput or lower cost than on-line systems. However, their applicability is more limited than an on-line system. Even for applications where batch-processing is acceptable, on-line processing is often deemed more desirable than batch processing. Recent advances in both price and performance have made on-line processing feasible and cost-effective for all but a few exceptionally large applications. Hence, in the remainder of this book, we assume that the transactions are processed on-line. However, the techniques discussed in this chapter are equally applicable to batch-processing systems.

The performance of Relational Database Management Systems for OLTP applications has been a controversial topic since the introduction of RDBMS products over a decade ago. Until very recently most, if not all industry-standard benchmarks have used OLTP as the primary basis for comparing the performance of RDBMS products. Consequently, several RDBMS and hardware vendors have spent a great deal of effort to tune their products for OLTP performance. This is both good and bad news for you.

The good news is that the you can buy products off the shelf that are highly tuned for OLTP. The bad news is that each comes with sufficiently many knobs and dials to baffle even the most dedicated DBA. Even worse, some products incorporate **benchmark specials:** features and techniques that have limited or no applicability other than in the standard benchmarks. We discuss techniques that you can actually use.

Understanding the architecture and idiosyncracies of SQL Server can help you get the most performance out of your application. Doing so beyond the bounds of reason can be counterproductive and may compromise the portability and maintainability of your application. Of course, the bounds of reason depend on your desire for performance. We spend most of our time on techniques that are fundamental to the performance of SQL Server on transaction processing applications and do not require any more than a general familiarity with SQL Server.

10.1 CONFIGURING FOR OLTP

10.1.1 Checkpoint and Recovery

The frequency and duration of checkpoint is extremely important to the performance of transaction processing applications that perform a lot of `insert`, `delete`, and `update` statements. Inserts, updates, and deletes dirty pages in memory. Checkpoint writes out dirty pages to disks. Frequent checkpoints ensure quick recovery from crashes. However, they may do so at the cost of throughput and response. To see this, consider a *hot* page that is updated very frequently. The LRU buffer replacement tries to keep this page in memory. As long as this page is kept in memory, updates to this page do not cause additional I/O operations. However, every checkpoint forces this page to be written out to the disk. Thus, checkpoints increase the number of writes to disks.

Generally speaking, the writes caused by checkpoints in OLTP applications by SQL Server are *random writes*. That is, even if the same checkpoint process eventually writes out several blocks on the same track on the disk, it rarely does so in an order that minimizes the movement of the disk head. The order in which pages of a table or index are written out by the checkpoint process is determined by the chronological order in which they were dirtied and not by their physical address. The additional random writes to the disks can affect throughput and/or response time if I/O performance is a bottleneck.

There is an additional dimension to the performance of checkpoints: their **intensity**. An intense checkpoint process takes over the entire I/O bandwidth of the server for a short period of time while it writes out all the dirty pages to disks as fast as possible. The effect of such a checkpoint on the throughput and response of concurrent OLTP is drastic, but short-lived. A less intense, controlled checkpoint process limits itself to only a part of the I/O bandwidth of the server. Such a checkpoint takes longer, but its impact on the throughput and response of concurrent OLTP is minimal.

SQL Server supports only the controlled checkpoint. Before System 11 SQL Server the checkpoint process is limited to 10 concurrent asynchronous writes. This ensures that the impact of checkpoint on the I/O subsystem is limited to 10 asynchronous I/O operations. System 11 SQL Server can issue more than 10 asynchronous writes, depending on the configuration and number of named caches. We discuss checkpoints on System 11 SQL Server in Chapter 12, *Batch Processing Performance*.

You may want to tailor the frequency and timing of checkpoints to the requirements of your application. For example, you may want to checkpoint databases after, not during, certain critical operations. Or the characteristics of your application may allow you to trade frequency of checkpoints for performance. You can control the frequency and timing of checkpoints using the configuration options `recovery interval in minutes` and `trunc log on chkpt`. The frequency of automatic checkpoints depends on the above two configuration options as follows:

SQL Server examines each database once every minute to see whether it needs to be checkpointed. The database option `trunc log on chkpt`, if set, causes SQL Server to perform a checkpoint (and truncate the log) on the database in question once every minute, regardless of the recovery interval configuration value. Therefore, if your intention is to control the frequency of automatic checkpoints on a database, you must set the above option to false for the database using `sp_dboption`.

Assuming `trunc log on chkpt` is set to false, SQL Server decides whether or not to initiate a checkpoint on the database in question depending on the estimated time to recover from a failure at that instant. If the estimated time to recover exceeds the value of the configuration parameter `recovery interval in minutes`, then a checkpoint process is started. Thus, the value of this configuration option is inversely related to the frequency of checkpoints. A value of 5 (the default value) indicates that SQL Server initiates a checkpoint on every database that has seen a sufficient number of updates, inserts, or deletes since the last checkpoint to warrant an estimated recovery interval of over five minutes. You can reduce the frequency of checkpoints by setting this configuration parameter to a higher value.

A value as high as 2000 (minutes) effectively disables automatic checkpoints and can be used to take complete control over the timing and frequency of checkpoints. If you use such a high value, you should make very sure that your application or the DBA does not forget to perform periodic checkpoints on all databases on SQL Server.

10.1.2 Memory Management

The total amount of memory available to SQL Server is denoted by the configuration parameter `total memory` and is measured in 2048 byte pages. To change the amount of memory available to SQL Server, you need to change the value of this configuration parameters following the procedure described in Appendix B, *SQL Server Configuration* and reboot SQL Server. Part of this memory is used to store stack, extent i/o buffers, and sort buffers (used during index creation), buffers used to hold incoming and outgoing network packets, and several other internal data structures. SQL Server uses the remaining memory to store compiled stored procedures and cache data and index pages. Having sufficient memory and apportioning it appropriately among alternative usages is critical to performance. Figure 10.1 shows some of the lines logged by SQL Server in the errorlog file that denote memory usage.

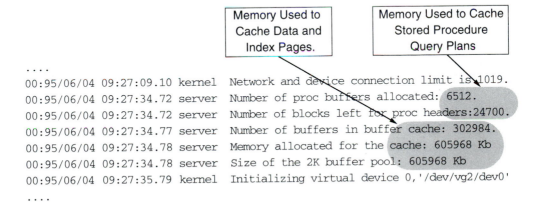

Figure 10.1   Buffer information from SQL Server errorlog file - - - - - - - - - - - - - -

Figure 10.2 shows the values of some of the configuration parameters that determine memory usage by SQL Server.

```
1> sp_configure
2> go
name                             minimum     maximum    config_value run_value
----------------------------  ----------- -----------  ------------ ----------
.... (selected lines only)
user connections                       5  2147483647            60         60
memory                              1000  2147483647        350000     350000
locks                               5000  2147483647         10000      10000
procedure cache                        1          99             2          2
stack size                         20480  2147483647             0      28672
additional netmem                      0  2147483647        737280     737280
default network packet size          512      524288             0        512
maximum network packet size          512      524288          4096       4096
extent i/o buffers                     0  2147483647            33         33
```

Figure 10.2   Part of the output from sp_configure -

Procedure Cache

The configuration parameter procedure cache denotes the fraction of the remaining memory used for storing compiled stored procedures, expressed as a percentage. For example, if your SQL Server is left with 10000 pages after allocating memory for stack, network, extent i/o buffers, etc., and procedure cache is 20, SQL Server uses 2000 pages of memory to store compiled stored procedures. Although the configuration parameters express the amount of memory in procedure cache as a fraction of the total memory, there is no reason the former should scale with the latter. Therefore, if you alter the total amount of memory in your SQL Server, you should consider changing the above fraction as well.

The amount of memory needed to store compiled stored procedures depends only on the size and number of stored procedures *in use* simultaneously and not on the total number of stored procedures in the database. Further, it increases with the number of concurrent invocations of the stored procedures. You should consider resizing the procedure cache if either the number of users or the size or number of active stored procedures changes.

Essential to the process of sizing the procedure cache is the ability to judge whether you have too much or too little procedure cache. You can determine this by the monitor counter `procedure reads`, which indicates the number of times SQL Server had to read a procedure off the disk, following the instructions in Chapter 8, *Monitoring SQL Server*. You have sufficient procedure cache if the number of procedure reads is zero or a small number. If so, you may want to decrease the size of the procedure cache until you see an increase in the number of procedure reads.

Buffer Cache

SQL Server needs to have sufficient memory in order to keep the most frequently accessed indexes and/or tables in cache. The **logical reads** generated by the optimizer and the access methods are requests for pages. If the requested pages are not found in memory, the buffer manager performs **physical reads** to read them off the disk. The number of physical and logical reads is critical to the performance of transaction processing, and can be monitored using the techniques described in Chapter 8, *Monitoring SQL Server*, and Chapter 9, *Instrumenting SQL Code*.

You may be able to improve the performance of your application by ensuring that SQL Server is caching appropriate indexes and table. The brute-force approach is to throw more memory at the problem. However, the real challenge is to use the available memory more effectively. The example in Figure 10.3 illustrates the effect of caching index and data pages on OLTP performance.

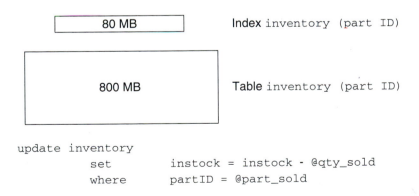

```
update inventory
        set         instock = instock - @qty_sold
        where       partID = @part_sold
```

Figure 10.3   Effect of caching index and data pages on OLTP- - - - - - - - - - - - -

Table inventory tracks the quantity in-stock for a large number of parts and is updated very frequently by a large number of salespersons using a nonclustered index on `partID`. Suppose this is the only activity on SQL Server, we have 100MB of buffer cache, and the sizes of the tables and indexes are as indicated in Figure 10.3.

First, let us assume that the distribution of `partID` updates is uniformly random over the range of all values for `partID`. For best performance, the optimal solution is to cache the entire index. With the entire index cached, each select reads at most one data page from disk. That is, the expected number of cache misses per transaction is less than 1. However, SQL Server most likely uses a significant part of the buffer cache to cache data pages from the inventory table, since the least recently used (LRU) buffer replacement policy does not differentiate between data and index pages. If so, the performance is suboptimal. To see this, assume that SQL Server caches 50MB each of data and index.[1] Then, approximately $(80 - 50)/80 = 3/8$ of the accesses to the leaf-level page of the index need to read an index page from the disk, and approximately $(800 - 50)/800 = 15/16$ of the accesses to the data pages need to read a data page from the disk. Thus, the expected number of pages read per update is $3/8 + 15/16 = 21/16$, or over 1.31. Recall that the optimal value is less than 1.

One way to improve performance in the above scenario is to increase the size of the buffer cache. For example, suppose you increased the size of the buffer cache to 200MB, thus enabling SQL Server to cache all 80 MB of index and 120MB of data. Then, the number of data pages read per update is again less than 1. Alternatively, you could keep the size of buffer cache at 100MB and improve performance by instructing SQL Server to extend preferential treatment to index pages. By preferential treatment, we mean overriding the default LRU buffer replacement policy to keep certain pages in memory even if they happen to be among the least recently used ones. We discuss ways to accomplish this in "Index and OAM Trips" on page 328, and "Using Named Caches to Improve Cache Hit Ratio" on page 311.

Now, let us address the more realistic scenario where the distribution of `partID`s being updated is not uniform over the range of all values for `partID`. Let us assume a skewed distribution, with 5% of the data pages and 20% of the leaf-level index pages[2] accounting for over 80% of all the updates. Then, SQL Server is

---

[1.] This assumes that all but the leaf-level pages of the index are always in cache. This is often the case.

likely to keep most of the $800 \times 0.05 + 80 \times 0.2 = 56$ MB of *hot* pages in buffer cache in its standard configuration. In this case, it does not pay to force SQL Server to provide preferential treatment to index pages.

To summarize, you need to ensure that the buffer cache is large enough to cache the most frequently accessed indexes and tables. However, the size of the buffer cache in itself is not a guarantee that all the intended objects are cached. Depending on the characteristics of your application, you may need to alter the configuration of individual tables and indexes, as described later in this chapter, to achieve optimal performance.

Wash Size

Transaction processing applications often perform a large number of operations that dirty pages, including inserts, updates, and deletes. Using the write-ahead log (WAL) protocol, SQL Server keeps dirty pages in memory instead of writing them to disk even after the transaction that dirtied those pages has committed. This reduces the number of writes to disks when several transactions dirty the same page. Except for certain notable exceptions (e.g., page splits and rollbacks), SQL Server does not write dirty pages to disk until they age out of memory or a checkpoint flushes them out. The mechanism used for aging out dirty buffers is known as **bufwash**. The configuration parameter `cbufwashsize` in System 10 and earlier versions of SQL Server is the measure of the number of least recently used buffers that SQL Server attempts to keep clean. That is, if the wash size is 256, then SQL Server automatically initiates a write on a dirty page as soon as it ages to become one of the 256 least recently used buffers. An increase in the wash size has the following effects:

1. **An increase in the supply of clean buffers** — This can be an advantage if your application may suddenly need a large supply of clean buffers. Examples include creation of large temporary objects while scanning tables that are already in caches, table scans, scans using clustered indexes, and use of super-fast disks such as SSD and nvRAM.

2. **An increase in the number of writes to disks** — In its attempt to keep a large supply of clean buffers, SQL Server is forced to write out some dirty buffers that are likely to be used again or deleted before they become the least recently

---

[2.] Typically, the effect of skew is more obvious when there are fewer entries per page. Index pages typically contain more entries per page than data pages.

used buffer. Examples include creation and deletion of tables and indexes in `tempdb` and large worktables. A large wash size may force them to be written to disk, whereas with the default bufwash configuration they would not involve any I/O operations at all.

3. **A reduction in the time to checkpoint** — Since there are fewer dirty pages to write out, checkpoint has less work to do. To make a significant difference in the time to checkpoint, wash size has to be of the same order of magnitude as the total number of buffers. There are almost always better alternatives to improving checkpoint time than to use an inordinately large wash size.

If your application has the additional property of occasionally requiring a large supply of clean buffers, then the default was size of 256 may not suffice. Such cases are extremely rare. Suppose the time to complete a disk write is 10ms. Then a wash size of 256 allows your application to use up clean pages at a steady rate of 256 buffers every 10ms, or over 50MB/sec. If a bottleneck at any one disk can occasionally cause a disk write to take (say) 100ms, then this number reduces to 5MB/sec. This may not be sufficient if your application uses clean buffers in short bursts rather than steadily. The real solution to this problem is to alleviate the bottleneck at the slowest disk. An increase in the size of the wash area is a short-term solution.

While a larger supply of clean buffers may improve response, it generally does not improve throughput. This is because all a larger value of bufwash does is to initiate the writing of a page earlier than otherwise, it does not reduce the absolute number of I/O operations. However, an unusually small value of bufwash can result in a situation where the least recently used buffer, the buffer SQL Server wants to use next, is still in the process of being written out. This is highly undesirable, because SQL Server must freeze all activity in the database until this write completes. This, of course, has a rather drastic and adverse effect on all aspects of performance. Thus, the ground rule in terms of sizing the wash area is to make it large enough to prevent the above situation from occurring. Any value larger than that is a waste. The default value of 256 suffices for most applications.

10.1.3 Memory Management with System 11 SQL Server

Starting with System 11, SQL Server supports multiple named caches and multiple buffer pools within each named cache. Tables, indexes, and databases can be bound to specific named caches. Pages from a table, index, or database are cached only in the named caches that they are bound to. We discuss the process of creating and managing named caches later in Chapter 13, *Advanced Topics*. In the remainder of this section, let us discuss some of the ways that named caches can be used to improve performance of transaction processing applications.

Using Named Caches to Improve Cache Hit Ratio

As illustrated by the example in the previous section, cache utilization can benefit from tailoring the buffer replacement policies to the characteristics of specific tables and indexes. You can control the caching of specific tables, indexes, and databases by binding them to named caches and sizing the named caches appropriately. For example, you may be able to reduce the number of I/O operations drastically by binding a small index or table that is used very frequently to a named cache large enough to contain all hot pages. If your application creates a lot of temporary objects, then you may stand to gain by binding `tempdb` to its own cache and making it large enough to preclude I/O on temporary objects. One of the simplest and yet most effective applications of this technique is to put frequently used indexes into named caches large enough to hold the entire index.

Using Named Caches to Reduce Impact of Checkpoints

The performance of checkpoint and its effect on the performance of concurrent transaction processing depends largely on the number of dirty pages in memory. For certain applications the LRU buffer replacement policy tends to keep dirty pages in memory longer than necessary. Besides deteriorating cache utilization this has the adverse effect of exacerbating the cost of checkpoints as the I/O subsystem is under utilized between checkpoints and overutilized during checkpoints. Named caches may be able to help you control the residency of dirty pages in memory. For example, consider an application where transactions keep inserting rows into a table. As this table grows, new pages are created. After a new page is full, LRU replacement keeps it in memory until it ages to become the least recently used page in cache. If this table grows fast enough, a substantial fraction of your buffer cache may be used up by dirty pages from this table.[3] In this case, the cost of a checkpoint can be rather high.

---

[3] The log is a special case of such a table, although log pages are usually written to disk long before they are aged out by the LRU replacement policy. Events that cause log pages to be written out include commit, rollback, and page splits.

You can use named caches to alleviate the above and similar problems. The trick is to bind the offending table to a named cache and size the named cache and its wash area so that the dirty pages are written to disk sooner rather than later. This causes SQL Server to write out dirty pages continually rather than saving them for the checkpoint.

Using Named Caches to Improve Scalability

One of the factors that limits the scalability of SQL Server to multiple engines/CPUs on high-volume transaction processing applications is the sequential nature of the data structures used by the buffer manager in enforcing the LRU buffer replacement policy. Basically, SQL Server needs to maintain a queue that lists the buffers in chronological order of their most recent use. The need to maintain strict chronological order forces engines to synchronize their usage of buffers. This synchronization limits scalability.

Named caches can alleviate this problem by binding the most frequently used tables, indexes, or databases to separate named caches. This eliminates the need to maintain a single queue for all pages in cache, since we now have a separate queue for each named cache. You should assess the number of logical reads on individual tables and indexes in your application and partition them among named caches in such a way that no one cache accounts for a disproportionate number of logical reads. Beware that the actual number of logical reads may not be intuitive. For example, assuming there is a clustered index on `T(x)`, the simple `select` statement:

```
select * from T where x between 5 and 10
```

most likely performs $k-1$ logical reads on the clustered index on `T`, and p logical reads on the table `T`, where k is the depth of the clustered index and p is the number of pages that contain matching rows. If most of your SQL statements access only one page, then the number of logical reads on the index may outnumber the number of logical reads on the table by a factor equal to the number of levels in the index. If such is the case, it may make sense to put the most frequently accessed index in a cache by itself.

Among the most frequently accessed pages in almost any transaction processing application on SQL Server are the pages holding `sysindexes` and the clustered index on `sysindexes`. It often helps performance to create a small named cached specifically for these two database objects.

10.1.4 Other Server Configuration Parameters

There are several other configuration options that influence the performance of SQL Server on transaction processing applications. Figure 10.4 shows part of the output from `sp_configure`. The values for the parameters shown here are provided only as examples. The values you need to use to optimize SQL Server to your application depend on the exact nature of your application.

```
name                        minimum      maximum     config_value run_value
--------------------------- -----------  ----------- ------------ -----------
user connections                     5  2147483647           60          60
locks                             5000  2147483647        10000       10000
open objects                       100  2147483647            0         500
fill factor                          0         100            0           0
time slice                          50        1000            0         100
nested triggers                      0           1            1           1
devices                              4         256           60          60
remote connections                   0  2147483647            0          20
pre-read packets                     0  2147483647            0           3
max online engines                   1          32            7           7
min online engines                   1          32            1           1
engine adjust interval               1          32            0           0
additional netmem                    0  2147483647       737280      737280
default network packet size        512      524288            0         512
maximum network packet size        512      524288         4096        4096
extent i/o buffers                   0  2147483647           33          33
identity burning set factor          1     9999999         5000        5000
...
```

Figure 10.4   Example sp_configure output -

Let us discuss the role of these configuration parameters on performance.

- **User/remote connections** — Maximum number of concurrent logins to SQL Server. Each user connection uses over 50KB of memory and `additional network memory` at the expense of buffer cache. Therefore, it does not pay to overconfigure SQL Server in terms of the number of concurrent logins. We discuss the number of user connections later in this chapter in "Managing a Large Number of Users" on page 343.

- **Devices** — Maximum number of devices on your SQL Server. The performance of the I/O subsystem of SQL Server depends more on the actual number of devices used than on the value of this parameter and the value of this parameter does not have any significant impact on memory usage.

- **Default/maximum network packet size, additional network memory** — SQL Server uses 512-byte packets by default. You can change that in System

10 and later versions of SQL Server by changing the configuration parameter `default network packet size` or by appropriate API calls (e.g., DBSETLPACKET) from your client. In either case, you need to alter two other configuration parameters for the intended effect. These are `maximum network packet size` and `additional network memory`. The former, of course, needs to be at least as large as the desired packet size. The latter is calculated as $3 \times n \times p$, where n is the maximum number of concurrent users and p is the desired packet size. You can examine the size of the network packets in use by active users by the command:

```
select
          spid, status, hostname, network_pktsz
from
          sysprocesses
```

- **Locks, open objects** — Maximum number of locks and concurrent accesses to tables and indexes. You may consider increasing these values depending on the number of concurrent users.

- **Max online engines** — These configuration parameters limit the number of engines in SQL Server. The maximum allowable value varies from one version of SQL Server to another and depends on the choice of the hardware platform. The release notes contains information specific to your choice of hardware.

- **Min online engines, engine adjust interval** — These configuration parameters are not used in System 11 or previous versions of SQL Server. In the future, they may be used to control dynamically the number of engines online and the frequency of adjustment.

- **Time slice** — Used to identify and abort runaway tasks. The value of this configuration parameter is the maximum number of **clock ticks** (100ms for most platforms) a task is allowed to use the CPU at a time. Tasks that do not perform I/O operations or do not run into semaphore contention on a regular basis need to worry about this parameter. If your application is designed to perform a lot of uninterrupted in-memory processing (e.g., a `count(*)` on a cartesian product between a pair of thousand-page tables), then you may need to increase the value of this parameter.

- **Fill factor, OAM trips** — We discuss the role of **fill factor** in the creation of indexes in "Clustered Indexes and Page Splits" on page 334 and the role of **OAM trips** on page allocation and deallocation in "Index and OAM Trips" on page 328. These parameters let you set a global default for all tables on SQL

Server. We strongly urge you to leave these parameter at the default value of zero and configure the corresponding options on individual tables.

- **Extent i/o buffers** — Extent I/O buffers are large (16K) buffers used to accelerate I/O in certain batch operations, most notably index creation. This parameter sets aside a number of large buffers for this purpose. We discuss the role of extent i/o later in Chapter 12, *Batch Processing Performance*. This parameter should be set to a small value, unless creation of indexes is a significant part of your transaction processing application.

- **Identity burning set factor** — In System 10 and later versions of SQL Server you can make one column in a table an identity column. Successive inserts to the table are automatically assigned successive values for this column with few exceptions, the most notable being that ranges of values for this column may be skipped by the recovery following a crash. For example, if this column contains values 1 through 43, the range size is 100, and SQL Server crashes, then the recovery skips the remaining values in the current range (1,100), and returns 101 as the next identity value. The value of this parameter has a very small negative correlation with performance of inserts on tables having an identity column. Setting the configuration value to n causes SQL Server to divide the range of all values for the identity column into $10^7/n$ ranges of equal size. Our recommendation is to use a large value so that the gaps in the values in your identity columns resulting from a crash and recovery are small. The impact on performance is minimal.

Figure 10.5 shows some additional configuration parameters that influence the performance of SQL Server in transaction processing. These configuration parameters are not accessible via the `sp_configure` system stored procedure in System 10 and earlier versions of SQL Server. System 11 SQL Server allows you to configure the `cbufwashsize` for every buffer pool. These require a fair amount of knowledge about the internals of SQL Server; please use due caution.

```
cnblkio=500
cnblkmax=500
cnalarm=200
cschedspins=2000
cbufwashsize=1500
```

Figure 10.5   Other useful configuration parameters -

- **cnblkio, cnblkmax** — These two parameters limit the number of asynchronous I/O operations that SQL Server can have outstanding. These numbers are closely tied to the number of concurrent I/O operations that the operating system and the hardware (controllers, disks, etc.) can process efficiently. In a nutshell, SQL Server imposes flow control on the flux of asynchronous I/O operations to the operating system and the hardware devices. Increasing and decreasing the value of these parameters has the effect of relaxing or tightening this flow control. Consider changing the values of these parameters only if you are absolutely convinced that there is a mismatch between the configured values and the bandwidth supported by the hardware platform.

- **cnalarm** — This parameter limits the number of concurrent timed sleeps on SQL Server. If, for example, your application can have a large number of users executing `waitfor delay` statements concurrently, you may need to increase the value of this parameter. Timed sleeps are used internally by SQL Server for various purposes, including Replication Server support, so do not set this value lower than the default.

- **cschedspins** — This configuration parameter determines how eagerly SQL Server waits for the completion of I/O operations. A large value of this parameter optimizes response time on multiprocessors by having SQL Server use up a proportionate number of idle cycles to poll for completion of I/O operations. A small value causes SQL Server to yield idle CPU cycles to other processes running on the system. Beware, $0 = \infty$ in this case, and causes SQL Server to never yield any idle CPU cycles to other processes.

  You should consider changing the `cschedspins` parameter if your application has other processes sharing the CPU with SQL Server and their performance is critical to the overall performance of your application. In certain situations, these other processes may include the operating system threads that execute requests whose completion SQL Server is polling for. More often, a non-SQL Server part of your application, such as `bcp` or `isql` scripts, are sharing CPUs with SQL Server. In such cases, a small, non-zero value for this parameter (e.g., 1 to 10) may help performance.

- **cbufwashsize** — We have discussed the topic of bufwash earlier in this section. System 10 and earlier versions of SQL Server have a single bufwashsize for SQL Server since there is only one buffer cache. System 11 and later versions of SQL server allow you to set the value of this parameter separately for each named cache.

10.2   DATABASE DESIGN FOR OLTP

Databases are rarely used exclusively for online transaction processing or exclusively for decision support processing. More often than not, you will find yourself designing the schema of a database to meet performance goals in both domains. To say the least, that is not an easy task. In this section, we outline the issues in the design of the schema of your database that is of special interest to transaction processing. Keep in mind that while some of these issues are orthogonal to the performance of complex queries, most are not. We discuss the optimization of the database schema for processing of complex queries in Chapter 11, *Query Processing Performance*.

10.2.1   Constraints and Triggers

Application designers use constraints and triggers to enforce data integrity and business logic. Because constraints and triggers impose extra processing on your data, their presence can have a negative impact on the performance of your application. However, that is no argument for eliminating critical constraints and triggers from your application.

In this section we discuss the impact of constraints and triggers on the performance of transaction processing. Our objective is to make constraints and triggers an integral part of our database schema, not an afterthought. This allows you to consider the impact on performance of constraints and triggers during design, thereby leading to a design that achieves your performance goals without compromising data integrity. We discuss the three broad classes of constraints and triggers in increasing order of their impact on performance.

Uniqueness Constraints

A uniqueness constraint ensures that the uniquely constrained columns are distinct and have no duplicates in the table. The uniqueness constraint is enforced using an index. They are declared explicitly as in `create unique index ...`, or implicitly[4] as illustrated by the examples in Figure 10.6.

---

4. Supported only in System 10 and later versions of SQL Server.

```
create table foo (                      create table bar (
      x           integer,                    x           integer unique,
      y           integer,                    y           integer,
      junk        char(255),                  junk        char(255)
      unique (x,y)                       )
)
```

Figure 10.6   Examples tables -

In both of the examples, SQL Server creates a unique index on the appropriate columns. The effect of the implicit declaration of uniqueness constraints is no different from the explicit creation of the appropriate indexes.

Uniqueness constraints are associated with *no* performance penalty. The presence of an uniqueness constraint may in fact improve performance by helping the optimizer obtain accurate estimates of the sizes of intermediate results and by enabling the optimizer to consider certain join orders that would be semantically incorrect if it were not for the uniqueness constraints. This is especially true for processing of certain classes of quantified subqueries. We discuss the role of uniqueness constraints in query optimization in Chapter 11, *Query Processing Performance*.

Check Constraints

Check constraints restrict the domain of allowable values for columns. The example in Figure 10.7 illustrates the use of a declarative check constraint. You can also implement check constraint using user-defined datatypes and rules.

Observe that the query plan is not affected by the presence of a check constraint. The access methods detect the presence of a check constraint on a table at run time and perform the necessary checks. The presence of the check constraint on the table is shown in Figure 10.8 as the column Rule_name in the sp_help output.

```
1> create table bar (x integer check ( x between 1 and 100))
2> go
1> insert into bar values (10)
2> insert into bar values (90)
3> go
1> update bar set x=x+20
2> go
QUERY PLAN FOR STATEMENT 1 (at line 1).
    STEP 1
        The type of query is UPDATE.
        The update mode is direct.
        FROM TABLE
            bar
        Nested iteration.
        Table Scan.
        Ascending scan.
        Positioning at start of table.
        Using I/O Size 2 Kbytes.
        With LRU Buffer Replacement Strategy.
        TO TABLE
            bar
Msg 548, Level 16, State 1:
Line 1:
Check constraint violation occurred, dbname =  'testdb',
table name = 'bar',
constraint name = 'bar_x_1794105432'.
Command has been aborted.
```

Figure 10.7   Example check constraint -

The overhead of a check constraint is limited to a few additional instructions executed by the CPU. It does not add any logical or physical page accesses and it does not affect the synchronization or scheduling of tasks.

```
1> sp_help bar
2> go
Name                     Owner                    Type
-------------------      --------------------     ----------------------
bar                      dbo                      user table
Data_located_on_segment        When_created
---------------------------    --------------------------
default                              Jun  6 1995  1:25PM
(1 row affected)
Column_name  Type       Length Prec Scale Nulls Default_name     Rule_name
-----------  ---------- ------ ---- ----- ----- --------------- ----------------
x            int             4 NULL  NULL     0 NULL            bar_x_1794105432
Object does not have any indexes.
No defined keys for this object.
```

Figure 10.8 sp_help output for table with check constraint - - - - - - - - - - - - - - -

Referential Integrity Constraints

Referential integrity constraints enforce inter-table dependencies. The example in Figure 10.9 shows an implementation of a referential integrity constraint.

```
1> create unique index bar_non1 on bar(x)
2> go
1> create table foo(x integer, foreign key (x) references bar(x))
2> go
1> insert into foo values(10)
2> insert into foo values(90)
3> go
1> update foo set x=x+80
2> go
Msg 546, Level 16, State 1:
Line 1:
Foreign key constraint violation occurred, dbname = 'testdb', table name = 'foo',
constraint name = 'foo_1906105831'.
Command has been aborted.
```

Figure 10.9 Example referential integrity constraint -

The presence of an integrity constraint causes the optimizer to embed additional calls to the access methods in the plan for the query. These additional calls enforce the referential integrity specified in the constraint by accessing the referenced table. The showplan output in Figure 10.10 illustrates how the referential integrity constraint is enforced in the plan generated for the previous `update` statement.

```
QUERY PLAN FOR STATEMENT 1 (at line 1).
    STEP 1
        The type of query is UPDATE.
        The update mode is deferred.
        FROM TABLE
            foo
        Nested iteration.
        Table Scan.
        Ascending scan.
        Positioning at start of table.
        Using I/O Size 2 Kbytes.
        With LRU Buffer Replacement Strategy.
        FROM TABLE
            bar
        Index : bar_non1
        Ascending scan.
        Positioning by key.
        Index contains all needed columns. Base table will not be read.
        Keys are:
            x
        Using I/O Size 2 Kbytes.
        With LRU Buffer Replacement Strategy.
        TO TABLE
            foo
```

Figure 10.10 Showplan for update with a referential integrity constraint - - - - - - - -

The overhead of referential integrity constraints includes additional calls to access methods, additional logical reads, and potential for additional physical reads. However, the additional logical and physical reads are, in some sense, the least one can do short of not enforcing the constraint at all. The cost of a referential integrity constraint is small, compared to the benefits of maintaining the proper referential integrity of the database.

Triggers

Like referential integrity constraints, triggers cause the optimizer to generate additional steps in the plan for the query. In this case, the additional code includes the stored procedure that comprises the body of the trigger. Figure 10.11 shows an example table and update trigger. The showplan output in Figure 10.12 illustrates the effect of the presence of a trigger on the plan for an update statement.

```
1> create table foo(x integer, y integer)
2> go
1> create trigger foo_x on foo for update as
2>      if update(x)
3>              select * from deleted
4> go
```

Figure 10.11 Example table with update trigger- -

The optimizer attaches the plan for the trigger to the plan for the query. The body of the trigger is executed only if the conditional that identifies the specified column is updated. As the plan for the update statement shows, SQL Server can use direct updates even in presence of a trigger. However, it must store both the pre- and post-update contents of the entire row in the log. These log records represent the inserted and deleted pseudo-tables that are present in the trigger. This can be seen in the plan for the body of the trigger, where we expect to find the entire pre-update image of the row by scanning the log. This additional traffic to the log is the overhead of having a trigger on the table.

SQL Server goes to great lengths to minimize the number of bytes written to the log in case of a direct update. We discuss this in "Order of Columns" on page 326 in greater detail. Suffice it to say that the compactness of the log entries enhances performance. However, the presence of a trigger causes SQL Server to bypass this optimization and write entire rows to the log. The addition of a trigger to a table that sees a large number of in-place updates increases the flux to the log and may hurt overall performance. On the other hand, the addition of a trigger to a table that already sees a lot of deferred updates does not change the behavior of the application significantly. Because deferred updates already log the pre- and the post-update contents of the entire row as a result of the delete and the update.

```
QUERY PLAN FOR STATEMENT 1 (at line 1).
    STEP 1
        The type of query is UPDATE.
        The update mode is direct.
        FROM TABLE
            foo
        Nested iteration.
        Table Scan.
        Ascending scan.
        Positioning at start of table.
        Using I/O Size 2 Kbytes.
        With LRU Buffer Replacement Strategy.
        TO TABLE
            foo
QUERY PLAN FOR STATEMENT 1 (at line 2).
    STEP 1
        The type of query is COND.
QUERY PLAN FOR STATEMENT 2 (at line 3).
    STEP 1
        The type of query is SELECT.
        FROM TABLE
            foo
        Nested iteration.
        Log Scan.
        Ascending scan.
        Positioning at start of table.
        Using I/O Size 2 Kbytes.
        With MRU Buffer Replacement Strategy.
QUERY PLAN FOR STATEMENT 3 (at line 0).
    STEP 1
        The type of query is GOTO.
```

Figure 10.12 Showplan output for an update with an update trigger - - - - - - - - -

One limitation of triggers is that the decision to log the entire row is not contingent on what columns are affected by the update. In the previous example, the showplan output for the two statements:

```
update foo set x=10
update foo set y=10
```

are virtually identical, even though the trigger refers only to column x. In other words, the optimizer does not take advantage of the fact that the trigger does not do any work in the second statement and results in the same logging behavior as the first statement. That is, attaching a trigger to one column of a table increases the flux to the log not just for update statements that change that column, but for all update statements on the table. If you have a table that has two disjoint sets of columns that are updated by separate SQL statements and you need to attach a trigger to a column in one set, you should consider vertically partitioning the table.

In a nutshell, if you do a lot of in-place updates and care about log throughput, pay very close attention to the use of triggers.

10.2.2 Designing Tables for Transaction Processing

Normalization

As a rule of thumb, normalization helps the performance of updates, inserts, and deletes by eliminating duplication of data. A denormalized table can have a functional dependency from one set of columns to another and the former set cannot be used as a unique key for the table. The denormalized table design in Figure 10.13 helps illustrate this definition.

```
/* Denormalized table design */
create table Parts (
        PartID     integer,
        SuppID     integer,
        SuppPhone char(30))
create table Supplier (
        SuppID     integer,
        SuppAddr   char(255))
```

Figure 10.13 Denormalized table design- -

Suppose table Parts stores one row for each supplier of a part (parts and suppliers are identified by unique IDs), and that there is a functional dependency from SuppID to the supplier's phone and address. The denormalized table design in the example stores the phone number of the supplier in the table Parts itself. The motivation to do so may stem from the desire to reduce the cost of looking up the

phone number of a supplier given a `PartID`. This has the unfortunate consequence of burdening the application logic with the task of enforcing the functional
dependency. If the phone number of a supplier changes, the application must
ensure that the column `SuppPhone` is updated for all parts supplied by the supplier. There are several methods for implementing this in SQL Server, an update
trigger being one of the more efficient ones. As discussed earlier in this chapter,
triggers affect the performance of all updates on the denormalized table, including
those that do not involve the column in question.

The normalized table design in Figure 10.14 stores `SuppPhone` in the `Supplier`
table. This relieves the application logic of the burden of enforcing the said functional dependency.

```
/* Normalized table design */
create table Parts (
        PartID                  integer,
        SuppID                  integer)
create table Supplier (
        SuppID                  integer,
        SuppPhone               char(30),
        SuppAddr                char(255))
```

Figure 10.14 Normalized table design -

Variable-Length Data

In System 10 and previous versions of SQL Server, updates that involve variable-
length columns are performed in deferred mode rather than in-place. Deferred
updates can be substantially more expensive than in-place updates. Hence, it helps
to eliminate the use of variable-length datatypes from columns that are updated
frequently. SQL Server treats all columns that allow `NULL` as variable length columns. For example, `CHAR(n) NULL` is treated the same as `VARCHAR(n)`. The following code segment can help you identify variable length columns in your
database.

```
select   o.name TableName, c.name ColumnName, c.length
Length
         from     sysobjects o, syscolumns c
         where    o.id = c.id
         and      c.offset<0
         and      o.name not like 'sys%'
```

Figure 10.15 Query to find variable length columns -

System 11 and later versions of SQL Server relax the restrictions on in-place updates by performing in-place updates that involve variable-length datatypes, provided there is no trigger, the table is not replicated, and there is enough room on the page to store the updated row. When a trigger is present or the table is replicated, SQL Server generates log records as for a deferred update, however, if there is enough room on the existing page to store the updated row, an in-place update is performed on the page.

The presence of variable length rows also makes the number of pages required to store a given set of rows dependent on the order of rows. For example, a change in the order in which the rows are loaded or the creation of a clustered index can affect the mapping of rows to pages as well as the total number of pages.

Order of Columns

The order of the columns within a table does have some impact on the performance of updates. Basically, it helps to juxtapose columns that are updated by the same SQL statement. The example in Figure 10.16 illustrates the reason.

The table design on the left has the columns x and z, which are updated by the same SQL statement, separated by column y. SQL Server generates a log entry in response to this update. One way to log this change would be to log the old and the new value of the entire row. However, that can be very inefficient if only a few columns have changed. Instead, SQL Server logs the old and the new values of only those parts of the row that have changed.

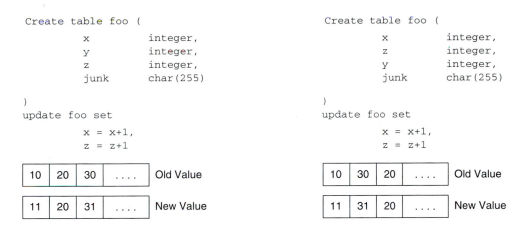

Figure 10.16 Order of columns -

The size of this log entry depends on the order of columns. For the sake of simplicity, let us view the log entry as a set of quadruples $<s,l: o/n>$, where s is the byte offset of the starting point of a change, l is the length of the region affected by the change, o is the old value, and n is the new value. Assuming that integers are 4 bytes in size, the following two log quadruples can be used to log the change in the table design on the left in the example: $<0,4:(10)/(11)>$, $<8,4:(30)/(31)>$. On the other hand, the following, more compact, log entry suffices for the table design on the right: $<0,8:(10,30)/(11,31)>$. Thus, the order of columns can influence the volume of log generated by your application. If the size or the performance of the log is of concern to you, you should revisit the most frequently used update statements in your application and ensure that the affected columns are physically contiguous. There are three caveats to the ordering of columns:

1. SQL Server uses an additional optimization to reduce the size of the log entries in the case that successive changes are separated by eight or fewer bytes. In the case of the design on the left in the example, an equivalent but more compact log entry is the single quadruple $<0,12:(10,20,30)/(11,20,31)>$. Even though the column y is not affected by this change, we are better off logging it as if it did change. However, this log entry is still larger than the one produced by the design on the right.

2. The physical order of columns is not necessarily the same as the order of columns in the `create table` statement, although there is a strong correlation. SQL Server stores all fixed length columns before all variable length columns. Further, the bit columns are packed into single-byte fields. For example, if your create table statement intersperses fixed length columns (f1,f2, ...) and variable length columns (v1, v2, ...) in any order that maintains order within each group, then the physical order of the columns is (f1,f2,....,v1,v2,...). If we throw a few bit columns (b1, b2, ...) into the mix, the situation is a bit more complex. Each group of eight successive bit columns are packed into a byte, which is positioned at the location where a fixed length column declared in place of the first of the eight bit columns would have been positioned.

3. SQL Server is smart enough to optimize the log entry for the case that the update statement whose execution does not actually change the contents of a column. For example, if we were to replace the update statement in the example by:

```
update foo set x=x+1, z=30
```

then SQL Server generates the compact log entry *<0,4:(10)/(11)>* in both of the above two designs. Further, the update statement:

```
update foo set x=10, z=30
```

does not generate a log entry at all. Observe that the size of the log entry is determined at query execution time, not at query compile time, since the query compiler cannot determine whether or not the update changes the contents of the row.

4. SQL Server compares rows without regard to the column definitions. As a result, the byte order of your platform and even the data itself can have an effect on the number and size of log records.

Index and OAM Trips

As mentioned earlier in this chapter, your application may benefit by having SQL Server treat different tables and indexes differently. The same applies to OAM (Object Allocation Map) pages. The OAM for an object is a linked list of bitmaps that encodes the allocation of extents to the object. System 10 and earlier versions of SQL Server scan this chain multiple times for every allocation and deallocation of an extent. If your application performs a lot of insert and/or delete operations on a table, it pays to extend preferential treatment to the OAM pages for this table.

By default, the buffer replacement policy used by SQL Server treats data, index, and OAM pages equally. You can force SQL Server to extend preferential treatment to index and/or OAM pages for certain tables in SQL Server versions 4.9.x and later by using the table-specific configuration parameters `index trips` and `oam trips`. The value of index trips for a table is a measure of the priority of the indexes on this table when it comes to buffer replacement. The default setting of 0 instructs SQL Server to treat an index page for this table the same as any other page. The larger the value of index trips for a table, the harder SQL Server tries to keep the index pages for this table in memory. A value as large as 1000 effectively locks every index page for the table in memory the very first time it is accessed.

There are several caveats to the use of index trips and OAM trips:

1. There is no way to extend this kind of preferential treatment to data pages.

2. There is no way to extend preferential treatment to one index on a table without extending it to all other indexes on the table, including those yet to be created.

3. As in politics and government, excessive use of index trips and OAM trips has the same undesirable effect as extending preferential treatment to too many: it defeats the purpose and the overall performance degrades.

10.2.3 Designing Indexes for Transaction Processing

The addition of an index to a table that is updated frequently may involve a trade-off. The index allows efficient access to rows in the table, thus enhancing the performance of selects. It also increases the cost of updates, inserts, and deletes, since these operations may need to update the index in addition to updating the table itself. The example in the following pseudo-code illustrates some of the trade-offs:

```
create table ufo_sighting (
        state    char(2), /* As in 'AL', ... , 'WY' */
        est      datetime,/* Eastern Standard Time */
        details  char(255))
create clustered index us_clu
        on ufo_sighting(state, est) with allow_dup_row
```

Suppose the reports about UFO sighting are inserted into the above table at peak rates of up to 100 per minute. About once every hour, you need to run the following query to report all sightings within the last five minutes.

```
select est, state, details
        from ufo_sightings
```

```
        where est > dateadd(minutes, getdate(), -5)
```

Since this query is being forced to scan the table, it may make sense to add a non-clustered index to help this query.

```
create nonclustered index us_non1 on ufo_sighting(est)
```

Surely, the query runs faster, but inserts pay a price. Each insert now needs to get a lock on the last leaf page of the nonclustered index and insert an entry there. We have just added more work and a bottleneck to the application. How about switching the order of columns in the clustered index instead of adding a nonclustered index?

```
create clustered index us_clu
        on ufo_sighting(est, state) with allow_dup_row
```

This index can be used by the query since the search argument specifies a non-empty prefix of the index. Naturally, the query runs faster than it did with the original clustered index. But observe what this does to the inserts: because the clustered index orders the rows of the table by time, all the 100 inserts in a minute must now be inserted on the last page of the table. Further, we have effectively lost the state name as a useful search argument for ad hoc queries.

Another alternative is to keep the original clustered index and rewrite the query as follows. This works well until the 51st state joins the union:

```
create proc in_state @state char(2) as
select est, state, details
        from ufo_sightings
        where est > dateadd(minutes, getdate(), -5)
        and state = @state

exec in_state 'AL'
....
exec in_state 'WY'
```

The purpose of this example is to give you a taste of the trade-offs involved in adding an index to a table that gets updated often. Potential implications range from several orders of magnitude improvements in query performance to crippling lock contentions. In the remainder of this section, we discuss some of these implications.

Impact of Nonclustered Indexes

Insert and delete operations require inserts and deletes to the affected nonclustered indexes. An in-place update may or may not require indexes to be updated, depending on whether or not any of the columns in the index is updated. Only those indexes that include one or more of the columns updated by the `update` statement are changed to reflect the new values of the columns. For each such nonclustered index, the effect of an update on the table is similar to that of a delete and an insert on the index. In turn, the delete and insert may involve splitting and shrinking of index pages. Also, the choice and order of columns in the nonclustered index may cause severe lock contentions, as shown by the previous example. Thus, the decision to include a column that is frequently updated in a nonclustered index should not be taken lightly.

Impact of Clustered Indexes

We need to pay special attention to the cost of updating a column that is part of the clustered index. An update that *may* change the value of a column in the clustered index is necessarily deferred, irrespective of whether or not the execution of the update statement actually changes the value of this column. In other words, as long as the SQL statement indicates that a column in the clustered index can be updated, the optimizer chooses a deferred update, instead of delaying the choice between deferred and in-place until run-time. This, in turn, forces two updates to each nonclustered index present on the table: one for the delete and another for the following insert.

The maintenance of the clustered index itself to reflect inserts and deletes on the table has very interesting performance characteristics. In certain cases, inserts and deletes to a table having only a clustered index can actually be cheaper than inserts and deletes to a table having only a nonclustered index. The clustered indexes contain only the range of values of the indexed columns for the rows within each page not all of the values of the indexed columns for each row on the page. Hence, if the range of values of the columns of a clustered index on a page does not change as a result of the insert or the delete, no change is required to the clustered index. This, for example, is the case when one page of a table having a clustered index on a single integer column contains values 1, 3, and 5 of the indexed column and we insert a row having value 4 for the indexed column (and this does not cause a page split).

There are less obvious cases where SQL Server does not require an update to a clustered index as a result of an insert or a delete operation. Unfortunately, there is no simple rule to determine what fraction of your insert and delete operations require updates to the clustered index. In contrast, a nonclustered index must store the values of the indexed columns for every row on every page. Therefore, every insert and delete to a table having only nonclustered indexes must update every nonclustered index.

The worst case of an insert or a delete to a table having a clustered index happens when the splitting or shrinking of a page is involved. We discuss page splits in greater detail later in this section. However, we should note here that the relocation of rows due to a page split requires the nonclustered indexes to be updated. Thus, having nonclustered indexes on a table which has a clustered index that is frequently subjected to inserts, deletes, and/or deferred updates is yet another design decision that should not be taken lightly.

In general, if you have a table with only a clustered index, you need to be concerned only about the frequency of page splits and shrinks. If the table has a clustered index in addition to nonclustered indexes, you need to be aware that the splitting and shrinking of pages may require a substantial amount of updates to the nonclustered indexes.

Duplicate Keys in Clustered Indexes

The presence of duplicate key values in a clustered index can have some interesting consequences on the performance of insert operations. Duplicate key values means that two or more rows agree on all columns of the clustered index, not just any one column in the clustered index. SQL Server uses an overflow page chain for each group of duplicate key values. The overflow page chains hang off the chain of data pages (leaf level of the B-Tree that comprises the clustered index and the table), as illustrated by the following example.

Suppose we have a clustered index on a single column having datatype integer, and that each data page holds up to 4 rows. The example in Figure 10.17 shows the overflow chain when the value 25 of the indexed column occurs multiple times in the table. Only the key values are shown for each row contained on each page. SQL Server puts the rows having the duplicate key value in an overflow page chain. The pages in the overflow page chain can only contain rows having the duplicate key value. However, not all rows having this key value are located in the overflow chain; some of them may be contained in the previous page in the data page chain. In the example, that would be the page containing key values (20,22,25,25). This page cannot contain a key value greater than the duplicate key value. At most one overflow page chain can hang off any one page in the data page chain. Two or more duplicate key groups may share a page on the data page chain, but there can only be one overflow chain. The overflow chain contains a unique duplicate key value, hanging off of the data page pointed to by an index page.

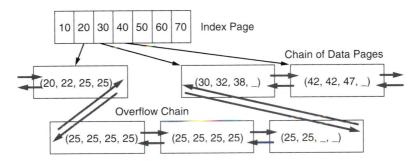

Figure 10.17 Duplicate keys in clustered indexes -

Using overflow page chains ensures that the range of key values for every page pointed to by the index pages are disjoint. However, they can also have an adverse impact on the performance of transaction processing:

1. The performance of the insertion of a key value depends on the number of duplicates already present for that key value. In the previous example, inserting a row having the key value 35 accesses only one data page: the one containing key values (30,32,38,_). However, inserting a row having the key value 25 causes SQL Server to scan the entire overflow page chain to find the last page on the overflow page chain, thus accessing three pages on the overflow page chain in addition to the one page on the data page chain. The length of the over-flow chain grows linearly with the number of duplicates and the number of page accesses to insert n duplicates grows quadratically with n.

2. The storage density may be adversely affected by the presence of a very large number of key values, each of which has a small number of duplicates. For example, if each page holds 3 rows and we have 100 distinct key values, each value is repeated four times. In the absence of a clustered index, the number of

pages is $\lceil 400/3 \rceil = 134$. If we create a clustered index on this table, each group of duplicate keys requires two pages: one on the data page chain and one on the overflow chain. The number of pages has grown from 134 to $100 \times 2 = 200$: an increase of almost 50%.

Clustered Indexes and Page Splits

Inserting a row into a table with a clustered index causes SQL Server to split a data page if the new row does not fit on the page to which it is being inserted. A new page is allocated, part of the data is left on the existing page and the rest is moved to the new page. The new page is linked between the existing page and the next page in the chain. The increase in the number of index entries due to the splitting of the data page may cause the index pages above it in the clustered index to split. A single insert may cause all pages in the path from the root page to the data page to split and may even add a level to the B-Tree. Similarly, deleting the last row in a page causes a **page shrink**: the elimination of a page from the chain of data pages.

Splitting a page is an expensive operation. As mentioned in the previous two sections, the relocation of rows from an existing page to the new page may involve updates to multiple index pages in the nonclustered indexes on the table. In this section, we discuss the impact of a page split on the clustered index only. We should also note that the index pages in the nonclustered indexes themselves undergo splits and shrinks similar to data pages in a table having a clustered index. However, split and shrink operations on the pages of a nonclustered index are handled differently than those on the data pages of a table having a clustered index.

In the absence of a page split, inserting a row to a table having a clustered index only causes the data page and some or none of the index pages on the path from the root to this page to become dirty. This may or may not result in additional writes to the disk, depending on frequency of page replacements and checkpoints relative to the next access to this page. In other words, an insert to a clustered index that does not cause the data page to split is an inexpensive operation. However, if the same insert causes the data page to split, the cost is substantially greater. The example in Figure 10.18 illustrates the changes in the clustered index performed by the page split.

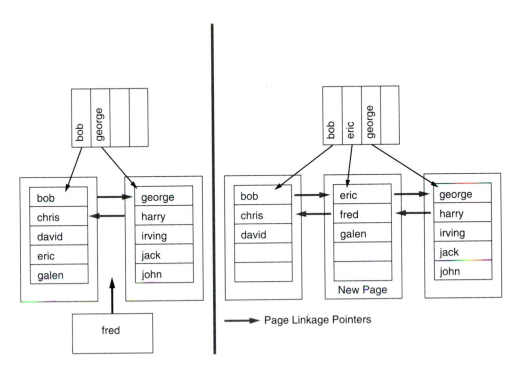

Figure 10.18 Inserting rows into table having a clustered index- - - - - - - - - - - - -

The cost of updating a clustered index to reflect a page split may include:

1. An additional traversal of the path from the root page to the data page.[5] The first pass determines whether the data page needs to be split. The second pass splits the index pages on the way down, if necessary.

2. The allocation of a new page.

3. Linking the new page into the page chain. SQL Server acquires an exclusive lock on the page that follows the page being split in the page chain, which, in turn increases lock contention and the potential for deadlocks.

[5.] This is new in System 10 SQL Server. 4.9 SQL Server traverses only once, but this results in a greater potential for deadlocks during index page splits.

4. Relocation of some rows from the existing data page to the new page. This, in turn, causes both the pages and the log to be flushed to the disk immediately.

5. An update of the index entries to reflect the relocation of rows and the existence of a new row.

Thus, in addition to increasing lock contention and potential for deadlocks, each page split *dirties* at least four pages, two of which are flushed to disk immediately along with the log.[6] If your application inserts data sequentially to a table having a clustered index (i.e., in ascending order of the clustered index), the immediate flushing of dirty pages to disk doubles the number of writes to disk. That is, inserting 100 pages of data causes 200 pages to be written to disk.

Fortunately, page splits occur only when a page is full, not on every insert to the table. Therefore, the average cost of inserts to a table having a clustered index is somewhere between the cost of an insert that does not require a page split and one that does. The higher the number of rows per data page, the closer the average cost is to the former rather than the latter. Short of eliminating clustered indexes or rewriting your application to perform fewer inserts to tables having clustered indexes, there are several things you can do to minimize the cost of page splits:

1. Minimize the number of nonclustered indexes on tables that have a clustered index and are subjected frequently to insert, delete, or deferred update operations.

2. Minimize the frequency of page splits by decreasing the size of rows through normalization and vertical partitioning. The frequency of page splits is inversely related to the number of rows on a page. Of course, vertical partitioning does not help if the primary key is the clustered index, since you now perform page splits on two tables, albeit each less frequently than the single table.

3. Minimize the frequency of page splits by leaving some empty space on data pages. You can do so using the `fillfactor` feature of the `create index` statement. A low fill factor reduces the number of page splits during inserts. But it does so only at the cost of increasing the number of pages (and hence disk space, memory, and number of I/O operations) required to store the same number of rows. There are two caveats to the use of fill factors: they are most helpful when the distribution of the key values among the rows being inserted is uniformly random, and the effect of fill factor diminishes with time. The

---

[6]   System 11 SQL Server reduces this overhead in certain special cases.

empty space created by the use of the fill factor feature in the `create index` statement is progressively used up by inserts. To re-establish the desired fill factor, you must periodically rebuild the clustered index.

4. System 11 SQL Server does not flush the dirty pages and the log to the disk on page splits if the key values are being inserted to the table in ascending order. This reduces the number of writes to disk by up to a factor of two when the value of the clustered index increases monotonically, such as a clustered index on an identity column or on a time-dependent series like invoice numbers.

5. If the key values being inserted are comprised of ascending subsequences, then System 11 SQL Server allows you to use the table configuration option `ascinserts` to optimize the performance of page splits. The example in the following code segment illustrates the occurrence of ascending subsequences in multi-column indexes.

```
create unique clustered index t_clu
        on trades (account, trade)
```

Suppose you have 4 accounts (A, B, C, D) and the trade number increases monotonically within each account. For example, the key values in the rows being inserted could be as follows.

```
B1, B2, C1, A1, A2, D1, C2, D2, D3, A3, B3, ...
```

The above sequence is composed of the ascending subsequences:

```
(A1, A2, A3, ...),
(B1, B2, B3, ...),
(C1, C2, ...),
(D1, D2, D3, ...)
```

Ascending subsequences are very common in applications having multi-column clustered indexes where the value of the right-most column in the clustered index grows with time. If a table having a clustered index exhibits this behavior, you should consider use of the `ascinserts` configuration option (see Chapter 13, *Advanced Topics*).

10.2.4 Logging and Group Commits

The performance of the log device is often a limiting factor in the overall performance of SQL Server on transaction processing application. Each database in SQL Server has a transaction log represented by the `syslogs` table. All the log information for the database must be written to the log device. The following basic rules govern the writing of log pages to the log device.

1. Rows or log entries can only be appended to the end of the log, in chronological order.

2. A transaction cannot commit until the log records for the transaction have been written to the disk.

3. A dirty data page cannot be written to disk until the log entries that record the changes made to this page are written to the disk.

The second of these three rules seems to suggest that log entries should be written out to disk as soon as possible, since a transaction cannot release the locks it holds until it has committed. SQL Server can write no less than 2K to disks at a time. Since the commit record is not necessarily the last entry on a log page, SQL Server faces the following dilemma: delay the commit of the transaction or write the log page before it is full. Figure 10.19 shows the performance trade-off between these two cases.

If SQL Server chooses to wait until the fourth transaction, D, adds its record to the log before starting the log write, when the log write completes, all four transactions, A to D, can commit. A must wait until three more transactions add their changes to the log, in addition to the time it takes to write the log page, before committing.

If SQL Server writes the log page after every transaction adds a change to the log, the same page is written over and over again as it fills up. No transaction waits more than the time it takes to write the log page before committing, but a transaction that wants to add a record to the log page just after the log page write begins must wait for the log page write to complete before adding its record to the log page.

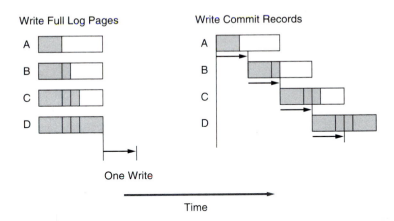

Figure 10.19 Group Commit: response time, throughput trade-off - - - - - - - - - - -

The example in Figure 10.19 offers two extreme examples. Either we write the last log page every time a transaction adds a commit record to the log, or we wait until the log page is full before writing the page. If SQL Server waits until the log page is full before writing the page, the delaying of a commit can add to the lock contention as the transaction waiting to commit cannot release locks. In the worst case, this can cause a deadlock. If SQL Server writes the log page every time a transaction wants to commit, the same log page may be written to the disk multiple times as more changes are recorded on that page. If SQL Server were to write out the last page of the log on every commit, performance is limited by the following problems:

1. The commit rate is limited by the throughput of the log disk. An average disk drive can field 60 operations per second. If SQL Server writes out the last log page for every new log record, the application is limited to 60 transactions per second.

2. Assuming asynchronous I/O operations are used, access to the last log page by other transactions while it is in the process of being written by the committing transaction can have some adverse implications on performance on certain hardware platforms.

3. Repeated writing of the log page (or any other page) uses up precious bus bandwidth and throughput of the I/O subsystem.

SQL Server uses an adaptive mechanism that combines some of the benefits of both extremes, while avoiding most of the pitfalls. When there are many active tasks on the system, it is likely to write mostly full log pages. This is called **group commit** or **commit sharing**. When there are many transactions modifying the database simultaneously, log pages fill quickly, and group commit benefits throughput with little response time penalty. On the other hand, if there is very little concurrent activity in the database, SQL Server is likely to write out the log page as soon as a commit record is added to it. Often, throughput is not an issue with low levels of concurrency and hence it makes sense to minimize response time.

There are two characteristics of applications that affect the performance of the group commit mechanism.

- **Frequency of page splits** — A page split acts somewhat like a commit in that the log entry needs to be written to disk. This has the effect of increasing the effective commit rate and hence the demand on the log device. System 11 SQL Server alleviates this problem somewhat as discussed in "Clustered Indexes and Page Splits" on page 334.

- **Transaction rollbacks** — A transaction rollback needs to read the log pages that contain the log entries for the transaction. For transactions of reasonable lengths, these pages are still in cache. If not, pages are read from the log disk. You can observe whether this is happening in your application by monitoring the log disk. If so, log throughput is affected by the random access to the log disk. Further, the undo operations caused by the rollback cause data pages to be written to disk, not unlike a page split. This can have an adverse impact on efficiency of group commit.

You can measure group commit activity by comparing the rate of growth of the log with the number of writes to the log disk. In order to get a correct assessment, you need to turn off automatic checkpointing and truncation of the log as discussed in "CONFIGURING FOR OLTP" on page 303, and then use the tools discussed in Chapter 8, *Monitoring SQL Server* to monitor the size and growth of the log. For example, suppose you monitor the server at x transactions per second and find the log growing at y pages/sec, and z writes to the log disk per second. Then, you can determine the need for and the effectiveness of group commits as follows.

- If $y \geq x$, then there is no need for group commits.
- If $x > z$, then group commits are working, and x/z denotes the average number of transactions per group.
- If $z > y$, then some log pages are being written to the log disk more than once. This may be inevitable in a low throughput or single user situation. However, this should not occur in high-throughput, multi-user applications.

In general, you should not need to worry about group commit mechanism. There are no configurable parameters for the group commit mechanism. However, there are a few reasons why you may want to know the performance of the group commit mechanism in your application.

Correct Assessment of Log Device Performance

Suppose a combination of factors such as low concurrency, high throughput, and desire for quick response is causing SQL Server to write some or most log pages multiple times. You may need to factor this into the selection of a controller and a disk drive for your log device. For example, disks from two vendors may offer the same rotational and seek latency and/or sustained throughput. However, one of them may outperform the other by a large margin when the sequence of writes to the disk contains a lot of repetitions. The following example exemplifies a typical sequence of block numbers written to the log disk when the group commit mechanism decides to write log pages before they are full.

```
100, 101, 101, 101, 102, 103, 104, 104, 104, 105, 106, 107, 107, ...
```

Special Disks as Log Devices

The need for higher log throughput has caused some users to use very high performance devices such as solid-state disks, non-volatile RAM, disk arrays with large persistent caches, and even file systems[7] as log devices. One of the characteristics of writes to such devices is an extremely short turn-around time. For example, a smart caching controller may signal the completion of a write as soon as the last byte of the write request is received. The impact of such behavior on the adaptive nature of the SQL Server group commit mechanism needs to be evaluated on a per device and per application basis. In the worst case, the overall effect of having a superfast log disk is repeated rewrites to the same log page with no little or no

---

[7.] The first and foremost issue in use of such devices is recoverability. You need to make sure that the device ensures the persistence of writes to the device. This is not true for most file systems.

gain in performance. If you choose to use such a device as your log disk, you may want to compute the fraction of writes to log pages that are repeated as shown. If the last log page is re-written many times, you may not see much performance gain out of the fast log disk.

Large Log Buffers with System 11 SQL Server

System 11 SQL Server can write to the log in units larger than a page. If log throughput is of concern for your application, you should certainly consider using log buffers larger than 2K. However, the effectiveness of the larger buffer size is limited if your application performs a large number of last log page re-writes. Repeated writing of 16K buffers is no more efficient than repeated writing of 2K buffers. If you find that an increase in the size of the log buffer results only in an increased number of repeated writes to the log disk and not in improved performance, you have two options: rewrite application to improve group commit or reduce the size of the log buffers.

Multi-Database Transactions

Transactions that span more than one database add log entries in the log of each database they touch. If run in single user mode, a multi-database transaction involving *n* databases requires *2n-1* writes to the log devices — one for the database where the `begin transaction` was executed and two for each of the other databases involved in the transaction. In a multi-user environment, some or all of these writes may be grouped with other writes to the log devices through the group commit mechanism, reducing the number of additional writes to log devices. Multi-database transactions do perform more writes to log devices than single database transactions and should not be used without regard for their impact on performance.

If your application must use multi-database transactions, you may still have the option of chosing one database over another to start the multi-database transaction. Since the number of writes to the log device of a database depends on whether or not the transaction was started in the database, this choice may affect performance.

10.3   APPLICATION DESIGN

We discussed several general guidelines for designing client/server application for high performance in Chapter 7, *Application Development*. Let us continue that discussion with some aspects of application design that are of special interest to transaction processing.

10.3.1 Managing a Large Number of Users

User Connections and Memory

SQL Server allocates memory for user connections at boot time. This is determined by two configuration parameters: `number of user connections` and `additional network memory`. If your application allows a large number of users to log into SQL Server, you are forced you to set aside a large portion of memory for user connections. This memory is not available to cache data, index, or procedures, even if the actual number of concurrent users is smaller than the number of user connections configured at boot time. A large disparity between the maximum and average number of concurrent logins can have a negative impact on performance. Here are some options you may want to explore in minimizing the configured number of user connections.

- **Flow control at application level** — Suppose the number of concurrent logins on SQL Server can be very large for short periods of time and that business logic permits you to refuse logins during peak hours (or more like peak minutes). Then, one solution is to configure the system for a number of user connections that suffices for all but the highest peaks. Of course, such a solution is effective only if such peaks are brief and rare.

- **Transaction monitors** — You may be able to multiplex a large number user contexts into a few user connections through the use of a transaction monitor. Commercial transaction monitors such as Tuxedo, Top End, and Encina provide this capability and a host of other features useful in complex transaction processing systems. On the other hand, multiplexing of user contexts is only a small part of the functionality provided by the commercial transaction monitors. If multiplexing is all you need, then you may be able to write your own transaction monitor as an Open Server application.

- **Length of sessions** — As discussed in Chapter 7, *Application Development*, your client applications should log out of SQL Server if they expect to be idle for an extended period. Also, you may be able to work with fewer user connections by introducing breaks at appropriate points during a client session.

- **Avoid livelocks** — When SQL Server refuses a connection request from a client because the maximum number of concurrent users is reached, it retains no memory of which clients were refused connections. This raises the possibility of livelocks. Suppose several clients are polling SQL Server for connections, some more frequently than others. Then the polite clients may be starved out. To prevent this from happening, you may want to add queueing logic to your application.

Using Stored Procedures

Stored procedures are practically indispensable for performance of transaction processing applications on SQL Server. Compared to ad hoc SQL, stored procedures save the effort of parsing, compiling, and optimizing SQL statements, as well as the effort of resolving access privileges etc. Dynamic SQL in Client-Library is translated into stored procedures. Disregarding the frequency of Dynamic SQL prepare commands, applications that use Dynamic SQL also enjoy most of the benefits of stored procedures. Approaches that require recompilation of SQL statements for every execution of a transaction (e.g., a `dbcmd ()` .. `dbsqlexec()`) may see poorer performance.

Sharing Stored Procedures

We discussed the granularity of the interaction between the clients and SQL Server in Chapter 7, *Application Development*. Transaction processing applications are no exception to the rule that too much or too little interaction between the clients and SQL Server can hurt performance. The size and nesting of stored procedures can be used to tailor the frequency of this interaction. In this section, we discuss a different aspect of stored procedures that is of special interest to transaction processing since it pertains to large number of users: **sharing of procedure cache**.

The stored procedures in SQL Server are not re-entrant. That is, if two users are executing a stored procedure concurrently, SQL Server maintains two copies of the compiled query in the procedure cache. If a lengthy stored procedure is used by multiple users concurrently, then you may be forced to set aside a large portion of the main memory in SQL Server for use as procedure cache. This can have an adverse impact on performance by reducing the number of buffers available to cache data and indexes.

If the size of the procedure cache is an issue in the performance of your application, there are a few techniques that may help you reduce the amount of procedure cache required by your application. Of course, the first opportunity to explore is a reduction in the length of the stored procedures through better reuse of code. T-SQL constructs such as nested procedure calls and iterators may help you in reusing code. However, often the length of a stored procedure is due to the complexity inherent in the application. In such cases, one option is to split your stored procedures to isolate the parts that are used concurrently.

The example in the following pseudo-code shows a stored procedure that is over a thousand lines long and takes 100 seconds to execute. Suppose this stored procedure is used concurrently by several users. Then, SQL Server is forced to maintain multiple copies of this stored procedure in procedure cache.

```
proc takes_100_seconds
begin
        /* 500 lines, 5 seconds */
        /* 10 lines, 90 seconds */
        /* 500 lines, 5 seconds */
end
```

Now, let us assume that only 10 lines in the stored procedure account for 90% of the time taken. Such is often the case when a loop, lock contention, or a complex SQL statement use up a disproportionate amount of time. In this case, we may be able to reduce the amount of procedure cache required by splitting off the large chunks of the stored procedure that take little time into separate stored procedures. The following pseudo-code shows how.

```
proc takes_100_seconds
begin
        exec first_five_seconds
        /* 10 lines, 90 seconds */
        exec last_five_seconds
end
proc first_5_seconds
begin
        /* 500 lines, 5 seconds */
end
proc last_5_seconds
```

```
begin
        /* 500 lines, 5 seconds */
end
```

Now, SQL Server needs to maintain multiple copies of a significantly smaller stored procedure. The bulk of the code is now contained in the two new stored procedures which are less likely to be used by as many concurrent users as the original stored procedure because they take very little time to execute.

Temporary Tables

Using temporary tables to hold intermediate results is very common. Unfortunately, creating and dropping temporary tables and indexes can be a bottleneck with a high number of users because both actions require exclusive access to the system tables in `tempdb`. The following code segment illustrates the problem.

```
create proc P @w int as
begin transaction
        create table #T(x int)
        insert into #T select x from Q where y=@w
        select sum(x) from #T
commit transaction
```

Suppose we have a lightweight stored procedure P that stores a few rows in a temporary table #T. As the number of users invoking P increases, the creation and (implicit) dropping of #T becomes a bottleneck. An alternative is to store the intermediate results in a persistent table, instead of a temporary table, as illustrated by the following code segment.

```
create table T (u int,x int)
create clustered index T_clu on T(u)
create proc P @w int as
begin transaction
        /* generate unique token @u */
        insert into T select @u, x from Q where y=@w
        select sum(x) from T where u=@u
        delete from T where u=@u
commit transaction
```

Since multiple concurrent users may be storing their temporary results in this table, we need to distinguish between the rows stored by separate invocations of P. We do so by adding an indexed column u to the table and requiring that all concurrent invocations of the stored procedure use distinct values of @u. The generation of a unique token may follow naturally from application logic. For example,

346

if @w or any other variable in the stored procedure is guaranteed to be distinct among all concurrent users (e.g., @@spid), you can use it as the unique token. If all else fails, you can generate a unique token using the @identity feature.

The above alternative eliminates contention on the system tables in tempdb, but does so only at the expense of expensive inserts and deletes, their log entries, page splits and shrinkages, and index maintenance. If you know the maximum number of concurrent invocations of P and the number of rows inserted into #T, you can improve the above solution by using updates instead of inserts and deletes. This alternative is illustrated by the following pseudo-code.

```
create table T (u int, i int, x int)
create clustered index T_clu on T(u)
for (@u=0; @u<maxusers; @u++)
        for (@i=1; @i<maxrows; @i++)
                /* maximum number of rows selected is known */
                insert into T values (@u,@i,nullvalue)
create proc P @w int, @u int as /* unique token @u */
declare @x int, @i int
begin transaction
declare c cursor for select x from Q where y=@w
for (@i=0, open c, fetch c into @x; @@sqlstatus == 0; @i++, fetch c
into @x)
        update T set x = @x where u = @u and i = @i
select sum(x) from T where u=@u and i<@i
commit transaction
```

We load the table T with the appropriate number of rows. Then, each invocation of P identifies its private set of rows in T using a unique token and uses updates instead of inserts and deletes to store its intermediate results in T. There can be many other variations on the above theme. The idea is to avoid frequently creating and dropping tables, as these operations can become serialized on the system tables. Furthermore, you should use in-place updates over inserts and deletes on a shared table, as in-place updates are faster than inserts and deletes.

10.3.2 Access Methods for Transaction Processing

Certain coding styles are better suited than others for transaction processing applications. In this section we discuss some simple, local optimizations that can make your code more efficient. They can make a substantial difference in the performance of your application. However, they are not a substitute for the more general issues discussed earlier in this chapter and elsewhere in this book. An attempt to improve performance by rephrasing your SQL statements can be a frustrating and fruitless experience if the problems are more general in nature. Therefore, we must start this section with a word of caution: do not spend any time fine-tuning your SQL statements until you have a complete picture of how the performance of your SQL statements affects the overall performance of your application.

For any reasonably large application, it is impossible to apply peephole optimization to every SQL statement. We need some way to identify parts that need the most work. Those of you who are familiar with tuning C and C++ programs may be disappointed to find there is no profiler for Transact-SQL. Chapter 9, *Instrumenting SQL Code*, discusses several techniques that may help you identify trouble spots. One simple technique that we have found useful is to run each of the most frequently executed stored procedures once in showplan mode, save the output in a text file, and then look for telltale signs of problems. Keywords and phrases such as `Table scan` or `Update mode is deferred` spell trouble. Chapter 9, *Instrumenting SQL Code*, contains a complete list of such keywords and phrases.

Select Statements

If you have two `select` statements you may want to merge them into one. Example:

```
select @total = 0.0
select @i = 0
```

should be replaced by:

```
select @total = 0.0, @i = 0
```

Merging two single-table `select` statements into one two-way join requires more thought, but may be worth the effort. For example:

```
select @buyer = c_name from customer where c_id = @c_id
select @seller = s_name from salesperson where s_id = @s_id
```

can be merged into:

```
select @buyer = c_name, @seller = s_name
       from customer, salesperson
       where    c_id = @c_id
       and      s_id = @s_id
```

if `c_id` and `s_id` are unique indexes on respective tables. The benefits of doing this is even more pronounced when the `select` statements are inside a cursor, for we reduce the number of `open` and `fetch` statements by a factor of two. However, beware: if the optimizer picks a join order different from the original order of statements, then you need to be concerned about possibility of deadlocks. More on this later in this chapter.

The time to compile a statement grows quadratically with the number of columns. This is not a major issue for stored procedures that are not compiled repeatedly. However, if you are using ad hoc SQL in your OLTP application, you need be concerned about the time to compile your SQL statements. One option is to break up a `select` statement having a long list of columns into two `select` statements, each having half the number columns. This may help in the sense that $x^2 + y^2 < (x + y)^2$ for all $x > 1$ and $y > 1$. However, by having two `select` statements instead of one, you may be trading compilation time for execution time.

Using Cursors Effectively

ANSI SQL compliant server cursors, introduced in System 10 SQL Server, can help performance in several ways. We illustrate the use of cursors to improve efficiency of transaction processing applications using three case studies.

1. **Positioned updates** — Often we need to identify a row or a set of rows before applying an update to it. Suppose you need to locate the row for a given member of a tennis club and check his membership status before you can update his balance to reflect a charge for today's use of the facilities.

```
select @m_status = m_status,
        @m_balance = m_balance,
        @m_creditlimit = m_creditlimit
        from    members  HOLDLOCK
        where   m_id = @m_id
if (@@row_count = 0) goto RequestEnrollment
if (@m_status <>'Active') goto RequestActivation
if (@m_balance > @m_creditlimit) goto RequestPayment
update members set m_balance = m_balance + @current_charge
        where m_id = @m_id
```

The above implementation traverses the index only once to look up the membership status and balance and once again to update the balance. The following cursor-based implementation traverses the index only once.

```
declare m_cursor cursor for select
        m_status, m_balance, m_creditlimit
        from    members
        where   m_id = @m_id
```

```
                for update of m_balance
        open m_cursor
        fetch m_cursor into @m_status, @m_balance, @m_creditlimit
        if (@@sqlstatus <> 0) goto RequestEnrollment
        if (@m_status <> 'Active') goto RequestActivation
        if (@m_balance > @m_creditlimit) goto RequestPayment
        update members set m_balance = @m_balance + @current_charge
                where current of m_cursor
```

One of the techniques commonly used by developers for the 4.9 SQL Server is to maintain two connections to SQL Server. One connection scans rows to read their content into local variables at the client and the other follows on its heels, updating rows. In addition to the overhead of multiple connections and scans, this method can also requires the application developers to manage lock contention between the two connections. The use of cursors is both easier and more efficient for positioned updates.

2. **Running averages and cumulative aggregates** — If your application requires computation of running averages (e.g., the monthly average of the closing price of an equity for every day of the last year) or cumulative aggregates (e.g., list of shareholders in descending order of the number of shares owned and a running total of the number of shares listed so far in the report), cursors can help you phrase the query far more efficiently than you can otherwise. The following pseudo-code illustrates implementations of the above example queries using cursors.

```
        /* Running average */
        declare a cursor
                for select closing from prices
                where symbol=@sym and date = @x
                order by date
        declare b cursor
                for select closing from prices
                where symbol=@sym and date = @x + one month
                order by date
        select @x = today - one year
        select @sum = sum(closing) from prices
                where symbol=@sym and
                        date between @x and @x + one month
        for (open a, open b, fetch a into @old, fetch b into @new;
                @@sqlstatus==0;
                        fetch a into @old, fetch b into @new)
                select @x + one month, (@sum += (@new - @old))/30
```

```
/* Cumulative aggregate */
declare cursor c
        for select name, shares from shareholders
        order by shares desc
@sum=0; open c
for (fetch c into @name,@shares;
                @@sqlstatus==0;
                fetch c into @name,@shares)
        select @name, @shares, (@sum += @shares)
```

3. **Reducing number of scans** — Sometimes limitations in the semantics of SQL or Transact-SQL may force you to scan the same table or evaluate the same expression more than once. Suppose for your tennis club application you need to display each inactive member's phone number without the area code if they live in the local area code and their complete phone number otherwise.

```
select m_name, m_phone
        from      members
        where     m_status <> 'Active'
        and       m_phone not like '(510)%'
select m_name, substr(m_phone, 5, 10)
        from      members
        where     m_status <> 'Active'
        and       m_phone like '(510)%'
```

Cursors enable you to accomplish this in a single scan of the table.

```
declare m_cursor cursor for select m_name, m_phone
        from      members
        where     m_status <> 'Active'
open m_cursor fetch m_cursor into @name, @phone
while (@@sqlstatus = 0) begin
        if (charindex('(510)', @phone) <> 0)
                select @name, substr(m_phone, 5, 10)
        else
                select @name, @phone
        fetch m_cursor into @name, @phone
end
```

Performance of Cursors

There are a few issues related to the efficiency of cursors on SQL Server that you should be aware of:

1. Cursors continue to hold locks even after the transaction has committed or aborted. If lock contention is an issue, you should close all open cursors as early as possible after the transaction has committed.

2. There is some overhead associated with the processing of a query using a cursor rather than as a single SQL statement. Therefore, SQL statements should be rephrased using cursors only when the resultant savings in the number of scans justifies this overhead.

3. Cursors disable certain optimization features, most notably the OR optimization strategy and the use of non-unique index in scanning a table. We discuss these issues in greater detail in Chapter 11, *Query Processing Performance*.

4. The performance of a fetch statement is inversely related to the number columns in the select list for obvious reasons. This dependence is more pronounced in System 10 SQL Server than in System 11 SQL Server. If your application uses cursors having very long select lists, then you may see some performance advantage by either reducing the length of the select list, or by migrating to System 11 SQL Server.

5. System 11 SQL Server can better optimize cursors when both of the following conditions are met: no table is accessed concurrently by more than one cursor and all cursors in a command batch or stored procedure use fetch cursor `INTO` `@variable` rather than `select @variable = column`.

Insert and Delete Statements

The key to the performance of `insert` statements often lies in the declaration of the table and indexes rather than in the phrasing of the `insert` statement itself. "Designing Indexes for Transaction Processing" on page 329 discusses the design of indexes. Also, "Granularity of Locks" on page 355 discusses the reduction of lock contention in applications that insert many rows into the same table. In the remainder of this section, we address only the phrasing of the `insert` statement itself.

The choice between `select .. into y from x` and `insert into y select ... from x` can have a significant impact on log throughput. The latter is ANSI standard SQL. Unfortunately, its semantics forces SQL Server to log the rows inserted. The former is a SQL Server extension[8] and does not log the rows

---

[8.] `Select into` requires the dboption `select into/bulkcopy` to be set true on the database in question.

inserted. If log throughput is a concern, consider using `select into` for `insert` statements that insert large number of rows. Similarly, `truncate table` is faster than `delete from` for deleting all rows from a table, since it does not log the deletes.

The explicit listing or the order of column names in the `insert` statement has no impact on performance. For example, the following three statements have identical performance characteristics.

```
insert into employees values (10, 20)
insert into employees(x,y) values (10,20)
insert into employees(y,x) values (20,10)
```

If you are counting on deletes to make pages available for subsequent inserts, you may be interested to know that a page deleted from one table is not necessarily available for inserting into another table. Deleting all rows from a page does not make the page available for allocation to a different table. However, it does make this page available for reallocation to the same table. Deleting all rows from all pages in an extent makes the extent available for allocation to any table. However, all extents within and allocation unit exhibit some affinity toward the tables that already own extents on the allocation unit. That is, table `employees` owns an extent in allocation unit **A** but not in **B**, and both **A** and **B** have free extents available, the next allocation of an extent for `employees` comes from **A** and not **B**.

10.3.3 Distributed Transactions

The performance of distributed transactions is largely determined by the semantics of the distributed transactions. The more demanding the semantics, the harder it is to improve performance. One of the more demanding is the notion of two-phase commits and among the less demanding are various types of replication. The choice among them should be determined by *all* the requirements of your application, not just performance.

Remote Procedure Calls

SQL Server has a remote procedure call mechanism. One SQL Server may execute a stored procedure on another SQL Server and read some results. There are a variety of restrictions on remote procedure calls:

1. **Remote procedure calls are not part of a transaction** — In particular, a rollback on the local SQL Server does not imply a rollback on the remote SQL Server. This can be used to your advantage for some applications. For example, you may have an auditing operation that you want to record regardless of the fate of the transaction. Since the work performed by the remote procedure call does not rollback with a transaction rollback, you can use remote procedure calls to effect changes to data outside the context of the transaction.

2. **A remote procedure call must be a complete unit of work** — You cannot use one remote procedure call to begin a transaction on the remote SQL Server and use another to complete it.

3. **The calling SQL Server can only use some of the return information from a remote procedure call** — Remote procedure calls may return messages, columns, and row data, but the calling SQL Server can only read the return status and values returned in output parameters.

Keeping connections open to a remote server has no significant impact on the performance of SQL Server, other than the memory configured for the remote connections. Establishing the connection for the site handler can be time consuming as it involves opening the interfaces file, finding the remote server's entry in the file, translating the network address of the remote server (e.g., using Network Information Services), and logging into the remote server. Disabling the site handler time-out feature means the connection is formed only once and the connection cost is borne only by the first remote procedure call to the remote server. Subsequent remote procedure calls to the remote server are handled through the existing connection. Disabling the time-out can improve the performance of applications that make infrequent use of RPCs, at the cost of a network connection that cannot be used for a user login. Applications that make frequent use of RPCs do not benefit from a long time out as they are using the site handler frequently enough to keep it from timing out and dropping the connection.

Two Phase Commits

Two phase commit requires three SQL Servers: the two SQL Servers sharing the transaction and a third to mediate the commit or rollback of the transaction. The SQL Server acting as the commit server uses a single database table to store the commit information. The commit information is appended to the end of this table. At very high throughput of two phase commits, the heap inserts into this table can be a bottleneck in the prepare and commit stages. If your application performs a large number of two-phase commits and you have identified the commit server as the bottleneck, you should distribute the workload of commit service among multiple commit servers. There is no reason why each database server cannot also play a dual role as a commit server; although you need to program a protocol into your application by which any subset of SQL Servers can elect one SQL Server as a commit server.

10.4   LOCKING AND CONCURRENCY

Performance of transaction processing systems is especially susceptible to lock contention. Often one can reduce lock contention without compromising data or transactional integrity by either altering the schema of the database or by rewriting parts of the application. The basic techniques are straightforward.

1. Lock at the smallest granularity possible.
2. Eliminate single points of contention.
3. Use the lowest level of locks possible.
4. Minimize the duration locks are held.
5. Acquire locks in an order that avoids deadlocks.

In the remainder of this section we discuss how these techniques apply to SQL Server. However, let us begin with a statement of the obvious: reducing contention enhances the performance only if lock contention is a problem. Some of the techniques that reduce lock contention, such as locking at smaller granularity may increase the overhead of lock management while reducing lock contention. Therefore, they should be used only if lock contention is a problem. If overhead is a problem, these techniques may exacerbate your performance dilemma. The methods discussed in Chapter 8, *Monitoring SQL Server* may help you to determine whether this is the case.

10.4.1 Granularity of Locks

SQL Server locks data in units of pages and tables. Row-level locks are not supported. This poses an additional challenge for the developer: how to live with page-level locks when row-level locks are called for.

Emulating Row-Level Locks

Small tables often account for most of the lock contention. A transaction may obtain an exclusive lock on a row in the master table to process the detail rows (e.g., lock the master row for a flight while scanning the 400 seat assignments within the flight). Another example is an application that maintains on-line aggregates by having each transaction increment one of a few rows of aggregates. In such cases, SQL Server can emulate row level locks by putting one or very few rows on each page. You can force SQL Server to do so by creating a clustered index with a low fill factor. A fill factor of one guarantees that no page contains more than one row. However, you must create the clustered index after all the rows have been loaded, since inserts do not preserve fill factor. System 11 SQL Server adds an additional configuration parameter for tables: `max_rows_per_page`. If reducing lock contention on a small table is your only reason for having a clustered index with a small fill factor, you should consider using this configuration parameter instead.

Avoiding Table-Level Locks and Lock Escalation

Table locks can hurt performance by prohibiting concurrent access to tables. Typically, they are acquired only by batch operations such as creating a clustered index. Such operations should not be performed concurrently with transaction processing. However, even an on-line transaction can escalate page locks to a table lock after the number of page locks acquired by a single SQL statement exceeds a certain threshold. This threshold is fixed at 200 for System 10 and earlier versions of SQL Server and is a configurable parameter in System 11 SQL Server. We should note that lock escalation occurs when the number of distinct pages locked at the same level (e.g., shared, exclusive) by one reference to a table in a single SQL statement exceeds the threshold. For example, the following cases do not cause an escalation to a table lock, assuming the threshold is set at 200, and all `select` statements are executed with keyword `HOLDLOCK`.

1. An SQL statement scans 300 rows over 100 pages.

2. A transaction has two SQL statements, each of which locks a disjoint set of 150 pages.

3. A `select` statement has two references to a table, each of which scans 150 pages in the table.

Here are examples of cases when SQL Server attempts to escalate page locks to a table lock. Assume that the lock promotion threshold is set at 200:

1. An SQL statement scans over 200 pages.

2. An update statement locks 180 pages in update mode and 50 in exclusive mode.

3. A SQL Server cursor scans over 200 pages.

An attempt to escalate page locks to a table lock succeeds only if a table lock does not conflict with page locks on the same table held by another concurrent transaction. The following pseudo-code illustrates a case where an attempt to escalate page locks to a table lock fails:

```
begin transaction T1
update foo set x = 5 where pkey = 10001
                           /* matches one row on page# 1000 */
waitfor delay '1:00:00'
rollback transaction T1
```

Suppose T1 has already started and it holds a single exclusive page lock on page 1000 in table foo as well as an exclusive intent lock on table foo. Now we start T2:

```
begin transaction T2
select * from foo HOLDLOCK where pkey < 5000
                          /* scans pages 1 through 500 */
commit transaction
```

Transaction T2 attempts to escalate its collection of shared page locks on foo to a table-level lock for every new page it scans, starting with page 201. However, its request for a shared table lock on foo conflicts with the exclusive intent lock on table foo that is held by T1.

If successful, lock escalation can improve performance for queries that access many pages from one table. The overhead of acquiring and managing the page locks is bypassed once the transaction has a table lock. On the other hand, SQL Server's lock escalation strategy can hurt performance in two ways:

1. **Successful escalation can increase contention** — The query now has a lock on the entire table rather than on only the selected pages in the table. As a result, other transactions cannot modify any pages in the table, even if they want to modify pages in the table that the transaction with the table lock does not care about.

2. **Unsuccessful attempts at escalation increase overhead of lock management**
— Managing locks is strictly overhead and the time it takes increases the duration of your query. Traversing the lock structures in SQL Server takes time. This time is wasted if the lock escalation fails.

If successful lock escalation is a source of lock contention in your application, then your options in System 10 and earlier versions of SQL Server include a work around similar to the example above. You can add two dummy pages to the table, and have two dummy transactions that take turns locking one of the two pages, ensuring that at least one of the two pages is locked at any given point in time. This works better than a more straightforward implementation of the above example, since a single long-running dummy transaction can disable the truncation of the log. System 11 SQL Server provides a much cleaner solution by making the threshold for lock escalation a configurable parameter.

If a large number of unsuccessful attempts at lock escalation is a concern, your options in System 10 and earlier versions of SQL Server are limited. The configurable threshold for escalation in System 11 SQL Server, of course, is a clean and effective cure for this malady.

10.4.2 Eliminating Single Points of Contention

If several concurrent transactions need a lock on a single page or table and at least one of them needs an update or exclusive lock, we have an obvious source of lock contention. Such cases may be disguised in various forms and shapes. We discussed one such case in "Temporary Tables" on page 346. Unfortunately, we cannot provide you with an exhaustive laundry list that covers all such cases. The techniques discussed in Chapter 8, *Monitoring SQL Server* and Chapter 9, *Instrumenting SQL Code*, may assist you in identifying if and when a single page or table becomes a source of lock contention. In the remainder of this section, we discuss one specific case that occurs in many transaction processing applications.

Heap Inserts and Clustered Indexes

A heap is a table that does not have a clustered index. Inserts to such a table are always directed to the very last page of the table. If your application has multiple transactions appending rows to a single table, such as a daily log of transactions or an audit trail, and this table does not have an appropriate clustered index, the last page of this table may be a source of lock contention.

Short of rewriting your application to distribute heap inserts among multiple heaps, your options in System 10 and earlier versions of SQL Server are limited to adding an appropriate clustered index to the heap. The example in the following pseudo-code illustrates this approach.

```
create table trail (account int, amount money)
create proc payment @account int, @amount money as
        insert into trail (account, amount)
                values (@account, @amount)
```

In the above situation, the last page of the table trail is a potential source of contention. The following pseudo-code shows one solution to this problem.

```
create table trail (account int, amount money, hashkey smallint)
create clustered index trail_clu on trail(hashkey) with allow_dup_key
create proc payment @account int, @amount money as
        select @hashkey = hash(@account) /* hash to range 1:10000 */
        insert into trail (account, amount, hashkey)
                values (@account, @amount, @hashkey)
```

The above solution adds an artificial key to the heap, one that is computed by applying a hash function to some application variable that does not stay fixed at any one value. The effect of this change is to direct the inserts to one of 10000 points of insertions in the table. If the values of `@account` and the hash function ensure that the value of `@hashkey` is random, then there is no single source of lock contention. You may not need to add artificial columns to your heap. Often, keys that decluster inserts occur naturally in the application. The above example could include the identification of the salesperson receiving the payment in the table `trail`. This is a natural choice as a key for eliminating contention between salespersons who access the database concurrently since two different users never share a value of this key.

System 11 adds a much cleaner solution to the heap insert problem in the form of **partitioned tables**. We discuss the use of partitioned tables for heap inserts in Chapter 13, *Advanced Topics*, "Performance of Concurrent Inserts" on page 520.

10.4.3 Duration of Locks and Isolation Levels

The relationship between the duration transactions hold locks and contention for locks is easy to see. The longer a transaction holds a lock, the greater the chances another transaction may end up waiting on it. In general, transactions should acquire locks as late as possible and release them as soon as possible. The example in the following pseudo-code illustrates how one may rewrite a transaction to reduce the duration of locks.

```
create proc foo as
begin transaction
        select @x=x from foo HOLDLOCK where = 20
        /* Code block A: Does not use the value of @x */
        if (@x<100) ... else ....
        /* Code block B */
commit transaction
```

The transaction in the example above acquires a lock on `foo` long before it needs it. If lock contention at `foo` limits performance, you can rewrite the stored procedure as follows to acquire the lock on `foo` *after* the code block A.

```
create proc foo as
begin transaction
        /* Code block A: Does not use the value of @x */
        select @x=x from foo HOLDLOCK where = 20
        if (@x<100) ... else ....
        /* Code block B */
commit transaction
```

Or, we could simply omit the keyword `HOLDLOCK`, in which case the lock on `foo` is not held during the execution of code block A. It is tempting to conclude that a transaction should only acquire a lock on a page when it is absolutely needed, and release the lock as soon as it is done with the page. Unfortunately, the implications of both late acquisition and early release of locks reach farther than the previous example indicates.

Late Acquisition of Locks and Deadlocks

Deadlocks can result from a circular dependency between lock contentions. Suppose task t_i is waiting for a lock held by t_{i+1} for $i = 1 ... (n-1)$, and t_n is waiting for a lock held by t_1. This is a deadlock as no task can make progress. Deadlocks can affect the performance of transaction processing applications, not just because of the additional work of aborting and retrying a transaction to break a deadlock, but also because of the overhead of the additional application code needed to detect and handle deadlocks. Simply put, deadlock avoidance is important for performance.

A technique commonly used to avoid deadlocks is to impose a total order on all the resources in the database and acquire locks on the objects in that order. The purpose of the total order is to preclude the circular dependency illustrated above. For example, if you have three tables $\langle A, B, C \rangle$ and 100 pages in each table, you could require that every transaction acquires locks in the order:

$\langle A, A1, A2, ..., A100, B, B100, B99, ..., B1, C, C1, C2, ..., C100 \rangle$

where X denotes a table-level lock on table X and Xi denotes a page lock on page i of table X. If a transaction needs locks x and y, and x precedes y in the total order, then the order only implies that the transaction must acquire the lock x before attempting to acquire a lock y and not that the transaction must acquire all locks that occur between x and y in the total order. Note that table locks precede all page locks on all pages in the table. This is a specific instance of the more general rule that if lock x covers lock y, in the sense that any transaction that has the lock x does not need lock y, then x must precede y in the total order. For example, since a table lock covers all page locks on pages of the table, it must precede them. Similarly, an exclusive lock on a resource must precede an update lock on the same resource, which in turn must precede a shared lock on the same resource.

If the above explanation seems daunting, rest assured. The actual task of ensuring that your transactions follow such a total order is a lot easier than suggested by the above formalization and may even follow naturally from business logic. However, its implications may be contradictory to our earlier discussion about acquiring locks as late as possible. For example, if you have two transactions that use pages A and B in opposite order, then you must either violate whatever total order you adopt, or have one transaction acquire a lock earlier than needed. There is no firm rule on which of these two options is better for performance. Intuitively, if the need for the additional concurrency outweighs the likelihood or cost of a deadlock, then you should make an exception to the total order. Otherwise, you should have one transaction acquire a lock earlier than it needs to. In either case, document your assumptions and decisions; your DBA will thank you for it.

The example in the following pseudo-code illustrates a common source for deadlocks prior to the availability of cursors in System 10 SQL Server:

```
create proc positioned_update @x int
begin transaction
        select @y = y from foo HOLDLOCK where x = @x
        select @y = /* some complex function of @x and @y */
        update foo set y = @y where x = @x
```

```
commit transaction
```

Suppose two users invoke the above stored procedure concurrently and that their arguments select rows on the same page in the table. Then, it is possible that both acquire a shared page lock on the said page and cause a deadlock while trying to upgrade their shared page locks to exclusive page locks. Observe that this stored procedure violates the requirement on total order from our earlier discussion by acquiring a shared lock on a page before trying for an exclusive lock on the same page. The following pseudo-code illustrates how use of cursors eliminates this problem.

```
create proc positioned_update @x int
declare a cursor for select y from foo where x = @x for update of y
begin transaction
        open c fetch c into @y
        select @y = /* some complex function of @x and @y */
        update foo set y = @y where current of a
commit transaction
```

The above stored procedure forces a transaction to acquire update page locks before upgrading them to exclusive page locks. Since two transactions cannot get an update lock on the same page, the lock upgrade cannot cause a deadlock. One may argue that the above implementation limits concurrency to avoid deadlocks. You could, of course, omit the FOR UPDATE OF . . . clause from the cursor declaration. This causes each transaction to acquire shared locks first and then upgrade them to exclusive locks. However, observe that this change does not improve concurrency between two instances of the same transaction since whenever two transactions do get shared page locks on the same page, one of them must abort. This change improves concurrency between this transaction and other transactions that only read the page in question. The following example shows another form of deadlocks common when you use cursors:

```
create proc positioned_update @x int
declare b cursor for select y from foo where x = @x for update of y
declare c cursor for select z from bar where x = @x for update of y
begin transaction
        open b fetch c into @y
        open c fetch c into @z
        select @y = /* some complex function of @y and @z */
        update foo set y = @y where current of b
commit transaction

create proc read_only @x int
```

```
begin transaction
        select @y = y from bar HOLDLOCK where x = @x
        select @y = y from foo HOLDLOCK where x = @x
commit transaction
```

In the above example, the two stored procedures acquire locks in opposite order on two tables — a clear violation of total order requirement discussed earlier. A deadlock results if `read_only` acquires a shared page lock on `bar`, while `positioned_update`, holds update locks on both pages, but has yet to upgrade to an exclusive lock.

Early Release of Locks and Isolation Levels

The default mode of operation in SQL Server releases shared locks on pages before a transaction has committed. The exact point in time when locks are released depends on several factors including the use of cursors and the query plan chosen by the optimizer. You can force transactions to hold shared locks until commit either by using the keyword `HOLDLOCK` in `select` statements or by using the statement `set transaction isolation level 3` in a session. There is no mechanism for releasing update and exclusive locks before commit. They are always held until the transaction commits.

As an application developer, you do not need to do anything special to release shared locks early. The default mode of SQL Server does that for you. However, releasing a lock before a transaction commits can compromise transactional integrity. The ANSI Standard for SQL defines several levels of isolation. Generally speaking, the higher the isolation level, the larger the scope of locking. Isolation level 3 ensures repeatability of reads, serializability of transactions, and no phantoms. Level 2 implies repeatability of reads.[9] If your application requires serializability of transactions and repeatability of reads, you must override the default behavior of SQL Server to ensure that transactions do not release shared locks before commit.

Holding shared locks until commit may seem like a hefty price to pay for transactional integrity. Let us explore the need for holding read locks and the serializability of transactions using the example in Figure 10.20.

---

[9] The ANSI standard definition of Level 2 isolation does not guarantee repeatable reads. However, the implementation of Level 2 isolation by most major RDBMS vendors does guarantee repeatable reads. See Melton, et al. in Proceedings of the ACM SIGMOD Conference on Management of Data, 1995 for a very interesting exposition on isolation levels.

```
          begin transaction xfer
          update savings
                  set balance = balance-@sum
                  where customer = @cust
②  update checking
                  set balance = balance+@sum
                  where customer = @cust
          commit transaction xfer
```

```
          begin transaction fees
①  select @sav = balance from savings
                  where customer = @cust
③  select @chk = balance from checking
                  where customer = @cust
          if (@sav+@chk < 5000.00)
                  exec proc charge_fee @cust
          commit transaction fees
```

Figure 10.20 Serializability -

Transaction `xfer` transfers a specified sum from a customer's savings account to his checking account. Transaction `fees` checks if the sum of his two balances is less than $5000, and if so, charges a monthly fee. Transactional integrity requires that `fees` should see the correct sum of the accounts even while `xfer` is moving money from one account to another. Serializable repeatable reads ensure that the transactions behave as expected, even when they work concurrently. However, if we relax the requirement for serializability repeatable reads, the above transactions may not behave as expected. To see this, consider the following scenario:

1. Transaction `fees` reads the savings balance for a customer — `fees` acquires a shared lock on the page in savings containing the row for the customer's account and releases the lock when the read is complete.

2. Transaction `xfer` updates both savings and checking for the same customer — `xfer` acquires exclusive page locks on the pages in savings and checking containing the rows for the customer's two accounts and releases all locks when the transaction commits.

3. Transaction `fees` reads the (updated) checking balance — `fees` acquires a shared lock on the page in checking containing the row for the customer's account and releases the lock when the read is complete.

Transaction fees has combined the customer's savings balance from before the transfer with his checking balance after the transfer to come up with a wrong assessment of the customer's worth. Level 3 isolation would cause SQL Server to hold onto the shared locks on pages read by the query until the transaction commits. In this example, `xfer` is blocked until `fees` commits because `xfer` cannot acquire an exclusive lock on the needed pages until `fees` releases its shared locks.

The above example illustrates that serializability of transactions can be essential for transactional integrity. If your transactions release shared locks before commit, then you need to weigh the potential for inconsistency against the reduction in concurrency due to serializability.

10.4.4 Other Issues in Locking

Avoiding Livelocks

You may be able to reduce the potential for livelocks in your application by controlling the order in which locks are released. Transactions in SQL Server release locks in the order that they were acquired. The order locks are released can determine the order of the tasks that are waiting for those locks resume execution.

Conversational Transactions

Conversational transactions involve interaction with users as part of the transaction. If a user starts a transaction, acquires a few locks and then goes to lunch, we may see a severe degradation in performance because of lock contention. There is no easy solution for the lock contention caused by conversational transactions. If your application involves interaction with end-users, you should consider writing your application such that no such interactions are performed within the scope of transactions.

Dirty Reads

System 10.1 SQL Server and System 11 SQL Server support isolation level 0. This topic is discussed in Chapter 13, *Advanced Topics*, "Isolation Level 0" on page 525.

Chapter 11

Query Processing Performance

The earliest proponents of relational database systems touted ad hoc query processing as the primary strength of the relational model — not transaction processing. Interestingly, transaction processing has played the dominant role in the wide commercial acceptance of relational database management systems — not query processing. However, query processing has regained some of the lost ground in the recent years. All major relational and some object-relational vendors have added cost-based optimizers and the capability to handle very large databases to their products. New benchmarks such as TPC-D have increased the competition among hardware and software vendors. The steady improvement in the price and performance of CPUs and memory over the last decade and the rather drastic improvement in the price and capacity of disks over the last few years have all but eliminated the cost of storing data. The promise of parallel query processing has whetted the users' appetite for enormous data warehouses. Now, all that remains is for the application developers to put it all together and make it work.

Unfortunately, this is where the going gets tough. The functionality and capability of products vary widely. Performance of complex queries is often highly sensitive to the phrasing of the queries and the database schema. A minor change in the syntax of a query can affect its performance by several orders of magnitude. Almost every product has its own variant of SQL, replete with extensions and hints. Even when two products agree on the syntax and semantics of a query, their performance may vary substantially. If your application processes complex queries, porting it from one RDBMS to another is far from trivial. In fact, the same product may have widely different performance on two separate invocations of the same query.

We have discussed various aspects of query processing by SQL Server in previous chapters. The architecture of SQL Server, discussed in Chapter 4, *SQL Server — Form and Structure*, and Chapter 5, *SQL Server — Methods and Features*, determines how SQL Server organizes data on disks, how memory is used to reduce the amount of disk access, and how tables are indexed. Chapter 7, *Application Development*, describes how to structure your client-server application. Chapter 8, *Monitoring SQL Server*, and Chapter 9, *Instrumenting SQL Code*, show how to monitor SQL Server and view the query plans. This chapter provides more details about query plans, how they are optimized, and what you can do to ensure the generation of optimal plans for your queries.

11.1   MYTH VERSUS REALITY

Let us start by clearing up some common misconceptions about query processing in SQL Server.

11.1.1 Creating a Stored Procedure Generates the Plan

A common misconception is to assume that the query plan is generated when the stored procedure is created. In fact, when a stored procedure is created, all SQL Server does is to check the body of the stored procedure for correctness, and store the text and parse tree in system tables. This makes the stored procedures persistent. However, the optimizer still needs to generate the query plan from the parse tree. This is done on an as-needed basis at run time, and is known as the **compile** or **recompile** step. Once the stored procedure is compiled, the plan generated by the optimizer is cached in procedure cache. It is not uncommon to have the optimizer invoked only once at start-up time for every stored procedure. In the normal course of usage, this plan is cached in the procedure cache, and reused on successive invocations. This approach to compilation of stored procedures has two advantages.

1. Caching of stored procedures improves transaction processing performance by eliminating the need to invoke the optimizer during normal transaction processing.

2. Since the values of the arguments to a stored procedure are available during compilation, the optimizer uses them in estimating the cost of alternative plans.

The latter can lead to unpredictable performance characteristics. Consider a stored procedure where the choice of the optimal plan depends on the values of the arguments. For example, a stored procedure that counts the number of customers who have placed an order in a given time interval could benefit by using index scan for small intervals and table scan for large intervals. If the first and only compilation of this stored procedure is for a small interval, the generated plan may perform poorly on subsequent invocations of the stored procedure for large intervals.

If you suspect that the choice of the optimal plan varies over the range of arguments to the stored procedure generated by your application, you may need to force a recompile of the stored procedure, either globally or every time a change in the distribution of the arguments necessitates a recompile. You can force a recompile by creating or invoking the stored procedure with the `with recompile` option.

Automatic Recompile of Stored Procedures

You need to pay special attention to automatic recompile of stored procedures. Certain activities on SQL Server cause an automatic recompile of stored procedures, including those created and invoked without the `with recompile` option.

When a stored procedure is invoked, SQL Server checks the system table entries for every table accessed by the stored procedure to decide whether a recompile is necessary. Relevant columns include `schemacnt` and `indexdel` in `sysobjects`. An operation that modifies the characteristics of a table also updates the system table entries for the table if the modification is significant enough to warrant a recompile of stored procedures that depends on the table. You need to be aware of such activities for two reasons: repeated recompiles can be expensive and an inappropriate recompile may replace a good query plan by a bad one.

The system stored procedure `sp_depends` shows which stored procedures depend on which tables, constraints, indexes or triggers, and vice-versa. The following is a list of some of the activities that force a recompile of stored procedures, either by incrementing `schemacnt` or `indexdel`, or by other means:

- **SQL Server shutdown** — The contents of the procedure cache are lost when SQL Server is shutdown. Naturally, the first invocation of every stored procedure after a cold start of SQL Server requires a recompile.

- **Deletion/alteration of tables/indexes** — `Alter table` increments the `schemacnt` for the table, and `drop index` increments `indexdel` for the table. Both cause all stored procedures that reference this table to be recompiled on the next invocation.

- **Creation/deletion of triggers and constraints** — As we observed in Chapter 10, *Transaction Processing Performance*, the query plan is influenced by the presence of triggers and constraints. If you create a trigger or constraint or drop a constraint on a table, all stored procedures that reference the table are recompiled on the next invocation.

- **Capacity miss in procedure cache** — If your application requirements exceed the configured size of the procedure cache, then invocation of other stored procedures may cause a less frequently used stored procedure to be purged from the procedure cache. Then, the next invocation of the infrequently used stored procedure causes a recompile.

- **Cache configuration** — The optimizer uses the count of database buffers in optimizing queries. Until System 11 SQL Server, the number of buffers available to a query could not change dynamically. Thus, there was no need to recompile queries to account for a change in the number of buffers. In System 11 SQL Server, certain cache configuration operations can be changed dynamically, such as `sp_bindcache` and `sp_poolconfig`. We discuss cache configuration in Chapter 13, *Advanced Topics*. Suffice it to say that some cache configuration operations, including `sp_bindcache`, force a recompile of all stored procedures that reference affected databases, tables, and indexes.

While an automatic recompile can cause problems, sometimes a recompile is necessary to enhance performance. Just as it is important to know what causes a recompile, it is also important to note that certain events do *not* cause stored procedures to be recompiled:

- **Adding an index** — Adding an index to a table does not increment its `schemacnt`. Therefore, if you add an index to enhance the performance of a stored procedure that has been invoked recently, you may need to execute it once with the `with recompile` option before you can see the benefits of the index.

- **Update statistics** — The `update statistics` command does not force an automatic recompile of affected stored procedures. This may seem counterintuitive in that the primary objective of `update statistics` is to provide more up-to-date and accurate information to the optimizer. You need to be aware that `update statistics` does not influence the plans for stored procedures until the next recompile.

- **Different parameters**— It is difficult, if not impossible, to know when the differences in the values of parameters justify a recompile. SQL Server does not consider a change in the value of parameters as ample enough reason to recompile a stored procedure.

11.1.2 Query Processing is Read-Only

There are several reasons why your read-only query may result in writes to disks. Let us examine some of the more common ones.

- **Intermediate results** — The query may create temporary tables to store intermediate results. Creation of such tables may be explicit (e.g., `select ...  into #temp`) or implicit (e.g., worktable created by optimizer). In either case, if the size of the temporary table is sufficiently large, the buffer manager is forced to write out pages of the temporary table to disk in order to maintain a supply of clean pages. Writing of intermediate results to disks is not essential for integrity and every attempt should be made to eliminate them. System 10 and earlier versions of SQL Server provide only one option for eliminating disk I/O for intermediate results: add more main memory. System 11 SQL Server provides two additional options: replacement strategy and named caches. We discuss these options later in this chapter and in Chapter 13, *Advanced Topics*.

- **Other queries' dirty laundry** — Each user task in SQL Server shares in the burden of writing out dirty pages to disk to maintain a supply of clean buffers, whether or not it is responsible for dirtying the pages. Thus, the execution of a truly read-only query may be forced to write out pages dirtied by other activities on SQL Server. Short of discouraging other users from dirtying pages, pre-System 11 SQL Servers provide no method for eliminating this overhead. System 11 SQL Server adds two options that may help in relieving read-only queries from the burden of writing dirty pages to disk: named caches and the housekeeper task. Both are discussed in Chapter 13, *Advanced Topics*.

- **Dynamic SQL** — As discussed in Chapter 7, *Application Development*, SQL Server creates and drops stored procedures in `tempdb` to process Dynamic SQL, which modifies system tables and generates log entries in `tempdb`. Thus, a read-only query executed using Dynamic SQL performs writes to the log device for `tempdb`.

- **Offset information** — SQL Server creates a temporary data structure called the **offset table** to optimize access through indexes. It comprises of pointers to the beginning of rows on a page and is a natural part of index traversal whenever rows of variable length are involved. Instead of recomputing the offset table for a page every time it is traversed, SQL Server attempts to save the offset table to persistent store. The writing of such pages may introduce disk writes to an otherwise read-only activity. However, this should not be detrimental to performance. The following three conditions must be met before the offset optimization introduces an additional write:

1. The table/index must contain variable-length rows.[1]

2. The database must not be in read-only mode.

3. The I/O subsystem is not overloaded.

If you suspect that your read-only queries are performing unnecessary writes to disks, consider using `sp_dbpotion` to put your database in a read-only mode. Of course, this is only possible if your application does not require write access to the database.

11.1.3 Plan Depends on the Order of Tables or Clauses

SQL Server does not consider all possible join orders when more than four tables are involved in a join. However, in general, the join order or indexes selected by the optimizer do *not* depend on the order of the tables in the `from` list, the order of conjunctions and disjuntions in the `where` clause, or the order of operands in comparisons. For example, the following pairs of SQL constructs are indistinguishable from each other as far as the optimizer is concerned:

```
from T1, T2, T3 where T1.x=T2.y and T2.y>10
from T2, T3, T1 where 10<T2.y and T2.y=T1.x
```

Since the optimizer does not care about the ordering of tables, clauses, or comparisons, you should not expect to influence the choice of a query plan by re-ordering the phrasing of the query. There are very few exceptions to the above rule:

- **Forced join order** — Application developers can force the join order by using undocumented features. Then, the ordering of tables in the `from` clause matters.

- **Multiple subqueries** — If a query involves two or more subqueries, then the relative order of the subqueries may influence the order in which they are processed.

---

[1] System 10 and 4.9 SQL Server fail to recognize the absence of variable-length columns in tables and indexes under certain circumstances, including the creation of indexes on an empty table and the loading of data into an empty table using normal BCP. This causes SQL Server to compute offset information unnecessarily, thus imposing a minor performance penalty. This situation is easily corrected by executing `dbcc checktable` on the table in question. While System 11 SQL Server recognizes the absence of variable-length columns correctly on newly created tables and indexes, upgrading a database containing such a table or index to System 11 requires the `dbcc checktable`.

- **Multiple materialized views** — If the query contains multiple instances of materialized views (discussed later in "Common Subexpression" on page 429), then the order in which these tables are materialized depends on the order of their occurrence in the query text.

- **Identical cost** — If two different join orders have identical estimated costs and this cost turns out to be the least among all join orders considered, then the optimizer breaks the tie by picking the first join order. Such coincidences are rare.

- **Single-Row Tables** — A table is called a **single-row** when the query text and the uniqueness constraints imply that no more than one row of the table contributes to the result of the query. Such tables are always put before all other tables in the join order. When the query contains two or more such tables, the relative order of those tables in the join order is the same as their order of occurrence in the from clause. In the example below, T1 and T3 are both known to be single-row tables and hence the join order begins with T1 and T3, in that order:

```
unique index T1(x)
unique index T3(z)

select ...
        from T1, T2, T3, T4
        where T1.x = 5
        and   T2.z = 10
        and ...
```

This is not to say that rephrasing of the query does not influence the optimizer. The optimizer is not very good at algebra yet. For example, it cannot tell that the clauses T1.x=@x+100 and T1.x-100=@x are identical or that T1.x=T2.x and T2.x=T3.x implies T1.x=T3.x. We discuss how such rephrasing of queries influences the optimizer later in this chapter. However, let us put to rest the notion that we can change the query plan by merely reordering tables, clauses, or comparisons.

11.1.4 Plan Depends on Schema, Statistics, and Phrasing

Application developers and DBAs are often upset when a seemingly inconsequential change in the context of an SQL statement causes its performance to change drastically. It is true that the database schema, statistics about indexes, the phrasing of the query are the three most influential factors in the optimization of the query. However, there are several other factors that influence the selection of indexes and join orders. Let us identify some of the more common ones as such, lest they be mistaken for inconsequential changes:

- **Use of cursors** — Often, the same query text produces a different plan when used through a cursor. This is especially true when the most appropriate index is not unique or when an optimizable OR clause is involved.

- **Use of stored procedures** — The same query text may result in different plans depending on whether it is invoked as an ad-hoc query or as part of a stored procedure. Even within a stored procedure, the plan for a query may depend on whether the variables used in the where clause are local variables or parameters to the stored procedure. We discuss this behavior in greater detail later in this chapter.

- **Configuration of database buffers** — As discussed elsewhere in this chapter, the number of database buffers relative to the size of the tables influences the choice of plans. Differences in the number of database buffers or the size of tables between two instances of the same database schema can cause the query plan to be different.

11.1.5 There is One Optimal Plan

The optimizer in SQL Server optimizes for total resource cost. That is, it attempts to minimize a certain combination of the I/O cost and the CPU cost of the plan. This may not necessarily optimize your measure of performance, especially if it includes impact on other concurrent users or the time to the first row of results. For example, the optimal plan for a join may involve caching the inner table. If your application requires this query to share database buffers with multiple concurrent users, you may prefer a plan that uses less memory to the "optimal" plan. Another example is the case that the time to the first row of result is as important as the time to the completion of the query. The optimizer in SQL Server attempts to minimize the total resource cost for the entire query. This may not be optimal for time to first row.

There is no single measure that best describes what is optimal. You need to be aware that the measure used by the optimizer in SQL Server may not be the same as that used by your application. For example, the optimizer assumes that a certain fraction of the buffer cache is available for query processing. This assumption may or may not be valid for your application, depending on the number of concurrent users and the type of queries they use. While the recognition of such differences does not necessarily lead to an immediate resolution, it is an important step in tuning the performance of query processing.

There is another reason why you may not want to insist on the "optimal" plan. The choices made by the optimizer are based on estimates. Often, there are multiple alternative query plans for a query, all of which are comparable in cost to the optimal plan. In such cases, the optimizer may make a wrong choice among them. However, this is not catastrophic, except perhaps in competitive benchmark situations. If your objective is to meet preset performance goals as opposed to wringing out every last bit of performance, it suffices to have optimizer choose one of several good plans.

11.2   HOW THE OPTIMIZER VIEWS QUERIES

The choice of indexes and join order are the two most influential factors in the efficiency of a query plan. SQL Server, like most other RDBMS products, uses a combination of **cost-based** and **heuristic** optimization for the selection of both.

1. **Cost-based optimization** — The optimizer selects a plan having the lowest estimated cost among all possible plans for the query. The selection process typically involves enumeration of a large number of alternative plans. Cost-based optimization relieves application developers of the burden of specifying how to access data. Developers identify the data they need only by specifying the criteria it must meet in the `where` clause. The cost-based optimizer uses this information and statistics about the data to select an optimal access method for retrieving the data.

2. **Heuristic optimization** — Heuristic optimization bases its choice of access methods on a set of general guidelines. Heuristics tend to perform well on most queries. However, the application developer is responsible for avoiding pitfalls — the cases where the heuristics perform poorly. Here are examples of some heuristics:[2]

- Prefer or force join orders that resemble the order of tables in the `select` list.
- Base choice of indexes on the relative order of predicates in the `where` clause.

[2.] We mention these heuristics only as examples. The actual heuristics used by the optimizer in SQL Server are more sophisticated.

- Do not consider join orders that require a join between two tables not connected by any join clauses.

It may appear that cost-based optimization has the edge over heuristic optimization across the board. Nevertheless, all RDBMS vendors use a combination of the two, rather than using cost-based optimization only. The reason lies in the complexity of cost-based optimization. The number of alternative query plans grows exponentially with most measures of the complexity of the query and the schema, including the number of tables in the select list, the number and types of indexes, and the number and types of predicates in the `where` clause. This renders cost-based optimization intractable even for queries and database schemas of moderate complexity. To optimize complex queries in a reasonable time, the optimizer uses heuristics to limit its search to a more tractable number of query plans. The intent is to combine the efficiency of heuristic optimization with the advantages of cost-based optimization.

The impact of this hybrid optimization process on the guidelines for tuning SQL statements is as one might expect. Largely, application developers are isolated from the internals of SQL Server in that they can get by without specifying how to access data. However, there are cases when the heuristics or the cost functions mislead the optimizer. Therefore, it pays to understand the process and heuristics used by the optimizer in choosing a plan for the query. We do not recommend that the phrasing of queries be tied very closely to the internals of the optimizer. Our objective in this section is to develop some general guidelines that can assist you in avoiding major pitfalls.

Some of the techniques listed here go beyond avoiding pitfalls. You may use them to fine-tune critical queries. However, the optimizer is continually evolving. Therefore, some of these techniques may not apply to future versions of SQL Server. If your phrasing of queries is based on any undocumented behavior of the optimizer, you should identify such dependencies in your application code by comments or otherwise.

11.2.1 An Overview of the Process

Selection of indexes and join order is a complex process. It is counterproductive for an application developer to attempt to master every nuance of the algorithms used by the optimizer. Instead, we would like to use this section to develop a model for how the optimizer and the lower layers of SQL Server view the query text created by you. Our hope is to provide you with a framework rather than long lists of do's and don'ts.[3] Let us use the following query to introduce some of the concepts used in the remainder of this chapter. Or better yet, get your scratch pad out, jot down your favorite query (or least favorite, if you are an end-user) and use it as a working example throughout the remainder of this chapter.

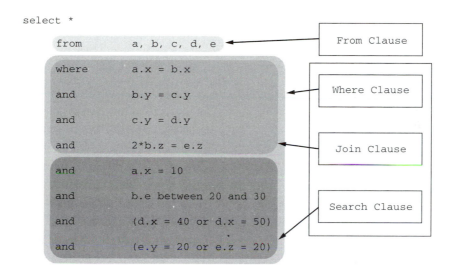

Figure 11.1   Example query -

Search and Join Clauses

The clauses that connect two different tables are called **join clauses** and the clauses that restrict the values of columns within a single table are called **search clauses**. In the query in Figure 11.1, the clauses a.x = 10 and b.z between 20 and 30 are examples of search clauses and the clause a.x = b.x is an example of a join clause.

---

3.   Unfortunately, we will see such lists in the remainder of this chapter. We hope that this framework will make such lists shorter and easier to understand.

Join Graph

The join graph for a query denotes the tables as nodes, join clauses by dotted edges, and search clauses by solid edges. Figure 11.2 shows the join graph for the query in the above example.

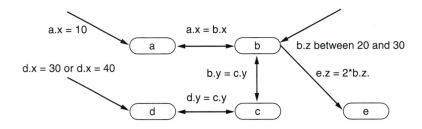

Figure 11.2 Example join graph -

The edges into a node denote information that may be valuable in limiting the scope of the search on the table represented by the node. For example, we could use the search clause `b.z between 20 and 30` in conjunction with an index on `b(z)` to limit the scope of our search for rows in b. Alternatively, we could use the join clause `a.x = b.x` in conjunction with an index on `b(x)` to find rows in b that match a given row in a.

Asymmetric Join Clauses

Note that all but one of the four join clauses in the join graph are bidirectional. The join clause `2*b.z = e.z` is represented in the above join graph by a directed edge rather than a bidirectional edge because it is used by SQL Server only for identifying rows in e that match a row in b, and not vice-versa. Often, such cases are forced by datatype conversions implied by the database schema rather than the query text. For example, if the join clause `d.y = c.y` were to involve a datatype mismatch between a `float d.y` and an `int c.y`, then it has the same impact on index selection and join order as the join clause `d.y = f(c.y)`, where `f()` converts `int` to `float`. We discuss other instances of asymmetric join clauses later in conjunction with subqueries and outer joins.

Unoptimizable Clauses

Notice that the clause `d.y = 20 or e.z = 30` does not appear in the join graph at all, whereas the clause `d.w = 40 or d.x = 50` has been labeled as a search clause. The clause `d.y = 20 or e.z = 30` is not an optimizable search clause. An OR clause can be optimized only if all the operands of the OR are optimizable clauses involving columns of the same table. While not included in the example, joins involving inequalities (e.g., `b.x < d.x`) are not very influential in the choice of indexes and join order. As a result they are not represented in the join graph.

Connected Queries and Cartesian Products

A query is called connected if and only if the join graph is **connected**.[4] A cartesian product is a join between two tables that does not benefit from any optimizable join clause. For example, if we were to start the evaluation of the query in the above example by joining a with e, then we would need to match every row in a with every row in e. If the join graph for a query is connected, there is at least one plan for the query that does not involve a cartesian product.

Join Order

A join order is an ordering on the set of tables that denotes the order in which tables are accessed. For example, Figure 11.3 shows the join order `(c,d,b,e,a)` for the join graph in Figure 11.2.

The join order instructs SQL Server to look up all rows in c. For each such row, it then looks up all matching rows in d. For each such row, it looks up all matching and qualifying rows in b. For each such row, it looks up all matching rows in e. Finally, for each such row, it looks up all matching and qualifying rows in a. We denote this join order as `((((d,c),b),e),a)`, or simply as `(d,c,b,e,a)` assuming that join orders are left-associative.

Note that this join order does not involve a cartesian product. That is, at every step, we have an optimizable join clause that can be used to identify matching rows in the next table. An example of a join order involving a cartesian product is `(d,c,a,b,e)`. This is because there is no optimizable join clause for the join

---

4. We use the term connected somewhat loosely. The traditional definition of connected component in a directed graph requires that for every pair of nodes x and y, there is at least one directed path from x to y *and* one from y to x. We settle for a path in either direction, instead of both directions.

between (d,c) and a. Absence of a cartesian product does not necessarily mean that every pair of tables adjacent in the join order is related by an optimizable join clause. The only requirement is that there be an optimizable join clause for every step implied by the join order. For example, consider the join order (c,b,d,e,a). Although none of the pairs of tables (b,d), (d,e), and (e,a) are related by optimizable join clauses, each of the joins ((c,b),d), ((c,b,d),e), and ((c,b,d,e),a) has an optimizable join clause. Each step in the join order is optimizable as long as the next table is connected to at least one of the previous tables, not necessarily the last table.

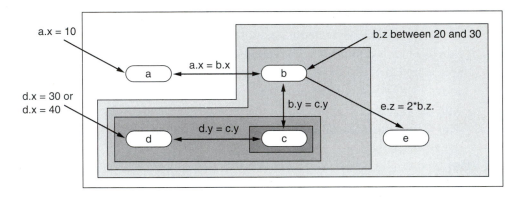

Figure 11.3   Join order- -

11.2.2 Statistics and Cost Estimation

The optimizer needs to estimate the cost of alternative plans. For example, the join order shown in Figure 11.3 requires SQL Server to access all matching rows in b for every row in the result of joining c and d. To estimate the total cost of accessing b, the optimizer needs to estimate the **number of accesses**, and the **cost per access**. The number of accesses is the number of rows in the result of joining c and d. At each step in the join order, the optimizer estimates the number of rows in the intermediate result and uses it in estimating the number of rows at the next step. The cost per access depends on the choice and selectivity of indexes. In this case, we have two clauses that may be of help: b.y=c.y and b.z between 20 and 30. At each step, the optimizer uses a combination of **statistics**, **uniqueness constraints**, and **heuristics** to estimate the **selectivity** of search and join clauses.

The selectivity estimates are then used in combination with the database schema and **cost functions** to estimate the cost of the step. Figure 11.4 shows the process for cost estimation.

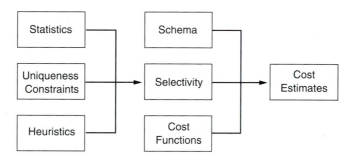

Figure 11.4   Process for query cost estimation -

Search and Join Selectivities

The selectivity of a search clause is the ratio of the number of rows for which the search or join clause is true to the total number of rows in the table. For example, if the search clause `b.z between 20 and 30` is true for 100 of the 1000 rows in b the selectivity of the search clause is $100/1000 = 0.1$. The selectivity of a join clause is the ratio of the number of matching rows to the number of rows in the previous step. For example, if, on average, every row resulting from the join between d and e matches 10 rows in b, the join selectivity for this step is 10. The search and join selectivities enable the optimizer to estimate the number of rows and number of accesses at each step in the query plan.

Statistics

The statistics on tables and indexes are used by the optimizer in estimating selectivities. For example, the estimation of the selectivity of the search clause in the above example requires statistical information on the number of rows in b for which the clause `b.z between 20 and 30` holds true. Similarly, the estimation of the selectivity of the join clause `b.y = c.y` requires statistical information on the number of duplicates in `b.y`. SQL Server maintains two types of statistics for every index — **distribution** and **density**. Both are computed by `create index` and `update statistics <table> [<index>]` commands. Neither is updated automatically to reflect changes to the table due to `update`, `insert`, or `delete` commands. You can check for the availability of statistics on the indexes for a given table with the query:

```
select          o.name, i.indid, i.name, i.distribution
        from     sysobjects o, sysindexes i
        where    o.id = i.id
        and      o.name = "<table name>"
```

The availability of statistics for an index is denoted by a non-NULL value for `distribution`. Typically, statistics are not available if the table contained no rows when the index was created. Currently, there is no way to turn statistics off, in the sense that once the `update statistics` command has been executed on a table, there is no way to tell the optimizer to ignore the statistics on that table.

Distribution

The distribution statistics are used to estimate selectivity of search clauses in two steps. In the first step, SQL Server estimates what fraction of the table matches the value using only the first column of the index. If this fraction is less than a pre-defined threshold, statistics about the remaining columns of the index are used in conjunction with statistics about the number of duplicates to derive a more accurate estimate of the selectivity of the search clause.

Density

Density statistics are used to estimate selectivity of join clauses. SQL Server maintains density information for each non-empty prefix of the index.[5] For each prefix of the index, the density is an intentionally approximate measure of the average number of duplicates in the prefix. For example, if we have an index `T(x,y,z)`, then we have densities for `T(x)`, `T(x,y)`, and `T(x,y,z)`. The density for `T(x)` is related to the number of duplicates in `T(x)`, and that for `T(x,y,z)` to the number of duplicates in `T(x,y,z)`. For any join clause, the density for the longest prefix of the join clause is used to estimate selectivity. For example, the join clause `T.x = T2.x and T.y = T2.y` would use density for `T(x,y)`, whereas the join clause `T.x = T2.x` would use that on `T(x)`.

---

[5] This feature was introduced in System 10 SQL Server. 4.9 and earlier SQL Servers used the density on the entire index for estimating selectivity of join clauses that used only a prefix of the index. This often caused the optimizer to be overly optimistic about the join selectivities.

Uniqueness Constraints

Suppose the database schema in the above example contained a unique index on b(y). Then, the optimizer does not need statistics on this index to estimate the join selectivity, since the constraint already guarantees that each value of c.y matches at most one row of in b. For the purposes of index selection for cursors, an index which contains an identity column as part of its key is considered unique even if it is not declared as unique.

Uniqueness constraints, whenever applicable, have a greater impact on query optimization than statistics. By definition, statistics are approximate, whereas the uniqueness implied by a constraint is exact. But there is a more important factor that distinguishes the role of uniqueness constraints in optimization from that of statistics. This role is best illustrated by the following example.

```
create table foo (x int unique, y char(255))
select count(distinct x) from foo.
```

Without the uniqueness constraint on foo(x), the optimizer is forced to eliminate duplicates before counting. Elimination of duplicates adds a potentially expensive sort step to the plan for the query. The uniqueness constraint as stated obviates elimination of duplicates, and hence the sort step. Observe that statistics, however accurate, could not obviate duplicate elimination. Even if the statistics could guarantee uniqueness at the time the query is compiled, SQL Server needs a uniqueness constraint to ensure that this condition remains valid through the lifetime of the query plan. Uniqueness constraints enable the optimizer to consider additional alternative plans for the query, whose correctness depends on the uniqueness constraints. We discuss the impact of uniqueness constraints in greater detail in "SUBQUERIES AND OUTER JOINS" on page 414 and "VIEWS AND AGGREGATES" on page 429.

Heuristics

In the absence of statistics and uniqueness constraints, the optimizer is forced to guess the selectivity of search and join clauses. Table 11.1 lists some of the heuristics used by the optimizer in estimating selectivity in absence of statistics.

Table 11.1   Heuristics for selectivity estimation

Clause	Selectivity	Comments
Equality search clause	0.10	
Inequality search clause	0.33	Excludes <>, which is not optimizable.
Range search clause	0.25	The clauses `x>=5` and `x<=10` and `x between 5 and 10` are equivalent.
Equality join clause	$1 \leftrightarrow n/m$	m and n are the numbers of rows in the two tables, $n > m$.
Size of temp tables	100 rows, 10 pages	Includes worktables.

The heuristic for equality join clause is based on the assumption of a master-detail relationship between the two tables being joined. That is, if one table contains m rows and the other $n \gg m$, then this heuristic models the case that the former table is a master table, the latter table is a detail table, and each row in the former matches an average of n/m rows in the latter.

A very common use of heuristics is for optimization of queries involving temporary tables and worktables or command batches that query a table created within the same batch. Since these tables do not exist when the query is compiled, the optimizer must resort to guessing their sizes. The numbers it uses are 100 rows and 10 pages. This assumption can cause performance problems. If you suspect this to be the case, here is a work around you may want to try: Move the offending query into a separate stored procedure and invoke this stored procedure from the original query text. Since this temporary table has already been populated by the time this stored procedure is invoked, the optimizer can use actual statistics on this table. But beware, this work around causes the query to be recompiled each time it is executed.

Recompilations forced by changes in the database schema that involve only temporary tables comprise a special case. The output from such a recompilation is not very likely to be useful in the future, since the next invocation of the same stored procedure most likely will force yet another recompilation. System 11 SQL Server recognizes this special case and does not write the output from the recompilation to disk. Thus, the use of temporary tables to pass information between stored procedures is somewhat more efficient in System 11 SQL Server than in the earlier versions of SQL Server.

Cost Functions

Cost functions are crude models for the complex internals of the RDBMS engine and the hardware. For example, the cost of accessing a data or index page depends not only on the performance of the I/O subsystem and the CPU, but also on whether the page is already in cache, the availability of database buffers, other concurrent activity on SQL Server, layout of data on this disk, and so on. The cost model is a simplified view of a very complex system. Fortunately, it does not need to be very accurate for the optimizer to distinguish good plans from bad ones. The cost functions used by the optimizer are platform-independent and work well for a very wide class of platforms.

The cost functions *can* mislead the optimizer when non-traditional I/O subsystems (e.g., solid-state disks) are used. We discuss the use of such devices in greater detail in Chapter 13, *Advanced Topics*.

11.2.3 Accuracy of Estimates

Usually, the process of estimating index and join selectivities as described in the previous section provides estimates that are accurate enough for the optimizer to tell bad plans from good ones. Unfortunately, there are also cases when the optimizer is fooled by inaccurate statistics. Let us discuss a few common scenarios that cause the optimizer to make very large errors in estimates.

Out-Of-Date or Missing Statistics

The lack of proper statistics is a relatively straightforward problem. Creating an index automatically computes statistics on the indexed columns. Should these statistics lose accuracy as indexed columns are affected by updates, inserts, and deletes, you can update the statistics with the `update statistics` command.

The computation of statistics requires a scan of the table (or the leaf pages in a nonclustered index) so updating statistics on large tables and indexes should be scheduled carefully.

Missing Indexes

Statistics are maintained on indexes only — not on all columns in the table. We must create indexes before the optimizer can use the statistics. Sometimes, you may need to create an index on a small table just so the optimizer has the statistics it needs, even though it may decide not to use the index. The example in Figure 11.5 shows such a case.

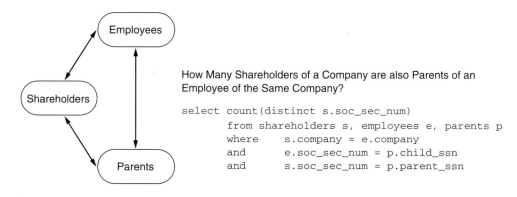

How Many Shareholders of a Company are also Parents of an Employee of the Same Company?

```
select count(distinct s.soc_sec_num)
        from shareholders s, employees e, parents p
        where    s.company = e.company
        and      e.soc_sec_num = p.child_ssn
        and      s.soc_sec_num = p.parent_ssn
```

Figure 11.5   Example query -

Suppose we have 10 companies, 2000 shareholders, and 1000 employees. Then each company has an average of 200 shareholders and 100 employees. It is highly undesirable to use the join clause `s.company = e.company` since that would amount to enumerating all $100 \times 200 = 20000$ employee-shareholder pairings for each company and then looking up the `parents` table to see whether a parent-child relationship exists. This notion may be intuitive to the application developer, but in the absence of indexes and statistics on `shareholder(company)` and `employee(company)` the optimizer invokes the heuristic for equality join clause listed in Table 11.1 to incorrectly assume a master-detail relationship between employees and shareholders of record. That is, it assumes that each employee matches exactly two shareholders. This assumption makes the join orders that start by joining `employees` with `shareholders` appear far more cost effective than they really are. Should such an error cause the optimizer to select a suboptimal join order you may need to create the indexes on `employees(company)` and `shareholders(company)` just so that the optimizer has access to statistics. Observe that these indexes may not actually be used in the optimal query plan — their primary purpose is to provide the optimizer with statistics.

Selectivity of the First Column

The first column of a composite index has a greater influence on the estimation of selectivity for search clauses than other columns in the index. For example, if you have an index on `employee(gender, ssn)`, where `gender` has poor selectivity and `ssn` has excellent selectivity, then the optimizer may be overly pessimistic in estimating selectivity for the search clause `gender = 'M'` and `ssn = '555-55-5555'`. If you identify errors in estimation of selectivity for search clauses on composite indexes as a performance bottleneck, you should consider reordering columns in the index to make the most selective column the first column of the index. Of course, as discussed in Chapter 4, *SQL Server — Form and Structure*, "INDEXES" on page 92, the order of columns in indexes influences the very ability of queries to use the indexes. Hence, such reordering should be done only after studying its impact on all other uses of the index.

Parameters versus Local Variables

As discussed earlier in this chapter, stored procedures are compiled only when invoked for the first time and the values of the parameters are used in the optimization process. This can lead to some unexpected behavior, as illustrated by the example in Figure 11.6.

```
create proc foo @x int as          create proc bar @x int as
select *                           declare    @y         int
        from T                     select @y = @x
        where T.x = @x             select *
                                           from T
                                           where T.x = @y
```

Figure 11.6   Stored procedure with parameters and variables - - - - - - - - - - - - -

Procedures `foo` and `bar` are identical except that `bar` uses a local variable in the search clause whereas `foo` uses a parameter. Suppose there is an index on `T(x)`, and that available statistics indicate this index to be highly selective. Then, `foo` gets an accurate estimate of the selectivity, whereas `bar` is forced to use heuristics to estimate the selectivity. The reason for this difference is that at the time of compilation the value of the parameter `@x` is known, but that of the local variable `@y` is unknown. Such differences can cause the optimizer to choose the wrong plan based on incorrect estimates.

Of course, it is impossible to replace all instances of local variables in `where` clauses by parameters — you should attempt to do so only when necessary. Figure 11.7 shows a work around for such cases.

```
create proc foo as              create proc foo1 @x int as
declare @x int                  select * from T
....                                        where x = @x
select * from T                 go
        where x = @x            create proc foo as
....                            declare @x int
go                              ....
                                exec foo1 @x
                                ....
                                go
```

Figure 11.7   Stored procedure work around -

Of course, this work around works as shown only for queries that do not retrieve values into local variables. Such cases require additional code. Further, there is the overhead of an additional procedure call. Hence, this workaround should not be used indiscriminately.

Concurrent Activity on SQL Server

The optimizer cannot anticipate the state and workload of the system during execution. For example, it does not know whether data or index pages are in cache, the number of concurrent users, and the availability of clean database buffers. It assumes that none of the data or index pages are already in cache when the execution begins and that the execution of the plan can use up to 85% of the database buffers to cache inner tables in a join. This assumption is appropriate for a single-user application on a cold start. In the case of an application that has been running long enough to cache a few frequently accessed pages in memory, or one that involves multiple concurrent users, this assumption can cause SQL Server to be overly pessimistic about the cost of reading pages from *hot* tables and overly optimistic about the availability of database buffers.

11.2.4 Worktables

A worktable is an internal temporary table created by SQL Server as part of processing the query. The worktable is created, populated, queried, and dropped during the execution of the query. Certain query processing operations are simplified through the use of worktables. Examples of such operations include:

- **Order By and Distinct** — Processing `order by` and `distinct` often[6] requires a sort operation to order the result rows in the correct order or eliminate duplicate values. SQL Server accumulates the rows to be sorted in a worktable. The sort manager reads its input from this worktable. The number of rows in the worktable is the number of rows being sorted.

- **Group By** — SQL Server uses a worktable to hold the groups as they are being constructed. There is one row for each group in the result set. This worktable has a clustered index on the grouping columns.

- **View and Subquery Materialization** — We discuss the materialization of views and subqueries later in this chapter. Suffice it to say that some of them are materialized into worktables.

- **Reformatting** — We discuss the reformat operation in "Reformatting" on page 404. The reformat operation transfers selected rows and columns into a worktable and then invokes the sort manager to build an index on it.

Output from `showplan` indicates when a worktable is created in the query. In System 10 and earlier SQL Servers, the showplan output does not identify worktables individually. This makes the task of reading showplan output unsavory when the query plan uses more than one worktable. System 11 SQL Server identifies worktables by name, making it easier to understand the showplan output for query plans that involve more than one worktable.

[6.] Exceptions include the use of an index to eliminate duplicates or to scan rows in sorted order.

Worktables are always created in `tempdb`. Unlike temporary tables, they do not create entries in the system catalogs in `tempdb`. Hence, you need not worry about concurrency issues related to system catalogs in `tempdb` as far as worktables are concerned. However, you do need to pay close attention to the size of `tempdb`, and the caching of worktables.

Sizing *tempdb*

The size of `tempdb` is a correctness issue more than a performance issue. You need to make `tempdb` large enough to hold the worktables for all concurrent users. In assessing the size of `tempdb` you need to pay special attention to the `order by`, `distinct`, reformat, and materialization operations that involve a large number of rows and `group by` operations that involve a large number of groups.

Caching Worktables

Ideally, there should be no I/O in `tempdb`. This is indeed the case whenever there are enough database buffers to hold the entire worktable. Operations on worktables are not logged[7] since worktables are not persistent. The data and index pages for the worktables are deallocated at the end of the query and need not be written to disk at all. If there are sufficient database buffers to hold the entire worktable in memory until deallocation, there is no I/O on the worktable.

On the other hand, if there are not enough database buffers to hold all active worktables, SQL Server is forced to write out dirty pages from the worktable and indexes on worktables to disk. This can hurt performance since each page in the worktable accounts for at least two I/O operations — one to write the newly created dirty page to disk and another to read it when needed. Sorting of large worktables can cause a significant number of I/O operations if the value of the configuration parameter number of sort buffers (see Appendix B, *SQL Server Configuration*) is too small. You can easily determine when your application is performing I/O for worktables by using the monitoring tools described in Chapter 8, *Monitoring SQL Server*. For example, `set statistics io on` shows whether or not any physical reads were performed for any worktables.

---

7. This is not true for all operations in `tempdb`. See "Using Temporary Tables to Simplify Queries" on page 439.

If you do find that your application performs I/O in `tempdb`, then System 11 SQL Server provides two options to remedy the situation: named caches and the fetch-and-discard buffer replacement strategy. The named caches feature and the implications of the fetch-and-discard buffer replacement strategy are discussed in Chapter 13, *Advanced Topics*.

11.3 INDEX SELECTION

The choice of indexes depends on the choice of join order and the choice of join order depends on the selectivity of indexes. Hence, it is impossible to discuss either in isolation. One way to view the process of index selection is exemplified by Figure 11.8, which builds on the example from Figure 11.1. The optimizer labels each search clause and each direction of every join clause in the join graph with the identity of the index estimated to be the most appropriate and the estimated number of rows and pages accessed if this index is used.

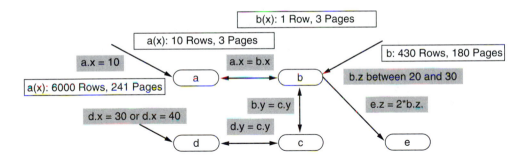

Figure 11.8   Example query -

Figure 11.8 shows only the labels for the clauses `a.x = 10`, `a.x = b.x`, and `b.z between 20 and 30`. For `a.x = 10`, the optimizer has estimated that an index scan using `a(x)` is the best option, and accesses 6000 rows and 241 pages. For the search clause `b.z between 20 and 30`, the optimizer has estimated that a table scan on `b` is the best option and that it must access 430 rows and 180 pages. For the join clause `a.x = b.x`, the optimizer needs to consider both the directions. On table `a`, the optimizer has estimated that an index scan using index `a(x)` is the best option and that each scan must access 10 rows and 3 pages. On table b, the optimizer has estimated that an index scan using index b(x) is the best option and that each scan must access 1 row and 3 pages. All other clauses can be labeled similarly.

Estimating Numbers of Rows

The number of matching rows is estimated by using uniqueness constraints and statistics whenever available and heuristics otherwise. For example, the estimate of 430 rows for the search clause b.z between 20 and 30 is computed using the distribution information discussed in the previous section.

Estimating Number of Pages

Estimating the number of pages is somewhat more involved. It depends on several factors including: the total number of rows and pages in the table, the number of levels in the index, whether the index is clustered or covering, and the number of database buffers available. The following guidelines can help you estimate the number of pages for the three most frequently used access methods. These are not necessarily the estimates used by the optimizer:

1. For table scans, the number of pages is estimated as the total number of pages in the table.

2. For clustered index scans, the number of pages is estimated as $(n \times p/m) + (y-1)$, where n is the estimated number of rows, p is the number of pages in the table, m is the total number of rows in the table, and y is the number of levels in the clustered index.

3. For nonclustered index scans, the number of pages is estimated as $n + (n \times p/m) + (y-1)$, where n is the estimated number of rows, x is the number of pages in the index, m is the total number of rows in the table, and y is the number of levels in the index; but with the following exception: If the innermost table is small enough to fit in cache, then the estimate is lowered to account for cache hits.

In the example above, the estimate of 3 pages for the access to b using the join clause a.x = b.x depends on the number of levels in the index b(x). The choice of the table scan on b for the search clause b.z between 20 and 30 becomes more interesting if we assume the presence a nonclustered index on b(z). The number of pages in a range scan using a nonclustered index often exceeds the total number of pages in a table unless the index is highly selective.

For example, suppose the total number of rows and pages in b are 1290 and 180, respectively, the number of pages in the nonclustered index b(z) is 20, and the search clause b.z between 20 and 30 has a selectivity of 1/3. Then, an index scan using the nonclustered index b(z) accesses $1290 \times 1/3 = 430$ rows and, hence $430 + 20 \times 430/1290 + (3 - 1) = 439$ pages. In comparison, the table scan accesses only 180 pages.

11.3.1 Clustered and Nonclustered Index Scans

The optimizer prefers a clustered index scan to a table scan even for search clauses having very poor selectivity. To see why, observe that for all but the smallest tables, $(n \times p/m) \leq p$ whenever the selectivity n/m is less than 1. That is, a query that is able to use a clustered index scan almost always reads fewer pages than one using a table scan. The cost functions used by the optimizer recognize the advantage of clustered index scans and prefer clustered index scans to table scans even when the query is not very selective.

On the other hand, the optimizer prefers a table scan to a nonclustered index scan except for highly selective search or join clauses. To see this, observe that $n + (n \times p/m) < p$ implies $n < p$, which holds true only if the selectivity n/m is smaller than p/m, the reciprocal of the number of rows per page. For example, a nonclustered index scan on a table having 10 rows per page actually reads more pages than a table scan unless the selectivity of the search clause is numerically smaller (i.e., more selective) than 1/10. Again, the cost functions used by the optimizer take this into account and prefer nonclustered index scans to table scans only when justified by the estimated values of selectivity and the number of rows per page.

The use of larger than 2K I/O in System 11 SQL Server adds to the relative advantage of clustered indexes and table scans over nonclustered indexes. The larger units of I/O reduce the number of I/O operations for clustered index scans and table scans, but not for nonclustered index scans. A nonclustered index scan performs more I/O operations than a table scan if the selectivity is numerically greater (i.e., less selective) than the reciprocal of the number of rows per unit of I/O. Until System 11 SQL Server, the unit of I/O was a page. If you enable large I/O in System 11 SQL Server (say 16K), the optimizer most likely uses large I/O for clustered index scans and table scans but not for nonclustered index scans.

If you expect to use index scans to accelerate the performance of a range query, your best bet is to use a clustered index that includes as much of the search clause as possible as a prefix. For example, if a bookstore needs to frequently list all books for a given author and publisher, you should consider using a clustered index that begins with the `authorid` and `publisherid` (in any order), rather than using, say, the ISBN number as the clustered index. As a thumb rule, expect to use nonclustered indexes only when the search clause is highly selective.

Nonclustered indexes can be as efficient, if not more efficient, than clustered indexes for a very special class of queries. We discuss them later in "Index Covering" on page 400.

11.3.2 Joins and Composite Indexes

One of the problems with the way the optimizer estimates selectivities of indexes is that indexes are evaluated with respect to individual join clauses and not their conjunction. This can lead to overly pessimistic estimates for selectivity of the indexes. The example in Figure 11.9 illustrates such a case.

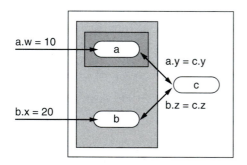

```
unique clustered index aw on a(w)
unique clustered index bx on b(x)
unique clustered index cyz on c(y,z)
select count (*)
          from      a, b, c
          where     a.w = 10
          and       b.x = 20
          and       a.y = c.y
          and       b.z = c.z
```

Figure 11.9   Query where optimizer is pessimistic about selectivity - - - - - - - - -

Consider the join order (a,b,c), as shown in the example in Figure 11.9. Suppose the join clause $a.y = c.y$ is not very selective. The join clause $b.z = c.z$ does not have any useful index, since z is not a prefix of the index $c(y,z)$. However, their conjunction, $a.y = c.y$ and $b.z = c.z$, has excellent selectivity — in fact, it guarantees uniqueness. Unfortunately, given the way the optimizer estimates selectivities, it never considers[8] the conjunction of these two join clauses in estimating selectivity. This property can cause the optimizer to overestimate the cost of some excellent plans. In order to remedy the situation, the optimizer uses a special heuristics while selecting the join order to compensate for such overestimation. We discuss this heuristic later in this chapter.

Notwithstanding the use of this heuristic, this problem often surfaces in the context of the so called **multi-dimensional** database schemas. Typically, the schema of a multi-dimensional database is comprised of one large table having a composite index, where each of the columns in this composite index has a foreign key reference to one of a collection of smaller **dimension** tables. The optimizer tends to underestimate the usefulness of the composite index in the same manner as in the above example.

There are two ways to work around this problem. One is to add more composite indexes, each a different permutation of the same set of columns. This approach has obvious disadvantages in terms of creating and maintaining these indexes. The second solution is to force the optimizer to use a join order that visits the large table last. Notice that the problem lies only in estimating the selectivity of the composite index, not in its use in the execution of the query plan. Should the optimizer decide to use the optimal join order as shown in the above example, the index scan on c uses the values of both the indexed columns to limit the scope of the search to the unique qualifying row.

11.3.3 Like Optimization

Optimization of `like` clauses depends on the value of the pattern. If the first occurrence of a wildcard in the pattern is preceded by a non-null string, the optimizer uses this string to derive additional search clauses. The following example illustrates how `like` clauses are optimized.

```
select ssn, lastname, firstname
        from    authors
        where   lastname like 'Roy%'
```

Assuming there is an index on `author(lastname)`, the optimizer adds two additional search clauses to this query, internally transforming it into:

---

8. The conjunct of two or more search clauses on the same table are considered a single search clause and the conjunction of two or more join clauses between the same two tables is also considered a single join clause. This discussion applies only to the conjunction of two join clauses that join one table to two different tables.

```
select ssn, lastname, firstname
        from      authors
        where     lastname like 'Roy%'
        and       lastname >= 'Roy'
        and       lastname <= 'Roy\255'
```

where '\255' denotes a special character that follows all other characters in the sort order. Note that this transformation is internal and is not visible through showplan. Now, let us consider the case when the first character in the pattern is a wildcard. The following example shows a minor variation on the query from the previous example that can lead to a major difference in performance:

```
select ssn, lastname, firstname
        from      authors
        where     lastname like '%Roy%'
```

The optimizer cannot add search clauses to this query. Hence, this query most likely does not use the index on `lastname`. To promote the use of index scans in conjunction with `like` clauses, you need to ensure that the pattern begins with an adequately selective prefix rather than a wildcard.

Unfortunately, this optimization is disabled for `like` clauses that use a parameter of a stored procedure for the pattern. For example, consider the `like` clause in the following example:

```
create procedure foo @lastname as
        select ssn, lastname, firstname
        from      authors
        where     lastname like @lastname

exec foo 'Roy%' with recompile
```

If the optimizer were to add the additional search clauses to the compiled query plan as discussed above, a subsequent invocation of the compiled plan with the argument 'Sugiyama%' would yield incorrect results. Hence, `like` clauses using parameters for patterns cannot benefit from this optimization.

11.3.4 OR and IN Optimization Strategy

The search clauses involving the IN construct but not a subquery are processed as a list of OR clauses. For example, the clause:

```
x in (5,10,20)
```

is internally translated into the clause:

```
x = 5 or x = 10 or x = 20
```

The repertoire of access methods available to the optimizer is somewhat limited in case of OR clauses. The optimizer considers an index for OR clause only if *both* operands of the OR can use an index on the table. As illustrated by the example in "An Overview of the Process" on page 376, an index on d(x) can be used in conjunction with the clause d.w = 40 or d.x = 50. However, the OR clause d.y = 20 or e.z = 30 cannot be optimized since it involves two different tables, even if each operand of the OR can use an index. In the former case, if the optimizer chooses a query plan that uses index d(x) as mentioned, SQL Server performs the scan in two phases:

1. Perform an index scan for each operand of the OR, building a list of the rowid's of all matching rows, then merge the two lists. For example, suppose d.w = 40 matches rows (100, 101, 102, 103, 105) and d.x = 50 matches (104, 106), the merged list contains (100, 101, 102, 103, 104, 105, 106).

2. Scan the data pages in ascending order of the rowids, selecting only the rows whose rowid is contained in the list constructed in the previous step.

While potentially improving cache hit ratio, the above approach for processing IN and OR clauses can have some unexpected implications on performance.

Unnecessary Duplicate Elimination

The first step in the OR optimization strategy involves merging multiple lists of rowids. This step involves duplicate elimination and amounts to a sort under the covers. This is unfortunate, since the semantics of the OR and IN clauses often eliminate the need to eliminate duplicates. For example, the lists of rowids for d.x=40 and d.x=50 are necessarily disjoint. However, the optimizer does not avoid the duplicate elimination step in these special cases.

Unoptimizable Join Clauses

As we shall see in "Joins Under OR Clauses" on page 405, join clauses under an OR clause cannot be optimized. Since the optimizer translates IN clauses into OR clauses, the same applies to joins involving IN clauses. For example, while the join clause t1.x = t2.y may be optimizable, t.x in (t2.y, t2.z) is not.

Cursors and OR/IN Strategy

The OR optimization strategy cannot be used in conjunction with cursors. For example, while the statement:

```
select y from t where t.x=@x1 or t.x=@x2
```
may be able to use the OR optimization strategy on the index t(x), the statement:
```
declare x cursor for select y from t where t.x=@x1 or t.x=@x2
```
cannot use the index on t(x) and performs a table scan instead.

11.3.5 Cursors and Index Selection

The choice of indexes available to queries inside cursors is limited. The limitations depend on whether or not the cursor is updatable, on whether or not it may update a column in an index, and on whether or not the index is unique. If a cursor *may* update a column in some index, it cannot use this index.

- FOR READ ONLY — A cursor can use any index if it is declared with the FOR READ ONLY option or contains an aggregate such as GROUP BY or ORDER BY, a subquery, or a union (and hence is not updatable by definition). All other cursors are assumed to be updatable, whether or not declared with the FOR UPDATE option. This includes cursors involving joins. Updatable cursors cannot use indexes that are not declared to be unique. This limits the updatable cursors to using either a table scan or a unique index.

- FOR UPDATE OF — Cursors declared with the FOR UPDATE OF ... option cannot use indexes that are either not unique or include any of the columns listed as being updatable.

- FOR UPDATE — The choice is even more limited for the cursors declared with the FOR UPDATE option, but without a list of columns to be updated. Such cursors can only use unique indexes. They cannot use a table scan. An error is raised if such a cursor is declared on a table that does not have any unique indexes.

Even when a cursor has a choice between unique indexes and a table scan, the optimizer prefers unique indexes to table scans. If a cursor is updatable but not specified as FOR UPDATE, any unique index is chosen over a table scan.

Your best bet is to declare a cursor as FOR READ ONLY if it is read only and with an explicit list of columns updated otherwise. If the optimizer still fails to choose the best index, you can force the optimizer to do so using the methods discussed in "Forcing the Use of Indexes and Join Orders" on page 434. If you choose to do so, you need to be aware of the following implications of forcing a cursor to use an index.

- If there is no `FOR UPDATE` clause, the cursor becomes read only.

- If there is a `FOR UPDATE` clause and the user specifies an index that is either not unique or contains any of the columns listed as being updatable, SQL Server may close the cursor on update. This possibility is indicated by a warning message generated at the time of compilation.

11.3.6 `MAX` and `MIN` Strategies

The optimizer uses indexes to process `MAX` and `MIN` aggregates whenever possible. For example, the query `select min(x) from t` can be processed efficiently using an index on `t(x)` by selecting the first row. Similarly, `max(x)` can be computed efficiently using index `t(x)` by selecting the last row.

This optimization becomes more risky when there is a `where` clause involved. For example, the query `select min(x) from t where y=10` can be processed using an index on `t(x)`, but we need to find the first row qualifying row, not just the first row. The efficiency of this access method depends on the selectivity of the `where` clause. The more selective the `where` clause, the longer we expect to scan the index before we find the first qualifying row. In such cases, we may have been better off using an index on `t(y)` instead. The `MIN` optimization can be counterproductive in conjunction with a highly selective `where` clause. The `MAX` optimization is not used in conjunction with a `where` clause. The following rules determine the use of the `MIN` and `MAX` optimizations.

- The expression inside the `MAX` or `MIN` must be the first column of an index.

- The `MAX` or `MIN` expression must be the only element in the select list.

- The `MAX` expression cannot be optimized when used in conjunction with a `where` clause.

- The query cannot involve a `GROUP BY` aggregate.

Enabling `MAX/MIN` Optimization

You need to separate the `MAX` and `MIN` expressions into a separate statement to avail of these optimizations. For example, you may need to rephrase the statement `select max(x), min(x) from t` as a combination of the statements `select max(x) from t` and `select min(x) from t`.

Disabling *MIN* Optimization

As mentioned above, sometimes, the MIN optimization can backfire when used in conjunction with a highly selective where clause. In such a situation, you can disable the use of the MIN optimization by including a (redundant) aggregate in the select list. For example, you can rephrase select min(x) from t where y = 10 as select min(x), max(x) from t where y = 10.

11.3.7 Index Covering

A nonclustered index on a table is said to cover a query if all the columns of the table that are used in the query are included in the index. For example, an index on t(x,y) covers the queries select x from t where x=10 and select count(*) from t, t2 where x=5 and y=10 and t.x = t2.z, but not the query select x, y from t where z=5. The occurrence of count(*) in select list can be ignored when determining whether or not an index covers a query. Notice that a covering index is not required to include *all* the columns used in the query, only those that belong to the table that owns the index. Hence, one query may be covered by multiple indexes on multiple tables.

A query plan accessing a table through a covering index need not access the data pages for the table. Thus, the presence of a covering index can substantially enhance the performance of a query. The optimizer recognizes this opportunity and factors it into its choice of indexes and join orders. On some occasions, the selection of a covering index may not be based on its covering property. For example, the choice of this index may be forced due to semantics or by the application developer. Even in these cases, the optimizer recognizes its covering property and eliminates the access to data pages.

The benefits of covering indexes can be significant. This is especially true when the inner table of a large join is covered by an index on the join key. For example, consider the following query:

```
select t1.x, t2.y from t1. t2
        where     t1.x between 5 and 10
        and       t1.x = t2.x
```

Suppose the optimizer chooses the join order (t1, t2) and there is an index on t2(x). The optimizer accesses the index once for each row selected from t1. For every matching row found in the index, it accesses a data page to determine the value of t2.y in the row, causing a lot of random I/O on t2. Now, consider replacing the index on t2(x) by an index on t2(x,y). The optimizer recognizes that the value of y is available in the index itself and eliminates the access to the data pages of t2.

One of the most common uses of covering indexes is in processing statements of the form select count(*) from t. The optimizer makes a cost-based decision between a table scan and an index scan on each index on the table. Typically, the smallest index is used and the data pages are not accessed.

Until System 11 SQL Server, there was no documented method for determining whether or not an index covered the query. The showplan output displayed the choice of indexes, but not whether the indexes cover the query. As discussed in Chapter 8, *Monitoring SQL Server*, System 11 SQL Server enhances the showplan output to display information on the covering of indexes.

11.4   JOIN ORDER SELECTION

The choice of join order is probably the single most important factor in the performance of query processing. Tools and tricks to force a join order are perennially popular topics in newsgroups and user conferences. We, too, soon join the fray when we discuss ways to work around the optimizer. In this section, however, we work on giving the optimizer a chance to make the right decision.

The optimizer chooses join orders by enumerating a subset of all possible join orders and then choosing the one having the lowest estimated cost among those enumerated. There are basically two reasons why the optimizer may miss the optimal join order:

1. The optimizer fails to consider the optimal join order.

2. Errors in selectivity estimates cause the optimizer to prefer an inferior plan to the optimal join order.

It is tempting to assume that the former is the case and force a join order. However, the latter reason is more common than you may think. Often the selection of a wrong join order is merely a symptom of a problem elsewhere. More often than not, the root cause for selecting a wrong join order can be traced back to an error in the estimation of selectivities, such as those discussed in "Accuracy of Estimates" on page 385 and "Joins and Composite Indexes" on page 394. In such cases, the optimizer may have considered the optimal join order only to reject it because of inaccurate estimates. The best way to deal with such problems is to work on the source of the misinformation. The accuracy of estimates has already been discussed earlier in this chapter. We spend the remainder of this section discussing the heuristics used by the optimizer in enumerating join orders. However, we encourage you to give the optimizer a chance before you force a join order. Please check these heuristics to check whether the join order you want is being considered. If so, you may want to revisit the previous section and make sure that the cost estimates are accurate.

11.4.1 Join Processing Strategies

The basic strategy for joins is the one we discussed in "An Overview of the Process" on page 376 and is called the **nested loops** join strategy. The join is computed by performing a depth-first search of the join order. Figure 11.10 presents a simplified model of the nested loops join strategy.

The join order determines not only the size of intermediate results but also the usability and selectivity of indexes, the efficiency of I/O on the tables and indexes, whether or not a sort step is required at the end of the join, and so on. Let us discuss some of the implications of join order on the processing of the join.

Usability of Indexes

Often, the join strategy can use more columns of an index than envisioned by the optimizer while choosing the index. For example, suppose the optimizer has chosen the join order (a, b, c) for the query in Figure 11.9 and has decided to use an index on $c(y, z)$ for locating matching rows in c. For reasons discussed later in this section, the optimizer does not know that the value of z is known when the query looks for matching rows in c. This may cause the optimizer to use a pessimistic estimate for the selectivity of this index and may even pick a worse plan instead. We discuss ways to deal with such situations later in this section. However, assuming the optimizer has picked this join order for whatever reason, the actual execution of the query plan uses as much of the index as possible. In this example, even if the optimizer had based its choice of the index $c(y, z)$ on the first column of the index only, the execution of the query plan uses values for both the columns of the index, perhaps to get a better selectivity than the optimizer anticipated.

Thus, the selection of a query plan and its execution are somewhat isolated from each other. If you can get the optimizer to select the correct join order and the correct indexes, the execution engine gets the most mileage out of the query plan.

On the other hand, it is important that the plan use both the correct join order and the correct set of indexes. For example, suppose the table c in the above example had two indexes c(x) and c(z), instead of the composite index c(y, z). Once the optimizer has chosen to use the index c(z), the execution engine cannot decide to use the index c(x) instead of c(z) even if c(x) has a better selectivity than c(z).

```
join (current_row, list_of_tables)
{
        if (list_of_tables == NULL)
        {
                output current_row;
                return 1;
        }
        this_table = head(list_of_tables);
        remaining_tables = tail(list_of_tables);
        row_count = 0;
        for each (this_row in this_table that matches current_row)
        {
                /* fix values of columns of this_table in current_row
                        using values from this_row; */
                current_row = fix_values(this_row, current_row);
                /* proceed to the next table in join order */
                row_count += join(current_row, remaining_tables);
        }
        return row_count;
}
```

Figure 11.10 Pseudo-code for join strategy- -

Order of Traversal

The order in which rows in the inner table are accessed is determined by the choice of the index and the order in which join keys are generated by the outer table. For example, suppose the inner table is clustered on the join key and the join keys are being generated in ascending order from the scan on the outer table. Then, the pages in the inner table are accessed sequentially resulting in fewer (and most likely very efficient) I/O operations. The same analysis applies to the I/O operations for the index pages in case of a nonclustered index.

The optimizer does not factor in the order of traversal in estimating the cost of doing I/O operations for the inner tables of a join. Instead, it bases its choice of join order and indexes on the pessimistic assumption that all accesses to rows in the inner tables occur in random order. Often, this causes the optimizer to neglect join orders and indexes whose efficiency is derived from the order in which join keys are generated. This is often the case when the first few columns of a composite clustered index on the inner table are a foreign key reference to the outer table. If you suspect that the optimizer is failing to exploit the order of join key, you may need to force the optimizer to use the correct join order.

Again, the isolation between the generation and the execution of the query plan comes to our aid. Even if the optimizer did not factor in the sequential nature of the access to the inner table, the execution engine can exploit this opportunity to perform fewer I/O operations than estimated.

Reformatting

The term **reformat** describes the creation of an index on a table during the execution of the query. Sometimes, the cost of executing the query without an index far outweighs the cost of creating a useful index as part of the query's execution. For example, consider the query:

```
select count(*) from a, b where a.x = b.x
```

where table a contains 10^6 rows in 10^4 pages, table b contains 10^3 rows in 10^3 pages, and the 4-byte join key has no usable index on either table. Without any indexes, the join order (b, a) performs $10^{(3+4)}$ I/O operations on the inner table and the join order (a, b) performs $10^{(6+3)}$ logical reads on the inner table. Instead, the optimizer may choose to reformat table b using the column b.x, in other words, create an index on b(x). SQL Server first builds a small worktable by selecting only the relevant columns from the table into a worktable and then sorts it by creating a clustered index on the specified columns. In this example, that would result in a worktable containing only 10^3 rows of 4 bytes each which has a clustered index on the join key. Next, SQL Server can scan the outer table a and look up matching rows in the (cached) worktable using a clustered index.

Reformat extracts only the relevant rows and columns from a table into a worktable and constructs an index on it using the join keys. It is most effective when the inner table is small but not tiny and the size of the columns accessed from the inner table adds up to a small fraction of the size of the rows.

Often, the key to performance using reformat lies in convincing the optimizer to consider reformatting. The optimizer considers reformatting a table only if it is the inner table of a join and there are *no* usable indexes on the table. For example, if we had a nonclustered index on `b(x)` in the above example, the optimizer would not even consider reformatting table `b`. Instead, it would choose to scan the inner table using the nonclustered index even if the inner table did not fit in memory.

Joins Under OR *Clauses*

The optimizer cannot optimize join clauses that are under an OR. For example, the optimizer can optimize the join `t1.x = t2.x` and the join `t1.x = t2.x and t1.y = t2.y`, but not the join `t1.x = t2.y or t1.y = t2.y` or the join `t1.x = t2.y or t1 = 10`. An unoptimizable join clause cannot use an index on the join key on the inner table and hence is usually very inefficient. Therefore, you should avoid having a join clause under an OR clause.

If the optimization of an OR clause turns out to be a performance bottleneck in your application, you should consider rephrasing the OR as a UNION or a UNION ALL. For example, you may be able to rephrase the query:

```
select     t1.z, t2.z from t1, t2
           where     t1.x = t2.x
           or        t1.y = t2.y
as
select     t1.z, t2.z from t1, t2
           where     t1.x = t2.x
union [all]
select     t1.z, t2.z from t1, t2
           where     t1.y = t2.y
```

Notice that neither of these two ways to rephrase the query guarantees the same set of duplicates as the original query. The rephrasing using UNION ALL preserves duplicates that the original query would eliminate, whereas the rephrasing using UNION eliminates the duplicates that the original query would preserve. You need to make sure that your rephrasing produces same set of duplicates as the original query or that the difference is acceptable to the application logic.

11.4.2 Join Order Heuristics

The exhaustive approach to discovering the optimal join order is to enumerate all possible join orders and for each, cost the execution of the query. For queries that involve a large number of joins, but in the end involve very little access to the database, the cost of enumerating and estimating the cost of all possible join orders may exceed the cost of executing the query.

The number of join orders of n tables is exponential in n. Even the number of linear join orders or permutations of tables is $n!$. Hence, the optimizer is forced to use heuristics to limit its quest for the optimal plan to a subset of join orders. The intent of these heuristics is to limit the number of join orders enumerated *without* omitting the optimal join order in the process. Unfortunately, heuristics are fallible by definition. Let us discuss some of these join-order heuristics to see whether the optimal join order for your query may be overlooked by the optimizer. Earlier in this chapter, we developed a model for the process of selection of indexes and join orders. This discussion builds on that model.

Single-Row Tables First

The optimizer extends special preference to a table if it is known that only one row is accessed from this table. Simply put, the optimizer puts single-row tables as early in the join-order as the semantics permit. This heuristic is never a bad idea by itself. Moving a single-row table up in the join order does not affect either the number or the pattern of accesses to the other tables. It may in fact reduce the number of accesses to other tables significantly if the number of rows selected is 0 rather than 1 or if the row provides highly selective values for the join clauses that relate this table to other tables.

In some sense, single-row tables are thereby eliminated from join-order considerations. In the remainder of this section, we assume that all tables estimated to produce no more than one row have already been put at the very beginning of the join order and limit our discussion only to the tables estimated to produce multiple rows.

No Implied Join or Search Clauses

Transitivity of equality and certain inequalities can be used to derive new join and search clauses. For example:

```
T1.x = T2.y and T2.y = T3.z
```

implies:

```
T1.x = T3.z
```

and:

```
T1.x <= T2.y and T2.y = 10
```

implies:

```
T1.x <= 10.
```

However, the optimizer does not derive or otherwise exploit implied join and search clauses.[9] This limitation can cause the optimizer to miss optimal plans, especially if the implied clauses have better selectivity than the stated clauses. Whenever you have a choice, you should state the join and search clauses in the most selective form possible. Figure 11.11 shows an example of such a choice.

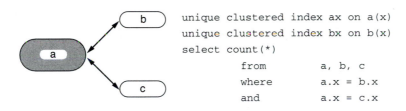

```
unique clustered index ax on a(x)
unique clustered index bx on b(x)
select count(*)
        from      a, b, c
        where     a.x = b.x
        and       a.x = c.x
```

Figure 11.11 Stating highly selective join and search clauses - - - - - - - - - - - - - - -

Suppose the implied join clause b.x = c.x has far better selectivity than the stated join clauses a.x = b.x and a.x = c.x. Then, you should rephrase this query by adding b.x = c.x as a third join clause or by replacing the less selective of the two stated join clauses with b.x = c.x.

However, there are several good reasons why you should not add implied clauses indiscriminately. First, this can be a lot of work and makes applications harder to maintain due to the redundancy. Second, verification of redundant clauses burns up valuable CPU cycles. Third, the optimizer may take longer, since it must evaluate a significantly larger number of join orders. Fourth, in the worst case, more join orders could mean more opportunities for the optimizer to make mistakes.

---

9. The optimizer in SQL Server 11.0.1 derives implied search clauses but not implied join clauses.

On the other hand, you can use this property to enforce join orders without resorting to explicit hints. Suppose you want to enforce the join order (b,c,a) in the example in the above figure. You can accomplish that by rephrasing the `where` clause as `c.x = b.x and a.x = b.x`. In other words, you can force the optimizer's hand by stating a minimal superset of the join and search clauses you would like it to use.

(Almost) No Cartesian Products

A cartesian product between two tables a and b means matching every row of a with every row of b and often produces a result far larger than either operand. The cartesian product of two tables containing 1000 rows each contains 1,000,000 rows. Naturally, a plan involving a cartesian product is rarely a win. The optimizer considers join orders involving cartesian products only in the following cases:

1. The join graph is not connected. A cartesian product is inevitable in this case.

2. The join involves six or fewer tables.

3. The estimated number of rows in the intermediate result so far is 25 or less.

The last case is an exception to the no-cartesian-products heuristics specifically designed to handle queries that benefit from cartesian products between tables and intermediate results having few rows. We have seen an example of such a query in Section "Joins and Composite Indexes" on page 394.

In all other cases, the optimizer eliminates a join order from consideration if it involves a cartesian product. If you would like the optimizer to select a join order involving a cartesian product and your query does not fit any of the above cases, your options are limited to either rephrasing the query or forcing a join order through optimizer hints.

No Bushy Joins

The optimizer considers only **linear join orders** or permutations of the given set of tables. It does not consider **bushy joins**. The example in Figure 11.12 illustrates the difference.

A linear join order accesses the tables in a linear order — starting from the outermost table and finishing at the innermost table. At each step it refines the intermediate result[10] by joining it with the next table. By contrast, a bushy join divides the set of tables into two subsets, computes the joins of each subset recursively, and then computes the result by joining the two intermediate results.

This heuristic reduces the number of join orders significantly since the optimizer needs to enumerate only the permutations of the given set of tables, not all possible recursive partitioning schemes. However, it may also cause the optimizer to overlook some very efficient join orders. Bushy joins may be in order when a large subset of the tables being joined can be joined to produce a result significantly smaller than the tables themselves. For example, suppose c+d is much smaller than any of a, b, c and d in Figure 11.12. Then only two of the three joins in the bushy join involve large tables whereas all three joins in the linear order involve a large table.

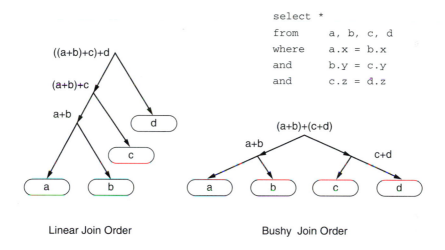

```
select  *
from     a, b, c, d
where    a.x = b.x
and      b.y = c.y
and      c.z = d.z
```

Linear Join Order   Bushy Join Order

Figure 11.12 Linear join orders versus bushy join orders - - - - - - - - - - - - - - - - -

If you suspect that the join order chosen by the optimizer generates bigger intermediate results than necessary, you may stand to gain by rephrasing the join query. You need to identify a subset of tables whose join contains very few rows, select this join into a temporary table in one statement and then join this temporary table with the rest of the tables in another statement. For example, you could rephrase the query in Figure 11.12 as shown in Figure 11.13.

[10.] We use the term intermediate result only to explain the concept. The intermediate results are never really materialized.

```
select  *
          from    c, d
          into    #cd
          where   c.z = d.z
select  *
          from    a, b, #cd cd
          where   a.x = b.x
          and     b.y = cd.y
```

Figure 11.13 Rephrasing to demonstrate a bushy join - - - - - - - - - - - - - - - - - -

Using `select into` a temporary table has some implications for I/O to `tempdb`. For example, pages dirtied by the `select into` may be flushed to disk even though the table is temporary (see Chapter 12, *Batch Processing Performance*, "select into" on page 472).

11.4.3 Join Order Enumeration

When the join involves more than four tables, the optimizer enumerates only a subset of all possible permutations. It does so by eliminating from consideration permutations that require expensive joins in the early phases. Like most other classical hill-climbing search algorithms, this approach runs the risk of eliminating the optimal solution from consideration just because it looks less than promising in the early phases. This heuristic is one of the least well understood aspects of the optimizer. Following is an excerpt from an excellent discourse on this topic by Peter F. Thawley presented at the Sybase Forum on Compuserve.

When you have more than four tables in the FROM clause, the optimizer will optimize each subset of four tables. Then it remembers the outer table from the best plan involving four tables, eliminates it from the set of tables in the FROM clause, and optimizes the best set of four tables taken out of the remaining tables. It continues with this until there are only four tables remaining, at which point it optimizes those four tables normally. For example, suppose you have a SELECT with the following FROM clause:

```
FROM T1, T2, T3, T4, T5, T6
```

It looks at all sets of four tables taken from these six tables. The sets are:

```
T1, T2, T3, T4      T1, T2, T5, T6      T2, T3, T4, T5
T1, T2, T3, T5      T1, T3, T4, T5      T2, T3, T4, T6
T1, T2, T3, T6      T1, T3, T4, T6      T2, T3, T5, T6
T1, T2, T4, T5      T1, T3, T5, T6      T2, T4, T5, T6
T1, T2, T4, T6      T1, T4, T5, T6      T3, T4, T5, T6
```

For each one of these combinations, it looks at all the join orders (permutations). For example, the join orders for T2, T3, T5, T6 are:

```
T2, T3, T5, T6      T3, T5, T2, T6      T5, T6, T2, T3
T2, T3, T6, T5      T3, T5, T6, T2      T5, T6, T3, T2
T2, T5, T3, T6      T3, T6, T2, T5      T6, T2, T3, T5
T2, T5, T6, T3      T3, T6, T5, T2      T6, T2, T5, T3
T2, T6, T3, T5      T5, T2, T3, T6      T6, T3, T2, T5
T2, T6, T5, T3      T5, T2, T6, T3      T6, T3, T5, T2
T3, T2, T5, T6      T5, T3, T2, T6      T6, T5, T2, T3
T3, T2, T6, T5      T5, T3, T6, T2      T6, T5, T3, T2
```

It remembers the best of all the join orders, for all the combinations. Let's say that the best join order is:

```
                        T5, T3, T6, T2
```

Once it has figured this out, it remembers the outer table of this join order (T5) as the outer-most table in the whole query. It eliminates this table from consideration as it chooses the rest of the join order. Now it has to decide where T1, T2, T3, T4, and T6 will go in the rest of the join order. It looks at all the combinations of four tables chosen from these five:

```
                    T1, T2, T3, T4
                    T1, T2, T3, T6
                    T1, T2, T4, T6
                    T1, T3, T4, T6
                    T2, T3, T4, T6
```

It looks at all the join orders for each of these combinations. It remembers that T5 is the outer table in the join when it makes this decision. Let's say that the best join order is T3, T6, T2, T4. It remembers T3 as the next table after T5 in the join order for the entire query, and eliminates it from consideration as it chooses the rest of the join order. The remaining tables are:

$$T1, \quad T2, \quad T4, \quad T6$$

Now we're down to four tables, so it looks at all the join orders for all the remaining tables. Let's say the best join order is:

$$T6, \quad T2, \quad T4, \quad T1$$

This means that the join order for the entire query is:

$$T5, \quad T3, \quad T6, \quad T2, \quad T4, \quad T1$$

Note that the four outermost tables are NOT *the first four tables in the FROM clause. As you can see, even though we look at the join orders for only four tables at a time, the fact that we do this for all combinations of four tables taken out of the FROM clause makes the order of tables in the FROM clause irrelevant.*

This heuristic tends to prefer join orders that start with small, or highly selective tables.[11] While this works well in practice on the vast majority of queries, there are some cases where the optimizer gets lured away from the optimal solution by an inferior join order having a lower starting cost. Following are some scenarios that may fool the optimizer. In the following join diagrams, shaded ovals denote large tables and the plain ovals denote small tables.

The kite

We have a join between one large table and a sequence of joins between smaller tables. Assume that the large table is not clustered on the join key.

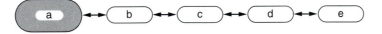

Figure 11.14 The kite -

---

[11] In this context, the qualification "small" applies only to the part of the table that is estimated to be accessed. For example, if a statistics or uniqueness constraints indicate that only a few rows are accessed from a large table, this table is considered to be a small table for the purposes of join order selection.

The optimizer may be tempted by the relatively inexpensive join (b,c,d,e), and pick one of them as the outermost table. Once this decision is made, the order in which rows in a are accessed is determined by the order in which the join keys are generated by the outer tables. This is unfortunate, since the optimizer could have chosen to start with a as the outermost table, in which case we would be doing a sequential scan on a. Instead, we end up doing a random read for every row.

The Dumbbell

We have a join involving two large tables and a number of smaller tables.

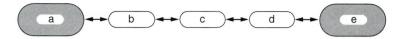

Figure 11.15 The dumbell -

The optimizer considers (a,b,c,d) and (b,c,d,e) separately, and makes a choice between them depending on whichever is cheaper. Assume without loss of generality that it picks (a,b,c,d), probably because a is smaller than e. Then, it is forced to scan e in whichever order the join key is generated. This may be inefficient compared to a join order that has e as the outermost table and hence can perform a sequential scan on e instead of a large number of random reads.

The Branch

If the join graph is shaped like Y, the chosen plan may end up scanning large tables more often than necessary. Suppose the optimizer has already picked a as the outermost table in the following join graph. While choosing the next table, the optimizer can only consider subsets of four tables and only those subsets that do not involve a cartesian product.

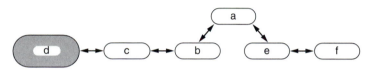

Figure 11.16 The branch -

In this case, there is only one such set of 4: `(b,c,e,f)`. Notice that in deciding to consider only these four tables in the next step, we have conveniently postponed the more difficult task of joining `d`. Suppose the next table to be picked is `e` and that the average number of matches in `e` is 10. This is unfortunate, since when we must eventually get around to joining `d`, we must access each row 10 times more often than we would had we decided to put `c` and `d` before `e` in the join order. A similar situation arises when the two ends of the Y are linked by a join clause to form a loop.

System 11 SQL Server adds an option to relax the 4-table heuristic. You can use the command `set table count <n>` to have the optimizer consider all permutations of subsets of up to n tables, for n is less than or equal to eight. Changing the maximum table count should be done with caution. The complexity of optimization is exponential in this quantity. You should limit the use of the `table count` option only to the queries where the 4-table heuristic is causing the optimizer to choose a suboptimal query plan.

11.5 SUBQUERIES AND OUTER JOINS

For System 11 SQL Server, the processing and performance of subqueries have undergone more extensive changes than any other aspect of query processing. The System 10 SQL Server strategy for subquery processing supplemented the 4.9 SQL Server strategy with compatibility with the ANSI SQL-89 standard and fixes for several correctness bugs. System 11 SQL Server introduces a radically different strategy for subquery processing.

11.5.1 Introduction to Subqueries

Let us view queries involving subqueries as being composed of multiple blocks. Figure 11.17 shows an example of a subquery composed of two blocks.

While the scope of column names and hence the parsing of subqueries is aligned with the block structure of the query, the processing is not necessarily so. As we shall see, often the optimizer flattens the query by merging the two blocks. Hence, we should use block structure of a query only to understand its semantics. Let us define some of the terminology we can use to analyze the optimization of subqueries.

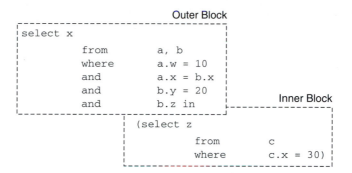

Figure 11.17 Subquery example -

Correlated Subqueries

A subquery is said to be correlated if it contains a reference to a table from an outer block or is semantically equivalent to one that does. Correlation is easy to spot. For example, the inner block in the query:

```
select  *  from manager m
        where m.salary <
                (select   avg(e.salary)
                 where    e.mgr_id = m.id
```

is a correlated subquery because it contains a reference to table m in the outer block. Sometimes, correlation may be less obvious. For example, the inner block in the query in Figure 11.17 is semantically equivalent to:

```
select x
        from     a, b
        where    a.w = 10
        and      a.x = b.x
        and      b.y = 20
        and      exists (select *
                         from     c
                         where    c.x = 30
                         and      c.z = b.z)
```

Quantified and Expression Subqueries

A subquery is called quantified if it is connected to the outer block through a quantified predicate such as IN, NOT IN, EXISTS, NOT EXISTS, ANY, and ALL. Otherwise it is called an expression subquery.

Subquery Materialization

Subquery materialization is a method for processing a query involving a subquery that first involves computing the result of the inner block into a local variable or a worktable and then using the result of the materialization instead of the subquery in the evaluation of the outer block.

Existence Joins

An existence join is a variant of the relational join operator. An existence join between tables a and b finds, for each row in a, at most one matching row in b. The scan on the inner table of an existence join stops as soon as the first matching and qualifying row is found. It is not necessary to identify all rows that match and qualify, simply that at least one such row does. The difference between a standard relational join and an existence join can be visualized in Figure 11.10 by inserting the statement:

```
if (row_count>0) break;
```

just before the end of the for loop. Notice that, unlike an equijoin, an existence join is not symmetric with respect to its operands. We use the notation =E to denote an existence join.

Subquery Unnesting

Subquery unnesting is another method for processing subqueries. Often, the schema of the database and the semantics of the query allow the optimizer to eliminate a subquery by moving all of the tables in the inner block to the outer block. For example, an existence subquery can be converted into an existence join in the outer block.

Subquery Flattening

A special case of unnesting is the availability of uniqueness constraints that enable the optimizer to flatten a subquery into a normal join instead of an existence join. For example, suppose there is a unique index on `c(z)` in the above query. Then, the existence join between `b` and `c` can be replaced by an equi-join since the index guarantees uniqueness.

11.5.2 Subquery Processing: 4.9 and System 10 SQL Server

The basic infrastructure for processing subqueries is the same in 4.9 and System 10 SQL Servers and is based on two strategies: **unnesting** and **inside-out**. There are some significant differences between these two versions of SQL Server in certain aspects of subquery processing. We discuss the infrastructure in the context of System 10 SQL Server in this section and highlight the differences between 4.9 and System 10 SQL Server in a separate subsection.

Unnesting

Whenever possible, the optimizer replaces the inner block of a query by an existence join. For example, the processing of the query in Figure 11.17 is converted into an existence join between `b` and `c`. SQL Server finds for each row in `b`, at most one row in `c` that qualifies on both the search and join clauses `c.x = 30` and `c.z = b.z`. This strategy works for IN, ANY, and EXISTS subqueries, unless the subquery is part of an OR clause.

Inside-Out

First, the inner block is computed as a special aggregate into a worktable, grouped by the correlation columns from the outer block. This step involves a join between the inner block and the correlation tables in the outer block. Next, this worktable is joined back to tables in the outer block. The special aggregation operations include GROUP BY ALL, ANY, and ONCE. The ANY and ONCE aggregates are used only internally. That is, they are not available as extensions in Transact-SQL. Their use is best illustrated through examples.

Example: NOT IN Subquery

The query:

```
select x from t1 where x not in (select x from t2 where y=10)
```

is computed in the following two steps:

```
select x, enny=ANY(x) into #work from t1, t2
        where    (t1.x is null or t1.x=t2.x or t2.x is null)
        and      y=10
        group by all t1.x
select t1.x from t1, #work where t1.x = #work.x and #work.enny=0
```

The first step joins the inner block with the correlation tables from the outer block, groups all qualifying rows from t2 by the correlation column t1.x, and stores the result in a worktable. The ANY() aggregate checks for existence. The second step joins this worktable with the outer block to check for non-existence.

Example: Expression Subquery

The query:

```
select * from t1 where t1.x = (select t2.x from t2 where t2.y=t1.y)
```

is computed in the following two steps:

```
select t1.y, ONCE(t2.x) into #work(y,wunce) from t1, t2
        where t2.y=t1.y group by t1.y
select t1.* from t1, #work where t1.y=#work.y and t1.x=#work.wunce.
```

The first step joins the inner block with the correlation tables from the outer block, groups them by the correlation column t1.y, and stores the result in a worktable. The aggregation operator ONCE has one special property — it detects and flags duplicates. This is required by the ANSI semantics for expression subqueries. The second step joins this worktable with the outer block.

Differences Between 4.9 and System 10 SQL Server

System 10 SQL Server corrected several bugs in the processing of subqueries. Several of these bugs were related to incompatibility with the ANSI semantics for handling of NULL values and empty tables. Let us discuss only a few of the changes that have the most impact on performance. Please refer to Sybase documentation for a complete list of changes.

Subquery Flattening

The query `select * from t1 where t1.x in (select x from t2)` cannot be flattened into `select t1.* from t1 where t1.x=t2.x` because the former eliminates duplicate from `t2`, whereas the latter does not. System 10 SQL Server recognizes this limitation and refuses to flatten existence subqueries into equi-joins and uses an existence join instead. One of the implications of the use of existence joins instead of equi-joins is that the optimizer can no longer use a join order where a table from the inner block precedes one from the outer block. In certain cases this can cause a performance regression when moving from 4.9 to System 10 SQL Server.

Handling of *NOT IN* and *NOT EXISTS*

The ANSI semantics for quantified subqueries require the NOT IN and NOT EXISTS clauses be considered true if either the outer block generates the NULL value and the inner block is non-empty or if the inner block contains the NULL value. This forces the System 10 SQL Server optimizer to process NOT IN subqueries by adding OR clauses. We have seen an example of this under "Example: NOT IN Subquery" on page 418. As we discussed in "Joins Under OR Clauses" on page 405, joins under OR are not optimized. This can cause the performance of NOT IN subqueries to be significantly worse in System 10 SQL Server than in the 4.9 SQL Server.

Another implication of the inefficient handling of NOT IN and NOT EXISTS in System 10 SQL Server is that you may need to rephrase their use by IN and EXISTS expressions whenever possible. For example, you should replace:

```
if not exists (select * from foo where foo.x = @x) then
        /* Do this */
else
        /* Do that */
```

by:

```
if exists (select * from foo where foo.x = @x) then
        /* Do that */
else
        /* Do this */
```

even in the case that the `/* Do that */` part is a no-op.

Performance Issues

Certain aspects of the inside-out strategy for processing subqueries can cause poor performance. Part of the reason is that most application developers (and the ANSI semantics) tend to view subqueries **outside-in** and not **inside-out**. That is, we tend to think of the inner block as being executed once for each matching row in the outer block. If you found the above description of the inside-out strategy counter-intuitive, you are not alone. Let us discuss some implications of the inside-out strategy on performance of subqueries.

Overhead of the Inside-Out Strategy

The correlation tables in the outer block are joined twice — once with the inner block and then again with the worktable. The GROUP BY ALL aggregate requires an extra pass over the grouping table. A subquery under an OR clause is converted into a join that is not optimized.

Copying Search Clauses

The performance of a subquery depends on the selectivity of the search and join clauses in the inner block. For example, consider the query:

```
select lastname, firstname from authors a
       where      lastname like 'Roy%'
       and        not exists
                  (select * from titles t
                          where      t.author_id = a.author_id
                          and        t.subject like '%database%')
```

The first step in the inside-out strategy joins titles with authors from the outer block. The performance of this step can benefit from the selectivity of the search clause lastname like 'Roy%'. However, this search clause is not part of the inner block. The optimizer recognizes this opportunity and copies search clauses on correlation tables from the outer block into the inner block. In the above example, the optimizer copies the said search clause into the first step of the plan to arrive at the following:

```
select ANY(*) into #work(enny) from titles t, authors a
       where      t.author_id = a.author_id
       and        t.subject like '%database%'
       and        a.lastname like 'Roy%'
       group by all a.author_id
```

The addition of this search clause can improve performance by reducing the number of rows scanned from both the tables, as well as the number of rows in the worktable.

Join Clauses Are NOT Copied

Unlike search clauses, join clauses from the outer block are not copied from the outer block into the inner block. For example, consider the following variation on the query in the above example:

```
select lastname, firstname from city c, authors a
        where    cityname = 'Palo Alto'
        and      c.cityid = a.cityid
        and      not exists
                 (select * from titles t
                         where    t.author_id = a.author_id
                         and      t.subject like '%database%')
```

Now, the optimizer is forced to choose between copying into the inner block either both or neither of the table `city` and the search/join clause on it. It chooses to copy neither — for good reasons. However, the first step in the plan for this variant of the query lacks the selective search clause, as shown below:

```
select ANY(*) into #work(enny) from titles t, authors a
        where    t.author_id = a.author_id
        and      t.subject like '%database%'
        /* Missing: Search and join clauses on city */
        group by all a.author_id
```

Thus, you may see a big difference in the performance of the above two queries, even though their complexities may be comparable in the sense that the number of authors residing in a given city may not be any larger than the number of authors having a given last name.

If the optimizer's decision not to copy join clauses into subqueries is responsible for poor performance, you can rephrase the query to copy the table as well as the search and join clauses on it into the subquery, as shown below for the query in the above example:

```
select lastname, firstname from city c, authors a
        where    cityname = 'Palo Alto'
        and      c.cityid = a.cityid
        and  .   not exists
                 (select * from titles t, city c2
                         where    t.author_id = a.author_id
```

```
and      t.subject like '%database%'
and      cityname = 'Palo Alto'
and      c2.cityid = a.cityid)
```

11.5.3 Subquery Processing: System 11 SQL Server

System 11 SQL Server uses a fundamentally different strategy for processing subqueries. It employs an **outside-in** strategy where earlier versions of SQL Server
would have employed the inside-out strategy. There are many other improvements. Let us discuss some of the important features of the subquery processing
strategy in System 11 SQL Server.

Outside-In Processing

The inner block is evaluated once for every row generated by the outer block. This
immediately solves several performance and correctness problems with the
inside-out strategy.

- The overhead of creating and scanning potentially large worktables is eliminated. This can make a substantial difference in the performance of NOT
  EXISTS and NOT IN query if they used to do a lot of I/O on tempdb.

- We no longer need to worry about copying search and join clauses from the
  outer block to the inner block. The selectivity of the search and join clauses in
  the outer block is made available to the processing of the inner block through a
  reduction in the number of times the inner block needs to be evaluated.

- There is no need for the GROUP BY ALL aggregate used by System 10 and earlier versions of SQL Server to process NOT EXISTS subqueries. The outside-in
  processing of NOT EXISTS subqueries obviates the slow GROUP BY ALL
  aggregates by computing the non-existence of each row as it is generated by the
  outer table.

- There is no need to add OR clauses to handle NULL values in order to conform
  to the ANSI standard since the ANSI semantics follow naturally from the outside-in strategy. Further, subqueries under an OR no longer translate into a join
  that cannot be optimized unless the correlation columns are nullable. Instead,
  the outside-in processing computes the subquery when needed (see "Short Cir-
  cuiting" on page 424).

Subquery Caching

One potential disadvantage of outside-in processing is recomputation of the inner block. Consider the first example query in "Copying Search Clauses" on page 420 and assume that `author_id` is not unique in table `authors`. Without any further optimization, the outside-in strategy evaluates the subquery multiple times for the same `author_id`. Observe that such duplicates were eliminated automatically in the inside-out strategy by grouping the results of the inner block on the correlation columns.

If the rows generated by the outer block contain a sufficiently large number of duplicate values in the correlation columns, the outside-in strategy can end up evaluating the inner block multiple times for the same set of values in the correlation columns. To prevent this, System 11 SQL Server supplements the outside-in strategy with an in-memory cache for storing the values generated by evaluation of the inner block. For each row generated by the outer block, SQL Server first checks the subquery cache to determine whether it already knows the value for the inner block for the generated values of the correlation columns. The inner block is evaluated only if no match is found in the subquery cache.

The caching of subquery is most effective when the computation of the inner block is expensive. Here are two cases when the subquery caching is the most effective:

1. The outer block generates lots of rows, but few distinct values in the correlation columns. In this case, the subquery cache gets populated by the results of the subquery for each of the distinct values early on during the processing of the query. From then on the inner block is rarely executed.

2. The outer block generates lots of rows, lots of duplicates, *and* lots of distinct values for the correlation columns, but it generates those values in sorted order. In this case, the subquery cache remembers the values of the correlation columns and the result from only the most recent execution of the inner block. On the other hand, if the values are generated in random order, the cache hit ratio in the subquery cache is poor since it cannot hold all the distinct values for the correlation columns.

The subquery cache is *not* shared between concurrent users or between different subqueries within one SQL statement. The memory used for the subquery cache is allocated out of the procedure cache. The size of the subquery cache is fixed at 2048 bytes. The number of results of the subquery that can be stored in the subquery cache is determined by the number of bytes needed to store the values of all the correlation columns and the result of the subquery. To compute this number, imagine a table having all correlation columns and the result of the subquery as columns. Use the method for calculating the number of rows in a data page as described in Chapter 6, *Physical Database Design*, with one modification: replace 2016 by 2048 in the formula.

If the number of distinct values for the correlation columns generated by the outer block exceeds the capacity of the subquery cache, duplicate values may result in repeated evaluations of the inner block. The command:

```
set statistics subquerycache on
```

shows the size and the hit ratio in the subquery cache. If you see a poor hit ratio in a query where the outer block generates lots of duplicate values, you may need to alter the join order in the outer block so that the values of the correlation columns are generated in sorted order.

Short Circuiting

Whenever a query contains a `where` clause that involves a subquery along with other search and join clauses that do not involve subqueries, the `where` clauses are shuffled to move the clauses involving subqueries to the end of the list of `where` clauses. For example, the query:

```
select * from t1
        where    t1.x = (select t2.x from t2 where t2.y<5)
        and      t1.y = 10
```

is translated internally into:

```
select * from t1
        where    t1.y = 10
        and      t1.x = (select t2.x from t2 where t2.y<5)
```

This optimization makes the evaluation of the subqueries conditional on all other conditions being evaluated first. In the above example, the inner block is evaluated for only those rows from the outer block satisfying the search clause. This can be a significant performance benefit for queries that contain a highly selective search or join clause along with a subquery clause under an AND, or a search or join clause having very poor selectivity along with a subquery clause under an OR. With the outside-in strategy, the subquery is executed only when the highly selective clause is true in the former case and only when the non-selective clause is false in the latter case.

In the case of search clauses, the short-circuit optimization is the counterpart of the optimization involving copying search clauses in the inside-out strategy (see "Copying Search Clauses" on page 420). However, outside-in processing with short-circuiting is more efficient since it does not involve the additional overhead of including the correlated tables from the outer block in the join for the inner block.

In the case of join clauses, the short-circuiting optimization has no counterpart in the inside-out strategy, since the inside-out strategy does not copy join clauses. In such cases, outside-in processing with short-circuiting should outperform the inside-out strategy by a wide margin, since the inside-out strategy is forced to evaluate the inner block for all rows in the outer blocks — not just the rows for which the subquery result is required in the computation of the outer block.

Improved Subquery Flattening

Expression, IN, and EXISTS subqueries are flattened into equi-joins if the uniqueness of the values returned by the subquery is guaranteed either by a uniqueness constraint on the correlation column in the inner block or through the correlation clause. For example, the query:

```
select t1.x from t1 where t1.y =
        (select t2.y where t2.z = t1.z)
```

is flattened into the query:

```
select t1.x from t1, t2
        where     t1.y = t2.y
        and       t1.z = t2.z
```

provided there is a unique index on t2(z).

If a unique index on a table in the inner block is covered by the correlation columns, then uniqueness is guaranteed. The optimizer recognizes that there is no reason not to flatten the subquery into an equi-join. You can help the optimizer flatten existence subqueries by ensuring that the uniqueness conditions implied by business logic are declared in the schema.

Improved Ordering of Existence Joins

System 11 SQL Server flattens IN, ANY, and EXISTS subqueries into existence joins unless the subquery contains an aggregate or is part of an OR clause. System 11 SQL Server is better at optimizing existence joins than System 10 and earlier versions of SQL Server. As mentioned in "Existence Joins" on page 416, existence joins are asymmetric in that they require one of the operands to precede the other in the join order. For example, consider the processing of the query:

```
select * from t1 where t1.x in (select t2.x from t2)
```

This query is flattened into the existence join:

```
select t1.* from t1, t2 where t1.x =E t2.x
```

The optimizer must put t1 before t2 in the join order, since we are checking t2 for the existence of values found in t1 and not vice-versa. System 10 and earlier versions of SQL Server enforced this by requiring the right operands of existence joins follow all other tables in the join order. System 11 SQL Server relaxes this rule by requiring only that for each existence join, its right operand follow its left operand in the final join order. This gives the optimizer a greater number of possible join orders to choose from and an opportunity to come up with better join orders than System 10 SQL Server.

The effect of this improvement in the ordering of existence joins is most obvious in the case of correlated subqueries where the outer table is comprised of a large join and the inner block is highly selective. For example, consider the following query:

```
select name,
        from    titles t, publishers p
        where   t.publisher_id = p.publisher_id
        and     t.author_id in
                (select a.authorid from authors a
                        where    a.org = 'Stanford University')
```

Since there is an existence join from t to a, System 10 and earlier versions of SQL Server cannot consider any join order in which a was not the innermost table. System 11 SQL Server has the option of choosing the join orders (t,a,p), which may turn out to be optimal if most of the organizations fail to qualify the search clause in the subquery.

Other Improvements

System 10 and earlier versions of SQL Server used a sort step to process distinct expression subqueries. For example, the query:

```
select * from t1 where t1.x <
        (select distinct t2.x from t2 where t2.y = 5)
```

causes the processing of the inner block to sort the rows to eliminate duplicates. System 11 SQL Server eliminates the sort step from the processing of such queries.

As discussed in "Handling of NOT IN and NOT EXISTS" on page 419, System 10 SQL Server is not very efficient at processing queries involving NOT EXISTS and NOT IN. System 11 SQL Server all but eliminates this problem by limiting the introduction of the unoptimizable OR clauses that were responsible for the poor performance. These OR clauses are required only if the correlation columns can contain NULL values. The optimizer recognizes this and does not introduce the OR clauses if the correlation columns are declared as NOT NULL. If you are concerned about the performance of NOT IN subqueries in System 11 SQL Server, make sure that the correlation columns are declared as NOT NULL. We should note that NOT NULL *is* the default for most datatypes.[12]

Potential for Performance Regressions

While System 11 SQL Server is more efficient than its predecessors at processing most subqueries, there are a few cases where it may perform slower than its predecessors. We have seen one potential case of performance regression in "Subquery Caching" on page 423, when the values for the correlation columns generated by the outer block contain lots of duplicates as well as lots of distinct values, thereby defeating the caching of subquery results.

Let us discuss one more potential for regression. Consider the following query, assuming that huge is a large table, t is a tiny table, and both h_x and t_x are highly selective but non-unique indexes.

```
select * from huge h where h.h_x in
          (select t.h_x from tiny t where t.t_x = 10)
```

The inside-out strategy preferred by System 10 and previous versions of SQL Server works well for this query. The first step finds a few matching rows to store in the worktable which is then joined back to the big table using a highly selective index in the second step. In contrast, the outside-in strategy preferred by System 11 SQL Server scans the big outer table, performing an existence search on the inner table for every row in the outer table. Of course, all but a few of those existence searches fail.

[12.] Unless you change the default database options. When the database option allow nulls by default is true, NULL values are allowed. Setting allow nulls by default to true is required for ANSI compatibility.

Notwithstanding a few special cases of regression in performance (which are likely to be fixed as SQL Server continues to mature), the subquery processing strategy in System 11 SQL Server provides significant improvements in both quality and performance over its predecessors.

11.5.4 Outer Joins

Although subqueries and outer joins may seem unrelated, there is a good reason to discuss them in one section. The semantics of outer and existence joins impose similar restrictions on the join orders. Simply stated, the inner table in an outer join,[13] like the existence table in an existence join, must follow the other operand of the join in the join order. Let us discuss this restriction and its implications on performance in view of the example in Figure 11.18.

```
select *
         from    a, b, c, d
         where        a.x = b.x
         and          b.y = c.y
         and          b.z *= d.z
```

Figure 11.18 Outer join example -

The values of the columns of d in the output depend on whether or not the row matches some selected row in b. Hence, the outer join from b to d requires that b precede d in the final join order. The optimizer ensures this by considering only those join orders that put all other tables ahead of all tables that are inner tables of an outer join. That is, the optimizer considers only those plans in which d is the last table in the join order. Observe that this restriction is stronger than it needs to be. For example, a join order that puts d before other tables in the join order is semantically correct as long as d is not put before b in the join order.

[13.] The inner table in an outer join is the table that may return a matching value or NULL if there is no matching value in the table. In the outer join a.z =* d.z, a is the inner table.

11.6   VIEWS AND AGGREGATES

The performance of queries involving views depends on the definition of the views. In certain cases the view needs to be materialized. When a view is materialized, its performance is comparable in efficiency to replacing the view definition with a `select ... into #temp`. In some other cases the definition of the view is incorporated into the plan for the query as if the use of the view in the query were to be replaced by the definition of the query.

11.6.1 View Materialization

Views involving vector aggregates are materialized into worktables. Those involving scalar aggregates (e.g., MIN, MAX, AVG) are materialized into local variables. Views are materialized when the query is executed not when the view is defined. Figure 11.19 illustrates the process.

```
create view foo(x, ay) as   select    x, avg(y)
select    x, avg(y)                    into       #work(x,
          from       bar               ay)
          where      z = 10            from       bar
          group      by x             where      z = 10
select    count(*)                     group      by x
          from foo         select     count(*)
          where x = 20                 from #work
                                       where x = 20
```

Figure 11.19 Example of view materialization -

While two concurrent users can share the definition of a view, they cannot share the materialization. For example, if two users were to execute the `select` statement using the view in Figure 11.19 concurrently, each would populate and scan its own private version of the same worktable.

11.6.2 Common Subexpression

Some competitive compilers for 3GL languages such as C and FORTRAN perform common subexpression elimination as part of optimization. For example, the evaluation of the expression $x \times f(x) + y \times (1 - f(x))$ evaluates the common subexpression $f(x)$ only once. Unfortunately, common subexpressions in Transact-SQL are evaluated as many times as they are used. This is not a severe penalty for inexpensive common subexpressions. However, if the common subexpressions involve expensive view materializations, redundant evaluations can hurt performance. For example, observe the evaluation of the view `regional_sales` in the following example:

```
create view regional_sales as
select    rs.region, sum(rs.sales) sales
          from      retail_sales rs
          group by region
select region, sale
          from      regional_sales rs1
          where     sales > (select avg(sales) from regional_sales)
```

You may expect the two usages of the materialized view `regional_sales` in the `select` statement to share a single materialization of the view. Unfortunately, the optimizer does not yet perform common subexpression elimination. The view is materialized twice, once for each time it is used. You should pay special attention to multiple usage of materialized views within a command batch. If you identify redundant materializations as a performance problem, you may consider replacing views by temporary tables. For example, the above query can be rewritten as follows:

```
select rs.region, sum(rs.sales) sales
          into      #regional_sales
          from      retail_sales rs
          group by region
select region, sale
          from      #regional_sales rs1
          where     sales > (select avg(sales) from #regional_sales)
```

11.6.3 Scalar Aggregates

The optimization of the MIN and MAX aggregates has been discussed in "MAX and MIN Strategies" on page 399. All other scalar aggregates are processed using local variables that maintain a running aggregate as rows are generated by the execution of the query plan. The discussion in "Common Subexpression" on page 429 applies to scalar aggregates as well. For example, the execution of the query:

```
select    avg(sales), avg(sales)/avg(commission)
          from      retail_sales
```

computes $avg(sales)$ twice (although it only scans the table once).

11.6.4 Group By and Having

The performance of queries involving the group by aggregate depends on the cardinality[14] of the aggregate. Let us use the two examples in Figure 11.20 to illustrate how. The first example groups deposits by the types of accounts (e.g., Checking, Savings). The second example groups deposit by account numbers, of which there may be thousands.

Low-cardinality aggregate

```
select     accttype, count(*), sum(amount)
           from        deposits
           where       time between '8-20-1995' and
           '8-31-1995'
           group by accttype
```

High-cardinality aggregate

```
select     acctno, count(*), sum(amount)
           from        deposits
           where       time between '8-20-1995' and
           '8-31-1995'
           group by acctno
```

Figure 11.20 Group by query example

SQL Server processes such queries by creating a worktable that contains one row for each group. A clustered index is created on the grouping columns. SQL Server starts by creating an empty worktable having a clustered index on the grouping column. Each qualifying row generated by scanning the base table is entered into the appropriate group using this clustered index. If the group (row in worktable) already exists, the non-key columns in the worktable are updated as appropriate. If the group has not been created yet, a new row is inserted into the worktable.

---

[14] In this case, the cardinality of the query is the number of groups returned.

If the number of groups is large and the worktable does not fit in memory, SQL Server needs to perform physical reads on worktable pages. The `set statistics io on` command, discussed in Chapter 8, *Monitoring SQL Server*, can be used to determine whether this is the case. There are two opportunities to reduce the number of physical reads:

- **Order of Generation** — We can modify the query plan to generate the rows ordered by the groups. For example, if the table `deposits` in the second example in Figure 11.20 is sorted by `acctno`, we may stand to gain by using a table scan instead of an index scan using an index on `deposits(time)`. This causes the rows to be generated in ascending order of the groups, thus limiting all accesses to the worktable to the last page of the worktable. Then, only the last page of the worktable (plus a few index pages) needs to stay in cache.

- **Cache Utilization** — We can use the **named cache** or **fetch-and-discard** features of System 11 SQL Server to keep the worktable in cache. See Chapter 13, *Advanced Topics*.

If the number of groups is small, the worktable is held in cache. In this case, the aggregate computation is often not the dominant factor in performance. The number of index scans and logical reads on the worktable is proportional to the number of rows generated (not the number of groups), and is often the dominant factor in the performance of low-cardinality aggregates. System 11 SQL Server optimizes the implementation of `group by` to reduce the number of index scans and logical reads for the following two cases:

1. Low-cardinality aggregates.

2. High-cardinality aggregates where the generation of rows is ordered by the grouping columns.

11.6.5 Order By and Distinct

Here we discuss the performance-related issues in the execution of queries involving `order by`.

Sort Avert

If the choice of indexes and join orders implies that the rows are generated in the order specified by the `order by` clause, the optimizer bypasses the sort step. For example, consider the query:

```
select lastname, firstname
```

```
from      authors
where     lastname like 'Roy%'
order by lastname
```

If the optimizer decides to scan table `authors` using an index on `authors(lastname)`, the sort step is redundant since the rows are generated in ascending order of `lastname` already. In System 10 and earlier SQL Servers, the optimizer does not consider the benefits of avoiding the sort step while choosing indexes and join order. Thus, **sort avert** is by serendipity rather than a planned optimization. If you suspect that the optimizer is missing an opportunity to avoid the sort step, you should try forcing your choice of indexes and/or join order. System 11 SQL Server considers the cost of the sort step in choosing indexes and join orders. It should be able to avail itself of this optimization automatically.

The optimizer is fairly good at recognizing cases where the sort step is not necessary. It can keep track of the order of generation through joins. However, there are a few cases that can fool the optimizer. Suppose we have an index on `authors(lastname, firstname)`, and consider the following query:

```
select lastname, firstname
          from      authors
          where     lastname = 'Roy'
          order by firstname
```

If the index `authors(lastname, firstname)` is used to scan `authors`, the sort step is not required since the search clause and the choice of indexes implies that the rows are generated in sorted order. However, the optimizer fails to consider the implications of such conjunctions. In such cases, you need to help the optimizer by rephrasing the query to include all the columns in the relevant index in the `order by` clause. For example, rephrasing the query as follows causes the optimizer to recognize the redundancy of the sort step:

```
select lastname, firstname
          from      authors
          where     lastname = 'Roy'
          order by lastname, firstname
```

Worktable and Cache

SQL Server always copies the rows and columns to be sorted into a worktable before invoking the sort manager. This copying is highly inefficient if your query sorts all or most of a table. Unfortunately, there is no workaround yet. However, you may be able to eliminate I/O from this process by caching the worktable in cache. See the discussions on fetch-and-discard and named cache feature of System 11 SQL Server in Chapter 13, *Advanced Topics*.

Efficiency of Sorting

The algorithm for sorting worktables is the same as the algorithm used for creating indexes, except that worktable sorts cannot use extent I/O buffers. We discuss the sort step in greater detail in Chapter 12, *Batch Processing Performance*. System 11 SQL Server introduces one feature that can help the performance of large sorts — large I/O. We discuss this in greater detail in Chapter 13, *Advanced Topics*.

11.7 OVERRIDING OPTIMIZER DECISIONS

Sometimes you need to override the optimizer's decisions. There are several reasons why you may need to resort to overriding SQL Server's optimizer. It could be that the heuristics used by the optimizer are not appropriate for your application. Or it could be that your application has no room for the overhead required to provide the optimizer with accurate estimates (e.g., frequent updating of statistics, frequent recompiles, additional procedure calls, additional indexes, and redundant clauses). We assume that you have already investigated all other options discussed earlier in this chapter.

11.7.1 Forcing the Use of Indexes and Join Orders

The method for forcing the use of an index was not documented or supported by Sybase until System 11 SQL Server. There are two ways to force the use of an index in System 11 SQL Server:

```
from <tablename> [<alias>] [(index <indexname>)] [HOLDLOCK]
from <tablename> [<alias>] [(<indid>)] [HOLDLOCK]
```

In the second format, `indid` is an identifier for the index that identifies it uniquely within the context of the table. This value is 1 for the clustered index (if any) and between 1 and 255 (exclusive) for nonclustered indexes. The `indexes` stored procedure in Appendix G, *Reference and Scripts*, lists the `indid` for all indexes on a given table. In the first format, `indexname` is the logical name of an index and need not be qualified by the table name (e.g., <tablename>.<indexname>)

since the syntax already associates the index with the table. You can force a table scan by using `<tablename>` in place of `<indexname>` in the former format and `0` in place of `<indid>` in the second format.

We strongly recommend the former format over the latter, since the `indid` of an index may change when the table or the index is dropped and recreated. Further, if the number of indexes in your application is customized by the someone other than you, identifying indexes by their `indid`'s is not an option. The latter syntax makes application immune to the dropping and creating of indexes. If you need to maintain compatibility with System 10 or 4.9 SQL Servers, the second format is your only option. Beware that the second format is not documented or supported by Sybase for any version of SQL Server.

You can force the optimizer to use the order in which the tables are listed in the `from` clause by enclosing the SQL statement by the following two undocumented commands:

```
set forceplan on
set forceplan off
```

This causes the optimizer to refrain from enumerating alternative join orders and use the order in which the tables are listed in the `from` clause as the join order. Again, please be aware that the use of `forceplan` is not documented or supported by Sybase.

11.7.2 What You Cannot Force

Some of decisions made by the optimizer are not easy to override. Let us identify some of them up front, lest we waste valuable time looking for fruitless ways to override optimizer decisions. In the next section, we discuss some things you can do to influence the optimizer's decisions; however, they do not give you direct control over any of the decisions listed here.

- **Join order on worktables** — Since worktables are not listed in the `from` clause, using `forceplan` has no effect on their position in the join order.

- **Indexes on updates** — The `update` command does not include a `from` clause, so you cannot force indexes on updates.

- **Use of reformat** — There is no way to tell the optimizer to reformat a table.

- **Subquery attachments** — There is no way to tell the optimizer to attach a subquery to a specific table on the outer block.

- **Subquery and view materializations** — There is no way to tell the optimizer whether or not to materialize a subquery or a view.

11.7.3 Subtle Ways to Influence the Optimizer's Decisions

In case you are expecting a list of undocumented and impossible to maintain ways to work around the optimizer, let us start this section by discussing why you may prefer these indirect methods to hardcoding optimizer decisions into your application. Using the forceplan and forceindex features transfers the responsibility of query optimization completely to you. You may not want that responsibility. Often, all you need is to guide the optimizer away from choosing the less optimal query plans. For example, you may want to instruct the optimizer to stay away from a particular index if its presence is causing the optimizer to choose a poor query plan, but you may not want to hardcode the choice of the index yourself. The responsibility of choosing the correct query plan still lies with the optimizer. All you have done is instruct the optimizer not to consider a certain class of query plans. The optimizer can still make a cost-based choice among the rest of the plans.

Please note that while these techniques do not rely on undocumented commands, they *do* rely on undocumented behavior of SQL Server. Please document each use of these techniques diligently — doing so can save someone the trauma of reverse engineering the optimization during an upgrade sometime in the future.

Disabling an Index

As discussed in "An Overview of the Process" on page 376, the optimizer is not good at algebra. You can keep it from using an index by enclosing the occurrence of an indexed column in a search or join clause by a unary operator that does not change the value of its operand. For example, you can rephrase the search clause `t.x between @x and @x+100` as `t.x+0 between @x and @x+100` to disable the use of an index on `t(x)`. Similarly, you can rephrase the join clause `t1.y=t2.z` as `t1.y+""=t2.z` to keep the optimizer from putting `t2` before `t1` in the join order. This causes the optimizer to be pessimistic about plans that lookup `t1(y)` for values found in `t2.z`.

Choosing Your Join Clauses Carefully

As discussed in "No Implied Join or Search Clauses" on page 406, the optimizer prior to SQL Server 11.0.1 does not derive implied join or search clauses using the transitive properties of the clauses. Whenever you have a choice, you should use clauses that pertain to selective indexes and efficient joins. Two examples in Figure 11.21 illustrate this concept.

```
select count(*)                 selectcount(*)
      from      a, b                  from      a,b,c
      where     a.x = @x              where     a.x = b.x
      and       a.x = b.x             and       b.x = c.x
      /* and    b.x = @x */           /* and    c.x = a.x */
```

Figure 11.21 Implied search and join clauses -

In the first example, we have a choice between two search clauses and have chosen a.x = @x over b.x = @x because we know the index on a(x) is more selective than the index on b(x). In the second example, we have a choice of two out of three join clauses and have chosen not to use the clause c.x = a.x because we know this join clause has poor selectivity.

The optimizer in SQL Server 11.0.1 derives the implied search clause b.x = @x in the first example, but not the implied join clause c.x = a.x in the second example.

Even for a moderately sized application, it can be a lot of work to identify such opportunities in every query. Here are a few rules that are generally useful:

1. Prefer join clauses that are along foreign key relationships to those that are not. This brings your application more in line with one of the heuristics used by the optimizer (see "Equality Join Clause" in Table 11.1 on page 384).

2. Do not break up an equality clause on a composite index across foreign key relationships. For example, if b(x) is a foreign key reference to a(x) and b(x,y) is a unique index on b, then supplement a.x=10 and a.x=b.x and b.y=20 with the additional implied search clause b.x=10. This allows the optimizer to consider join orders where b precedes a and perhaps come up with

a better overall plan. We recommend that you supplement rather than replace a.x=10 by b.x=10 unless you are very sure that b precedes a in the optimal join order.

3. Prefer search clauses that imply uniqueness or have excellent selectivity. The choice of search clauses that is the most natural to the application is not necessarily the most selective.

Encouraging Interesting Join Orders

As discussed in "JOIN ORDER SELECTION" on page 401, the choice of indexes on the outer table can determine the order in which rows in the inner table are scanned. This can have a significant effect on the performance of the query. In the absence of an appropriate search clause, the optimizer fails to consider the use of an index in terms of efficiency of I/O on the inner tables. In such cases, you can encourage the optimizer to use an index on the outer table that generates the join keys in ascending order by adding a dummy search clause that is true for all qualified rows. Figure 11.22 illustrates this with an example.

Figure 11.22 Encouraging the optimizer to consider better access patterns - - - -

The optimizer does not consider the use of an index on a(y) for the outer table a, since there is no search clause involving a.y. This is unfortunate as the query plan that scans outer table a using index a(y) may have the lowest cost if the inner table b is clustered on b(y). Since the join keys are generated in ascending order the I/O on table b is sequential. You can encourage the optimizer to consider using the index a(y) in scanning the outer table by adding the search clause a.y < ∞, where ∞ is guaranteed to be larger than all values of a.y.

Using Temporary Tables to Simplify Queries

You can assume greater control over the generation of query plans and their execution by breaking a query into multiple queries and using temporary tables to pass intermediate results between them. In this chapter, we have seen several reasons to simplify complex queries by breaking them up into simpler queries:

- Simulate bushy joins (see "No Bushy Joins" on page 408).

- Provide the optimizer with better estimates by using parameters instead of local variables in search clauses (see "Accuracy of Estimates" on page 385).

- Avoid multiple redundant materialization of views (see "Common Subexpression" on page 429).

Using temporary tables in query processing can also improve the modularity of your application by allowing modules to exchange data through temporary tables. For example, suppose one module extracts summary data into temporary tables to be used by several other modules for analysis. Separating the business logic needed to extract data into a separate module improves modularity by reducing code duplication and improves performance by reducing the number of times the extraction process is executed.

No matter your reasons for using temporary tables, here are some guidelines for ensuring good performance while using temporary tables.

Logging in `tempdb`

Insert, update, and delete operations on temporary tables *are* logged. This is true for the temporary tables created with the prefix "#" (local temporary tables), as well as for those created with the prefix "`tempdb..`" (scope not limited to the stored procedure that creates them). You may wonder whether it is necessary to log the changes to temporary tables. The reason is simple: The temporary tables *are* persistent in the sense that they may be created and accessed by different transactions. Therefore, all operations on temporary tables must be as recoverable as those on any other table. Therefore, you need to keep in mind both the overhead of logging and the size of the log segment in `tempdb` while designing temporary tables into your application.

Usually, the overhead of logging is the most severe for the initial population of temporary tables. If the semantics of your application permit, you may be able to eliminate logging from this step by using `select ... into` instead of the more conventional `insert into ... select from`. The insert operations performed by the former are not logged, whereas those by the latter are logged, irrespective of whether or not the target is a temporary table. To avoid any confusion, we should emphasize that the use of `select ... into` does not compromise the recoverability or integrity of transactions in any way. However, there are some limitations on combining `select ... into` with other statements in a command batch or stored procedure. Please consult appropriate Sybase documentation for further details.

Contention on System Catalogs in `tempdb`

Creating and dropping temporary tables causes updates to the system catalogs in `tempdb`. If your application involves a large number of concurrent users, please consult Chapter 10, *Transaction Processing Performance*, "Temporary Tables" on page 346 for ways to deal with contention on system catalogs in `tempdb`.

Sizing `tempdb`

The issues here are essentially the same as those discussed in the context of worktables in "Sizing tempdb" on page 390. You need to ensure that `tempdb` is large enough to hold all the temporary tables and indexes that may exist on SQL Server at any given point in time.

Caching `tempdb`

Again, the issues here are essentially the same as those discussed in the context of worktables in "Caching Worktables" on page 390. However, there is a difference between the default buffer replacement policies for worktables and temporary tables in System 11 SQL Server. In the case of worktables, the optimizer knows the last time the worktable is accessed and can use the fetch-and-discard buffer replacement strategy on the last pass through the worktable. With temporary tables, the optimizer cannot know whether a particular access to a temporary table is the last access. Hence, the optimizer does not generate the **fetch-and-discard** buffer replacement policy for temporary tables. As the application developer, you are likely to know the last time you are going to access a temporary table and you can force the optimizer to choose the fetch-and-discard buffer replacement strategy. See Chapter 13, *Advanced Topics*, for details.

Chapter 12

Batch Processing Performance

Batch processing refers to periodic and long-running activities on the database server. Unlike on-line transactions and queries, batch processes can often be scheduled during off-peak hours to lessen their impact on other activities on SQL Server. Examples include:

- backing up databases and/or transaction logs
- indexing data
- downloading data from an external source
- database consistency checks

For some applications, you can separate the issue of the performance of batch operations from the impact they have on the performance of other activities on SQL Server. For example, if your application permits scheduled down time for batch operations, you need not be concerned about the interference between batch operations and transaction/query processing as long as the batch operations can be completed within the scheduled down time. In this case, your objective is to optimize the performance of the batch operations, without regard for other operations your application performs outside the scheduled downtime.

However, more often than not, scheduled down time is undesirable if not unacceptable. In this case, batch processing must share SQL Server resources with concurrent query/transaction processing. Given this, the optimization of batch processing performance must include its impact on that of other activities on SQL Server.

In this chapter, we discuss two aspects of the performance of batch operations:

1. Performance of batch operations assuming we can use all the resources on the server hardware.

2. Ways to minimize the impact of batch operations on other concurrent activities on SQL Server.

12.1 GENERAL GUIDELINES

12.1.1 Concurrent Batch Operations

Not all batch processes can be performed concurrently with each other or with query and transaction processing. Before getting into the optimization of individual operations, we should make sure that the schedule for their invocation is optimal with respect to their ability to share resources on SQL Server. Here, we list some of the more common batch operations and identify whether or not they can be performed concurrently.

Bulk Copy

The bulk copying of data into a table from an external source acquires exclusive locks on all pages touched by each batch. Combining bulk copy into a table with any other operation on the same table, including another concurrent bulk copy can have an unexpected impact on performance. In the absence of other concurrent operations, bulk copy data into SQL Server escalates its exclusive page into a table lock, provided the batch size is sufficiently large for the configured level of lock escalation threshold. In the presence of other concurrent activities, attempts at lock escalation fail, and both activities proceed concurrently. If that is your intent, you should disable lock escalation on the table in question and either reduce the bulk copy batch size or increase the number of locks in SQL Server. Generally speaking, it is best not to bulk copy data into SQL Server concurrently with any other operations on the same table.

The bulk copying of data from a table to an external source acquires only a shared lock on one page at a time, and can be performed concurrently with other accesses to the table.

These properties of bulk copy do not depend on whether the fast or the normal version of BCP is used or on whether the copying is invoked through an API or the BCP utility. Bulk copying of data in or out of one table in a database has no impact on the accessibility of other tables in the same database.

Creating Indexes

Creating a clustered index on a table acquires an exclusive lock on the table and therefore cannot be performed concurrently with any other access to the table. Creating a nonclustered index on a table acquires a shared table lock on the table and can be performed at the same time as other read-only accesses to the table. Dropping any index requires exclusive access to the table.

Backup

Backups performed using Backup Server (rather than the Bulk Copy utility) do not acquire any locks on tables or other database objects and therefore can be performed concurrently with updates/deletes/inserts. Certain operations, including fast bulk copy and `select into`, influence your ability to dump the transaction log without dumping the database itself. You cannot access a database while you are loading the database or transaction log of the database.

Recovery

When SQL Server boots, it recovers all of the databases. You cannot access a database until it has recovered. On the other hand, there are no restrictions on accessing a recovered database while other databases on the same SQL Server are in the process of recovery.

DBCC

In general, `dbcc` commands can be used concurrently with other activities on SQL Server. The `dbcc` commands `checktable`, `checkdb`, `tablealloc`, and `indexalloc` obtain shared locks on tables (one table at a time for `checkdb`). The `dbcc` commands involving system catalogs, `dbcc checkalloc` with `fix` option, and `dbrepair` require SQL Server to be in single user mode. The `dbcc checkalloc` command without the `fix` option does not obtain any locks on SQL Server.

12.1.2 Host-Based Communication

Some batch operations require the transfer of a significant amount of data in or out of SQL Server. Obvious examples include dump/load and bulk copy in/out. Other interesting examples include statistical analysis, data mining, and ledger posting.

It makes sense to spare the network by having the client and SQL Server share a machine. Let us discuss some options for configuring SQL Server for such a mode of operation.

Network Communication

There are two parts to network overhead — the raw bandwidth of the network and the overhead of the network protocols. Currently, the only way to avoid the latter in case of SQL Server is to go through Backup Server. All other communication to SQL Server must go through one of the supported transport layer protocols (e.g., TCP/IP, IPX/SPX), even if the client and SQL Server run on the same machine. However, we can avoid the overhead of the raw network by running the client on the same machine as SQL Server. There are two opportunities to optimize communication in such a configuration.

1. Choose and configure your implementation of the transport layer protocol (e.g., TCP/IP) for maximum efficiency. You may find the configuration parameter `maximum network packet size` and the option TCP_NODELAY of interest (see Appendix B, *SQL Server Configuration*).

2. Minimize the overhead of the name service provided by the transport layer protocol. You can use **loopback** to have your client session communicate with SQL Server when the client and SQL Server are on the same host. Appendix C, *Network Configuration*, discusses the loopback mechanism for TCP/IP.

Backup Server

The Backup Server is *the* most efficient method for transferring data in and out of SQL Server. It transfers data to and from disks in larger units than SQL Server without the overhead of network protocols. Whenever your application permits, you should prefer the Backup Server to any other means of getting large volumes of data in or out of SQL Server.

Sharing CPUs

As discussed in Chapter 3, *Sybase Product and Feature Overview*, SQL Server is rather finicky about sharing memory and CPUs. Here are some guidelines for configuring SQL Server to share CPUs and memory with processes other than the Auxiliary Servers:

1. Make sure that SQL Server has exclusive access to as many CPUs as the configured number of engines and as much physical memory as specified by the configuration parameter `total memory`. For example, if your default configuration for SQL Server employs 6 engines on a 6-CPU machine and you need to run two CPU-intensive client threads on the same machine, you may want to reduce the number of engines to 4. Further, if the virtual memory consumed by the clients causes page faults in SQL Server, you may need to reduce the memory used by SQL Server.

2. If you must share CPUs between clients and SQL Server, you may need to change the SQL Server configuration parameter `cschedspins` to a small positive value like 10 (see Appendix B, *SQL Server Configuration*).

12.1.3 Divide and Conquer

Currently, most batch operations supported by SQL Server operate on databases or tables and their running time and resource utilizations are proportional to the size of the database or the table. For example, Backup Server can only backup or load an entire database and not selected tables from a database. The `dbcc` utilities operate on entire tables and not on part thereof. If you have one database or one table that is exceptionally large, you may need to partition it into smaller units to perform batch operations in parallel.

Often, the rationale for partitioning databases or tables follows naturally from application logic. For example, if your application is comprised of a few large read-only tables and several smaller tables that are updated, you may want to put the tables that are updated into a separate database, thereby reducing the processing requirements for backup and recovery. Another example is horizontal partitioning of tables based on business requirements such as geographic location or classification of data.

System 11 SQL Server adds the capability to partition tables. This sets a framework for parallel batch (and interactive) operations on partitioned tables likely to be supported in future versions of SQL Server. If parallelism is your sole objective in manually partitioning tables, you should consider using the table partitioning feature in System 11 SQL Server instead.

12.1.4 Data Loading and Indexes

There is a trade-off between the overhead of:

- loading data with indexes in place and maintaining the indexes while loading data.

- loading data without indexes in place and rebuilding indexes after the load completes.

If you are loading data into an empty table, it is almost always better to first load the data and then build the indexes. One exception to this — clustered indexes and sorted data — is discussed later in "Clustered Indexes" on page 479. The more interesting case is loading data into a table that already has many rows and a few indexes. You need to make a choice between dropping the indexes only to rebuild them after loading data and loading data with the indexes in place. As a general rule, if the percentage increase in the number of rows due to the load exceeds 5%, you should consider dropping and rebuilding all nonclustered indexes on the table. Of course, the break-even point depends on the application.

12.1.5 Server Configuration

SQL Server configuration for optimal performance on batch processing is often suboptimal for concurrent query/transaction processing, and vice-versa. If your application allows down time for batch processing, you should use two or more different configurations, each optimized for one mode of operation. On the other hand, if your application requires batch operations to be performed concurrently with normal query and transaction processing, you should take that into account in choosing a configuration for SQL Server. For example, if your application requires SQL Server to share a machine with a CPU intensive client program occasionally, then you should consider configuring SQL Server with fewer engines than the total number of CPUs in the system.

The following configuration file shows values for some of the configuration parameters for various batch operations on System 11 SQL Server. Not all of them may be useful for any one batch operation. You should experiment with subsets of these settings instead of trying to use all of them at once.

```
############################################################
#
#         Configuration File for the Sybase SQL Server
#
############################################################


[Configuration Options]

[General Information]

[Backup/Recovery]
        recovery interval in minutes = 2000
# A large recovery interval disables automatic checkpointing.
# Use this with caution.
# Does not have any effect if the dboption "trunc. log on chkpt"
# is set to true.

[Cache Manager]
        number of oam trips = 10
# Keeps allocation pages in memory. Use for loading
# multi-gigabyte tables.
        number of index trips = 10
# Keeps index pages in memory. Use for loading data into tables
# having nonclustered indexes. # Do not use if the 2K pool in
# default data cache is too small.

[Named Cache:default data cache]
        cache size = 56M
        cache status = default data cache

[2K I/O Buffer Pool]
        pool size = 40M
        wash size = 2048 K
# Make this pool large for the following purposes:
#        - recovery (it is the only pool used by recovery)
#        - loading data with indexes in place
#        - create index with large number of sort buffers

[16K I/O Buffer Pool]
        pool size = 16M
        wash size = 4096 K
# The size of this pool is less important than its presence.
# Usage includes the following
```

```
#          - log for normal BCP (use sp_logiosize to enable 16K
#               log writes)
#          - data pages while loading, dbcc check operations,
#               create index, long reports etc.
#               must use dbcc iosize to force 16K io)


[Disk I/O]

[Network Communication]
        max network packet size = 4096
# Make this large (up to 12K) for operations that transfer
# a lot of data to/fro SQL Server.


[O/S Resources]
        max async i/os per engine = 1012
        max async i/os per server = 1012
# You may need to increase these for multiple concurrent
# i/o intensive operations.


[Physical Resources]

[Physical Memory]
        total memory = 40000
# Must be large enough to accommodate default data
# cache plus other in-memory structures.
        additional network memory = 737280
# Set to 3 * <number of user connections> *
# <maximum network packet size>


[Processors]
        max online engines = 2
        min online engines = 2
# These should depend on the number of concurrent
# batch operations.


[SQL Server Administration]
        number of sort buffers = 1024
        sort page count = 1200
        number of extent i/o buffers = 200
# Above three parameters are useful for creating indexes
# on large tables.
        housekeeper free write percent = DEFAULT
# The housekeeper should be used at its default setting of
```

```
# 1% for most batch operations.
        lock promotion HWM = 1000
        lock promotion LWM = 1000
        lock promotion PCT = 100
# Disable lock promotion only if you are doing multiple
# concurrent BCP into the same table.
# Do not change defaults for lock promotion otherwise.

[User Environment]
        number of user connections = 60
        user log cache size = 4096
# Increase the user log cache size for operations that log
# a lot of data (e.g., normal bcp).
# Need not be a power of 2. You need not make this any
# larger than the size of the log writes.

[Lock Manager]
        number of locks = 10000
# Increase this value only if you are doing multiple
# concurrent BCP into the same table.
```

12.2   DUMP, LOAD, AND RECOVERY

The use of dump and load utilities generally falls into two categories:

- **Making copies of a database** — Your application may require you to dump a database to a tape, make several copies of it, ship it to different customers or sites, and have them load the tape to rebuild a copy of your database. In a data warehouse environment, you could use the same mechanism to download data from the SQL Server performing your transaction processing to one or more decision-support SQL Servers. Or, you could use the dump and load mechanism to upgrade to a more recent version of SQL Server.

- **Protection against failure** — You may need to dump the entire database or the transaction log to an archive at regular intervals to ensure that you can recover from a disaster or just to have the option to recreate a past state of the database.

The requirements and performance criteria of these two classes of usages differ. For example, the performance of load is as important as the performance of dump (if not more important) in the former class of applications. In the latter case, the emphasis is on the impact of the dump on the performance of the normal activities on SQL Server. However, both share a common set of mechanisms and tuning parameters. Let us keep the diversity of usages in mind as we discuss the performance of dump and load utilities.

Additional memory does not benefit the performance of database dump and load. However, additional memory in the form of data cache (number of database buffers in System 10 and earlier versions of SQL Server and the size of the 2K pool in the default data cache in System 11 SQL Server) can enhance the performance of loading the transaction log and hence, that of database recovery.

SQL Server dumps databases and database transaction logs page by page. Dump does not understand that databases contain tables, indexes, and other objects. Instead, it sees only pages containing data and pages containing log. As a result, it is not possible to use the dump and load facilities to dump a single table or database object. Furthermore, dump and load does not perform any defragmentation or consolidation of the data in your database.

12.2.1 Dump

The more frequently you dump a database, the less information you are likely to lose in the event of a failure. The trade-off is that dump increases activity on the server system, affecting the performance of SQL Server and your application. You need to strike a balance between time to recovery and application performance. Mission critical applications, a trading system or a car rental reservation application, have strict availability requirements. Time that the application is down is revenue lost from your business. Unfortunately, failures occasionally occur. You should not allow an unlikely hardware or software failure to become an unforeseen reality. For this reason, a coherent disaster recovery plan is an essential part of your mission critical application. Part of this plan is minimizing the impact of hardware or severe software failure. This means understanding how to get back on-line quickly, but at the same time, not crippling your application by encumbering it with an overabundance of safety features.

Transaction Log Dumps

The transaction log contains a history of all logged modifications made to a database. This log is the first line of defense against a hardware or software failure. If SQL Server crashes, you are assured that all transactions committed before the crash are safely recorded in the database. When SQL Server boots, it runs recovery on the databases to synchronize the data pages of the database with the transaction log.

Dumping the transaction log saves a record of the changes made to the database since the last dump of the database or the transaction log. Generally, dump transaction is faster than dump database because it dumps only the transaction log and not the entire database. If your application involves relatively few logged operations on a large database, dump transaction may be significantly faster than dump database. There are a few restrictions on the usage of dump transaction:

- Dump tran is allowed only if no unlogged operations are performed on the database since the last dump database or dump tran. Unlogged operations include select into, truncate table, and fast BCP.

- You can only use dump tran if you have a complete transaction log. If you dump tran with no_log or dump tran with truncate_only after dumping the database or transaction log, you cannot use dump tran and expect to recover your database. You must use dump database instead.

- Dump tran is permitted only if the transaction log is on separate database devices from the data. You arrange this by creating the database with the log on option or by manipulating the segments so that the logsegment is on its own disk.

- Create index logs only page allocation. It does not log any of the data stored in the index. Recovering from a transaction log dump after creating an index takes nearly as much time as the create index in the first place. As a result, you should always perform a dump database after creating a large index.

For the best possible recoverability, you should always be in a position to run dump tran. Even if a disk drive used by a database fails, you can still dump the transaction log of the database to recover the transactions committed since the last dump database or dump transaction. When you recover, you can recover your data right up to the point of failure.

Database Dumps

While the transaction log mechanism protects you from momentary hardware or software problems, it cannot protect you from more permanent problems. If the disk drive containing the transaction log fails, you obviously cannot recover data from the broken disk drive. Saving extra copies of the database and transaction log protect you from these failures. The dump command makes a copy of the database and/or transaction log to an archive. Load recovers the dump image into a usable database.

A database dump image contains copies of all the allocated pages in the database. Unallocated pages are not dumped. A large database with very little data results in a small dump image. The dump image is a snapshot of the database when the dump completed. When you load the database, the loaded data appears as it did just as the dump finished. To achieve this, dump may have to save several copies of a page if the data on the page changes between the time dump first records the page and the time that dump completes.

Impact of Dump on Transaction Processing

Users can continue to use a database while it is being dumped. The performance impact of dump in 4.9 SQL Server is moderate, mostly due to SQL Server's handling of the tape drive. For System 10 and System 11 SQL Server, the impact is negligible. Because dump is handled exclusively by Backup Server, very little synchronization is required between SQL Server and Backup Server. The fact that dump does not affect SQL Server's data cache combined with the lack of synchronization means SQL Server's transaction processing capabilities are not hindered by the dump database or dump transaction log operations. There is, of course, some impact on the I/O subsystem of the system. Dump adds more I/Os to your database devices.

Dump activity may throw off any carefully planned I/O subsystem balancing you have performed. Dumping a database also dumps the transaction log. This may affect your log disk I/O rate calculations while the dump is being performed. Because of dump's impact on the I/O subsystem, it is a good idea to dump databases and transaction log during lulls in the usage of the system. Perhaps your application is most heavily used during business hours, allowing a night-time window of inactivity for dumping the database. It may also be that your application runs around the clock at very high volume. In this case, as you plan the physical design of your database, you should leave yourself some I/O bandwidth on the data and log devices to perform database and transaction log dumps.

Table and Database Organization

SQL Server is optimized for databases where the transaction log is in a separate segment from data. In addition, you can only dump the transaction log if the log is in a separate segment. If you cannot dump the transaction log separately from data, your ability to recover transactions after a disk failure is limited. For these reasons, it is a good idea to put the transaction log of a database in a separate segment.

Dump deals with databases. A dump cannot store anything more granular. This means you cannot use dump and load to recover the contents of a single table without restoring the entire database (see "POPULATING A DATABASE" on page 467). This can be frustrating when only a small table in a large database is damaged.

It is unlikely that a read only (or read mostly) database gets damaged by applications or SQL Server. Highly active tables are more likely to be damaged. For this reason, if quick recovery is a goal, you might consider putting active tables together in one database and read only, static tables in a different database. This reduces the dump and load time by limiting the data that is dumped and loaded to the data that is changing. There is no reason to make many dumps of data that is not changing.

12.2.2 Load

If you are making a copy of a database, you most likely load only a dump of the database. During recovery from media failure or severe software failure, you probably load the last dump of the database and follow with the dumps of the transaction logs.

Because you are loading a consistent snap shot of the database, you can employ some operating system tricks to improve performance that are otherwise inadvisable. If something goes wrong, you can always start the load operation again. For example, if your operating system and hardware permit, you may turn on write-caching on the database devices involved in the load. This improves performance by allowing the software on the disk drive to schedule the best time to write data. Once the load operation is complete, you should turn off write caching on the disk drives. Otherwise a power failure may result in an inconsistent database.

In all versions of SQL Server, a database being loaded is not available until after the load is complete. When the load completes, all of the unallocated database pages are zeroed. With System 10 and later versions of SQL Server, Backup Server is responsible for zeroing the database pages that are mixed in with the allocated pages while SQL Server is responsible for zeroing the pages beyond the end of the dumped database. The time to zero the unallocated database pages may be high if this is an extremely large database and the dump of the database is small.

If you are loading the database as part of failure recovery you probably need to load dumps of the transaction log after loading the dump of the database. You load the dumps of the transaction log in sequence. This means the time to load the database is the sum of the time it takes to load the database dumps and each of the transaction dumps. You cannot load the transactions dumps in parallel. Each transaction dump must be loaded separately, in the order of the dump. There is a certain amount of overhead associated with each load operation. You must mount the tapes. The tape drives may have to rewind the tapes and position the heads at the beginning of the correct file on the tape. Given this fixed overhead cost per load command, you want to minimize the number of load commands that are needed to recover the database. Thus, you want to dump the database periodically in order to minimize the number of transaction log dumps you need to load. For example, if you dump the database once a day and the transaction log once an hour, at most you have 23 load commands to perform (load database followed by 22 load transactions). If you choose to dump the database twice a day, your worst case drops to 11 load commands (dump database followed by 10 load transactions).

12.2.3 Using Dump and Load to Copy a Database

There are a variety of issues to be aware of when you use dump and load to make a copy of a database:

1. You should create the database with the same device fragment layout and segment maps as the dumped database. Neglecting to do so could lead to various problems with data on the log segment or log on the data segment. Your carefully planned disk I/O balancing scheme may also be at risk.

2. The default character set of SQL Server loading the database must match the default character set of the SQL Server that created the dump image. SQL Server stores all character and text data in the default character set. Because

dump and load work on database pages, they are unaware of the format of the data stored on each page and cannot perform the appropriate character set conversions.

3. The sort order of SQL Server loading the database must match the sort order of SQL Server that created the dump image. Among other things, the sort order defines the order of indexes. Indexes must be reorganized if the SQL Server loading the dump image has a different sort order than the SQL Server that created the dump image. Again, because dump and load work with database pages, they cannot understand that some of the pages are for indexes. If you need to move a database between two SQL Servers that must have differing sort orders, you must use BCP to copy the data in and out of SQL Server. In addition, when loading the data into SQL Server, be aware that the data may no longer be sorted from the point of view of the SQL Server being loaded.

4. The SQL Server that created the dump image must be running on the same hardware and operating system as the SQL Server that loads the dump image. Sybase does not officially support cross-vendor dump and load although certain combinations are known to work reasonably well. We do not recommend relying on cross-vendor dump and load.

5. System 10 and earlier versions of SQL Server cannot read dump images written by other versions of SQL Server. For example, after an upgrade to System 10 SQL Server, you must make new dump images of your databases if you want dumps that System 10 can use. System 11 SQL Server drops this restriction and can read dump images created by System 10 SQL Server, but not dumps created by versions of SQL Server earlier than System 10 SQL Server.

12.2.4 Recovery

The transaction log in each database records all of the changes made to the database. SQL Server does not write out modified data pages until it is convenient or compelled to do so. When the system crashes, the cached copies of the data pages are lost. During recovery, SQL Server reconstructs the contents of the lost data pages and updates the database pages to reflect the changes recorded in the transaction log. Recovery is an I/O bound operation, so the amount of time it takes to run recovery on a database is proportional to the number of log pages that are read and the number of database pages that are updated.

Frequency of Checkpoints

When SQL Server checkpoints a database, all modified pages are flushed to disk. A checkpoint record in the transaction log indicates that all pages modified before the checkpoint record are recorded on disk, so there is no need to check them during recovery. If a system crash occurs shortly after a checkpoint, the number of log pages to scan and the number of data pages to update is relatively small. As a result, the recovery time is short. Hence, frequent checkpoints reduce the time it takes to run recovery.

SQL Server automatically checkpoints the database to prevent long recovery times. The frequency of checkpoints is indirectly controlled by the `recovery interval` configuration value. `Recovery interval` is the number of minutes you are willing to wait for SQL Server to recover all databases. The larger the `recovery interval`, the less frequent are checkpoints and the longer it takes to run recovery. Frequent checkpoints interfere with transaction processing. Infrequent checkpoints result in long recovery times. You need to find the balance appropriate to your application.

SQL Server judges the time it takes to run recovery by counting the number of log records since the last checkpoint. A checkpoint is performed when the number of log records is large enough that recovery would take longer than the `recovery internal`. Because SQL Server does not take current activity into account, the checkpoint might occur during a period of peak usage, slowing your application when it needs to be its fastest.

You can avoid automatic checkpoints by setting an extremely large `recovery interval` and performing checkpoints manually. In this way, you can schedule checkpoints when they are convenient to your application. Perhaps your application load is uneven, with bursts of activity every hour, but lulls at other times. You prefer checkpoints during the lulls and not during the bursts of activity, you should turn off automatic checkpoints, and either write a program that performs checkpoints at regular intervals (e.g., a `cron` job), or use the housekeeper in System 11 SQL Server. This may result in a less predictable recovery time, but provide better performance for your application without entirely sacrificing the benefits of checkpointing the database.

Bypassing Recovery

SQL Server recovers databases in the order of their `dbid`. This means `master`, `model`, and `tempdb` are recovered first. User databases follow. Users may log into SQL Server as soon as the `master` database is recovered. Users may begin using individual databases once they are recovered. You do not have to wait for all databases in SQL Server to recover before restarting your application. You should order your databases so that the most critical databases are recovered first. You can do this by creating the databases in the correct order.[1]

SQL Server does not start additional engines until after recovery completes in all databases. This means there is only one engine running before recovery completes in all databases. If SQL Server begins servicing applications after only one of several databases are recovered, the recovery of the other databases may be slowed by the applications' activity on SQL Server.

If recovery of a particular database is problematic, you can bypass the recovery of the database in one of two ways:

1. Boot SQL Server with the recovery bypass flag, allow updates to system tables, set the bit with the value 256 in the status of the database in sysdatabases (e.g., `set status = (status | 256)`, disallow updates to the system tables, shutdown SQL Server, and boot again. Recovery of the one database is skipped.

2. If there is a database device that is used only by the one problem database, you can change the permissions on the device file such that SQL Server cannot open the device file. When SQL Server boots it cannot open the database device, marks the database as suspect, and does not run recovery on the database.

Choice of Devices

While dump and load generally refer to dump and load to tape, this is not absolutely required. Depending on your needs, some archive devices may be more appropriate than others. Use of disks as archive devices provides the same level of protection against failures as tapes, but with higher performance and cost. Also, disks have lower capacity than tapes. Use of operating system files as archive

---

[1] You may also update the `sysdatabases` system table and arrange the `dbids` so the most important databases have the lowest `dbid` values. At the same time, you must also update other system tables that join on `dbid`. Try out your reorganization procedures on a test database before doing these changes to the production system.

devices can combine the performance benefits of disks with ease of management. For example, you can use utilities such as `ftp` to copy dump images to remote sites for added protection against failures.

12.2.5 Dump and Load with 4.9 SQL Server

Dump and load are handled directly by 4.9 and previous versions of SQL Server, without the benefit of Backup Server. This limited the performance and flexibility of dump and load. For example, 4.9 SQL Server:

- Supports a limited set of backup devices
- Can only put one dump image per disk file or tape
- Has a cumbersome dump device name mapping mechanism
- Relies on asynchronous tape I/O which sometimes prevented the tapes from streaming properly
- Does not support network dumps and loads

For best performance, we recommend scheduling dumps during periods of limited activity on SQL Server. Furthermore, dumps to operating system files, when the databases are small enough, provides reasonable performance. This assumes you have sufficient disk space to make this possible. Once you have a dump image in an operating system file, you can use operating system tools to dump the file to an archive device. An easy way to manage the dump image files is to create two dump devices for each database, one for dump database and another for dump transaction log. You can write a script to initiate the dump command and then rename or archive the dump image file. The performance of the dump is limited by how quickly you can write to the dump image. Loading using the scheme requires you to read the appropriate dump images from the archive using the operating system tools. Then you can use the load database or load transaction commands to load the database from the file. For best dump and load performance, however, we strongly recommend upgrading to System 10 or System 11 SQL Server.

Given the limited performance of 4.9 SQL Server dump and load, it might be faster for you to recreate the data than to load the data from tape. If this is the case, you may not want to perform dumps if it is more economical to recreate the lost data from scratch. This might be the case for applications that use programs to generate data or download data from other database systems.

12.2.6 Dump and Load Using OS Tools

While it is possible to use operating system programs to dump and load the database device files directly, we strongly recommend against this practice. There are several reasons why SQL Server's dump and load facilities are better:

- You must shutdown SQL Server while you dump database device files using operating system tools. The operating system tools do not understand that some of the files hold data and others hold log information. If SQL Server is running while the operating system dump takes place, the data devices are not kept synchronized with the log devices. As a result, it is impossible to recover a consistent picture of the database.

- Operating system tools do not understand the structure of the database device files. SQL Server dump and load only dumps or loads the parts of the database that contain data. Operating system tools cannot distinguish between the parts of the file that contain data and those that are still empty and dump the entire file. This is a waste of time and tape.

- SQL Server dumps databases, operating system dumps files. A database device may contain parts of many databases, and a database may occupy parts of many database devices. Operating system tools do not understand the relationship of database devices to databases.

- SQL Server allows you to dump only the transaction log. This means you are dumping only the changes made to the database since the last `dump database` or `dump transaction`. In most cases, this is much less data than the entire database. This might not be the case if the database is small but extremely active.

If you have particular reasons to use operating system dump utilities, you can dump databases to operating system files, then dump those files using the operating system tools. Recovery is then a two step process. First you recover the operating system files, then recover the database from these files.

12.3 PERFORMANCE OF BACKUP SERVER

The SQL Server/Backup Server combination introduced with System 10 offers significant performance improvements over 4.9 SQL Server. System 10 and later versions of SQL Server assign the dump and load tasks to Backup Server. Backup Server is an auxiliary server.

Backup Server reads SQL Server's database devices directly, so it must run on the same machine as SQL Server. If you have more than one SQL Server running on one machine, it is only necessary to have one Backup Server for the machine. You do not need a separate Backup Server for each SQL Server.

12.3.1 Architecture of Backup Server

Improvements over 4.9 SQL Server

Backup Server in conjunction with System 10 and System 11 SQL Server gives many improvements to the dump and load operation of SQL Server:

- Backup Server supports a wider variety of dump devices than 4.9 SQL Server. In addition, it is designed to make it easier to incorporate new, specialized devices (e.g., automatic tape loaders).

- Backup Server can write many dumps to a single tape or file. This was impossible to do in previous versions of SQL Server.

- Prior to System 10 SQL Server, archive volume change requests were handled through the `console` program. SQL Server sends a message to the `console` program prompting the operator to change a tape. In System 10 and later versions of SQL Server, the `dump` command itself prompts for tape changes. The operator uses the `sp_volchange` stored procedure to tell SQL Server (and hence Backup Server) that a new tape is ready. This is significantly less cumbersome than the `console` program and it is now possible to write scripts that handle tape changing.

- Archive device management in System 10 SQL Server is improved significantly over 4.9 SQL Server. For example, you can specify the physical name of the file or tape drive to dump to with the `dump database` command. It is no longer necessary to set up a database dump device with the `sp_adddumpdevice` stored procedure.

- Backup Server allows you to dump databases across the network. This makes it possible for a SQL Server to dump or load a database using a tape drive that is not physically attached to the computer running SQL Server.

- Backup Server can dump a database or its transaction log to many devices simultaneously. This is called device striping. This feature significantly shortens the time it takes to dump (and load) a database.

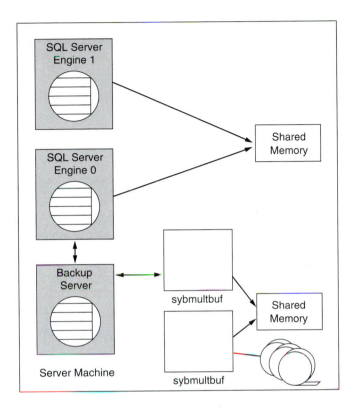

Figure 12.1   Unix Backup Server architecture -

Process Structure

On most Unix-based platforms, Backup Server uses a helper program called `syb-multbuf` to facilitate the transfer of data from archive devices to database devices (for load) and vice versa (for dump). Two copies of `sybmultbuf` run for every dump stripe. One instance of `sybmultbuf` is responsible for reading data, the other for writing. The two processes communicate via a shared memory segment. An additional shared memory segment is used for communication between Backup Server and the `sybmultbuf` pair. Hence, each dump stripe results in two shared memory segments. A small segment (generally 2K) to facilitate communication between Backup Server and `sybmultbuf` and a larger segment (generally 104K) for buffer space between the `sybmultbuf` reader and writer. You should add the memory required by Backup Server and the `sybmultbuf` programs to system configuration calculations if you plan to use dump and load on your SQL Server. If memory on your system is tight, you should check for paging activity during a database dump or load to the largest number of stripes you are considering.

On other platforms, Backup Server is responsible for all dump and load I/O activity and does not rely on a helper program. In this case, there are no additional shared memory segments or memory requirements.

Dump and Load Stripes

Whereas 4.9 SQL Server can dump to only one archive device at a time, Backup Server can dump to many devices simultaneously. This is called dump striping. Taking advantage of dump stripes significantly reduces the time it takes to perform a dump. Loads also may be performed using dump stripes, although this is not mandatory. You may load a dump with fewer tape drives than were used to create the dump.

When performing a striped dump, Backup Server chooses which pages of the database are written to which archive devices. The algorithm is such that even in a sparsely populated database, each stripe has an equal share of the database to archive. I/O activity is coordinated in such a way that archive devices and database devices are kept busy doing I/O in parallel. This is true even in cases where there are more archive devices than database devices or vice versa.

Remote Backups

A Backup Server may dump data to an archive device controlled by a remote Backup Server, allowing SQL Server database dumps across the network. Each dump stripe on a remote Backup Server is given a network connection. The dump image is passed from the local Backup Server (the Backup Server reading the database devices) to the remote Backup Server (the Backup Server writing the archive devices) using the RPC mechanism. Throughput is limited by network bandwidth and the overhead of RPCs. Unless you have an extremely fast network, dumping to local devices provides better performance. When performing a dump to a remote Backup Server, Backup Server always handles local I/O directly, regardless of operating system.

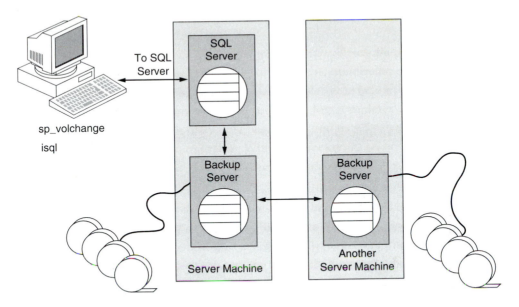

To SQL
Server

sp_volchange

isql

Figure 12.2   System 10 and System 11 SQL Server dump/load architecture - - -

Data Compression

Backup Server only dumps allocated pages. The size of the archive, and hence the performance of the backup, depends on the number of allocated pages in a database and not the total number of pages in the database. However, while loading a database, Backup Server first loads all the allocated pages and then zeroes out all unallocated pages. Hence, the performance of load can be substantially worse than that of the dump if the database contains a large number of unallocated pages or if you are loading a dump from a small database into a large database.

Backup Server does not compress data. Instead, it relies on compression provided by the archive devices. You should enable compression on archive devices whenever available. In general, you can expect about a 50% compression rate on tape drives that include on board data compression. The compression rate is higher if the allocated pages of your database contain very little data (e.g., you created a clustered index with a low fill factor). Any reduction in the size of the backup through the use of data compression can reduce the demands not only on the capacity of the archive devices but also on their performance.

12.3.2 Performance of Dump

Backup Server, `sybmultbuf`, and the SQL Server engines all run as separate processes on your server. While they are designed to work together, it is sometimes possible for SQL Server to starve Backup Server and the associated `sybmultbuf` processes for CPU time.

You can check for starvation by examining CPU utilization of SQL Server. If the CPU utilization is 100%, Backup Server and `sybmultbuf` may be starved for CPU. Check the process status of the Backup Server and `sybmultbuf` processes, they should appear to be waiting for I/O or running. If they are waiting in the runnable queue they are being starved for CPU time. You can adjust the SQL Server `cschedspins` configuration parameter to reduce SQL Server's utilization of the system. This generally frees more CPU time for the auxiliary servers like Backup Server. However, the performance of dump and load is often limited by the I/O capacity of your archive devices and not by the performance of the CPU. In a machine with a high capacity data bus and well balanced I/O channels, Backup Server should be able to stream data to several tape drives simultaneously. Streaming to a tape drive provides maximum throughput because the tape does not have to stop and start for each block of data.

In an inactive database, the time to dump scales more or less linearly with the number of allocated pages in the database and the number of dump stripes. With an active database, the dump takes longer. Pages that are changing may be dumped more than once so that the dump image stays current with the database.

Let us assume that a tape drive can write data at 500K per second. `sp_spaceused` reports the amount of space consumed by tables, indexes, and log in the database. Summing these, you have an estimate of the amount of data written during dump database. The time it takes to dump the database is given by $p/s/r$ where p is the amount of data to dump, s is the number of stripes (i.e., number of tape drives participating in the dump), and r is the rate at which each tape drive writes data. For example, suppose you have a 2Gb database, of which 1,468,006K is allocated, and you are dumping to four tape drives, each of which writes data at 500K per second:

$$p/s/r = (1468006K)/4/\left(500\frac{K}{s}\right) = 734s$$

or about 12.5 minutes. A single tape drive with a write rate of 500K per second can dump this database in about 50 minutes. Assuming linearly scaling, with 16 tape drives at 500K per second, you can dump roughly 28 Gb per hour. With compress, the rate increases to over 50 Gb per hour. In a Backup Server benchmark, using 16 tape drives on a well balanced Sun Microsystems computer system, Backup Server achieved a 47.5 Gb per hour sustained dump throughput, demonstrating near linear scaling of Backup Server with regards to number of stripes.

12.3.3 Mitigating Impact on OLTP Performance

The primary impact on SQL Server performance is through the I/O operations initiated by the Backup Server. Backup Server tries to minimize its impact on the I/O subsystem by initiating I/Os on database devices in such a way that the I/O rate does not exceed that of the device writing data. In addition, the I/Os are scheduled so that there is never more than one archive device trying to read data from a particular database device at a time. This is true even if there are more archive devices than database devices in the database.

The monitoring tools discussed in Chapter 8, *Monitoring SQL Server*, do not monitor Backup Server I/O. You can use operating system tools to monitor disk activity instead. You should check that Backup Server is not impacting the performance of SQL Server by monitoring SQL Server's disk activity. SQL Monitor shows the number of I/O from SQL Server that are rejected by the operating system. If the I/O rejection rate increases when Backup Server is running, the database or transaction log dump is taxing the I/O subsystem of your system.

You can trade-off the performance of Backup Server with its impact on the performance of SQL Server by changing the number of dump stripes. With many stripes, data flux through the system is higher, increasing the impact of the dump related I/O on system performance. With fewer stripes, the data flux is lower, decreasing the impact of the dump, but affecting the system for a longer time. The best choice depends on your application's usage pattern. If you only have one hour in the day when the activity is less than peak, you need to use enough stripes to get through the dump in that time. If you have no time during the day when a dump is convenient, maybe fewer stripes is better. It takes longer to do the dump, but the impact on the system is lessened.

12.4 CREATE AND ALTER DATABASE

The `create database` command initializes all data pages in the database by writing zeroes onto all of the pages in the database. This can be a lot of disk writes for a large database, and accounts for the lion's share in the time and resource consumption by create database. The `alter database .. on ..` command is similar to the `create database` command in that it needs to zero out all pages on the new devices.

12.4.1 Improvements in System 10 SQL Server

System 10 SQL Server includes two enhancements to the performance of `create database`.

1. The `create database` command writes an extent (16K) at a time rather than a page (2K) at a time, provided SQL Server has been configured with I/O extent buffers. The default configurations of System 10 and later versions of SQL Server include 10 I/O extent buffers.

2. The `create database` command writes to up to 6 devices in parallel, provided there are as many devices and as many I/O extent buffers available. If I/O extents are not available, `create database` uses regular page-sized buffers. For example, consider the command:

```
create database mydb
        on d1=100,d2=100,d3=100,d1=100
        log on log1=100
```

where d1, d2, d3 are database devices used for data pages and log1 is a database device used for log pages. For best performance, you should have at least four I/O extent buffers available when the above command is executed. One I/O extent buffer is assigned to each device and the I/Os to different devices are performed in parallel, reducing the time it takes to zero all of the pages.

You should have one I/O extent buffer available for each database device participating in the `alter database` command. The total number of database devices in the database is irrelevant. Only the number of database devices the database is growing onto is important.

12.4.2 Ordering of Devices

The `create database` command in System 10 and later versions of SQL Server performs sequential writes to multiple devices. If your application maps multiple devices to the same physical disk or the same set of volumes, `create database` may be slowed down due to the interference between two streams of sequential writes to the same spindle. For example, if d2 and d3 in the above example are mapped to the same physical disk, `create database` subjects this physical disk to two streams of sequential writes.

Notice that this problem arises only if more than one device maps to the same physical disk. We advise against using such a setup for reasons other than the performance of `create database`. However, if you map multiple logical devices to the same physical disk, you should make sure that the order of devices in the `create database` commands puts such logical devices as far from each other as possible.

12.4.3 Create Database for Load

The `create database .. for load` command bypasses the page initialization step of `create database`. As the database is about to be loaded, there is no need to first initialize all of the pages. Some initialization is performed, however. The allocation pages of the database are initialized. There is one allocation for every 256 pages of the database. Nevertheless, `create database .. for load` is significantly faster than `create database` and should be used whenever you are creating a database as a preamble to loading the database with the `load` command.

12.5 POPULATING A DATABASE

There are several methods to populate a database with data. Table 12.1 lists the more popular ones in descending order of efficiency.

Table 12.1   Relative performance of populating a table

Method	Applicability	Performance Issues
load database	From dump database	Backup Server is very efficient.
select into	From existing tables	Not logged.
fast BCP	No indexes or triggers	Not logged.
normal BCP	No restrictions	Needs memory to cache indexes.
insert statements	No restrictions	Needs application tuning and memory to cache indexes.

We have already discussed the topic of loading a database from a dump in "Load" on page 453 and noted that it is the most efficient method for loading data into SQL Server. We discuss each of the other four methods in this and the following sections after discussing a few issues that are common to all. These issues are related to the general problem of transferring large volumes of data into SQL Server.

12.5.1 General Issues

Logged versus Unlogged Methods

The inserts are not logged for `select into` and fast `BCP` and are logged for normal `BCP` and `insert` statements. The use of nonlogged methods does not compromise the integrity of the database. However, as discussed in "Dump" on page 450, the execution of a nonlogged operation on a database prevents you from dumping the transaction log until after the next database dump. Depending on the schedule for backups, the use of one or more nonlogged operations may force you to perform a `dump database` instead of the relatively inexpensive `dump transaction`. You should factor this difference into your comparison of alternative methods for loading data.

The allocation and deallocation of pages to tables and indexes is logged even for nonlogged operations. This is necessary to ensure the integrity of the allocation map for the database. Thus, even nonlogged operations generate log entries, albeit at a significantly lower rate than the logged operations.

Transaction Log

For the logged methods, make sure the log is on its own, fast disk drive. If the amount of data you need to load is larger than the log, you cannot load all of the data in a single transaction and you should provide some mechanism to truncate the log periodically so it does not become full. Running out of log space stops your data population tasks immediately. Various mechanisms are available to you to truncate the transaction log:

- Turn on the `truncate log on checkpoint` option in the database. Turning on this option causes SQL Server to truncate the log once per minute when the internal checkpoint task checks whether or not an automatic checkpoint is needed in the database. The `truncate log on checkpoint` has negative performance implications. Unless absolutely necessary, you should leave this option disabled.

- Periodically issue `dump tran` commands as you are loading data. You can do this every so many rows or as often as needed to keep you from running out of log space.

- Program the `sp_thresholdaction` stored procedure to truncate the log. SQL Server executes this stored procedure whenever the amount of free space in the log segment falls below a preset threshold.

Batch Size

The batch size is the number of rows inserted into the table per transaction. A `select into` statement cannot be split into multiple transactions. However, the batch size can be specified for both fast and normal BCP, and can be programmed for `insert` statements.

On each commit, SQL Server needs to write out all the log pages to disk. In the case of nonlogged operations, SQL Server needs to write out the data pages as well as log pages. Thus, load data pauses briefly after each batch while the disk activity completes. The length of this pause depends on the batch size and on whether or not the operation is logged. In general, a larger batch size improves throughput. But increasing the batch size beyond the point of diminishing returns can be counterproductive since it limits your ability to handle log full conditions. The ideal batch size depends on the nature of your application. Generally, batch sizes larger than 1000 rarely improve performance.

Data Transfer

SQL Server cannot load data any faster than the rate at which it receives data. Generally, the delivery of data to SQL Server is rarely the performance bottleneck. But, it may be worthwhile to make sure that the process for supplying data to SQL Server is not the bottleneck. If the source of data is a file system, you should make sure that its operation does not interfere with SQL Server's usage of disks, CPUs, and virtual memory. A large network packet size is recommended for transmission of data to SQL Server (see Appendix B, *SQL Server Configuration*).

The datatype conversions should be performed at the client if SQL Server is the bottleneck in performance and on SQL Server otherwise. Even more important, there should be at most one datatype conversion, not two. For example, consider the following statement.

```
dbfcmd(dbproc, "insert into foo(x) values (%d)", &x);
```

The client program is converting data from binary to ASCII, only to have SQL Server convert it back to binary.[2] The BCP library routines eliminate this overhead by transferring data from client to SQL Server in native format. If the limitations of the BCP interface make it impossible to use in your application, consider enclosing the insert statement in a stored procedure and using the RPC interface.

If the source of data is an application rather than an utility such as BCP, you should make sure that it is using the application programming interface efficiently. Of course, you are not limited to general-purpose utilities such as isql and BCP. Custom applications using the BCP library routines can minimize the overhead by focusing only on the datatypes and delimiters that are important to your application. Make sure that the binding of local variables to columns is done once for each table and not once for each row. If your client application passes data to stored procedures that insert the data into tables, you should make sure that the calls to the stored procedures are efficient. The discussion on application programming in Chapter 7, *Application Development* may be of interest here.

Number of Engines

Configuring SQL Server with more engines does not necessarily improve the performance of data loading, especially if that means taking a CPU away from the process supplying data to SQL Server. The load database operation does not use more than one engine. The select into and BCP operations are single-threaded for each instance and do not stand to gain from the availability of multiple engines. As far as the performance of loading one large table is concerned, the first four methods cannot benefit from more than one or two engines.

Here are two opportunities for improving the performance of data loading by increasing the number of engines:

1. If you need to load multiple tables, you can use select into or BCP on multiple tables concurrently.

---

[2] The overhead of compiling the SQL statement once for each inserted row does not help performance either.

2. If you are loading data by having multiple sessions perform `insert` statements on one table, there may be some benefit to having more engines. See the discussion on heap inserts in Chapter 10, *Transaction Processing Performance*, and on partitioned tables in Chapter 13, *Advanced Topics*.

Number of Database Buffers

The number of database buffers is extremely important to the performance of loading data in the presence of indexes. We discuss this topic later in "CREATING INDEXES" on page 474. In the absence of any indexes, there is little motivation to use more database buffers than what is needed to hold one batch of data, plus the overhead of log and allocation pages. You may be able to make the initial stage of loading go faster by using large batches and lots of database buffers. However, this does not necessarily translate to better performance overall. Figure 12.3 illustrates why.

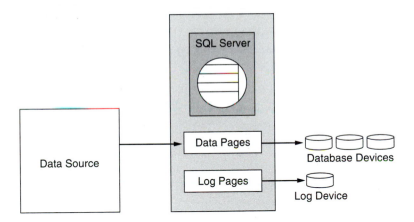

Figure 12.3   Many database buffers may not improve overall throughput - - - - -

SQL Server delays the writing of the newly created data pages. If SQL Server has a large supply of clean buffers when the loading begins, SQL Server does not write any data pages to disk until the end of the batch in the case of nonlogged operations and until it has used up all the clean buffers in case of logged operations. The throughput of loading during this phase is higher than the more realistic and sustainable throughput that is seen during the remainder of the load process.

Use of large batches and more memory may in fact hurt overall performance by leaving SQL Server with the task of writing out a large number of dirty pages to disk after the source has finished supplying the last batch. We revisit this issue in Chapter 13, *Advanced Topics*, "Housekeeper" on page 528.

12.5.2 select into

One of the most efficient methods to create and populate a table from other tables is to use the `select .. into` feature of Transact-SQL. There are several restrictions on the use of this feature:

1. It can be used only to create and populate a table. It cannot be used to add data to an existing table. Further, the table cannot be created with any indexes, triggers, or partitions.

2. The database option `select into/bulk copy` must be set to true on the database that contains the table.

3. A `select .. into` statement cannot be used inside a user-defined transaction.

The `select .. into` operation does not log inserts. Hence it is highly efficient. On the other hand, like other nonlogged operations, this statement cannot be combined with statements in a transaction, it flushes all dirty pages to disk before completion, and it prohibits dumping of the transaction log until after the next database dump. The flushing of dirty pages to disk may seem redundant in case of temporary tables, but is essential for transactional integrity.

12.5.3 Fast BCP

BCP has two modes, referred to as **fast** BCP and **normal** BCP. As the names suggest, fast BCP is more efficient than normal BCP. There are certain restrictions on the usability of fast BCP:

1. Fast BCP may only be used in databases where the `select into/bulkcopy` option is enabled.

2. Fast BCP may only be used on tables that do not have any indexes or triggers.

Here are some of the factors that influence the performance of fast BCP.

- **Unlogged** — Fast BCP is not logged. Like other unlogged operations, it cannot be part of a user-defined transaction, it flushes all dirty pages to disk before completion, and it prohibits dumping of the transaction log until after the next database dump.

- **Simpler code path** — The implementation of the fast BCP feature exploits the absence of indexes and logging to use a simpler code path. Expect the CPU utilization for fast BCP to be lower than that for other methods.

- **Table size** — As the table increases in size, the amount of time it takes SQL Server to allocate fresh pages to the table increases. This table size related performance degradation is significant in System 10 and earlier versions of SQL Server. System 11 SQL Server uses an improved algorithm for allocating pages to tables and performs significantly better.

- **Disk speed** — The disk subsystem is often the determining factor in the performance of data loading. A smaller latency usually leads to better performance. The discussion on the use of write-caching in Chapter 13, *Advanced Topics* may be of interest here as well.

- **Batch size** — Batch size determines how frequently SQL Server pauses to flush the data pages to disk and write allocation information to the log. Larger batch sizes generally mean better performance.

- **oamtrips configuration** — If you are populating a large table, set the configuration parameter oamtrips for the table to 100. This encourages SQL Server to keep the Object Allocation Map (OAM) pages in memory, thereby eliminating physical I/O from page allocation. Improvements in the algorithm for page allocation in System 11 SQL Server have all but eliminated the need for this parameter.

- **Housekeeper configuration** — Housekeeper, introduced in System 11 SQL Server, can help the performance of data loading by writing data pages to disk asynchronously with respect to the batch size. The default setting of 20% free writes should work well for loading data. More on this in Chapter 13, *Advanced Topics*.

12.5.4 Normal BCP

If the table has a trigger or is indexed, SQL Server uses the normal version of BCP instead of fast BCP. The select into/bulkcopy database option does not have to be enabled to use BCP if the table has a trigger or index.[3] Normal BCP logs all inserts and is implemented using mechanisms similar to those used by insert statements.[4] However, normal BCP is more efficient than insert statements at reading in large amounts of data from the client, since it eliminates data conversion, command parsing, and compiling. You can take advantage of this efficiency by using the BCP utility program or by coding your own specialized BCP program using the BCP library routines in DB-Library or Client-Library.

All but the first two of the factors listed in "Fast BCP" on page 472 (*Table size*, *Disk speed*, *Batch size*, *oamtrips configuration*, and *Housekeeper configuration*) are applicable to normal BCP as well. However, normal BCP flushes only the log pages to disk at every batch, not the data pages. The data pages are written out to disk by the standard buffer replacement process, checkpoint, or the Housekeeper.

Indextrips Configuration

If the table has nonclustered indexes, for best performance you should have a data cache large enough to hold all of the nonclustered index pages. Nonclustered indexes are much larger than the clustered-index pages. A Nonclustered index contains copies of the indexed columns from every row in the table. If you have sufficient memory to keep all nonclustered indexes in cache, you should set the configuration parameter indextrips for the table to 10 to encourage SQL Server to keep the index pages in memory. More on this in "LOADING DATA INTO INDEXED TABLES" on page 478.

12.6   CREATING INDEXES

Creating an index involves two steps:

1. **Sort** — Scan the table, extracting the index columns. Sort the columns into runs and store the runs on disk.

2. **Merge** — Merge the runs and build the index.

The performance characteristics of creating a clustered index differs significantly from that of creating a nonclustered index. In addition to sorting data and creating a B-Tree-like structure for a nonclustered index, creating a clustered index requires relocation of the rows in the base table.

[3.]   Strangely, if the table is not indexed and has no trigger, you must enable the select into/bulk copy database option to BCP data into the table.

[4.]   The primary difference is that any triggers on the table are not executed.

12.6.1 Nonclustered Indexes

The lion's share of the time and resource requirements in creating nonclustered indexes is in the sort and merge steps, which includes the building of the B-Tree structure for the index. The amount of data sorted depends only on the number of rows and on the size of the columns in the index — not on the size of the columns not included in the index. The performance of scanning the base table in the sort phase depends on the overall size of the table, including the columns that are not indexed. The performance of the sort itself and that of the merge depend only on the number of rows and the size of the indexed columns rather than on all of the columns. Thus, for a given table, the time it takes to create an index is related to the number and sizes of columns in the index.

There are several things you can do to make the sort and merge steps more efficient.

Exploit Available Sort Order

If the data rows are already sorted in the order of the index, you should use the `with sorted_data` option. However, this option can only be used if there are no duplicate keys in the nonclustered indexes.

Use Extent I/O Buffers

System 10 and later versions of SQL Server use the extent I/O buffers in the sort step. The default value for the configuration parameter `number of extent I/O buffers` is zero. For creating indexes on large tables, you should increase this value. The recommended value is 10.

Use More Memory

SQL Server employs a multistage merge sort whose default configuration is conservatively optimized for small memory configurations. The size of the runs generated by the sort phase, and hence the number of levels in the merge phase, depends on the number of sort buffers used. In the default configuration, SQL Server uses 50 sort buffers. System 10 and later versions of SQL Server can be configured to use more memory by using the configuration parameter `number of sort buffers` (see Appendix B, *SQL Server Configuration*). The recommended value is $max(100, \sqrt{n})$, where n is the number of data pages in the table.

12.6.2 Clustered Indexes

Creating a clustered index on a table involves five steps:

1. All nonclustered indexes on the table are dropped.

2. The rows are sorted in ascending order of the index key and relocated to a new set of pages.

3. The B-Tree for the clustered index is built with respect to the new set of pages.

4. The old pages are deallocated.

5. The nonclustered indexes dropped in step 1 are rebuilt.

Given that nonclustered indexes are rebuilt after a clustered index is created, you should always create the clustered index before creating any nonclustered indexes. The sort step for clustered indexes is similar to that for nonclustered indexes. Hence, the discussion in "Nonclustered Indexes" on page 475 on configuring SQL Server for large sorts applies to creating clustered indexes as well. However, unlike nonclustered indexes, the `with sorted_data` option can be used to create clustered indexes that are not unique.

The sort step for creating a clustered index involves a lot more data movement than that for nonclustered indexes. When creating a clustered index, SQL Server needs to relocate the rows in the table to order them by the index key. The database must have enough free space to accommodate the copy of the table as the index is built. The amount of free space that is needed is 120% of the size of the table being indexed. For example, if you need to create a clustered index on a 10 Gb table, then the database must contain 12 Gb of free space. This space is used only during the creation of the clustered index and is returned to the pool of free space afterwards.

The relocation of rows and pages and hence the 120% space overhead is required even when the clustered index is created with the `with sorted_data` option. You may be wondering why, since there seems to be no need to relocate rows when the data is already sorted. In the general case that the clustered index contains duplicate keys, the presence of duplicates may require the addition of overflow pages to the table (see Chapter 4, *SQL Server — Form and Structure*, "Clustered Index and Duplicate Keys" on page 93) and the relocation of rows to overflow pages. Also, the use of the `fillfactor` option may require the relocation of rows and pages.

12.6.3 Creating Indexes Concurrently

You can create multiple indexes concurrently with the restriction that creating a clustered index acquires an exclusive lock on the table. You can create any combination of indexes on any number of tables concurrently as long as it does not include a clustered and a nonclustered index on the same table. Such concurrency can significantly reduce the total time to index a database. Here are some issues in concurrency of index creation that can affect performance:

Extent I/O Buffers

Only one `create index` command can use the extent I/O buffers. Hence, if you issue multiple `create index` commands, all but the first performs I/O in 2K units. Therefore, you should issue the most resource-intensive `create index` command first.

Sort Buffers and Procedure Cache

Each `create index` command allocates the configured number of sort buffers (default is 50) from the data cache. If you have configured a large number of sort buffers or have a small supply of data cache buffers, the `create index` commands may run short of database buffers. Each `create index` command also allocates some memory from the procedure cache. Hence, the same consideration also applies to the size of the procedure cache. The amount of memory allocated from the procedure cache by each `create index` command is proportional to the configured number of sort buffers — 36 bytes times the number of rows of data that fit in the configured number of sort buffers. For example, if each sort buffer holds 100 rows and there are 50 sort buffers, $36 \times 50 \times 100 = 180000$ bytes are allocated from the procedure cache.

Interference in I/O Subsystem

The efficiency of `create index` depends on the sequential nature of the I/O performed during index creation. Interference between two concurrent `create index` commands on the same table, or on two tables on the same disk, can cause performance problems. You should avoid such situations whenever possible. The indexes you create concurrently should not share database devices.

12.7 LOADING DATA INTO INDEXED TABLES

We discussed various methods of loading data in "POPULATING A DATA-BASE" on page 467. Two of the discussed methods, normal `BCP` and `insert` statements, can insert rows into tables having indexes. We also discussed the performance of creating indexes in "CREATING INDEXES" on page 474. This brings us to the obvious question — should indexes be created before or after the loading of data? There are three factors that make loading data with indexes slower than otherwise:

- **Logging** — Both the methods for loading data with indexes in place require that all inserts be logged. Some developers may know ways to turn off logging. This mechanism is strictly for the purpose of testing and cannot guarantee recoverability. We do not discuss any such mechanisms in this book and urge you not to turn off logging on any production database. Our only options, then, are to either load data using one of the unlogged methods before creating indexes, or pay the overhead of logging while loading data with indexes in place. The remainder of this section assumes the latter.

- **Lack of extent I/O buffers** — Fast BCP uses the extent I/O buffers to perform I/O in units of 16K rather than 2K. Normal `BCP` and `insert` statements cannot use extent I/O buffers.

- **Non-sequential nature of inserts** — Loading data without any indexes means that rows can be put anywhere. This leads to sequential writes to the data disk, which can be highly efficient depending on the I/O subsystem. On the other hand, loading data into a table that already has one or more indexes can generate random access to data and index pages. In the absence of sufficient buffer cache, this can lead to a large amount of random I/O.

In order to make the performance of loading data with indexes competitive with that of loading data without indexes, we need to address each of the above three issues. Again, we need to make a distinction between clustered and nonclustered indexes.

12.7.1 Clustered Indexes

One of the problems with creating clustered indexes on large tables is the requirement that the database contain free space to the amount of 120% of the size of the table. This may rule out the option of creating the clustered index after loading data. Even when adequate free space is available, the overhead of relocating rows makes creating the index after loading data less than desirable.

Order of Inserts

The performance of loading data into a table having a clustered index depends on the order in which the keyed columns are inserted. If the data to be loaded is already sorted by the index key, then no relocation of rows takes place. On the other hand, if the data is not sorted by the index key, then inserting a row to a page frequently causes relocation of some of the rows to a new page. We use the examples in Figure 12.4 to illustrate how page splitting and the relocation of rows to a new page depends on the order in which keys are inserted into the table.

As data is inserted and the table grows, SQL Server must allocate fresh pages to the table. In the presence of a clustered index, new pages are created by splitting existing pages. The examples in Figure 12.4 assume that exactly 4 rows fit in each page and show the values of the indexed column for the rows in each page. Splitting a page entails the introduction of a new page following the current page in the page chain and the relocation of some or none of the rows from the current page to the new page. Figure 12.4 denotes the splitting of a page by having two edges connect a page to its after-image and the new page. Labels along the edge, if any, denote rows that are relocated from the current page to the new page.

When the data is loaded in sorted order, every insert is at the very end of the table — as the last row on the last page. SQL Server recognizes this as a special case and does not relocate any rows to the new page. The first example in Figure 12.4 shows the page splits when data is loaded in sorted order. No rows need to be relocated and the current page remains full after the split. As a result, the pages are densely packed and the number of page allocations and page splits is as small as possible. On the other hand, if the data is inserted out of sorted order, page splits require the relocation of rows. The second example in Figure 12.4 shows that when data is inserted in random order, most page splits require relocation of rows causing the pages to be sparsely populated, thereby increasing the number of pages and page splits.

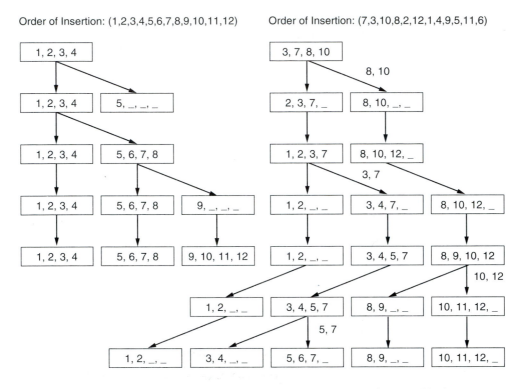

Order of Insertion: (1,2,3,4,5,6,7,8,9,10,11,12)   Order of Insertion: (7,3,10,8,2,12,1,4,9,5,11,6)

Figure 12.4   Ordered versus unordered insert with a clustered index - - - - - - - -

Additional Disk Writes

In System 10 and earlier versions of SQL Server, a page split caused by a logged operation forces the new page to be written to disk as soon as it is created. If loading data into a table having a clustered index creates n new pages, SQL Server writes each of these n pages to disk once when they are created and again as part of normal buffer replacement. In other words, to load n pages of data to a table having a clustered index, SQL Server writes data pages to disk at least $2n$ times.

System 11 SQL Server avoids some unnecessary disk writes in the special case that the data is loaded in sorted order. We discuss this issue in greater detail in Chapter 13, *Advanced Topics*, "Ascending Inserts" on page 525.

Enhancements in System 11 SQL Server

The two enhancements in System 11 SQL Server — the use of larger than 2K writes and the elimination of the additional disk write after splits — cannot be used to speed up loading a table with a clustered index unless the data is loaded in sorted order. If you must load data into a table that already has a clustered index, we recommend that you:

- Load data in sorted order, and
- Use large I/O

12.7.2 Nonclustered Indexes

As each row is inserted into a table, all nonclustered indexes on the table must be modified to account for the inserted row. The modification of each nonclustered index requires SQL Server to search the index to locate the leaf page for the new row, add a new entry to this page, and split index pages as needed. Typically, each nonclustered index adds three or four logical reads, one physical read, and up to one physical write for each row inserted into the table. There are two ways to eliminate the additional I/O needed to modify the index:

- **Use lots of memory** — If the nonclustered indexes fit in memory, you may be able to avoid the physical I/O. You may find the discussion on `indextrips` in Chapter 10, *Transaction Processing Performance* useful in reducing the amount of memory required to cache the index.

- **Load data in sorted order** — If the data is loaded in ascending order of the nonclustered index, the amount of memory required for the index is lower. However, the relative advantage of loading in sorted order is not as great for a nonclustered index as for a clustered index.

12.7.3 Recommendations

Here is a common scenario: You need to load a table and build several indexes on it, including a clustered index. Let us discuss your options in the context of System 11 SQL Server.

Sorted by the Clustered Index

If the data is already sorted by the clustered index or you have the option of sorting it by the clustered index, you should:

1. Create the table and the clustered index.

2. Load data in sorted order using normal BCP, but with large I/O on data as well as log, and then ...

3. Create the nonclustered indexes using the optimizations discussed in "Nonclustered Indexes" on page 475.

Not Sorted by the Clustered Index

If the data is not sorted by the clustered index and you do not have the option of sorting it, you should:

1. Create the table but not any indexes.

2. Load data in given order using fast BCP.

3. Create the clustered index using the optimizations discussed in "Clustered Indexes" on page 476, and then...

4. Create nonclustered indexes using the optimizations discussed in "Nonclustered Indexes" on page 475.

12.8   MISCELLANEOUS BATCH OPERATIONS

12.8.1 Checkpoints

Checkpoint is the process of writing out all dirty buffers. This helps limit the time it takes to recover the database from the transaction log should SQL Server shut down suddenly.

Time and Resource Utilization

The number of disk writes performed by a checkpoint is closely tied to the number of buffers that are dirty at the time the checkpoint command is issued. Buffers dirtied during the checkpoint do not affect the number of disk writes. Checkpoint writes out the dirty buffers chronologically. This order often causes checkpoint writes to be random rather than sequential. In general, we should assume random writes in assessing the time and resource utilization for checkpoints.

Impact on Concurrent Activity on SQL Server

Checkpoint is an I/O intensive operation and can effect the performance of concurrent query/transaction processing on SQL Server. If this poses a problem, you should consider replacing the automatic checkpoints by planned checkpoints that work around periods of peak activity. There are two ways a checkpoint can affect performance of other activity on SQL Server:

1. If the I/O subsystem is already saturated, the checkpoint process may add the last straw and break the camel's back. The checkpoint process moderates the load on the I/O subsystem by having no more than a certain number of outstanding I/O requests at any given time. With System 10 SQL Server, the maximum number of outstanding I/O requests for checkpoint is 10. In System 11 SQL Server, this is a configurable parameter (see Appendix B, *SQL Server Configuration*).

2. No other task can update a data or index page that is in the process of being written to disk. The checkpoint process performs all writes for one table before proceeding to the next table. If your application contains a small (but not tiny) table that is updated *very* frequently, then you may see a substantial impact on performance of concurrent activity on SQL Server while the checkpoint process writes the pages of this table to disk. In such cases, you may want to stripe such tables across multiple disks to minimize this impact. Note that using more memory to cache this table does not help the performance of checkpoints.

12.8.2 DBCC Commands

The complexity of SQL Server and the applications that use it make it inevitable that tables and indexes are occasionally corrupted by a transient hardware fault or an error in SQL Server's data manipulation routines. The DataBase Consistency Checker (DBCC) commands help catch those errors that are difficult to find on the fly. Periodic use of the DBCC commands help assure that your databases are in a consistent state. Dump and load do not do these checks. If the database is corrupted when it is dumped, a fresh load of the database is also corrupted.

Running the DBCC commands periodically against your databases is good insurance against unexpected down time. Depending on the nature of the database corruption, certain rows of tables may become inaccessible to your applications, or in the worst cases, SQL Server may crash whenever it tries to access data in the corrupted portion of the database. There is no way to discover a corruption in a database without stumbling across it while reading data out of the database. If your application touches only a small portion of the data on a regular basis, a database corruption may be lurking in a seldom used part of the database. As soon as your application tries to access this data, SQL Server detects the corruption and your application availability suffers.

The DBCC commands check databases by examining all of the pages containing data in the database. Links between the pages and between the pages and control structures are checked for consistency with one another.

More specifically, the DBCC commands perform the following consistency checks on a database:

- Information in system tables is self-consistent.

- Pages used by a table or index are recorded as allocated in the allocation pages, OAM pages for the object, and GAM pages.

- All pages recorded as allocated are used by a table, index, or text/image column page chain.

- Pages are properly linked together to form tables, indexes, and text/image columns.

- Data on index pages matches the data on the child index or data pages, that is, the row data in the table is consistent with the copies of the information in the leaf pages of the nonclustered indexes and in the non-leaf pages of all indexes on the table.

- Indexes are sorted correctly.

SQL Server has six DBCC commands that check for database consistency. The differences in the commands are in their scope (i.e., what database objects are checked) and consistency domain (i.e., what kinds of checks are performed on the objects):

- **checkcatalog** — verify that the information in the system tables is self-consistent.

- **checkdb** — check the consistency of an entire database.

- **checktable** — check the consistency of a single table and its indexes.

- **checkalloc** — check the page allocation information for the entire database.

- **tablealloc** — check the page allocation information for a single table.

- **indexalloc** — check the page allocation information for a single index.

Many DBCC commands update control information on data pages or in special control pages. As a result, you may see disk writes from some DBCC commands even though there does not appear to be any problem with the tables or indexes that needs to be repaired.

Appendix D, *DBCC Commands*, describes the DBCC commands in detail. Table 12.2 below shows the locks acquired by the commands. This can be helpful in assessing the impact of the various DBCC commands on concurrent activity in the database.

Table 12.2   DBCC command locks

Command	Lock
checkcatalog	shared page locks on system tables.
checktable	shared table lock on the table being checked.
tablealloc	When fix is given: exclusive table lock on the table being checked When nofix is given: shared page locks on the table being checked.
indexalloc	shared table lock on the table being checked.

Optimizing DBCC Commands

Extent I/O

The performance of sequential table and index scans is critical to the performance of DBCC commands. Most DBCC commands perform I/O in units of extents rather than pages in System 10 and later versions of SQL Server. SQL Server preallocates eight extent sized buffers for use by DBCC commands.[5] Hence, up to eight concurrent DBCC commands can perform I/O in units of 16K. The rest perform I/O in units of 2K — just as 4.9 and earlier versions of SQL Server. No warning or other message is returned to notify the administrator when a DBCC command is forced to perform I/O in 2K units.

[5.]   This is separate from the extent I/O buffers used by `create index`.

fix/nofix

Use of the `fix` option with `dbcc checkalloc` causes it to acquire table locks. If the impact on the performance of other concurrent activity is of concern, you should first try the command with the default setting of `nofix` and repeat with `fix` only when necessary.

checktable/checkdb

You should tailor the frequency of `dbcc check` operations on individual tables to the frequency at which they are updated and the impact of the unavailability of the table. If a large table is rarely updated or if the essential parts of the application cannot run while this table is not available, you should perform `dbcc checktable` on this table less frequently than on other tables.

skip_ncindex

The time it takes to check the consistency of a nonclustered index is comparable to the time it takes to drop and create the index. We recommend that you use the `skip_ncindex` option with `dbcc checktable` and `dbcc checkdb` commands. A corrupted nonclustered index does cause loss of data. All of the data in a nonclustered index is copied from the underlying table.

12.8.3 Long-Running Reports

You may not always be able to schedule the execution of the dreaded "queries-from-hell" or other long running reports during off-peak hours or scheduled down time. We discussed the topic of tuning the performance of such queries in Chapter 11, *Query Processing Performance*. Let us discuss our options in minimizing their impact on other concurrent activity on SQL Server.

I/O and Buffer Management

Large table scans tended to use up more than their fair share of data cache buffers in System 10 and earlier versions of SQL Server. The pages read in by a table scan would cause pages already in cache to be flushed out. Thus, a batch operation could have a severe impact on concurrent online activities on SQL Server. System

11 SQL Server reduces the number of data cache buffers used by table scans and other similar operations (see Chapter 13, *Advanced Topics*). Large table scans no longer flush hot pages out of cache.

Some other queries commonly found in reports still remain very demanding on system resources. Examples include `order by` and `distinct` elimination over a large number of rows, `group by` involving a large number of groups, joins with large outer tables, and joins that require reformatting of tables. If impact on other concurrent activity is of greater concern than the response time for any such query, you should consider using a kinder and gentler query plan that is less demanding on system resources. Often, you can trade the fastest query plan for one that uses less memory by exploiting existing orders on tables to minimize their impact on the I/O subsystem. The discussions in Chapter 11, *Query Processing Performance*, "Order of Traversal" on page 403, Chapter 11, *Query Processing Performance*, "Group By and Having" on page 431, and Chapter 11, *Query Processing Performance*, "Sort Avert" on page 432 may be of interest here.

Isolation Level and Cursor Locks

You should execute long running reports at the lowest isolation level permitted by your application. If lock contention holds up other concurrent activity on SQL Server, consider breaking up long transactions into shorter transactions. Note that the cursor locks are held beyond transaction boundaries. Close cursors as soon as appropriate.

Lock Escalation

Lock escalation can sometimes work in your favor. At other times, it works against you. Escalation to a table lock reduces the total number of locks held on SQL Server. On the other hand, it can stall concurrent activity through lock contention. System 11 SQL Server provides mechanisms for tuning lock escalation on a per-object basis. In System 10 and earlier versions of SQL Server, you may be able to prevent lock escalation by having a dummy long running transaction hold an exclusive page lock on a redundant page in the table.[6]

[6.] The idea here is to have one task hold an exclusive lock on a page of the table which prevents other tasks from acquiring a shared table lock. This essentially blocks escalation from shared page locks to a shared table lock. The hazard here is that the task acquiring read locks cannot try to read the page with the exclusive lock held by the other task.

Truncating the Log

One problem with long-running transactions is that the log cannot be truncated beyond the oldest active transaction. System 11 SQL Server provides some additional methods for dealing with this problem (see Chapter 13, *Advanced Topics*, "Oldest Active Transaction" on page 522).

12.8.4 Defragmentation

We use the term fragmentation to denote the following two conditions:

Pages are Sparsely Populated

Often pages end up containing fewer than the optimal number of rows. This can happen as a result of page splits, deletions, and deferred updates. This condition is detrimental to performance since more physical and logical I/O operations and more memory are needed to access a given set of rows. See Chapter 13, *Advanced Topics*, "Ascending Inserts" on page 525 for a discussion of how this can happen as a result of inserts only.

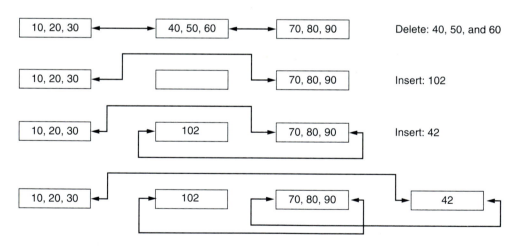

Figure 12.5   Fragmenting a table -

Page Chain is Crooked

Performance suffers when the page chain is not aligned with the physical location of pages on disk. Examples of situations where this may occur include:

- Multiple tables and/or indexes allocate pages from the same segment.
- Multiple segments share a device.
- Inserts, deletes, and deferred updates are applied to nonclustered indexes and tables having clustered indexes.

The examples in Table 12.5 show how the page chain can become crooked as a result of inserts and deletes on a table having a clustered index. Each page holds three rows and rows are denoted by the value of the clustered index.

Avoiding Fragmentation

Before we discuss methods for defragmentation, let us discuss how we may be able to minimize fragmentation in our application. The algorithm for allocation and deallocation of pages attempts to keep the page chain aligned with the physical location of pages on disk. It does so by allocating the page from the same extent or allocation unit as the page this page will be linked to. We may be able to use this property to reduce fragmentation:

- **Object-Segment mapping** — The algorithm for the allocation and deallocation of pages attempts to keep the page chain aligned with the allocation units and devices. When you map multiple tables and indexes into the same segment, the pages allocated to them may come from the same allocation unit. If two tables/indexes sharing a segment take turns in allocating and deallocating pages, then the same allocation unit contains extents for both (see Chapter 4, *SQL Server — Form and Structure*, "DEVICES, SEGMENTS, AND PAGES" on page 77). If your application contains two tables or indexes both of which are subjected to inserts, deletes, and/or deferred updates, you should put them on different segments. Note that a table and its nonclustered indexes can be put on different segments. If you are loading data with nonclustered indexes in place, you should put the table and each of the nonclustered indexes on different segments.

- **Use Fillfactor** — Using fillfactor when creating indexes leaves some room on each page for growth. This gives page allocation some headroom in terms of the number of insert, delete, and deferred updates you can perform before pages are allocated or deallocated.

- **Use BCP** — Both fast and normal BCP leave some unused space in every allocation unit. As shown Figure 4.13, "Pages, extents, and allocation units," on page 87, the first extent of each allocation unit contains the allocation page. Since BCP allocates pages an extent at a time, it skips such extents. When you load a table using (normal) BCP, 7 pages (approximately 3%) are left unused in every allocation unit. Then, the presence of these unallocated pages in every allocation unit enables SQL Server to keep the page chain aligned within allocation units, although not within extents. This can help the performance of table scans by improving the cache hit ratio of disk controllers and other buffered devices.

- **Use Ascinserts** — Chapter 13, *Advanced Topics*, "Ascending Inserts" on page 525 describes a configuration parameter for increasing the density of rows on pages. This is a new feature in System 11 SQL Server.

Correcting Fragmentation

There is no command to perform defragmentation.[7] However, defragmentation can be performed as a result of operations that rebuild the page chain. The efficiency of these operations should benefit from the use of large I/O in System 11 SQL Server.

The following methods can be used to defragment a table:

- **BCP Out/In** — You can BCP the contents of a table out to external media, truncate the table, and then BCP the contents back into the table. You may want to drop the nonclustered indexes before truncating the table and rebuild them after you BCP in the contents of the table.

- **select * into and/or sp_rename** — You can copy the contents of a table into a new table using select * into. You need to drop the original table and rebuild any needed indexes on the new table.

- **Drop and create the clustered index** — You can drop and rebuild the clustered index. Creating the clustered index automatically rebuilds all nonclustered indexes as well.

[7.] Dump and load do *not* defragment a database.

Chapter 13

Advanced Topics

Do not let the tag "advanced" conjure up images of disclaimers like "Don't try this at home" and "Professional driver on closed course". The topics and methods discussed in this chapter are quite mundane.

This chapter contains two broad classes of topics. First, it describes methods and topics whose applicability spans all of query processing, transaction processing, and batch processing. Second, this chapter details some of the new features in System 11 SQL Server.

13.1 HIGH PERFORMANCE I/O SUBSYSTEMS

The performance of most SQL Server applications is limited by the performance of the I/O subsystem. You may be able to improve performance by augmenting traditional disk-based I/O subsystem with performance supplements such as caching disk controllers or with replacements such as file system files for database devices or by using solid-state disks.

13.1.1 Implications of I/O Performance

There are three parts to the cost of an I/O operation:

- **CPU cycles for issuing the I/O** — The number of cycles spent by SQL Server and the operating system in issuing and completing an asynchronous I/O request varies from one hardware platform to another. I/O operations can have a significant impact on overall performance of the system, especially if your application is I/O intensive.

- **Seek and data transfer** — The characteristics of the disks and disk controllers determine the throughput and response of the I/O subsystem. Potential improvements include disk controllers with larger and/or smarter caches, disks with lower latencies, and disk arrays.

- **I/O congestion due to delayed completion** — A delay in the completion of an I/O request can create a traffic jam of I/Os in SQL Server. For example, a transaction cannot release the transactional locks it holds until the log page that contains the commit record is written to disk.

The second and third parts provide the motivation to employ high performance I/O subsystems such as write-caching, disk arrays, and solid-state disks. The first part of the cost cannot be helped by changes in the I/O subsystem. Let us discuss how high performance I/O subsystems can be used to enhance the performance of SQL Server.

Query Processing and `tempdb`

The caching of worktables and temporary tables in query processing is discussed in Chapter 11, *Query Processing Performance*, "Query Processing is Read-Only" on page 371, "Caching Worktables" on page 390, and "Using Temporary Tables to Simplify Queries" on page 439. If worktables and temporary tables holding intermediate results are too large to cache in memory, the performance of reads and writes on the device that holds `tempdb` becomes critical to performance. In such cases, your first preference should be to rephrase queries to minimize the size of intermediate results. Failing that, you should consider putting `tempdb` on high-performance I/O devices.

The performance of writes to the log device for `tempdb` is not usually critical, since operations on worktables are not logged. However, as mentioned in Chapter 11, *Query Processing Performance*, "Using Temporary Tables to Simplify Queries" on page 439, inserts, deletes and updates to temporary tables are logged. Also, as mentioned under Chapter 7, *Application Development*, "Dynamic SQL" on page 186, using dynamic SQL causes some traffic to the log in `tempdb`. If you are making extensive use of temporary tables or dynamic SQL and find that log traffic in `tempdb` is a performance bottleneck, placing `tempdb` on high performance I/O devices may be of some benefit.

Transaction and Batch Processing and the Log Device

The performance of the log device can be critical to the performance of transaction processing applications. In this case, you should consider placing the log segment on a high performance I/O device. Here are some factors that may influence your decision to do so:

Large I/O

Writes to the log device are sequential. You may be able to improve the performance of the traditional log disk simply by using writes larger than 2K. See "NAMED CACHES AND BUFFER POOLS" on page 500 before resorting to exotic database devices for the log.

Group Commits

As mentioned in Chapter 10, *Transaction Processing Performance*, "Logging and Group Commits" on page 338, at sufficiently high levels of concurrency and throughput, SQL Server minimizes the writing of partially full log pages by delaying writes to the log device. The algorithm for group commit adapts to the response from the log device. Simply put, a quick response from the log device encourages SQL Server not to delay the next write. This behavior, while intuitive, may nullify the benefits of a high-performance log device. In the worst case, the effect of an increase in the performance of the log device translates into an increase only in the number of times a log page is written before it is full and not the overall throughput. Response time, however, may be improved because SQL Server is not waiting very long for the log page writes.

Group commits occur only with a large number of concurrent users and high throughput and not in batch processing. "Logging and Group Commits" on page 338 describes how to measure the effectiveness of group commits. If your application does not benefit from group commits, you need not worry about the failure of group commits.

Data Devices

There are two motivations to use high-performance devices for data:

- **Efficient access to medium and large tables and indexes** — Performance of I/O is important for frequently accessed tables and indexes that are too large to be cached in database buffers. For truly large tables, the decision to use high-performance devices involves a trade-off between cost and performance. The use of such devices may be easier to justify for indexes on large and medium-sized tables. Another interesting case is skewed access pattern on large tables. If, for example, 5% of the pages in a large table account for 80% of the accesses to the table, I/O subsystems having large and intelligent caches may help performance.

- **Duration of checkpoints** — As discussed in Chapter 10, *Transaction Processing Performance*, "Checkpoint and Recovery" on page 303 and Chapter 12, *Batch Processing Performance*, "Checkpoints" on page 482, a checkpoint may affect the performance of concurrent transaction processing while the dirty pages of a hot table are being written to disk. If you observe a sharp drop in the performance of transaction throughput during checkpoint, you should consider putting small tables that are updated very frequently on high-performance devices.

13.1.2 Caching by the I/O Subsystems

Most disk controllers cache reads. If SQL Server issues a request to read 2K from a disk, the disk or the disk controller often holds in its cache the region adjacent to the requested 2K. You can verify this for your system by performing a table scan (e.g., `select count(*) from foo (0)` on a table having few rows per page) with `set statistics io on` and `set statistics time on`. If the reads are not cached, the scan performance is limited by the rotational latency of the disk. With a 5400 RPM disk, you should expect to perform 90 reads or 180 KB every second. However, scan performance for a single disk typically exceeds 800KB/sec. Most read requests result in cache hits in the disk or the controller and only a few requests need to read information off the disk.

The caching of reads by the I/O subsystems is always safe to use. We discuss how the use of bigger and smarter caches in the I/O subsystem can improve performance. On the other hand, the caching of writes has implications on consistency and recoverability. The caching of writes means that the I/O subsystem only copies data into cache before signalling the completion of the disk write. The actual writes to the disk occur later.

When is Write Caching Safe?

With write caching, the disk controller or disk drive can decide when it is convenient to write data to disk. It can schedule for optimal disk head travel and plan for the rotational latency of the disk platter. This improves the performance of disk writes because the process that initiates the write does not have to wait for the write to complete. Most disk controllers do not cache writes in their default mode of operation. There is a very good reason for this: recoverability. SQL Server assumes disk writes are persistent. If the disk controller were to hold the disk page in cache while SQL Server believes that the write has completed, the database is unrecoverable should a failure such as loss of power or disk crash prevent the controller from completing the write.

We should emphasize that SQL Server assumes writes are persistent not just on the log device but on *all* devices. To see why, consider the completion of checkpoint. Suppose the write of a dirty page to device is held in cache while the write of the "checkpoint completed" record to the log completes. Should the power or the disk fail before the dirty data page is written to persistent store, the database may be rendered unrecoverable. With the checkpoint record in the log, SQL Server assumes that all pages changed by transactions prior to the checkpoint are stored on disk.

Some I/O subsystems guarantee that the cached writes are completed despite any single failure by using an interruptible power supply (UPS) in conjunction with mirroring or RAID (1 through 5). You need to make sure that the conditions under which the I/O subsystem guarantees that cached writes are completed are acceptable to your application. If your application requires that the database survive any combination of two failures simultaneously, you cannot use write-caching that handles single failures only. Some caching controllers require the power supply to be restored within a certain number of hours to ensure recovery from power failures. This is typically tied to properties of the UPS or the non-volatile memory used by the cache. You also need to make sure that the time and resources required by the disk subsystem to recover from a failure are in line with the requirements of your application.

Desperately Seeking Write Caching

Write caching can make a significant difference in the performance of certain batch operations, including `create database`, `load database`, `BCP`, and `create index`. If your application performs these operations in stand-alone mode and unrecoverable failures are acceptable in this mode of operation, you may be able to use write caching with less stringent requirements. Some disk controllers allow you to turn write caching on and off mid-flight, and some file systems provide a **sync** command that flushes all cached writes to the disks. If your I/O subsystem provides such mechanisms, you may be able to use write-caching as follows:

1. If necessary, dump and archive the database. This is your point of recovery in case something goes wrong. You may not need this step for the creation or initial population of the database.

2. Put SQL Server in stand-alone mode. Turn on write caching on the disk drives you are using.

3. Perform the batch operation.

4. Turn off write caching. You need to make sure that this flushes all cached writes to persistent media.

If all of the above steps succeed, you can resume normal activity on SQL Server. You may want to perform a checkpoint between steps 3 and 4 to flush the dirty pages created by the batch operation to disk. This checkpoint does not guarantee recoverability; its purpose is to exploit write caching in cleaning up the database buffers.

13.1.3 Representative I/O Subsystems

There are two broad classes of technologies that are used to build high-performance I/O subsystems:

- **Large and smart caches** — Some high-performance I/O subsystems supplement an array of traditional disks with large caches that are used to cache either reads or both reads and writes. There is a wide variety of such products that differ in the size and resilience of the cache as well as in the choice of algorithms for caching.

- **Persistent random access store** — Some high-performance I/O subsystems replace traditional disks with radically different technologies that provide both random access and persistence. Their performance is closer to semiconductor memory technologies than to traditional disks. Unfortunately, so is their price.

Let us outline some of the representative high-performance I/O subsystems. This discussion is not an endorsement or rejection of any products and technologies. Each of them has strengths and weaknesses. Their relevance to an application depends on the characteristics of the application and the acceptable costs to your organization. Further, there are new technologies on the horizon that cannot be classified with our framework.

Buffered File Systems

Some operating systems cache both reads and writes to file systems in main memory. The discussion on recoverability in "When is Write Caching Safe?" on page 494 is relevant to the use of such file systems as database devices.

It can be tempting to use operating system files for SQL Server database devices. File system files are easier to manage than raw partitions and often query performance appears to be better. The operating system buffers data between SQL Server and the disk drives. This means SQL Server does not read and write to the disks but to buffers managed by the operating system. However, raw partitions, if properly tuned, can have an edge over buffered file systems in performance by obviating the additional processing the operating system performs to buffer I/O operations.

If you have a choice between using additional main memory as buffers for file systems and using it as SQL Server database buffers, the discussion in "Implications of I/O Performance" on page 491 and "When is Write Caching Safe?" on page 494 indicate why the latter may be a safer bet. One reason to leave memory in the operating system rather than using it in SQL Server is if this additional memory needs to be time-shared between SQL Server and other applications on the same machine.

Disk Striping and Logical Volume Managers

Even distribution of workload across I/O devices is essential to performance. This can be a difficult task if the I/O pattern in the application is stable and it can be impossible otherwise. It is not uncommon to find the performance of a single device out of scores of devices used by SQL Server to be the limiting factor in performance.

Most operating system vendors provide mechanisms for striping devices across multiple spindles using logical volume managers or smart disk controllers. In general, the use of such techniques does not imply caching of writes and hence does not have any implications on the recoverability of the database. There is a small overhead involved in having the operating system translate addresses within logical volumes to physical addresses on disk.

If you observe one or a few disks to be the bottleneck in performance, you should consider using logical volume managers to stripe the devices across multiple spindles.

Caching Disk Controllers

As mentioned in "Representative I/O Subsystems" on page 496, most disk controllers cache reads but not writes. Some provide the option to cache writes, but you need to pay close attention to recoverability before enabling caching on writes.

There is another aspect to the caching in controllers that has some implications on their use on log or data devices. Often SQL Server issues multiple asynchronous writes to adjacent pages on the same device. We discussed one such situation in "Logging and Group Commits" on page 338, where successive writes to the log disks are sorted by page number, with some duplicates. Another case is the flushing of newly created pages to disk after a batch operation such as `BCP` or `select .. into`. Pages are allocated and dirtied in ascending order of page number. They are also written to disk in ascending order of their physical location.

Some smart controllers can coalesce multiple writes into a single write. For example, some may be able to coalesce concurrent asynchronous writes to pages numbered:

```
(100), (101), (102), (201), (202), (103), (104), (203)
```

into two writes to pages numbered:

```
(100-104), (201-203)
```

This improves performance by reducing the number of I/O operations performed by the disk drive. In addition, the single operation avoids the possibility of missing the block as the platter spins around and having to wait for an entire rotation of the platter.

Disk Arrays with Large Caches

Several vendors package arrays of disks with large caches and smart controllers. The controller caches reads as well as writes and ensures persistence of writes by using a combination of UPS, RAID, mirroring, and non-volatile memory technologies. There are a wide variety of products in this class.

The implications of the use of disk arrays on performance depends on both the algorithms used by the controller and on the characteristics of the application. There are no simple rules or guidelines that we are aware of to help make decisions. Here are some of the factors you need to consider in deciding whether they are appropriate for your application:

- The discussion in "Caching by the I/O Subsystems" on page 494 applies to arrays of disks as well.

- Generally speaking, the efficiency of read caching used by products in this class is superior to the read caching used by traditional disk controllers. For example, if two concurrent table scans access pages from the same disk, traditional disk controllers may under utilize the cache. Suppose the two scans are accessing pages (100, 101, 102, ...) and (200, 201, 202, ...). A smart controller should be able to reserve two separate regions in its cache to store both the sequences, instead of alternately filling the entire cache with one sequence and then the other.

- Some products in this class guarantee persistence of cached writes under fairly extensive failure scenarios.

Solid State Disk Devices

Solid state disks (SSD) use semiconductor memory to store information but are attached to your computer like a disk drive. SSDs have a number of advantages over mechanical disk drives. There is no read/write head or disk platter to move so random access to data is extremely fast. Data transfer is not limited by the rotation speed of the platters so data transfer is very fast. There are no moving parts in the SSD so they can be very reliable. Unfortunately, SSDs are also very expensive. The cost of SSD is closer to that of RAM than to that of traditional disks.

The concerns about recoverability from "When is Write Caching Safe?" on page 494 do not apply to SSDs, since their performance is not based on caching of writes. However, the persistence of the contents of the device is often tied to the reliability and longevity of the UPS technology used in the product.

Some hardware platforms provide proprietary versions of solid state disks that can be plugged directly on the memory bus of the server. The names of such devices vary from one vendor to another. These devices enjoy all the advantages of the SSDs, except that they are proprietary rather than industry standard. In addition, they eliminate one of the potential bottlenecks in the use of SSDs — the bandwidth of the I/O bus and/or the disk controller.

13.2   NAMED CACHES AND BUFFER POOLS

System 10 and earlier versions of SQL Server treat the collection of database buffers as a single monolithic entity. Your ability to control the memory utilization for specific objects is limited to the configuration of such parameters as `index-trips` and `oamtrips`. System 11 SQL Server allows you to group database buffers into multiple named caches, bind tables, indexes, and databases to named caches, and enable variable-size I/O on named caches. With these features you can control the use of memory by each table, object, and database. Figure 13.1 illustrates the use of these features.

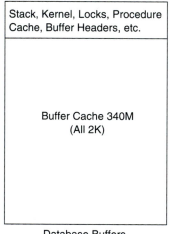
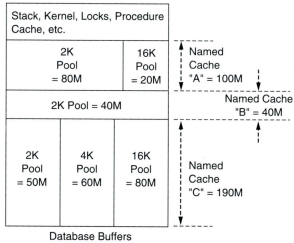

Figure 13.1   Named caches -

We partitioned the monolithic 2K buffer pool of size 350M from System 10 SQL Server into three named caches: "A", "B", and "C" of sizes 100M, 40M, and 190M, respectively. Further, we have created multiple buffers pools within each named cache. Each buffer pool is associated with a size that denotes the unit of

I/O used in that buffer pool. Named cache "A" contains a 2K pool of size 80M, and a 16K pool of size 20M. We can bind tables, indexes, and databases to named caches. Table 13.1 shows the bindings for the example in Figure 13.1.

Table 13.1   Objects bound to name caches

Named Cache	I/O Sizes	Tables, Indexes, and Databases
"A"	2K, 16K	table db1..T1, table db2..T2, clustered index T1(x), nonclustered index T1(y)
"B"	2K	tempdb
"C"	2K, 4K, 16K	table T3, nonclustered index T1(z), clustered index T2(x), db1..syslogs

Let us list some of the options and limitations in configuring named caches and buffer pools and in binding objects to caches. This list is intended only to highlight the choices available to us, not to act as a reference manual for buffer configuration. Please consult the Sybase documentation for SQL Server for a complete list of all the options and limitations.

- Each buffer pool in a named cache is associated with a unique unit of I/O. The sizes of the buffer pools within each named cache add up to the size of the named cache. If the sum of the configured sizes of the buffer pools is smaller than the size of the named cache, the remainder is put into the 2K pool. Every named cache must contain a 2K buffer pool.

- The sizes of the named caches in System 11 SQL Server adds up to somewhat less than the size of the buffer pool in System 10 and earlier versions of SQL Server. The size of the buffer header has increased by approximately 2.5% of the size of the buffer itself.

- Tables, indexes, and databases are bound to named caches and not to buffer pools. All the units of I/O for all the buffer pools in a named cache are available to all the tables, indexes, and databases bound to the named cache. In the above example, the optimizer can choose between 2K and 16K I/O for db1..T1, and between 2K, 4K and 16K for the log on database db1. Two different accesses to the same table/index/database may choose different units of I/O.

- There are very few restrictions on the binding of tables, indexes, and databases to named caches. You can bind a table, the clustered index on this table, and a nonclustered index on this table to three different named caches. However, binding a database or its system tables to a named cache can be performed only when the database is in single user mode.

The following code segment shows the entries required in the System 11 SQL Server configuration file to generate the configuration shown in Figure 13.1:

```
# The first character in the configuration file must be a #
[Configuration Options]

[General Information]

[Cache Manager]
        procedure cache percent = 2

[Named Cache:A]
        cache size = 100M
        cache status = mixed cache

[2K I/O Buffer Pool]
        pool size = 80M
        wash size = DEFAULT

[16K I/C Buffer Pool]
        pool size = 80M
        wash size = DEFAULT

[Named Cache:B]
        cache size = 40M
        cache status = mixed cache

[2K I/O Buffer Pool]
        pool size = 40M
        wash size = DEFAULT

[Named Cache:C]
        cache size = 190M
        cache status = mixed cache

[2K I/O Buffer Pool]
        pool size = 50M
```

```
        wash size = DEFAULT

[4K I/O Buffer Pool]
        pool size = 60M
        wash size = DEFAULT

[16K I/O Buffer Pool]
        pool size = 80M
        wash size = DEFAULT

[Physical Resources]

[Physical Memory]
        total memory = 200000
```

13.2.1 Managing Named Caches and Buffer Pools

System 11 SQL Server provides several utilities for monitoring and managing named caches and buffer pools.

sp_poolconfig

The number and sizes of named caches cannot be changed dynamically. Creating or dropping named caches or increasing or decreasing the amount of memory contained in a named cache requires a reboot of SQL Server. However, the following system stored procedures can be used to reconfigure dynamically the sizes and wash areas of the buffer pools within each named cache without rebooting SQL Server:

```
sp_poolconfig <cache name>, "[2|4|8|16]K", <amount> [, <source pool>]
```

For example, the command:

```
sp_poolconfig "A", "16K", "10M", "4K"
```

resizes the 16K pool to 10Mb. If this means an increase in the size of the target pool then the deficit is taken from the source pool. If this means a decrease in the size of the target pool then the surplus is returned to the source pool. The 2K pool is used if the source pool is omitted from the arguments.

The discussion on wash sizes in Chapter 5, *SQL Server — Methods and Features*, "Dirty Buffers" on page 104 and "Buffer Replacement Policies" on page 518 applies to each buffer pool in each named caches. You can configure the wash size for each buffer pool either by using the configuration file or by using the following alternate form of the sp_poolconfig stored procedure:

```
sp_poolconfig <cache name>, "[2|4|8|16]K", "wash size = <?>[K|M]"
```

For example, the command:

```
sp_poolconfig "A", "4K", "wash=1024"
```

sets the size of the wash area in the 4K pool of cache A to 1024 pages.

sp_bindcache

Once multiple named caches and multiple buffer pools are configured within each named cache, we need to bind databases, tables, and indexes to named caches before the application can benefit from the use of named caches. The syntax for binding databases, tables, and indexes and to a named cache is as follows:

```
sp_bindcache <cache name>, <database name>
        [,<table name> [, <index name>]]
```

Note that databases, tables, and indexes can only be bound to a named cache and not to a specific buffer pool within the named cache. If the named cache contains multiple buffer pools the optimizer chooses among them.

Binding databases, tables, and indexes to named caches can be performed dynamically and does not require a reboot of SQL Server. However, a database must be in single user mode before it or its system catalogs can be bound to a named cache. The following examples illustrates the typical sequence of commands involved in binding of databases, tables, and indexes to named caches. Here is how to bind user tables and indexes to a named cache:

```
sp_bindcache "my cache A", "mydb", "tableA"
go
sp_bindcache "my cache AI", "mydb", "table A", "indexAclu"
go
sp_bindcache "my cache B", "mydb", "tableB"
go
sp_bindcache "my cache B", "mydb", "tableB", "indexBnon1"
go
```

Here is how to bind system tables (e.g., log and sysindexes) to a named cache:

```
use master
```

```
go
sp_dboption mydb, "single user", true
go
use mydb
go
checkpoint
go
sp_bindcache "my log cache", "mydb", "syslogs"
go
sp_bindcache "my system cache", "mydb", "sysindexes"
go
sp_bindcache "my system cache", "mydb", "sysindexes", "sysindexes"
go
use master
go
sp_dboption mydb, "single user", false
go
use mydb
go
checkpoint
```

Here is how to bind an entire database to a named cache:

```
use master
go
sp_dboption mytemp, "single user", true
go
use mytemp
go
checkpoint
go
sp_bindcache "my cache temp", "mytemp"
go
use master
go
sp_dboption mytemp, "single user", false
go
use mytemp
go
checkpoint
go
```

A word of caution regarding dynamic binding of databases, tables, and indexes to named caches: Binding a database, table, or index to a named cache causes all pages of this object to be flushed from the cache that the object was previously bound to. If any of those pages are dirty, they are written to disk. This can cause a sharp drop in performance of ongoing activities on SQL Server. Even after the binding is completed, it may take a while for the new named cache to be warmed up with the hot pages from the bound object. Again, performance may be lower during this warm-up period. Hence, you should avoid changing the binding of databases, tables, and indexes to named caches during peak periods of activity on SQL Server.

The `sp_bindcache` command can help tune queries in a rather unusual way. Suppose you are trying out different ways of phrasing a complex query or experimenting with things like optimizer hints and buffer sizes by executing the query repeatedly and comparing the response times. Your observations may be distorted by the partial caching of data pages in memory. For example, the second execution of a query may run a lot faster than the first thanks to the pages that were read into memory by the first execution. In such cases, you can use `sp_bindcache` to simulate a cold start. After each execution, bind all relevant databases, tables, and indexes to the named caches that they were bound to in the first place. This causes the cached pages to be flushed out of the cache, without changing the bindings.

sp_cacheconfig

The `sp_cacheconfig` stored procedure can be used to display cache configuration options using the following syntax:

```
sp_cacheconfig ["<cache name>"]
```

Following is a sample output from sp_cacheconfig for a configuration having 10 named caches:

Cache Name	Status	Type	Config Value	Run Value
cache C	Active	Mixed	1.00 Mb	1.00 Mb
cache CI	Active	Mixed	108.00 Mb	108.00 Mb
cache log	Active	Log Only	6.00 Mb	6.00 Mb
cache O	Active	Mixed	28.00 Mb	28.00 Mb
cache OI	Active	Mixed	30.00 Mb	30.00 Mb
cache R	Active	Mixed	28.00 Mb	28.00 Mb
cache S	Active	Mixed	452.00 Mb	452.00 Mb
cache SI	Active	Mixed	108.00 Mb	108.00 Mb
cache tinyhot	Active	Mixed	18.00 Mb	18.00 Mb
default data cache	Active	Default	20.00 Mb	105.81 Mb
		Total	799.00 Mb	884.79 Mb

Observe that one of the caches is denoted as `log only` and that the run value for the size of the `default data cache` is larger than its configured value. Any memory left over after allocating memory to the other caches is given to the default data cache. If you are not sure about how large your named caches can be, you can start with a configuration which puts a minimal amount of memory into your named caches, boot SQL Server, and determine from the output of `sp_cacheconfig` how much memory can be moved from the default data cache into your named caches. Output from `sp_cacheconfig` also shows the configuration of each buffer pool in each named cache as follows:

```
Cache: cache C,    Status: Active,    Type: Mixed
       Config Size: 1.00 Mb,    Run Size: 1.00 Mb

  IO Size  Wash Size Config Size  Run Size
  -------- --------- ------------ ------------
     2 Kb     512 Kb      1.00 Mb      1.00 Mb
==================================================================
Cache: cache log,    Status: Active,    Type: Log Only
       Config Size: 6.00 Mb,    Run Size: 6.00 Mb

  IO Size  Wash Size Config Size  Run Size
  -------- --------- ------------ ------------
     2 Kb     512 Kb      1.00 Mb      1.00 Mb
     4 Kb    4096 Kb      5.00 Mb      5.00 Mb
==================================================================
[Output omitted]
Cache: cache tinyhot,    Status: Active,    Type: Mixed
       Config Size: 18.00 Mb,    Run Size: 18.00 Mb

  IO Size  Wash Size Config Size  Run Size
  -------- --------- ------------ ------------
     2 Kb     512 Kb     18.00 Mb     18.00 Mb
==================================================================
Cache: default data cache,    Status: Active,    Type: Default
       Config Size: 20.00 Mb,    Run Size: 105.81 Mb

  IO Size  Wash Size Config Size  Run Size
  -------- --------- ------------ ------------
     2 Kb    1024 Kb     16.00 Mb    101.81 Mb
    16 Kb    2048 Kb      4.00 Mb      4.00 Mb

(return status = 0)
```

sp_helpcache

The current databases, tables, and indexes named cache bindings can be displayed
with the following system stored procedure:

```
sp_helpcache ["<cache name>"]
```

Following is a sample output from `sp_helpcache` that shows the binding of
some user and system tables and indexes to the named caches listed in the above
output from `sp_cacheconfig`:

```
Cache Name            Config Size Run Size    Overhead
------------------    ----------- ----------  --------
cache C               1.00 Mb     1.00 Mb     0.11 Mb
cache CI              108.00 Mb   108.00 Mb   5.56 Mb
cache log             6.00 Mb     6.00 Mb     0.34 Mb
cache O               28.00 Mb    28.00 Mb    1.44 Mb
cache OI              30.00 Mb    30.00 Mb    1.53 Mb
cache R               28.00 Mb    28.00 Mb    1.44 Mb
cache S               452.00 Mb   452.00 Mb   23.19 Mb
cache SI              108.00 Mb   108.00 Mb   5.56 Mb
cache tinyhot         18.00 Mb    18.00 Mb    0.97 Mb
default data cache    20.00 Mb    105.81 Mb   5.46 Mb


Memory Available For Memory Configured
Named Caches         To Named Caches
------------------   -------------------
 897.75 Mb             799.00 Mb


There is 98.75 Mb of memory left over that will be allocated to the
default cache


------------------ Cache Binding Information: ------------------

Cache Name            Entity Name          Type             Index Name
------------------    -------------------  ---------------  ----------
cache C               mydb.dbo.tableC      table
cache C               mydb.dbo.tableC      clustered index  indexCclu
cache CI              mydb.dbo.tableC      index            indexCnon1
cache log             mydb.dbo.syslogs     table
cache O               mydb.dbo.tableTiny4  clustered index  indexTiny4
cache O               mydb.dbo.tableO      table
cache O               mydb.dbo.tableTiny4  table
```

```
cache OI            mydb.dbo.tableO      clustered index indexO
cache R             mydb.dbo.tableR      clustered index indexRclu
cache R             mydb.dbo.tableR      table
cache S             mydb.dbo.tableS      table
cache SI            mydb.dbo.tableS      clustered index s_clu
cache tinyhot       mydb.dbo.sysindexes clustered index sysindexes
cache tinyhot       mydb.dbo.tableTiny1 clustered index indexTiny1
cache tinyhot       mydb.dbo.tableTiny2 clustered index indexTiny2
cache tinyhot       mydb.dbo.tableTiny3 clustered index indexTiny3
cache tinyhot       mydb.dbo.sysindexes table
cache tinyhot       mydb.dbo.tableTiny1 table
cache tinyhot       mydb.dbo.tableTiny2 table
cache tinyhot       mydb.dbo.tableTiny3 table
default data cache mydb.dbo.tableH      table
(return status = 0)
```

Observe that some caches contain both tables and indexes, and others (e.g., cache OI and cache SI) contain only indexes. Typically, indexes that are accessed the most frequently are best put in separate named caches. Also, observe that the cache declared as `log only` contains only the log, and that the relatively small cache, cache `tinyhot`, contains a few user and system tables and indexes, where the user tables are named tiny. The cache `tinyhot` illustrates the process for locking a few hot and tiny tables into memory.

13.2.2 Why Partition Memory?

Let us discuss two fundamental reasons why you may want to partition memory into named caches and assign tables, indexes, and databases into different named caches, and one reason why you may not want to partition memory.

Reducing Physical I/O

Assigning part of the memory to tables, indexes, and databases gives you control over how they are cached. You can use this flexibility to improve cache hit ratio and reduce physical I/O. Here are some options you should consider.

Lock Hot Tables/Indexes/Databases in Memory

You can lock any set of tables/indexes/databases in memory by configuring a named cache that is larger than the sum of the sizes of the items bound to the cache. Here are examples of some tables/indexes/databases you should consider locking in memory.

- `tempdb`.
- Frequently used indexes (e.g., the index on the inner table of a join, indexes frequently used in random accesses). Observe that, unlike the `indextrips` configuration parameter, named caches allow you to extend preferential treatment to one out of several indexes on a table.
- Small tables that are updated frequently.

If you do not have sufficient memory to cache all of the table/index/database, it may pay to bind it to a cache that can accommodate a substantial fraction of the object in the following two cases:

- Access to the table/index/database is limited to a small working set at any given time, for example, if the access to a table or index is skewed in the sense that only a few pages account for most of the accesses to the table/index/database. Examples include `tempdb`, large inner tables in joins having a highly selective search clause on the outer table, and tables where the popularity of rows varies widely due to characteristics of the application.
- Not all of the bound tables/indexes/databases are accessed simultaneously and the access pattern does not change very frequently. If the named cache is large enough to accommodate all subsets of tables/indexes/databases that are used simultaneously, then the use of the named cache may be able to eliminate all I/O except those required when the access pattern changes.

Reclaim Memory from Cold Pages

Often the LRU buffer replacement policy tends to leave pages in memory longer than necessary. Here are some examples:

- Operations that access tables sequentially, such as selects and updates that use table scans, sequential loading of data, and joins that scan large inner tables sequentially.
- Random access to tables that are much too big to cache. There is little point in using up memory to cache (say) 5% of a table and have 95% of the accesses

result in cache misses. It may make more sense to use that memory more profitably elsewhere. We have seen an example of this in Chapter 10, *Transaction Processing Performance*, "Buffer Cache" on page 307, when we decided to cache all of the index and none of the table, instead of caching part of each.

System 11 SQL Server has mechanisms to detect some of the former situations (see "Buffer Replacement Policies" on page 518). However, it cannot detect all cases when a page is no longer needed. In such cases, you can force SQL Server to discard pages by binding the table/index/database to a named cache having a small amount of memory.

Improving SMP Scalability

If your application has the following combination of ingredients, the performance of SQL Server may be limited by contention on the shared data structures used by SQL Server in managing buffers:

- Four or more active CPUs.

- Large number of logical reads (= high throughput + good cache hit ratio).

- I/O subsystem and log are not bottlenecks.

If you find yourself in this situation, you may need to partition tables, indexes, or databases among multiple named caches to improve SMP scalability. You need to assess the frequency of logical reads for the most frequently accessed objects and assign them to named caches to balance the frequency of logical reads among named caches. System 11 SQL Monitor provides tools for measuring the frequency of accesses to tables and indexes. If you are without SQL Monitor, here are some guidelines for assessing the number of logical reads on tables and indexes:

- You should use your knowledge of the application to identify the SQL statements or stored procedures that account for the bulk of accesses to data and index pages.

- Use the `set statistics io` command (see Chapter 9, *Instrumenting SQL Code*, "IO Statistics" on page 294) to determine the number of logical reads performed by these SQL statements and/or stored procedures on the tables and indexes.

- `set statistics io` does not show the number logical reads on a table and index separately. Typically, indexes account for most of the logical reads in the case of random accesses and covered index scans. Tables account for most of the logical reads in case of table scans and large index scans.

- Certain system catalogs account for a large number of logical reads. Most notable is `sysindexes` for almost any application and `syscolumns` for applications that perform a lot of ad hoc SQL statements.

The objective here is only to preclude the possibility that one named cache accounts for the bulk of the logical reads and not to get an exact count for the number of logical reads. It suffices to identify a few of the most active tables, indexes, databases, and system catalogs, and bind them to different named caches.

Fragmenting Memory

We discussed two reasons to divide memory into multiple named caches. Let us discuss why you may not want to do so. A large monolithic pool of buffers is flexible in the sense that all of the memory is available to any table, index, or database that wants it. Consider the example in Figure 13.1 and a query whose performance is critically dependent on the ability to cache 300MB of some table in memory. The monolithic buffer pool of 340MB can outperform the fragmented collection of named caches by a wide margin.

Such cases are rare, but not implausible. While fragmenting memory into multiple buffer pools, you need to keep in mind the amount of memory required to cache individual objects and make sure that no table whose caching is critical to performance is starved for memory.

13.2.3 Impact of Buffer Sizes

There is a 1-to-1 correspondence between buffers and cached database pages in System 10 and earlier versions of SQL Server as each buffer can hold only one database page. With System 11 SQL Server, buffer sizes are variable, and one buffer can accommodate multiple database pages. This allows the optimizer and the application developers to perform I/O in units greater than one page at a time. Here are some of the factors that influence the choice of buffer sizes:

- The choice of buffer sizes for a table or index is limited to the buffer pools contained in the named cache it is bound to. In the example in Figure 13.1, accesses to table `T1` can be performed using 2K or 16K buffers and those to table `T3` using 2K, 4K or 16K buffers. System 11 SQL Server supports pools of buffers with buffer sizes of 2K, 4K, 8K, and 16K.

- A buffer can be shared only by an adjacent set of pages that does not span extent boundaries. Figure 13.2 and Table 13.2 show examples of sets of pages that can and cannot share a buffer.

Table 13.2   Pages and buffer sharing

Set of Pages	Can Share a Buffer?	Comments
(205)	Yes	Same as System 10 and earlier versions of SQL Server
(203, 204)	Yes	Adjacent, does not span extent boundary
(207, 208)	No	Spans extent boundary
(208,209)	Yes	
(208,209,210)	No	Needs 6K. Must be one of 2K, 4K, 8K, and 16K
(208-215)	Yes	

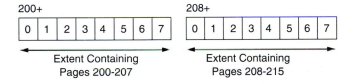

Figure 13.2   Pages sharing buffers -

- Different accesses to the same table and indexes can use buffers of different sizes, as long as they access disjoint sets of pages. For example, if pages 203 and 204 are already in a 4K buffer, SQL Server can read pages 208 – 215 into a 16K buffer, but not pages 200 – 203 into a new 8K buffer. In the latter case, it defaults to 2K buffers, and reads only the pages not already in cache.

• There is no dynamic coalescing or splitting of buffers. If SQL Server reads in pages 203 and 204 into one 4K buffer and pages 205 and 206 into another 4K buffer, it cannot coalesce them into a single 8K buffer. Similarly, it cannot divide the contents of an 8K buffer into two 4K buffers.

Why Use Large Buffers?

You can use large buffers to improve the efficiency of I/O. Typically, the cost of performing a 16K I/O is not much larger than the cost of performing a 2K I/O. We discussed three parts in the cost of an I/O operation in "Implications of I/O Performance" on page 491. Performing I/O in units of 16K rather than 2K means that we incur these fixed costs once for eight pages instead of once for every page.

However, large buffers should not be used indiscriminately. There are two potential disadvantages to using large I/O.

1. The cost of transferring a 16K buffer over a busy controller *can* be larger than that of a 2K buffer. If a controller has a peak throughput of 20MB/sec, transferring a 2K buffer takes 0.1ms, whereas a 16K buffer takes 0.8ms. At more realistic sustainable throughputs of 5MB/sec, this gap widens to 0.4ms vs. 3.2ms. This puts the transfer time in the same order of magnitude as seek time. It is tempting but misleading to assume that the I/O is free for all but the first page in a large buffer.

2. Using large buffers inappropriately can reduce the cache hit ratio. SQL Server reads a 2K page into a 2K buffer only when it needs to access this page. It reads eight pages into a 16K buffer when it knows that it needs to access one of those eight pages and *believes* that it may need to access one or more of the other seven pages. An inappropriate use of large buffers may fill up the buffer cache with pages that are rarely accessed. The optimizer is very conservative and chooses to use large buffers only when it is reasonably sure that it will need to access all of the pages in the buffer. However, you need to use care in overriding the optimizer's decisions when you force the use of large buffers.

Table 13.3 shows examples of operations that can benefit from large buffers.

Table 13.3   Operations that benefit from large buffers

Operation	Will Large Buffers Help?	Comments
Table scan	Yes, ..	.. provided the table is not badly fragmented and does not fit entirely in memory.
Random access	No	A query that accesses only one row or a few rows from the same page has no use for large buffers.
Clustered index scan	Yes, ..	.. provided the scan accesses multiple pages.
Nonclustered index scan	On the index, ..	.. provided the scan accesses multiple index pages. A covered index scan can use large buffers for index pages. In the special case that the data is sorted in the order of the nonclustered index, large buffers may be useful for the data pages as well.
BCP	Yes, except when ..	.. there is a clustered index on the table, and data is not being loaded in sorted order.
Create index	Yes for data, no for the index.	This provides the same benefits as the use of extent I/O buffers in System 10 SQL Server but without the restrictions on usability.
DBCC check commands	No	System 10 SQL Server already uses 16K I/O.
Insert statements	Yes, ..	.. provided there is no clustered index or the data is being inserted in ascending order of the clustered index. See "Ascending Inserts" on page 525.
Update and delete statements	Yes, ..	.. provided there is no `where` clause or the `where` clause meets the criteria specified in the first three items in this table.

Table 13.3   Operations that benefit from large buffers

Operation	Will Large Buffers Help?	Comments
Checkpoint	Yes	none.
Dump and load	No	I/O for dump and load is performed by Backup Server, not SQL Server. Thus, the cache sizes and configuration in SQL Server's data cache have no baring on the performance of dump and load.
Log	Yes	See "Log and Transaction Management" on page 521.

Forcing Buffer Sizes

The choice of buffer sizes is made automatically by the optimizer for SQL statements and utilities such as BCP, dbcc, and create index. There are three reasons why they may not automatically choose the optimal size for buffers:

1. The named cache may not contain a buffer pool of the appropriate size.

2. Some utilities may not take advantage of large buffers in the early versions of System 11 SQL Server.

3. The optimizer may not have enough information to justify the use of large buffers. This is frequently the case when SQL Server performs a sequential scan on a table or index without knowing that the scan is sequential. Examples include an index scan on a table that is sorted by the nonclustered index and joins where the inner table is sorted by the join key.

In such cases, you may need to force a buffer size, provided the named cache is configured with a buffer pool of the correct size. You can force the use of buffers of any given size either on specific references to tables/indexes in SQL statements or for all accesses to a table or index.

Forcing Buffer Size in SQL Statements

You can include the buffer size for specific tables and indexes in SQL statements using the keyword prefetch as illustrated by the following example.

```
select r.name, sum(amount) sales
```

```
from       retail_sales rs (index retail_sales prefetch 16),
           region r (index region prefetch 2)
group by r.name
```

You can specify a different buffer size for every occurrence of a table in the query. There is no way to specify different buffer sizes for a table and an index on the table. You cannot force a buffer size on one occurrence of a table without also forcing the use of an index. There is no mechanism for forcing a buffer size for worktables. However, the optimizer chooses large buffers for worktables whenever appropriate, provided the named cache that `tempdb` is bound to contains a pool of large buffers.

Forcing Buffer Size on Tables/Indexes

You can force the choice of buffer sizes on all accesses to a table or index in one of two ways:

1. You can limit the variety of buffer pools in the named cache that the table or index is bound to. Note that every named cache must contain a pool of 2K buffers. While you cannot force the use of large buffers by configuring named caches, you can limit the variety of large buffers the optimizer or utilities can choose from.

2. You can use the command:

```
dbcc iosize(<database name>,
            <object name[.<index name>]>,
            "[2|4|8|16]")
```

to force a buffer size on a table or index. However, beware that the effect of this command does not last beyond a SQL Server shutdown. You need to repeat this command after every reboot of SQL Server.

3. In the special case of the log, you can use the command:

```
sp_logiosize "[2|4|8|16]"
```

while using the database in question. Unlike that of `dbcc iosize`, the effect of this command is persistent. If this command is not used, SQL Server uses 4K buffers for log if the log is bound to a cache containing a 4K pool, and 2K buffers otherwise.

Overlap and Interference

The ability to have concurrent accesses to the same table or index perform I/O in different I/O units provides a great opportunity for performance tuning. For example, you can have index scans and random accesses on a table perform I/O in 2K units, while concurrent table scans and batch operations on the same table perform I/O in 16K units. This allows you to optimize the same configuration for performance over a wide range of applications having very different I/O requirements. On the other hand, using buffers of size greater than 2K can have two unexpected implications on performance:

• **Overlap** — Consider the example in Figure 13.2 and Table 13.2. Suppose the table is bound to a named cache that contains a 2K buffer pool and a 16K buffer pool and that page 205 is already cached in the 2K pool as a result of a recent index scan. An attempt to read pages 200 – 207 into the 16K pool (for example, prompted by a table scan) fails because there can be only one copy of page 205 in cache at any time. Instead, SQL Server reads each of the 7 pages other than page 205 into seven buffers in the 2K pool. This can affect performance in two ways. First, the table scan is slower since it cannot take advantage of large buffers. Second, the table scan may flood the 2K buffer pool with pages that were meant to be in the 16K buffer pool.

• **Interference** — Consider the example in Figure 13.2 and Table 13.2. Suppose the table is bound to a named cache that contains a 2K buffer pool and a 4K buffer pool and that pages 203 and 204 are cached in a 4K buffer. An attempt is made to read pages 204 and 205 into a 4K pool. Again, the attempt fails and only page 205 is read into the 2K pool. This situation and its effect are very similar to that of overlap.

Since every named cache must contain a 2K pool, there is no way to preclude interference short of disabling large buffers. However, you can avoid interference by configuring 2K and 16K pools only.

13.2.4 Buffer Replacement Policies

As discussed in Chapter 5, *SQL Server — Methods and Features*, "Buffer Replacement Strategy" on page 106, System 11 SQL Server provides two buffer replacement strategies: the Least Recently Used (LRU) strategy and the Fetch and Discard (MRU) strategy. You can force a particular buffer replacement strategy for `insert` and `delete` using the following syntax:

```
select * from
        T1 (index I1 prefetch 2 mru)
          where K1 = 5
delete T3
        from T3 (index I3 prefetch 2 mru)
          where K3 = 10
```

The keyword `mru` forces SQL Server to use the Fetch-and-Discard buffer replacement strategy, and the keyword `lru` forces SQL Server to use the standard Least Recently Used buffer replacement strategy.

13.3   OTHER ENHANCEMENTS

System 11 SQL Server adds a variety of enhancements in performance and scalability. The majority of these enhancements require no tuning or configuration. Here are some of the more visible ones.

13.3.1   Table Partitioning

System 11 SQL Server supports partitioned tables. You can partition a table using the command:

```
alter table <tablename> partition <number of partitions>
```

provided it does not have a clustered index. The complementary operation, to "unpartition" a table, is performed with the command:

```
alter table <tablename> unpartition
```

Currently, the performance benefits of partitioning tables is limited to concurrent inserts. However, the partitioning of tables provides an infrastructure for parallel processing of queries and batch operations in future versions of SQL Server.

Mapping of Partitions to Devices

When a table is partitioned, the allocation of space for the table is automatically distributed over the devices in the segment the table occupies. This improves the I/O throughput of the table by "striping" the table across many devices. Suppose a table has p partitions and occupies a segment that spans d devices. For the sake of simplicity, let us assume that one of p and d divides the other evenly.

- If $p > d$, then each device maps to a disjoint set of p/d partitions.
- If $p \leq d$, then each partition maps to a disjoint set of d/p devices.

In either case, this scheme ensures that the I/O operations due to concurrent operations on all the partitions of a table are distributed evenly across all the devices. If all the devices preferred by a partition are full, then SQL Server automatically starts stealing pages from one of the other devices used by the table.

Performance of Concurrent Inserts

We have discussed the performance of concurrent inserts and the use of clustered indexes to alleviate the heap-insert bottleneck in Chapter 10, *Transaction Processing Performance*, "Heap Inserts and Clustered Indexes" on page 358. Partitioning tables provides a simpler and more efficient solution than the use of clustered indexes. Each transaction that performs an insert on a partitioned table is assigned one partition of the table at random. All the inserts to this table by this transaction are directed to this partition. Thus, if your application has a large number of concurrent transactions inserting rows into a single table, you should consider partitioning the table.

System 11 SQL Server does not support partitioning of tables having clustered indexes. If your application relies on a clustered index for performance of concurrent inserts, then you need to choose between the following two options:

1. Continue using the clustered index in System 11 SQL Server.

2. Replace the clustered index by a nonclustered index (if the index is needed for some other aspect of the application) and partition the table.

If the clustered index is used solely to improve the performance of concurrent inserts and you decide instead to partition the table, you need not replace the clustered index with a nonclustered index. In such cases, the latter option is the obvious choice. However, if you need to replace it with a nonclustered index, you need to weigh the advantages of partitioning against the overhead of updating the nonclustered index.

Partitioning the table to avoid the heap-insert bottleneck has an advantage over using a clustered index in terms of distribution of I/O on devices. Suppose the table in question is contained in a segment that spans multiple devices. In the absence of partitioning, the allocation of pages to the table is not distributed evenly among the devices in the sense that all pages on one device are used up before the moving on to the next device. As a result, all the I/O is directed at only one device at any given time. On the other hand a partitioned table distributes the I/O evenly across all devices.

As a rule of thumb, you should partition any table that is subjected to concurrent inserts and/or deferred updates if it does not have a clustered index that is useful elsewhere. If this clustered index *is* used elsewhere, you have two choices: either continue using the clustered index and alleviate any I/O bottleneck (see "Disk Striping and Logical Volume Managers" on page 497) or replace it with a non-clustered index and partition the table. If the performance of disks is already an issue with the clustered index solution, you almost certainly gain some performance by using partitions instead of clustered indexes.

13.3.2 Log and Transaction Management

System 11 SQL Server makes several improvements in log and transaction management.

Buffer Management for Log

System 10 and earlier versions of SQL Server performed I/O to the log disk only in units of 2K. With System 11 SQL Server, the log can be bound to any named cache and configured to use any buffer size provided the named cache contains a buffer pool of the appropriate size. The default buffer size for log in System 11 SQL Server is 4K, provided the named cache that the log is bound to contains a 4K pool. You can configure the log to use buffers of a given size by binding the log to a cache that contains a buffer pool of the given size and executing the command:

```
sp_logiosize "[2|4|8|16]"
```

while using the database in question. If performance of the log device is an issue in your application, we recommend that you bind the log to a named cache that contains a pool of 4K, 8K, or 16K buffers, and designate this buffer as:

```
cache status = log only
```

in the configuration file. This buffer pool need not be very large. An exception is the case that an application needs to read the transaction log very frequently (e.g., reference to inserted and deleted in triggers, deferred updates and transaction rollbacks). You can monitor the log device using operating system tools to determine how frequently your application needs to read the log. If the number of reads on the log exceeds roughly 1% of the number of writes to the log device, you should increase the size of buffer pool and the wash size by the same amount.

Log Contention

The performance of logging is often limited by contention on the data structures that control the growth of the log in memory rather than by the throughput of the log device. The symptoms of this problem include poor performance during periods of high concurrency and a preponderance of tasks sleeping with the value 0 in the column blk in the output from sp_who. System 11 SQL Server reduces such contention by having transactions generate log entries in batches. Users accumulate their log entries in private areas called **user log cache** until they are ready to commit or the user log cache is full and then append all of the accumulated log entries to syslogs in one batch. No tuning is needed to enable this reduction in log contention.

The default size of the user log cache is 4096 bytes and can be changed using the configuration parameter user log cache size. You should not need to adjust this configuration value.

Read-Only Transactions

In System 10 and earlier versions of SQL Server, transactions, even read-only transactions, generate a pair of log entries — one for the begin tran and the other for the commit tran. System 11 SQL Server does not generate any log entries for read-only transactions. This may improve performance for transaction processing applications generated using PowerBuilder as it wraps a pair of begin and commit tran statements around every query.

Oldest Active Transaction

As mentioned in Chapter 12, *Batch Processing Performance*, the log cannot be truncated beyond the oldest active transaction. Hence, a long-running transaction can cause a log-full condition. System 11 SQL Server alleviates this problem in two ways:

- **Thinking philosophers** — In System 10 and earlier versions of SQL Server, long-running read-only transactions enter the begin tran in syslogs. This prevents the log from being truncated beyond this entry until this transaction commits. In System 11 SQL Server, the log entry for the begin tran is held in the user log cache. Hence, long-running read-only transactions such as reports and decision-support queries do not prevent the DBA from truncating the log.

- `syslogshold` **table** — The DBA needs to identify the oldest active transaction in `syslogs` in order to prevent a log-full condition. System 11 SQL Server adds a new system table `syslogshold` in `master` to help the DBA. You can identify the transaction that is blocking truncation of the log with the query:

```
select   h.spid, h.name
         from      master..syslogshold h, sysindexes i
         where     h.dbid = db_id()
         and       i.id = 8
         and       h.pages = i.first
```

13.3.3 Lock Management

System 11 SQL Server enhances performance and scalability of transaction processing applications in four ways.

Contention in Lock Management

In System 10 and earlier versions of SQL Server, the shared data structures used for lock management can become a performance bottleneck at high transaction rates and more than four engines. System 11 SQL Server alleviates this contention and improves the flexibility of the lock management by providing a number of new configuration parameters: `maximum engine freelocks`, `freelock transfer block size`, `page lock spinlock ratio`, `address lock spinlock ratio`, and `table lock spinlock ratio`.

Delayed Deadlock Detection

System 10 and earlier versions of SQL Server perform a search for deadlocks on every instance of contention for a lock. The vast majority of these searches turn up empty. System 11 SQL Server checks for deadlocks on a period basis rather than every time a lock request is blocked by another task. The configuration parameter `deadlock checking period` controls the frequency of the deadlock checks. One consequence of this change is that, unlike System 10 SQL Server, System 11 SQL Server does not detect deadlocks immediately as they occur. The detection is delayed by up to the `deadlock checking period`. While two tasks are in a deadlock situation, neither can proceed. This could cause additional contention on locks already held by the tasks that are deadlocked.

Lock Escalation

As discussed in Chapter 10, *Transaction Processing Performance*, System 10 and earlier versions of SQL Server attempt to escalate page locks into table locks after the first 200 page locks acquired by the same statement. System 11 SQL Server includes configuration parameters that allow you to configure the threshold for lock escalation at three levels: SQL Server-wide, per-database, and per-table. The following commands are used to adjust the lock escalation thresholds.[1]

```
sp_lockpromote "PCT|LWM|HWM", <value>, "server"
sp_lockpromote "PCT|LWM|HWM", <value>|NULL, "DATABASE",
        <database name>
sp_lockpromote "PCT|LWM|HWM", <value>|NULL, "TABLE",
        <table name>
```

Parameters LWM and HWM denote the low and high water marks for lock escalation threshold. When LWM and HWM are equal, the PCT parameter is ignored and the value for LWM is used as the threshold for lock escalation. When $1 < LWM \leq HWM \leq (2^{31} - 1)$, the threshold for lock escalation is determined as a percentage of the total number of pages in the table, subject to a minimum of LWM and a maximum of HWM.

- By default, SQL Server has both LWM and HWM set to 200. This mimics the lock escalation behavior of System 10 and earlier versions of SQL Server.

- You can change the threshold for lock escalation to a different fixed value by setting both LWM and HWM to this value. When LWM and HWM are the same value, the value of PCT is not used.

- You can set the threshold for lock escalation on each table to a fixed percentage of the number of pages in the table by setting PCT to the percentage, LWM to 2, and HWM larger than the number of pages in the table.

- You can use set the threshold for lock escalation to a percentage of the number of pages in the table subject to some reasonable bounds by setting PCT to the percentage, and LWM and HWM to the lower and upper bounds.

- Check the value of the configuration parameter number of locks before using a high threshold for lock escalation. If you set a high lock escalation threshold, you might run out of locks.

---

1. System 11 SQL Server calls this **lock promotion** rather than **lock escalation**.

Isolation Level 0

System 10 SQL Server version 10.1 and later provide the option of reading uncommitted data. The default behavior of SQL Server is not to read uncommitted data. You can override the default behavior by the following methods:

- **Session level** — Use the command:

```
set transaction isolation level <0|read uncommitted>
```

- **Statement level** — Append to the `select` statement:

```
at isolation level <0|read uncommitted>
```

- **Table within a statement** — Follow the table name with the keyword:

```
NOHOLDLOCK
```

Reading uncommitted data can improve the performance of queries but does not maintain many of the transactional consistency semantics we are used to with high isolation levels.

13.3.4 Index Management

Max Rows per Page

We discussed the topic of reducing lock contention by using `fillfactor` in conjunction with a clustered index to reduce the number of rows on a page in Chapter 10, *Transaction Processing Performance*, "Emulating Row-Level Locks" on page 356. System 11 SQL Server provides a simpler alternative. You can specify the maximum number of rows per page for a table or index using the configuration parameter `max_rows_per_page` in the `create` or `alter` statement for the table or index. This method has two advantages over the use of `fillfactor`:

1. Unlike using `fillfactor`, insert, delete, and deferred updates maintain `max_rows_per_page`. The `fillfactor` value is only used when the index is created.

2. You can limit the number of rows per data page without creating a clustered index on the table.

Ascending Inserts

We discussed the implications of the order in which data inserted into a table with a clustered index in Chapter 12, *Batch Processing Performance*, "Order of Inserts" on page 479. The example in Figure 12.4 on page 480 shows that inserting rows in ascending order into an empty table having a clustered index minimizes the number of pages and page splits. This provides us with a method for optimizing batch loading of data into tables having clustered indexes. However, we may encounter more pages and page splits if the table was not empty when we started the inserts. The examples in Figure 13.3 illustrate why, using the example in Figure 12.4 on page 480 as a base.

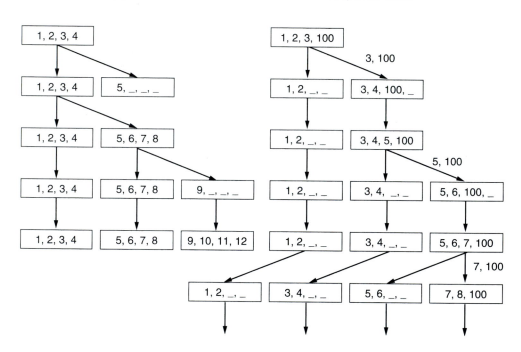

Order of Insertion: (1,2,3,4,5,6,7,8,9,10,11,12) Starting with an Empty Table.

Same Order of Insertions. Starting with the Row 100 Already in the Table.

Figure 13.3   Ascending inserts -

The presence of a row in the table that follows the values being inserted in sorted order can cause the number of pages and page splits to increase. This situation can occur with composite indexes when the successive inserts increase the value of the right-most column only. For example, consider the clustered index:

```
invoice(department_number, invoice_number)
```

If your application inserts invoices numbered 40, 41, 42, 43, and 44 for department E, and the table already contains invoices for department F, the effect is similar to that in the second example in Figure 13.3.

System 11 SQL Server provides a method for reducing the number of pages and page splits in such cases. You can optimize the performance of such inserts on specific tables by turning the **ascinserts** mode on for those tables. The command:

```
dbcc tune (ascinserts, <1|0>, <table name>)
```

turns on the **ascinserts** mode if the second argument is a 1 and turns it off otherwise. This mode has no impact on performance if the table does not have a clustered index, or when rows are inserted in sorted order at the end of the table (e.g., loading data in sorted order into an empty table). It should be used only when the application inserts rows in ascending order of a clustered index into a table that already contains some rows and at least one of the existing rows follows the rows being inserted in the order imposed by the clustered index.

13.3.5 Page Allocation and Deallocation

With 4.9 and System 10 SQL Servers, performance of BCP can degrade as the table becomes very large. System 11 SQL Server improves the performance of large tables and databases by reducing the number of times OAM pages are scanned to allocate new pages to the growing table. The System 11 SQL Server configuration parameter page utilization controls the trade-off between scanning OAM pages to find reserved (but unused pages) and simply allocating new extents for the table. With this scheme, the unused pages are not wasted, their use is simply deferred until it is more convenient to use the pages. Setting page utilization to 100 mimics the 4.9 and System 10 SQL Server behavior of scanning OAM pages each time a new page must be allocated to the table. The default value for page utilization is 96. Increasing page utilization increases the likelihood that OAM pages are scanned to allocate a page to the table, however the table is more tightly packed into the database. Reducing page utilization increases the likelihood that new extents are allocated to the table, causing the table to be more dispersed through the database.

13.3.6 Housekeeper

System 11 SQL Server provides for the asynchronous execution of several house-keeping tasks using a new internal task called the **housekeeper**. The housekeeper is enabled by default. SQL Server configuration determines the range of activities performed by the housekeeper. One of the major functions of the housekeeper is to write dirty pages to disks asynchronously. It does so with minimal impact on the performance of other tasks on SQL Server by following these guidelines:

- The housekeeper runs at the lowest priority among all the tasks on SQL Server. The CPU cost of running the housekeeper is minimal — it uses up some of the idle cycles on SQL Server.

- It limits its impact on the I/O subsystem using the configuration parameter `housekeeper free write percent`. The value of this parameter limits the number of additional writes performed by the housekeeper, if any, as a fraction of the total workload on the I/O subsystem.

- The housekeeper does not start asynchronous writes on log pages. If a cache is designated as `log only`, the housekeeper ignores the cache.

The housekeeper can make a significant difference in the performance of some applications. For example, it can flush newly created pages to disk in the background during `BCP` in. It can use idle cycles on SQL Server to perform automatic checkpoints thus reducing the time to shutdown and the time to recover from a crash. It can also help the performance of transaction processing applications by relieving the user tasks of the burden of cleaning dirty pages. The housekeeper almost never has a negative impact on performance. Our recommendation is to use the default configuration for the parameter `housekeeper free max write percent` unless your application is heavily I/O bound. In the rare event that the housekeeper does have a negative impact on performance, there are two ways to turn it off:

1. Use `sp_configure` to change value of the configuration parameter `housekeeper max free write percent` to 0 (default is 1). The values of this parameter can be changed on-the-fly.

2. You can tell the housekeeper to ignore a specific named cache by adding `HK ignore cache` to the cache status in the configuration file. The following example illustrates:

```
[Named Cache:privacy please]
        cache size = 80M
```

```
                 cache status = mixed cache
                 cache status = HK ignore cache


    [2K I/O Buffer Pool]
              pool size = 40M
              wash size = 2048 K


    [16K I/O Buffer Pool]
              pool size = 16M
              wash size = 4096 K
```

The cache status `log only` implies `HK ignore cache`. Hence, there is no need to add `HK ignore cache` status to a cache already designated as `log only`.

Appendix A

General Configuration Practices

Here are some general tips for maximizing the performance of SQL Server:

1. **Avoid character set translation** — SQL Server supports several languages and hence a variety of possible collating sequences (also called sort orders).

2. **Avoid unnecessary datatype conversions** — Some datatype conversions are obvious, you are converting an integer column into a floating point value to perform some arithmetic. Other datatype conversions are less obvious. Sun SPARC systems and Intel-based systems represent integer data differently (the order of the bytes is reversed). Some data conversions are needed for a Sun SPARC system to send data to Intel-based systems. These data conversions impose a small amount of overhead on your client/server application.

3. **Use the binary sort order** — Binary sort order is very efficient as the characters can be compared to one another directly. Other sort orders require more complicated comparison operations, slowing sorting operations.

4. **Avoid running SQL Server from a remote mounted installation directory** — Many operating systems, like Unix, use a lazy loading strategy. This means the operating system only loads the executable part of the program when that part of the program is actually needed. In essence this means the operating system uses the program file to page in the executable part of the program. If the program file is on a remote mounted disk, the paging activity is over the network.

5. **Do not run SQL Server using remote mounted database or log devices** — Network mounted disks impose much more overhead than local disks. As a result, remote mounted disks are generally slower than local disks. In addition, recovery cannot be assured on any buffered device.

6. **Do not run client programs and SQL Server on the same machine unless you have more CPUs than engines or can set cschedspins to a small number** — SQL Server is not very gracious about sharing CPU resources. On the positive side, this helps minimize response time and maximize throughput.

The drawback is that other processes on the system are starved for CPU time. Setting cschedspins to a small number tells SQL Server to idle more quickly, giving other processes more CPU time. SQL Server cannot utilize more CPUs than you have configured max online engines. This means a four CPU system with a SQL Server configured with two engines has two CPUs available for client programs.[1]

7. **Avoid unnecessary work on your server** — Dedicate a machine to SQL Server, do not use this machine to supply your home directories and be a network name server.

8. **Eliminate unnecessary daemon processes from your server system** — If it is not mounting or advertising network disks, turn off NFS.

9. **Check for rogue processes on your server system** — SQL Server, the auxiliary servers, and any utility operating system programs needed to keep the computer running are all that are required on the server system. You should not be running other CPU or I/O intensive programs on the server system.

10. **If SQL Server goes down in an unusual way, make sure it has cleaned up its shared memory segment** — On some systems, shared memory segments may be pinned to physical memory. If nothing else, the shared memory segment is consuming virtual address space. Too many of these and the operating system may think that the system is starved for memory and swap rather than page processes.

---

[1] This is not entirely true for SQL Server on Windows/NT. On this operating system, operating system threads are used for disk and network I/O. These threads may run on any CPU and are running in addition to the engines. As a result, it is difficult to limit the number of CPUs utilized by SQL Server on Windows/NT.

Appendix B

SQL Server Configuration

SQL Server configuration parameters control the resource consumption and performance of SQL Server. The default values of the configuration parameters may or may not be suitable for your application. The values of some configuration parameters are obvious given the characteristics of your application, for example, the number of user connections and the number of database devices. The optimal values for some other configuration parameters are not so obvious. Examples include wash size and number of index trips. This appendix describes the performance-related configuration parameters available on SQL Server, how to set values, how to find out what values are currently set, and how to recover from a reconfiguration mistake.

The first three sections in this appendix discuss issues that are common to all configuration parameters — characteristics that determine their role, how to set them, and how to recover from configuration errors. The last three sections discuss the configuration parameters, starting with table/index-level parameters, and then moving on to database, and SQL Server-level parameters.

B.1 CONFIGURATION PROPERTIES

B.1.1 Scope

Some configuration parameters control the characteristics of the entire SQL Server; some control those of one specific database, and some others those of specific tables, indexes, named caches, and buffer pools. This appendix assumes that the scope of a configuration parameter is the entire SQL Server unless noted otherwise.

B.1.2   SQL Server Version

Newer versions of SQL Server support most, if not all, of the configuration parameters available in previous versions of SQL Server, and almost every new version of SQL Server adds new configuration parameters. While configuration parameters in two different versions of SQL Server may have the same name, the syntax and semantics of the configuration parameters may change from one version of SQL Server to the next.

The configuration manager in System 11 SQL Server has simplified the management of configuration parameters by providing a uniform interface. Some of the configuration parameters that were present in System 10 and earlier versions of SQL Server but not documented are now documented and supported in System 11 SQL Server.

B.1.3   Persistence

Changes to most configuration parameters are persistent in the sense that the changes are committed to disk and restored on reboot. The listing of configuration parameters in this appendix assumes that changes are persistent unless otherwise noted.

B.1.4   Dynamic versus Static

While the values of most configuration parameters can be changed on-line, changes to certain configuration parameters do not take effect until SQL Server is restarted. Configuration parameters which do not require a restart of SQL Server are called dynamic configuration parameters. Configuration parameters requiring a restart of SQL Server are called static configuration parameters. For most dynamic parameters, the effect of a change is realized at the next SQL statement, stored procedure invocation, or transaction. This appendix assumes that parameters are dynamic unless stated they are static.

B.1.5   Config Value versus Run Value

While SQL Server is running, each configuration parameter is associated with two values — **config value** and **run values**, as shown by the output of the `sp_configure` command. The run value is the value currently in use, and the config value is the value that is used after the next restart of SQL Server. In case of dynamic parameters, the two values are equal since changes in their values are effective immediately. In the case of static parameters, the two values should be equal at boot time, but the config value may be changed as a result of changing the configuration of SQL Server.

B.2 CHANGING SQL SERVER CONFIGURATION

There are several methods for changing values of the configuration parameters. These methods are outlined in Table B.1.

Table B.1   Methods for configuring SQL Server

Configuration Method	SQL Server Version	Comments
sp_configure	all	New syntax in System 11; no database/table/index-level parameters.
configuration file	System 11 only	Used at boot time; no database/table/index-level parameters.
buildmaster -y	4.9 and System 10 only	Used at boot time; no database/table/index-level parameters.
sp_dboption	all	Database level parameters only.
trace flags	all	Used either at boot time or at run-time.
dbcc tune	all	Currently the only method for certain configuration parameters.
sp_cacheconfig, etc.	System 11 only	For configuration of named caches.

B.2.1   sp_configure

The `sp_configure` command takes the form:

```
sp_configure ["<parameter name>" [, <value>]]
```

The use of `sp_configure` without any argument returns a list of all of the configuration parameters and their current and run values. If `parameter name` is specified but not `value`, the configured and run value for the configuration parameter is returned. You need not spell out the entire name of the configuration parameter — any substring that uniquely identifies the parameter suffices. If the substring fails to identify the configuration parameter uniquely, `sp_configure` returns the list of all configuration parameters whose names contain the argument as a substring.

In System 10 and 4.9 SQL Server, the process of changing configuration parameters is as follows.

```
1> sp_configure "parameter 1",value1
2> go
1> sp_configure "parameter 2",value2
2> go
1> reconfigure
2> go
```

It is only necessary to execute `reconfigure` once, after you have changed all of the configuration parameters you are interested in changing. The `reconfigure` command may report an error if the parameter values you provide are not self consistent. For example, you ask for 500 users and a stack space of 100k for each user, but only allow 10Mb memory for all of SQL Server. After a successful `reconfigure`, you need to reboot SQL Server before the new values for the static configuration parameter can take effect.

In System 11 SQL Server, the `reconfigure` command is not required.

B.2.2 Configuration File

System 10 and 4.9 SQL Server store the values of configuration parameters in the first page of the master device — often call the **configuration block**. System 11 SQL Server stores values of configuration parameters in text files known as **configuration files**. The configuration file can be specified as an optional argument to SQL Server at boot time using the flag `-c<config file>`. If a configuration file is not specified, SQL Server uses the file `$SYBASE/$DSLISTEN.cfg`.

The values of configuration parameters for System 11 SQL Server can be changed by editing the configuration file while SQL Server is not running. We recommend this method for static configuration parameters. The values of the dynamic parameters can also be changed by editing the configuration file, but for the changes to take effect before the next restart of SQL Server, you must use `sp_configure`.

All configuration changes made using `sp_configure` are made permanent by writing them out to the configuration file (System 11 SQL Server) or configuration block (4.9 and System 10 SQL Server). Hence, you should not edit the configuration file while SQL Server is running — your changes may be lost. Whenever SQL Server makes a change to the configuration file, it saves a copy of the old configuration file as file X.N, where X is the original name of the configuration file, and N is a three-digit integer whose value increases monotonically.

B.2.3 buildmaster -y

System 10 and 4.9 SQL Servers store their configuration in the configuration block, which is the first page of the master device. Unfortunately, there is no easy way to edit the configuration block with a text editor. One somewhat cumbersome way is to use the following two commands.

```
buildmaster <master device> -yall
buildmaster <master device> -y<parameter name>=<value>
```

The former command lists the configured values of all parameters, and the latter sets the value of a parameter. `buildmaster -y` is a poor substitute for `sp_configure` for changing configuration parameters. You should use `sp_configure` to change values of configuration parameters whenever possible. All configuration parameters are accessible using `sp_configure` in System 11 SQL Server, and hence `buildmaster -y` is no longer supported. However, not all 4.9 and System 10 SQL Servers configuration parameters are accessible through `sp_configure`. The shaded regions in Table B.7 lists the internal names as well as the System 11 (clear text) names for some such configuration parameters. We recommend that the use of `buildmaster -y` be limited to these parameters only. Table B.2 highlights some parameters that are important to performance-tuning work.

You should only run `buildmaster -y` on your master device when SQL Server is not running. No error checking is done on changes to the configuration parameters. It is important that you take special care when modifying parameters with `buildmaster -y` as there are some dependencies among the parameters in the configuration block. You should make sure that your change does not leave the configuration block in a state that prevents SQL Server from booting.

Table B.2   System 10 SQL Server buildmaster -y parameters

Configuration Parameter	Description
coamtrips	Large value attempts to keep allocation pages in memory.
cindextrips	Large value attempts to keep index pages in memory.
cnmaxaio_engine	Maximum number of outstanding asynchronous disk I/O operations per engine.
cnmaxaio_server	Maximum number of outstanding asynchronous disk I/O operations per server.
cclkrate	Number of microseconds per clock tick.
cschedspins	Determines how willing SQL Server is to yield the CPU to other processes on the system. A small value makes SQL Server "nice". Default is 2000. Beware: 0 means infinity.
cmaxscheds	Controls the maximum amount of time between checks for disk I/O completion.

B.2.4   sp_dboption

The database-level configuration parameters are changed by the `sp_dboption` system stored procedure. The new configuration parameter values do not take effect until you execute the `checkpoint` command in the database or restart SQL Server. Executing `sp_dboption` with no arguments lists the acceptable database configuration parameters. The `sp_helpdb` system stored procedure lists the options set on the database.

B.2.5   Trace Flags

Trace flags change the behavior of SQL Server by activating or deactivating special code paths within the executable.[1] Trace flags are not persistent which means that trace flags you turn on after SQL Server boots must be turned on again when you restart SQL Server. There are two ways to turn on trace flags.

1. The SQL Server executable binary takes an optional argument -T<x> on the command line to turn on trace flag <x>. A trace flag is a generally a three or four digit number. For example:

```
dataserver -dmaster.dat -T1603 -T1501
```

boots SQL Server with trace flags 1603 and 1501.

2. The Transact-SQL command dbcc traceon(<x>) turns on trace flag <x>. This works only for the dynamic trace flags and not for those that must be specified at boot time.

Once SQL Server is running there is no way to determine if a particular trace flag is on or off. To deactivate a trace flag you included in the command line, you must shutdown and restart SQL Server without including the trace flag on the command line. The trace flags turned on using the dbcc traceon() command can be turned off using the dbcc traceoff() command.

System 11 SQL Server continues to support trace flags. However, the more commonly used trace flags have been converted into SQL Server-wide configuration parameters accessible through sp_configure system stored procedure.

B.2.6   dbcc tune

Some of the configuration parameters in SQL Server can be set using only the dbcc tune command. This includes most of the table/index-level configuration parameters, and a few SQL Server-wide configuration parameters. The dbcc tune command has the following format:

```
dbcc tune(<parameter name>, <value> [, <table/index name>])
```

We expect all such parameters to be made accessible through the sp_configure interface in future releases of SQL Server.

---

[1] Trace flags are used internally by Sybase for testing that cannot be accomplished with regular SQL commands, for experimental new features, and for backward compatibility.

B.2.7   sp_cacheconfig, etc.

System 11 SQL Server provides several system stored procedures to manage named caches. Each stored procedure can be used to display the current configuration by omitting optional arguments. The syntax for these stored procedures in the final version of System 11 SQL Server may be different from the following. Please consult your Sybase documentation for correct syntax.

1. `sp_cacheconfig ["<cache name>"]` — Displays the configuration of the named cache.

2. `sp_poolconfig "<cache name>", "(2|4|8|16)K", "<pool size>" [,"(2|4|8|16)K"]` — Resizes the first pool, using buffers from or returning buffers to the second pool. If the second pool is not specified, the 2K pool is used.

   `sp_poolconfig "<cache name>", "(2|4|8|16)K", "wash size=<size>"` — Resizes the wash area for the named cache.

3. `sp_bindcache "<cache name>", "<database name>" [, "<table name>" [,"<index name>"]]` — Binds the specified database, table, or index to the named cache.

4. `sp_helpcache ["<cache name>"]` — Displays status and current bindings for the named cache.

B.3   MANAGING CONFIGURATION ERRORS

Configuring SQL Server can be a tricky business. Getting the right combination of total memory, connections, open objects, and the like can be difficult given the dependencies among parameters. Before changing the configuration, you should ensure that you can recover from a configuration error by restoring the previous configuration. In the worst case, SQL Server may not be able to boot with the modified configuration.

You should always save a copy of the current configuration before making any changes. System 11 SQL Server does this automatically for all changes made using `sp_configure` by saving a version-numbered copy of the current configuration file. Should a change render the configuration file unusable, you can revert to the most recent working version of the configuration file.

The same task is somewhat more challenging in the context of 4.9 and System 10 SQL Servers, since the configuration information is stored in a page on the master device. Hence, an unfortunate combination `sp_configure`/`reconfigure` commands followed by a shutdown can render SQL Server unfit to boot. This makes it hard to undo the configuration change as SQL Server has to be running in order to execute `sp_configure`/`reconfigure`.

The following guidelines will help ensure your ability to recover from configuration errors.

1. Keep a log of all changes made.

2. Change only one parameter (and all of its dependents) at a time.

3. Always save a copy of the current configuration. This is done automatically in System 11 SQL Server. Use the buildmaster -yall command for 4.9 and System 10 SQL Server.

4. If SQL Server fails to boot with the new configuration, restore the old configuration. In case of System 11 SQL Server, this means restoring the most recent working version of the configuration file. In case of 4.9 and System 10 SQL Server, you will need to compare the output from `buildmaster -yall` command with that from a working configuration, and use:

   ```
   buildmaster -y<name>=<value>
   ```

   commands to back out the offending changes.

5. If all else fails, you can restore the entire configuration block to its default values by using the command:

   ```
   buildmaster -d<master device> -r
   ```

   This command should not be taken lightly, since some of the default values may be inappropriate for your application. For example, your application may use more devices than default value for the maximum number of devices. If that is the case, you should follow up the buildmaster -r command with

   ```
   buildmaster -d<master device> -ycnvdisks=<value>
   ```

   Now you can boot SQL Server and use `sp_configure` to adjust the other configuration parameters back to your desired values.

B.4   TABLE AND INDEX CONFIGURATION

Table B.3 lists the configuration parameters associated with tables and indexes in SQL Server. Only the first two are available in 4.9 and System 10 SQL Server. The rest are new in System 11 SQL Server.

Table B.3   Configuration parameters for tables

Parameter	SQL Server Versions	Command	Comments
indextrips	4.9 System 10 System 11	`dbcc tune(indextrips, <value>, <table>)`	Number of times LRU replacement skips index pages. High value attempts to lock index pages in memory. Default is 0.
oamtrips	4.9 System 10 System 11	`dbcc tune(oamtrips, <value>, <table>)`	Number of times LRU replacement skips allocation pages. High value attempts to lock allocation pages in memory. Default is 0.
ascinserts	System 11	`dbcc tune(ascinserts, <value>, <table>)`	Value 1 optimizes tables having composite clustered indexes for inserts. Default is 0.
Lock escalation	System 11	See Chapter 13, *Advanced Topics*, "Lock Escalation" on page 524.	Determines lock escalation characteristics of the table.
Rows per page	System 11	See Chapter 4, *SQL Server — Form and Structure*, "Maximum Rows per Page" on page 98.	Determines number of rows per page.
Cache binding	System 11	`sp_bindcache`	Binds table or index to named cache.
I/O Size	System 11	`dbcc iosize("<database>", <io size in KB>, "<table[.index]>")`	Forces I/O to happen in the specified size. This configuration parameter is not persistent.

B.5   DATABASE CONFIGURATION

Table B.4 lists the database configuration parameters. These options are set using the `sp_dboption` system stored procedure.

Table B.4   Database configuration parameters

Configuration Parameter	Description
abort tran on log full	When true, transactions that try to write to the log after the last chance threshold is passed are aborted. When false, these transactions are suspended until more log space is available.
allows nulls by default	When true, columns that do not specify whether they allow nulls or not are assumed to allow nulls. When false, columns are assumed to not allow nulls. This changes the behavior of create table, for example.
auto identity	When true, tables that are created without a primary key or a unique constraint are automatically given an identity column. When false, tables are not automatically given an identity column. The presence of the identity column makes each row longer and provides a useful column for cursors.
dbo use only	When true, only the owner of the database may use the database. When false, any user-defined in the database may use the database.
ddl in tran	When true, data definition language commands such as create index are allowed within a user-defined transaction. When false, these commands are not allowed within a user-defined transaction. Using data definition language commands within a transaction locks certain system tables for the duration of the transaction. This can cause performance problems because many system tables must also be queried during read-only queries.
identity in nonunique index	When true, an index is created without the unique keyword on a table with an identity column, the identity column is added as the last key to the index. When false, the index is created as specified.
no chkpt on recovery	When true, SQL Server does not write a checkpoint record to the transaction log on the completion of recovery. When false, SQL Server writes a checkpoint record to the transaction log on the completion of recovery to indicate that transactions committed before recovery are already written to disk. This is useful for applications that expect to transfer transaction log dumps from one database to another.

Table B.4   Database configuration parameters

Configuration Parameter	Description
no free space acctg	When true, SQL Server does not perform free space accounting in non-log segments. When false, SQL Server performs free space accounting in all segments. Part of the recovery process involves computing the free space in each segment. Setting this option to true bypasses this step and speeds recovery. Free space accounting is also responsible for updating the rows per page column in sysindexes. As a result, when free space accounting is disabled, the rows per page value may not be accurate. Disabling free space accounting also prevents threshold actions on non-log segments from executing.
read only	When true, no changes may be made to the data in the database. When false, changes may be made to the data. SQL Server may write pages to a database that is not marked read only when executing a read only query (e.g., select). This is done to update certain control information in the database. When read only is true, no writes are allowed to the database.
select into/bulkcopy	When true, select into, fast BCP, and non-logged writetext are allowed to the database. When false, these non-logged commands are not permitted. A non-logged operation prevents you from dumping the transaction log. However, non-logged operations, such as fast BCP, are significantly faster than their logged equivalents.
single user	When true, only one user is allowed to use the database at a time. When false, any number of users may use the database simultaneously. This is generally used while you are trying to populate or reconfigure a database.
trunc log on chkpt	When true, the transaction log of the database is dumped every time the checkpoint task wakes up to check if it is time for a checkpoint. This is generally about once a minute. When false, the checkpoint task does not automatically dump the transaction log. Automatically truncating the log precludes you from dumping the transaction log. As a result, this option should probably be avoided in a production database where recovery of the data is important.

B.6 SERVER-WIDE CONFIGURATION

Table B.5 shows some of the trace flags that may be useful for performance tuning. The property of a trace flag as session-specific means that its effects are realized only by the user who turned the flag on and not by other users on the same SQL Server.

Table B.5   SQL Server trace flags

Trace Flag	Properties	Description
1204	Static	Print extensive information about deadlocks.
1501	Static	Perform all disk I/O on engine 0.
1502	Static	Exclude users tasks from engine 0.
1603	Static	Disable asynchronous disk I/O.
1610	Static	Do not delay transmission of TCP packets hoping to put more data into each packet. Improves network response at the cost of network throughput. Sometimes referred to as TCP no delay.
1611	Static	Lock shared memory segments into physical memory.[a]
302	Session-specific	Displays statistics used by optimizer in index selection.
310	Session-specific	Displays statistics used by optimizer in join order selection.
3604	Session-specific	Copies console messages generated by the user session to the user session. Use to observe effects of session-specific trace flags.
-1	Dynamic	Turns off all trace flags. New in System 11. Having all trace flags off is best for performance.

a.   Applicable only to operating systems that support this feature.

Table B.6 lists some configuration parameters that are currently accessible only through the `dbcc tune` command discussed in "dbcc tune" on page 539.

Table B.6   DBCC tune parameters

Parameter	Properties	Description
maxwritedes	not persistent	Determines intensity of checkpoints. See Table B.7 on page 547.
doneinproc	not persistent	Determines whether SQL Server should send debugging information to clients for every statement executed. Value 1 is required for operation with SQL Debug and similar client tools. Value 0 improves performance.

Table B.7 lists the SQL Server configuration parameters organized by System 11 SQL Server configuration parameter groupings. Each row of the table shows the System 11 SQL Server configuration parameter name, the closest System 10 SQL Server equivalent, some useful attributes of the configuration parameter, the units of the configuration parameter value, and a brief description of the parameter. Property "perf" means performance-related. Property "memory" means that the value of the parameter effects the total memory requirement of SQL Server. Shaded regions of the System 10 Configuration Parameter column indicate parameters that can be set only through `buildmaster -y` or are trace flags.

Table B.7   SQL Server configuration parameters

System 11 Configuration Parameter	System 10 Configuration Parameter	Properties	Unit	Description
Backup/Recovery				
recovery interval in minutes	recovery interval	perf	minute	Longest time you are willing to wait for recovery to complete. This controls the frequency of automatic database checkpoints.
print recovery information	recovery flags	reboot	N/A	Value determines the amount of information printed about a database during recovery.
tape reten- tion in days	tape reten- tion	reboot	day	Number of days a tape is retained before it can be reused for another dump.
Cache Manager				
number of oam trips	coamtrips	perf	count	Default oamtrips value. The larger this value the greater the preference given to OAM pages in the cache manager. In general it is safer to tune oamtrips on individual indexes and tables rather than adjust the system value.
number of index trips	cindextrips	perf	count	Default indextrips value. The larger this value the greater the preference given to index pages in the cache manager. In general it is safer to tune indextrips on individual indexes and tables rather than adjust the system value.
procedure cache percent[a]	procedure cache	reboot memory	percent	Percentage of buffer memory devoted to procedure cache. The rest of buffer memory is given to data cache.

Table B.7   SQL Server configuration parameters

System 11 Configuration Parameter	System 10 Configuration Parameter	Properties	Unit	Description
memory alignment boundary	none	reboot memory	byte	Controls the alignment of cache buffers in the system's memory space. Optimal alignment of SQL Server's internal data structures on certain address boundaries can improve performance. It is not necessary to adjust this parameter.
User-defined Cache[b]				
cache size	none	reboot memory perf	varies	Total size of the cache.
cachestatus	none		N/A	Indicates if the cache is only for data pages, only for log pages, or may contain a mix of data and log pages.
N k I/O Buffer Pool[c]				
pool size	none	perf	varies	Size of the buffer pool with this I/O size in the cache.
wash size	none	perf	varies	The wash size for the buffer pool with this I/O size. The wash size is the amount of clean buffer space that should be kept available at any given time.
Disk I/O				
allow sql serverasync i/o	-T1603[d]	reboot perf	N/A	Controls whether or not SQL Server uses asynchronous disk I/O. In general, you should enable asynchronous disk I/O in order to maximize performance.

Table B.7   SQL Server configuration parameters

System 11 Configuration Parameter	System 10 Configuration Parameter	Properties	Unit	Description
disk i/o structures	cnblkio	reboot perf	count	Number of I/O control structures available in SQL Server. SQL Server cannot have more than this number of I/O operations pending simultaneously. It is not necessary to change this parameter.
none[e]	cmaxwrit-edes	reboot perf	count	Maximum number of concurrent asynchronous I/O operations used by the checkpoint process. A large value causes checkpoint to be aggressive — faster, but with greater impact on other activities on the server. Default value of 10 may be too passive if you have more than 20 disks.
page utilization percent	none		percent	Controls how frequently SQL Server scans OAM pages looking for a free page. The alternative to scanning the OAM pages for a free page is to allocate a new extent. When set to 100, SQL Server always scans OAM pages when looking for a free page.
number of devices	devices	reboot memory	count	Maximum number of database devices that can be created.
Language				
default character set id	default character set id	reboot perf[f]	N/A	Identification value for the character set used by SQL Server to store character and text data.
default language id	default language		N/A	Language used by SQL Server when no other language is explicitly specified.

Table B.7   SQL Server configuration parameters

System 11 Configuration Parameter	System 10 Configuration Parameter	Properties	Unit	Description
number of languagesin cache	language in cache	reboot perf[g]	count	Number of languages to store in memory.
default sortorderid	default sortorder id	reboot perf	N/A	Identification value for the sort order used by SQL Server when creating indexes and sorting character data.
Network Communication				
default network packet size	default network packet size	reboot memory perf	bytes	Network packet size that is used when no other value is provided explicitly.
max network packet size	maximum network packet size	reboot perf	bytes	Maximum size of the network packet used by SQL Server.
remote server pre-read packets	pre-read packets	reboot memory perf	count	Number of extra packets to read from a RPC site handler.
number of remote connections	remote connections	reboot memory	count	Maximum number of connections permitted via RPC from other SQL Servers.
allowremote access	remote access	memory	N/A	Allow RPCs into this SQL Server. This must be set to 1 for backup server to work properly.
number of remote logins	remote logins	reboot memory	count	Number of connections allowed from this SQL Server to remote servers.
number of remotesites	remote sites	reboot memory	count	Number of connections allowed into this SQL Server from remote servers.

Table B.7   SQL Server configuration parameters

System 11 Configuration Parameter	System 10 Configuration Parameter	Properties	Unit	Description
max number network listeners	cmaxnet-works	reboot	count	Number of network listeners SQL Server can start. It is not necessary to adjust this parameter unless SQL Server must listen for connections on an unusually large number of network addresses.
tcp no delay	-T1610[h]	reboot perf	N/A	When set, enables the no delay option on TCP ports.
O/S Resources				
o/s file descriptors	none		count	Indicates the number of file descriptors available to SQL Server. This is a read only parameter.
o/s asynch i/o enabled	none	perf	N/A	Indicates whether or not asynchronous I/O is enabled. This is a read only parameter.
max async i/os per engine	cnmaxaio_engine	reboot perf	count	Maximum number of simultaneous outstanding asynchronous disk I/O operations permitted on each engine. This is useful for operating systems that place a limit on the number of asynchronous disk I/O operations that may be active at one time from a single process and the error handling is not graceful or light weight. In general, most operating systems have a system-wide limit rather than a per process limit.

Table B.7   SQL Server configuration parameters

System 11 Configuration Parameter	System 10 Configuration Parameter	Properties	Unit	Description
`max async i/os per server`	`cnmaxaio_ server`	reboot perf	count	Maximum number of simultaneous outstanding asynchronous disk I/O operations permitted on the system as a whole. This parameter assumes SQL Server is the only process performing asynchronous disk I/O. This is useful for operating systems that place a limit on the number of asynchronous disk I/O operations that may be active at one time on the system and the error handling is not graceful or light weight. If this is an operating system configuration value, you should set this parameter to match the operating system's value.
Physical Memory				
`total mem- ory`[i]	`memory`	reboot memory	2k pages	Amount of the computer's memory allocated to SQL Server.
`additional networkmem- ory`	`additional network memory`	reboot memory perf	byte	Memory used for larger network buffers.
`lock shared memory`	`-T1611`[j]	reboot perf	N/A	If the operating system supports this feature, lock the shared memory segments into physical memory. This improves the performance of SQL Server because SQL Server's internal data structures and buffers are never paged to system paging space. This can hamper the performance of the computer system as a whole if it becomes memory constrained because most of available memory is permanently consumed by SQL Server.

Table B.7   SQL Server configuration parameters

System 11 Configuration Parameter	System 10 Configuration Parameter	Properties	Unit	Description
Processors				
max online engines	max online engines	reboot memory perf	count	Number of engines running in this SQL Server.
min online engines	min online engines	N/A	N/A	Not used.
engine adjust interval	engine adjust interval	N/A	N/A	Not used.
none	-T1501	reboot perf	N/A	This trace flag forces all disk I/O to be performed through engine 0. This can sometimes improve performance on systems that use single threaded operating system kernels on symmetric multiprocessing systems.
none	-T1502[k]	static perf	N/A	This trace flag prevents user threads from executing on engine 0. This is useful with System 10 SQL Server as all network I/O is processed by engine 0. In addition, this can be used with "perform all disk i/o on engine 0" to eliminate user tasks from engine 0 when engine 0 is responsible for all disk activity.
SQL Server Administration				
number of openobjects	open objects	static memory	count	Maximum number of objects (e.g., tables) that can be open at one time in SQL Server.
number of open databases	open databases	static memory	count	Maximum number of databases that can be open at one time.

Table B.7   SQL Server configuration parameters

System 11 Configuration Parameter	System 10 Configuration Parameter	Properties	Unit	Description
`audit queue size`	`audit queue size`	static memory	count	The amount of auditing data buffered by SQL Server.
`default database size`	`database size`	static	Mb	The size of a database created when no size is given explicitly.
`identity burning set factor`	`identify burning set factor`	static perf	percent	Controls the fraction of the identity column that is released at one time. Making this value extremely small may have a minor negative performance impact on SQL Server.
`allownested triggers`	`nested trigger`	static	N/A	If set to 1, causes triggers to cascade. If set to 0, triggers do not cascade. This is provided for backward compatibility with older versions of SQL Server.
`allow updates to system tables`	`allow updates`		NA	Allow ad hoc changes to the system tables in the master database.
`print deadlock information`	`-T1204`[1]	perf	N/A	Print information to the errorlog about the tasks involved in a deadlock. This can significantly slow the processing of a deadlock.
`defaultfill factor percent`	`fillfactor`	static	percent	Fill factor to use when creating indexes when the fill factor is not explicitly specified.
`number of mailboxes`	`cnmbox`	static	count	Controls the number of mailbox data structures. It is not necessary to adjust this value.
`number of messages`	`cnmsg`	static	count	Controls the number of message data structures. It is not necessary to adjust this value.

Table B.7   SQL Server configuration parameters

System 11 Configuration Parameter	System 10 Configuration Parameter	Properties	Unit	Description
number of alarms	cnalarm	static	count	Controls the number of alarm data structures. Alarms are used for a variety of purposes, including the SQL waitfor command. You may need to increase this parameter if your application makes heavy use of the waitfor command, otherwise it is not necessary to adjust this value.
event buffers per engine	ceventbuf	static	count	Event buffers stored SQL monitoring information. It is not necessary to adjust this value.
cpu accounting flush interval	cpu flush	perf	ticks	Controls how frequently SQL Server updates the CPU accounting tables for charge back accounting. When a task accumulates cpu flush CPU time, SQL Server updates the syslogins table to reflect CPU usage. Making this value small has a small negative performance impact on SQL Server.
i/o accounting flush interval	i/o flush	perf	ticks	Controls how frequently SQL Server updates the I/O accounting tables for charge back accounting. When a task accumulates i/o flush I/Os, SQL Server updates the syslogins table to reflect the I/O usage. Making this value small has a small negative performance impact on SQL Server.
sql server clock tick length	cclkrate	static	micro-sec-onds	Length of SQL Server's internal clock tick. Do not change this value.

Table B.7   SQL Server configuration parameters

System 11 Configuration Parameter	System 10 Configuration Parameter	Properties	Unit	Description
runnable process searchcount	cschedspins	perf	count	Determines how willing SQL Server is to share CPU with other processes on the server. Small value (say 1) means very willing. Default is 2000. Beware: 0 means infinity.
time slice	ctimeslice	static	clock ticks	Number of clock ticks before a CPU-bound user is forced to yield the CPU to other users on every tick. Small value makes tasks nice.
cpu grace time	ctimemax	static	clock ticks	Number of times a CPU-bound user is forced to yield before it is assumed to be a run-away task and aborted.
i/o polling process count	cmaxscheds	perf	ticks	Controls the the amount of time between checks for disk I/O completion.
deadlock retries	none	perf	count	Controls how many times SQL Server attempts to acquire a lock once a deadlock is detected.
number of sortbuffers	csortbuf-size	perf	count	Number of extent sized buffers available for sort operations. Large value helps index creation.
sort page count	csortpg-count	perf	count	No longer used. Formally used to help index creation.
number of extent i/o buffers	extent i/o buffers	static memory perf	count	Number of large (8 page) buffers available on SQL Server. Large buffers are used by BCP, create database, and create index.
upgrade version	upgrade version		N/A	Version of SQL Server.

Table B.7 SQL Server configuration parameters

System 11 Configuration Parameter	System 10 Configuration Parameter	Properties	Unit	Description
size of auto identity column	none		preci-sion	Specifies the precision of the auto identity column that is automatically added to tables in a database if the database option auto identity is true.
identity grab size	none	perf	count	The number of identity values that each task may grab ahead of time. This reduces the synchronization overhead between tasks as they insert into an identity column but may result in gaps in the identity values.
lock promotion HWM	none	perf	page	The lock promotion threshold High Water Mark. If the computed lock promotion threshold is larger than the high water mark, lock promotion occurs at the high water mark.
lock promotion LWM	none	perf	page	The lock promotion threshold Low Water Mark. If the computed lock promotion threshold is less than the low water mark, lock promotion occurs at the low water mark.
lock promotion PCT	none	perf	percent	The lock promotion threshold percentage. The lock promotion threshold is computed by taking this percentage of the table size. This computed promotion threshold is compared against the lock promotion LWM and lock promotion HWM parameters to decide when to promote from page- to table-level locks.

Table B.7   SQL Server configuration parameters

System 11 Configuration Parameter	System 10 Configuration Parameter	Properties	Unit	Description
none	cbufwash-size[m]	perf	pages	Number of buffers to keep clean. When the number of clean buffers falls below this value, SQL Server begins washing buffers every time a buffer is dirtied. In general, you should only adjust this parameter when you have a clear reason to do so. The default value works reasonably well for most applications.
housekeeper free write percent	none	perf	percent	Controls how aggressive housekeeper is at writing out dirty buffers. When 0 housekeeper is disabled. When 100 housekeeper uses all free disk I/O write time to write out dirty buffers.
User Environment				
number of user connections	user connections	static memory	count	Maximum number of connections from clients.
stack size	stack size	static memory	byte	Size of the stack given to each task in SQL Server.
stack guard size	cguardsz	static memory	byte	Size of the guard area between task stacks. The larger the guard area, the less likely one task can corrupt the stack of an adjoining task, but the larger the stack guard, the less memory is available for buffers and other internal data structures.
systemwide password expiration	password expiration interval		days	Frequency that passwords expire.

Table B.7   SQL Server configuration parameters

System 11 Configuration Parameter	System 10 Configuration Parameter	Properties	Unit	Description
`user log cache size`	none	static perf	bytes	Amount of memory pre-allo-cated for each user connection to hold log entries. Larger values may reduce log contention.
`user log cache spinlock ratio`	none	static perf	count	Number of user connections sharing a certain low-level latch. Relevant only for extremely large number of users and engines.
Lock Manager				
`number of locks`	`locks`	static memory	count	Number of logical locks avail-able in SQL Server.
`deadlock checking period`	none	perf	ticks	Length of time between dead-lock checks. Set to 0 to mimic System 10 SQL Server behavior.
`freelock transfer block size`	none	perf	count	The number of locks moved between the global free lock list and an engine's free lock list during one transfer operation.
`max engine freelocks`	none	perf	count	The maximum number of free locks that can be associated with any one engine.

Table B.7   SQL Server configuration parameters

System 11 Configuration Parameter	System 10 Configuration Parameter	Properties	Unit	Description
`addresslock spinlock ratio`	none	static perf	N/A	Controls the number of spin-locks used to control access to address locks. The larger this number the smaller the number of spinlocks. More spinlocks consume additional memory but reduce contention in the management of address locks.
`page lock spinlock ratio`	none	static perf	N/A	Controls the number of spin-locks used to control access to page locks. The larger this number the smaller the number of spinlocks. More spinlocks consume additional memory but reduce contention in the management of page locks.
`table lock spinlock ratio`	none	static perf	N/A	Controls the number of spin-locks used to control access to table locks. The larger this number the smaller the number of spinlocks. More spinlocks consume additional memory but reduce contention in the management of table locks.

a.   Likely to change to "procedure cache size". Units measure size rather than a percentage.
b.   There is one such set of entries for the default cache and each user-defined cache.
c.   There is one such set of entries for each buffer pool defined within a cache.
d.   Disabling this parameter is the same as adding this trace flag to System 10 SQL Server.
e.   Use DBCC tune to adjust this parameter in System 11 SQL Server.
f.   There is a small performance penalty if SQL Server must perform character set translation.
g.   More languages in cache can help performance if you are using several languages.
h.   Enabling this parameter is the same as adding this trace flag to System 10 SQL Server.
i.   For System 11, memory is the amount of memory to allocate to cache and control information inside SQL Server. For System 10, memory includes these uses of memory plus the memory used to store the SQL Server executable image.
j.   Enabling this parameter is the same as adding this trace flag to System 10 SQL Server.
k.   Not available on System 11 SQL Server because all engines can perform network I/O in System 11.
l.   Enabling this parameter is the same as adding this trace flag to System 10 SQL Server.
m.   For System 11, this configuration parameter is on a per-cache basis, rather than system-wide.

Appendix C

Network Configuration

Clients must log into SQL Server before they can issue commands to SQL Server. The login process establishes a network connection between the client and the server.

C.1 INTERFACES FILE

Sybase clients and servers use the interfaces file to rendezvous on the appropriate network port number. The format of the interfaces file differs depending on the operating system, but the basic features of the file remain the same in all cases. The file is divided into entries. Each entry represents one rendezvous point in the network. SQL Server listens for connections on a network port specified by SQL Server's entry in the interfaces file. The client knows which host and port to connect to through the same or other entries in the interfaces file.

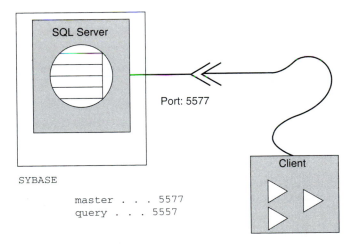

Figure C.1   Client/Server connection -

Table C.1 summarizes the various interfaces file types used by Sybase products.

Table C.1   Interfaces file formats

Format Type	Operating System	Example Entry

socket-style[a]	SunOS 4.x
	Digital Unix
	OpenVMS
	HP/UX[b]
	AIX
		SYBASE
		    query tcp ether cleo 5557
		    master tcp ether cleo 5557
		    console tcp ether cleo 5558[c]

TLI-style[d]	SunOS 5.x
	System V.4
		SYBASE
		    query tcp ether /dev/tcp 0x000215b5807a34a2
		    master tcp ether /dev/tcp 0x000215b5807a34a2
		    console tcp ether /dev/tcp 0x000215b6807a34a2

Windows/NT	Windows/NT	[SYBASE] $BASE$00=NLWNSCK,cleo,5557 MASTER=$BASE$00; $BASE$01=NLWNSCK,cleo,5557 QUERY=$BASE$01;

a.   Socket refers to the network programming interface used by SQL Servers that expect this style of interfaces file entry. The socket network interface is most common among Berkeley-derived Unix systems or systems that use the Berkeley networking code.
b.   Except for SPX/IPX which uses an TLI-style entry.
c.   The console line is only required with 4.9.1 SQL Server and before. SQL Server System 10 and later only need the master and query lines.
d.   TLI, or Transport Layer Interface, refers to the programming interface used by SQL Servers that expect this style of interfaces file entry. The TLI network interface is most common among System V.4 derived Unix systems.

The socket-style and TLI-style interfaces file entries have similar formats. The Sybase server name starts at the beginning of a line and may be followed to two numbers. The number indicate the retry count and time-out value. The retry count tells the client how many times it should try to connect to the Sybase server before giving up. The time-out value indicates how long the client should wait for the Sybase server to accept the connection. SQL Server itself ignores these numbers.

Following the Sybase server name are service lines. A service line starts with spaces or a tab character. Blank lines and comments are allowed in the interfaces file. A comment is a line that begins with the # character.

A service line has five fields. The first field is the service name. Valid services are: master, query, and console. Invalid services are ignored. The second field is the network protocol. The valid network protocols depend on the platform and SQL Server version. In general, tcp means TCP/IP, dnet means DECnet, and spx means SPX/IPX. The next field is generally platform-ether (where platform is the name of the platform running SQL Server). This field is ignored. The form of the remaining two fields depends on the interfaces file format.

For socket-style interfaces file entries, the remaining fields are the hostname and the port number. The host name is the name of the host on the network using the protocol mentioned on the line. The port number is a port number on the network.

For TLI-style interfaces file entries, the remaining fields are the network device endpoint and the network address for the listener port. The network device endpoint is a pseudo-device that acts as the interface between programs and the operating system kernel. The device endpoint for TCP/IP is normally /dev/tcp. For TCP/IP, the network address is a long hexadecimal number. It is relatively easy to translate the number into something that is easier to understand. The format of the number is:

```
0xnnnnppppphhhhhhhh
```

where nnnn identifies the format of the address, pppp is the port number, and hhhhhhhh is the host's address in the network. nnnn is either 0200 or 0002 depending on the byte order expected by the networking software. Note that this might differ from the byte order of the machine. This is meant to be the numeric value "2" which identifies the network address as a TCP/IP style address. pppp is the hexadecimal representation of the port number. 5557 is 15B5 in hexadecimal. For TCP/IP, network addresses generally appear as four numbers separated by periods. Each of these numbers is given by two digits in hhhhhhhh. For example, the network address 192.214.43.234 becomes C0D62BEA.

C.2   SQL SERVER'S INTERFACES FILE ENTRY

On Unix, SQL Server reads the DSLISTEN environment variable or the -s command line option to identify the name of SQL Server. On start up, SQL Server reads the interfaces file and locates the entry with the matching name. It then reads the `master` lines and starts a network listener on the host address and port number described on each `master` line. The host address must be a network address for the machine running SQL Server. SQL Server may listen for network connections at more than one port. This allows for two capabilities:

1. If the machine has more than one network connection, it has more than one legitimate network address. SQL Server may listen for network connections on multiple addresses, making it possible to increase the total network bandwidth available to SQL Server by having SQL Server listen and respond to connections on more than one physical network at a time. It is not necessary to route information from one network to the other for the benefit of SQL Server. Of course, there are other reasons why it might be useful to route information between the networks, failover, for example.

2. If the client machines are using heterogeneous network protocols, some TCP/IP others SPX/IPX, SQL Server can listen for network connections on each of the network protocols.[1] This makes it possible to have a single SQL Server simultaneously service a variety of client types.

SQL Server 4.9.1 and before also require a console line in the interfaces file entry. The console line indicates the network port used by SQL Server and the console program to communicate with one another. The console program is used during database and transaction dumps and loads to tell SQL Server when tapes are loaded into the tape drive. The console program was eliminated with System 10 SQL Server by the Backup Server and the `sp_volchange` stored procedure. System 10 SQL Servers do not require a `console` line in their interfaces file entry and they ignore a `console` line if one is present.

C.3   CLIENTS' INTERFACES FILE ENTRIES

On Unix, clients generally read the DSQUERY environment variable to identify the name of SQL Server to connect to. When the client needs to log into a SQL Server, it reads the interfaces file and locates the entry with the appropriate name. Clients read the `query` line rather than the `master` line to find the host address and port number. The client uses the first `query` line it finds in the interfaces file entry. If, for some reason, the client cannot connect to a SQL Server using the first

---

[1]   Not all network protocols are supported on every platform running SQL Server. Check the SQL Server Installation Guide and Release Bulletin and your hardware and/or operating system documentation for support of a particular network protocol if this is important to you.

query line, it looks for another query line in the same interfaces file entry. If it finds one, it tries to connect to a server at that network address and port. This process continues until it finally connects or runs out of query lines. This feature is useful for failover. You can add extra query lines for standby SQL Servers.

This behavior also means you cannot use a single interfaces file entry to communicate with a SQL Server over two different network addresses. To do this you must create an extra interfaces file entry that is an "alias" for the SQL Server. Suppose the SQL Server's main interfaces file entry has two master lines. The query line in the main entry matches the first master line. A server "alias" has just a query line that matches the second master line. Clients that want to connect to the SQL Server via the first listener use the SQL Server's main interfaces file entry. Clients connecting to the second listener must use the alias.

```
SYBASE
        master tcp ether cleo 5557
        master dnet ether cleo 98
        query tcp ether cleo 5557
SYBASE_alias
        query dnet ether cleo 98
```

C.4   USING LOOPBACK

The localhost or loopback address on TCP/IP allows two programs running on the same machine to communicate with one another through TCP/IP while avoiding much of the networking overhead. When localhost is use the operating system generally bypasses much of the networking software and handles the connection internally. This reduces the load on the network and reduces operating system overhead.

SQL Server and Sybase client programs can communicate through the localhost or loopback address as long as SQL Server and the clients are running on the same machine. Use localhost, loopback, or 127.0.0.1 as the machine address. You must still specify the other values for the interfaces file entry, including a port number. For example:

```
local_server
        query tcp ether localhost 3345
        master tcp ether localhost 3345
```

If clients elsewhere on the network also need to communicate with this SQL Server, you can add additional network listeners:

```
local_server
```

```
        query tcp ether localhost 3345
        master tcp ether cleo 5678
        master tcp ether localhost 3345
cleo_server
        query tcp ether cleo 5678
```

where `cleo` is the name of the machine running SQL Server. This interfaces file entry has SQL Server `local_server` listening for connections on the network port `cleo.5678` and on the port `localhost.3345`. Clients running on `cleo` should connect to `localhost.3345` to minimize network activity, while clients running on other machines can connect to `cleo_server`.

Appendix D

DBCC Commands

checkcatalog [(databasename)]

DBCC `checkcatalog` checks the data stored in the system tables for consistency. `checkcatalog` acquires shared page locks on the system tables as it reads the rows from the tables. In general, it verifies that information in one system table corresponds in a reasonable way with information in other system tables.

checkdb [(databasename [, skip_ncindex])]

DBCC `checkdb` performs a DBCC `checktable` (see "checktable({tablename|object_id} [, skip_ncindex])" for details) on every table in databasename or in the current database if databasename is not given. The tables are checked in order of their object id as listed in the `sysindexes` table. If `skip_ncindex` is given, `checkdb` does not check the nonclustered indexes on the tables for consistency. This reduces the amount of time it takes to perform the consistency check and may be a reasonable trade-off between a complete consistency check and the time it takes to perform the checks. You can always drop and create a nonclustered index if it later proves to be corrupted. No data is lost as the nonclustered index contains only a copy of the data in the table. If `skip_ncindex` is not given, `checkdb` checks all of the nonclustered indexes on every table in the database.

checktable({tablename|object_id} [, skip_ncindex])

DBCC `checktable` performs consistency checks on the table `tablename`. You may specify either the name of the table or the object id of the table. DBCC `checktable` checks that the pages of the table are linked together properly, that control information on the pages of the table is correct, that the clustered and nonclustered indexes are sorted in the correct order, that the pointers from nonclustered indexes to the table's data pages are correct, that the data stored in the nonclustered index is consistent with the data pages, and that the data pages of the table are consistent with information in `sysindexes` and (for System 11) `syspartitions`. When the `skip_ncindex` option is given, no checks are performed against the nonclustered indexes on the table. If `skip_ncindex` is not given, the nonclustered indexes are checked for consistency. The clustered index is always checked.

DBCC `checktable` acquires a shared table lock on the table being checked. This locks out changes to the data in the table by other threads, but does not affect other threads reading rows from the table.

You may see disk writes when you run DBCC `checktable`. DBCC `checktable` updates control information on the data pages of the table. In particular, it updates a status bit on the page that indicates if there are any variable length columns on the page. SQL Server optimizes access to data pages that have only fixed length columns. In addition, DBCC `checktable` updates control information for sliced tables.

checkalloc [(databasename [, fix|nofix])]

DBCC `checkalloc` performs a `tablealloc` (see "tablealloc({tablename|object_id}[, {full|optimized|fast|null} [, fix|nofix]])" for details) on every table in `databasename` or in the current database if `databasename` is not given. The `fix` option tells checkalloc to fix any allocation errors it finds while checking for page allocation consistency. If `nofix` is given, the errors are not corrected. If neither `fix` nor `nofix` is given, `nofix` is assumed.

DBCC `checkalloc` acquires a lock on the allocation pages to prevent other DBCC functions from running simultaneously against the same allocation pages. This means you cannot run two checkallocs against the same database simultaneously in two different login sessions. Also, it is not possible to run `checkalloc` at the same time as `tablealloc` or `indexalloc` in the same database.

tablealloc({tablename|object_id}[, {full|optimized|fast|null} [, fix|nofix]])

DBCC `tablealloc` checks the page allocation for a single table. The name of the table is given as tablename or by the object id of the table. In general, `tablealloc` makes sure that all pages allocated to the table are used by the table, all pages used by the table are allocated, and that all control information regarding the allocated pages is correct. If allocation errors are found, they are corrected with the `fix` option. If `nofix` is given, or no option is given, DBCC `tableal-loc` only reports allocation errors. It does not correct for the errors.

DBCC `tablealloc` checks only the data of the table and, if one is present, the table's clustered index.

The `full` option checks all page allocation information, including the OAM pages, allocation pages, and the page linkages. The `optimized` option checks only the allocation pages referenced by the table's OAM pages. This means the optimized check may miss errors for extents in allocation units controlled by allocation pages referenced in the table's OAM pages. The `fast` option only checks the consistency of the page linkage of the table. It does not check the page allocation against the allocation pages or the OAM pages. Specifying `null`, or not specifying any option, gives you the optimized check.

In all cases, DBCC `tablealloc` acquires a shared table lock on the table being checked. As with `checktable`, this locks out changes to the data in the table while `tablealloc` runs. It does not effect tasks reading rows from the table. Unlike DBCC `checkalloc`, `tablealloc` acquires a shared lock on the allocation pages, so it is possible to run several `tablealloc` and `indexalloc` commands simultaneously in the same database.

indexalloc({tablename|object_id}, index_id [, {full|optimized|fast|null} [, fix|nofix]])

DBCC `indexalloc` is similar to DBCC `tablealloc`, but it checks a nonclustered index rather than a table. The name of the table is given by `tablename` or the table's object id. The index is given by the index's id rather than the index's name. The `full`, `optimized`, `fast`, `null`, `fix`, and nofix options have the same meanings for `indexalloc` as for tablealloc.

DBCC `indexalloc` acquires a shared table lock on the table that has the index being checked.

Appendix E

Troubleshooting

The performance behavior of SQL Server can sometimes change unexpectedly. When a stored procedure query plan is cached, the new plan may not be optimal for all possible parameters (see Chapter 11, *Query Processing Performance*). Upgrading to a new version of SQL Server, even minor version changes or one-offs, can result in changes in behavior. A change made by Sybase to improve performance in a large number of situations may adversely affect the performance of your situation.

The symptoms of a performance problem are clear enough: a query takes too long; the report takes much longer to run today than it did last week; ever since the upgrade, the system's throughput has been poor. The solution to performance problems often is obvious once you have all the information you need. The difficulty is in understanding what information you need based on the symptoms your customers are observing. Symptom: query takes too long to execute. Do you need to look at disk I/O? How can you isolate the disk I/O from this one transaction from the others running on the system? Perhaps it is the interaction between this query and the others running at the same time that is causing the poor performance. Maybe it is not a disk I/O problem at all. Was the application changed?

When SQL Server does not perform as expected, a query that should take a few seconds takes hours, you can use the monitoring information and your understanding about how SQL Server works internally to identify the problem. For example, during the physical design of a database, you create an index on a large, frequently accessed table. You assume that SQL Server will use this index, rather than a table scan, to find rows in the table. As a result, you code several queries that should run fairly quickly. What you find, however, is that some of the queries take hours to run. Why? Monitoring SQL Server, you discover a large number of disk reads when the slow queries are executed. From this you can guess that SQL

Server is not taking advantage of the index. With this working hypothesis, you can go ahead and try to find possible solutions to the problem. Why do some of the queries use the index and others not?

This section discusses some common problem areas with regards to SQL Server applications and performance. We offer some tips on where to go for the information you need to resolve the performance problem.

Query Optimizer Chooses the Wrong Plan

SQL Server's query optimizer chooses a query plan based on:

- The tables involved in the query

- The join clauses

- The search clauses

- Indexes on the tables

- Statistics on the indexes

- Buffer cache configuration

- Forced join order and/or index selection

Changing any of these characteristics of the query may affect the optimizer's estimated cost of possible query plans, and hence its choice of the best query plan. Prior to System 11 SQL Server, SQL Server uses a 32 bit integer value to store the estimated cost of a query plan. For certain very expensive plans, the cost could exceed the largest 32 bit value, causing an overflow error. While this error does not cause SQL Server to abort the plan, it does make very expensive plans look cheaper than they should, causing the optimizer to sometimes choose the wrong plan. System 11 SQL Server corrects this problem by using a floating point value to store estimated query plan costs.

If SQL Server consistently chooses the wrong plan, your only recourse is to force SQL Server to use the correct plan. You can do so by mandating a certain join order and/or insisting on the use of particular indexes. See Chapter 11, *Query Processing Performance*, for more details.

Sql Server Upgrade Slows Down Queries

Major and even minor upgrades of SQL Server sometimes cause certain applications to perform poorly after the upgrade. Often this is the result of changes to SQL Server's query optimizer. Sybase periodically makes minor tweaks to the query compiler and optimizer, improving performance in general cases, but perhaps adversely affecting performance in some specific cases.

- **Check query plans** — Have the query plans changed substantially? Are your assumptions for index utilization still true? Try rewriting queries or using force plan to coerce the right access methods. For this to be useful you will either need to keep copies or documentation about the query plans you are expecting or you will need both the old and new SQL Servers running at the same time so you can make comparisons.

- **Check disk utilization patterns** — You can determine changes to the query plans indirectly by checking on disk I/O. After the upgrade is there substantially more I/O to a particular database device? Try examining showplan output and show statistics io output of suspect queries to further isolate the problem.

- **Check stored procedures** — If the performance of stored procedures is in question, try re-compiling the stored procedures. Sometimes changes to the query compiler are made in conjunction with changes elsewhere in SQL Server, adversely affecting existing query plans. This can be corrected by re-compiling the stored procedures.

- **Check SQL Server memory utilization** — If this is a major upgrade, check the amount of memory devoted to procedure and data cache. The amount of memory consumed by SQL Server for things other than procedure and data cache may have changed. Try configuring SQL Server to use more memory or adjusting the proportions of memory devoted to different purposes within SQL Server.

Operating System Upgrade Slows Down Queries

Operating system vendors tweak the performance of the system software in order to improve the performance for general users. Database engines do not impose typical loads on a computer system, so tweaks that help many users compiling programs may not help you as a database administrator.

- **Verify that SQL Server is using asynchronous disk I/O** — Check SQL Server's errorlog and verify that asynchronous I/O is still enabled. Make sure the operating system is configured to allow asynchronous disk I/O.

- **Use the operating system to monitor overall system performance** — Has the maximum disk I/O rate changed? Has the CPU utilization changed? Is SQL Server still getting the same amount of CPU time as before? Look for new daemon processes or other changes to the system that might affect SQL Server.

- **Check for system paging** — Complex operating systems like Unix generally have a number of daemon, or utility programs, that run in the background. Are the utility functions in the new version of the operating system consuming more memory and/or CPU than before? Try disabling the daemons you do not need.

- **Check the system configuration** — Is the system configuration the same? Has the upgrade modified configuration changes you made to improve performance of SQL Server? Have the configuration values reverted to default values? Verify all of the system configuration values.

Performance Degrades with Large Number of Users

When the number of users of any system increases, a gradual decline in the performance of the system is expected. Ideally, the performance degradation is of the form of gradually lengthening response time, while the system's throughput remains constant. Often one finds this to be the case to some point, then performance drops off dramatically as the number of active users passes some threshold.

- **Check for lock contention** — Use `sp_who` and `sp_lock`. Is contention on certain tables, or even certain pages in a table, throttling the overall performance of your application? Are there many demand locks? This may mean queries are holding onto locks for too long.

- **Check disk utilization** — Is the application I/O bound? Use SQL Monitor to check on the I/O rates to the database devices. Is one device a bottleneck? Try spreading the I/O over more devices or increasing the amount of memory for SQL Server's data cache.

- **Check tempdb utilization** — Is there enough memory to hold all the worktables and temporary tables?

Performance Degrades with Few Users

When there are only a few users on the system, one should expect fast response time at low throughput. With few users, throughput may be limited by the small number of clients rather than a bottleneck within SQL Server. If the response time increases or fails to decrease with a decrease in the number of users, then there are some opportunities for investigating the performance degradation.

- **Check group commits** — If the response time is determined by a sequence of short transactions, then each log page may be written to disk multiple times. This hurts throughput, but improves response time.

- **Check network traffic** — The transport layer may not be taking full advantage of lower throughput. Try using TPC no delay.

- **Check for excessive idle time** — Is there enough work to keep system completely busy? If not, the client may be a limiting factor in performance.

- **Check for excessive disk reads** — Sometimes, accesses to data and indexes pages by other users improve cache hit ratio. Check whether the total number of disk operations per user is greater with fewer users.

Performance Does Not Scale with the Number of Engines or CPUs

Scalability to a large number of CPUs is not assured on any shared memory hardware or with any database system. Ideally, adding another CPU or engine adds that much more to the maximum throughput and contributes to a reduction in response time. In practice, scaling is reasonable to a point. Beyond some threshold, adding more CPU or engines contributes nothing to performance and may actually degrade performance of the system.

- **Check the number of users** — Are enough users running simultaneously to take advantage of engines? Each login to SQL Server is a task. A task may only run on one engine at a time. This means a single query can only utilize one engine. If there are more engines than active users, some engines will always be idle. An idle engine does not contribute to throughput or reduced response time.

- **Check that the configured number of engines matches the number of CPUs** — The configured number of engines should never exceed the number of CPUs. On some systems it is useful to leave one CPU for operating system tasks. This is particularly important on operating systems that rely on separate operating system threads to handle I/O operations.

- **Check system monitors** — Is there a bottleneck on some other aspect of the system? Eliminating the other bottleneck, be it network I/O or I/O to a single disk drive, can improve scalability.

Ad Hoc Queries Work Fine, But Stored Procedures Performance is Poor

This is a frequently asked question. SQL Server optimizes stored procedures the first time they are executed. The optimized query plan it chooses for the stored procedure depends on the parameters passed into the procedure. This can be a problem when part of the where clause is parameterized. For example:

```
create proc examplep @p1 int as
select col1, col2 from table1 where col3 = @p1
```

Here the choice of the best query plan depends on the selectivity and indexes for `table1.col3`. Suppose the first time `examplep` is executed 80% of the rows in `table1` have `col3` = `@p1` (i.e., `@p1` is not selective). SQL Server will choose a table scan as the most efficient way of accessing the rows in `table1`. This plan is stored in the procedure cache. The next time `examplep` is executed `@p1` is given a new value and only 1 row of `table1` has `col3` = `@p1` (i.e., `@p1` is highly selective). SQL Server still performs a table scan even though the access method is to read table1 through the index on `col3`. A table scan is chosen because the cached query plan for `examplep` says to perform a table scan, not an index scan. You can use showplan to examine the plan chosen by SQL Server. You can force SQL Server to recompile the stored procedure by using the with recompile option when the stored procedure is created or executed.

Appendix F

Industry Standard Benchmarks

Benchmarks provide a way to comparison shop. Standardized benchmarks abound, though more likely than not, your application is not at all like the standard benchmarks used to compare hardware and database software performance. Few application developers can afford the time and effort involved to create their own personalized benchmark. For very critical applications or major architectural decisions, personalized benchmarks can be very important. Most people, however, have to content themselves with comparing benchmark results from the industry standard benchmarks.

There are a number of standard benchmarks that are typically applied to computer systems: Dhrystone, LINPACK, SPEC[1] (see Table F.1).

Table F.1   Industry standard benchmarks

Benchmark Name	Description	Applicability
Dhrystone	Small benchmark representative of integer programming	Systems programming
LINPACK	Floating point matrix operations	Simulations, models of physical systems
SPECcint92	Integer benchmark	Systems programming
SPECcfp92	Floating point benchmark	Simulations, models, computer graphics

---

[1]   Standard Performance Evaluation Corporation.

Unfortunately for database buyers, these benchmarks generally focus on mathematical operations for engineering or scientific applications. None captures the essence of database systems.

F.1   TRANSACTION PROCESSING COUNCIL

In 1988 the major database software and hardware vendors formed the Transaction Processing-performance Council (TPC). This council designs and monitors industry standard database benchmarks. Of course, each vendor wants its products to have the best benchmark performance, so depending on the political winds prevalent at the council, some TPC benchmarks may favor one vendor over another.

The benchmarks try to mimic applications typically run on databases. As the use of relational databases has changed, so too has the character of the TPC benchmarks. The TPC frowns upon "benchmark specials," special features that benefit only the benchmark but are generally not useful to customers with real applications. As a result, the engineering efforts of the hardware and software vendors to obtain good benchmark performance generally benefit the broader user community.

These benchmarks differ substantially from one another. Therefore, it is not possible to compare directly the results from one kind of benchmark with the results from another.

F.2   TPC-A AND TPC-B

The TPC-A benchmark models a simple transaction processing environment by mimicking transactions from a bank teller machine. The benchmark is comprised of a single transaction that alters the balance of a randomly chosen customer and logs the change in a history table. Both the size of the database and the number of tellers are required to scale linearly with the throughput. TPC-B is a variant of TPC-A which reduces the cost of running the benchmark by allowing the transactions to be processed in a batch mode rather than interactively from terminals. The reported metrics are the transaction rate (transactions per second) and the cost per transaction per second.

TPC-A and TPC-B are the first widely-accepted industry-standard benchmarks for transaction processing systems. They represent a major advance in the discipline (or lack thereof) of performance evaluation for database systems. Even after being rendered obsolete by the TPC in June 1995, they continue to be used for internal testing by most vendors because of their relative simplicity.

Both TPC-A and TPC-B suffer from two fundamental limitations that eventually led to their demise. First, they are based on an overly simplistic transaction that touches only four pages in most implementations. This enabled vendors to make unrealistic claims about performance by optimizing their products and benchmark implementations for unrealistically short and simple transactions. Second, rapid advances in the cost and performance of database servers made the TPC-A pricing model unrepresentative of most customers needs. For example, dumb terminals account for nearly 70% of the total cost of the system in some of the later TPC-A results.

F.3   TPC-C

In 1992, TPC released version 1.0 of their third benchmark, TPC-C. TPC-C is conceptually unrelated to TPC-A and TPC-B and models a moderately complex order entry transaction environment. The database has nine tables holding information about districts, warehouses, orders, items, stock, and customers. There are five transactions that relate to processing orders and managing inventory levels. The amount of data scales linearly with the performance. Performance is reported as the transaction rate (transactions per minute) and the cost per transaction per minute.

TPC-C has been used by most major vendors for measuring transaction processing performance. TPC-C corrects a major flaw in TPC-A and TPC-B by using five transactions of varying complexities instead of a single, simple transaction. As the cost and performance of the database servers kept improving, the pricing model for TPC-C, which was based on that for TPC-A, starting losing relevance to reality in the same vain as the TPC-A pricing model. TPC has moved to keep the pricing model for TPC-C realistic by dropping the price of terminals from version 3.0 of TPC-C in February 1995.

The strength of TPC-C lies in its complexity. In an article published in Open Systems in August 1994, Walter Baker of Informix compares tuning the TPC-C benchmark to pushing a balloon in at one end, only to have it come out at the other. Unlike TPC-A and TPC-B, it is difficult, if not impossible, to relate the performance of TPC-C to the performance of any one feature or component within the database system. An unscrupulous vendor attempting to gain an unfair advantage in TPC-C through a quick fix to their product, is likely to run into problems elsewhere in TPC-C. Part of the complexity of TPC-C is its requirement for ANSI Level 2 isolation between most transactions, which prevents vendors from trading data and transactional integrity for performance.

F.4   TPC-D

TPC-D, released in April 1995, is the first benchmark from TPC which addresses performance of complex queries rather than transaction processing. TPC-D models applications that perform complex business oriented queries concurrently with updates in a multi-user environment. The 17 queries and two updates in TPC-D mimic a multinational wholesale supplier coordinating the placement and execution of orders among thousands of suppliers and millions of customers. The 17 queries are designed to push the database server's abilities in optimizing and parallel execution of complex queries and cover a wide variety of relational operators and access methods. The two updates are designed to keep the database server honest in transactional semantics and data integrity.

Queries and updates are phrased in SQL. Vendors are not allowed to use optimizer hints or to rephrase queries to enhance performance. This effectively restricts participation to products that support SQL. Updates represent the need to keep the decision-support database closely synchronized with an on-line production database. This, and the 7x24 availability requirement, differentiate TPC-D from applications that perform read-only query processing on data downloaded from elsewhere and effectively preclude products that do not handle concurrent updates.

TPC-D reports three metrics: Response in single user test, throughput in multi-user test, and the cost to performance ratio, where performance is a combination of the other two metrics. All metrics include the size of the database, which can be chosen from a finite number of steps between 1GB and 1TB.

No one benchmark can represent all the needs of all applications in the highly diverse world of decision-support, and TPC-D has its limitations.

1. TPC-D precludes products that do not support concurrent updates and those that do not support SQL.

2. The synthetic data in TPC-D is evenly distributed and contains no skew or correlation. As a result, the performance and choice of the optimal plan for a query do not depend on the values of the constants and variables in the query.

3. The queries are not ad-hoc. The vendors have come to know the 17 queries in TPC-D quite intimately over the five years it took TPC to complete the TPC-D specification. Vendors have had far more time to tune their performance on these 17 queries than you will ever get to tune the performance of your query.

Despite its shortcomings, TPC-D fulfills the long-standing need for a reliable benchmark for query processing performance and is likely to gain wide acceptance as the standard in decision support performance. It remains to be seen whether subsequent releases of TPC-D eliminate some of its limitations.

Table F.2   TPC benchmark summary

Benchmark	Description	Applicability
TPC-A	Bank Teller	Simple on-line transaction processing; short simple queries with limited data exchange.
TPC-B	Bank Teller - essentially the same as TPC-A	Simple on-line transaction processing; short simple queries with limited data exchange.
TPC-C	Inventory Control	Moderately complex on-line transaction processing.
TPC-D	Multi-national wholesale supplier	Large database, complex queries, decision support.

F.5   TPC BENCHMARK RESULTS

Benchmark results are audited, reported, and available from vendors. Full specifications for the benchmarks are available from the Transaction Processing-performance Council.[2] Each benchmark result includes a full disclosure describing in

---

2. See the FAQ for comp.benchmarks. As of this writing, TPC documents are available via anonymous FTP from ftp.dg.com.

excruciating detail the configuration of the system used to obtain the result. This is useful should you want to repeat the exact benchmark and try to recreate the results.

Appendix G

Reference and Scripts

G.1   USEFUL FUNCTIONS

SQL Server includes a number of built-in functions that are useful for writing performance monitoring tools for your application (see Table G.1). Table G.2 lists queries report the number of pages used and reserved by a table, index, or text page.

Table G.1   Useful SQL Server functions

Function Prototype	Description
object_name(id,[dbid])	Returns the name of the object id. This saves a join with sysobjects. When used with dbid, object_name returns the name of objid in dbid. This is indispensable when you want to query tables system tables such as syslocks that give you dbid and the object id, and want to get the object name.
object_id(name)	Returns the id of the object in the current database.
data_pgs(id,doampglioampg)	Returns the number of pages allocated to a table or index.
used_pgs(id,doampg,ioampg)	Returns the number of pages used by a table and its clustered index.
reserved_pgs(id,doampglioampg)	Returns the number of pages reserved by a table or index.
rowcnt(doampg)	Returns an estimated row count for the table.

Table G.2   Page usage reports

Description	Query
| Table without a clustered index. Tables without a clustered index have sysindexes.indid of 0. | ```
select
    object_name(sysindexes.id),
    data_pgs(sysindexes.id, doampg),
    reserved_pgs(sysindexes.id, doampg)
from
    sysindexes
where
    sysindexes.id > 100 and indid = 0
``` |
| Table with a clustered index. Tables with a clustered index have an sysindexes.indid of 1. | ```
select
    object_name(sysindexes.id),
    used_pgs(sysindexes.id, doampg, ioampg),
    reserved_pgs(sysindexes.id, doampg)
from
    sysindexes
where
    sysindexes.id > 100 and indid = 1
``` |
| For the text chain of a table. Text chains have an sysindexes.indid of 255. | ```
select
    object_name(sysindexes.id),
    data_pgs(sysindexes.id, doampg),
    reserved_pgs(sysindexes.id, doampg)
from
    sysindexes
where
    sysindexes.id > 100 and indid = 255
``` |
| For the nonclustered index on a table. Nonclustered indexes have a sysindexes.indid more than 1 and less than 255. | ```
select
    object_name(sysindexes.id),
    data_pgs(sysindexes.id, ioampg),
    reserved_pgs(sysindexes.id, ioampg)
from
    sysindexes
where
    sysindexes.id > 100 and
    indid > 1 and indid < 255
``` |

The `rowcnt()` function returns an estimate of the row count for the table. While the count is an estimate, it is much faster to calculate the row count with `rowcnt()` than with `count(*)` when the table does not contain an index. For example:

```
select
    object_name(sysindexes.id),
    rowcnt(doampg)
from
    sysindexes
where
    sysindexes.id > 100 and (indid = 0 or indid = 1)
```

returns the estimated page counts for every user table in the current database.

G.2   SQL SCRIPTS

Sybase provides a rich set of system stored procedures that help you monitor SQL Server and examine the tables, indexes, and other database objects you create in it.

At times these stored procedures do not present information in the most convenient form for performance work. Here are some stored procedures and views that we find handy when working on the performance of SQL Server. In general it is worth remembering that SQL Server system stored procedures are written entirely in T-SQL and Sybase does not pull any special tricks to get the stored procedures to work. If you need to produce a report that is similar to, but not exactly like a system stored procedure, start with the system stored procedure that generates the report most like the report you want, use `sp_helptext` to examine the stored procedure, and start writing your own.

Table G.3   Useful system stored procedures

Procedure Prototype	Description
sp_configure *parameter, value*	Set the configuration parameter *parameter* to *value*. When value is not given, the current value for *parameter* is returned. This is useful for understanding how SQL Server is currently configured.
sp_depends *object-name*	Report all of the objects that *object-name* depends on and all of the objects that depend on *object-name*. For example, a stored procedure depends on the tables it uses. A view depends on the tables the view is constructed from and may have stored procedures that depend on it. This is useful for understanding how objects in the database are related to one another.
sp_estspace *table-name, number-of-rows, fill-factor, use-maximum-length, text-image-length, io-rate*	Report how much space is needed by *table-name* and its indexes when there are *number-of-rows* rows in the table and the indexes are created with the fill factor *fill-factor*. sp_estspace also reports how long it will take to create the indexes after the data is loaded into the table. By default, sp_estspace assumes that variable length columns are on the average half the maximum length of the column. *use-maximum-length* is a comma separated list of variable length columns sp_estspace should assume are filled to the maximum length of the column. *text-image-length* is the average length of text and/or image columns for each row of the table. By default, sp_estspace assumes the database device files containing the table can perform 30 I/O operations per second. *io-rate* allows you to change this value if you are using faster hardware.
sp_help *object-name*	Reports a variety of information about the object. For tables, this includes the owner, segment, the data types and sizes for the columns, and any indexes.
sp_helpindex *table-name*	Lists the indexes on *table-name*.
sp_lock	Returns the locks currently acquired on database pages and tables.

Table G.3   Useful system stored procedures

Procedure Prototype	Description
sp_monitor	Reports system-wide statistics about the operation of SQL Server including CPU utilization, network traffic, and disk activity.
sp_placeobject *segment-name*, *object-name*	Tell SQL Server to place new pages allocated to *object-name* on the segment *segment-name*.
sp_recompile *table-name*	Cause all stored procedures that depend on the table *table-name* to be recompiled the next time they are executed. This is useful when the statistics on *table-name* are updated or useful index is added to *table-name*.
sp_reportstats	Lists the amount of CPU and I/O performed by each user of the system as well as the total CPU and I/O counts. Use sp_clearstats to start a new accounting period for the statistics. This is useful for identifying heavy users of the system.
sp_spaceused	Reports the amount of space consumed in the current database. The report includes the size of the database, the amount of reserved space, the amount of space consumed by data and index, and the free space. This is useful in estimating the amount of time needed to perform a dump database. When a database is dumped, only pages containing control information, data, and indexes are dumped. Free space is not dumped.
sp_spaceused table-name	Reports the amount of space consumed by the table table-name in the current database. The report lists an estimate of the row count and the amount of reserved space, data space, and index space consumed by the table. sp_spacedused syslogs lists the size of the database's transaction log and is useful in estimating the amount of space needed to perform a dump transaction log.
sp_sysmon[a]	Reports a variety of statistics about the operation and performance of SQL Server. The sp_sysmon stored procedure provides much more detailed information than sp_monitor.
sp_who	Lists the users currently logged into SQL Server and their current activity. This is useful in determining who is logged into the system and if some users are blocked by locks held by other users.

a.   Introduced with System 11 SQL Server.

G.2.1 Locks

The stored procedure locks combines the information in `sp_lock` and `sp_who` to show the login name, the lockname, the database name, the object name, and the number of locks of that type held on the object in the database by the login.

Table G.4   locks output description

Column	Description
login	Login name.
locktype	Type of lock held by login. Corresponds to the locktypes reported by sp_lock.
database	Name of the database the lock is held in.
table	Name of the table in the database the lock is held on.
count	Number of locks of this type held by this login on this table in this database.

```
create procedure locks as
create table #lockname (type int, name char(20))
insert #lockname values(1,"ex_table")
insert #lockname values(2,"sh_table")
insert #lockname values(3,"ex_intent")
insert #lockname values(4,"sh_intent")
insert #lockname values(5,"ex_page")
insert #lockname values(6,"sh_page")
insert #lockname values(7,"update")
insert #lockname select type+256,name + "-blk"
        from #lockname
        where type >= 1 and type <= 7
insert #lockname select type+512, name + "-demand"
        from #lockname where type >= 1 and type < = 7
insert #lockname select type+256+512, name + "-demand-blk"
        from #lockname
        where type >= 1 and type <=7

select
        "login" = syslogins.name,
        "locktype" = #lockname.name,
        "database" = db_name(syslocks.dbid),
        "table" = object_name(syslocks.id,syslocks.dbid),
        "count" = count(page)
from
        master..syslogins syslogins,
        #lockname,
        master..syslocks syslocks,
        master..sysprocesses sysprocesses
where
        syslogins.suid = sysprocesses.suid and
        sysprocesses.spid = syslocks.spid and
        #lockname.type = syslocks.type
group by
        syslogins.name,
        #lockname.name,
        db_name(syslocks.dbid),
        object_name(syslocks.id,syslocks.dbid)
```

Figure G.1   Stored procedure locks -

G.2.2 Row Size

While working out the physical design of the database, it is often important to know the number of bytes in a table row and the number of rows that may fit on one page. The stored procedure `rowsize` calculates the number of bytes per row and the minimum number of rows per page for a table that exists in the current database. `Rowsize` takes the name of the table. If the name of the table is not given, `rowsize` reports on all of the user tables in the current database. Columns of type bit confuse `rowsize`.

Table G.5   rowsize output description

Column	Description
name	Table name.
bytes	Maximum number of bytes per row for this table excluding overhead.
overhead	Number of bytes of overhead in each row. Overhead is 4 bytes for tables with only fixed length columns and 6 bytes for tables with one or more variable length columns.
rowsPerPage	Minimum number of rows per page.

```
create proc rowsize @table_name varchar(30) = NULL as
select
        o.name,
        bytes = sum(c.length),
        overhead = 5 - sign(min(c.offset)),
        rowsPerPage = 2016/(sum(c.length)+ 5 - sign(min(c.offset)))
from
        sysobjects o, syscolumns c
where
        (@table_name = NULL or o.name = @table_name) and
        o.type = 'U' and o.id = c.id
group by o.id
```

Figure G.2   Stored procedure rowsize -

G.2.3   Space Used

The stored procedure spaceused runs `sp_spaceused` on every user table in the current database.

```
create proc spaceused as
declare @table_name char(30)
declare @eot_so int
declare c_msu_so cursor for
        select
                name
        from
                sysobjects
        where
                id>9999 and type = 'U'
begin
        open c_msu_so
        select @eot_so = 0
        while (@eot_so = 0) begin
                fetch c_msu_so into @table_name
                if (@@sqlstatus > 0) begin
                        select @eot_so = 1
                        break
                end
                exec sp_spaceused @table_name
        end
end
```

Figure G.3   Stored procedure spaceused -

G.2.4 Columns

The stored procedure `columns` shows the columns, length, and datatype number for each column in a table.

Table G.6   columns output description

Column	Description
name	Name of the column.
length	Number of bytes in the column.
type	Data type number.
prec	Precision — only useful for numeric columns.
scale	Scale — only useful for numeric columns.

```
create proc columns @table_name varchar(30) as
select
        c.name, c.length, c.type, c.prec, c.scale
from
        sysobjects o, syscolumns c
where
        o.name = @table_name and
        o.type = 'U' and
        o.id = c.id
```

Figure G.4   Stored procedure columns -

G.2.5 Devices View

The `disk init` command requires a `vdevno`. Each database device must have a unique `vdevno`, but it is often difficult to figure out which `vdevno` values you have already used. The `devices` view lists the `vdevno` value and the name of the database device using that `vdevno`.

```
create view devices(vdevno, name) as
select
        low/16777216,name
from
        master..sysdevices
where
        cntrltype=0
```

Figure G.5   devices view -

G.2.6   Indexes

The stored procedure `indexes` returns the names of the indexes on a table, the index id, and index trips value.

```
create procedure indexes @table_name varchar(30) = NULL as
select
        "table" = object_name(id),
        name,
        indid,
        ipgtrips
from
        sysindexes
where
        (@table_name = NULL or @table_name = object_name(id)) and
        id >1000 and
        indid > 0
group by
        object_name(id)
order by
        object_name(id)
```

Figure G.6   Stored procedure indexes -

G.2.7   Statistics

The stored procedure `statistics` returns the names of the indexes on a table, the index ID, and the distribution page. The distribution page holds the statistics for the index. If the distribution page is NULL there are no statistics stored for this index.

```
create procedure indexes @table_name varchar(30) = NULL as
select
        "table" = object_name(id),
        indid,
        name,
        distribution
from
        sysindexes i
where
        @table_name = NULL or @table_name = object_name(id)
group by
        object_name(id)
order by
        object_name(id), indid
```

Figure G.7   Stored procedure indexes -

G.2.8 Last Log Record

You cannot truncate the transaction log beyond the oldest active transaction. With SQL Servers before System 11 it was difficult to determine the oldest transaction. System 11 SQL Server adds a new system table `syslogshold` in the master database to help you find the oldest active transaction. You can identify the transaction that is blocking truncation of the transaction log with the query in Figure G.8.

```
select    h.spid, h.name
          from    master..syslogshold h, sysindexes i
          where   h.dbid = db_id()
          and     i.id = 8
          and     h.pages = i.first
```

Figure G.8   Finding the oldest active transaction -

G.3   SQL SERVER DATATYPES

Table G.7   SQL Server datatypes

Class	Type	SQL Type Name	Closest C Equivalent	Length in Bytes	Description/Remarks
Exact Numeric	integer	tinyint	unsigned char	1	Single byte integer value.
		smallint	short	2	Two byte integer value.
		int	int	4	Four byte integer value.
	decimals	numeric(p,s)	none	2–17	Exact numeric type. p and s determine the precision and scale (e.g., number of significant digits and number of digits to the right of the decimal point).
		decimal(p,s)	none	2–17	Same as numeric.
Approximate Numeric	float	float(p)	float/double	4 or 8	Floating point value. Use of float or double C equivalent depends on the value for p (e.g., precision).
		double precision	double	8	Double precision floating point value.
		real	float	4	Single precision floating point value.
Money		smallmoney	none	4	Four byte fixed point value.
		money	none	8	Eight byte fixed point value.
Date		smalldatetime	none	4	Four byte date/time value.
		datetime	none	8	Eight byte date/time value.

Table G.7   SQL Server datatypes

Class	Type	SQL Type Name	Closest C Equivalent	Length in Bytes	Description/Remarks
Character		char(n)	char []	n	Character data stored in SQL Server's default character set padded with spaces to fill out all n bytes.
		varchar(n)	char []	length of value	Character data stored in SQL Server's default character set. n defines the maximum length.
		nchar(n)	char []	n * @@nchar-size	National character data stored in SQL Server's default character set. Useful when the size of a character is more than one byte. Value is padded with spaces to occupy all n characters.
		nvarchar(n)	char []	length of value	National character data stored in SQL Server's default character set. Useful when the size of a character is more than one byte. n defines the maximum length.
Binary data		text	char []	multiple of 2 Kb	Character data stored in SQL Server's default character set using 2 Kb chunks. Must use readtext and writetext functions to access more than the first 255 characters.
		binary(n)	char []	n	Binary data padded with 0 to n bytes.
		varbinary(n)	char []	length of value	Binary data with maximum length n bytes.
		image	char []	multiple of 2 Kb	Binary data stored in 2 Kb chunks. Must use readtext and writetext functions to access more than the first 255 bytes.

Table G.7   SQL Server datatypes

Class	Type	SQL Type Name	Closest C Equivalent	Length in Bytes	Description/Remarks
Bit		bit	none	1	Boolean value. 8 bits are grouped into a single byte for storage in SQL Server. The ninth bit column starts the second bytes worth of bit columns. bit column cannot allow null.

G.4   SYSTEM TABLES

SQL Server uses system tables to store meta-information about the database — the names of tables, indexes, and columns, the datatypes of the columns, even information about the locks acquired and the users logged into SQL Server. Some of the system tables are not actually stored on disk. These tables are materialized on the fly when you select from them. Many system tables have special properties which make it impossible to add triggers or constraints. Listed in this section are some of the system tables we feel are useful in performance work. SQL Server manuals include a full list of all system tables.

syscolumns

The `syscolumns` system table has one row for every column in a table, every column in a view, and every parameter in a stored procedure.

Table G.8   syscolumns

Column	Description
offset	Position within the row. When positive, the column is a fixed length column. When negative, the column is a variable length column.
name	Column or parameter name.

sysdepends

The `sysdepends` system table has one row for every procedure, view, or table that is used by a procedure, view, or trigger.

Table G.9   sysdepends

Column	Description
id	obj_id of this object.
depid	obj_id of the object that depends on this object.
resultobj	1 if this object is updated by depid.
readobj	1 if this object is read by depid.

sysindexes

The `sysindexes` system table has one row for each page chain in the database. There are separate page chains for a table with a clustered index, a table without a clustered index, a nonclustered index, and text or image column.

Table G.10   sysindexes

Column	Description
name	Name of the index or table.
id	obj_id of this object.
indid	0 for the table, 1 for the clustered index, 2 to 254 for nonclustered index, 255 for a text or image page chain.
oampgtrips	oamtrips value for this table or index.
igtrips	indextrips value for this index.
rowpage	Maximum number of rows per page.
distribution	Location of the distribution page.

Table G.10   sysindexes

Column	Description
minlen	Minimum size of a row.
maxlen	Maximum size of a row.
maxirow	Maximum size of a non-leaf index row.

sysobjects

The `sysobjects` system table has one row for each table, view, stored procedure, rule, default, trigger, check constraint, and referential integrity constraint in the database.

Table G.11   sysobjects

Column	Description		
name	Name of the object.		
id	obj_id of the object.		
uid	Owner of the object.		
type	Kind of object.		
		S	System Table.
		U	User Table.
		V	View.
		L	Log.
		P	Stored Procedure.
		R	Rule.
		D	Default.
		TR	Trigger.
		RI	Referential Integrity Constraint.

Table G.11   sysobjects

Column	Description
indexdel	Index delete count. This value is incremented each time an index is deleted from the table. SQL Server uses this column to decide if it should recompile stored procedures that use this table.
schemacnt	Certain changes to the schema increment this column. SQL Server uses this column to decide if it should recompile stored procedures that use this table.

sysdevices

The `sysdevices` system table has one row for each dump device and database device.

Table G.12   sysdevices

Column	Description
low	Virtual page number for the first page on the device. This is vdevno times `16777216`.
high	Virtual page number for the last page on the device. high minus low gives the size of the device.
name	Logical name of the device (i.e., the name used with create database).
phyname	Physical name of the device (i.e., the name of the file).

sysengines

The `sysengines` system table has one row for each engine participating in this SQL Server.

Table G.13   sysengines

Column	Description
osprocid	Operating system process id.
osprocname	Operating system process name.
cur_kpid	SQL Server task that is currently running on this engine.

syslocks

The `syslocks` system table has one for each lock acquired in SQL Server.

Table G.14   syslocks

Column	Description
id	The lock is acquired on this obj_id.
dbid	The lock is acquired on obj_id in this database.
page	The lock is acquired on this page

Table G.14   syslocks

Column	Description		
type	The kind of lock		
	1		Exclusive table lock.
	2		Shared table lock.
	3		Exclusive intent lock.
	4		Shared intent lock.
	5		Exclusive page lock.
	6		Shared page lock.
	7		Update lock.
	+256		Lock is blocking another task.
	+512		Lock is a demand lock.
spid	The task number that holds this lock.		
class	If this lock is held by a cursor, the name of the cursor that holds this lock.		

sysprocesses

The `sysprocesses` system table has one row for each task running in SQL Server.

Table G.15   sysprocesses

Column	Description
spid	SQL Server task number.
enginenum	Engine that is currently executing this task.

Table G.15   sysprocesses

Column	Description	
status	Status of this task.	
	infected	Task is in the process of printing a stack trace and terminating.
	recv sleep	Task is sleeping waiting to read data from the network.
	send sleep	Task is sleeping waiting to write data to the network.
	alarm sleep	Task is sleeping on an alarm. For example, tasks executing the waitfor command are sleeping on an alarm.
	lock sleep	Task is sleeping waiting to acquire a lock.
	sleeping	Task is sleeping for some other reason. For example, the task may be waiting for data to be read from disk.
	runnable	Task can run, but there is no engine available to run the task.
	running	Task is running on an engine.
	bad status	Task is not reporting a valid status.
	log suspend	Task is waiting for log space to become available.
hostname	Name of the host running the client associated with this task (set with [ct...]).	
program_name	Name of the program the client is using (set with [ct...]).	
cmd	Command task is currently executing.	
cpu	Number of CPU ticks consumed by this task.	
physical_io	Number of physical I/O operations attributable to this task.	
memusage	Amount of memory currently allocated to this task.	
blocked	spid of a task that is blocking this task. For example, the other spid may hold locks that this spid requires.	
dbid	Current database for this task.	
uid	User who owns this task.	
tran_name	Name of an active transaction owned by this task.	
time_blocked	Number of seconds this task has been blocked from executing.	
network_pktsz	Network packet size used by this task.	

Glossary

ad hoc queries   Unplanned queries that are given to SQL Server. The contents of the queries is not known when the database is designed and optimized.

blocked   A task that is blocked is prevented from executing because another task or activity stands in its way. For example, if one task holds an exclusive lock on some data, when another task tries to acquire a lock on the data it is said to be blocked by the first task.

buffer replacement   Algorithm used to re-use buffers in the data cache. See Least Recently Used and Most Recently Used.

cache   Memory used to buffer recently used data. Also refers to the process of buffering recently used data.

cache hit   Data is found in cache memory. Contrast with cache miss.

cache hit rate   Percentage of time that data is found in the cache. Data that is not found in the cache must be retrieved from disk.

cache miss   Data is not found in cache memory and must be retrieved from another (slower) source. Contrast with cache hit.

check constraint   Check that the data item is in the correct format. A check constraint is similar to a rule.

CISC   Complex Instruction Set Computer — processor design characterized by a small set of registers and a complex and asymmetric instruction set. Newer CISC designs incorporate some of the same performance enhancements seen in RISC chips.

client-side cursor Cursor implemented in the client library. See cursor.

clustered index Index on a table in which the data rows are physically ordered by the order of the index.

commit sharing See group commit.

commodity products When referring to computer systems, commodity products are systems built with industry standard components, typically derived from the PC marketplace. An alternative is a system built from hardware available from only one hardware vendor.

composite index An index built on more than one column of the table.

configuration block The first block of the master device is used to store SQL Server configuration information. This is called the configuration block. System 10 and earlier versions of SQL Server use the configuration block to store all SQL Server wide configuration. System 11 and later versions of SQL Server store only a small amount of information in the configuration block. See configuration file.

configuration file System 11 and later versions of SQL Server use a configuration file to store configuration information. The configuration file is stored in the Sybase release directory and can be modified using a regular text editor.

correlated subquery Subquery that refers to tables and columns from the outer query.

covering index See index covering.

cursor Place holder in a query result set. Allows the client program to process rows in a result one (or a few) at a time rather than all at once.

data cache Memory used to store copies of data and index pages.

data page Page of a database devoted to holding data (e.g., from a table).

default A value given to a column when no value is provided explicitly.

deferred update A deferred update is performed by first deleting and then inserting the data. Deferred update mode means SQL Server first logs the change to the database before applying the change to the table. Deferred updates on insert and update generally occur when the statement updates a column with a unique index. See direct update.

demand lock A lock that has been passed over several times without being granted. A demand lock does not allow other locks to be granted ahead of it.

Direct Memory Access A controller with direct memory access can access the computer's memory directly without involving the CPU. If the controller does not have direct memory access, the CPU is responsible for reading and writing information on behalf of the controller. This impacts the performance of the system as the CPU must spend time servicing the controllers and has less time to run user programs.

direct update A direct update, also called an update in place, is an update that changes the contents of the table directly, rather than through a delete and insert. Direct updates are much faster than deferred updates. Direct update means SQL Server changes the contents of the table at the same time that the changes are logged. See deferred update.

DMA See Direct Memory Access.

duplicate keys A key column with duplicate keys allows many copies of the same value in the column.

exclusive lock A task with an exclusive lock on some piece of data prevents other tasks from accessing the same data.

fill factor Specifies how full index pages (including clustered index data pages) are made when the index is created.

gigabyte 2^{30} bytes, 1,024 megabytes, 1,048,576 kilobytes, 1,073,741,824 bytes.

group commit

A transaction does not commit until the transaction is written to the transaction log. SQL Server may consolidate several transactions into a single write to the transaction log. Many transactions then commit simultaneously. This is called group commit.

index covering

The leaf pages of a nonclustered index cover for the data pages because the query does not access columns other than the columns participating in the nonclustered index.

index page

Page of a database devoted to an index.

infected

An infected process is a task that has received an unexpected signal or is otherwise assumed to be in a bad state. SQL Server generally prints a stack trace to the errorlog for tasks that are infected.

intent lock

Tasks acquire intent locks on tables that correspond to locks the tasks have acquired on pages in the table. For example, a task with an exclusive page lock in a table also holds an exclusive intent lock on the table that contains the page.

join clause

A join clause is the part of a where clause that connects two tables through the key columns of the tables.

kilobyte

2^{10} bytes, 1,024 bytes.

language cursor

See native cursor.

leaf index page

Lowest level of an index. In a nonclustered index leaf pages contain copies of the indexed columns. In a clustered index, leaf pages are the data pages of the table.

Least Recently Used

The least recently used item in a list of items is the item that was used furthest in the past.

lock

As a verb, to protect an item so that it cannot be accessed or changed by another user of the item. As a noun, some entity that is used to control access to an item.

logical read	SQL Server reads data from the data cache rather than the database devices.
LRU	See Least Recently Used.
megabyte	2^{20} bytes, 1,024 kilobytes, 1,048,576 bytes.
microsecond	One millionth of a second.
millisecond	One thousandth of a second. A car traveling 60 miles per hour travels about 1 inch in a millisecond.
Most Recently Used	The most recently used item in a list of items is the item that was used closest to the present.
MRU	See Most Recently Used.
nanosecond	One billionth of a second.
native cursor	Cursor implemented in the server. See cursor.
nonclustered index	The leaf pages of the index contain pointers to the data pages containing the data rows. The data rows are not physically ordered by this index.
non-leaf index pages	Pages of an index that are not the lowest level of the index. Non-leaf index pages contain page pointers to the next layer of the index.
page	Smallest allocatable unit in a SQL Server database. Pages are 2K on most platforms.
page lock	A lock on a page in the database.
paging	The act of exchanging information in the computer's main memory for information stored on disk in the page or swap area. This allows a computer with a limited amount of main memory to simulate a computer with much more memory.

physical memory   The main memory (RAM) of the computer.

physical read   SQL Server reads data from the database devices. The data was not found in the data cache.

prefix   The prefix to an index refers to the first N columns of a composite index built on M columns, where N is less than M. For example, an index built on columns a,b,c has a and a,b as prefixes.

procedure cache   SQL Server memory set aside to store optimized query plans.

recovery   The process of reconstructing the last known state of the databases in SQL Server.

referential constraint The values in one table must in another table.

reformatting   SQL Server creates an index on a worktable to improve the overall performance of the query.

release directory   Directory where Sybase SQL Server and other Sybase supplied software is installed. Generally, the path to this directory is stored in the SYBASE environment variable.

RISC   Reduced Instruction Set Computer — processor design characterized by many registers, a simple and orthogonal instruction set, and various pipelining and other performance enhancements.

RPM   Revolutions Per Minute.

rule   Similar to a check constraint, except that rules may be applied to user-defined datatypes. Rules check the format of the data, but may not check the content of the data with respect to other columns or tables.

runnable   The task is not blocked and will run the next time it is assigned to an engine.

running   The task is currently executing on an engine.

SCSI Small Computer System Interconnect, a standard interface for connecting peripherals like disk drives and tape drives to computer systems.

search clause The part of a where clause that restricts the values of particular columns within a single table.

Seek Time Amount of time to move the head of a disk drive from one track to another.

self join A join of a table with itself.

server-side cursor See native cursor.

shared lock Many users may acquire a shared lock on a particular item.

shared memory Memory that is shared between several processes running on the same computer.

showplan output Output produced after `set showplan on` is executed.

sleeping The task is waiting for some resource to become available.

stored procedure A named sequence of T-SQL statements stored in SQL Server.

subquery Query that appears as part of another query's `where` clause.

swapping See paging.

table lock Lock acquired on an entire table.

table scan Act of reading every row of a table.

terabyte 2^{40} bytes, 1,024 gigabytes, 1,048,576 megabytes, 1,073,741,824 kilobytes, 1,099,511,627,776 bytes.

terminating The task is being killed.

transaction	An atomic unit of work to the database. All statements in the transaction must execute or none of the statements in the transaction must execute.
Transfer Rate	Rate at which information moves from one place to another. Typically applied to hardware devices like disk drives and tape drives.
trigger	A named sequence of T-SQL statements that executes when a table is modified.
TPC	Transaction Processing Council. This organization defines industry standard benchmarks.
TPM	Transactions per minute.
TPMC	Transactions per minute measured with the Transaction Processing Council's standard benchmark TPC-C.
TPS	Transactions per second.
uniqueness constraint	A column or columns of a table that are required to have unique values in each row.
update in place	The page of the table is modified directly, avoiding a delete and insert of the modified row.
worktable	Temporary table created by SQL Server to hold intermediate results while processing a query.
yielding	The task is giving up the engine to allow other tasks to execute.

Index